Forty Plus Four
1990-1993

First Supplement to the

Forty Years of Stock Car Racing

Series

By Greg Fielden

The Galfield Press
P.O. Box 15009
Surfside Beach, S.C. 29587
(803) 238-2404
Fax (803) 238-5452

About the Author:

Greg Fielden is recognized as one of the foremost historians of NASCAR Winston Cup stock car racing. He has been attending Winston Cup races since 1961 and has accumulated a vast library on America's greatest sport.

Fielden has documented the chronicle history of NASCAR's premier stock car racing division in the widely acclaimed "Forty Years of Stock Car Racing" series of books. "Forty Plus Four" traces the 1990-1993 seasons.

Forty Plus Four 1990-1993

The first Supplement to the Forty Years of Stock Car Racing series

First printing, March 1994

ISBN 1-885016-01-8

Other stock car racing publications by Greg Fielden:

Forty Years of Stock Car Racing

Volume I, The Beginning 1949-1958
Volume II, The Superspeedway Boom 1959-1964
Volume III, Big Bucks and Boycotts 1965-1971
Volume IV, The Modern Era 1972-1989

Rumblin' Ragtops, The History of NASCAR's Fabulous Convertible Division

High Speed At Low Tide

Additional stock car racing publication by the Galfield Press:

Tim Flock, Race Driver

Cover Photo: Davey Allison leads Alan Kulwicki into the first turn at Charlotte Motor Speedway in 1991. *Photo by Brian Czobat.*

Acknowledgements

The author wishes to extend a special thanks to P. J. Hollebrand, Brad Hoffner and photographers Brian Czobat, Kim Novosat and Bryan Hallman for their invaluable assistance in providing photographs for this publication.

Jim Ahmay
Larry Balewski
Lenny Batycki
Clyde Bolton
Tommy Britt
Steve Brown
Chris Browning
Bob Costanzo
Todd Crane
Greg Crisp
Steve Crumbacker
Dorothy Davis
Lynette Dudley
Gregg Feistman
Larry Fielden
Patricia Fielden
Jim Freeman
Donna Freismuth
Eddie Gossage
Donna Haas
Bill Hennecy
Tom Higgins
Don Hunter
Mike Joy
Jay Kainz
Kenny Kane
Doyle Kienel
Joseph Mattioli III
Bob Mauk
Jon Mauk
Jean McDuffie
Mike Mulhern
Graham Niven
Ty Norris
Yvonne Ordonez
Chris Percival
Benny Phillips
Sandy Roach
Al Robinson
Dave Rodman
Susan Russo
Kim Sanders
Ron Scalf
Brenda Schmidt
Hank Schoolfield
Frankie Smith
Sabrina Smith
Teddi Smith
Richard Sowers
Ken Squier
Russ Thompson
Bob Weeks
Fletcher Williams

Dedication

Davey Allison

Alan Kulwicki

J.D. McDuffie

Neil Bonnett

This publication is dedicated to the memories of Davey Allison, Alan Kulwicki, J.D. McDuffie and Neil Bonnett, four highly spirited individuals who contributed so much to NASCAR Winston Cup racing, and who paid the ultimate price for the sport they loved.

Table of Contents

Foreword

Forty Years of Stock Car Racing, Greg Fielden's masterful four-volume history, is regarded as the definitive account of NASCAR's Winston Cup series from its formation in June, 1949 through the end of the 1989 racing season. **Forty Plus Four 1990-1993**, Fielden's continuation of NASCAR's story, recreates the emotion and drama of four racing seasons since that time...years punctuated by tragedy and triumph.

The losses were great. An automobile accident took the life of Rob Moroso, a promising young driver who was awarded 1990 Rookie of the Year posthumously; J.D. McDuffie, the last of the independent drivers, was lost to turn five at Watkins Glen. Alan Kulwicki, the 1992 Winston Cup champion, died in a plane crash. Davey Allison, whose brother died the previous year in a Busch Grand National practice session at Michigan International Speedway, succumbed to injuries in a helicopter mishap. It was the end of a racing dynasty.

And NASCAR lost its founder and great visionary, William Henry Getty France.

While teams privately mourned, competition on-track was fierce. Racing technology had advanced to the degree that winning performances evolved as a delicate ballet between lift, drag, restricted engines and mandated spoiler heights. On the short tracks, time separations for an entire field could be measured in a blink of an eye.

In this highly readable book, Fielden lets us relive the defining moments: Mark Martin's "spacer caper" which cost the Arkansas native the championship in 1990; Kulwicki's narrow 10-point victory over Bill Elliott in the chase for the 1992 title; Dale Earnhardt posting three more championships in pursuit of Richard Petty's throne; and the King's final effort behind the wheel.

Unlike standard marketing publications that report only the face of NASCAR Winston Cup racing, **Forty Plus Four 1990-1993** stands out as a faithful chronicle of the day-to-day events that shape the sport – the ebb and flow of competition; the rough-and-tumble commentary; the soaring heights and the depths of heartbreak.

Forty Plus Four 1990-1993 is packed with Fielden's rich prose, his unerring eye for detail and accuracy of facts and figures, allowing a great sport to tell its own story.

Dorothy Davis
Motorsports Journalist

'The deaths of Alan Kulwicki and Davey Allison were losses to our future, but bigger losses to our heart. I'm really proud of the way our people picked themselves up, dusted themselves off and kept moving forward."

—NASCAR President Bill France, Jr.

1990 Winston Cup Season

Spacer Caper Foils Roush Racers; Earnhardt Bags Fourth Championship

SHOOTIN' INTO THE GROUND

While deer hunting after the close of the 1989 NASCAR Winston Cup season, Dale Earnhardt reflected on a year gone awry. He had won five races, won $1.4 million and had finished second in the final Winston Cup point standings. Supreme achievements. But he had failed to win his fourth Winston Cup title. That's what bugged him so much.

Rusty Wallace will go down in history for winning the championship in 1989. Actually, Earnhardt *lost* it.

Earnhardt led the point standings most of the season. After the Talladega 500 in late July, he and the RCR Enterprises team was 165 points ahead of Rusty Wallace. At that point in the season, it appeared the Kannapolis, N.C. rustler would cruise to his fourth championship. All he had to do was keep the wheels on his car, keep it between the fences and avoid any sort of mechanical trouble.

But Wallace, despite bickering with car owner Raymond Beadle over his contract, made a comeback. Earnhardt helped Wallace's cause with three poor efforts at Charlotte, North Wilkesboro and Rockingham.

Early engine failure put Earnhardt out of the 500-miler at Charlotte. At North Wilkesboro, he rebounded sharply and outran Wallace all day – until the final lap. Ricky Rudd had erased a 2.2-second deficit in the final half dozen laps and got under Earnhardt in the final lap. Earnhardt, determined not to let Rudd pass uncontested, tried to block the move. Rudd had already positioned himself and the two cars made contact. Both cars spun. Earnhardt fell from first to 10th in the last lap as Wallace finished seventh.

Dale Earnhardt lost the 1989 Winston Cup championship, but was determined to make amends in the 1990 NASCAR campaign.

Instead of picking up 47 points on Wallace and taking the point lead that day, he lost two points. His eyes were focused so much on the $47,000 first prize at North Wilkesboro that he temporarily lost sight of the $1 million that went with the title.

A week later at Rockingham, he was racing side-by-side with his friendly rival when Wallace slipped and knocked Earnhardt into a spin. More points lost.

Earnhardt trailed Wallace by 79 points entering the season finale at Atlanta. Dale won going away. But Wallace finished 15th and won the championship by 12 points.

And while all the thoughts got bottled up in his head while sitting out in the woods, Earnhardt found a suitable release. "The more I got to thinking about it, the madder I got. I'd be sitting in that deer stand and I'd shoot the ground just because I was mad."

Brian Czobat

Rusty Wallace was back to another run at the Winston Cup title.

Earnhardt and Wallace were expected to retain the favorites role in the 1990 chase for the Cup. Wallace had landed a new sponsor for what was to be his final season with car owner Raymond Beadle. "I know Dale is snorting like a rhinoceros like I was in 1988," said Wallace, who had finished an agonizing second to Bill Elliott in the Winston Cup standings. "But I'm going to be the best champion I can possibly be. I know Dale is going to come out blazing this year, but we're ready for him."

Earnhardt has had a history of bouncing back after a lackluster season. His 1986 championship, the second of his career and the first he shared with car owner Richard Childress, came after a dismal 1985 season. He failed to finish nine races that year, and his best effort on a superspeedway was a fourth.

But he got up off the floor, dusted himself off and promptly won back-to-back titles in 1986 and 1987.

For the 1990 season, Earnhardt was back behind the wheel of Richard Childress' Chevrolet Luminas, the seventh year they had been paired together. But there were over a dozen realignments for the 1990 campaign. The so-called 'silly season' is serious business, with drivers clawing for the best available seats.

JOHNSON SEEKS A NEW DRIVER

The dominos began to fall in the summer months of 1989. Terry Labonte, in his third and final year with Junior Johnson, tossed the first stone when he announced that he would leave Johnson and form his own Winston Cup team for the 1990 campaign. "I'll be running my own team with Oldsmobile in 1990 in a new facility," said the 1984 Winston Cup champion. I've been dodging the question. I haven't lied to people, I've just brushed it off.

"This isn't a sudden thing. I started working on it before Daytona in February. It's something I've wanted to do and now I have the opportunity. So I'm going to do it.

"One of the toughest things to do is get out of a car that is winning. I hope to win more. But I've contacted some people and some have contacted me. Once I give my word, I don't back off."

Johnson said Labonte's move did not catch him off guard. "I knew Terry had a deal with Oldsmobile and we want him to succeed. He's given us 100 percent. The team just never jelled. We wish him good luck. But we're going to try to whup him every race next year."

Immediately after Labonte and Johnson agreed to go their separate ways, the famed car owner from Ingle Hollow, N.C. began negotiations with Alan Kulwicki. It was no secret that Johnson wanted Kulwicki to drive his potent Fords.

KULWICKI TURNS DOWN OFFER

While the touring professionals were in Watkins Glen in August of 1989, Johnson offered Kulwicki an attractive three-year deal. Kulwicki asked for a few days to mull it over.

Kulwicki, a self-styled loner who came to NASCAR in 1985 with little more than a worn out race car, two full-time crew members and a vision that he would build his own championship team under his terms, only needed 24 hours to reach his decision.

He turned down an opportunity to drive for one of the legendary figures in NASCAR stock car racing. His decision jolted nearly everyone in the sport.

"Junior's offer was a helluva opportunity," said Kulwicki. "If anyone would have told me three years ago that I would pass up an opportunity to drive for him for the kind of money available, I would have told them they were crazy and go on down the road. Maybe now people will think I'm crazy for not accepting the offer. But I had to work hard for 15 years to get where I'm at and now I'm in my fourth season in Winston Cup racing.

"Now I'm used to working hard. Now, I don't mind it. And I believe the people I have with me now. Sure, things have been bad for us lately, but now I don't get down or as frustrated as I used to," he added, after going winless in 1989 and struggling to finish 14th in the Winston Cup standings. "The thinking on my team right now is 'We have a problem, so let's fix it.' And then we fix it.

"Time will tell if my decision is right or wrong. But I have never been a quitter in my life. Even as bad as things have been lately, if I joined another team, I would feel like I never stuck it out with what I have now. Down the road, I would never be able to say to myself that I have it my best shot. I would always second-guess myself.

"I want to thank Junior for offering me this opportunity. I know that he has great cars and people. I hope he will accept my respect for him and his team and understand that I made my decision solely on principle."

NEW FACES CHANGING PLACES

Following Kulwicki's decision, Sterling Marlin, Rick Wilson and Geoff Bodine loomed as the most likely candidates to take the Johnson ride. Marlin was still contracted to Billy Hagan, and Rick Wilson opted to leave Morgan-McClure to go to the RahMoc Motorsports operation headed by Bob Rahilly and Butch Mock.

Geoff Bodine, who had driven for Hendrick Motorsports since 1984, accepted Johnson's offer. Instead of a three-year package which was offered to Kulwicki, Bodine signed a one-year contract.

Alan Kulwicki turned down Junior Johnson's ride offer to stick it out with his own team, sponsored by Zerex.

Ricky Rudd left Kenny Bernstein's King Motorsports outfit to take the vacancy Bodine created on the Hendrick Motorsports team. Brett Bodine quit the Bud Moore Engineering team to join Bernstein; Morgan Shepherd took over Bud Moore's Ford ride; Dale Jarrett was released from Cale Yarborough Motorsports and accepted a position with the Baker-Schiff team, which never flew due to lack of sponsorship. Dick Trickle took the Yarborough Motorsports Pontiac ride.

In August, Phil Parsons announced he would be back with Richard Jackson's Precision Products Oldsmobile team for another year. But when Wilson departed from the Morgan-McClure Oldsmobile ride, Parsons rescinded on his verbal commitment and hooked up with car owner Larry McClure.

"It was a difficult thing to do, leaving Richard Jackson," said Parsons, who won at Talladega in 1988. "But after talking with Larry McClure and seeing the team's shops, I became convinced his team had the capability to win."

Terry Labonte's visions of becoming an owner-driver were derailed when he was unable to get a building permit for his new shops in Thomasville, N.C. He wound up taking the Precision Products ride. "Trying to start my own team turned into a disaster," said Labonte. "We couldn't build on some land I owned because it didn't perk properly for septic tanks. Then I bought a site in an industrial park in Thomasville, and the city wouldn't grant us a building permit. It turned out to be a big mess. I wouldn't build in the city of Thomasville now if they paid me."

Bobby Allison and partners Bob Bilby, Nathan Sims and Frank Plessinger, formed Bobby Allison Motorsports and hired Mike Alexander to drive the team's Buick. "It's great to be back actively," said Allison, whose career ended in a severe crash at Pocono in 1988. "I would like to have recuperated enough to drive myself, but that hasn't happened yet."

Bobby's son Davey was set to drive Fords for car owner Robert Yates, who had purchased the team from Harry Ranier a year earlier.

Kim Novosat

Richard Petty was hoping for some good news in the 1990 season.

Mark Martin was teamed with Jack Roush for the third year in a row. In 1988, the new team notched only three top five finishes. But in 1989, they made a solid stab at the championship and finished third on the strength of one victory and countless near-misses. "We have come together as a team," said Martin, "and we're ready to make another serious bid for the Winston Cup championship.

Richard Petty was back for his 33rd year. And he was hoping the 1990 season would be more fruitful than 1989. "This past year was the worst one I've ever had," said the King. "We ain't done nothing. I mean nothing. This has been one of those years you want to forget. We worked on the chassis all year long and we've made some progress. Now, we've got to do something about the engines."

GEARING UP FOR DAYTONA

Dale Earnhardt became an overwhelming favorite to win the elusive Daytona 500 once the teams arrived for Speedweeks. On pole day, Earnhardt qualified second to Hendrick Motorsports driver Ken Schrader, who racked up his third straight pole in the NASCAR's version of the Super Bowl.

Kim Novasat

Davey Allison would drive again for car owner Robert Yates.

The only reason Earnhardt didn't win the Busch Clash was because he was not in the field. He had failed to win a pole during the 1989 season.

But everything else fell Earnhardt's way during Speedweeks. He led most of the way in the Twin 125-mile qualifier, but pitted for fuel and tires during a caution flag. He was 12th in line for the restart with 10 laps to go. It only took him eight laps to roar through the pack and pass Dick Trickle for the win. "He hung tough," Earnhardt said of Trickle. "But I was going to go on by him. He knew that."

Geoff Bodine won the other Twin 125 by going the full 50 laps without a pit stop.

Brian Czobat

Derrike Cope drove the Bob Whitcomb Racing #10 Chevrolet to an upset victory in the Daytona 500.

Earnhardt poked a jab at Bodine and the strategic Junior Johnson crew. "If they run conservative in the 500 and worry about gas mileage, they're going to get their butts lapped," noted Earnhardt, who also won Saturday's Busch Grand National event.

ANOTHER 'HARDT-BREAKER' FOR DALE

Earnhardt was a formidable force in the Daytona 500. There was no driver in the field who could keep up with him. Earnhardt motored away from all rivals; they even had difficulty drafting him.

A late caution flag erased a 27-second lead and put a pack of cars within striking distance. Still, that was merely a minor inconvenience for Earnhardt – until the final lap.

He ran over debris on the backstretch and sliced a tire. Going into the third turn, Earnhardt fought for control as four challengers passed him. incredibly, Earnhardt did not knock down the wall. He held control and brought the car home fifth. Once again, Dale Earnhardt had come so close – yet failed – to win the race that has become the only sizable void in his illustrious career.

Derrike Cope won the Daytona 500 in only his third start. In September of 1989, Purolator announced they were not going to sponsor Cope's Bob Whitcomb Racing team in 1990. Shortly before Daytona, Purolator decided to keep their association with Whitcomb's promising team.

Not only was it his first career Winston Cup victory, it was also the first time he had finished in the top five.

THE SPACER CAPER

The second event of the 1990 season was at Paul Sawyer's Richmond International Raceway. On a terribly bitter cold day, Mark Martin ran down Rusty Wallace and Dale Earnhardt in the final 10 miles and throttled the Roush Ford to victory.

Martin had scored his second career victory. As he shook off the chill in the comfort of the press box following the race, the winning car was going through a routine post-race NASCAR inspection. During the tear-down, Technical Director Dick Beaty noticed that the carburetor on Martin's car was mounted on the engine's intake manifold with an aluminum block spacer half an inch thicker than the two inches allowed.

Engine specialists for other teams said a taller spacer would improve air flow and could increase horsepower.

NASCAR announced that Martin's victory would be

Brian Czobat

Mark Martin's Ford picked up the Folger's sponsorship in 1990 and was one of the favorites to challenge Earnhardt for the title.

Brian Czobat

Jack Roush and his team were docked 46 points after the controversial post-race inspection at Richmond.

upheld, but the team would be fined a record $40,000 and 46 Winston Cup points would be deducted from Martin. "At this point the victory stands," Beaty said about four hours after the conclusion of the race. "I don't know if it was an advantage or not."

Roush Racing team manager Steve Hmiel said spacers more than two inches thick have been allowed under NASCAR specifications as long as they are welded to the manifold, and that the engine was in violation because its spacer was bolted to the carburetor.

"It's a stupid rule," huffed Hmiel. "All you have to do is weld the spacer to the top of the manifold and it could be eight inches high, or whatever you want. Nobody would say anything."

Hmiel said crew chief Robin Pemberton installed the carburetor mounting which caused the penalty without informing Hmiel and misrepresented to Roush that the mounting had been approved by NASCAR.

Roush placed Pemberton on an immediate 30-day suspension without pay, but reversed his decision a day later in the wake of reaction from outsiders.

NASCAR spokesman Chip Williams said the victory stood because "the fans have a right to know who won the race when they leave the track. Our policy is not to disqualify anyone. We set it up so that's not to anyone's advantage to win by cheating."

Williams added that the penalty of 46 points was based on points which would have been earned if Martin had finished last in the leader's lap. Ten cars finished on the lead lap and had Martin finished 10th, he would have earned 46 fewer points.

Hmiel explained that the violation was a "communication problem within the (Roush Racing) company. It was really unfortunate for Robin. What happened is NASCAR lowered the engine ground clearance an inch and we needed to raise the carburetor equal amount to maintain proper air flow. We were caught in what we maintain is a gray area of the rules."

Ironically, Pemberton was co-crew chief when the former record fine of $35,000 was levied against Richard Petty for having an illegal big engine and improper tires on his car after winning at Charlotte in 1983.

Martin felt like his team "had received the death penalty for running a stop sign. People are going to say we are cheating to win, but it's not like that. I look at cheating as something that's done to get an unfair advantage. What was done on our car didn't give us an advantage on anybody. It wasn't like we had a big engine or illegal tires."

The 46-point penalty dropped Martin from sixth to 12th place in the Winston Cup standings as Dale Earnhardt took the lead. He had already dug himself a hole, trailing by 101 points after just two races.

PARSONS OUT, IRVAN IN

The first major shake-up occurred shortly after the season started. Phil Parsons, who accepted the Morgan-McClure ride after wriggling out of a verbal commitment to stay with Richard Jackson, got the axe after just three races. Parsons had been involved in three crashes – none of his making – through the first three races. Team owner Larry McClure made the announcement. "We just felt both Phil and our team were not progressing to where we all want to be, in the winner's circle," said McClure in a prepared statement. "We believe this change will be better for Phil and for us in the long run. Phil is a fine race car driver, but his driving style didn't mesh with our team.

"I saw things weren't going to work, so there was no use to put of making a change until later," said McClure.

Parsons expressed surprise at the hasty announcement. "I'm shocked more than anything else. I felt they might want to make a change, but I don't think three races was a fair amount of time to judge.

"I'm disappointed, but not bitter," added Parsons, who scored his only Winston Cup victory at Talladega in 1986. "I'm not going to throw mud around. I wish the team and I could have stayed together because I think we could have done really well this season."

Ernie Irvan, promising driver out of Modesto, Calif., was selected to replace Parsons. Irvan, a veteran of 61 Winston Cup races, had apparently been lined up with car owner Junie Donlavey for the 1990 season. Tru-Cure adhesives had agreed to sponsor the team, but the funds never came through. Donlavey allowed Irvan to seek another ride.

Kim Novosat

Ernie Irvan finished third at Atlanta in his first effort with Morgan-McClure.

Irvan had opened some eyes in recent months. He won the ARCA 500-kilometer race at Atlanta in November of 1989, and had won a qualifying race for the Daytona Busch Grand National event in spectacular fashion in the final lap.

"We like Ernie a lot and we feel he would do us a good job," said McClure, who has yet to win a Winston Cup race. "I like Ernie. I like what I've seen of him recently, and I would like to have him drive my car. The process of making him a permanent selection has been started."

Buddy Baker announced he was coming out of an injury-forced retirement to drive the Donlavey Ford in selected races.

IRVAN: JECKELL AND HYDE

In the Atlanta Motorcraft 500, Dale Earnhardt won and Ernie Irvan was sensational in his debut with Morgan-McClure. Time trials were rained out, so Earnhardt started on the pole as a result of his team's first place in the Winston Cup standings. Irvan was forced to start 30th, based on Morgan-McClure's position in the car owner standings.

Earnhardt won the race, passing Morgan Shepherd with two laps remaining. Irvan charged through the pack and finished a close third, outrunning Mark Martin and Ken Schrader in a spirited duel.

"Maybe this will close the book on the deal," said McClure. "Ernie drove a heck of a race. And he didn't surprise me a bit."

Irvan's next appearance was at Darlington. He wasn't sensational, but he did cause a spectacular crash that would sideline Neil Bonnett for over three years.

Irvan qualified third for Darlington's TranSouth 500. He chased Geoff Bodine and Dale Earnhardt for most of the early laps. While battling Bodine for second place in the 78th lap, Irvan spun his car off the fourth turn and slid the

Brian Czobat

Neil Bonnett suffered head injuries in a crash at Darlington. He would be forced out of the driver's compartment and into an advisory role for driver Jeff Purvis.

distance of the front chute. He was able to limp to the pits. Eventually, he fell 10 laps off the pace.

Later in the race, Irvan was on the inside front row for a restart. Urged by crew chief Tony Glover via radio, Irvan raced leader Ken Schrader into the fourth turn. As the pair rode door-to-door through the tight corner, Irvan's Chevrolet slipped sideways and bounced off Schrader's car.

With the cars tightly bunched up, 13 cars became involved in the crash. Bonnett, driving the Wood Brothers Ford, slowed down and glanced off a couple of other cars. When he was removed from the car, he had no recollection of who he was or where he was. The Hueytown, Ala. driver had suffered a concussion and a severe case of amnesia. Doctors recommended he sit out indefinitely.

The Wood Brothers looked at the available candidates to replace Bonnett and settled on Dale Jarrett. Jarrett had been left on the sidelines during the pre-season shuffle. He had inked a deal to drive for car owners Buddy Baker and Danny Schiff, but sponsorship never materialized.

Brian Czobat

Mark Martin made a solid run for the Winston Cup title, but came up a few points short.

EARNHARDT'S LEAD EVAPORATES

Earnhardt won the Darlington race, becoming the first driver to win two races in the 1990 season. Mark Martin had finished second, but he was logged in seventh place in the Winston Cup standings, 185 points behind.

Through the first 10 races of the season, Earnhardt was able to stay atop the Winston Cup standings. But in the late spring, his RCR Enterprises team hit a snag. In four straight races – Charlotte, Dover, Sonoma and Pocono – Earnhardt failed to log a single top 10 finish. In a flash, he had fallen from first to fifth in the standings.

Martin had overcome the 46-point penalty and early season misfirings to take the point lead as of the road course event at Sonoma, Calif. in June.

Earnhardt dug himself a hole in the title chase, trailing Martin by 136 points in the early summer. But the Intimidator roared back, winning three out of four races in less than a month. When Earnhardt won the Talladega 500 in July, he pulled to within a single point of Martin.

The race was on for the most sought after prize in NASCAR.

Martin repelled the mid-season Earnhardt challenge and kept the point lead. In late September, Martin held a slim 16 point lead as the tour completed the Goody's 500 at Martinsville – the 24th race of the 29-race schedule.

At that point in the season, Earnhardt had won eight races, while Martin had won twice. They both had 15 top five finishes. Earnhardt had won more than twice as much in official earnings, and he had outscored Martin 140-75 in bonus points. Earnhardt had led the most laps in seven races; Martin had led the most in one event.

Yet Martin was leading the point standings despite his 46-point penalty.

At North Wilkesboro, Earnhardt led most of the way but was beaten down the stretch by Martin. By winning the North Wilkesboro race, Martin was able to lock up his third win of the season, but picked up nothing in the point race. The margin with four races to go was still 16 points.

STUMBLING AT CHARLOTTE

Both title contenders hit the skids at Charlotte. Martin nursed a sputtering car to a 14th place finish, while Earnhardt was involved in two mishaps and a costly error in the pits. He finished 25th and fell 49 points behind Martin.

Martin said he was "fortunate to finish. I drove like I had an egg between my foot and the accelerator. It made noises and never did act happy when I got on the gas. Every engine I've ever had which shook like that took itself apart after a few laps. Our guys are building bulletproof stuff."

Earnhardt had started 15th, but never led. He was running comfortably in the lead lap when the second yellow flag unfurled after 100 laps. Earnhardt made a routine four-tire pit stop. The RCR Enterprises crew had changed the right side tires and made the move over to the left side when Ernie Irvan's Chevrolet spun on pit road, hitting the Earnhardt car.

The men behind the champ: Crew chief Kirk Shelmerdine and car owner Richard Childress.

"I never saw the car (Irvan) coming," said car owner Richard Childress. "All I saw was my boys going down, then all hell broke loose.It almost pinned them to the pit wall, and my boys mean more to me than any points."

Irvan had shot out of his pits into the path of Alan Kulwicki. The two cars hit and Irvan spun into Earnhardt's pits.

Additional repairs were made to the Earnhardt car. Six laps after the green flag waved again, Earnhardt spun off the fourth turn.

NO PENALTY FOR EARNHARDT

During the next pit stop, Earnhardt pulled out of his pits with the lug nuts missing on the left side wheels. He skidded to a halt in the first turn as the wheels came off.

The RCR Enterprises pit crew ignored NASCAR officials orders to refrain from running onto the track apron. With tools in hand, the crew sprinted to the car and changed the tires.

Although rules strictly prohibit any service from behind conducted on the track surface, Earnhardt did not receive any penalty from NASCAR. He got back into the race and finished 25th, 14 laps off the pace. It is doubtful that he would have lost any additional positions had he waited for a utility truck to bring the car back to the pits. The next car behind Earnhardt was an additional 17 laps behind.

The two gladiators struggled again at Rockingham. Earnhardt started 20th while Martin lined up 21st on the grid. Neither driver led in the race and Earnhardt was able to shave four points off the deficit by finishing 10th. Martin finished 11th.

MARTIN'S WHEELS FALL OFF AT PHOENIX

While Earnhardt's wheels literally flew off at Charlotte, Martin's wheels fell off figuratively at Phoenix. Entering the race with a comfortable 45-point lead, Martin was running fourth in the late stages. That would have been good enough to take a 20-point lead into the season finale at Atlanta.

But Martin's tires were wearing thin. During a six lap stretch of green between the seventh and eighth caution periods, Martin lost three more positions. With less than 15 miles remaining, he elected to pit under yellow.

With four new tires in place, Martin returned to the track running 12th. Another caution for five laps prevented him from moving up in the order.

When the final green flag waved with six laps to go, Martin was able to pass only two cars. He finished 10th. Earnhardt led virtually all the way and won in a romp. He left Phoenix with a six-point lead.

"As it turned out, track position meant more than new tires," said car owner Jack Roush.

"We had a better race car than a 10th place car," said

Kim Novosat

Dale Earnhardt and Mark Martin during a press conference before the season finale at Atlanta.

Martin. "But things don't always work out the way you planned. We did the racer's thing to do. The decisions we made were right. It just didn't work out right."

CHANGING HORSES

For the Atlanta event, Ford Motor Company pulled out all the stops. In extensive testing at Atlanta prior to race week, Martin had four cars at his disposal. Not all were Roush Racing cars.

One of the cars being tested was a Robert Yates-built Ford Thunderbird. "We'll try to duplicate what we learned from Robert's car and put it on ours," said Martin. "The only way to beat Dale for this championship is to outrun him. Maybe this will help us do that."

Earnhardt said the pressure was getting to his Ford rivals. "We've noticed all the Ford people, but that doesn't bother us," said Earnhardt. "It's a little late in the year to be doing all that engineering."

Crew chief Kirk Shelmerdine said the extra effort the Roush team was taking wouldn't help. "Either way, they'll still be in a Ford," he chided.

When it came time to check into Atlanta Motor Speedway, the Roush team had the Yates car. "It was just faster in testing," explained Martin. "It's a new Mike Laughlin car and it has a different design. We might have been able to do some things to our car to make it run this fast. But the tests are over and we're here with this car."

On pole day, Earnhardt qualified sixth while Martin was 11th fastest.

In the 500-miler, Earnhardt clearly had the upper hand all day. Only once did Martin pass Earnhardt on the track.

Earnhardt was able to run with the leaders and finish third. Martin ran out of gas twice, got lapped once and wound up sixth. The man in black had wrapped up his fourth point championship by 26 points.

FOUR TIME CHAMP

Earnhardt said his fourth championship was more meaningful than his first in 1980. "I was too young to realize what it meant to win the Winston Cup championship then. It gets harder every year to win the championship. It's tougher than winning the Super Bowl," said Earnhardt.

"This one was the toughest of them all," he added. "Roush and Martin really made us sweat for it. To come from behind and race them all the way to the end made the championship worth that much more."

Martin was a gracious loser. "We got beat by the best," he said. "We pushed 'em, and we pushed 'em hard."

Martin refused to speculate on the 46-point penalty at Richmond early in the year. "There are 29 races that make up the Winston Cup schedule, not just one. We put that one behind us long ago."

It was the second time in NASCAR major league history that a penalty has decided the outcome of he Winston Cup championship. In 1950, Lee Petty had been stripped of all 809 points he had earned through the spring and early summer. He had competed in a non-NASCAR sanctioned event and paid dearly for it. He accumulated enough points from scratch to finish third in the final standings.

Race #1

Cope Snares Daytona 500 in Final Lap; Dale Suffers 'Hardt-breaker'

DAYTONA BEACH, FL (Feb. 18) – The huge hand of fate swatted Dale Earnhardt out of the lead in the 499th mile of the Daytona 500 and dropped stock car racing's biggest prize into the lap of unheralded Derrike Cope.

Earnhardt had dominated the 32nd annual running of NASCAR's premier event, leading for 155 of the 200 laps around Daytona International Speedway. The Kannapolis, N.C. driver appeared to be well on his way to winning his first Daytona 500 when the right rear tire blew as he sped into the third turn.

Earnhardt's RCR Enterprises Chevrolet wobbled into the upper groove as Cope, Terry Labonte, Bill Elliott and Ricky Rudd hustled past.

Cope, making his third Daytona 500 start, held off Labonte's Oldsmobile by two car lengths to score his first Winston Cup triumph. Elliott was a close third with Rudd fourth. Earnhardt miraculously managed to keep his errant car out of the wall and limped home fifth.

"I ran over something in the second turn," lamented Earnhardt, who has won virtually everything except the Daytona 500. "I could tell on the backstretch that the right rear tire was going down. My only hope was to ride it out, but the tire shredded in turn three.

"We were so close," Earnhardt continued. "He (Cope) won the race but I outran everybody all day. He lucked into it."

Cope, who had never scored a top five finish in his Winston Cup career which began in 1982, had put his Bob Whitcomb Chevrolet among the front-runners for the entire race. Prior to the fateful final lap, the Spanaway, Wash. driver had led briefly on three occasions. Following the day's third and final caution period eight laps from the finish, caused by Geoff Bodine's spin in turn one, Cope picked up the lead. "I told Derrike not to pit," reflected crew chief Buddy Parrott. "There were seven cars on the lead lap and it was our best shot to score a top finish."

Earnhardt motored past Cope on the restart with five laps remaining. "There was no way I could handle Dale," admitted Cope. "I was just hanging on to stay behind him so he could pull me to second place. I wasn't exactly sure what happened to Dale, but it looked and sounded like a tire failure. I was amazed he could catch it like that without hitting the wall."

Cope became the fourth driver to score his initial victory in the Daytona 500. Others were Tiny Lund (1963), Mario Andretti (1967) and Pete Hamilton (1970).

"Not in my wildest dreams did I think we

ISC

Derrike Cope #10 authored one of stock car racing's biggest upsets in the Daytona 500. The unheralded youngster from Spanaway, Wash. took the lead in the final lap when overwhelming favorite Dale Earnhardt #3 cut a tire.

Derrike Cope enjoys the fruits of his first NASCAR Winston Cup victory.

could come here and win this race," said Cope, who pocketed $188,150 for his entrance into stock car racing history.

Runner-up Labonte was taking his first ride in the Precision Products Oldsmobile owned by Richard Jackson. "I was just hanging on the last lap. I tried to make a move on Cope, but I couldn't catch him. You really have to feel for Dale. He was the class of the field," said Labonte.

Earnhardt had little trouble stepping away from the field in what was a sleeper until the final mile. With less than 30 laps remaining, he had built up a 27 second lead. No driver had passed him under green flag conditions all afternoon.

With about 50 laps left in the race, Harold Elliott, engine builder for Rusty Wallace's Blue Max team, remarked, "I think the only way anybody will beat Dale Earnhardt today is to shoot his tires out."

Nobody shot Earnhardt's tires out, but the results were the same.

"What a heartbreaker," responded car owner Richard Childress. "To be a half-mile from something you've dreamed about all your life – man, that's awfully hard to take. But that's racing. It'll bite you when you least expect it."

Winston Cup Series Race No. 1
200 Laps at Daytona Int'l Speedway
Daytona Beach, FL
"Daytona 500"

500 Miles on 2.5-mile Superspeedway
February 18, 1990

Fin	St	No.	Driver	Team / Car	Laps	Money	Status
1	12	10	Derrike Cope	Bob Whitcomb Chevrolet	200	$188,150	Running
2	20	1	Terry Labonte	Precision Products Olds	200	117,800	Running
3	4	9	Bill Elliott	Harry Melling Ford	200	114,100	Running
4	19	5	Ricky Rudd	Hendrick Motorsports Chevy	200	77,050	Running
5	2	3	Dale Earnhardt	RCR Enterprises Chevrolet	200	109,325	Running
6	10	8	Bobby Hillin,Jr.	Stavola Brothers Buick	200	63,225	Running
7	38	27	Rusty Wallace	Blue Max Pontiac	200	59,682	Running
8	24	30	Michael Waltrip	Bahari Racing Pontiac	199	46,200	Running
9	3	11	Geoff Bodine	Junior Johnson Ford	199	80,950	Running
10	30	15	Morgan Shepherd	Bud Moore Eng. Ford	199	44,125	Running
11	31	21	Neil Bonnett	Wood Brothers Ford	199	38,400	Running
12	32	66	Dick Trickle	Cale Yarborough Pontiac	199	36,200	Running
13	18	90	Ernie Irvan	Junie Donlavey Ford	199	31,455	Running
14	9	17	Darrell Waltrip	Hendrick Motorsports Chevy	199	49,340	Running
15	6	57	Jimmy Spencer	Rod Osterlund Pontiac	199	41,050	Running
16	14	83	Lake Speed	Speed Oldsmobile	199	29,930	Running
17	33	26	Brett Bodine	King Motorsports Buick	199	27,160	Running
18	5	33	Harry Gant	Leo Jackson Olds	199	58,990	Running
19	21	94	Sterling Marlin	Billy Hagan Oldsmobile	198	26,070	Running
20	16	28	Davey Allison	Robert Yates Racing Ford	198	31,935	Running
21	7	6	Mark Martin	Roush Racing Ford	198	39,955	Running
22	17	98	Butch Miller	Travis Carter Chevrolet	198	22,100	Running
23	42	71	Dave Marcis	Marcis Auto Racing Chevy	197	22,995	Running
24	22	42	Kyle Petty	SabCo Racing Pontiac	196	21,640	Handling
25	23	47	Jack Pennington	Derick Close Olds	196	20,935	Running
26	27	32	Joe Ruttman	Chuck Wellings Pontiac	196	22,950	Running
27	26	16	Larry Pearson	David Pearson Buick	195	22,275	Running
28	29	02	Rich Bickle	Bickle Oldsmobile	195	19,120	Running
29	37	52	Jimmy Means	Means Racing Pontiac	195	19,090	Running
30	28	75	Rick Wilson	RahMoc Oldsmobile	193	21,260	Engine
31	39	53	Jerry O'Neil	Alan Aroneck Oldsmobile	193	17,805	Running
32	41	2	Eddie Bierschwale	US Racing Oldsmobile	191	20,125	Running
33	34	68	Hut Stricklin	Hendrick/Tri-Star Chevy	190	18,195	Running
34	11	43	Richard Petty	Petty Enterprises Pontiac	183	22,840	Running
35	25	7	Alan Kulwicki	AK Racing Ford	180	19,835	Running
36	13	14	A.J.Foyt	Foyt Enterprises Olds	115	18,380	Quit
37	40	80	Jimmy Horton	George Smith Ford	108	16,800	Dr Train
38	36	20	Rob Moroso	Dick Moroso Olds	82	15,595	Crash
39	35	73	Phil Barkdoll	Barkdoll Oldsmobile	64	15,610	Engine
40	1	25	Ken Schrader	Hendrick Motorsports Chevy	58	34,900	Engine
41	15	12	Mike Alexander	Bobby Allison Buick	42	17,750	Crash
42	8	4	Phil Parsons	Morgan-McClure Olds	41	25,100	Crash

Time of Race: 3 hours, 0 minutes, 59 seconds
Average Speed: 165.761 mph
Pole Winner: Ken Schrader - 196.515 mph
Lap Leaders: Geoff Bodine 1, Dale Earnhardt 2-27, Jimmy Spencer 28-31, Earnhardt 32-39, Bill Elliott 40, Earnhardt 41-44, Jack Pennington 45-50, Mark Martin 51-53, Derrike Cope 54, Earnhardt 55-90, Davey Allison 91-92, G.Bodine 93-95, Bobby Hillin, Jr. 96, Lake Speed 97-99, Harry Gant 100, Earnhardt 101-134, G.Bodine 135-137, Ricky Rudd 138, G.Bodine 139, Terry Labonte 140-146, Hillin, Jr. 147-149, Earnhardt 150-179, Cope 180, Earnhardt 181-193, Cope 194-195, Earnhardt 196-199, Cope 200.
27 lead changes among 13 drivers.
Cautions: 3 for 15 laps Margin of Victory: 1.5 car lengths

All-pro crew chief Kirk Shelmerdine added, "This is as bad as it gets. I'd hate to be our rivals the rest of the year because we're highly peeved."

The only driver who seemed poised to give Earnhardt a run for the money was Ken Schrader, who racked up his third straight Daytona 500 pole in qualifying. But Schrader was forced to start 40th in the 42 car field when he trashed his swift car in the final lap of Thurs-

ISC

Geoff Bodine, driving Junior Johnson's Ford, inherited the pole position when fastest qualifier Ken Schrader crashed in the Twin 125 and had to use a back-up car.

day's 125-mile qualifier.

According to NASCAR rules, a driver must start in the rear if a back-up vehicle replaces the primary car for the race. Curiously – and for the first time in NASCAR history – a driver retained credit for winning the pole despite running a back-up car. That also allowed Schrader to have a shot at winning the $212,800 bonus from Unocal for winning the race after starting on the pole.

NASCAR's decision to permit Schrader to keep the pole and have a shot at the bonus money brought a sharp response from Earnhardt, who had been the second fastest qualifier. "The pole car is out of the race and I should be moved up to have a shot at that bonus," said Earnhardt. "That's the way they did it a few years ago."

Earnhardt was right about that. In 1983, Cale Yarborough had won the Daytona 500 pole but wiped out his car in a reverse-flip. Although Cale had earned the inside front row spot, he lost credit for the pole when he was forced to bring in a back-up car. Ironically, the RCR Enterprises car then driven by Rudd assumed credit for the pole. "They must have changed the rules," said Childress, "but I didn't know they had done so. Now we don't have a

Derrike Cope #10 flashes across the finish line two car-lengths ahead of runner-up Terry Labone #1. Bill Elliott was a close third.

shot at the two hundred grand."

Schrader came from 40th to second place in the first 100-miles, but the engine blew in his Hendrick Motorsports Chevrolet in the 58th lap. The car was running real good, but something broke in the engine. I told the guys (his pit crew) that we didn't need any good luck to win this race. We didn't need any bad luck either, and that's what we got."

The yellow flag was out only three times, and only once for a multi-car tangle. Phil Parsons, taking his first ride in the Morgan-McClure Oldsmobile, snagged bumpers with rookie Rob Moroso in the 42nd lap. "I got clipped in the right rear and turned into the wall," said Parsons. "It was a screw-up on somebody's part." Alan Kulwicki and Mike Alexander were also involved.

Alexander was driving a Buick fielded by Bobby Allison, who was performing an active role for the first time since his disabling injury at Pocono in 1988. Allison was constantly greeted by well-wishers. "Everybody always asks me 'How are you'? Once in a while, I'd like to say 'I'm not worth a hoot'. But the fact is I'm slightly better than not worth a hoot."

Richard Petty authored the first caution when he looped his Pontiac in the second turn early in the race. Petty continued in the race and wound up 34th.

The highest finishing freshman driver in the race was Georgian Jack Pennington, a dirt track racer for more than a decade. Pennington led the race for six laps.

Sixth place went to Bobby Hillin,Jr., who excels on the ultra-fast superspeedways. Rounding out the top 10 were Rusty Wallace, Michael Waltrip, Geoff Bodine and Morgan Shepherd.

Cope averaged 165.761 mph in giving car owner Bob Whitcomb his first Winston Cup triumph.

ISC

Frantic pit work during the Daytona 500.

Race #2

Martin Fined and Docked 46 Points After Disputed Richmond Win

RICHMOND,VA (Feb. 25) – Mark Martin scampered out of the pits ahead of his rivals and led the final 16 laps to win the Pontiac Excitement 400 at Richmond International Raceway. It was the second career victory for the Batesville, Ark. Ford driver.

Following a lengthy post-race inspection performed by NASCAR technical officials, Martin and his Roush Racing team were fined a record $40,000 and stripped of 46 important Winston Cup points for an infraction in the carburetor of the winning car.

NASCAR Technical Director Dick Beaty said the carburetor on Martin's Ford was mounted on the engine's intake manifold with an aluminum block spacer half an inch thicker than the two inches allowed.

Martin's Team Manager Steve Hmiel said spacers more than two inches thick have been allowed if they are *welded* to the manifold, and that Martin's engine was in violation because its spacer was *bolted* to the carburetor.

"It's a stupid rule," Hmiel claimed. "All you have to do is weld the spacer to the top of the manifold and it

Winston Cup Series Race No. 2
400 Laps at Richmond Int'l Raceway
Richmond, VA
"Pontiac Excitement 400"

300 Miles on 0.75-mile Short Track
February 25, 1990

Fin	St	No.	Driver	Team / Car	Laps	Money	Status
1	6	6	Mark Martin	Roush Racing Ford	400	$59,150	Running
2	4	3	Dale Earnhardt	RCR Enterprises Chevrolet	400	42,600	Running
3	1	5	Ricky Rudd	Hendrick Motorsports Chevy	400	25,050	Running
4	17	9	Bill Elliott	Melling Performance Ford	400	16,650	Running
5	5	66	Dick Trickle	Cale Yarborough Pontiac	400	14,325	Running
6	18	27	Rusty Wallace	Blue Max Pontiac	400	15,400	Running
7	14	15	Morgan Shepherd	Bud Moore Eng. Ford	400	8,525	Running
8	10	26	Brett Bodine	King Motorsports Buick	400	8,025	Running
9	21	57	Jimmy Spencer	Rod Osterlund Pontiac	400	6,425	Running
10	13	25	Ken Schrader	Hendrick Motorsports Chevy	400	11,800	Running
11	7	42	Kyle Petty	SabCo Racing Pontiac	399	5,075	Running
12	8	17	Darrell Waltrip	Hendrick Motorsports Chevy	399	10,450	Running
13	11	94	Sterling Marlin	Billy Hagan Oldsmobile	399	6,725	Running
14	24	12	Mike Alexander	Bobby Allison Buick	397	3,275	Running
15	9	20	Rob Moroso	Dick Moroso Oldsmobile	397	4,400	Running
16	27	19	Chad Little	Chuck Little Ford	397	3,125	Running
17	35	71	Dave Marcis	Marcis Auto Racing Chevy	397	6,832	Running
18	32	52	Jimmy Means	Means Racing Pontiac	394	4,125	Running
19	29	01	Mickey Gibbs	Gibbs-West Ford	394	2,900	Running
20	31	28	Davey Allison	Robert Yates Racing Ford	393	9,650	Running
21	34	2	Rick Mast	US Racing Pontiac	392	5,825	Running
22	16	90	Ernie Irvan	Junie Donlavey Ford	387	2,775	Clutch
23	30	16	Larry Pearson	Pearson Racing Buick	386	5,550	Running
24	3	7	Alan Kulwicki	AK Racing Ford	358	7,025	Running
25	12	21	Neil Bonnett	Wood Brothers Ford	354	5,450	Battery
26	15	4	Phil Parsons	Morgan-McClure Olds	354	5,275	Running
27	23	30	Michael Waltrip	Bahari Racing Pontiac	350	5,275	Running
28	19	98	Butch Miller	Travis Carter Chevrolet	307	2,545	Crash
29	20	10	Derrike Cope	Bob Whitcomb Chevrolet	305	8,225	Crash
30	26	75	Rick Wilson	RahMoc Oldsmobile	283	6,100	Crash
31	28	8	Bobby Hillin,Jr.	Stavola Brothers Buick	230	4,475	Crash
32	25	1	Terry Labonte	Precision Products Olds	229	4,450	Engine
33	2	11	Geoff Bodine	Junior Johnson Ford	200	8,560	Engine
34	33	04	Bill Meacham	Charles Meacham Olds	87	2,425	Rear End
35	36	43	Richard Petty	Petty Enterprises Pontiac	83	2,425	Crash
36	22	33	Harry Gant	Leo Jackson Oldsmobile	75	8,250	Engine

Time of Race: 3 hours, 15 minutes, 18 seconds
Average Speed: 92.158 mph
Pole Winner: Ricky Rudd – 119.617 mph
Lap Leaders: Ricky Rudd 1-10, Alan Kulwicki 11-78, Geoff Bodine 79-119, Dale Earnhardt 120-130, Kulwicki 131-134, Rusty Wallace 135-136, Butch Miller 137, Wallace 138-174, Rudd 175-182, Earnhardt 183-204, Kulwicki 205-232, Wallace 233-257, Earnhardt 258-265, Wallace 266-294, Rudd 295-310, Dick Trickle 311-323, Rudd 324-329, Wallace 330-384, Mark Martin 385-400.
18 lead changes among 8 drivers.
Cautions: 12 for 75 laps Margin of Victory: 3.0 seconds

Brian Czobat

Mark Martin's victory at Richmond was tempered by heavy penalties handed down by NASCAR.

could be eight inches high." Hmiel added that the violation was the result of "a communication problem within our company. It's really an unfortunate thing for (crew chief) Robin (Pemberton). What happened is NASCAR lowered the engine ground clearance an inch and we needed to raise the carburetor an equal amount to maintain proper air flow. We got caught in what we think is a gray area of the rules."

Team owner Jack Roush suspended Pemberton for 30 days after the penalties were announced but reinstated him 24 hours later.

The fine was the largest in Winston Cup racing since Richard Petty was fined $35,000 (and lost 104 points) after his victory in the 1983 Charlotte 500. Ironically, Pemberton was Petty's crew chief that day.

"We didn't have time to do the welding. We were preoccupied and overlooked it. I hope it didn't cause too much embarrassment for the team, the sponsors or NASCAR," said Pemberton.

Martin's victory was upheld but he lost a big chunk of points which determine the national championship. Beaty said that 46 points were taken away from Martin because that was equal to the distance between first and 10th place, the finish position of the last car on the lead lap. "The violation might not have been discovered if they had finished fourth (or lower)."

Martin had started sixth on the grid and never led until

Crew Chief Robin Pemberton was suspended by team owner Jack Roush, but was reinstated a day later.

pit strategy put him at the front of the field following the day's 12th and final caution flag. With 10 cars on the lead lap, his rivals opted to change four tires under the yellow flag. Martin only got two new tires.

When the green flag came out with 13 laps to go, Martin motored away from the pack. He finished 3 seconds in front of runner-up Dale Earnhardt, who survived a bumping incident with Rusty Wallace in the final laps. Pole winner Ricky Rudd took third place with Bill Elliott and Dick Trickle completing the top five.

Earnhardt took the Winston Cup point lead by five points over Rudd. Martin would have jumped to fifth in the standings, 55 points behind Earnhardt. However, he was officially logged in 12th place, 101 points out of first place.

Richard Childress, owner of Earnhardt's Chevrolet, said the violation found on Martin's Ford did not have any bearing on the outcome of the race. "It didn't win the race for them," said Childress. "They won it with good strategy, making a two tire pit stop when the rest of us changed four."

Earnhardt's run into second place was nothing short of amazing. In Saturday's final practice session, he crashed the car beyond repair, forcing the RCR Enterprises team to bring in a back-up car designed for intermediate tracks. After posting the fourth best qualifying time, Earnhardt was forced to start the race at the rear of the field. It did not seem to hamper his charge to get to the front. By the 48th lap, he was in sixth place. He took the lead for the first time on lap 120. In all, Earnhardt led three times for 41 laps.

During the final 13 lap green flag run, Earnhardt and Wallace locked horns. Wallace, running second, was holding Earnhardt at bay until the cars came together off turn two. The contact knocked Wallace out of shape and he drifted back to a sixth place finish. Wallace had led the most laps – 148 – in the race.

""I bumped him a little bit," said Earnhardt. "I didn't mean to lay on him or anything, but it was getting too close to the end of the race to back off. I hope he's not too mad at me."

Wallace was angered but held his emotions. After the race ended, Wallace pulled his Pontiac nose-to-nose with Earnhardt's front bumper, remained in the car and glared at his opponent. "It was nothing special," said Wallace, biting his tongue. "We got together in turn two. We were just racing."

Alan Kulwicki, privateer trying to build his own team into a winner, led for 100 laps and was pulling away from the field when he tangled with Phil Parsons. Both had slipped in oil deposited by Bobby Hillin, Jr.'s blown engine in the 233rd lap. "I can't believe it happened," said Kulwicki. "My team doesn't deserve this kind of luck. The car was running great. We had everybody covered."

The race was viewed by a crowd of 50,000 which braved bitter weather conditions. Temperatures were hovering around the 20 degree mark with brisk winds dropping the chill factor to near zero.

Race #3

Kyle Rolls (Royce) To Victory at The 'Rock'; Wins $284,450

ROCKINGHAM, NC (March 4) – Kyle Petty led 433 of the 492 laps around the North Carolina Motor Speedway and romped to victory in the GM Goodwrench 500 to cash in on one of the biggest prizes in

Kyle Petty broke the bank at Rockingham.

NCMS

Kyle Petty earned $284,450 when he won the Goodwrench 500.

NASCAR Winston Cup racing.

Petty's third career triumph earned him $284,450 – padded considerably by Unocal's $220,400 bonus going to the winner of the pole and the race – and outdistanced runner-up Geoff Bodine by nearly a lap. Petty's overjoyed Team Owner, Felix Sabates, rewarded his young driver with a Rolls Royce after the victory.

Kyle's winning prize was erroneously reported as a record for NASCAR's premier division. Bill Elliott's single race earnings of $1,053,725 in the 1985 Southern 500 remains the all-time benchmark. Kyle's winnings were boosted by unclaimed rollover bonus money, which was available for one driver (Petty) to win one race. Elliott's Winston Million prize in 1985 was under a similar format – a prize unclaimed by other drivers and then available for one driver (Elliott) to win one race.

The outcome was hardly in doubt, although Petty admitted he had visions of Dale Earnhardt's Daytona heartbreaker dancing in his head during the final laps. " I did get a little nervous right there near the end," said Petty. "What happened to Dale on the last lap of the Daytona 500 is every driver's nightmare."

Kyle dashed off from his pole position to lead the first 52 laps. He ran away from the field and only lost the lead during pit stops – usually under the yellow flag. He had put the entire field a lap down until Bodine hustled past Kyle in the final 10 laps. "I just let him and Earnhardt go on that last restart," said

NCMS

The Prince of the Petty clan proudly shines in Victory Lane.

the third generation driver. "I thought it would be pretty foolish to wreck racing a couple of lapped cars."

Earnhardt struggled to finish 10th, three laps off the pace. He was able to emerge from Rockingham with an eight point lead over Rusty Wallace in the Winston Cup standings.

Ken Schrader came back from a savage practice crash to take third place honors. Schrader had "hit the wall a ton" on a practice session on February 22. Fourth place Sterling Marlin had earned the 10th starting position in qualifying, but he started at the rear following a practice crash which forced the use of a back-up car. Marlin, in Billy Hagan's Oldsmobile, wound up fourth. Fifth place went to Wallace.

Hut Stricklin drove in place of Davey Allison, who fainted in the garage area's men's room after playfully wrestling with a crewman two days before the race. Allison spent the night in a Charlotte hospital undergoing medical tests. NASCAR officials said he could start the race in order to receive championship points, but he could drive no more than a single lap.

Stricklin, who practiced in Allison's Robert Yates Racing Ford on Saturday, took over in the second lap.

Winston Cup Series Race No. 3
492 Laps at N.C. Motor Speedway
Rockingham, NC
"GM Goodwrench 500"
500.364 Miles on 1.017-mile Superspeedway
March 4, 1990

Fin	St	No.	Driver	Team / Car	Laps	Money	Status
1	1	42	Kyle Petty	SabCo Pontiac	492	$284,450	Running
2	8	11	Geoff Bodine	Junior Johnson Ford	492	31,825	Running
3	6	25	Ken Schrader	Hendrick Motorsports Chevy	491	24,575	Running
4	10	94	Sterling Marlin	Billy Hagan Oldsmobile	490	17,725	Running
5	7	27	Rusty Wallace	Blue Max Racing Pontiac	490	21,625	Running
6	5	17	Darrell Waltrip	Hendrick Motorsports Chevy	489	16,275	Running
7	27	15	Morgan Shepherd	Bud Moore Eng. Ford	489	10,975	Running
8	26	57	Jimmy Spencer	Rod Osterlund Pontiac	489	10,525	Running
9	28	1	Terry Labonte	Precision Products Olds	489	10,225	Running
10	4	3	Dale Earnhardt	RCR Enterprises Chevy	489	17,150	Running
11	19	33	Harry Gant	Leo Jackson Oldsmobile	488	12,775	Running
12	15	10	Derrike Cope	Bob Whitcomb Chevrolet	487	10,475	Running
13	37	98	Butch Miller	Travis Carter Chevrolet	486	5,832	Running
14	12	4	Phil Parsons	Morgan-McClure Olds	486	8,975	Running
15	31	01	Mickey Gibbs	Gibbs-West Ford	484	5,350	Running
16	30	12	Mike Alexander	Bobby Allison Buick	484	4,775	Running
17	24	8	Bobby Hillin,Jr.	Stavola Brothers Buick	483	8,425	Running
18	29	75	Rick Wilson	RahMoc Oldsmobile	482	8,075	Running
19	20	2	Rick Mast	US Racing Pontiac	479	7,575	Running
20	22	16	Larry Pearson	Pearson Racing Buick	477	8,000	Running
21	33	52	Jimmy Means	Means Racing Pontiac	470	4,925	Running
22	16	71	Dave Marcis	Marcis Auto Racing Chevy	461	6,800	Running
23	13	66	Dick Trickle	Cale Yarborough Pontiac	439	7,600	Crash
24	35	82	Mark Stahl	Stahl Racing Ford	434	3,675	Running
25	21	26	Brett Bodine	King Motorsports Buick	429	6,450	Running
26	2	6	Mark Martin	Roush Racing Ford	420	12,050	Valve
27	3	7	Alan Kulwicki	AK Racing Ford	415	6,800	T Chain
28	14	30	Michael Waltrip	Bahari Racing Pontiac	398	6,125	Engine
29	17	90	Ernie Irvan	Junie Donlavey Ford	397	3,375	Crash
30	9	20	Rob Moroso	Dick Moroso Olds	324	4,075	Engine
31	25	5	Ricky Rudd	Hendrick Motorsports Chevy	302	6,600	Oil Pan
32	32	43	Richard Petty	Petty Enterprises Pontiac	294	3,775	Engine
33	11	9	Bill Elliott	Melling Performance Ford	265	11,600	Crash
34	18	28	Davey Allison*	Robert Yates Racing Ford	263	10,950	Engine
35	36	70	J.D.McDuffie	McDuffie Racing Pontiac	171	2,825	Handling
36	23	21	Neil Bonnett	Wood Brothers Ford	95	5,350	Engine
37	34	93	Charlie Baker	Patsy Salmon Buick	49	2,725	Engine
38	38	91	J.T.Hayes	Junie Donlavey Ford	10	2,700	Flagged

Time of Race: 4 hours, 4 minutes, 21 seconds
Average Speed: 122.864 mph
Pole Winner: Kyle Petty – 148.751 mph
Lap Leaders: Kyle Petty 1-52, Rusty Wallace 53-55, K.Petty 56-82, Wallace 83-107, K.Petty 108-126, Ricky Rudd 127-136, Sterling Marlin 137-139, Bill Elliott 140, Dick Trickle 141, Terry Labonte 142, Geoff Bodine 143, K.Petty 144-169, Elliott 170, K.Petty 171-248, Rudd 249-253, Mark Martin 254, K.Petty 255-376, Martin 377-383, K.Petty 384-492.
18 lead changes among 9 drivers.
Cautions: 8 for 36 laps Margin of Victory: 26 seconds
*Relieved by Hut Stricklin

Winston Cup Series Race No. 4
328 Laps at Atlanta Int'l Raceway
Hampton, GA
"Motorcraft Quality Parts 500"
499.216 Miles on 1.522-mile Superspeedway
March 18, 1990

Fin	St	No.	Driver	Team / Car	Laps	Money	Status
1	1	3	Dale Earnhardt	RCR Enterprises Chevrolet	328	$85,000	Running
2	3	15	Morgan Shepherd	Bud Moore Eng. Ford	328	36,000	Running
3	30	4	Ernie Irvan	Morgan-McClure Olds	328	31,957	Running
4	14	25	Ken Schrader	Hendrick Motorsports Chevy	328	22,900	Running
5	17	6	Mark Martin	Roush Racing Ford	328	20,850	Running
6	5	42	Kyle Petty	SabCo Racing Pontiac	328	15,075	Running
7	10	11	Geoff Bodine	Junior Johnson Ford	328	19,250	Running
8	31	7	Alan Kulwicki	AK Racing Ford	327	11,625	Running
9	21	33	Harry Gant	Leo Jackson Oldsmobile	327	13,600	Running
10	9	94	Sterling Marlin	Billy Hagan Oldsmobile	326	12,300	Running
11	15	26	Brett Bodine	King Motorsports Buick	326	9,495	Running
12	7	9	Bill Elliott	Melling Performance Ford	326	13,875	Running
13	28	28	Davey Allison	Robert Yates Racing Ford	326	12,155	Running
14	11	66	Dick Trickle	Cale Yarborough Pontiac	326	9,935	Running
15	6	57	Jimmy Spencer	Rod Osterlund Pontiac	325	8,680	Running
16	16	8	Bobby Hillin,Jr.	Stavola Brothers Buick	325	8,545	Running
17	29	75	Rick Wilson	RahMoc Oldsmobile	324	8,235	Running
18	27	21	Neil Bonnett	Wood Brothers Ford	322	7,625	Running
19	34	19	Chad Little	Chuck Little Ford	322	4,415	Running
20	18	98	Butch Miller	Travis Carter Chevrolet	321	4,970	Running
21	22	90	Buddy Baker	Junie Donlavey Ford	319	4,135	Running
22	20	71	Dave Marcis	Marcis Auto Racing Chevy	317	7,050	Running
23	25	12	Mike Alexander	Bobby Allison Buick	317	3,965	Running
24	2	27	Rusty Wallace	Blue Max Racing Pontiac	316	14,930	Engine
25	32	43	Richard Petty	Petty Enterprises Pontiac	315	4,845	Running
26	8	17	Darrell Waltrip	Hendrick Motorsports Chevy	312	12,755	Running
27	4	5	Ricky Rudd	Hendrick Motorsports Chevy	307	6,545	Running
28	39	82	Mark Stahl	Stahl Racing Ford	300	3,660	Running
29	13	10	Derrike Cope	Bob Whitcomb Chevrolet	255	8,625	Engine
30	40	47	Jack Pennington	Derick Close Olds	253	4,290	Engine
31	23	52	Jimmy Means	Means Racing Pontiac	251	4,230	Engine
32	35	36	H.B.Bailey	Bailey Pontiac	214	3,480	Engine
33	36	20	Rob Moroso	Dick Moroso Olds	149	3,670	Engine
34	24	16	Larry Pearson	Pearson Racing Buick	135	6,095	Engine
35	26	2	Rick Mast	US Racing Pontiac	113	6,050	Engine
36	33	77	Ken Ragan	Marvin Ragan Ford	101	3,350	Valve
37	38	18	Hut Stricklin	Tri Star Motorsports Pontiac	84	3,330	Valve
38	19	30	Michael Waltrip	Bahari Racing Pontiac	53	5,960	T Chain
39	37	01	Mickey Gibbs	Gibbs-West Ford	40	3,285	Valve
40	12	1	Terry Labonte	Precision Products Olds	4	6,580	Engine

Time of Race: 3 hours, 10 minutes, 58 seconds
Average Speed: 156.849 mph
Pole Winner: No Time Trials
Lap Leaders: Rusty Wallace 1, Dale Earnhardt 2-56, Ken Schrader 57-61, Geoff Bodine 62-64, Darrell Waltrip 65, Earnhardt 66-110, G.Bodine 111-121, Sterling Marlin 122-123, Earnhardt 124-165, Schrader 166, G.Bodine 167-184, Earnhardt 185-219, Morgan Shepherd 220-227, Schrader 228-231, G.Bodine 232-234, Ernie Irvan 235, Kyle Petty 236-238, Earnhardt 239-275, G.Bodine 276-320, Shepherd 321-326, Earnhardt 327-328.
21 lead changes among 9 drivers.
Cautions: 3 for 10 laps Margin of Victory: 0.32 second

The driver change put Stricklin two laps behind.

Stricklin was able to make up a lap under green by passing Petty, but engine failure put him out after completing 263 laps. Bill Elliott bounced off Stricklin and hit the wall, ending his day.

Accidents also took out Ernie Irvan, who was in Junie Donlavey's Ford, and Dick Trickle, who had led for the second race in a row in Cale Yarborough's Pontiac.

Mark Martin's Ford dropped a valve in the final 100 miles and wound up 26th.

Petty ended a 69-race winless skid on the major league NASCAR touring series. "This win clears the air about my other two wins (at Richmond in 1986 and the World 600 at Charlotte in 1987). Everybody knows we won those races because of attrition. We didn't have the best car either time. It wasn't like that today. We dominated. It was totally cosmic the way we ran today," said Kyle.

The victory moved Petty into fifth place in the Winston Cup standings. Curiously, 11 of the top 12 in the Winston Cup point standings had not won a race.

Brian Czobat

Ernie Irvan donned a Kodak Film uniform for the first time at Atlanta and finished third.

Race #4

Earnhardt Snookers Shepherd; Captures Atlanta 500

HAMPTON, GA (March 18) – Dale Earnhardt made a daring three-abreast pass for the lead two laps from the finish and emerged victorious in the Motorcraft Quality Parts 500 at Atlanta International Raceway. It was the 40th Winston Cup career victory for the 38 year-old Kannapolis, N.C. driver.

Earnhardt had little trouble manhandling the 40 car field – leading for 216 laps – but a series of events late in the race changed the complexion. Earnhardt made a routine green flag pit stop with 52 laps remaining, but the RCR Enterprises team had trouble on the stop, taking 19.9 seconds to complete the 2-tire change. That left Earnhardt a lap behind leader Geoff Bodine.

Bodine pitted on lap 291 – allowing Earnhardt to get back into the lead lap – and was out in 13.2 seconds. When he resumed top speed, Bodine held a 6.8 second lead over Earnhardt.

Earnhardt chopped the deficit to a single car length when Rusty Wallace's blown engine brought out the second caution on lap 318. All cars on the lead lap took fresh tires with the exception of Morgan Shepherd, who had quietly put Bud Moore's Ford into contention.

On the restart, Shepherd led Mark Martin, whose pit crew work was the quickest under the yellow flag stops. Earnhardt and Bodine lined up fourth and fifth.

Only a lap of green was run before Bodine tangled with Bobby Hillin, Jr., who was three laps off the pace. Earnhardt scampered past Martin into second as the third caution came out.

"Cars a lap down won't let you race for the win," Bodine fumed afterwards. "That's just bad racing. I'm going to ask for a new rule – no double-file restarts in the last 10 laps of a race...not with guys acting like that."

The mishap knocked Bodine down to seventh in the final order.

For the final two-lap restart, Shepherd held command with the lapped car of Alan Kulwicki along side. Kulwicki raced Shepherd into the first turn, carrying Shepherd higher than he wanted. Earnhardt dived under Kulwicki and Shepherd in one fell swoop and emerged in the lead when the cars hit the backstretch.

Brian Czobat

Danny "Chocolate" Myers stands ready in Dale Earnhardt's pit.

"I didn't have time to look at what Alan and Morgan might have been doing," said Earnhardt. "The groove is wide over in that turn and I saw a hole open up on the inside. I think I went lower than I usually do but there was plenty of room."

Shepherd maintained Kulwicki interfered with his chance at victory. "He should have let me have the hole since I was racing for the win and he was a lap down," contended Shepherd, who was winner of this event in 1986 with Jack Beebe's team. "He slowed me up and let Earnhardt go under me."

Kulwicki claimed he did not cost Shepherd the race. "I don't think I did anything wrong. If Earnhardt got tires and he didn't, I don't see how Shepherd could have thought he would have won the race."

Brian Czobat

Buddy Baker ended a two-year retirement at Atlanta.

Shepherd was forced to settle for second, 0.32-second behind the winner. Ernie Irvan finished third in his maiden voyage in the Morgan-McClure Oldsmobile, replacing Phil Parsons. Ken Schrader edged Mark Martin for fourth after a motorized rubdown in the final lap.

Heavy rains washed out all qualifying and the starting grid was made up on team owner points. That put Irvan back in 30th place, but he drove through traffic like a seasoned veteran. "The way he handled that car didn't surprise me at all," said team owner Larry McClure. "This should lay to rest all speculation about why I hired him."

McClure had been fielding cars on the Winston Cup tour for seven previous years without a victory.

Buddy Baker took the vacancy in Junie Donlavey's Ford when Irvan shifted seats. It was Baker's first Winston Cup effort since 1988. Baker wound up 21st in the 40 car field.

Veteran car owner Donlavey hired Baker with a simple procedure. "I didn't have no 20-page contract to sign," said Donlavey. "We just shook hands and I told him to go racin'."

Earnhardt stretched his Winston Cup lead to 58 points over Shepherd, who moved past Wallace into second. Martin was still buried in 13th place in the standings, 175 points behind Earnhardt.

Race #5

Earnhardt Tames Darlington; Bonnett Hurt

DARLINGTON, SC (April 1) – Dale Earnhardt continued his mastery of Darlington Raceway – disregarding the slogan that the crusty old racing palace is 'Too Tough To Tame' – by motoring to a convincing victory in the TranSouth 500. It was Earnhardt's second straight win at the 1.3660-mile oval and his fifth in the last nine races.

Brian Czobat

Dale tamed Darlington again.

Neil Bonnett was transported to a Florence Hospital suffering from head injuries and severe amnesia following a multi-car collision in the 212th lap. Ernie Irvan, in his second start with the Morgan-McClure team, triggered the pile-up when he skidded into leader Ken Schrader. Irvan was 10 laps behind at the time.

Irvan, who started third, spun early in the race and was hopelessly out of contention. On a restart following the sixth caution of the day, Irvan was battling new leader Schrader to get one of his laps back. Coming off the fourth turn, Irvan's Oldsmobile slipped sideways and whacked Schrader, setting off a wild melee that eventually involved 13 cars.

Bonnett's Wood Brothers Ford was caught in the middle of the wreck, but did not seem to sustain any hard knocks. The extent of Bonnett's injuries was largely a mystery.

Irvan's exploits brought sharp responses from several other drivers. "I'd like to know what in the heck somebody 10 laps down is doing up there in the first place," barked Sterling Marlin. "He was in over his head. It was really stupid."

"Ernie needs to calm down a little," said Schrader, who recovered to finish 10th, one lap behind. "You don't need to do that stuff when you're 10 laps down."

Irvan said he was surprised the leader of the race was running so hard. "I didn't think Schrader would race

Winston Cup Series Race No. 5
367 Laps at Darlington Raceway
Darlington, SC
"TranSouth 500"

501.322 Miles on 1.366-mile Superspeedway
April 1, 1990

Fin	St	No.	Driver	Team / Car	Laps	Money	Status
1	15	3	Dale Earnhardt	RCR Enterprises Chevrolet	367	$61,985	Running
2	2	6	Mark Martin	Roush Racing Ford	367	34,460	Running
3	13	28	Davey Allison	Robert Yates Racing Ford	367	25,795	Running
4	1	11	Geoff Bodine	Junior Johnson Ford	367	28,110	Running
5	19	15	Morgan Shepherd	Bud Moore Eng. Ford	367	17,610	Running
6	20	33	Harry Gant	Leo Jackson Oldsmobile	367	14,880	Running
7	17	9	Bill Elliott	Melling Performance Ford	367	15,070	Running
8	4	26	Brett Bodine	King Motorsports Buick	367	11,675	Running
9	9	30	Michael Waltrip	Bahari Racing Pontiac	367	11,140	Running
10	6	25	Ken Schrader	Hendrick Motorsports Chevy	366	14,585	Running
11	16	17	Darrell Waltrip	Hendrick Motorsports Chevy	366	14,155	Running
12	22	8	Bobby Hillin,Jr.	Stavola Brothers Buick	365	7,050	Running
13	8	42	Kyle Petty	SabCo Racing Pontiac	363	9,780	Running
14	28	1	Terry Labonte	Precision Products Olds	361	8,590	Running
15	34	71	Dave Marcis	Marcis Auto Racing Chevy	360	9,892	Running
16	32	19	Chad Little	Chuck Little Ford	360	4,215	Running
17	31	98	Butch Miller	Travis Carter Chevrolet	360	4,085	Running
18	11	27	Rusty Wallace	Blue Max Pontiac	359	14,900	Running
19	35	12	Mike Alexander	Bobby Allison Buick	356	3,790	Crash
20	29	47	Jack Pennington	Derick Close Olds	354	5,635	Running
21	25	43	Richard Petty	Petty Enterprises Pontiac	349	5,390	Engine
22	21	66	Dick Trickle	Cale Yarborough Pontiac	298	8,120	Engine
23	14	7	Alan Kulwicki	AK Racing Ford	295	6,750	Crash
24	10	5	Ricky Rudd	Hendrick Motorsports Chevy	294	6,480	Running
25	33	57	Jimmy Spencer	Rod Osterlund Pontiac	280	6,385	Running
26	12	20	Rob Moroso	Dick Moroso Olds	234	3,470	Handling
27	24	10	Derrike Cope	Bob Whitcomb Chevrolet	224	8,170	Engine
28	5	94	Sterling Marlin	Billy Hagan Olds	211	6,570	Crash
29	26	75	Rick Wilson	RahMoc Racing Olds	211	5,910	Crash
30	18	21	Neil Bonnett	Wood Brothers Ford	209	5,775	Crash
31	38	52	Jimmy Means	Means Racing Pontiac	208	3,665	Crash
32	3	4	Ernie Irvan	Morgan-McClure Olds	201	6,680	Crash
33	40	36	H.B.Bailey	Bailey Pontiac	168	2,870	Flagged
34	39	38	Dick Johnson	Down Under Ford	95	2,835	Handling
35	37	70	J.D.McDuffie	McDuffie Racing Pontiac	82	2,800	H Gasket
36	27	51	Hut Stricklin	Hendrick Motorsports Chevy	82	2,765	Flagged
37	7	46	Greg Sacks	Hendrick Motorsports Chevy	61	2,730	Cranksha
38	36	01	Mickey Gibbs	Gibbs-West Ford	53	2,715	Engine
39	23	2	Rick Mast	US Racing Pontiac	42	5,350	Engine
40	30	90	Buddy Baker	Junie Donlavey Ford	9	2,650	Engine

Time of Race: 4 hours, 2 minutes, 26 seconds
Average Speed: 124.073 mph
Pole Winner: Geoff Bodine – 162.996 mph
Lap Leaders: Geoff Bodine 1-23, Alan Kulwicki 24-25, Mickey Gibbs 26, G.Bodine 27-53, Dale Earnhardt 54-78, Jimmy Spencer 79, Earnhardt 80-99, G.Bodine 100-170, Bill Elliott 171-173, G.Bodine 174-205, Ken Schrader 206-211, G.Bodine 212, Morgan Shepherd 213-223, Earnhardt 224-247, Shepherd 248-275, Dick Trickle 276-280, Brett Bodine 281, Shepherd 282-306, Earnhardt 307-348, Shepherd 349, Earnhardt 350-367.
20 lead changes among 10 drivers.
Cautions : 10 for 51 laps Margin of Victory: 0.25-second

Greg Fielden

Mark Martin ran a strong second at Darlington.

me that hard," said Irvan in a bold statement. "I was trying to get one of my laps back and Kenny was racing me awfully hard. I just got loose and spun and Kenny spun, too. It was just hard racing."

Pole sitter Geoff Bodine, who had been the class of the field until the crash, suffered damage to his Junior Johnson Ford and never contended again. "I saw it coming and backed off," he said. "I thought I'd made it okay but someone hit me in the back end. It was never really right the rest of the day.

Earnhardt pushed his RCR Enterprises Chevrolet past Morgan Shepherd's Ford with about 80 miles to go and led all but one lap thereafter. Mark Martin was a close second but couldn't muster enough horsepower to challenge Earnhardt down the stretch. Third place went to Davey Allison, who recovered from a couple of wall-banging incidents. Bodine finished fourth after leading the most laps and Shepherd drifted to fifth after glancing off the fourth turn wall late in the event.

"We didn't get into any trouble and the work of the guys in the pits won the race for us," said Earnhardt, who had started 15th on the grid. "That deal (the Irvan-Schrader crash) was close for me. I jumped off the corner and found a hole, but I just as easily could have been involved. But this is Darlington, and I was cautious when I got out of bed this morning."

The triumph boosted Earnhardt's point lead to 78 points over Shepherd. "We didn't need all those cautions toward the end of the race," said the Conover, N.C. driver, who led four times for 65 laps. "Our car ran better under long green flag conditions. We haven't finished out of the top 10 this year, but if we're to challenge Earnhardt for the championship, we need to win some races."

Third place Allison survived two bouts with the wall. "If I hadn't kept running into the wall, maybe I could have had something for Earnhardt at the finish," he remarked.

The Hendrick Motorsports team fielded five cars in the race – two were added for drivers Greg Sacks and Hut Stricklin. The extra two cars were painted up like racers in the upcoming film "Days of Thunder", which proved to be one of the most dreadful Hollywood productions demeaning the sport of stock car racing.

Stricklin and Sacks wound up 36th and 37th after mechanical problems sidelined them.

Race #6

Allison Nips Martin at Bristol; Rudd and Marlin Feud

BRISTOL, TN (April 8) – Davey Allison overcame a crash with Rob Moroso, a decided disadvantage of having to pit on the backstretch, and held off Mark Martin in a stirring finish to capture the Valleydale Meats 500 at Bristol International Raceway.

It was Allison's first win since July 1, 1989 when he won at Daytona, and the seventh of his career.

Allison qualified 19th in the field of 32, which forced his Robert Yates team to set up pits on the back chute. Ironically, that played a major role in the victory for the Hueytown, Ala. driver.

Considering track position more important than fresh tires after the 13th and final caution of the day, Allison took the lead for the first time with 109 laps remaining. "We decided against pitting because we had gotten tires about 30 laps earlier, and we knew our car ran just as fast after 50 laps as on new tires. And pitting on the back would have put us at the tail end of the line."

Allison held several challengers at bay during the final

Winston Cup Series Race No. 6
500 Laps at Bristol Int'l Raceway
Bristol, TN
"Valleydale Meats 500"

266.5 Miles on .533-mile Short Track

April 8, 1990

Fin	St	No.	Driver	Team / Car	Laps	Money	Status
1	19	28	Davey Allison	Robert Yates Racing Ford	500	$50,100	Running
2	3	6	Mark Martin	Roush Racing Ford	500	31,300	Running
3	13	5	Ricky Rudd	Hendrick Motorsports Chevy	500	19,775	Running
4	14	1	Terry Labonte	Precision Products Olds	500	13,500	Running
5	25	75	Rick Wilson	RahMoc Racing Pontiac	500	13,857	Running
6	17	25	Ken Schrader	Hendrick Motorsports Chevy	500	11,675	Running
7	5	94	Sterling Marlin	Billy Hagan Olds	500	8,850	Running
8	7	15	Morgan Shepherd	Bud Moore Eng. Ford	499	8,475	Running
9	10	17	Darrell Waltrip	Hendrick Motorsports Chevy	499	25,500	Running
10	4	42	Kyle Petty	SabCo Racing Pontiac	499	11,900	Running
11	12	21	Dale Jarrett	Wood Brothers Ford	493	8,300	Running
12	8	2	Rick Mast	US Racing Pontiac	489	8,225	Running
13	6	66	Dick Trickle	Cale Yarborough Pontiac	488	7,950	Running
14	32	98	Butch Miller	Travis Carter Chevrolet	486	4,000	Running
15	16	71	Dave Marcis	Marcis Auto Racing Chevy	471	7,025	Running
16	1	4	Ernie Irvan	Morgan-McClure Olds	471	8,800	Running
17	11	9	Bill Elliott	Melling Performance Ford	465	10,850	Running
18	26	57	Jimmy Spencer	Rod Osterlund Pontiac	456	6,050	Running
19	9	3	Dale Earnhardt	RCR Enterprises Chevrolet	451	10,990	Running
20	20	30	Michael Waltrip	Bahari Racing Pontiac	442	6,725	Running
21	15	8	Bobby Hillin,Jr.	Stavola Brothers Buick	433	5,725	Running
22	18	26	Brett Bodine	King Motorsports Buick	421	5,620	Running
23	29	12	Mike Alexander	Bobby Allison Buick	399	3,400	Running
24	2	11	Geoff Bodine	Junior Johnson Ford	383	11,225	Running
25	31	33	Phil Parsons	Leo Jackson Olds	342	9,080	Running
26	28	43	Richard Petty	Petty Enterprises Pontiac	328	3,900	Engine
27	30	70	J.D.McDuffie	McDuffie Racing Pontiac	290	3,210	Engine
28	23	27	Rusty Wallace	Blue Max Pontiac	220	12,375	Crash
29	27	52	Jimmy Means	Means Racing Pontiac	202	3,745	Camshaft
30	24	20	Rob Moroso	Dick Moroso Olds	169	3,850	Crash
31	21	7	Alan Kulwicki	AK Racing Ford	126	4,600	Oil Pan
32	22	10	Derrike Cope	Bob Whitcomb Chevrolet	56	7,300	Crash

Time of Race: 3 hours, 3 minutes, 15 seconds
Average Speed: 87.258 mph
Pole Winner: Ernie Irvan – 116.157 mph
Lap Leaders: Ernie Irvan 1-16, Geoff Bodine 17-48, Bobby Hillin, Jr. 49-89, Dale Jarrett 90-128, G.Bodine 129-136, Kyle Petty 137-191, Sterling Marlin 192-222, Dave Marcis 223, Darrell Waltrip 224-355, Marcis 356, D.Waltrip 357-391, Davey Allison 392-500.
11 lead changes among 9 drivers.
Cautions: 13 for 65 laps   Margin of Victory: 8 inches

Bryan Hallman

Davey Allison #28 skids into a spinning Rob Moroso #20 in Bristol's Valleydale 500.

Ricky Rudd wound up third after knocking Sterling Marlin to a spin in the final lap. Terry Labonte wound up fourth and Rick Wilson came from 25th to finish fifth.

Marlin and Rudd were running directly behind Allison and Martin as the quartet of cars whipped off the second turn on lap 500. Rudd tapped Marlin's Oldsmobile, which went spinning into the inside retaining barrier. The mishap knocked Marlin down to seventh

Kim Novasat

Davey Allison nipped Mark Martin by inches in close Bristol finish.

60-mile run. Darrell Waltrip challenged Allison for 40 laps before a flat tire ruined his bid with 25 laps left. Martin began reeling Allison in and made a move to the inside off turn four of the final lap. The cars crossed the finish line door-to-door – and official declaration of the winner was not announced until NASCAR officials studied the television replay. Official margin of victory – according to the naked eye – was eight inches.

Kim Novosat

Dale Jarrett #21 spins off Bristol's fourth turn as Sterling Marlin #94 scoots past.

place.

After the checkered flag dropped, Marlin waited on Rudd to come around. Rudd stopped his car and the two drivers played a game of cat and mouse before both came around to the front pits.

Marlin took his complaints directly to the Rudd truck. One of Marlin's crewmen, Tony Shoemaker, waved a sledgehammer during the scuffle. He was later suspended for three weeks by NASCAR for "conduct detrimental to racing".

After cooler heads prevailed, Marlin said, "All I know is that he (Rudd) spun me out. It's really frustrating for something like this to happen, especially on the last lap."

Rudd said that the "94 car was holding me up all day. I'm sorry things turned out the way they did, but that was the last lap and I wasn't holding back."

The Marlin-Rudd bashing was simply the final rubdown in a day filled with incidents.

Ernie Irvan, who notched the first pole of his career, led the first 16 laps, but spun off turn two moments after the restart. The caution did not come out and Irvan lost three laps getting four new tires.

Less than five laps later, Dale Earnhardt looped his Chevrolet in the same spot Irvan had spun. Earnhardt nicked the inside wall and had to retreat to the pits for lengthy repairs.

Irvan pinched Derrike Cope into the wall in the 60th lap, putting Cope out of the race.

Highly touted newcomer Rob Moroso, suffering through a rough freshman season, clobbered the wall in the 171st lap and slid into the path of Allison, who continued despite considerable body damage.

Two substitute drivers also experienced a rough road on the slick track. Dale Jarrett, filling in for the injured Neil Bonnett, tangled with Irvan in the 354th lap while battling for fourth. The incident knocked Jarrett a lap

Kim Novosat

A heavy crash sidelined Rusty Wallace.

off the pace and he eventually wound up 11th. He had led for 39 laps in his first drive for the Wood Brothers.

Phil Parsons drove Leo Jackson's Oldsmobile in place of Harry Gant, whose father had passed away. Parsons started in the back row but made a move to the front. He was taken out of contention when he slammed the wall on lap 162 following a tap from Jarrett.

Rusty Wallace was eliminated in a crash just before the half-way point.

In all, the caution flag was out 13 times for 65 laps. Allison's winning speed was held to 87.258 mph.

All the wrecks weren't the fault of the drivers," said Geoff Bodine, reflecting on the racing surface which peeled up during the race. "No one in the world should race in these conditions. It's like trying to drive on roller bearings. We shouldn't be out there."

Passing was a definite problem late in the race. "I just held my line," said Allison about his close duel with Martin. "I didn't mirror drive. I gave him some room to race. I knew Mark would be tough, but I was going o make him earn it if he got it."

Most pleasant sight of the day was the fact that Michael Waltrip started the race. In the Busch Grand National race the day before, Waltrip's car was sliced in two after striking the gate at the crossover entrance in turn two. Waltrip wound up 20th, 58 laps off the pace.

Earnhardt finished 19th and lost a chunk of his point lead. Morgan Shepherd, who finished eighth, closed to within 42 points in the Winston Cup standings. Martin came from seventh to third in the standings, 121 behind Earnhardt.

Kim Novosat

A crunched fender ended Ernie Irvan's bid for victory.

Winston Cup Series Race No. 7
400 Laps at North Wilkesboro Speedway
North Wilkesboro, NC
"First Union 400"
250 Miles on .625-mile Short Track
April 22, 1990

Fin	St	No.	Driver	Team / Car	Laps	Money	Status
1	20	26	Brett Bodine	King Motorsports Buick	400	$50,682	Running
2	7	17	Darrell Waltrip	Hendrick Motorsports Chevy	400	31,625	Running
3	4	3	Dale Earnhardt	RCR Enterprises Chevrolet	400	21,775	Running
4	8	5	Ricky Rudd	Hendrick Motorsports Chevy	400	12,775	Running
5	21	15	Morgan Shepherd	Bud Moore Eng. Ford	400	12,100	Running
6	1	6	Mark Martin	Roush Racing Ford	400	18,975	Running
7	22	27	Rusty Wallace	Blue Max Pontiac	400	12,825	Running
8	2	11	Geoff Bodine	Junior Johnson Ford	400	10,075	Running
9	17	28	Davey Allison	Robert Yates Racing Ford	400	8,600	Running
10	5	42	Kyle Petty	SabCo Racing Pontiac	399	10,850	Running
11	10	7	Alan Kulwicki	AK Racing Ford	399	6,675	Running
12	18	71	Dave Marcis	Marcis Auto Racing Chevy	399	6,350	Running
13	27	33	Harry Gant	Leo Jackson Oldsmobile	399	8,050	Running
14	16	21	Dale Jarrett	Wood Brothers Ford	399	5,975	Running
15	12	1	Terry Labonte	Precision Products Olds	398	6,325	Running
16	9	4	Ernie Irvan	Morgan-McClure Olds	398	5,675	Running
17	32	12	Mike Alexander	Bobby Allison Buick	397	4,125	Running
18	13	9	Bill Elliott	Melling Performance Ford	397	9,100	Running
19	6	25	Ken Schrader	Hendrick Motorsports Chevy	397	7,800	Running
20	15	57	Jimmy Spencer	Rod Osterlund Pontiac	396	6,025	Running
21	26	10	Derrike Cope	Bob Whitcomb Chevrolet	393	7,675	Running
22	11	75	Rick Wilson	RahMoc Racing Olds	384	5,000	Running
23	29	2	Rick Mast	US Racing Chevrolet	384	6,925	Running
24	3	66	Dick Trickle	Cale Yarborough Pontiac	372	8,600	Engine
25	30	98	Butch Miller	Travis Carter Chevrolet	333	3,350	Running
26	28	36	Kenny Wallace	Randy Hope Pontiac	315	2,550	Crash
27	19	30	Michael Waltrip	Bahari Racing Pontiac	309	4,675	Trans
28	25	52	Jimmy Means	Means Racing Pontiac	306	3,100	Oil Cooler
29	23	43	Richard Petty	Petty Enterprises Pontiac	201	2,475	Crash
30	31	8	Bobby Hillin,Jr.	Stavola Brothers Buick	183	3,925	Crash
31	14	94	Sterling Marlin	Billy Hagan Olds	150	3,925	Crash
32	24	20	Rob Moroso	Dick Moroso Olds	9	3,175	Crash

Time of Race: 2 hours, 58 minutes, 46 seconds
Average Speed: 83.908 mph
Pole Winner: Mark Martin – 117.475 mph
Lap Leaders: Mark Martin 1-103, Darrell Waltrip 104-179, Dale Earnhardt 180-186, Brett Bodine 187-249, Earnhardt 250-314, D.Waltrip 315-317, B.Bodine 318-400.
6 lead changes among 4 drivers.
Cautions: 10 for 68 laps Margin of Victory: 0.95-second

Race #7

Scoring Flap Fails to Alter Brett Bodine's North Wilkesboro Win

NORTH WILKESBORO, NC (April 22) – Brett Bodine was credited with leading the final 83 laps and emerged victorious in a disputed North Wilkesboro Speedway's First Union 400 marred by a scoring mistake. It was Bodine's first Winston Cup career win and it came in his 79th major league start.

Bodine also gave car owner Kenny Bernstein his first win on an oval. Ricky Rudd had posted two road course wins for Bernstein before Bodine took the wheel this year.

Bodine's Buick finished 0.95-second ahead of a fast closing Darrell Waltrip. Third place went to Dale Earnhardt, who struggled early and eventually made up a lost lap. Ricky Rudd took fourth and Morgan Shepherd was fifth.

NASCAR officials said after the race they had erred when they put Bodine in the lead after he stopped and got a change of tires in the 10th and last caution period with about 50 miles remaining.

Kenny Wallace, making his Winston Cup debut, crashed his Pontiac in the 320th lap, three laps after race leader Waltrip had made his final pit stop for fresh tires. Other cars in the lead lap had also made their final pit stop under green. With the caution out, NASCAR officials instructed the pace car to pick up Earnhardt as the leader.

Brian Czobat

Brett Bodine led the final 83 laps to win at North Wilkesboro.

Bodine, the actual leader, was running directly in front of Earnhardt. That let Bodine go around the track to the rear of the line, gaining nearly a lap on the field. Bodine made his final pit stop as rival crews lodged a barrage of complaints to officials.

Brett Bodine – The end of a long dry spell.

Waltrip, Earnhardt, Shepherd, Mark Martin and other drivers on the lead lap stayed on the track. Bodine pitted for four new tires and rejoined the race at the rear of the pack.

The caution was extended for a total of 18 laps while officials reviewed the scoring tapes. They determined that Bodine had been the leader when the yellow flag came out and the pace car had been misplaced.

The cars on the lead lap were waved past the pace car and sent around the track to the rear of the line, enabling them to regain the lost distance to Bodine. But that didn't negate the advantage Bodine gained by getting tires changed before the error was corrected.

The 31 year-old Chemung, N.Y. driver was left in the lead for the restart and led the final 62 laps under green.

Discussion and arguments between officials and pit crews continued for almost two hours. Finally, Les Richter, NASCAR Vice-President and Director of Competition, declared that Bodine was the official winner of the race. Richter said officials made "judgement call" errors which were "not correctable."

"We made a mistake when the pace car picked up the wrong car on lap 319," said NASCAR's David Hoots, who was in the control tower during the race. "By the time we caught it, pit road had opened up. Once we opened it up there was no way to correct it. Bodine was the leader, and you can't penalize him for pitting. We couldn't tell him to go back to the pits and put his old tires on."

Bodine said he "knew I was leading before the caution came out. I was going crazy in the car, but NASCAR finally got it straightened out. I didn't know the others didn't pit (during the yellow), so I really can't talk about that. I had a feeling if we ever got to the front, we'd stay there. Having track position was the key and new tires helped."

Waltrip and Earnhardt felt the incidents affected the outcome. "If Brett had lined up behind us, he would never have been a factor. Letting him be the leader was a big advantage.

"But I've been down this road before," Waltrip continued. "It's a no-win situation. They (NASCAR) knew when they began moving some cars around and not others, they were opening the door. They knew a lot of people would be standing at the door when the race was over."

"Darrell should have won the race," declared Earnhardt, who extended his point lead to 57 points over Shepherd. "I thought we could have won the race, but we should have run second."

The scoring foul-up accented the need for computerized scoring in NASCAR Winston Cup events.

"There seems little doubt a computer would help," said Publisher Hank Schoolfield. "The idea that it would eliminate mix-ups is an invitation to severe disappointment.

"Computers process information put into them by humans," added Schoolfield. "Two things are doubted by hardly anybody: 1- The human brain still is the most sophisticated computer known; and 2- Humans make errors.

"The ultimate remedy for excluding (scoring errors) is there probably isn't one, unless somebody figures a way to have auto races without humans."

Crashes took out a number of competitors, including rookie Rob Moroso, who collided early with Richard Petty; Sterling Marlin, who was the victim of a spinning Jimmy Spencer; Bobby Hillin,Jr. who crashed with Jimmy Means; and Petty, who was sidelined after a second crash on lap 204.

Winston Cup Series Race No. 8
500 Laps at Martinsville Speedway
Martinsville, VA
"Hanes Activewear 500"
263 Miles on .526-mile Short Track
April 29, 1990

Fin	St	No.	Driver	Team / Car	Laps	Money	Status
1	1	11	Geoff Bodine	Junior Johnson Ford	500	$95,950	Running
2	17	27	Rusty Wallace	Blue Max Pontiac	500	36,800	Running
3	12	15	Morgan Shepherd	Bud Moore Eng. Ford	500	19,750	Running
4	7	17	Darrell Waltrip	Hendrick Motorsports Chevy	500	19,600	Running
5	2	3	Dale Earnhardt	RCR Enterprises Chevy	499	20,800	Running
6	6	25	Ken Schrader	Hendrick Motorsports Chevy	498	12,875	Running
7	4	6	Mark Martin	Roush Racing Ford	498	14,000	Running
8	23	30	Michael Waltrip	Bahari Racing Pontiac	497	10,657	Running
9	9	66	Dick Trickle	Cale Yarborough Pontiac	497	10,800	Running
10	13	9	Bill Elliott	Melling Performance Ford	497	14,925	Running
11	21	57	Jimmy Spencer	Rod Osterlund Pontiac	496	8,085	Running
12	8	26	Brett Bodine	King Motorsports Buick	495	7,100	Running
13	10	20	Rob Moroso	Dick Moroso Olds	495	5,050	Running
14	28	71	Dave Marcis	Marcis Auto Racing Chevy	495	7,700	Running
15	3	4	Ernie Irvan	Morgan-McClure Olds	490	8,075	Running
16	15	42	Kyle Petty	SabCo Racing Pontiac	490	9,200	Running
17	14	10	Derrike Cope	Bob Whitcomb Chevrolet	489	7,600	Running
18	18	98	Butch Miller	Travis Carter Chevrolet	485	4,600	Running
19	30	52	Jimmy Means	Means Racing Pontiac	484	4,400	Running
20	22	43	Richard Petty	Petty Enterprises Pontiac	484	4,875	Running
21	26	8	Bobby Hillin, Jr.	Stavola Brothers Buick	458	5,300	Running
22	19	28	Davey Allison	Robert Yates Racing Ford	456	8,550	Running
23	11	5	Ricky Rudd	Hendrick Motorsports Chevy	417	5,100	Running
24	24	76	Bill Sedgwick	Wayne Spears Chevrolet	359	2,750	Running
25	20	7	Alan Kulwicki	AK Racing Ford	332	5,725	Pump Belt
26	27	33	Harry Gant	Leo Jackson Olds	305	8,250	Running
27	29	75	Rick Wilson	RahMoc Racing Olds	301	4,675	Crash
28	31	12	Jeff Purvis	Bobby Allison Buick	247	3,300	Crash
29	32	2	Rick Mast	US Racing Pontiac	246	4,400	Trans
30	5	21	Dale Jarrett	Wood Brothers Ford	171	4,050	Clutch
31	16	1	Terry Labonte	Precision Products Olds	91	3,750	Engine
32	25	94	Sterling Marlin	Billy Hagan Olds	12	3,750	Camshaft

Time of Race: 3 hours, 23 minutes, 49 seconds
Average Speed: 77.423 mph
Pole Winner: Geoff Bodine – 91.726 mph
Lap Leaders: Dale Earnhardt 1-21, Geoff Bodine 22-114, Rusty Wallace 115-151, G.Bodine 152,Alan Kulwicki 153-154, Darrell Waltrip 155-160, Wallace 161-254, Kulwicki 255, Wallace 256-297, G.Bodine 298-336, Wallace 337-363, G.Bodine 364-500.
12 lead changes among 5 drivers.
Cautions: 10 for 44 laps Margin of Victory: 4.5 seconds

Race #8

Martinsville Win is Bittersweet For Geoff and Junior

MARTINSVILLE, VA (April 29) – Geoff Bodine parlayed excellent pit work by the Junior Johnson crew into a convincing victory in the Hanes Activewear 500 at Martinsville Speedway. It was Bodine's first win since joining legendary car owner Junior Johnson.

The 4.5-second triumph was laced with emotion as Brent Kouthen, a member of the Johnson team, was fatally injured two days before in a highway accident. "He was just like our boy," said Johnson. "For the last 18 years, it'd been just like he was ours. I didn't want

Kim Novosat

Derrike Cope spins at Martinsville as Ricky Rudd slips by on the low side.

Brian Czobat

Geoff Bodine leads Ernie Irvan, Chad Little and Kyle Petty through Martinsville's tight first turn.

to much come up here today. It really upset us."

Bodine started on the pole and led four times for a total of 270 laps. The 41 year-old New York native paced the final 137 laps after his pit crew beat Rusty Wallace's in a battle of pit stops. "We had a 19.6 second stop and that was good enough to beat Rusty's guys," said Bodine. "That gave me the lead and that made a big difference. It's so difficult to pass here. And my car ran great after the last stop. I was watching Rusty in the mirror and I think he was a little loose coming off the turns."

Beating Wallace in the pits and on the track was particularly satisfying for the winner. Bodine had complained that Wallace's Blue Max Racing team was letting tires run askew during pit stops – maybe not accidentally. "After running over one of their tires at North Wilkesboro and hitting one on my final stop today, I think that maybe they're rolling them out there to slow others down. I don't think what they're doing is very good sportsmanship. But it wasn't as bad today. Dick Beaty said NASCAR would allow another man over pit wall to watch the loose tires. That's a good deal," said Bodine.

The back-to-back Winston Cup victories by the Bodine Brothers enabled them to become the first brothers to pull the trick since Donnie and Bobby Allison won in succession at Atlanta and Ontario in 1978. "It's been a great week for the Bodines," said Geoff. "It's so ironic that our family can be going through such a good time and Junior and his family are having it so rough. I'm torn both ways."

Morgan Shepherd ran down Darrell Waltrip in the final 20 laps to take third place. Waltrip wound up fourth and Dale Earnhardt came home fifth.

Earnhardt departed Martinsville with a 52 point cush-

Kim Novosat

Dale Earnhardt #3 and Morgan Shepherd race door-to-door at Martinsville.

Kim Novosat

Jeff Purvis drove the Bobby Allison Buick at Martinsville in his first Winston Cup start.

ion over Shepherd in the Winston Cup standings.

Geoff Bodine moved into third place ahead of Martin, who finished seventh.

Bodine pocketed $95,950 for his eighth career Winston Cup victory, boosted by $38,000 of Unocal bonus money.

Mike Alexander, driving the Bobby Allison Buick, crashed in practice on Friday, then climbed out of the car. Alexander's recovery from a brain injury in a non-NASCAR short track race at Pensacola, Fla. had been slow. "I don't feel I'm getting the most out of the car," said Alexander. "I still have some lingering effects from the crash. I didn't know how bad until a couple of months ago. My confidence is down, but I'm not going to give up hope."

Brian Czobat

Geoff Bodine in Victory Lane.

Ironically, it was Alexander who was tabbed to replace Allison in the Stavola Brothers car when Allison was injured at Pocono the same year.

Dirt track ace Jeff Purvis was hired to replace Alexander and he suffered a couple of spins. The Clarksville, Tenn. driver wound up 28th in the 32 car field.

For Bodine, it was his 11th career victory – including Modified and Sportsman races. "Yep, win number 11 in car number 11," beamed Bodine. "And I think there were 11 raisins in my cereal this morning."

Race #9

Earnhardt Handles Pesky Sacks in Talladega's Winston 500

TALLADEGA, AL (May 6) – Dale Earnhardt turned back the challenge from pesky Greg Sacks and won the Winston 500 at Talladega Superspeedway.

It was the third win of the season for Earnhardt, who padded his Winston Cup lead to 90 points over Morgan Shepherd.

Earnhardt led 107 of the 188 laps around Talladega's 2.66-mile oval, but could not shake Sacks, who was in one of the Hendrick Motorsports Chevrolets. Rick Hendrick announced that he had a new association with actor and IndyCar owner Paul Newman. Sacks had started 17th but whipped his way into contention early.

The 500-mile contest was essentially a three-car duel. Ken Schrader, in another of the Hendrick Motorsports cars, showed muscle but departed on lap 154 with engine problems.

Pole sitter Bill Elliott was never a factor after running nearly 200 mph in qualifying. NASCAR inspectors made Elliott's Melling Performance crew adjust their rear spoiler – leaving Elliott ineffective. He eventually wound up 22nd, 13 laps off the pace.

Mark Martin and Ernie Irvan had a spirited duel for third place, which Martin captured by less than a car length. The Martin-Irvan duel took place 6.5 seconds behind the leaders. Fifth place went to Michael Waltrip, who enjoyed his best run of the season and his first top five finish in nearly two years. Terry Labonte finished sixth, the only other driver on the lead lap.

Shepherd wound up eighth to maintain his string of top 10 finishes in every race during the 1990 NASCAR campaign.

Bryan Hallman

Greg Sacks #18 was an unexpected challenger to Dale Earnhardt at Talladega.

Earnhardt started fifth but snared the lead in the second lap. Sacks bolted through the field and latched onto Earnhardt's rear bumper, taking the lead for the first time on lap 20. With occasional interludes from Schrader, Earnhardt and Sacks hooked up and engaged in a private two-car struggle. Other top teams found it nearly impossible to merely draft the Chevrolet tandem.

"We didn't have anything from the guys up front," conceded Martin. "I'll tell you what, the 18 car (Sacks) could really push the 3 car. I don't think *anybody* could keep up with them. There were a few times when we could hang on, but it was for dear life. We couldn't even draft them."

Once the two leaders separated themselves from the field, it became a one-on-one battle for top honors. "When we were racing, I was watching him in the mirror," said Earnhardt. "When he started falling off in the second corner, I knew he was testing me. I started falling off, too, just playing a game of cat and mouse. On the last lap, I didn't back off and it might have caught him off guard."

Sacks, who recorded his first top five finish since winning the 1985 Daytona Firecracker 400, said, "The best two cars finished first and second, what can I say?" I felt I had a shot at him on the last lap, but we came up on (the lapped car of) Elliott and that hurt me. Maybe I should have made my move a lap earlier," said Sacks, who led four times for 41 laps.

Hut Stricklin, new driver for the Bobby Allison Buick team, clipped fenders with Rusty Wallace shortly past the half-way point, triggering a wild wreck. Dale Jarrett, Phil Parsons and Ricky Rudd were eliminated. Elliott, Buddy Baker and Bobby Hillin, Jr. were also involved. Wallace lost five laps getting his Pontiac repaired. Stricklin continued and finished ninth.

Elliott had won the pole at 199.388 but never led a lap. "My day wasn't worth a flip. I never got a decent break. One time I pitted, thinking I had a flat tire. It wasn't flat. Then I go back out and cut down a tire. It was a long day," he said.

Rookie Jack Pennington had moved up to seventh place late in the race. When the final restart occurred

Winston Cup Series Race No. 9
188 Laps at Talladega Superspeedway
Talladega, AL
"Winston 500"

500.08 Miles on 2.66-mile Superspeedway

May 6, 1990

Fin	St	No.	Driver	Team / Car	Laps	Money	Status
1	5	3	Dale Earnhardt	RCR Enterprises Chevrolet	188	$98,975	Running
2	17	18	Greg Sacks	Hendrick Motorsports Chevy	188	46,900	Running
3	6	6	Mark Martin	Roush Racing Ford	188	39,050	Running
4	4	4	Ernie Irvan	Morgan-McClure Olds	188	30,150	Running
5	10	30	Michael Waltrip	Bahari Racing Pontiac	188	26,425	Running
6	31	1	Terry Labonte	Precision Products Olds	188	20,657	Running
7	11	42	Kyle Petty	SabCo Racing Pontiac	187	20,950	Running
8	21	15	Morgan Shepherd	Bud Moore Eng. Ford	187	17,200	Running
9	18	12	Hut Stricklin	Bobby Allison Buick	187	13,400	Running
10	3	17	Darrell Waltrip	Hendrick Motorsports Chevy	187	24,725	Running
11	32	47	Jack Pennington	Derick Close Olds	187	9,870	Running
12	24	26	Brett Bodine	King Motorsports Buick	187	12,540	Running
13	7	7	Alan Kulwicki	AK Racing Ford	186	12,010	Running
14	29	71	Dave Marcis	Marcis Auto Racing Chevy	186	11,405	Running
15	38	19	Chad Little	Chuck Little Ford	186	7,975	Running
16	37	98	Butch Miller	Travis Carter Chevrolet	186	8,510	Running
17	34	2	Rick Mast	US Racing Pontiac	186	9,570	Running
18	35	35	Bill Venturini	Venturini Chevrolet	183	6,255	Running
19	40	01	Mickey Gibbs	Gibbs-West Ford	183	6,040	Running
20	22	27	Rusty Wallace	Blue Max Pontiac	183	17,575	Running
21	20	52	Jimmy Means	Means Racing Pontiac	181	6,565	Running
22	1	9	Bill Elliott	Melling Performance Ford	175	16,570	Running
23	33	8	Bobby Hillin,Jr.	Stavola Brothers Buick	171	8,310	Running
24	23	11	Geoff Bodine	Junior Johnson Ford	170	13,655	Running
25	8	28	Davey Allison	Robert Yates Racing Ford	162	13,275	Running
26	15	94	Sterling Marlin	Billy Hagan Olds	159	7,945	Engine
27	25	66	Dick Trickle	Cale Yarborough Pontiac	158	8,790	Running
28	2	25	Ken Schrader	Hendrick Motorsports Chevy	154	13,735	Valve
29	39	43	Richard Petty	Petty Enterprises Pontiac	137	5,630	Running
30	36	73	Phil Barkdoll	Barkdoll Racing Olds	121	4,875	Clutch
31	30	90	Buddy Baker	Junie Donlavey Ford	115	5,420	Handling
32	12	57	Jimmy Spencer	Rod Osterlund Pontiac	114	7,340	Engine
33	14	5	Ricky Rudd	Hendrick Motorsports Chevy	104	7,285	Crash
34	16	21	Dale Jarrett	Wood Brothers Ford	103	7,230	Crash
35	26	72	Phil Parsons	Barkdoll Racing Olds	101	4,600	Crash
36	9	33	Harry Gant	Leo Jackson Olds	83	11,570	Engine
37	13	20	Rob Moroso	Dick Moroso Olds	79	4,740	Piston
38	28	83	Lake Speed	Speed Oldsmobile	41	4,435	Engine
39	19	75	Rick Wilson	RahMoc Racing Oldsmobile	9	6,380	Engine
40	27	10	Derrike Cope	Bob Whitcomb Chevrolet	3	9,350	Engine

Time of Race: 3 hours, 8 minutes, 2 seconds
Average Speed: 159.571 mph
Pole Winner: Bill Elliott – 199.388 mph
Lap Leaders: Ken Schrader 1, Dale Earnhardt 2-19, Greg Sacks 20-25, Earnhardt 26-40, Kyle Petty 41, Buddy Baker 42, Geoff Bodine 43-44, Morgan Shepherd 45, Darrell Waltrip 46-48, Shepherd 49-52, Earnhardt 53-59, Schrader 60-76, Earnhardt 77-97, Sacks 98-108, Earnhardt 109-113, Schrader 114-115, Sacks 116-123, Mark Martin 124-127, Ernie Irvan 128, Earnhardt 129-131, Sacks 132-147, Earnhardt 148-163, Terry Labonte 164, Michael Waltrip 165-166, Earnhardt 167-188.
25 lead changes among 12 drivers.
Cautions: 7 for 28 laps Margin of Victory: 2 car lengths

with 18 laps to go, the Augusta, Ga. driver had difficulty getting up through the gears. He eventually wound up 11th, but it was the fourth straight race he had placed ahead of highly regarded freshman Rob Moroso.

Neil Bonnett, sidelined with amnesia since the Darlington crash, held a news conference and told reporters he would not attempt to drive again in 1990. "Since Darlington, I've been going through extensive testing and I didn't find out a total evaluation until this week," said the winner of 18 Winston Cup races in a career that began in 1974.

"This is the first time I've felt comfortable enough to be around you guys," Bonnett told a gathering of reporters. "Desire or wanting to doesn't enter into this decision. It's a medical decision."

Sitting beside Bonnett was long time friend Bobby Allison, who suffered a brain injury two years ago at Pocono. "Bobby was the first guy who stopped by my house," said Bonnett. "We were sitting there on the couch. Between Bobby trying to say what he was thinking and me trying to remember what he was saying, it was a helluva conversation."

Winston Cup Series Race No. 10
400 Laps at Charlotte Motor Speedway
Concord, NC
"Coca-Cola 600"
600 Miles on 1.5-mile Superspeedway
May 27, 1990

Fin	St	No.	Driver	Team / Car	Laps	Money	Status
1	9	27	Rusty Wallace	Blue Max Pontiac	400	$151,000	Running
2	7	9	Bill Elliott	Melling Performance Ford	400	67,450	Running
3	2	6	Mark Martin	Roush Racing Ford	400	51,700	Running
4	20	30	Michael Waltrip	Bahari Racing Pontiac	400	32,600	Running
5	4	4	Ernie Irvan	Morgan-McClure Olds	400	28,350	Running
6	3	7	Alan Kulwicki	AK Racing Ford	400	23,775	Running
7	6	28	Davey Allison	Robert Yates Racing Ford	400	24,400	Running
8	24	15	Morgan Shepherd	Bud Moore Eng. Ford	400	18,100	Running
9	11	10	Derrike Cope	Bob Whitcomb Chevrolet	400	18,750	Running
10	13	11	Geoff Bodine	Junior Johnson Ford	400	23,125	Running
11	1	25	Ken Schrader	Hendrick Motorsports Chevy	400	63,100	Running
12	14	66	Dick Trickle	Cale Yarborough Pontiac	399	15,000	Running
13	42	1	Terry Labonte	Precision Products Olds	399	14,257	Running
14	28	18	Greg Sacks	Hendrick Motorsports Chevy	398	8,668	Running
15	27	90	Buddy Baker	Junie Donlavey Ford	398	10,465	Running
16	35	71	Dave Marcis	Marcis Auto Racing Chevy	398	10,850	Running
17	41	42	Kyle Petty	SabCo Racing Pontiac	397	13,900	Running
18	18	98	Butch Miller	Travis Carter Chevrolet	396	7,890	Running
19	21	75	Rick Wilson	RahMoc Racing Olds	395	9,370	Engine
20	37	47	Jack Pennington	Derick Close Olds	395	7,775	Running
21	26	57	Jimmy Spencer	Rod Osterlund Pontiac	394	8,800	Running
22	16	17	Darrell Waltrip	Hendrick Motorsports Chevy	393	14,800	Running
23	33	80	Jimmy Horton	George Smith Ford	389	5,400	Running
24	25	19	Chad Little	Chuck Little Ford	385	5,200	Running
25	15	33	Harry Gant	Leo Jackson Oldsmobile	383	12,100	Running
26	10	20	Rob Moroso	Dick Moroso Olds	356	5,600	Engine
27	30	43	Richard Petty*	Petty Enterprises Pontiac	352	5,650	Oil Leak
28	34	5	Ricky Rudd	Hendrick Motorsports Chevy	320	7,450	Camshaft
29	5	26	Brett Bodine	King Motorsports Buick	317	8,950	Engine
30	12	3	Dale Earnhardt	RCR Enterprises Chevrolet	262	13,950	Running
31	36	2	Rick Mast	US Racing Pontiac	251	7,000	Engine
32	19	21	Dale Jarrett	Wood Brothers Ford	241	7,120	Engine
33	39	89	Rodney Combs	Mueller Brothers Pontiac	226	4,190	Engine
34	17	8	Bobby Hillin, Jr.	Stavola Brothers Buick	208	6,800	Crash
35	22	94	Sterling Marlin	Billy Hagan Olds	201	6,750	Engine
36	40	72	Tracy Leslie	Tex Powell Oldsmobile	195	4,100	Engine
37	23	12	Hut Stricklin	Bobby Allison Buick	173	4,680	Oil Line
38	38	83	Lake Speed	Speed Oldsmobile	113	4,060	Crash
39	8	68	Bobby Hamilton	Diamond Ridge Pontiac	102	4,540	Crash
40	31	06	Terry Byers	Kathryn Byers Pontiac	40	4,020	Engine
41	32	77	Ken Ragan	Marvin Ragan Ford	5	4,520	Engine
42	29	88	Larry Pearson	Bill Edwards Racing Pontiac	2	4,520	Engine

Time of Race: 4 hours, 21 minutes, 32 seconds
Average Speed: 137.650 mph
Pole Winner: Ken Schrader – 173.963 mph
Lap Leaders: Ken Schrader 1-4, Mark Martin 5-16, Schrader 17-33, Rusty Wallace 34-55, Brett Bodine 56-59, Davey Allison 60, Harry Gant 61, Darrell Waltrip 62-63, Geoff Bodine 64-66, Wallace 67-170, Dale Jarrett 171-174, Wallace 175-263, Schrader 264-305, Derrike Cope 306-307, G.Bodine 308-309, Wallace 310-400.
15 lead changes among 10 drivers.
Cautions: 11 for 48 laps Margin of Victory: 0.17-second
*Relieved by Sterling Marlin and Hut Stricklin

Race #10

Rusty Waters Victory Drought With Dominant 600 Triumph

CONCORD, NC (May 27) – Rusty Wallace drove his Blue Max Pontiac to an overwhelming victory in Charlotte Motor Speedway's Coca-Cola 600, although the triumph on paper was by only two car lengths.

Wallace started ninth and scooted into the lead for the first time on lap 34. From that point on, there was no doubt that Wallace would win if he held his car between the walls.

A late caution for oil on the track deposited by Rick Wilson's Oldsmobile set the stage for a one lap shootout. Wallace got the jump on Bill Elliott and easily outdistanced the other 10 cars which were running on the lead lap.

Wallace collected $151,000 for his first win of the season and the 17th in his career.

Mark Martin grabbed third place, Michael Waltrip enjoyed another strong run by taking fourth and fifth place went to Ernie Irvan, who made up two lost laps during the race.

"I was getting off the corners so quick that it felt like I had rockets in the tailpipes," said Wallace. "It feels really good to win. People have been counting us out. We might have been down this year, but never out. There's nothing bad about this team."

Wallace has publicly stated that he will leave the Raymond Beadle owned operation at the end of the year.

Wallace had one close call during the final stages. When Wilson sprayed the third turn with oil, Wallace nearly lost his advantage over Elliott. "When I got into that oil, I took a pretty good ride. The car slid from the bottom of the track to the top. But I never touched the wall."

Brian Czobat

All lanes of the wide pit road at Charlotte Motor Speedway are utilized.

Elliott ducked under Wallace in turn three but couldn't make the pass. On the restart with a single lap to go, Elliott never made a stab at Wallace, seemingly more concerned about keeping third place Martin at bay. "That last caution didn't make any difference," said Elliott, who did not lead a lap. "I couldn't get enough momentum. I'm pleased we run second."

Dale Earnhardt started 12th and was bitten by ill Charlotte luck once again. The right rear tire popped on lap 103 and his Chevrolet darted into Bobby Hamilton and then struck the wall.

"We were riding seventh and holding our own," said Earnhardt. "We needed a caution. Unfortunately, we were the caution."

Repair work took over an hour, and Earnhardt returned to the track running 38th, nearly 120 laps behind. "I was only worried about the points I was going to lose. The crew did a good job of putting it back together," he said.

Earnhardt managed to complete 262 laps, good enough for 30th place. He picked up eight positions and 24 points by returning to the race.

Morgan Shepherd finished eighth and closed to within 21 points in the Winston Cup standings. "We should have run third, but the last set of tires were so tight we fell back. We need to win a race to prove we are championship material. It was unfortunate Dale had to have bad luck for us to close the gap. But that's the only way you can catch up in the point race."

Richard Petty suffered through a long day. The King became fatigued and called for relief from Sterling Marlin midway in the race. Marlin said he had difficulty breathing the way Petty's seat was mounted and had to get out. Petty briefly got back in before Hut Stricklin ran the car until it developed an oil leak. Petty got credit for finishing 27th.

Hamilton, competing in his second Winston Cup

Bryan Hallman

Dale Earnhardt #3, Bill Elliott #9, Rusty Wallace #27 and Derrike Cope #10 in a close duel in Charlotte's Coca-Cola 600.

event, started a surprising eighth in the Diamond Ridge Pontiac owned by Gary Bechtel. His fine run was curtailed when Earnhardt had the tire failure.

Ken Schrader won the pole and led three times for 63 laps. He faded in the closing laps and wound up a disappointing 11th.

The qualifying field was separated by less than one second in one of the most competitive fields in Charlotte history. But Wallace doused the competitive spirit by thoroughly dominating the event.

Darrell Waltrip was bidding for a third straight 600 triumph, but he lost a cylinder and limped to a 21st place finish, seven laps off the pace.

Brett Bodine enjoyed a strong run early, but the engine in his Buick blew after completing 317 laps.

Winston Cup Series Race No. 11
500 Laps at Dover Downs Int'l Speedway
Dover, DE
500 Miles on 1-mile Superspeedway
June 3, 1990

Fin	St	No.	Driver	Team / Car	Laps	Money	Status
1	15	10	Derrike Cope	Bob Whitcomb Chevrolet	500	$55,050	Running
2	10	25	Ken Schrader	Hendrick Motorsports Chevy	500	34,575	Running
3	1	66	Dick Trickle	Cale Yarborough Pontiac	500	29,125	Running
4	2	6	Mark Martin	Roush Racing Ford	500	23,575	Running
5	16	94	Sterling Marlin	Billy Hagan Olds	500	16,325	Running
6	14	15	Morgan Shepherd	Bud Moore Eng. Ford	500	12,275	Running
7	11	4	Ernie Irvan	Morgan-McClure Olds	500	11,325	Running
8	8	9	Bill Elliott	Melling Performance Ford	500	16,025	Running
9	6	42	Kyle Petty	SabCo Racing Pontiac	500	15,575	Running
10	5	27	Rusty Wallace	Blue Max Pontiac	500	19,825	Running
11	20	5	Ricky Rudd	Hendrick Motorsports Chevy	499	9,025	Running
12	17	21	Dale Jarrett	Wood Brothers Ford	498	8,425	Running
13	19	1	Terry Labonte	Precision Products Olds	498	8,075	Running
14	29	98	Butch Miller	Travis Carter Chevrolet	493	6,682	Running
15	3	11	Geoff Bodine	Junior Johnson Ford	492	12,850	Running
16	31	8	Bobby Hillin, Jr.*	Stavola Brothers Buick	491	7,100	Running
17	27	28	Davey Allison**	Robert Yates Racing Ford	491	11,750	Running
18	9	26	Brett Bodine	King Motorsports Buick	490	6,800	Running
19	25	17	Darrell Waltrip	Hendrick Motorsports Chevy	489	12,650	Running
20	32	80	Jimmy Horton	George Smith Ford	485	4,375	Running
21	23	43	Richard Petty***	Petty Enterprises Pontiac	478	4,550	Running
22	30	52	Jimmy Means	Means Racing Pontiac	477	3,500	Running
23	24	75	Rick Wilson	RahMoc Racing Pontiac	441	6,400	Running
24	7	7	Alan Kulwicki	AK Racing Ford	413	6,250	Running
25	34	70	J.D. McDuffie	McDuffie Racing Pontiac	411	3,450	Valve
26	21	30	Michael Waltrip	Bahari Racing Pontiac	369	7,550	Running
27	22	12	Hut Stricklin	Bobby Allison Buick	325	3,950	Camshaft
28	26	2	Rick Mast	US Racing Pontiac	237	5,875	Clutch
29	18	20	Rob Moroso	Dick Moroso Olds	167	4,550	Engine
30	33	74	Mike Potter	Bobby Wawak Pontiac	161	3,100	Oil Leak
31	4	3	Dale Earnhardt	RCR Enterprises Chevrolet	159	12,600	Engine
32	28	57	Jimmy Spencer	Rod Osterlund Pontiac	151	6,625	Engine
33	35	85	Bobby Gerhart	Gerhart Chevrolet	151	2,950	Fatigue
34	13	33	Harry Gant	Leo Jackson Oldsmobile	139	91900	Camshaft
35	12	71	Dave Marcis	Marcis Auto Racing Chevy	3	5,400	Engine
36	36	48	Freddie Crawford	Hylton Engineering Chevrolet	6	2,775	Cylinder

Time of Race: 4 hours, 2 minutes, 1 second
Average Speed: 123.960 mph
Pole Winner: Dick Trickle – 145.814 mph
Lap Leaders: Dick Trickle 1, Mark Martin 2-18, Bill Elliott 19-24, Harry Gant 25-36, Elliott 37-96, Martin 97-100, Kyle Petty 101-104, Martin 105-122, Gant 123-138, K.Petty 139-159, Derrike Cope 160-194, K.Petty 195-231, Trickle 232-275, Ken Schrader 276-278, Cope 279-280, Rusty Wallace 281-331, K.Petty 332-336, Sterling Marlin 337-346, Trickle 347-364, Cope 365, Wallace 366-445, Cope 446-500.
22 lead changes among 9 drivers.
Cautions: 5 for 32 laps Margin of Victory: 1.24 seconds
*Relieved by Jim Sauter **Relieved by Hut Stricklin ***Relieved by Larry Pearson

Race #11

Derrike Dazzling at Dover; Shepherd Takes Point Lead

DOVER, DE (June 3) – Derrike Cope ran down Rusty Wallace with 55 laps remaining and held off a fast closing Ken Schrader to win the Budweiser 500 at Dover Downs International Speedway. It was the second 500-mile win of the season for the Spanaway, Wash. Chevrolet driver.

Cope, surprise last lap winner of the Daytona 500, used snappy pit service and a strong motor on lease from Hendrick Motorsports to cash in on the $55,050 first prize before 72,000 spectators at the one-mile oval.

Morgan Shepherd finished sixth and took the lead in the Winston Cup point standings. Dale Earnhardt, who held a 21 point lead entering the event, rolled to the garage area with a blown engine after just 22 laps. NASCAR rules prohibit teams from changing engines, so the RCR Enterprises crew practically rebuilt the engine, including the replacement of a cam shaft and several rods.

Earnhardt got back in after a repair job of an hour and 45 minutes and ran a total of 159 laps before the engine blew again.

Earnhardt got credit for 31st place in the 36 car field. He picked up 12 additional points by getting back into the race. The three-time national champion fell to third in the standings, 59 points out of first place. Shepherd took a 32 point lead over Mark Martin, who wound up fourth.

Dick Trickle started on the pole for the first time in his career and wound up third, just ahead of Martin. Fifth place went to Sterling Marlin.

Cope was in front four times for 93 laps. He had pushed his Bob Whitcomb Chevrolet to the front on lap 160 and held it for 35 laps before running out of gas. His Buddy Parrott-led pit crew serviced him without losing a lap, but attention was shifted to the front where Schrader, Trickle, Kyle Petty and Wallace swapped the lead.

During the fifth and final caution flag, Parrott's crew got Cope in and out of the pits with a 20.1 second pit stop, moving him from seventh to third in line for the restart. "We ran out of gas, but I knew we could come back. We just miscalculated," said the winner.

"We just had too many horses to feed," explained Parrott, who notched his 23rd Winston Cup victory as a crew chief. "But we knew we could catch up if we stayed on the lead lap."

Cope's car was equipped with an engine built in the Hendrick Motorsports shops.

Dover Downs

Dover winners Derrike Cope and crew chief Buddy Parrott share in the Victory Lane ceremonies.

Cope became the only multiple winner other than Earnhardt during the 1990 campaign, but still found himself buried in 19th place in the point standings, logged solidly behind 11 drivers who had not won a race.

Three drivers called on relief drivers. Richard Petty, for the second race in a row, gave way to Larry Pearson, who ran only a few laps before he had to climb out. "Richard had his seat adjusted so much it was terrible," said Pearson, echoing a similar comment heard from Sterling Marlin, who spelled Petty at Charlotte. ""He sits crooked in the car, probably because of all his past injuries. The sides were so close they cut off the circulation."

Cope edged Hendrick driver Ken Schrader by 1.3 seconds, gaining a measurable degree of respect for his young team. "We're young, we're inexperienced, but we have a lot of heart," said Cope. "I was hustling that ol' girl. She was really running. I could run the bottom of the racetrack in both corners."

Trickle's hopes for his first Winston Cup victory were foiled by a flat tire, which caused a spin on lap 386. "I had a flat tire and got sideways," said the veteran driver. "The 42 car tapped me into a spin. But it was my fault because I had a flat tire and was all over the place.

Jim Sauter relieved Bobby Hillin, Jr. and Hut Stricklin filled in for Davey Allison for the second time this year.

Allison was mired in a slump, having posted only two top five finishes all year. There were reports of grumbling within the Robert Yates Racing camp. Allison had threatened to possibly quit the team, "unless a legitimate crew chief can be found."

Alan Kulwicki continued his run of sour luck by placing 24th, 87 laps off the pace. The Greenfield, Wisc. driver has yet to finish in the top five in 1990.

"We had the fastest car on the track until we broke a shock absorber (in the spin). After that, I was just riding around," said Trickle.

Wallace led the most laps – 131 – and was poised to make it two wins in a row. He was on the point for the final restart with 73 laps to go.

The Pontiac driver kept the lead for 19 laps before Cope whizzed by. "Our car handled good all day until we put the last set of tires on," explained Wallace. "Cope ran me down and went on. That was it. He did a good job, but where in the heck did he come from?"

Wallace drifted to a 10th place finish, the final car on the lead lap.

Kim Novosat

Derrike Cope #10 was able to handle Dale Earnhardt without benefit of a tire failure this time.

Race #12

Wallace Scores at Sonoma For 5th Road Course Win in Last 7 Starts

SONOMA, CA (June 10) – Rusty Wallace nudged Ricky Rudd out of the way in the 60th lap and breezed to victory in the Banquet Frozen Foods 300 at Sears Point International Raceway before a record crowd of 66,000. It was the fifth win in the last seven Winston Cup road races for the St. Louis, Mo. driver.

Wallace and Rudd, acknowledged masters of the road courses, were expected to battle for top honors – and they did exactly that. Rudd, who earned the pole position with a track record 99.743 mph, led the first 11 laps. A tire went flat on Rudd's Hendrick Motorsports Chevrolet and a wild scramble took place as rivals were trying to scoot by his limping machine. Bill Elliott, Dale Earnhardt and Mark Martin all banged together, forcing all to the pits under the green flag.

Ernie Irvan took the lead in the 12th lap and headed the field until Rob Moroso authored a scary single car crash in the 18th lap. A tire blew on Moroso's family-owned Oldsmobile and he sailed over a guard rail and smashed into a chain link fence. "I was going into a turn when a tire blew and spun me around," said the 21 year-old freshman driver. "The next thing I knew I was flying through the air. The car landed so far up in the sticks I don't know how we'll get it back."

Wallace didn't take the lead until the 23rd of the 74 laps, but he was only out of the lead for 10 laps after

Brian Czobat

Rusty Wallace, NASCAR's Road Warrior.

Winston Cup Series Race No. 12
74 Laps at Sears Point Int'l Raceway
Sonoma, CA
"Banquet Frozen Foods 300"
186.48 Miles on 2.52-mile Road Course
June 10, 1990

Fin	St	No.	Driver	Team / Car	Laps	Money	Status
1	11	27	Rusty Wallace	Blue Max Pontiac	74	$69,100	Running
2	5	6	Mark Martin	Roush Racing Ford	74	34,000	Running
3	1	5	Ricky Rudd	Hendrick Motorsports Chevy	74	28,675	Running
4	26	11	Geoff Bodine	Junior Johnson Ford	74	20,650	Running
5	31	8	Bobby Hillin,Jr.	Stavola Brothers Buick	74	17,007	Running
6	17	94	Sterling Marlin	Billy Hagan Olds	74	12,475	Running
7	2	4	Ernie Irvan	Morgan-McClure Olds	74	12,700	Running
8	28	0	Irv Hoerr	Precision Products Olds	74	7,000	Running
9	20	30	Michael Waltrip	Bahari Racing Pontiac	74	10,600	Running
10	14	75	Rick Wilson	RahMoc Racing Olds	74	12,225	Running
11	21	7	Alan Kulwicki	AK Racing Ford	74	9,400	Running
12	16	12	Hut Stricklin	Bobby Allison Buick	74	6,800	Running
13	19	10	Derrike Cope	Bob Whitcomb Chevrolet	74	10,000	Running
14	10	21	Dale Jarrett	Wood Brothers Ford	74	5,800	Running
15	37	09	Terry Fisher	Dick Midgley Pontiac	74	4,575	Running
16	13	42	Kyle Petty	SabCo Racing Pontiac	74	10,925	Running
17	36	18	Stan Barrett	Hendrick Motorsports Chevy	74	3,850	Running
18	7	25	Ken Schrader	Hendrick Motorsports Chevy	74	10,825	Running
19	41	33	Harry Gant	Leo Jackson Olds	74	10,800	Running
20	29	73	Bill Schmitt	Sylvia Schmitt Chevrolet	74	6,650	Running
21	4	9	Bill Elliott	Melling Performance Ford	74	12,600	Running
22	42	2	Jim Bown	US Racing Chevrolet	73	6,675	Running
23	35	99	John Krebs	Krebs Pontiac	73	4,600	Running
24	15	28	Davey Allison	Robert Yates Racing Ford	72	10,580	Running
25	38	23	Mike Chase	Don Freymiller Buick	72	3,575	Running
26	32	43	Richard Petty	Petty Enterprises Pontiac	71	4,420	Running
27	40	57	Jimmy Spencer	Rod Osterlund Pontiac	71	6,300	Running
28	43	24	Butch Gilliland	Gear Engineering Chevrolet	71	4,200	Running
29	8	15	Morgan Shepherd	Bud Moore Eng. Ford	70	6,165	Engine
30	33	93	Troy Beebe	Allen Beebe Buick	70	3,475	Running
31	30	98	Butch Miller	Travis Carter Chevrolet	68	4,075	Running
32	22	71	Dave Marcis	Marcis Auto Racing Chevy	67	6,025	Running
33	12	17	Darrell Waltrip	Hendrick Motorsports Chevy	65	12,375	Running
34	3	3	Dale Earnhardt	RCR Enterprises Chevy	65	12,650	Running
35	9	1	Terry Labonte	Precision Products Olds	62	5,935	Clutch
36	34	76	Bill Segdwick	Wayne Spears Chevrolet	61	3,305	Running
37	23	19	Chad Little	Chuck Little Ford	60	3,295	Running
38	6	40	Tommy Kendall	Marc Reno Chevrolet	46	4,025	Crash
39	27	66	Dick Trickle	Cale Yarborough Pontiac	41	6,250	Engine
40	44	44	Jack Sellers	Adel Emerson Buick	41	3,225	Running
41	18	26	Brett Bodine	King Motorsports Buick	38	5,225	Crash
42	24	20	Rob Moroso	Dick Moroso Olds	17	3,975	Crash
43	39	34	Ted Kennedy	Karen Kennedy Oldsmobile	11	3,225	Oil Line
44	25	04	Hershel McGriff	Bob Lipseia Pontiac	2	3,225	Engine

Time of Race: 2 hours, 41 minutes, 35 seconds
Average Speed: 69.245 mph
Pole Winner: Ricky Rudd – 99.743 mph
Lap Leaders: Ricky Rudd 1-11, Ernie Irvan 12-18, Mike Chase 19-22, Rusty Wallace 23-30, Tommy Kendall 31-34, Wallace 35-53, Bobby Hillin, Jr. 54-57, Rudd 58-59, Wallace 60-74.
8 lead changes among 6 drivers
Cautions: 9 for 24 laps   Margin of Victory: Under Caution

that.

Rudd was able to stay on the lead lap following his tire puncture and, with the help of nine caution periods, worked his way back into contention.

The Chesapeake, Va. driver led the 58th and 59th lap before Wallace rubbed Rudd in turn seven of the 2.52-mile road course. "I just let him know I was back there and that I do remember that corner," said Wallace, referring to the year before when Rudd washed Wallace off the course in a battle for the win. "It's very hard to pass on that hairpin turn. You need the whole track to get by."

Dover Downs

Davey Allison chats with crew member Tony Price.

Mark Martin drove past Rudd with three laps remaining to take second place. His bid to overtake Wallace was foiled when a two car tangle involving Terry Labonte and Davey Allison forced the race to end under the yellow flag.

Rudd held onto third despite fading brakes and a second green flag pit stop to replace another flat tire. Geoff Bodine claimed fourth spot and Bobby Hillin, Jr. notched his best career effort on a road course by taking fifth spot.

Martin was able to move atop the Winston Cup standings when Morgan Shepherd, who was running in the top five, blew the engine in his Bud Moore Engineering Ford with just over three laps to go.

"We had a good strong run going," said Shepherd, but when we ate breakfast this morning and the bill came to $13, I said 'Ooh-no! Not here on Sunday'."

Shepherd was left with a 29th place finish and 62 points behind Martin.

Dale Earnhardt suffered problems for the third race in a row and dropped to fourth place in the standings, 136 points behind Martin. Earnhardt encountered transmission problems that knocked him nine laps off the pace.

"We've had our share of problems the last few weeks, but there's nothing to do but keep plugging. Maybe we'll be able to finish a race next time without having to take a time out."

Wallace moved into third place in the standings.

"Just a few weeks ago, Earnhardt led me by almost 300 points, and now I'm ahead of him," said Wallace. "This team is on a roll. Now we've just got to stay out of trouble. One little problem and you can lose a ton of points."

Trans Am champion Tommy Kendall drove a Marc Reno Chevrolet and qualified sixth. He ran with the leaders and led for four laps but ran into a spinning Chad Little, departing on lap 46.

Hollywood stunt driver Stan Barrett drove the Hendrick Motorsports Chevrolet which Greg Sacks ran second at Talladega, finishing 17th on the lead lap – just ahead of Hendrick running mate Ken Schrader.

A total of 21 of the 44 starters finished on the lead lap. Wallace averaged only 69.245 mph, the slowest Winston Cup race on a road course since Parnelli Jones won a 72-mile event at Bremerton, Wash. at an average speed of 38 mph.

Race #13

Ol' Man Gant Ends Famine; Grabs Loot at Pocono

LONG POND, PA (June 17) – Harry Gant recovered from an early spin and outran his younger rivals to win the Miller Genuine Draft at Pocono International Raceway. Gant became the oldest winner in NASCAR Winston Cup history, notching his 11th career win at the age of 50 years, 158 days. Bobby Allison had held that distinction before the race, winning the 1988 Daytona 500 at the age of 50 years, 73 days.

Greg Crisp

Harry Gant grins in Pocono's Victory Lane.

Gant drove his Leo Jackson Oldsmobile around Rusty Wallace with 12 laps remaining and hustled to a 2-second triumph. Wallace held off

Jay Kainz

Harry Gant's Oldsmobile leads Darrell Waltrip, Brett Bodine and Richard Petty into Pocono's first turn.

Geoff Bodine for runner-up honors. Fourth place went to Brett Bodine and Davey Allison came home fifth.

An assortment of problems played havoc with a number of front-runners, including Gant. In the 113th lap, Gant skidded into the infield in the first turn. "I had just passed the 21 car (Dale Jarrett) and either him or somebody else ran into the back of me. It turned me crossways and I went through the grass," said Gant.

Until the mishap, Gant had never run in the top 10. "The green never stayed out long enough to show what the car could do," he reasoned.

While he was able to stay on the lead lap, the front grille area of Gant's Olds suffered cosmetic damage. Team owner Leo Jackson said the aluminum air duct which channels air into the radiator was bent beneath the car. "I wouldn't have given you a plug nickel for our chances half-way through the race," said Jackson.

"It got so hot I was a couple of laps from parking the car," Gant reflected. "It got up to 250 degrees and I didn't see any sense in tearing up a good engine. But the caution came out about then and we were able to do some work on it under the caution. The caution flags definitely helped us today."

A track record 13 caution flags slowed the action for 44 laps and reduced Gant's winning speed to 120.600 mph. The frequent caution periods bunched the field often enough that 22 cars finished on the lead lap, tying an all-time record established at Watkins Glen in 1988.

Wallace led the most laps and overcame a stop-and-go penalty for passing too early on one of the restarts. "I went absolutely brain-dead," admitted Wallace. "I passed on the left. I couldn't believe I forgot about the rule and I messed up big time."

Point leader Mark Martin struggled to finish 14th, but retained his lead by 53 points over Morgan Shepherd, who was fortunate to finish 11th.

Shepherd was overcome by heat and fumes after his Ford blew a tire and ripped the inside fender well panel. That let an extraordinary amount of heat in the car, "and it just cooked him," said Bud Moore Engineering team member Greg Moore. Shepherd had to be treated at the infield hospital after the race.

Dick Trickle, who started on the front row, also required medical attention after his Pontiac crashed in the final lap. He suffered a shoulder injury but declined a trip to a local hospital.

Michael Waltrip demolished his Pontiac in practice and took a bumpy trip to the hospital to check out back

Kim Novasat

Rob Moroso #20 leads Alan Kulwicki #7 during middle stages of Pocono's 500. Both drivers led the race; both drivers crashed.

pains. "The ride to the hospital was worse than the wreck," said Michael. "You drive 30 miles strapped to a piece of plywood over rough roads, and then they ask me if my back hurts."

Rob Moroso led for four laps before being passed by Alan Kulwicki. Three laps after losing the lead and still holding down to second place, Moroso crashed hard on lap 134.

Kulwicki broke out of his season-long slump by leading 34 laps, but he wiped out his Ford when a tire blew, sending him into the wall.

Richard Petty's Pontiac went into the wall off the tunnel turn on lap 95. He was unhurt.

Dale Earnhardt was not a factor, although his RCR Enterprises pit crew gave him the lead with a lightning fast pit stop 31 laps from the finish. When the green flag came out, Earnhardt couldn't keep up with the lead pack and eventually wound up 13th. He fell to fifth in the Winston Cup standings, 133 points behind leader Martin.

Ernie Irvan started on the pole and led for a total of 18 laps, but he was not a factor in the end and wound up 17th.

A total of 16 different drivers led the race, a Pocono record.

J.D.McDuffie #70, Jack Pennington and Rick Wilson #75 battle down home stretch at Pocono International Raceway.

Winston Cup Series Race No. 13
200 Laps at Pocono Int'l Raceway
Long Pond, PA
"Miller Genuine Draft 500"
500 Miles on 2.5-mile Superspeedway
June 17, 1990

Fin	St	No.	Driver	Team / Car	Laps	Money	Status
1	16	33	Harry Gant	Leo Jackson Olds	200	$54,350	Running
2	24	27	Rusty Wallace	Blue Max Pontiac	200	37,307	Running
3	4	11	Geoff Bodine	Junior Johnson Ford	200	30,750	Running
4	20	26	Brett Bodine	King Motorsports Buick	200	19,850	Running
5	12	28	Davey Allison	Robert Yates Racing Ford	200	20,700	Running
6	21	12	Hut Stricklin	Bobby Allison Buick	200	11,425	Running
7	5	18	Greg Sacks	Hendrick Motorsports Chevy	200	11,050	Running
8	9	17	Darrell Waltrip	Hendrick Motorsports Chevy	200	15,925	Running
9	7	94	Sterling Marlin	Billy Hagan Olds	200	10,675	Running
10	14	42	Kyle Petty	SabCo Racing Pontiac	200	15,350	Running
11	29	15	Morgan Shepherd	Bud Moore Eng. Ford	200	9,850	Running
12	17	10	Derrike Cope	Bob Whitcomb Chevrolet	200	10,550	Running
13	6	3	Dale Earnhardt	RCR Enterprises Chevrolet	200	14,150	Running
14	11	6	Mark Martin	Roush Racing Ford	200	13,150	Running
15	8	25	Ken Schrader	Hendrick Motorsports Chevy	200	12,525	Running
16	3	9	Bill Elliott	Melling Performance Ford	200	13,450	Running
17	1	4	Ernie Irvan	Morgan-McClure Olds	200	15,125	Running
18	35	19	Chad Little	Chuck Little Ford	200	4,650	Running
19	19	30	Michael Waltrip	Bahari Racing Pontiac	200	8,425	Running
20	27	1	Terry Labonte	Precision Products Olds	200	8,975	Running
21	33	47	Jack Pennington	Derick Close Olds	200	4,925	Running
22	31	71	Dave Marcis	Marcis Auto Racing Chevy	200	7,675	Running
23	26	98	Butch Miller	Travis Carter Chevrolet	199	5,775	Running
24	34	38	Jim Sauter	Down Under Ford	199	3,925	Running
25	2	66	Dick Trickle	Cale Yarborough Pontiac	198	7,075	Crash
26	36	54	Tommy Riggins	Hakes-Welliver Oldsmobile	196	3,825	Running
27	38	52	Jimmy Means	Means Racing Pontiac	194	3,775	Running
28	40	70	J.D.McDuffie	McDuffie Racing Pontiac	188	3,725	Running
29	25	8	Bobby Hillin,Jr	Stavola Brothers Buick	180	6,675	Engine
30	23	57	Jimmy Spencer	Rod Osterlund Pontiac	172	6,575	Crash
31	13	21	Dale Jarrett	Wood Brothers Ford	171	6,425	Crash
32	15	5	Ricky Rudd	Hendrick Motorsports Chevy	169	6,275	Running
33	28	13	Randy LaJoie	Linro Motorsports Buick	167	3,450	Crash
34	10	7	Alan Kulwicki	AK Racing Ford	165	6,850	Crash
35	18	75	Rick Wilson	RahMoc Racing Oldsmobile	150	6,025	Engine
36	30	20	Rob Moroso	Dick Moroso Olds	134	4,950	Crash
37	39	2	Troy Beebe	US Racing Pontiac	119	5,875	Crash
38	22	43	Richard Petty	Petty Enterprises Pontiac	94	3,825	Crash
39	32	80	Jimmy Horton	George Smith Ford	65	3,200	Engine
40	37	53	Jerry O'Neil	Alan Aroneck Oldsmobile	22	3,150	Crank

Time of Race: 4 hours, 8 minutes, 25 seconds
Average Speed: 120.600 mph
Pole Winner: Ernie Irvan – 158.750 mph
Lap Leaders: Ernie Irvan 1-2, Greg Sacks 3-24, Jimmy Spencer 25, Geoff Bodine 26-36, Sacks 37-40, Michael Waltrip 41, Kyle Petty 42-53, Irvan 54-69, G.Bodine70-71, Jack Pennington 72, Mark Martin 73-76, G.Bodine 77-82, Rusty Wallace 83-84, Brett Bodine 85-96, Morgan Shepherd 97-114, Derrike Cope 115-117, G.Bodine 118-127, Rob Moroso 128-131, Alan Kulwicki 132-151, G.Bodine 152, Kulwicki 153-161, G.Bodine 162, Sacks 163-165, Harry Gant 166-168, Dale Earnhardt 169-171, Wallace 172-188, Gant 189-200.
26 lead changes among 16 drivers.
Cautions: 13 for 44 laps Margin of Victory: 2 seconds

Race #14

Elliott Blows; Earnhardt Nips Irvan in Michigan 400

BROOKLYN, MI (June 24) – Bill Elliott's blown engine 15 laps from the finish set up a frantic duel at Michigan International Speedway, and Dale Earnhardt nipped Ernie Irvan at the finish of the Miller Genuine Draft 400.

Elliott started eighth and took an early backseat to the

MIS

Dale Earnhardt #3, Bill Elliott #9 and Rusty Wallace #27 battle for the lead at Michigan International Speedway.

speedy Mark Martin, who led 59 of the first 61 laps from the pole. After the second caution period, Elliott tracked down his rivals and took the lead for the first time on lap 71. From there on, he led a total of 102 laps before the engine in his Melling Performance Ford blew as he motored down the front chute.

"An oil fitting broke off and the motor began to suck air," said a dejected Elliott. "The oil pressure started going down after the last caution period. I didn't think the engine would last."

Elliott led through the 171st lap when the fourth and final caution appeared. During the yellow flag, members of the Melling team tried to repair the damage.

Quick pit work enabled Elliott to return to the track running fifth – 19 cars were still on the lead lap.

Ken Schrader took the lead for the first time by virtue of having the quickest pit stop.

Kim Novosat

Big and Little Dale; Earnhardt and son Dale, Jr. share a relaxing moment before the race.

Terry Labonte lined up second for the final green flag restart with Earnhardt third, Irvan fourth and Elliott fifth.

Earnhardt zipped around Schrader on lap 178. A lap later, Schrader limped to the garage area with a blown engine.

Elliott shot past leader Earnhardt with 18 laps to go and was pulling away when the engine gave up. ""I was surprised I got back to the front after the last caution as fast as I did," said Elliott. "Earnhardt and those guys are not easy to pass."

Elliott's departure put Earnhardt back in front for two laps, but Irvan made it interesting.

Irvan shoved his Morgan-McClure Oldsmobile into the lead and made a strong bid for his first career victory. He was able to hold off Earnhardt for seven laps before losing first place in the second turn.

Earnhardt grabbed the lead for good with six laps to go and the record crowd of 85,000 was treated to an electrifying finish to a race that had otherwise been rather dull.

"It looked like Elliott had us covered today," said Earnhardt. "He was going on and leaving me and Ernie to race for second. But you've got to be there at the end.

"I kept playing Ernie and I saw I could beat him in the middle of the turns," continued Earnhardt. "I got beside him and went on. We bumped fenders a couple of times.

"I probably cut him off on the last last lap, but I was trying to win as hard as he was."

Irvan settled for runner-up position, 0.22-second behind Earnhardt at the stripe. "Dale didn't drive dirty," said Irvan. "He got behind me and figured out my weak points. "He knew where to pass me. I could have won on the last lap by taking Dale out, but that's not racing."

Geoff Bodine ran in contention all day, but did not lead a lap. He squeezed the nose of his Ford past Martin in the final lap to take third. "We made an adjustment on the last stop and it worked," said Bodine. "We caught the leaders and for a minute I thought I might be able to win the thing."

Dave Marcis leads a pack of cars into Michigan's high-banked first turn.

Winston Cup Series Race No. 14
200 Laps at Michigan Int'l Speedway
Brooklyn, MI
"Miller Genuine Draft 400"
400 Miles on 2-mile Superspeedway
June 24, 1990

Fin	St	No.	Driver	Team / Car	Laps	Money	Status
1	5	3	Dale Earnhardt	RCR Enterprises Chevrolet	200	$72,950	Running
2	11	4	Ernie Irvan	Morgan-McClure Chevrolet	200	41,000	Running
3	4	11	Geoff Bodine	Junior Johnson Ford	200	33,375	Running
4	1	6	Mark Martin	Roush Racing Ford	200	25,400	Running
5	19	33	Harry Gant	Leo Jackson Oldsmobile	200	23,425	Running
6	24	7	Alan Kulwicki	AK Racing Ford	200	17,125	Running
7	17	1	Terry Labonte	Precision Products Olds	200	15,550	Running
8	6	42	Kyle Petty	SabCo Racing Pontiac	200	17,450	Running
9	13	5	Ricky Rudd	Hendrick Motorsports Chevy	200	13,800	Running
10	27	75	Rick Wilson	RahMoc Racing Olds	200	15,225	Running
11	29	43	Richard Petty	Petty Enterprise Pontiac	200	10,375	Running
12	18	10	Derrike Cope	Bob Whitcomb Chevrolet	200	13,100	Running
13	2	15	Morgan Shepherd	Bud Moore Eng. Ford	200	11,550	Running
14	12	26	Brett Bodine	King Motorsports Buick	200	11,000	Running
15	9	17	Darrell Waltrip	Hendrick Motorsports Chevy	200	16,525	Running
16	34	20	Rob Moroso	Dick Moroso Olds	200	9,282	Running
17	3	27	Rusty Wallace	Blue Max Pontiac	200	18,400	Running
18	14	94	Sterling Marlin	Billy Hagan Olds	199	9,325	Running
19	22	71	Dave Marcis	Marcis Auto Racing Chevy	199	9,010	Running
20	21	57	Jimmy Spencer	Rod Osterlund Pontiac	199	9,470	Running
21	16	30	Michael Waltrip	Bahari Racing Pontiac	199	8,450	Running
22	36	29	Phil Parsons	Diamond Ridge Pontiac	199	5,485	Running
23	23	98	Butch Miller	Travis Carter Chevrolet	198	6,125	Running
24	15	66	Dick Trickle	Cale Yarborough Pontiac	198	8,965	Running
25	8	9	Bill Elliott	Melling Performance Ford	185	27,105	Engine
26	32	18	Greg Sacks	Hendrick Motorsports Chevy	180	4,995	Running
27	7	25	Ken Schrader	Hendrick Motorsports Chevy	179	12,685	Engine
28	20	8	Bobby Hillin,Jr.	Stavola Brothers Buick	164	7,550	Running
29	33	23	Eddie Bierschwale	Don Bierschwale Olds	151	4,765	Mtr Mount
30	38	35	Bili Venturini	Venturini Chevrolet	142	4,705	Camshaft
31	28	2	Troy Beebe	US Racing Pontiac	132	7,240	Engine
32	25	12	Hut Stricklin	Bobby Allison Buick	130	5,155	Engine
33	35	83	Lake Speed	Speed Oldsmobile	120	4,470	Whl Studs
34	26	21	Dale Jarrett	Wood Brothers Ford	101	7,010	Trans
35	39	91	Ed Cooper	Cooper Oldsmobile	77	4,350	Engine
36	10	28	Davey Allison	Robert Yates Racing Ford	65	11,310	Engine
37	37	70	J.D.McDuffie	McDuffie Racing Pontiac	57	4,285	Rock Arm
38	31	47	Jack Pennington	Derick Close Olds	54	4,510	Crash
39	30	52	Jimmy Means	Means Racing Pontiac	28	4,250	Engine
40	40	89	Rodney Combs	Mueller Brothers Pontiac	15	4,225	Piston

Time of Race: 2 hours, 39 minutes, 46 seconds
Average Speed: 150.219 mph
Pole Winner: No Time Trials
Lap Leaders: Mark Martin 1-21, Butch Miller 22, Harry Gant 23, Martin 24-61, Dale Earnhardt 62-70, Bill Elliott 71-108, Gant 109-110, Elliott 111-132, Gant 133, Elliott 134-171, Earnhardt 172, Ken Schrader 173-177, Earnhardt 178-181, Elliott 182-185, Earnhardt 186-187, Ernie Irvan 188-194, Earnhardt 195-200.
16 lead changes among 7 drivers.
Cautions: 4 for 16 laps Margin of Victory: 0.22 second

Martin finished fourth and saw his point lead increase to 94 points over Morgan Shepherd, who wound up 13th. Fifth place went to Harry Gant and Alan Kulwicki came from 24th to place sixth.

Martin was disappointed with his fourth place effort after dominating the early stages. "Not much to say. We wound up fourth. We had a good race, but for some reason we had real inconsistency in our tires from set to set."

Earnhardt's triumph enabled him to move to within 118 points of leader Martin, though still logged in fifth place. "We've got to win some races and try to catch back up," said Earnhardt. "The main thing is we have to keep from having trouble."

Race #15

Earnhardt Wins 400 as 'Days of Thunder' Crash Wipes Out Field

DAYTONA BEACH, FL (July 7) – Dale Earnhardt avoided a massive 24-car collision at the outset of the Pepsi 400 and breezed to his first 'official' win at Daytona International Speedway.

The big crash – the largest at the Big D since the 1960 Modified & Sportsman race which involved 37 cars –

was triggered when Richard Petty, Greg Sacks and Derrike Cope were racing three abreast for most of the opening lap. Cope and Sacks made contact in the tri-oval and their cars got crossed up in front of the entire field. They were battling for seventh at the time of the mishap.

"Three idiots wrecked," barked Geoff Bodine, one of dozens whose cars were mangled in the crash. "They saw the damn movie," he added, alluding to the horrid movie release "Days of Thunder" which depicted that NASCAR drivers deliberately steer into rivals and intentionally cause big crashes.

ISC

Dale Earnhardt stayed out of trouble and earned a trip to Victory Lane at Daytona.

Winston Cup Series Race No. 15
160 Laps at Daytona Int'l Speedway
Daytona Beach, FL
"Pepsi 400"
400 Miles on 2.5-mile Superspeedway
July 7, 1990

Fin	St	No.	Driver	Team / Car	Laps	Money	Status
1	3	3	Dale Earnhardt	RCR Enterprises Chevy	160	$72,850	Running
2	12	7	Alan Kulwicki	AK Racing Ford	160	38,700	Running
3	6	25	Ken Schrader	Hendrick Motorsports Chevy	160	31,400	Running
4	8	1	Terry Labonte	Precision Products Olds	160	23,450	Running
5	13	94	Sterling Marlin	Billy Hagan Olds	160	21,250	Running
6	23	8	Bobby Hillin,Jr.	Stavola Brothers Buick	160	16,832	Running
7	16	33	Harry Gant	Leo Jackson Oldsmobile	160	17,400	Running
8	24	21	Dale Jarrett	Wood Brothers Ford	160	13,500	Running
9	11	20	Rob Moroso	Dick Moroso Olds	160	11,000	Running
10	10	42	Kyle Petty	SabCo Racing Pontiac	159	16,875	Running
11	2	6	Mark Martin	Roush Racing Ford	158	14,490	Running
12	22	52	Jimmy Means	Means Racing Pontiac	158	7,300	Running
13	9	5	Ricky Rudd	Hendrick Motorsports Chevy	158	10,135	Running
14	25	27	Rusty Wallace	Blue Max Pontiac	158	17,020	Running
15	33	57	Jimmy Spencer	Rod Osterlund Pontiac	157	10,030	Running
16	27	30	Michael Waltrip	Bahari Racing Pontiac	155	8,950	Running
17	5	17	Jimmy Horton*	Hendrick Motorsports Chevy	155	14,495	Running
18	36	47	Jack Pennington	Derick Close Olds	152	5,495	Running
19	30	66	Dick Trickle	Cale Yarborough Pontiac	151	9,125	Running
20	34	71	Dave Marcis**	Marcis -McDuffie Pontiac	140	8,570	Engine
21	40	96	Philip Duffie	Duffie Racing Buick	139	4,710	Running
22	20	26	Brett Bodine	King Motorsports Buick	138	7,515	Running
23	37	98	Butch Miller	Travis Carter Chevrolet	134	5,270	Running
24	17	28	Davey Allison	Robert Yates Racing Ford	133	12,325	Running
25	15	11	Geoff Bodine	Junior Johnson Ford	119	12,730	Running
26	21	12	Hut Stricklin	Bobby Allison Buick	118	4,860	Running
27	32	19	Chad Little	Chuck Little Ford	114	4,140	Running
28	18	10	Derrike Cope	Bob Whitcomb Chevrolet	100	8,920	Running
29	4	9	Bill Elliott	Melling Performance Ford	95	12,525	Running
30	35	90	Buddy Baker	Junie Donlavey Ford	71	3,730	Crash
31	26	73	Phil Barkdoll	Barkdoll Racing Olds	17	3,675	Crash
32	29	01	Mickey Gibbs	Gibbs-West Ford	13	3,645	Crash
33	14	4	Ernie Irvan	Morgan-McClure Olds	6	6,310	Crash
34	31	15	Morgan Shepherd	Bud Moore Eng. Ford	2	6,260	Crash
35	38	2	Charlie Glotzbach	US Racing Pontiac	2	6,205	Crash
36	7	43	Richard Petty	Petty Enterprises Pontiac	1	4,900	Crash
37	1	18	Greg Sacks	Hendrick Motorsports Chevy	1	6,995	Crash
38	19	14	A.J.Foyt	Foyt Enterprises Olds	1	3,480	Crash
39	23	75	Rick Wilson	RahMoc Racing Olds	1	6,060	Crash
40	39	06	Terry Byers	Byers Racing Pontiac	1	3,505	Crash

Time of Race: 2 hours, 29 minutes, 10 seconds
Average Speed: 160,894 mph
Pole Winner: Greg Sacks – 195.533 mph
Lap LEaders: Dale Earnhardt 1-31, Jimmy Spencer 32-34, Earnhardt 35-61, Sterling Marlin 62-76, Ken Schrader 77, Rob Moroso 78-79, Earnhardt 80-92, Bobby Hillin, Jr. 93-95, Earnhardt 96-134, Hillin, Jr. 135-138, Harry Gant 139, Schrader 140, Alan Kulwicki 141, Moroso 142-143, Earnhardt 144-160.
15 lead changes among 8 drivers.
Cautions: 4 for 14 laps Margin of Victory: 1.47 seconds
*Relieved by Greg Sacks **Relieved by J.D.McDuffie

Sacks had earned the pole at 195.533 mph, but his car was closely scrutinized following qualifying. "NASCAR took his manifold gadget," explained Earnhardt, who started third and immediately drew away from Sacks at the start. "Either that or he was afraid to use it. I think the start of the race showed the difference in his car. He wasn't as fast as when he qualified, was he?"

Sacks was trapped in the center groove when King Richard, who started seventh, and Cope, who started 18th, drew beside the Hendrick Motorsports driver. By the middle of the backstretch, the three were distantly behind the front six, who had pulled away.

Contact was made several times before the big crash occurred. "You can't win a race on the first lap," retorted Petty, "and they're a bunch of us in the garage area to prove that."

Sacks claimed that "Richard got into me a little bit and I got into Derrike and it sort of felt like a pinball effect. I wasn't hitting Derrike until I got hit."

Petty had a different view. "I got hit in the right rear and it spun me the wrong way. That looks like yellow paint, don't it?" Sacks drove a yellow and white car.

Cope said that Sacks "hit me going into turn three. I moved up and told myself to relax. I got hit again in turn four and I said 'come on guys, calm down'. Sacks hit me again and I hit the wall. Evidently, he must have bounced off me and hit King. I guess we all got into a situation we couldn't get out of. You can't back off. You get out of shape and you have 30 or 40 other guys right behind you."

Many observers, including some drivers, said Sacks and possibly others had lowered their angle of spoiler to a dangerous degree. "Every other car has a 33-degree spoiler and he (Sacks) had a 25," said Ernie Ir-

Brian Czobat

Tapestry of Terror; skid marks leave graphic evidence of big first lap pile-up.

van, another of the victims in the mishap. "Something told me he was going to be loose. I could go fast with a 25 degree spoiler, but I knew I might not be around at the finish."

The race was red-flagged for 36 minutes and 7 seconds while the wreckage was cleared.

When the race finally resumed, there was little competition left for Earnhardt. He would lead for 127 of the 160 laps and only lost the lead during pit stops.

Bobby Hillin, Jr. emerged as Earnhardt's most serious threat. The young Midland, Tex. driver, looking for his first win since the 1986 Talladega 500, put the Stavola Brothers Buick up front twice for seven laps. But he lost all chances of victory when he spun entering the pits for his final routine green flag stop. "I just blew it," confessed Hillin, Jr. "I let the guys on the crew down, and I feel bad. I came in too hard and spun it out."

Hillin, Jr. recovered, but was only able to salvage sixth place. He had started 28th.

Earnhardt outran Alan Kulwicki to the finish line by 1.47 seconds. The final three laps had been run under green following the fourth and final caution flag. Kulwicki was no match for the speedy Earnhardt. "For a change, we weren't in the wrong place at the wrong time," said that hard-luck owner-driver. "Everything happened behind me today. The wreck took out some good cars, but we beat some real good cars at the end."

Ken Schrader led twice for two laps and settled for third. Terry Labonte was fourth after having to start at the rear, and Sterling Marlin was fifth.

Mark Martin wound up 11th, quite an achievement since he was also heavily involved in the early wreck. He held his point lead by 63 points over Earnhardt, who vaulted from fifth to second.

Darrell Waltrip suffered serious leg injuries when his car was crunched by Dave Marcis in a practice crash. A.J.Foyt's Oldsmobile had blown an engine, dropping oil off the fourth turn. Labonte, Martin, Irvan, Phil

ISC

The beginning of the big 24-car crash.

Barkdoll and Bill Elliott were also involved.

Marcis also suffered a broken leg.

Jimmy Horton replaced Waltrip in the 400-miler, but was caught up in the early wreck. He eventually finished 17th.

Marcis had to borrow a Pontiac from J.D. McDuffie to start the race. He got out after the pace lap and McDuffie drove the rest of the way.

Winston Cup Series Race No. 16
200 Laps at Pocono Int'l Raceway
Long Pond, PA
"AC Spark Plug 500"
500 Miles on 2-mile Superspeedway
July 22, 1990

Fin	St	No.	Driver	Team / Car	Laps	Money	Status
1	4	11	Geoff Bodine	Junior Johnson Ford	200	$58,500	Running
2	6	9	Bill Elliott	Melling Performance Ford	200	33,650	Running
3	8	27	Rusty Wallace	Blue Max Pontiac	200	30,000	Running
4	11	3	Dale Earnhardt	RCR Enterprises Chevrolet	200	22,800	Running
5	15	28	Davey Allison	Robert Yates Racing Ford	200	25,950	Running
6	1	6	Mark Martin	Roush Racing Ford	200	21,050	Running
7	13	5	Ricky Rudd	Hendrick Motorsports Chevy	200	12,650	Running
8	26	98	Butch Miller	Travis Carter Chevrolet	200	10,582	Running
9	24	43	Richard Petty	Petty Enterprises Pontiac	200	8,675	Running
10	22	1	Terry Labonte	Precision Products Olds	200	12,450	Running
11	2	25	Ken Schrader	Hendrick Motorsports Chevy	200	12,750	Running
12	17	8	Bobby Hillin,Jr.	Stavola Brothers Buick	200	9,550	Running
13	12	10	Derrike Cope	Bob Whitcomb Chevrolet	200	11,350	Running
14	5	33	Harry Gant	Leo Jackson Olds	200	12,150	Running
15	23	66	Dick Trickle	Cale Yarborough Pontiac	199	10,325	Running
16	21	26	Brett Bodine	King Motorsports Buick	199	8,650	Running
17	9	7	Alan Kulwicki	AK Racing Ford	199	8,350	Running
18	18	21	Dale Jarrett	Wood Brothers Ford	198	7,950	Running
19	29	57	Jimmy Spencer	Rod Osterlund Pontiac	197	7,625	Running
20	25	17	Darrell Waltrip*	Hendrick Motorsports Chevy	197	14,175	Running
21	37	52	Jimmy Means	Means Racing Pontiac	197	4,175	Running
22	30	22	Rick Mast	U S Racing Pontiac	196	4,075	Running
23	28	30	Michael Waltrip	Bahari Racing Pontiac	193	6,975	Running
24	36	77	Ken Ragan	Marvin Ragan Ford	190	3,925	Crash
25	39	74	Mike Potter	Bobby Wawak Pontiac	189	3,975	Running
26	10	4	Ernie Irvan	Morgan-McClure Olds	181	6,775	Running
27	35	58	Brian Ross	Ken Schrader Pontiac	175	3,775	Engine
28	34	71	Dave Marcis**	Marcis Auto Racing Chevy	172	6,575	Running
29	20	12	Hut Stricklin	Bobby Allison Buick	167	4,425	Engine
30	16	94	Sterling Marlin	Billy Hagan Olds	155	6,825	Crash
31	19	75	Rick Wilson	RahMoc Racing Olds	154	6,250	Crash
32	7	20	Rob Moroso	Dick Moroso Olds	138	4,825	Crash
33	3	18	Greg Sacks	Hendrick Motorsports Chevy	137	14,950	Crash
34	31	53	Jerry O'Neil	Alan Aroneck Olds	134	3,650	Crash
35	14	42	Kyle Petty	SabCo Racing Pontiac	131	10,350	Oil Pan
36	27	15	Morgan Shepherd	Bud Moore Eng;. Ford	121	5,925	Crash
37	33	54	Tommy Riggins	Hakes-Welliver Oldsmobile	120	3,250	Crash
38	38	13	Randy LaJoie	Linro Motorsports Buick	10	3,225	Engine
39	22	38	Dick Johnson	Down Under Ford	4	3,200	Crash
			Rich Vogler	Ray & Diane DeWitt Chevrolet	-	-	DNS

Time of Race: 4 hours, 1 minute, 48 seconds
Average Speed: 124.070 mph
Pole Winner: Mark Martin – 158.264 mph
Lap Leaders: Ken Schrader 1-3, Greg Sacks 4-23, Geoff Bodine 24-29, Jimmy Spencer 30, Dale Earnhardt 31-36, G.Bodine 37, Sacks 38-41, G.Bodine 42-98, Sacks 99-107, G.Bodine 108-110, Rusty Wallace 111-113, G.Bodine 114-120, Wallace 121-123, Kyle Petty 124-126, Davey Allison 127-139, G.Bodine 140-142, Derrike Cope 143-146, G.Bodine 147-162, Allison 163-173, G.Bodine 174-178, Wallace 179, G.Bodine180-200.
22 lead changes among 9 drivers.
Cautions: 10 for 35 laps Margin of Victory: 1.22 seconds
*Relieved by Jimmy Horton **Relieved by J.D.McDuffie

Race #16

Bodine Best in Pocono Fuel Duel; Earnhardt Closes In Point Race

POCONO, PA (July 22) – Geoff Bodine hit the jackpot with a gamble on fuel consumption and Dale Earnhardt continued to chip away at Mark Martin's point lead in the AC Spark Plug 500 at Pocono International Raceway.

Pocono Int'l

Geoff Bodine grabbed his second win of the season at Pocono.

Bodine notched his second win since joining the Junior Johnson Ford team by outlasting Harry Gant and sprinting away from Bill Elliott in the final lap. Ken Ragan's crash in the final stages set up a one lap dash to the checkered flag.

Bodine led the final 21 laps after taking the lead in a spirited duel with Davey Allison and Rusty Wallace. All three drivers led during the 180th lap, but Bodine was in front at the start-finish line.

Bodine's gamble was set up when Sterling Marlin clipped the wall in the tunnel turn, bringing out the

Greg Crisp

The Junior Johnson pit crew swings into action.

ninth of the day's 10 caution flags. All contenders pitted for fresh tires and fuel. Bodine, with crew chief Tim Brewer calculating the fuel mileage, was intent on trying to go the final 107.5 miles without pitting. Most other teams felt they would have to pit for a splash of fuel if the race ran green the rest of the way.

Notable exceptions were Elliott, who pitted on lap 159 – under the yellow flag – and Gant, whose Leo Jackson team was rolling the dice with Bodine.

Most of the 14 cars on the lead lap took on fuel between laps 188 and 192.

Pocono Int'l

The first turn awaits the roaring pack in Pocono's 500-miler.

Bodine, who led 119 of the 200 laps, was running just ahead of Gant and Elliott when the green and white flags flew simultaneously starting the final lap. "My heart stopped when my engine sputtered," said Bodine, who won for the ninth time in his career that has spanned 11 years. "I yelled (on the radio) 'we're out of gas'. But it caught again and I took off. But that fuel gauge was jumping around the whole last lap."

After Bodine rolled into victory lane, NASCAR officials checked the fuel tank and reported that six-tenths of a gallon was left in the tank. "We weren't going to give the race away," declared crew chief Brewer. "We knew we were beat if we had stopped. I told Geoff to find a line and go. If we ran out, we ran out."

Gant's Oldsmobile coughed and sputtered in the final lap, which gave Bodine a clear run. Gant's fuel supply had gone dry and he coasted across the finish line in 14th place. "We needed about another half gallon," said the dejected Gant. "We lacked about a mile or so."

Elliott, whose bid was foiled by the late caution, finished second, 1.22 seconds behind Bodine's Ford. Rusty Wallace had difficulty clearing Dick Trickle's lapped Pontiac in the final lap and settled for third. Fourth place went to Dale Earnhardt and Allison took fifth. Sixth place went to pole sitter Mark Martin, who faded at the outset and never led a lap.

Earnhardt was able to slice 15 points off of his deficit and now trails Martin by 48 points.

Morgan Shepherd suffered his fourth straight DNF and fell 258 points behind in the Winston Cup standings. He had led the points just four races earlier.

Greg Sacks started

Jay Kainz

Mark Martin and Ken Schrader lead fast Pocono field.

third in one of four Chevrolets entered by the Hendrick Motorsports team. The Mattituck, NY driver ran with the leaders until being involved in two wrecks six laps apart. Rob Moroso, having a horrible freshman season on the big league NASCAR series, was also involved in two wrecks.

Jerry O'Neil was taken to the hospital complaining of headaches following a crash with Sacks.

Darrell Waltrip and Dave Marcis were able to start the race despite painful injuries suffered in a practice crash at Daytona. Waltrip made one lap before turning over the wheel to relief driver Jimmy Horton. The three-time Winston Cup champ had to be pulled from the car and Horton was nearly two laps down when he got back into the fray. He eventually finished 20th, three laps behind.

Marcis had long-time friend Jim Sauter take the wheel of his Chevrolet after the first lap. Sauter wound up 28th in the final rundown.

Bodine averaged 124.070 mph before a record audience estimated at 100,000 by local police.

Rich Vogler, highly acclaimed USAC Sprint and Midget champion, had qualified for the 32nd starting spot in a Chevrolet entered by new team owners Ray and Diane DeWitt. Vogler was killed in a Sprint car race at Salem, Ind. the night before the race. The car was withdrawn and the spot remained vacant on the pace lap. Only 39 cars started the 500-mile race.

Big crash on lap 156 depleted the field at Pocono.

Race #17

Dale Delivers at 'Dega; Trails Martin by 1-point in Standings

TALLADEGA, AL (July 29) – Dale Earnhardt zipped past Bill Elliott with 20 laps remaining and sped to victory in the DieHard 500 at Talladega Superspeedway. The $152,975 triumph was the sixth of the year for the 42 year-old Kannapolis, N.C. Chevrolet driver, who managed to close to within one point of Winston Cup leader Mark Martin.

Earnhardt started on the pole and dominated the proceedings – leading six times for 134 laps. He could have led more. Confronted with the possibility of running out of gas in the final stages, Earnhardt drafted eventual runner-up Bill Elliott for 18 laps before moving to the front for good.

"It was a move to save fuel," said Earnhardt, who had made his final pit stop on lap 148, leaving 106.4 miles to go. "I asked Richard (Childress, team owner) if I could make it the rest of the way. He said maybe I could if I drafted Bill for awhile.

"I asked Richard if I could go to the front (with 22 laps to go). After I didn't get an answer for a couple of laps, I went ahead to the front. I'm always more comfortable in front. I felt we had the strongest car and could handle Bill," said the winner.

Elliott wound up second, but never made an offensive move in the final lap. "I knew I couldn't do anything with him," admitted Elliott. "If it had been somebody else, I might have been able to do something. But not him (Earnhardt)."

Sterling Marlin finished a distant third in Billy Hagan's Oldsmobile. Alan Kulwicki ran a strong fourth and Ricky Rudd was fifth.

Martin had given Earnhardt the hardest run, but he was forced to pit for gas with nine laps remaining. He finished ninth, the final car on the lead lap. "We ran good all day," said Martin, who was able to pull five seconds ahead of the field while running with Earnhardt. "But all we got out of it was a dry gas tank and a ninth place finish."

Earnhardt led the most laps of the Talladega DieHard 500 since Pete Hamilton led 157 laps en route to victory in 1970.

Earnhardt bagged a $68,800 bonus from Unocal for winning the pole and the bonus. It was his first pole

Bryan Hallman

Jimmy Spencer gets upside down after tangling with Ken Schrader during final lap of Talladega 500.

since early in the 1987 season.

Davey Allison qualified second and led the first three laps, but the young Alabama star struggled and eventually finished 20th, two laps down.

Stanley Smith, another Alabama native, entered his first Winston Cup race and qualified a stunning 12th in George Bradshaw's Tri-Star Motorsports Pontiac. Smith was involved in a pit road mishap with Tracy Leslie in the 55th lap. Smith's car got squeezed into the tri-oval grass, then spun and slid into Leslie's Oldsmobile, which was just exiting his pit stall.

"I was in the lane nearest the grass," explained Smith. "A car (Jim Sauter, in relief of Dave Marcis) came out and hit my front end. The next thing I knew I was spinning."

Bryan Hallman

Spencer continued after his crash and finished 24th.

Winston Cup Series Race No. 17
188 Laps at Talladega Superspeedway
Talladega, AL
"DieHard 500"

500.08 Miles on 2.66-mile Superspeedway
July 29, 1990

Fin	St	No.	Driver	Team / Car	Laps	Money	Status
1	1	3	Dale Earnhardt	RCR Enterprises Chevy	188	$152,975	Running
2	9	9	Bill Elliott	Melling Performance Ford	188	48,390	Running
3	14	94	Sterling Marlin	Billy Hagan Olds	188	34,050	Running
4	5	7	Alan Kulwicki	AK Racing Ford	188	24,750	Running
5	25	5	Ricky Rudd	Hendrick Motorsports Chevy	188	22,050	Running
6	16	4	Ernie Irvan	Morgan-McClure Chevrolet	188	16,325	Running
7	21	10	Derrike Cope	Bob Whitcomb Chevrolet	188	16,350	Running
8	3	42	Kyle Petty	SabCo Racing Pontiac	188	16,350	Running
9	4	6	Mark Martin	Roush Racing Ford	188	18,570	Running
10	17	8	Bobby Hillin,Jr.	Stavola Brothers Buick	187	14,075	Running
11	39	83	Lake Speed	Speed Oldsmobile	187	8,537	Running
12	6	20	Rob Moroso	Dick Moroso Oldsmobile	187	7,950	Running
13	15	17	Jimmy Horton	Hendrick Motorsports Chevy	187	15,980	Running
14	41	12	Hut Stricklin	Bobby Allison Buick	187	8,710	Running
15	7	33	Harry Gant	Leo Jackson Olds	187	14,185	Running
16	24	25	Ken Schrader	Hendrick Motorsports Chevy	186	13,500	Crash
17	13	11	Geoff Bodine	Junior Johnson Ford	186	14,735	Running
18	38	18	Greg Sacks	Hendrick Motorsports Chevy	186	6,230	Running
19	33	19	Chad Little	Chuck Little Ford	186	6,050	Running
20	2	28	Davey Allison	Robert Yates Ford	186	15,075	Running
21	32	30	Michael Waltrip	Bahari Racing Pontiac	186	9,480	Running
22	30	01	Mickey Gibbs	Gibbs-West Ford	186	5,550	Running
23	27	47	Jack Pennington	Derick Close Olds	186	5,695	Running
24	31	57	Jimmy Spencer	Rod Osterlund Pontiac	186	8,790	Running
25	28	35	Bill Venturini	Venturini Chevrolet	185	5,135	Running
26	10	15	Morgan Shepherd	Bud Moore Eng. Ford	185	8,235	Running
27	29	14	A.J.Foyt	Foyt Enterprises Olds	185	4,865	Running
28	35	71	Dave Marcis*	Marcis Auto Racing Chevy	183	7,895	Running
29	42	43	Richard Petty	Petty Enterprises Pontiac	183	5,725	Running
30	23	52	Jimmy Means	Means Racing Pontiac	180	5,605	Out of Gas
31	40	82	Mark Stahl	Stahl Racing Ford	178	4,585	Running
32	26	27	Rusty Wallace	Blue Max Pontiac	149	15,465	Engine
33	18	26	Brett Bodine	King Motorsports Buick	148	7,295	Engine
34	19	98	Butch Miller	Travis Carter Chevrolet	144	5,150	Engine
35	37	75	Rick Wilson	RahMoc Oldsmobile	133	7,055	Engine
36	20	66	Dick Trickle	Cale Yarborough Pontiac	132	7,985	Running
37	12	68	Stanley Smith	Tri-Star Motorsports Pontiac	54	4,285	Pit Crash
38	34	72	Tracy Leslie	Tex Powell Olds	54	4,990	Pit Crash
39	22	21	Dale Jarrett	Wood Brothers Ford	51	7,005	Engine
40	36	90	Buddy Baker	Junie Donlavey Ford	47	4,150	Ignition
41	8	29	Phil Parsons	Diamond Ridge Pontiac	25	4,150	Crash
42	11	1	Terry Labonte	Precision Products Olds	6	6,775	Engine

Time of Race: 2 hours, 52 minutes, 1 second
Average Speed: 174.430 mph
Pole Winner: Dale Earnhardt – 192.513 mph
Lap Leaders: Davey Allison 1-3, Dale Earnhardt 4-27, Butch Miller 28, Bobby Hillin,Jr. 29-31, Michael Waltrip 32, Earnhardt 33-54, A.J.Foyt 55-58, Sterling Marlin 59-64, Earnhardt 65-95, Marlin 96-99, Allison 100, Rob Moroso 101, Rusty Wallace 102, Geoff Bodine 103-104, Harry Gant 105, G.Bodine 106, Earnhardt 107-140, Kyle Petty 141-143, Bill Elliott 144-146, Hillin,Jr. 147, Earnhardt 148-150, Elliott 151-168, Earnhardt 169-188.
23 lead changes among 13 drivers.
Cautions: 2 for 12 laps Margin of Victory: 0.26 second
*Relieved by Jim Sauter

Leslie, a rookie out of Mt.Clemens, MI., made a brilliant move that perhaps saved the lives of several pit crewmen. "I looked in my mirror and saw a car spinning toward me," said Leslie. "I let out the clutch to get away, but it was too late."

Four crewmen were treated for injuries. Art Presnell, Robin Metdepennigan, Joey Britt and Eric Dunn were the men hurt in the collision, but if Leslie had not been aware of the impending peril, it could have been worse.

Jimmy Spencer and Ken Schrader crashed on the backstretch of the final lap. Michael Waltrip's Pontiac ran out of gas and slowed abruptly. Schrader plowed into Waltrip, who was pushed into the path of Spencer. "Schrader caught him in the quarter-panel," said Spencer, who was driving Rod Osterlund's Pontiac. "Then Waltrip bounced into me and I went barrel-rolling down the track."

Spencer's car landed on its wheels and he limped back around to finish 24th. Schrader got credit for 16th.

Darrell Waltrip, injured at Daytona, stepped out of his car and let substitute driver Jimmy Horton take the wheel of the Hendrick Motorsports Chevrolet. He responded with his personal best effort in Winston Cup racing – a 13th place finish.

With 12 races remaining, Earnhardt stands poised to win his fourth NASCAR championship. But he will have to fight an uphill battle in a championship which fails to reward winning races. Thus far in the 1990 season, he has won 600% more races than Martin, has more top five finishes, led the most races, led the most laps and has earned nearly twice as much money as his closest adversary in the standings.

Jim Ahmay

Road racer Sarel van der Merwe drove the Hendrick Motorsports Chevrolet in place of injured Darrell Waltrip at Watkins Glen.

Race #18

Rudd Survives at the Glen; Hagan Chases Kendall with a Cane

WATKINS GLEN, NY (Aug. 12) – Ricky Rudd overcame an early spin-out, three flat tires and the loss of an 11.1-second lead by a late yellow flag, and won the Budweiser at the Glen event at Watkins Glen International before a reported record audience of 120,000. It was the third win in the last five road course events for the Chesapeake, Va. driver and the triumph ended famines for himself and car owner Rick Hendrick.

Rudd finished 6.54 seconds ahead of runner-up Geoff Bodine to score his first win since June of 1989. It also removed the

Rusty Wallace #27 gets turned around in crash with Geoff Bodine #11 and Dale Jarrett.

Winston Cup Series Race No. 18
90 Laps at Watkins Glen International
Watkins Glen, NY
"Budweiser at the Glen"
218.52 Miles on 2.428-mile Road Course
August 12, 1990

Fin	St	No.	Driver	Team / Car	Laps	Money	Status
1	12	5	Ricky Rudd	Hendrick Motorsports Chevy	90	$55,000	Running
2	5	11	Geoff Bodine	Junior Johnson Ford	90	33,900	Running
3	13	26	Brett Bodine	King Motorsports Buick	90	22,490	Running
4	8	30	Michael Waltrip	Bahari Racing Pontiac	90	16,980	Running
5	3	6	Mark Martin	Roush Racing Ford	90	20,790	Running
6	23	15	Morgan Shepherd	Bud Moore Eng. Ford	90	12,775	Running
7	1	3	Dale Earnhardt	RCR Enterprises Chevrolet	90	22,380	Running
8	10	40	Tommy Kendall	Marc Reno Chevrolet	90	6,570	Running
9	11	25	Ken Schrader	Hendrick Motorsports Chevy	90	13,040	Running
10	18	0	Irv Hoerr	Precision Products Olds	90	7,775	Running
11	9	7	Alan Kulwicki	AK Racing Ford	90	10,040	Running
12	6	9	Bill Elliott	Melling Performance Ford	90	13,400	Running
13	19	20	Rob Moroso	Dick Moroso Olds	90	5,360	Running
14	2	1	Terry Labonte	Precision Products Olds	90	8,270	Running
15	17	94	Sterling Marlin	Billy Hagan Olds	90	8,555	Running
16	25	8	Bobby Hillin,Jr.	Stavola Brothers Buick	89	7,660	Running
17	14	42	Kyle Petty	SabCo Racing Pontiac	89	10,940	Running
18	28	43	Richard Petty	Petty Enterprises Pontiac	89	5,120	Running
19	21	28	Davey Allison	Robert Yates Racing Ford	89	12,165	Running
20	26	21	Dale Jarrett	Wood Brothers Ford	88	7,445	Running
21	27	33	Harry Gant	Leo Jackson Olds	85	10,335	Running
22	38	70	J.D.McDuffie	McDuffie Racing Pontiac	84	3,225	Running
23	16	12	Hut Stricklin	Bobby Allison Buick	82	4,130	Crash
24	20	17	Sarel van der Merwe	Hendrick Motorsports Chevy	77	12,070	Crash
25	40	98	Butch Miller	Travis Carter Chevrolet	75	4,085	Engine
26	36	2	Jerry O'Neil	US Racing Pontiac	74	2,975	Running
27	15	38	Dick Johnson	Down Under Ford	67	2,915	Handling
28	22	4	Ernie Irvan	Morgan-McClure Chevrolet	65	5,705	Running
29	31	57	Jimmy Spencer	Rod Osterlund Pontiac	63	5,545	Engine
30	33	66	Dick Trickle*	Cale Yarborough Pontiac	60	5,435	Trans
31	30	71	Dave Marcis	Marcis Auto Racing Chevy	52	5,250	Throttle
32	29	75	Rick Wilson	RahMoc Racing Olds	50	5,160	Brakes
33	32	54	Tommy Riggins	Hakes-Welliver Olds	48	2,390	Trans
34	4	27	Rusty Wallace	Blue Max Pontiac	46	15,590	Engine
35	7	10	Derrike Cope	Bob Whitcomb Chevrolet	45	7,330	Engine
36	35	22	Rick Ware	Bobby Jones Pontiac	42	2,295	Brakes
37	37	13	Orna Kimbrough	Linro Motorsports Buick	40	2,240	Oil Leak
38	39	04	John Alexander	Ford	35	2,210	Oil Leak
39	34	52	Jimmy Means	Means Racing Pontiac	33	2,805	Trans
40	24	18	Greg Sacks	Hendrick Motorsports Chevy	14	2,145	Crash

Time of Race: 2 hours, 21 minutes, 49 seconds
Average Speed: 92.452 mph
Pole Winner: Dale Earnhardt – 121.190 mph
Lap Leaders: Dale Earnhardt 1-8, Rusty Wallace 9-17, Irv Hoerr 18-20, Wallace 21-39, Ricky Rudd 40-41, Earnhardt 42-44, Geoff Bodine 45-49, Mark Martin 50-65, Rudd 66-73, Hut Stricklin 74, Alan Kulwicki 75-80, Rudd 81-90.
11 lead changes among 8 drivers
Cautions: 5 for 15 laps Margin of Victory: 6.54 seconds
*Relieved by Dorsey Schroeder

Brian Czobat

Billy Hagan and his trusty cane.

goose-egg from car owner Rick Hendrick's win column in 1990. Despite a potent four-car team, Hendrick's cars had not scored in 72 cumulative entries on the Winston Cup Series dating back to the fall of 1989.

"Any win is good, but this one is special for our team," declared Rudd, who won for the 11th time in his career. "It makes it a lot easier at the shop Monday, not having to answer those phone calls about why you ran second, third or wherever."

Rudd started 12th and was served his first dose of bad luck when he spun on lap 10 after rubbing fenders with Geoff Bodine. "Each time we had problems, the caution would come and gave us a chance to regroup. On a day like today, it comes down to pit strategy and a lot of luck. Toward the end of the race, we didn't have any tire trouble and the others did."

The Bodine brothers, from nearby Chemung, battled for second place, with Geoff prevailing. Michael Waltrip took fourth place and Mark Martin wound up fifth.

Martin had the lead with 25 laps to go, but encountered several flat tires which threatened to knock him out of the Winston Cup point lead. "We had the godawfulest luck I've ever seen in my life. Three flat tires in the last 19 laps. I can't believe we came back to finish fifth."

Martin finished two positions ahead of Dale Earnhardt to push his slim lead in the Winston Cup standings to 10 points.

Kim Novasat

Jimmy Spencer loops his Pontiac at Watkins Glen.

Earnhardt survived a scuffle with Rusty Wallace to finish seventh. Earnhardt was leading in the 44th lap when Wallace's Pontiac snagged the rear quarter-panel at the entrance to turn one. "I was a little too eager to pass Earnhardt down there," said Wallace. "I got into the turn in good position and slowed up. I slowed right into him. But I blew up a lap later. I guess me and Earnhardt are even."

Earnhardt didn't necessarily agree with Wallace about being even. "I haven't got any comment on that deal with Rusty," Earnhardt growled. "Let's just say I'll handle it myself".

Brian Czobat

Tommy Kendall finished eighth, then had to dodge Billy Hagan's cane.

Billy Hagan, team owner of the Oldsmobile driven by Sterling Marlin, encountered a little disagreement with road racing specialist Tommy Kendall after he and Marlin collided in the last lap while battling for fifth place. The mishap dropped Marlin to 15th while Kendall was able to salvage ninth.

After the race, Hagan, who walks with a cane – a result of a 1985 sports car crash – charged after Kendall. "(Bill) Elliott went into the turn a little deep and Sterling tried to pass him on the inside," said Kendall, who was driving Marc Reno's Chevrolet. "I got to the left and shot to the inside. Elliott got a wheel off in the dirt, came back on the track and knocked Sterling into me. I was driving past them and got drilled in the side.

"Sterling came over afterwards and asked me why I wrecked him," continued Kendall. "Then his car owner (Hagan) chases me around my own car a couple of times, swinging that cane at me. I guess that's part of being the new kid on the block."

Hut Stricklin led a single lap and was holding down second place when he hit the lapped car of Sarel van der Merwe with seven laps to go. The crash sidelined both drivers. The assignment in the Hendrick Motorsports Chevrolet had been given to van der Merwe while Darrell Waltrip was still on the sidelines. He was five laps down at the time of the wreck.

California newcomer Troy Beebe had lined up Junie Donlavey's Ford in his quest to make the starting field. Beebe spun at the top of the esses and was clobbered by Dick Trickle and Mark Martin in rapid succession. Beebe had to be cut from his car and was transported by helicopter to Packer Hospital in Sayre, Pa. He suffered a concussion and a fractured pelvis. He was listed in serious condition. Beebe was discharged from the hospital 15 days later.

Trickle suffered numerous bruises, a cut chin and an ankle injury. He competed in the Sunday race wearing a size 11 shoe on his swollen right foot and a size 8 1/2 on his left. Martin was shaken but unhurt.

"I firmly believe we almost got killed up there," commented Martin.

Race #19

Martin Masters Michigan; Takes Aim at Earnhardt

BROOKLYN, MI (Aug. 19) – Mark Martin sprinted away from his rivals in the second half of the Champion Spark Plug 400 and increased his narrow advantage

Winston Cup Series Race No. 19
200 Laps at Michigan Int'l Speedway
Brooklyn, MI
"Champion Spark Plug 400"
400 Miles on 2-mile Superspeedway
August 19, 1990

Fin	St	No.	Driver	Team / Car	Laps	Money	Status
1	5	6	Mark Martin	Roush Racing Ford	200	$71,200	Running
2	8	17	Greg Sacks	Hendrick Motorsports Chevy	200	41,600	Running
3	6	27	Rusty Wallace	Blue Max Pontiac	200	33,900	Running
4	2	9	Bill Elliott	Melling Performance Ford	200	27,000	Running
5	39	5	Ricky Rudd	Hendrick Motorsports Chevy	200	20,607	Running
6	10	28	Davey Allison	Robert Yates Racing Ford	200	19,325	Running
7	9	11	Geoff Bodine	Junior Johnson Ford	200	18,750	Running
8	7	3	Dale Earnhardt	RCR Enterprises Chevrolet	200	19,400	Running
9	21	15	Morgan Shepherd	Bud Moore Eng. Ford	200	13,550	Running
10	16	21	Dale Jarrett	Wood Brothers Ford	200	14,825	Running
11	1	7	Alan Kulwicki	AK Racing Ford	200	13,000	Running
12	38	98	Butch Miller	Travis Carter Chevrolet	200	9,600	Running
13	11	33	Harry Gant	Leo Jackson Olds	200	14,300	Running
14	36	1	Terry Labonte	Precision Products Olds	200	10,900	Running
15	20	12	Hut Stricklin	Bobby Allison Buick	200	9,075	Running
16	18	42	Kyle Petty	SabCo Racing Pontiac	200	13,250	Running
17	12	26	Brett Bodine	King Motorsports Buick	200	11,900	Running
18	41	71	Dave Marcis	Marcis Auto Racing Chevy	199	9,150	Running
19	13	10	Derrike Cope	Bob Whitcomb Chevrolet	199	10,650	Running
20	4	94	Sterling Marlin	Billy Hagan Olds	199	9,450	Running
21	17	8	Bobby Hillin,Jr.	Stavola Brothers Buick	198	8,225	Running
22	14	19	Chad Little	Chuck Little Ford	198	5,125	Running
23	30	90	Buddy Baker	Junie Donlavey Ford	198	5,025	Running
24	27	68	Mike Chase	Tri-Star Motorsports Pontiac	198	4,925	Running
25	40	57	Jimmy Spencer	Rod Osterlund Pontiac	197	7,875	Running
26	26	20	Rob Moroso	Dick Moroso Olds	197	5,425	Running
27	25	52	Jimmy Means	Means Racing Pontiac	195	5,475	Running
28	31	35	Bill Venturini	Venturini Chevrolet	192	4,575	Running
29	19	75	Rick Wilson	RahMoc Racing Olds	186	7,225	Steering
30	34	30	Michael Waltrip	Bahari Racing Pontiac	181	7,125	Engine
31	28	48	Ben Hess	Hylton Engineering Pontiac	169	4,275	Crash
32	15	66	Dick Trickle	Cale Yarborough Pontiac	162	7,900	Crash
33	22	43	Richard Petty	Petty Enterprises Pontiac	128	4,725	Engine
34	23	89	Rodney Combs	Mueller Brothers Pontiac	127	4,025	Oil Line
35	3	4	Ernie Irvan	Morgan-McClure Chevrolet	113	6,775	Engine
36	32	22	Rick Mast	Bobby Jones Pontiac	103	3,950	Engine
37	33	77	Ken Ragan	Marvin Ragan Ford	102	3,925	Crash
38	29	47	Jack Pennington	Derick Close Olds	73	4,150	Oil Pan
39	24	50	Ted Musgrave	DeWitt Racing Chevrolet	65	3,890	Valve
40	35	25	Ken Schrader	Hendrick Motorsports Chevy	19	10,875	Engine
41	37	91	Ed Cooper	Cooper Oldsmobile	17	3,875	Rock Arm

Time of Race: 2 hours, 52 minutes, 53 seconds
Average Speed: 138.822 mph
Pole Winner: Alan Kulwicki – 174.982 mph
Lap Leaders: Bill Elliott 1-22, Dale Earnhardt 23, Dave Marcis 24, Brett Bodine 25-33, Earnhardt 34-67, Rusty Wallace 68, Mark Martin 69-70, Greg Sacks 71-72, Geoff Bodine 73-74, Richard Petty 75-79, Earnhardt 80, Wallace 81, Earnhardt 82-88, Wallace 89, Earnhardt 90-94, Wallace 95-123, Martin 124-154, Sacks 155-156, G.Bodine 157, Earnhardt 158-159, Morgan Shepherd 160, Kyle Petty 161, Martin 162-200.
23 lead changes among 11 drivers.
Cautions: 6 for 26 laps Margin of Victory: 1.7 seconds

Brian Czobat

Mark Martin regained momentum with Michigan victory.

over Dale Earnhardt to 48 points.

Martin kept his Roush Racing Ford in contention throughout the early portions of the 200-lap contest around Michigan International Speedway's two-mile oval, then throttled to a convincing triumph by leading 70 of the final 77 laps.

At the finish, Martin outdistanced Greg Sacks by 1.7 seconds. Rusty Wallace was a distant third with Bill Elliott fourth and Ricky Rudd fifth.

Earnhardt was one of the primary contenders early in the race, but he slipped to eighth in the final rundown.

"We had a race car today that we've been looking for," said Martin after his third career win. "We've been looking for some momentum to beat that black car (Earnhardt) for the Winston Cup championship."

Brian Czobat

Pole sitter Alan Kulwicki #7 leads Jimmy Spencer #57 and Chad Little at Michigan.

Brian Czobat

Greg Sacks #17 pairs up with Davey Allison at Michigan International Speedway.

Martin picked up 38 points in the battle for top honors and the estimated $1.3 million awards that go with the title. "We didn't really gain that much, but with this win everybody is going to stand up and say this team is serious," said Martin.

Alan Kulwicki earned his first pole of the season, but he never led. Elliott led the first 22 laps before giving up first place in the first round of pit stops. He never led after that.

Earnhardt and Wallace moved to the front and treated the crowd of nearly 100,000 to a terrific duel. From lap 23-123, the two hard chargers led all but 22 laps. "Dale and I racing side-by-side was what the fans paid to see," said Wallace. "Unfortunately, both of us had problems. One of my exhaust pipes fell off and I know I lost 20-30 horsepower."

Earnhardt said he was slowed by tire problems during the late stages.

Richard Petty led for five laps – the first time he has led a Winston Cup race since the Atlanta 500 in March of 1989.

Martin thundered past Wallace in the 124th lap and was threatened only by Sacks for the rest of the race.

"After the half-way point, I didn't think I could lose unless something went wrong," said Martin. "I decided it was time to go and drove on into the lead."

Sacks, the third substitute driver for the injured Darrell Waltrip in the last three races, turned in a fine per-

MIS

Mark Martin #6 ducks under Bill Elliott en route to victory at Michigan.

formance. "Martin just had too much under the hood for me," he confessed. "But this is a good run for this team. I've got four or five more races with this team before Darrell comes back. I think we can win one in that time."

Jeff Hammond, crew chief on the Hendrick Motorsports Chevrolet team, said he wasn't surprised at how well Sacks performed. "Sacks is capable of winning races. We have an opportunity to work with a driver who knows all the tracks we're going to. He's a seasoned driver."

Brett Bodine led for nine laps in Kenny Bernstein's King Motorsports Buick, but was foiled by a loose tail pipe in the waning laps. "Evidently the straps on the tailpipe broke and somebody behind us must have turned us in (to NASCAR). Lady luck got us in the end," said the younger Bodine.

Bodine was running in fourth place with 15 laps to go when he was blackflagged to the pits for repairs. He wound up 17th in the final rundown, the final car on the lead lap.

Race #20

Irvan Prevails in Bristol 500 For First Winston Cup Victory

BRISTOL, TN (Aug. 25) – Ernie Irvan drove past Dale Earnhardt with 90 laps to go and held off Rusty Wallace in a stirring duel to win the Busch 500 at Bristol International Raceway. It was the first win for the 31 year-old Modesto, Calif. driver and the first for the Morgan-McClure team.

Irvan, making his 17th start for the Abington, Va. based Chevrolet team, nipped Wallace at the stripe by about a car length. Mark Martin padded his Winston Cup point lead on the strength of a third place effort. Terry Labonte came home fourth and Sterling Marlin was fifth.

Dale Earnhardt started on the pole and led 350 of the first 410 laps. Following a restart, Earnhardt was battling with the lapped car of Ricky Rudd and cut down a tire after scrubbing fenders. "A damned lapped car cut me off," snorted Earnhardt, whose altercation opened the door for Irvan. "It's a shame we had to lose that way. The car was perfect."

Irvan breezed into the lead as Earnhardt peeled into the pits. Earnhardt lost a lap but blasted through the pack and salvaged eighth place. He fell 61 points behind Martin in the battle for the Winston Cup championship.

Wallace spent most of the evening running in the pack, but sprinted into contention and challenged Irvan over the final 50 laps. The two ran bumper-to-bumper virtually the rest of the way and Wallace pulled along side of Irvan a couple of times. "All he had to do was tap me and I would have spun out," reflected Irvan, whose first win came in his 179th start. "He gave me plenty of room, and if it ever comes down to us again, I'll remember it."

Wallace said he felt fatigued in the final laps. "I don't like to admit this," he said, "but I was getting a little

Bristol Int'l

Ernie Irvan misses a spinning Alan Kulwicki by inches at Bristol.

Brian Czobat

Jimmy Means' Pontiac was badly damaged in a practice wreck at Bristol.

tired in the end. I used all my energy just to catch him. He started making mistakes and I was making mistakes, too."

Earnhardt garnered his third pole of the season and dominated until his scuffle with Rudd. Most of his rivals spent the evening chasing the black #3 Chevrolet and spent considerable time running into each other.

Greg Sacks, hot off a sparkling effort at Michigan, was involved in three wrecks in the Hendrick Motorsports Chevrolet. Rookie Rob Moroso was knocked out in his second crash of the evening, then took over for a fatigued Davey Allison. Moroso spun Allison's Ford once and limped to a 23rd place finish.

Derrike Cope looped his Chevrolet off the fourth turn early in the race and scooped up Morgan Shepherd, Bobby Hillin, Jr. and Sacks. Despite substantial damage, all were able to continue.

Alan Kulwicki had run second a good part of the time, but he spun late in the race after a tap from Irvan. "We got up to second and were running just as fast as Earnhardt," said Kulwicki, who eventually finished sixth. "Then we had a problem in the pits and that nudge from Ernie spun us out. It was just a case of bad breaks tonight."

The humidity reached epic proportions that sapped the strength out of many drivers.

Three drivers called on relief and two cars had to be parked when substitutes could not be located. Richard Petty found himself in the unusual position of having to pull out of the race due to fatigue – when no suitable replacement could be found – then providing brief relief work for his son Kyle. Richard summoned for relief midway in the race. A call was made for Chad Little, who had been unable to earn a starting berth. But when Little could not be found, J.D.McDuffie was called in. McDuffie strapped himself into the King's car, but had difficulty reaching the floorboard controls due to the difference in height.

Brian Czobat

Ernie Irvan broke the ice and scored his first Winston Cup win at Bristol.

Eddie Bierschwale and Rick Wilson were considered, but Bierschwale had not practiced any car and was thus ineligible under NASCAR rules. Wilson was regarded as too short and would have problems similar to McDuffie. Finally, Petty parked the car.

Eventually, Little showed up when a plea was aired over MRN radio. With Petty's car parked, Little got into Brett Bodine's Buick.

Kyle was eventually felled by the heat and Richard drove the SabCo Racing Pontiac for a few laps before pulling behind the wall.

Irvan averaged 91.782 mph before a packed house of 58,200.

Winston Cup Series Race No. 20
500 Laps at Bristol Int'l Raceway
Bristol, TN
"Busch 500"
266.5 Miles on .533-mile Short Track
August 25, 1990

Fin	St	No.	Driver	Team / Car	Laps	Money	Status
1	6	4	Ernie Irvan	Morgan-McClure Chevrolet	500	$49,600	Running
2	4	27	Rusty Wallace	Blue Max Pontiac	500	32,850	Running
3	2	6	Mark Martin	Roush Racing Ford	500	22,830	Running
4	16	1	Terry Labonte	Precision Products Olds	500	14,150	Running
5	13	94	Sterling Marlin	Billy Hagan Olds	500	12,900	Running
6	10	7	Alan Kulwicki	AK Racing Ford	500	10,325	Running
7	9	21	Dale Jarrett	Wood Brothers Ford	499	9,850	Running
8	1	3	Dale Earnhardt	RCR Enterprises Chevrolet	499	30,125	Running
9	27	30	Michael Waltrip	Bahari Racing Pontiac	499	9,157	Running
10	7	5	Ricky Rudd	Hendrick Motorsports Chevy	499	10,100	Running
11	11	11	Geoff Bodine	Junior Johnson Ford	498	11,750	Running
12	19	25	Ken Schrader	Hendrick Motorsports Chevy	497	9,825	Running
13	8	9	Bill Elliott	Melling Performance Ford	497	11,550	Running
14	26	41	Larry Pearson	Larry Hedrick Chevrolet	497	4,100	Running
15	28	8	Bobby Hillin, Jr.	Stavola Brothers Buick	496	7,325	Running
16	31	98	Butch Miller	Travis Carter Chevrolet	495	5,600	Running
17	3	66	Dick Trickle	Cale Yarborough Pontiac	494	7,650	Running
18	30	57	Jimmy Spencer	Rod Osterlund Pontiac	493	6,200	Running
19	18	71	Dave Marcis	Marcis Auto Racing Chevy	490	6,050	Running
20	25	17	Greg Sacks	Hendrick Motorsports Chevy	485	12,175	Running
21	22	12	Hut Stricklin	Bobby Allison Buick	483	4,275	Running
22	32	52	Jimmy Means	Means Racing Pontiac	479	4,175	Running
23	12	28	Davey Allison*	Robert Yates Racing Ford	474	10,350	Running
24	24	22	Rick Mast	Bobby Jones Pontiac	463	3,375	Running
25	14	26	Brett Bodine**	King Motorsports Buick	396	5,575	Brakes
26	21	33	Harry Gant	Leo Jackson Olds	395	8,800	Running
27	15	10	Derrike Cope	Bob Whitcomb Chevrolet	379	8,775	Rear End
28	5	42	Kyle Petty***	SabCo Racing Pontiac	331	8,750	Fatigue
29	20	43	Richard Petty	Petty Enterprises Pontiac	215	3,800	Fatigue
30	17	20	Rob Moroso	Dick Moroso Olds	188	3,900	Crash
31	29	15	Morgan Shepherd	Bud Moore Eng. Ford	123	4,650	Crash
32	23	75	Rick Wilson	RahMoc Racing Olds	122	4,650	Engine

Time of Race: 2 hours, 54 minutes, 13 seconds
Average Speed: 91.782 mph
Pole Winner: Dale Earnhardt – 115.604 mph
Lap Leaders: Dale Earnhardt 1-67, Ernie Irvan 68-96, Dale Jarrett 97-121, Earnhardt 122-296, Irvan 297, Earnhardt 298, Geoff Bodine 299, Jarrett 300-303, Earnhardt 304-410, Irvan 411-500.
9 lead changes among 4 drivers.
Cautions: 10 for 47 laps Margin of Victory: 0.21 second
*Relieved by Rob Moroso **Relieved by Chad Little ***Relieved by Richard Petty

Winston Cup Series Race No. 21
367 Laps at Darlington Raceway
Darlington, SC
"Heinz Southern 500"
501.322 Miles on 1.366-mile Superspeedway
September 2, 1990

Fin	St	No.	Driver	Team / Car	Laps	Money	Status
1	1	3	Dale Earnhardt	RCR Enterprises Chevrolet	367	$210,350	Running
2	11	4	Ernie Irvan	Morgan-McClure Chevrolet	367	35,900	Running
3	8	7	Alan Kulwicki	AK Racing Ford	367	23,340	Running
4	2	9	Bill Elliott	Melling Performance Ford	367	24,380	Running
5	7	33	Harry Gant	Leo Jackson Olds	367	21,340	Running
6	10	6	Mark Martin	Roush Racing Ford	367	16,825	Running
7	5	5	Ricky Rudd	Hendrick Motorsports Chevy	367	12,755	Running
8	3	11	Geoff Bodine	Junior Johnson Ford	367	17,545	Running
9	9	10	Derrike Cope	Bob Whitcomb Chevrolet	366	12,105	Running
10	6	26	Brett Bodine	King Motorsports Buick	366	13,455	Running
11	15	66	Dick Trickle	Cale Yarborough Pontiac	365	11,360	Running
12	16	75	Rick Wilson	RahMoc Racing Olds	365	10,025	Running
13	22	20	Rob Moroso	Dick Moroso Olds	365	9,085	Running
14	24	1	Terry Labonte	Precision Products Olds	365	9,475	Running
15	12	28	Davey Allison	Robert Yates Racing Ford	364	14,290	Running
16	17	71	Dave Marcis	Marcis Auto Racing Chevy	364	8,875	Running
17	29	41	Larry Pearson	Larry Hedrick Chevrolet	363	5,415	Running
18	23	94	Sterling Marlin	Billy Hagan Olds	362	8,370	Trans
19	28	29	Phil Parsons	Diamond Ridge Pontiac	362	5,120	Running
20	34	12	Hut Stricklin	Bobby Allison Buick	361	7,792	Running
21	14	15	Morgan Shepherd	Bud Moore Eng. Ford	358	7,645	Running
22	32	47	Jack Pennington	Derick Close Olds	357	4,840	Running
23	36	57	Jimmy Spencer	Rod Osterlund Pontiac	355	7,345	Running
24	19	22	Rick Mast	Bobby Jones Pontiac	354	4,375	Running
25	13	42	Kyle Petty	SabCo Racing Pontiac	332	12,630	Running
26	30	30	Michael Waltrip	Bahari Racing Pontiac	272	6,890	Crash
27	39	2	Charlie Glotzbach	US Racing Pontiac	255	6,050	Engine
28	18	21	Dale Jarrett	Wood Brothers Ford	241	6,655	Crash
29	25	98	Butch Miller	Travis Carter Chevrolet	239	4,540	Crash
30	26	17	Greg Sacks	Hendrick Motorsports Chevy	227	12,810	Crash
31	20	8	Bobby Hillin,Jr.	Stavola Brothers Buick	227	6,315	Crash
32	27	83	Lake Speed	Speed Oldsmobile	175	3,605	Engine
33	40	82	Mark Stahl	Stahl Racing Ford	112	3,550	Handling
34	33	43	Richard Petty	Petty Enterprises Pontiac	93	4,120	Engine
35	35	19	Chad Little	Chuck Little Ford	91	3,420	Crash
36	31	52	Jimmy Means	Means Racing Pontiac	91	3,975	Crash
37	38	96	Philip Duffie	Duffie Racing Buick	52	3,320	Handling
38	37	36	H.B.Bailey	Bailey Pontiac	39	3,265	Crash
39	21	25	Ken Schrader	Hendrick Motorsports Chevy	31	10,710	Crash
40	4	27	Rusty Wallace	Blue Max Pontiac	14	14,400	Engine

Time of Race: 4 hours, 4 minutes, 16 seconds
Average Speed: 123.141 mph
Pole Winner: Dale Earnhardt – 158.448 mph
Lap Leaders: Dale Earnhardt 1-42, Dave Marcis 43, Geoff Bodine 44-48, Bill Elliott 49-80, Marcis 81-82, G.Bodine 83-119, Butch Miller 120, G.Bodine 121-154, Ernie Irvan155-156, G.Bodine 157-160, Irvan 161-212, G.Bodine 213-220, Elliott 221, Dale Jarrett 222, Irvan 223-230, Elliott 231-295, Earnhardt 296-298, Irvan 299-306, Ricky Rudd 308-313, Earnhardt 314-367.
20 lead changes among 8 drivers
Cautions: 10 for 51 laps Margin of Victory: 4.19 seconds

Race #21

Earnhardt Manhandles Darlington; Schrader Snaps

DARLINGTON, SC (Sept. 2) – Dale Earnhardt wrestled his ill-handling Chevrolet to an impressive victory in Darlington Raceway's Southern 500 for his seventh win of the season.

Earnhardt stormed into the lead 54 laps from the finish and outran runner-up Ernie Irvan by 4.19 seconds despite the effects of what the winner felt was a deflating tire. "It felt like I was dragging a cow around or had a tree hung up under the car," declared Earnhardt, who reduced his deficit in the Winston Cup standings to 26 points behind Mark Martin. "Richard Childress talked me through it, though. He kept giving me Irvan's lap times and told me to keep my cool. My hands were getting numb from the vibration of the steering wheel. We

Bryan Hallman

Ken Schrader #25 steered into Morgan Shepherd, causing both of them to crash in Darlington's Southern 500.

were fortunate a tire didn't blow."

Irvan was in sight of Earnhardt when the final round of green flag pit stops began with just under 100 miles remaining. Earnhardt pitted with 67 laps to go, getting four tires in 20.3 seconds. Instead of pitting with Earnhardt, Irvan elected to stay on the track for another five laps. "That probably cost us the race," said Tony Glover, Irvan's crew chief. "Dale gained seven seconds on us while we stayed out."

When Irvan finally made his final pit stop, he returned to the track running in third place behind Alan Kulwicki. "By the time Ernie got around Kulwicki," said Glover, "we had used our tires up."

Kulwicki held on to finish third. Bill Elliott managed to finish fourth and Harry Gant was fifth.

Point leader Mark Martin survived two spin-outs – one with Kulwicki in the opening laps. "I had a couple of close calls," said Martin. "The guys in the pits were great. They kept working with the car and we got a top 10 finish. That was kind of a miracle."

Jack Roush, owner of Martin's Ford, expressed shock that Earnhardt was able to run 67 laps on his last tankful of gas. "I don't know how they keep doing it," said Roush. "It's amazing how much fuel mileage he can get at the end of the race."

While Earnhardt was able to keep his cool under pressure, Ken Schrader clearly lost his. Schrader, mired in a winless season after such high expectations, had started 21st and made a quick move at the start of the race. In the 25th lap, he tried to pass Morgan Shepherd on the high side of turn two and ran out of room. His Hendrick Motorsports car grazed the wall and had to come to the pits for a 40 minute repair.

Moments after Schrader returned to the track, he yanked his car into the side of Shepherd's Bud Moore Ford, sending both hard into the wall.

The move – right out of the current film "Days of Thunder" – incensed the Bud Moore Engineering crew. "That was a stupid thing that boy (Schrader) did," growled car owner Moore "Maybe we ought to go over there and work that boy's head over with a hammer."

"Morgan just run us up into the fence," reasoned Schrader on the first incident. He declined comment on the second altercation, preferring to sequester himself in the back of the transporter.

Greg Moore, a member of the Moore Engineering team, said, "I never get angry, but that was uncalled

Bryan Hallman

Mark Martin #6 and Alan Kulwicki spin in early stages of Southern 500.

Brian Czobat

Dale Earnhardt, the master of Darlington, takes the checkered flag again.

for. That was the most flagrant thing I've ever seen. A man 50 laps down deliberately comes back on the track and wrecks a man."

Shepherd averted the controversy by saying, "It's a bad deal, but I had better not comment on it right now."

NASCAR Competition Director Dick Beaty said he would have a session with both parties. "The only two people who know what really happened are Kenny and Morgan," said Beaty. "But I will talk to everyone involved."

Michael Waltrip was running in the top five when a tap from Earnhardt spun him around. "Whoever was behind me (Earnhardt) just turned me around," he huffed.

Kyle Petty, running directly behind Earnhardt and in a position to score his first win since Rockingham, plowed into the spinning Waltrip car. "Just goes to show you how quickly a good day can get messed up in a hurry," said Kyle.

Earnhardt admitted he tapped Waltrip's Pontiac. "I got into him, but he jammed on the brakes and that got him into the wall."

Earnhardt won a $100,000 bonus from Winston for winning two of the four Crown Jewel races. Had it not been for the tire failure in the final lap of the Daytona 500, he would have been only the second driver to cash in on the Winston Million. "We know we should have won the Million," said Earnhardt, who scored his third straight win at Darlington. "But we're thankful to win two of the four races. And winning the pole position here was a surprise to us."

Racing scribe Benny Phillips said that perhaps it was time to bury the track slogan Darlington uses. "Until a more proper time, let's forget this nonsense about Darlington being 'Too Tough To Tame'," said Phillips. "Let's wait until after Dale retires. Or let us remember that it is Earnhardt who is 'Too Tough To Tame', and not Darlington Raceway.

Race #22

Earnhardt Racks Up Richmond Win; Still Trails in Point Race

RICHMOND, VA (Sept. 9) – Dale Earnhardt stretched his fuel supply, received an assist from Harry Gant and nipped Mark Martin in a confusing Miller Genuine Draft 400 at Richmond International Raceway. For Earnhardt, it was his eighth win of the season – compared to Martin's two victories – yet he still trails in the Winston Cup standings by 16 points.

Earnhardt's 47th career victory was the product of exceptional fuel mileage and a weird restart with three laps to go.

Rusty Wallace and Mark Martin had given up the lead in the final 50 miles by having to pit for fuel while Earnhardt was able to motor on in his RCR Enterprises Chevrolet. Wallace brought his Blue Max Racing Pontiac into the pits on lap 346 and dropped well back in the field.

Martin took the lead at that point and built up an eight second cushion. But he was forced to retreat to the pits

Kim Novosat

Davey Allison #28 and Terry Labonte #1 pair up at Richmond.

for a splash of fuel with 25 laps left. Earnhardt breezed into the lead and was holding down a five second advantage over Martin when Ernie Irvan brought out the ninth and final caution with five laps to go.

The caution only lasted two laps and cars on the lead lap were getting in position for the quick restart.

Harry Gant, driving the Rod Osterlund Pontiac in relief for virus-stricken Hut Stricklin, was holding down ninth place a lap behind. But with the radio not working, Gant thought he was in the lead lap.

Kim Novasat

Dale Jarrett's Wood Brothers Ford on the hook after he clobbered the inside wall at Richmond.

He positioned himself on Earnhardt's rear bumper as Martin and others desperately tried to get in their proper position for the restart.

At the green flag with three laps left, Earnhardt shot away from the pack and Martin struggled with Gant. When the checkered flag flew, Earnhardt was nearly a full second in front of runner-up Martin.

Darrell Waltrip, making his return from serious leg injuries in July, wound up an impressive third. Bill Elliott came across the line in fourth spot with Wallace fifth.

"We were lucky to win this one," said Earnhardt. "Mark and Rusty had faster cars and Mark would have

Winston Cup Series Race No. 22
400 Laps at Richmond Int'l Raceway
Richmond, VA
"Miller Genuine Draft 400"

300 Miles on .75-mile Short Track
September 9, 1990

Fin	St	No.	Driver	Team / Car	Laps	Money	Status
1	6	3	Dale Earnhardt	RCR Enterprises Chevrolet	400	$59,225	Running
2	7	6	Mark Martin	Roush Racing Ford	400	30,550	Running
3	27	17	Darrell Waltrip	Hendrick Motorsports Chevy	400	25,107	Running
4	16	9	Bill Elliott	Melling Performance Ford	400	16,950	Running
5	11	27	Rusty Wallace	Blue Max Pontiac	400	19,525	Running
6	9	42	Kyle Petty	SabCo Racing Pontiac	400	11,875	Running
7	5	66	Dick Trickle	Cale Yarborough Pontiac	400	9,900	Running
8	14	5	Ricky Rudd	Hendrick Motorsports Chevy	399	8,350	Running
9	10	11	Geoff Bodine	Junior Johnson Ford	399	10,850	Running
10	3	25	Ken Schrader	Hendrick Motorsports Chevy	399	15,930	Running
11	30	8	Bobby Hillin, Jr.	Stavola Brothers Buick	399	7,450	Running
12	1	4	Ernie Irvan	Morgan-McClure Chevrolet	399	13,875	Running
13	31	12	Hut Stricklin*	Bobby Allison Buick	399	5,350	Running
14	2	30	Michael Waltrip	Bahari Racing Pontiac	398	6,725	Running
15	23	71	Dave Marcis	Marcis Auto Racing Chevy	397	6,975	Running
16	8	28	Davey Allison	Robert Yates Racing Ford	396	9,550	Running
17	12	1	Terry Labonte	Precision Products Olds	396	6,100	Running
18	24	52	Jimmy Means	Means Racing Pontiac	396	4,450	Running
19	34	98	Butch Miller	Travis Carter Chevrolet	395	4,225	Running
20	19	75	Rick Wilson	RahMoc Racing Olds	394	6,325	Running
21	26	43	Richard Petty	Petty Enterprises Pontiac	394	4,075	Running
22	32	90	Charlie Glotzbach	Junie Donlavey Ford	394	3,100	Running
23	29	18	Greg Sacks	Hendrick Motorsports Chevy	384	3,075	Running
24	17	94	Sterling Marlin	Billy Hagan Olds	383	5,225	Running
25	33	56	Ron Esau	Marc Reno Chevrolet	383	3,050	Running
26	4	7	Alan Kulwicki	AK Racing Ford	354	5,905	Running
27	25	57	Jimmy Spencer	Rod Osterlund Pontiac	318	5,055	Running
28	37	20	Rob Moroso	Dick Moroso Oldsmobile	273	4,225	Crash
29	13	21	Dale Jarrett	Wood Brothers Ford	272	4,355	Crash
30	18	15	Morgan Shepherd	Bud Moore Eng. Ford	270	5,100	Engine
31	15	26	Brett Bodine	King Motorsports Buick	242	4,310	Crash
32	21	19	Chad Little	Chuck Little Ford	239	3,480	Crash
33	38	2	D.K.Ulrich	US Racing Pontiac	185	4,265	Engine
34	28	01	Mickey Gibbs	Gibbs-West Ford	160	2,805	Crash
35	20	10	Derrike Cope	Bob Whitcomb Chevrolet	120	7,355	Engine
36	22	33	Harry Gant	Leo Jackson Oldsmobile	12	8,855	Engine

Time of Race: 3 hours, 8 minutes, 21 seconds
Average Speed: 95.567 mph
Pole Winner: Ernie Irvan – 119.872 mph
Lap Leaders: Ernie Irvan 1-33, Alan Kulwicki 34-76, Mark Martin 77-78, Kulwicki 79-101, Ken Schrader 102-123, Rusty Wallace 124-163, Dale Earnhardt 164-236, Wallace 237-240, Earnhardt 241-276, Wallace 277-287, Earnhardt 288-303, Wallace 304, Earnhardt 305-310, Wallace 311, Earnhardt 312-328, Wallace 329-346, Martin 347-375, Earnhardt 376-400.
17 lead changes among 6 drivers.
Cautions: 9 for 55 laps Margin of Victory: 0.85 second
*Relieved by Harry Gant

Kim Novasat

Darrell Waltrip, making his return to racing at Richmond, chats with Hendrick Motorsports teammate Ken Schrader.

probably beaten me if he had been on my bumper for the restart. And we cut it close on fuel mileage. It was sputtering the last couple of laps."

Wallace was still scratching his head well after the race ended. "I'm so sick of running out of gas I don't know what to do," he lamented. "I can't believe we were out of sync by 60 or 70 laps. It's getting frustrating. We were so much quicker than any car out there. It's ridiculous we have to pit 60 laps ahead of the other cars. I just don't get it."

Martin stretched his fuel supply as long as he could, but didn't have nearly enough juice to run to the end. "We just couldn't make it. Wasn't even close. But we probably would have still won if I could have gotten on Dale's bumper where I should have been. I'm not going to complain, though. We did the best we could," said Martin.

Gant crossed the finish line in 10th place, but was penalized three positions by NASCAR for not getting out of the way in the final stretch duel. "He was seriously out of position on the restart," said a NASCAR official.

A rash of wild crashes interrupted the 300-miler. Dale Jarrett, in the Wood Brothers Ford, tangled with Rob Moroso's Oldsmobile, sending Jarrett through the inside guard rail on the backstretch. The crash, which occurred on lap 281, brought out the red flag for 31 minutes, 42 seconds so repairs could be made to the guard rail.

Chad Little suffered a concussion when his Ford slammed head-on into the wall after getting tangled with Brett Bodine. Ken Schrader nipped Bodine's rear bumper, sending Bodine's Buick spinning in front of a pack of cars.

Darrell Waltrip, who had hoped to return to the tour by late September, was able to get behind the wheel earlier than anticipated. "I about gave out in the first 75 laps, but once I relaxed and got a caution, I was back in business," he said. "The leg feels fine. The clutch was a lot testier than I remember it being. It gave me some problems getting in and out (of the pits), but I'm real proud of how everything worked out."

Earnhardt dedicated the win to Danny "Chocolate" Myers, whose grandmother passed away and was not in the RCR Enterprises pits.

Race #23

Elliott Ends Skid With Resounding Victory at Dover

DOVER, DE (Sept. 16) – Bill Elliott emerged from the depths of a winless famine and scored a convincing victory in the Peak AntiFreeze 500 at Dover Downs International Speedway.

The lanky Dawsonville, Ga. driver pushed his Ford to the front for 364 of the 500 laps around Dover's 'Monster Mile' and cruised to a 1.38 second triumph over Mark Martin.

Elliott's 32nd career victory was the first for the Melling Performance team since November of 1988 when it won at Phoenix.It also gave Mike Beam his first trip to victory lane as a crew chief. "I knew this was a strong team," said Elliott. "This win means a lot to this race team. We just needed a little luck and a few things finally going our direction. That's all it took."

Elliott started on the pole and led most of the way, but he had to sweat things out late in the race. "We were razor thin on gas, and I kept thinking we'd lose it all if we blew a tire or something." NASCAR officials measured Elliott's fuel tank in victory lane and it had only three-tenths of a gallon left, not to mention the right rear tire which went flat during the post-race ceremonies. "What a time to have a flat tire," Elliott said with a grin. "At least it happened after the race."

Rob Moroso experienced more bad times at Dover.

Winston Cup Series Race No. 23
500 Laps at Dover Downs Int'l Speedway
Dover, DE
"Peak AntiFreeze 500"
500 Miles on 1-mile Superspeedway
September 16, 1990

Fin	St	No.	Driver	Team / Car	Laps	Money	Status
1	1	9	Bill Elliott	Melling Performance Ford	500	$83,100	Running
2	6	6	Mark Martin	Roush Racing Ford	500	35,325	Running
3	3	3	Dale Earnhardt	RCR Enterprises Chevy	500	29,375	Running
4	8	33	Harry Gant	Leo Jackson Oldsmobile	499	19,425	Running
5	19	30	Michael Waltrip	Bahari Racing Pontiac	499	16,825	Running
6	11	21	Dale Jarrett	Wood Brothers Ford	499	13,675	Running
7	9	27	Rusty Wallace	Blue Max Pontiac	499	18,175	Running
8	15	42	Kyle Petty	SabCo Racing Pontiac	499	13,675	Running
9	7	28	Davey Allison	Robert Yates Racing Ford	499	14,075	Running
10	23	25	Ken Schrader	Hendrick Motorsports Chevy	498	14,875	Running
11	26	12	Hut Stricklin	Bobby Allison Buick	497	8,282	Running
12	18	94	Sterling Marlin	Billy Hagan Oldsmobile	497	8,625	Running
13	25	10	Derrike Cope	Bob Whitcomb Chevrolet	496	9,775	Running
14	21	8	Bobby Hillin,Jr.	Stavola Brothers Buick	495	8,025	Running
15	22	1	Terry Labonte	Precision Products Olds	495	8,350	Running
16	16	43	Richard Petty	Petty Enterprises Pontiac	494	5,600	Running
17	27	98	Butch Miller	Travis Carter Chevrolet	493	5,350	Running
18	30	57	Jimmy Spencer	Rod Osterlund Pontiac	493	7,000	Running
19	24	17	Darrell Waltrip	Hendrick Motorsports Chevy	492	12,650	Running
20	10	26	Brett Bodine	King Motorsports Buick	492	7,475	Running
21	29	18	Greg Sacks	Hendrick Motorsports Chevy	491	3,550	Running
22	14	71	Dave Marcis	Marcis Auto Racing Chevy	491	6,500	Running
23	12	66	Dick Trickle	Cale Yarborough Pontiac	478	7,400	Running
24	35	52	Jimmy Means	Means Racing Pontiac	461	4,250	Engine
25	13	15	Morgan Shepherd	Bud Moore Eng. Ford	441	6,200	Running
26	4	4	Ernie Irvan	Morgan-McClure Chevy	427	6,000	Running
27	31	75	Rick Wilson	RahMoc Racing Olds	395	5,925	Engine
28	17	20	Rob Moroso	Dick Moroso Olds	394	4,600	Crash
29	5	7	Alan Kulwicki	AK Racing Ford	342	5,775	Engine
30	34	80	Jimmy Horton	George Smith Pontiac	318	3,100	Engine
31	32	83	Tommy Ellis	Lake Speed Olds	285	3,050	Engine
32	20	5	Ricky Rudd	Hendrick Motorsports Chevy	246	5,600	Heating
33	28	51	Jeff Purvis	James Finch Chevrolet	222	2,950	Crash
34	33	2	Jim Sauter	US Racing Pontiac	203	4,900	Engine
35	38	48	James Hylton	Hylton Engineering Buick	202	2,800	Engine
36	2	11	Geoff Bodine	Junior Johnson Ford	175	12,825	Engine
37	40	09	Jerry Hufflin	Smith Racing Pontiac	130	2,750	Oil Leak
38	36	74	Mike Potter	Bobby Wawak Pontiac	113	2,700	Handling
39	37	54	Tommy Riggins	Hakes-Welliver Olds	105	2,675	Oil Pan
40	39	70	J.D.McDuffie	McDuffie Racing Pontiac	18	2,650	Trans

Time of Race: 3 hours, 58 minutes, 0 seconds
Average Speed: 125.945 mph
Pole Winner: Bill Elliott – 144.928 mph
Lap LEaders: Bill Elliott 1-43, Dale Earnhardt 44-53, Elliott 54-62, Earnhardt 63-86, Elliott 87-88, Geoff Bodine 89-90, Harry Gant 91, Earnhardt 92-152, Elliott 153-313, Earnhardt 314-320, Mark Martin 321-351, Elliott 352-500.
11 lead changes among 5 drivers.
Cautions: 6 for 29 laps Margin of Victory: 1.38 seconds

Dale Earnhardt finished in third place and lost only five points to Martin in the chase for the Winston Cup title. Martin clings to a 21 point lead with six races remaining.

Fourth place went to Harry Gant and Michael Waltrip took fifth spot.

Elliott led the first 43 laps before yielding the front position to Earnhardt. The two traded the lead several times – interrupted only by pit stops – and treated the crowd of 74,000 to a spine-tingling duel. As Elliott and Earnhardt performed their speedy struggle, they were running circles around most of the other hopefuls. "The first caution didn't come out for a while (lap 139) and

Bill Elliott ended a long drought at Dover Downs.

Kim Novosat

Jeff Purvis #51 takes the high side in duel with Tommy Ellis #83 at Dover.

we were able to put a lot of good cars a lap down," said Elliott. "After that, we only had to race with each other instead of the whole bunch."

Toward the waning stages, only Elliott, Earnhardt and Martin were left on the lead lap. Martin used the first caution flag – when Ernie Irvan's Chevrolet whacked the wall – to make up almost an entire lap. He was five seconds from going a lap down to Earnhardt when the yellow saved him.

Martin got his second wind late in the race, which played into the hands of Elliott. With Martin and Earnhardt racing side-by-side for second place, Elliott was able to scoot away to a comfortable lead. Martin finally swept past Earnhardt in the 450th lap and spent the rest of the day trying to chase down Elliott.

"Dale Earnhardt is the best race car driver I've ever laid eyes on," praised Martin. "He's a tough man to beat, and we did it today with a great car and a great crew. Maybe we can beat him again next week."

Jeff Purvis drove a Chevrolet entered by James Finch with Neil Bonnett listed as co-owner, but the former dirt track champion saw his day end when he cracked the wall in the 228th lap. He was five laps down at the time.

Tommy Ellis drove Lake Speed's Oldsmobile but was sidelined by engine failure. Speed crashed the primary car in practice, suffering a shoulder injury.

Alan Kulwicki started fifth, but wound up 29th with engine problems. Rookie Rob Moroso experienced more tough luck when he crashed his Oldsmobile after completing 394 laps.

Only five drivers led the event, and four of them occupied the first four positions. Geoff Bodine led twice during exchange of pit stops, but was sidelined early by a blown engine.

Race #24

Geoff Grabs Gold and Glory in Martinsville Slugfest

MARTINSVILLE, VA (Sept. 23) – Geoff Bodine rebounded from a late race spin, battled back into contention and outran Dale Earnhardt in the Goody's 500 at Martinsville Speedway. The 263-mile contest resembled a mechanical slugfest from start to finish.

Bodine's trip to victory lane was his third of the season. The Chemung, N.Y. Ford driver took the lead for good when he got around Mark Martin with 42 laps remaining. Dale Earnhardt nosed out

Kim Novasat

Bill Elliott closes on leader Dale Earnhardt in middle stages of Dover's 500-miler.

Kim Novasat

Hut Stricklin #12 leads Rusty Wallace in Martinsville's Goody's 500.

Martin for second place. Brett Bodine took fourth spot after starting 27th. Harry Gant finished fifth.

Bodine nearly threw his chance for victory out the window when he spun on lap 319 while trying to lap Terry Labonte. "I put my nose where I shouldn't have," admitted Bodine, who skidded into the infield in the second turn. "I got it chopped off, too."

Bodine plowed up a sizable acreage of Clay Earles' neatly manicured infield as he tried and succeeded in staying on the lead lap. With the caution flag out, Bodine was able to make a pit stop. He lined up 11th on the restart.

Bodine also said the trip over the curb and into the grass made his car handle better. "I don't know what could have happened, but after that I could drive deeper into the corners. Actually, it helped my mental attitude. I was determined to come back and win for the team after messing up."

Bodine was able to sprint away from the runner-up battle between Earnhardt and Martin. His margin of victory was 2.16 seconds.

Martin started on the pole but was hampered by a sputtering engine and fading brakes. A plug wire had fallen off during the early stages, but team manager Steve Hmiel and crew chief Robin Pemberton were

Brian Czobat

Terry Labonte spins his Oldsmobile as Alan Kulwicki squeezes past.

Winston Cup Series Race No. 24
500 Laps at Martinsville Speedway
Martinsville, VA
"Goody's 500"

263 Miles on .526-mile Short Track
September 23, 1990

Fin	St	No.	Driver	Team / Car	Laps	Money	Status
1	14	11	Geoff Bodine	Junior Johnson Ford	500	$53,850	Running
2	8	3	Dale Earnhardt	RCR Enterprises Chevrolet	500	30,550	Running
3	1	6	Mark Martin	Roush Racing Ford	500	24,450	Running
4	27	26	Brett Bodine	King Motorsports Buick	500	16,807	Running
5	3	33	Harry Gant	Leo Jackson Oldsmobile	500	18,100	Running
6	19	7	Alan Kulwicki	AK Racing Ford	500	10,975	Running
7	22	28	Davey Allison	Robert Yates Racing Ford	500	9,300	Running
8	10	9	Bill Elliott	Melling Performance Ford	500	14,150	Running
9	12	1	Terry Labonte	Precision Products Olds	498	9,100	Running
10	6	21	Dale Jarrett	Wood Brothers Ford	497	10,725	Running
11	9	4	Ernie Irvan	Morgan-McClure Oldsmobile	497	7,435	Running
12	15	94	Sterling Marlin	Billy Hagan Olds	495	6,850	Running
13	17	12	Hut Stricklin	Bobby Allison Buick	494	5,150	Running
14	13	71	Dave Marcis	Marcis Auto Racing Chevy	494	6,450	Running
15	2	27	Rusty Wallace	Blue Max Pontiac	493	19,275	Running
16	23	52	Jimmy Means	Means Racing Pontiac	491	4,650	Running
17	30	19	Chad Little	Chuck Little Ford	490	3,350	Running
18	29	57	Jimmy Spencer	Rod Osterlund Pontiac	488	5,750	Running
19	11	17	Darrell Waltrip	Hendrick Motorsports Chevy	487	10,850	Running
20	18	75	Rick Wilson	RahMoc Racing Olds	472	6,175	Running
21	28	20	Rob Moroso	Dick Moroso Olds	468	4,950	Running
22	20	66	Dick Trickle	Cale Yarborough Pontiac	466	6,025	Crash
23	5	42	Kyle Petty	SabCo Racing Pontiac	464	8,750	Running
24	31	10	Derrike Cope	Bob Whitcomb Chevrolet	450	6,900	Engine
25	25	15	Morgan Shepherd	Bud Moore Eng. Ford	402	4,875	T Chain
26	26	8	Bobby Hillin,Jr.	Stavola Brothers Buick	362	4,650	Trans
27	4	25	Ken Schrader	Hendrick Motorsports Chevy	289	10,150	Crash
28	16	5	Ricky Rudd	Hendrick Motorsports Chevy	289	6,200	Crash
29	21	43	Richard Petty	Petty Enterprises Pontiac	229	2,250	Engine
30	7	30	Michael Waltrip	Bahari Racing Pontiac	114	3,700	Engine
31	24	98	Rick Mast	Travis Carter Chevrolet	36	2,200	Crash

Time of Race: 3 hours, 26 minutes, 35 seconds
Average Speed: 76.386 mph
Pole Winner: Mark Martin – 91.571 mph
Lap Leaders: Rusty Wallace 1-39, Morgan Shepherd 40-72, Ken Schrader 73-85, Alan Kulwicki 86-125, Dale Earnhardt 126-127, Brett Bodine 128-146, Schrader 147-203, Ricky Rudd 204-288, Schrader 289, B.Bodine 290-291, Geoff Bodine 292-318, Bill Elliott 319-402, Earnhardt 403-425, B.Bodine 426-444, Mark Martin 445-458, G.Bodine 459-500.
16 lead changes among 10 drivers
Cautions: 11 for 57 laps Margin of Victory: 2.16 seconds

able to make repairs without losing a lap. Martin did not lead until the 445th lap.

Martin's third place showing allowed him to leave Martinsville with a 16 point lead.

Earnhardt also fought back from a stop and go penalty for jumping on a restart. "Ken Schrader (leader at the time) got on the gas then backed off," explained Earnhardt. "He snookered me. That hand will come back around."

Schrader and teammate Ricky Rudd were eliminated in a spectacular crash in the 290th lap. With Rudd leading, Schrader was trying to make the pass off the second turn. The cars made contact and fused together, then shot to the inside and clobbered the pit wall on the backstretch.

Harry Gant #33 and Jimmy Means #52 spin at Martinsville. Gant recovered to finish fifth.

"Kenny got loose and knocked me into the fence," said Rudd, who led the most laps despite running only a little over half the race. "I really don't know why he was racing that hard with over 200 laps to go. He would have gotten me in another couple of laps."

Schrader, seeking his third career victory in his 173rd start, said, "One of us lost it. I guess it depends on who you ask. I had been trying to pass him for three or four laps. It wasn't like he didn't know I was there. I think he got loose, came down and hit me."

Car owner Rick Hendrick went from a possible 1-2 finish to a heap of scrap metal in an instant. "This is something you worry about when you have more than one car," he said. "I hate it happened because we had a chance to win. The drivers have to race – and you have to let them race."

Two drivers were sent to NASCAR's penalty box for allegedly rough driving. Jimmy Spencer spent five laps in the 'box' for hitting Ernie Irvan.

Sterling Marlin was penalized five laps in a questionable decision by officials. Marlin tapped Bill Elliott into a spin in the 402nd lap. "Bill was right in front of me and he slowed a lot sooner than I thought he would," said Marlin, who eventually finished 12th in Billy Hagan's Oldsmobile. "I hit the brakes and my car started wheel hopping. I let off the brakes and hit Bill. It certainly wasn't intentional.

"We had a top five finish in hand," he added. "That's another one that was robbed from us."

Elliott admitted "there wasn't a lot Sterling could do. I wasn't running quite as fast as I had been. He hit me coming into the turn; and he hit me again. It was a chain reaction deal. He couldn't help it."

NASCAR's Dick Beaty explained the ruling: "We expect a certain degree of rubbing and banging. When someone loses his temper and the bumping becomes an attempt to spin another car, we have to take action."

Morgan Shepherd led 33 laps, but his Bud Moore Ford snapped a timing chain after completing 402 laps.

Race #25

Martin Wins North Wilkesboro; Gains Nothing in Point Race

N.WILKESBORO, NC (Sept. 30) – Enhanced by a mid-race chassis adjustment, Mark Martin charged past Dale Earnhardt in the final laps and won the Tyson Holly Farms 400 at North Wilkesboro Speedway. Despite winning the race, Martin picked up nothing in the battle for the lucrative Winston Cup championship race. It once again accented a huge flaw in the point structure which determines the seasonal champion. At times,

Winston Cup Series Race No. 25
400 Laps at North Wilkesboro Speedway
North Wilkesboro, NC
"Tyson Holly Farms 400"
250 Miles on .625-mile Short Track
September 30, 1990

Fin	St	No.	Driver	Team / Car	Laps	Money	Status
1	2	6	Mark Martin	Roush Racing Ford	400	$52,875	Running
2	8	3	Dale Earnhardt	RCR Enterprises Chevrolet	400	32,075	Running
3	12	26	Brett Bodine	King Motorsports Buick	400	18,750	Running
4	7	9	Bill Elliott	Melling Performance Ford	400	16,775	Running
5	9	25	Ken Schrader	Hendrick Motorsports Chevy	400	15,325	Running
6	23	4	Ernie Irvan	Morgan-McClure Olds	400	10,007	Running
7	11	17	Darrell Waltrip	Hendrick Motorsports Chevy	400	14,125	Running
8	16	27	Rusty Wallace	Blue Max Pontiac	400	13,325	Running
9	6	7	Alan Kulwicki	AK Racing Ford	400	7,125	Running
10	1	42	Kyle Petty	SabCo Racing Pontiac	399	18,025	Running
11	15	5	Ricky Rudd	Hendrick Motorsports Chevy	399	6,650	Running
12	26	15	Morgan Shepherd	Bud Moore Eng. Ford	399	6,350	Running
13	3	94	Sterling Marlin	Billy Hagan Olds	399	6,075	Running
14	18	8	Bobby Hillin,Jr.	Stavola Brothers Buick	399	5,875	Running
15	10	30	Michael Waltrip	Bahari Racing Pontiac	398	6,350	Running
16	19	11	Geoff Bodine	Junior Johnson Ford	398	9,950	Running
17	28	43	Richard Petty	Petty Enterprises Pontiac	397	4,025	Running
18	22	75	Rick Wilson	RahMoc Racing Olds	396	5,300	Running
19	4	21	Dale Jarrett	Wood Brothers Ford	396	5,150	Running
20	27	12	Hut Stricklin	Bobby Allison Buick	395	4,325	Running
21	32	20	Rob Moroso	Dick Moroso Olds	394	4,200	Running
22	25	10	Derrike Cope	Bob Whitcomb Chevrolet	393	6,900	Running
23	31	57	Jimmy Spencer	Rod Osterlund Pontiac	390	4,750	Running
24	29	19	Chad Little	Chuck Little Ford	390	2,600	Running
25	14	71	Dave Marcis	Marcis Auto Racing Chevy	383	4,775	Running
26	13	28	Davey Allison	Robert Yates Racing Ford	383	9,200	Running
27	5	1	Terry Labonte	Precision Products Olds	334	5,350	Running
28	17	33	Harry Gant	Leo Jackson Olds	327	8,150	Running
29	21	66	Dick Trickle	Cale Yarborough Pontiac	194	5,025	Crash
30	30	52	Jimmy Means	Means Racing Pontiac	128	2,375	Rock Arm
31	24	51	Jeff Purvis	James Finch Chevrolet	100	2,375	Brakes
32	20	98	Rick Mast	Travis Carter Chevrolet	17	2,375	Crash

Time of Race: 2 hours, 39 minutes, 53 seconds
Average Speed: 93.818 mph
Pole Winner: Kyle Petty – 116.387 mph
Lap Leaders: Mark Martin 1, Kyle Petty 2-65, Dale Earnhardt 66-234, Ken Schrader 235-240, Earnhardt 241-362, Martin 363-400.
6 lead changes among 4 drivers.
Cautions: 9 for 40 laps Margin of Victory: 3.63 seconds

winning races seems secondary.

Earnhardt finished second and led the most laps – and therefore scored an equal number of points that Martin did for winning the race. "We didn't pick up any points," said Martin, "but this win is important to this team. We came back and beat him when nobody expected us to." Martin held his 16 point lead in the Winston Cup point chase.

Brett Bodine finished in third place with Bill Elliott fourth and Ken Schrader fifth.

Martin led the opening lap, then Kyle Petty took over for 64 laps. Earnhardt, who started eighth, motored around Petty in the 66th lap and led through the 234th lap. It was during that runaway stretch for Earnhardt that the Jack Roush team decided to make a change. "We said enough is enough," said Martin. "He was gone and we had to gamble and try something. It was no fun watching him run away from everybody."

Martin said his crew removed a rubber spacer from a coil spring on the right front of his car during a caution brought out by Dick Trickle in the 194th lap. "We had to come down pit road twice to get it off," said Martin.

During the adjustment, Martin fell to 12th place but remained on the lead lap.

By lap 288, Martin had stormed into second place, but was still eight seconds behind the fleet Earnhardt. A recurring on-track duel between Ricky Rudd and Derrike Cope brought two additional yellow flags and gave Martin a chance to close on Earnhardt.

Martin dogged Earnhardt until the 363rd lap when he scrubbed Earnhardt during the decisive pass. Earnhardt was unable to challenge and wound up 3.63 seconds behind when the checkered flag fell.

"We got a tight set of tires," said Earnhardt. "The car wouldn't turn in the corners. Ol' Mark drove right by me. I hate tires had to decide a race like this, but give

Brian Czobat

Late race chassis adjustments by team manager Steve Hmiel contributed to Mark Martin's win at North Wilkesboro.

Brian Czobat

Rob Moroso finished 21st at North Wilkesboro in what turned out to be his final Winston Cup effort.

our guys credit. It's just these tires have been inconsistent all week."

The Rudd-Cope fracas stirred controversy but no action by NASCAR officials. Rudd said he "had a third or fourth place car if it hadn't been for the 10 car (Cope). I rubbed him unintentionally going into turn one. Then he hit me and spun me going into turn three and I backed into the wall. It would have been different if we had been racing for position. But he was three or four laps down," said Rudd.

Cope said that he "motioned for Ricky to pass on the outside. But he wanted the inside and smacked me. When we got to turn three, we got together again and up in the wall he went.

"I've been racing guys clean since I've been in Winston Cup, and they've got to start racing me clean," declared Cope.

Trickle had pushed Cale Yarborough's Pontiac into third position when a tire let go, putting him into the wall. "I felt a vibration just before it happened," said Trickle. "We were going to pit the next lap."

Other cautions were brought out by spins by Kyle Petty, Sterling Marlin, Hut Stricklin and Rob Moroso.

Moroso finished in 21st place, six laps off the pace. Following the race, Moroso ate dinner and consumed a few beers at a restaurant in Cornelius, N.C. He and his girlfriend, Debbie Bryan, left the restaurant following a delayed telecast of the race. Moroso, who had observed his 22nd birthday only days earlier, was killed when he lost control of his car on a turn while traveling at a high rate of speed and slammed into another vehicle driven by Tammy Williams. Bryan survived the collision.

The tragedy snuffed out the life and career of one of NASCAR's brightest future prospects, although his freshman season on the Winston Cup tour was riddled with wrecks and disappointments.

Brian Czobat

Richard and Kyle Petty run abreast through North Wilkesboro turn.

Race #26

Davey Scores at Charlotte; Title Contenders Struggle

CONCORD, NC (Oct. 7) – Davey Allison emerged as the winner of the Mello Yello 500 at Charlotte Motor Speedway after erstwhile leader Bill Elliott was foiled by brake problems.

Allison, who put the skids on a personal skid, led the

Winston Cup Series Race No. 26
334 Laps at Charlotte Motor Speedway
Concord, NC
"Mello Yello 500"
501 Miles on 1.5-mile Superspeedway
October 7, 1990

Fin	St	No.	Driver	Team / Car	Laps	Money	Status
1	5	28	Davey Allison	Robert Yates Racing Ford	334	$90,650	Running
2	33	15	Morgan Shepherd	Bud Moore Eng. Ford	334	51,800	Running
3	36	30	Michael Waltrip	Bahari Racing Pontiac	334	38,100	Running
4	20	42	Kyle Petty	SabCo Racing Pontiac	334	30,450	Running
5	41	7	Alan Kulwicki	AK Racing Ford	334	24,757	Running
6	16	5	Ricky Rudd	Hendrick Motorsports Chevy	334	18,425	Running
7	13	10	Derrike Cope	Bob Whitcomb Chevrolet	334	17,400	Running
8	1	26	Brett Bodine	King Motorsports Buick	334	35,600	Running
9	25	17	Darrell Waltrip	Hendrick Motorsports Chevy	334	18,900	Running
10	11	21	Dale Jarrett	Wood Brothers Ford	333	14,625	Running
11	14	75	Rick Wilson	RahMoc Racing Pontiac	333	11,350	Running
12	17	47	Jack Pennington	Derick Close Oldsmobile	333	7,650	Running
13	39	71	Dave Marcis	Marcis Auto Racing Chevy	331	10,800	Running
14	6	6	Mark Martin	Roush Racing Ford	331	13,600	Running
15	9	9	Bill Elliott	Melling Performance Ford	331	59,150	Running
16	21	94	Sterling Marlin	Billy Hagan Olds	330	7,925	Running
17	19	1	Terry Labonte	Precision Products Olds	330	7,475	Running
18	29	83	Phil Parsons	Lake Speed Oldsmobile	330	4,225	Running
19	22	41	Larry Pearson	Larry Hedrick Chevrolet	329	4,075	Running
20	18	43	Richard Petty	Petty Enterprises Pontiac	329	5,425	Running
21	24	01	Mickey Gibbs	Gibbs-West Ford	324	3,775	Running
22	37	23	Eddie Bierschwale	Don Bierschwale Olds	323	3,650	Running
23	30	44	Jimmy Horton	Group 44 Pontiac	323	3,525	Running
24	32	97	Chuck Bown	Tex Powell Chevrolet	322	3,450	Running
25	15	3	Dale Earnhardt	RCR Enterprises Chevy	320	12,275	Running
26	2	33	Harry Gant	Leo Jackson Olds	303	15,500	Engine
27	3	4	Ernie Irvan	Morgan-McClure Chevrolet	286	11,200	Running
28	28	68	Bobby Hamilton	Tri Star Motorsports Pontiac	277	3,200	Running
29	10	12	Hut Stricklin	Bobby Allison Buick	251	4,300	Engine
30	8	66	Dick Trickle	Cale Yarborough Pontiac	245	7,100	Crash
31	38	8	Bobby Hillin,Jr.	Stavola Brothers Buick	244	5,750	Crash
32	40	82	Mark Stahl	Stahl Racing Ford	244	3,000	Running
33	23	20	Jimmy Hensley	Dick Moroso Olds	240	3,625	Carb
34	27	98	Rick Mast	Travis Carter Chevrolet	235	3,550	Valve
35	4	25	Ken Schrader	Hendrick Motorsports Chevy	205	12,365	Engine
36	7	11	Geoff Bodine	Junior Johnson Ford	183	12,285	Camshaft
37	26	90	Buddy Baker	Junie Donlavey Ford	169	2,810	Rear End
38	12	27	Rusty Wallace	Blue Max Pontiac	133	11,995	Engine
39	35	52	Jimmy Means	Means Racing Pontiac	126	3,410	Heating
40	31	19	Chad Little	Chuck Little Ford	98	2,775	Crash
41	34	57	Jimmy Spencer	Rod Osterlund Pontiac	97	3,375	Crash

Time of Race: 3 hours, 38 minutes, 44 seconds
Average Speed: 137.428 mph
Pole Winner: Brett Bodine – 174.385 mph
Lap Leaders: Brett Bodine 1, Ernie Irvan 2-8, B.Bodine 9-10, Bill Elliott 11-63, Darrell Waltrip 64, Geoff Bodine 65-67, Elliott 68-234, Harry Gant 235, Elliott 236-258, Davey Allison 259-303, Morgan Shepherd 304-305, B.Bodine 306, Kyle Petty 307-309, Michael Waltrip 310-322, Allison 323-334.
14 lead changes among 10 drivers
Cautions: 6 for 37 laps Margin of Victory: 2.59 seconds

Brian Czobat

Robert Yates keeps a watchful eye on Davey Allison during Charlotte's Mello Yello 500

final 12 laps and outdistanced runner-up Morgan Shepherd by 2.59 seconds. Third place went to Michael Waltrip, who enjoyed one of his finest efforts of his career. Kyle Petty took fourth spot and Alan Kulwicki came from 41st on the starting grid to nail down fifth place.

Title contenders Mark Martin and Dale Earnhardt experienced numerous troubles on the balmy autumn afternoon. Martin wound up 14th on seven cylinders and took a 49 point lead in the Winston Cup standings after Earnhardt was involved in a pit road collision, a spin-out and a costly mistake in the pits. Earnhardt finished 25th, 14 laps behind. Neither driver led a lap.

Elliott's Melling Performance Ford was clearly the class of the field, leading for 243 of the first 258 laps. The only time he was not in the lead was when he was making routine pit stops.

Elliott surrendered the lead to Allison in the 259th lap when a brake caliper broke and friction generated heat

Brian Czobat

Davey Allison came on strong near the finish to score his second win of the 1990 season.

was damaging an inner liner in the right rear tire, causing it to deflate. "There's not much to say except that's the way things have been going this year," shrugged Elliott, who was able to salvage15th place, three laps off the pace. "I hate to give races away. We gave one away at Michigan (in June), and now this one."

Allison played the role of an opportunist when Elliott's misfortune changed the complexion of the race. "I don't know whether I could have challenged Bill or not," said Allison. "It doesn't matter now. Our car was loose at first. The crew worked on it and it finally felt good. I don't know what they did, but whatever it was it worked."

Allison gave praise to Jake Elder, who joined the team in July. "As soon as he joined the team, we got a top five," said Allison. "We've had such a bad year, but Jake put confidence right back in me. We need to work on our short track program. But I'm looking to the future now. We want the Winston Cup championship. That's our ultimate goal. Until we get that, we won't be satisfied."

The expected battle between Martin and Earnhardt never materialized. Martin's Ford ran on seven cylinders most of the day. "It was making all sorts of noises," said Martin. "I drove it like there was an egg between my foot and the gas pedal. We were fortunate to finish. Every engine I've ever had which shook like that took itself apart in a few laps. Our guys are building bullet-proof stuff."

ISC

Despite protests from NASCAR officials, the RCR Enterprises crew ran onto the track and changed Dale Earnhardt's tires.

Bryan Hallman

Dale Earnhardt spins his Chevrolet at Charlotte.

Earnhardt considered it lucky to lose only 33 points to Martin on a day which was filled with misfortune. During a pit stop at the 100 lap mark, Ernie Irvan and Alan Kulwicki collided on pit road. Irvan's Chevrolet spun into the RCR Enterprises Chevrolet - an instant after the crew moved to change left side tires. Had they still been on the right side, it could have been a tragic situation.

Kulwicki had made his pit stop and was preparing to drive back onto the speedway. "I was in my lane, far to the outside, and Irvan pulled out into my lane. There was no way I could stop for him. He ran me into the grass," explained Kulwicki.

"Kulwicki had a head of steam and decided he was going into the grass to get by me," claimed Irvan. "You can't run these cars in the grass. We're lucky nobody got hurt."

Earnhardt was on the pit lane and never saw the incident unfold. "Never saw him coming," said Dale. "We got hit on pit road and it messed the car up."

Once he returned to the track, Earnhardt spun out on lap 115. "It just got out from under me. It was because of that pit road deal."

Lightning struck a third time. During a pit stop following the spin, Earnhardt peeled out of pit road with the lug nuts loosened on the left rear tire. The tire flew off and he spun into the grassy infield in the first turn.

The RCR pit crew raced toward the car with tools in hand, but were motioned by a NASCAR official not to go toward the car. Rules strictly prohibit pit crews working on the car when it is on the track apron.

Despite the warning, the RCR Enterprises crew trotted past the NASCAR official.

Tires were secured in place and Earnhardt was able to rejoin the race without much lost time. NASCAR officials said they considered imposing a penalty for the infraction, but none was given.

Jimmy Hensley was tabbed to drive the Moroso Racing Oldsmobile in place of the late Rob Moroso. He was giving the car its finest run of the season - running 10th – when the car caught fire. He was given credit for a 33rd place finish.

Harry Gant had qualified second but was forced to use a back-up car after crashing in practice. The Taylorsville, N.C. driver made a strong run to the front – leading the 235th lap – but engine failure knocked him out in the closing laps.

Brett Bodine notched his first career pole and wound up eighth in Kenny Bernstein's Buick.

Bryan Hallman

Davey Allison cruises down pit road after winning Charlotte's 500.

Darrell Waltrip skids backwards at Rockingham.

Race #27

Kyle's Romp Fizzles; Kulwicki Stomps the 'Rock'

ROCKINGHAM, NC (Oct. 21) – Kyle Petty's bid for another romp at the 'Rock' was interrupted by engine woes and Alan Kulwicki gladly accepted the gift in the AC Delco 500 at North Carolina Motor Speedway.

Petty, who dominated the spring running of the GM Goodwrench 500, had picked up where he left off, leading 227 of the first 256 laps when the engine in his SabCo Racing Pontiac soured.

Kulwicki and Bill Elliott emerged as prime contenders, which Kulwicki won by heading the final 55 laps.

Elliott was running in second, eight car lengths behind, when Darrell Waltrip's spin with two laps to go forced the race to end under the yellow flag. Harry Gant wound up third. Geoff Bodine grabbed fourth spot when Ken Schrader surprisingly pitted under the yellow as the white flag came out.

It was a sweet victory for Kulwicki, who had not won in nearly two years. "I didn't think it would take this long to get our second victory," said the 35 year-old Wisconsin native, who will lose his sponsor Zerex after the season. "Maybe this win today will help us land a sponsor. I would have preferred for the race to end under the green flag, but the last caution did not affect the outcome. Whether I could have beaten Kyle, I don't know. We were getting stronger as the race went on. When he had his trouble, I thought we were about equal."

Kulwicki said he was tempted to take a Polish victory lap, but "I didn't want to get in hot water with the NASCAR officials." Kulwicki had been warned by NASCAR not to make another clockwise victory lap as

Winston Cup Series Race No. 27
492 Laps at N.C. Motor Speedway
Rockingham, NC
"AC Delco 500"
500.364 Miles on 1.017-mile Superspeedway
October 21, 1990

Fin	St	No.	Driver	Team / Car	Laps	Money	Status
1	3	7	Alan Kulwicki	AK Racing Ford	492	$53,300	Running
2	5	9	Bill Elliott	Melling Performance Ford	492	40,775	Running
3	4	33	Harry Gant	Leo Jackson Olds	492	23,575	Running
4	7	11	Geoff Bodine	Junior Johnson Ford	492	23,625	Running
5	1	25	Ken Schrader	Hendrick Motorsports Chevy	492	26,025	Running
6	29	94	Sterling Marlin	Billy Hagan Olds	491	12,882	Running
7	11	5	Ricky Rudd	Hendrick Motorsports Chevy	491	10,925	Running
8	28	17	Darrell Waltrip	Hendrick Motorsports Chevy	491	15,425	Running
9	9	4	Ernie Irvan	Morgan-McClure Chevrolet	490	10,325	Running
10	20	3	Dale Earnhardt	RCR Enterprises Chevrolet	490	19,750	Running
11	21	6	Mark Martin	Roush Racing Ford	490	13,350	Running
12	22	15	Morgan Shepherd	Bud Moore Eng. Ford	490	10,025	Running
13	12	1	Terry Labonte	Precision Products Olds	490	9,175	Running
14	27	8	Bobby Hillin,Jr.	Stavola Brothers Buick	490	8,875	Running
15	16	30	Michael Waltrip	Bahari Racing Pontiac	489	9,050	Running
16	10	21	Dale Jarrett	Wood Brothers Ford	489	8,525	Running
17	18	26	Brett Bodine	King Motorsports Buick	489	10,825	Running
18	17	75	Rick Wilson	RahMoc Racing Pontiac	487	7,475	Running
19	30	41	Larry Pearson	Larry Hedrick Chevrolet	487	4,275	Running
20	6	42	Kyle Petty	SabCo Racing Pontiac	485	13,850	Running
21	35	43	Richard Petty	Petty Enterprises Pontiac	485	5,350	Running
22	8	98	Rick Mast	Travis Carter Chevrolet	484	4,650	Running
23	25	71	Dave Marcis	Marcis Auto Racing Chevy	483	6,950	Running
24	31	47	Jack Pennington	Derick Close Olds	482	4,400	Running
25	26	19	Chad Little	Chuck Little Ford	479	3,675	Running
26	34	40	Tommy Kendall	Marc Reno Chevrolet	477	3,525	Running
27	38	57	Jim Bown	Rod Osterlund Pontiac	477	4,175	Running
28	39	52	Jimmy Means	Means Racing Pontiac	471	4,100	Running
29	2	28	Davey Allison	Robert Yates Racing Ford	470	14,700	Running
30	32	2	Rick Jeffrey	Doreen Jeffrey Chevrolet	467	5,300	Running
31	23	20	Jimmy Hensley	Dick Moroso Olds	452	3,850	Running
32	19	27	Rusty Wallace	Blue Max Pontiac	421	14,075	Engine
33	15	10	Derrike Cope	Bob Whitcomb Chevrolet	268	7,975	Valve
34	13	12	Hut Stricklin	Bobby Allison Buick	236	4,050	Engine
35	33	13	Mike Skinner	Thee Dixon Buick	230	2,825	Rear End
36	14	66	Dick Trickle	Cale Yarborough Pontiac	217	6,350	Engine
37	36	50	Ted Musgrave	DeWitt Racing Chevrolet	93	2,700	Engine
38	24	51	Jeff Purvis	James Finch Chevrolet	75	2,690	Engine
39	37	72	Tracy Leslie	Ron Parker Oldsmobile	67	2,650	Engine
40	40	93	Charlie Baker	Patsy Salmon Buick	35	2,600	Engine

Time of Race: 3 hours, 57 minutes, 25 seconds
Average Speed: 126.452 mph
Pole Winner: Ken Schrader - 147.814 mph
Lap Leaders: Ken Schrader 1-14, Davey Allison 15-25, Alan Kulwicki 26, Allison 27, Kulwicki 28, Schrader 29-30, Dave Marcis 31-32, Darrell Waltrip 33-35, Schrader 36-49, Kyle Petty 50-222, Kulwicki 223-225, Bill Elliott 226-230, Geoff Bodine 231-232, K.Petty 233-266, Kulwicki 267-330, Elliott 331-375, Kulwicki 376-402, Elliott 403-404, Schrader 405, G.Bodine 406-407, Elliott 408-437, Kulwicki 438-492.
21 lead changes among 8 drivers.
Cautions: 7 for 28 laps Margin of Victory: Under Caution

Brian Czobat

Alan Kulwicki's second career Winston Cup triumph was a long time coming.

he had done at Phoenix in 1988. "I didn't have Bill France, Jr. here to bail me out," responded Kulwicki.

The highly anticipated battle between Mark Martin and Dale Earnhardt for the Winston Cup point chase never materialized. Earnhardt qualified 20th and Martin was 21st. Both struggled for the second race in a row. Neither contender led a lap and Earnhardt finished 10th while Martin was 11th.

Steve Hmiel, Team Manager for the Roush Racing unit, perhaps summed it up best. "It was like sending two big home run hitters up against each other for a home run hitting contest and watching both bunt."

"It was just a bad day," said Earnhardt, who trimmed four points off his deficit and now trails Martin by 45 points with two races left. "Picking up four points is better than losing four points."

Martin had the third fastest overall time although he qualified on the second day. He was 25th fastest during opening day time trials. "We had a hoss of a motor, but it just wouldn't get around the race track. I feel fortunate I didn't wreck the car. I was out of control several times. I can't believe we ran as bad as we did."

A quick glance at the standings reveals an interesting flaw in the procedure in which the Winston Cup title is determined. Both Martin and Earnhardt have 16 top five finishes;

Kim Novosat

Dale Earnhardt and wife Theresa share a private moment.

each has as additional five efforts between sixth and 10th. The only notable difference is the victories – Earnhardt has eight and Martin three. But Earnhardt trails by 45 points and would have been woefully behind had Martin not been stripped of 46 points in the second event of the season at Richmond.

Petty was unable to finish better than 20th. He was seven laps off the pace when the checkered flag fell. He was so far behind he lost sight of the battle for the win. "Whoever won this race had a second place car. We had 'em covered today," said Petty.

Cal Lawson, a member of Kulwicki's crew, narrowly escaped serious injury when he was struck by Rusty Wallace during a pit stop. Wallace clipped Lawson, whose head hit Wallace's windshield so hard it cracked the glass. "I came out of the pits and this guy from Kulwicki's crew was right in front of my car," said Wallace. "I couldn't avoid hitting him."

NASCAR official Mike Howard was hit in the head by a bouncing tire in the backstretch pits. After treatment at the infield hospital, Howard returned to duty.

Race #28

Earnhardt Leaps to Top of Standings With Phoenix Win

PHOENIX, AZ (Nov. 4) – Dale Earnhardt turned the Checker 500 into a one man show and overhauled Mark Martin in the Winston Cup standings en route to a convincing victory at Phoenix International Raceway. Earnhardt took the lead in the 51st lap during a pit stop under the yellow flag and never looked back. It was the most lopsided superspeedway race since David Pearson led all but one lap in the 1973 Carolina 500 at Rocking-

Winston Cup Series Race No. 28
312 Laps at Phoenix Int'l Raceway
Phoenix, AZ
"Checker 500"
312 Miles on 1-mile Superspeedway
November 4, 1990

Fin	St	No.	Driver	Team / Car	Laps	Money	Status
1	3	3	Dale Earnhardt	RCR Enterprises Chevrolet	312	$72,100	Running
2	2	25	Ken Schrader	Hendrick Motorsports Chevy	312	32,900	Running
3	30	15	Morgan Shepherd	Bud Moore Eng. Ford	312	23,357	Running
4	10	17	Darrell Waltrip	Hendrick Motorsports Chevy	312	21,500	Running
5	12	9	Bill Elliott	Melling Performance Ford	312	19,775	Running
6	11	7	Alan Kulwicki	AK Racing Ford	312	12,225	Running
7	7	98	Rick Mast	Travis Carter Chevrolet	312	10,250	Running
8	13	11	Geoff Bodine	Junior Johnson Ford	312	14,950	Running
9	17	4	Ernie Irvan	Morgan-McClure Chevrolet	312	10,150	Running
10	8	6	Mark Martin	Roush Racing Ford	312	14,875	Running
11	4	28	Davey Allison	Robert Yates Racing Ford	312	13,350	Running
12	6	18	Greg Sacks	Hendrick Motorsports Chevy	312	4,850	Running
13	23	1	Terry Labonte	Precision Products Olds	312	8,650	Running
14	20	10	Derrike Cope	Bob Whitcomb Chevrolet	311	9,450	Running
15	16	26	Brett Bodine	King Motorsports Buick	311	8,625	Running
16	15	94	Sterling Marlin	Billy Hagan Olds	310	7,525	Running
17	19	71	Dave Marcis	Marcis Auto Racing Chevy	310	7,200	Running
18	40	73	Bill Schmitt	Sylvia Schmitt Chevrolet	310	4,875	Running
19	24	75	Rick Wilson	RahMoc Racing Olds	310	6,650	Running
20	32	76	Bill Sedgwick	Wayne Spears Chevrolet	310	5,300	Running
21	22	20	Chad Little	Dick Moroso Olds	309	4,50	Running
22	25	2	Ted Musgrave	Ray & Diane DeWitt Pontiac	309	5,375	Running
23	36	43	Richard Petty	Petty Enterprises Pontiac	308	4,300	Running
24	28	97	Chuck Bown	Tex Powell Oldsmobile	307	3,300	Running
25	42	52	Jimmy Means	Means Racing Pontiac	307	4,275	Running
26	18	12	Hut Stricklin	Bobby Allison Buick	306	4,175	Running
27	31	89	Rodney Combs	Mueller Brothers Pontiac	305	3,300	Running
28	41	57	Jim Bown	Rod Osterlund Pontiac	304	3,950	Running
29	38	69	Brad Kaeding	Gerald Smith Chevrolet	304	3,230	Running
30	21	21	Dale Jarrett	Wood Brothers Ford	299	6,395	Crash
31	43	99	John Krebs	Krebs Pontiac	293	3,835	Running
32	9	5	Ricky Rudd	Hendrick Motorsports Chevy	293	5,780	Running
33	39	29	Gary Collins	Marion Collins Oldsmobile	280	3,125	Running
34	33	72	Mark Reed	Jim Reed Chevrolet	269	3,100	Ignition
35	37	93	Troy Beebe	Beebe Racing Buick	263	3,085	Crash
36	34	51	Jeff Purvis	James Finch Chevrolet	256	3,055	Brakes
37	26	33	Harry Gant	Leo Jackson Olds	152	10,045	Tires
38	1	27	Rusty Wallace	Blue Max Pontiac	77	15,975	Engine
39	35	23	Mike Chase	Don Freymiller Buick	70	3,000	Crash
40	5	66	Dick Trickle	Cale Yarborough Pontiac	68	6,575	Engine
41	27	42	Kyle Petty	SabCo Racing Pontiac	48	9,975	Crash
42	14	8	Bobby Hillin,Jr.	Stavola Brothers Buick	47	4,975	Crash
43	29	30	Michael Waltrip	Bahari Racing Pontiac	47	4,975	Crash

Time of Race: 3 hours, 13 minutes, 25 seconds
Average Speed: 96.786 mph
Pole Winner: Rusty Wallace – 124.443 mph
Lap Leaders: Rusty Wallace 1-50, Dale Earnhardt 51-312.
1 lead change between 2 drivers.
Cautions: 9 for 48 laps Margin of Victory: 0.67-second

Brian Czobat

Dale and Ned Jarrett before the Phoenix race.

Brian Czobat

Bobby Hillin, Jr.'s Buick suffered a beating at Phoenix.

ham.

Ken Schrader was aided by nine caution flags and wound up second. He trailed the fleet Earnhardt by 0.67-second in a finish that was not nearly that close. Morgan Shepherd came from 30th starting position to finish third. Darrell Waltrip and Bill Elliott rounded out the top five.

Martin finished in 10th place and lost 51 points to Earnhardt. The Batesville, Ark. driver had been running sixth in the final 16 laps, which would have been good enough to take a 10 point lead to the season finale in Atlanta. But he elected to pit for new tires during the caution flag on lap 296 and was unable to make any appreciable gain during the final green flag laps.

"I thought Mark would have a top five finish and that would just about be it," admitted Earnhardt. "But with the way things turned out, we're making this point race pretty interesting. We were hoping to notch a few points off his lead and have a chance at Atlanta."

Martin scratched and clawed his way into fourth place with about 20 laps to go, but he used up the tires on his Roush Ford. He had fallen back to sixth when Chuck Bown's spin brought out the next to last caution flag. "I ran the tires off the car," explained Martin. "I was drifting back and would have gone further back under the final

Brian Czobat

Spectators fill the hillside at Phoenix International Raceway.

green flag laps. I had no choice but to pit."

To add insult to injury, Martin was involved in a crash after the checkered flag waved. "I slowed down after the race," said ninth-finishing Ernie Irvan, "and Mark didn't. That's about the size of it."

Rusty Wallace started on the pole and led the first 50 laps. But foul luck dogged the Blue Max Pontiac team as Wallace's engine failed after 77 laps. From that point on, Earnhardt was virtually unchallenged.

Troy Beebe, who was severely injured in a practice crash at Watkins Glen in August, made his return to Winston Cup racing and crashed again in the 264th lap.

Bill Schmitt finished 18th and edged 20th place finisher Bill Sedgwick by a single point in the Winston West final standings. Western drivers compete for both Winston West and Winston Cup points.

Winston Cup Series Race No. 29
328 Laps at Atlanta Motor Speedway
Hampton, GA
"Atlanta Journal 500"
499.216 Miles on 1.522-mile Superspeedway
November 18, 1990

Fin	St	No.	Driver	Team / Car	Laps	Money	Status
1	20	15	Morgan Shepherd	Bud Moore Eng. Ford	328	$62,250	Running
2	2	11	Geoff Bodine	Junior Johnson Ford	328	40,850	Running
3	6	3	Dale Earnhardt	RCR Enterprises Chevrolet	328	26,700	Running
4	21	21	Dale Jarrett	Wood Brothers Ford	328	17,225	Running
5	5	17	Darrell Waltrip	Hendrick Motorsports Chevy	327	22,300	Running
6	11	6	Mark Martin	Roush/Yates Racing Ford	327	14,700	Running
7	8	4	Ernie Irvan	Morgan-McClure Chevrolet	327	11,200	Running
8	3	7	Alan Kulwicki	AK Racing Ford	327	10,650	Running
9	1	27	Rusty Wallace	Blue Max Pontiac	327	20,700	Running
10	19	18	Greg Sacks	Hendrick Motorsports Chevy	326	7,625	Running
11	14	25	Ken Schrader	Hendrick Motorsports Chevy	326	11,750	Running
12	18	10	Derrike Cope	Bob Whitcomb Chevrolet	326	9,550	Running
13	15	12	Hut Stricklin	Bobby Allison Buick	326	6,450	Running
14	27	30	Michael Waltrip	Bahari Racing Pontiac	326	7,850	Running
15	9	9	Bill Elliott	Melling Performance Ford	326	37,800	Running
16	10	5	Ricky Rudd	Hendrick Motorsports Chevy	325	7,550	Running
17	22	43	Richard Petty	Petty Enterprises Pontiac	324	5,650	Running
18	7	26	Brett Bodine	King Motorsports Buick	323	7,250	Running
19	12	33	Harry Gant	Leo Jackson Olds	323	10,850	Running
20	29	65	Dave Mader III	Dick Bahre Pontiac	323	4,525	Running
21	24	1	Terry Labonte	Precision Products Olds	323	6,650	Running
22	31	8	Bobby Hillin, Jr.	Stavola Brothers Buick	323	6,475	Running
23	16	97	Chuck Bown	Tex Powell Chevrolet	322	3,400	Running
24	23	20	Steve Grissom	Dick Moroso Olds	322	4,275	Running
25	4	28	Davey Allison	Robert Yates Racing Ford	321	16,450	Running
26	26	2	Ted Musgrave	Ray & Diane DeWitt Pontiac	319	5,225	Running
27	37	19	Chad Little	Chuck Little Ford	318	3,200	Running
28	28	52	Jimmy Means	Means Racing Pontiac	316	4,025	Running
29	25	98	Rick Mast	Travis Carter Chevrolet	316	3,600	Running
30	38	89	Rodney Combs	Mueller Brothers Pontiac	315	3,125	Running
31	39	0	Jim Sauter	H.L.Waters Ford	310	3,050	Engine
32	33	29	Pancho Carter	Paul Romine Ford	298	3,040	Crash
33	34	75	Rick Wilson	RahMoc Racing Olds	291	5,705	Crash
34	36	71	Dave Marcis	Marcis Auto Racing Chevy	267	5,700	Engine
35	40	80	Jimmy Horton	George Smith Chevrolet	234	3,000	Rear End
36	32	47	Jack Pennington	Derick Close Olds	228	3,490	Engine
37	13	66	Dick Trickle	Cale Yarborough Pontiac	167	6,600	Engine
38	35	94	Sterling Marlin	Billy Hagan Olds	132	5,560	Steering
39	41	57	Jim Bown	Rod Osterlund Pontiac	56	3,530	Crash
40	17	68	Bobby Hamilton	Tri-Star Motorsports Pontiac	28	2,925	Engine
41	30	42	Kyle Petty	SabCo Racing Pontiac	12	9,925	Engine

Time of Race: 3 hours, 32 minutes, 34 seconds
Average Speed: 140.911 mph
Pole Winner: Rusty Wallace – 175.222 mph
Lap Leaders: Rusty Wallace 1, Davey Allison 2-14, Wallace 15-43, Dale Earnhardt 44-56, Alan Kulwicki 57-58, Geoff Bodine 59-103, Darrell Waltrip 104, G.Bodine 105, D.Waltrip 106-133, Derrike Cope 134-135, Bill Elliott 136-198, D.Waltrip 199-200, Morgan Shepherd 201-229, Earnhardt 230-233, Shepherd 234-239, Elliott 240-263, D.Waltrip 264-267, Earnhardt 268-292, Elliott 293-299, Shepherd 300-328.
19 lead changes among 9 drivers.
Cautions: 3 for 34 laps Margin of Victory: 2.47 seconds

Race #29

Earnhardt and Shepherd Win at Atlanta; Crewman Killed in Pits

HAMPTON, GA (Nov. 18) – Morgan Shepherd led the final 29 laps to win the Atlanta Journal 500 at Atlanta Motor Speedway as Dale Earnhardt was crowned the 1990 Winston Cup champion.

The festive atmosphere was tempered by the death of 32 year-old Mike Ritch, a crewman for Bill Elliott's Ford team, who died after behind crushed between two race cars in a tragic pit road accident late in the race.

Elliott, who led the most laps in the race, was leading in the 296th lap when Rick Wilson crashed to bring out the third and final caution of the afternoon. Elliott

Brian Czobat

Morgan Shepherd and daughter Shanda Renee in Victory Lane at Atlanta Motor Speedway.

Brian Czobat

Morgan Shepherd pushes his Bud Moore Ford around Bobby Hamilton en route to victory in the Atlanta Journal 500.

breezed down pit road and was being serviced by his Melling crew. Ricky Rudd's Hendrick Motorsports Chevrolet was approaching his pit – which was located directly in front of Elliott's pit stall – but lost control and spun past his pit. Rudd's car struck Elliott's as it was on the jacks. Jackman Tommy Cole was hit in the back by Rudd's car and he tumbled down the pit road. Ritch, busy changing the right rear tire, was crushed between the cars.

Ritch was airlifted to Georgia Baptist Hospital in Atlanta where he died two hours after undergoing surgery. Doctors said he had "unsurvivable" injuries.

Team owner Harry Melling mulled quitting the Winston Cup tour. "That's the second time this has happened to us," said Melling, referring to a 1987 pit accident at Riverside which injured crewman Steve Colwell and Chuck Hill. "I don't have to stay in this sport and I won't."

Cole was treated at trackside for minor injuries and released.

Ironically, Ritch and Cole were hired as replacements for Colwell and Hill.

"I don't know if I hit a grease spot or not," said Rudd. There wasn't anything I could do to avoid it. I'm really tore up about it. Nothing like this has ever happened to me before. It's one thing when you hit a car. When there's a human being between the cars, it's tragic."

Elliott limped to a 15th place finish, dismounted his car and immediately left the track. "I ain't got nothing to say about nothing," he told news reporters.

The tragedy put a damper on Shepherd's victory, which was his first on the premier NASCAR touring series in four years, and on Earnhardt, who claimed his fourth national driving championship.

Shepherd started 20th, but placed his Bud Moore En-

Brian Czobat

Darrell Waltrip #17 and Ernie Irvan battle at Atlanta.

gineering Ford into contention early. He led three times for 64 laps and outran runner-up Geoff Bodine by 2.47 seconds. Earnhardt claimed third spot while Dale Jarrett was fourth and Darrell Waltrip fifth. Martin wound up sixth in a Ford from the Robert Yates Racing stable.

Mark Martin makes a quick pit stop at Atlanta. His sixth place finish wasn't enough to overhaul Dale Earnhardt for the 1990 Winston Cup championship.

Earnhardt entered the race with a six point lead and won the title by 26 points – and gave Chevrolet it's eighth manufacturers championship. "It's been a tough year, really," said the four-time Winston Cup champ. "We've won races, but we got behind in the points. It's a hard fight to come back from where we did. I can't say enough for the team."

Earnhardt was irritated when one news reporter asked him to comment on the controversial 46-point penalty NASCAR handed the Martin-Roush team earlier in the year. "They cheated," snapped Earnhardt. "They got caught. That was a long time ago."

Martin took the defeat in stride, becoming only the second driver to lose the NASCAR championship on a penalty. Lee Petty lost the 1950 championship when he was stripped of all points during the season. "There were 29 Winston Cup races this year, not one," said Martin. "We put that Richmond deal behind us a long time ago."

Martin was driving a Ford Thunderbird built by Robert Yates instead of his usual Roush-built car. "We had to do something out of the ordinary. As long as we were ahead in the points, we didn't want to introduce something new into our system. But when we fell behind, we felt we had to do something because Earnhardt is so strong here. We tested some of our cars and the Yates car. The Yates car was clearly superior."

1990 NASCAR Season
Final Point Standings - Winston Cup Series

Rank	Driver	Points	Starts	Wins	Top 5	Top 10	Winnings
1	Dale Earnhardt	4,430	29	9	18	23	$3,308,056
2	Mark Martin	4,404	29	3	16	23	1,302,958
3	Geoff Bodine	4,017	29	3	11	19	1,131,222
4	Bill Elliott	3,999	29	1	12	16	1,090,730
5	Morgan Shepherd	3,689	29	1	7	16	666,915
6	Rusty Wallace	3,676	29	2	9	16	954,129
7	Ricky Rudd	3,601	29	1	8	15	573,650
8	Alan Kulwicki	3,599	29	1	5	13	550,936
9	Ernie Irvan	3,593	29	1	6	13	535,280
10	Ken Schrader	3,572	29	0	7	14	769,934
11	Kyle Petty	3,501	29	1	2	14	746,326
12	Brett Bodine	3,440	29	1	5	9	442,681
13	Davey Allison	3,423	29	2	5	10	640,684
14	Sterling Marlin	3,387	29	0	5	10	369,167
15	Terry Labonte	3,371	29	0	4	9	450,230
16	Michael Waltrip	3,251	29	0	5	10	395,507
17	Harry Gant	3,182	28	1	6	9	522,519
18	Derrike Cope	3,140	29	2	2	6	569,451
19	Bobby Hillin,Jr.	3,048	29	0	1	4	339,366
20	Darrell Waltrip	3,013	20	0	5	12	520,420
21	Dave Marcis	2,944	29	0	0	0	242,724
22	Dick Trickle	2,863	29	0	2	4	350,990
23	Rick Wilson	2,666	29	0	1	3	242,067
24	Jimmy Spencer	2,579	26	0	0	2	219,775
25	Dale Jarrett	2,558	24	0	1	7	214,495
26	Richard Petty	2,556	29	0	0	1	169,465
27	Butch Miller	2,377	23	0	0	1	151,941
28	Hut Stricklin	2,316	24	0	0	2	169,199
29	Jimmy Means	2,271	27	0	0	0	135,165
30	Rob Moroso	2,184	25	0	0	1	162,002
31	Rick Mast	1,719	20	0	0	1	112,875
32	Greg Sacks	1,663	16	0	2	4	216,148
33	Chad Little	1,632	18	0	0	0	80,140
34	Jack Pennington	1,278	14	0	0	0	95,860
35	Larry Pearson	822	9	0	0	0	72,305
36	Jimmy Horton	756	9	0	0	0	72,375
37	Mickey Gibbs	755	9	0	0	0	38,665
38	Mike Alexander	682	7	0	0	0	41,080
39	Phil Parsons	632	9	0	0	0	90,010
40	J.D.McDuffie	557	8	0	0	0	26,170
41	Buddy Baker	498	8	0	0	0	40,085
42	Lake Speed	479	6	0	0	0	75,537
43	Neil Bonnett	455	5	0	0	0	62,600
44	Mark Stahl	371	5	0	0	0	18,470
45	Bill Venturini	349	4	0	0	0	22,970
46	Rodney Combs	323	5	0	0	0	23,365
47	Irv Hoerr	281	2	0	0	2	14,775
48	Tommy Kendall	281	3	0	0	1	14,120
49	Ted Musgrave	280	4	0	0	0	17,190
50	Chuck Bown	276	3	0	0	0	10,150

1991 Winston Cup Season

Ernie Earns New Nickname; Gant Becomes Mr. September

SWEEPING PIT ROAD CHANGES

The 1991 NASCAR Winston Cup season was a multi-faceted offering. It began with sweeping changes regarding pit road procedures, triggered by the death of Melling Performance crewman Michael Ritch in the 1990 season finale at Atlanta.

NASCAR, maintaining its reputation of being a step ahead of other sanctioning bodies when it comes to safety, addressed the situation during the off-season. Pit road had become a crap shoot since mid-1989 when NASCAR ruled that pit stops could not begin during caution periods until the pace car had gone onto the track and picked up the leader.

In years past, when the caution flag dropped, many of the leaders whipped down pit road before the pace car picked up the field. That caused many scoring headaches – and occasionally, it affected the outcome of a race.

The scoring problems were eliminated when drivers were forced to line up behind the pace car. Pit road was opened and all cars on the lead lap hustled down pit road. In 1990, there were dozens of close calls on pit road; crew members getting grazed by on-rushing cars. "I think the price of men over the wall just went up," said Tim Brewer after a pit road crash at Charlotte Motor Speedway.

New pit road procedures would greet the NASCAR touring pros at Daytona. Through a series of trial-and-

ISC

Pit road looked much the same in the Daytona 500, but new procedures were made in the interest of safety.

Brian Czobat

Five cars were painted with military colors. Mickey Gibbs #24 (Air Force), Greg Sacks #18 (Navy), Alan Kulwicki #7 (Army), Buddy Baker #88 (Marines) and Dave Marcis #71 (Coast Guard) had their cars lined up on pit road before the Daytona 500.

mostly-error, procedures were changed through the first six events of the season. Confusion was underscored. Even the hardiest of racing veterans weren't sure what was going on.

At certain times, no tires could be changed during the yellow. That meant cars with flat tires had to continue running on the track. Another ruling limited pit stops under yellow to half the cars on the lead lap, depending on what color sticker a driver had on his windshield.

At Bristol, new rules created a multitude of lead changes under the yellow flag when the leader had not pitted. That constituted a physical impossibility.

The immediate result was a safer pit road but terribly boring races. Team strategies had to be planned over an entire 500-mile race. Caution periods no longer became a source of renewed strategy or an opportunity to make tire changes. Drivers often had to continue racing at full speed on worn tires, which became another safety concern altogether.

Eventually, NASCAR settled on an orderly pit road entrance with a strict speed limit. Tires could be changed once again.

ACCENT ON PATRIOTISM

By the time the Winston Cup teams arrived in Daytona, the United States was involved in a confrontation with Iraq. Air strikes were a daily news item. Extra security was in force at Daytona.

Inside the confines of the 2.5-mile Daytona International Speedway, teams were getting ready for the big race. With the economy in a slight dip, many drivers were operating on limited finances.

Sports Marketing Enterprises, the motorsports branch of R.J. Reynolds sponsorship program, backed five unsponsored drivers in the Daytona 500. Alan Kulwicki was fitted with Army colors, Dave Marcis' car was painted in Coast Guard livery, Greg Sacks had Navy on his Chevrolet, Buddy Baker was painted in Marine colors, and Mickey Gibbs carried the flag for the Air Force – all in the name of patriotism for America's Desert Storm war effort.

Kulwicki had drawn much attention. Determined to field his own Winston Cup team, Kulwicki had turned down an offer to drive for Junior Johnson in 1990. Johnson then settled on Geoff Bodine for a year.

Although Kulwicki managed to win one race during the 1990 campaign, it was a tough struggle for the Wisconsin native. "We got off to a rough start in 1990," said Kulwicki. "We had a lot of things go wrong. Other people would crash in front of us, or someone would blow an engine. We'd get in their oil, or something like that...things we had no control over."

Kulwicki did not make it into the top 20 in points until mid-season, but he came on strong and wound up ninth in the point parade.

Toward the end of the year, Kulwicki was informed that Zerex AntiFreeze would not be returning as his sponsor. He had several prospects, the most promising was Maxwell House coffee. But car owner Johnson was expanding his operation to include a second team and had Maxwell House in his hip pocket.

Johnson again made the offer to Kulwicki. And as he had done the year before, Kulwicki turned him down. "I have a sponsor lined up," Kulwicki told Johnson. When the discussion centered around Maxwell House,

Johnson advised Kulwicki that he should carefully consider his offer, that the firm wasn't necessarily going to back Kulwicki.

Two weeks later, Johnson announced that Maxwell House had agreed to sponsor Johnson's second car to be driven by Sterling Marlin. Kulwicki was really left out in the cold.

Undaunted, Kulwicki went to Daytona with no sponsor, but grateful for Winston's one-race financial support.

Bryan Hallman

Junior Johnson's Ford carried #97 for four races. Johnson was suspended for four races when NASCAR found an oversized engine after The Winston all-star event. Johnson transfered temporary ownership to his wife Flossie and was able to compete with a different car number.

EARNHARDT IS THE FAVORITE

During the shake-down runs at Daytona, it was quite clear that Dale Earnhardt was once again the overwhelming favorite to sweep Speedweeks. His performance in the Busch Clash was remarkable – a dazzling display of speed and power that had become the subject at every lounge and bar in Daytona.

Earnhardt had come from sixth to first in a lap and won the first 10-lap segment of the 20-lap, 50-mile sprint for 1990 pole winners. Under a new format, the race was flagged at half-way and the cars were lined up in reverse order. This put Earnhardt at the rear of the 14-car field.

Brian Czobat

Dale Earnhardt lost the Daytona 500 but won another Winston Cup championship.

It only took Earnhardt a little over a lap to overhaul the entire field. He won the second 10-lapper without challenge. "It was awesome, wasn't it," Earnhardt said with a grin.

Other drivers shuddered at Earnhardt's accomplishments. "I don't see anybody beating him," confessed Bill Elliott. "Anybody who can come from last to first in less than two laps...I mean, you have to understand, he's *bad*!"

Mark Martin said it was "disappointing to see him come out here and dominate like that."

One motorsports reporter wrote, "Cancel the (1991) NASCAR season. Judging by what Dale Earnhardt did in the Busch Clash, there's no sense in having one."

True to form, Earnhardt rattled the cages in Speed-

Dover Downs

Darrell Waltrip and Ernie Irvan chat before the start of a race. Irvan's relentless driving style and his involvment in big wrecks made him the object of criticism.

weeks, winning the Clash, the Twin 125 and Saturday's Busch Grand National event. He was all set to end his 0-for-12 losing streak in the Daytona 500.

IRVAN PULLS SURPRISE

Earnhardt shot from his second row starting spot to take the lead from Davey Allison in the second lap. He easily led until the first caution flag.

As the new pit road rules trapped some drivers and assisted others, Earnhardt fell from the lead during the middle stages. But as yellow flags and timely green flag pit stops for tires drew the field together, Earnhardt was poised for his run toward the checkered flag.

When a green flag restarted the 500 with 12 laps to go. Earnhardt bolted around Rusty Wallace and took first place. Another late caution interrupted the brisk pace for four laps.

Two laps after the final restart, Ernie Irvan parked his Morgan-McClure Chevrolet on Earnhardt's rear bumper. Earnhardt was unable to pull away. The packed house watched in awe as Irvan made a surprise move on Earnhardt with six laps left. Running low on fuel and riding on worn tires, Irvan had passed the unpassable.

Davey Allison, who had started on the pole, drew alongside of Earnhardt and challenged for second place. The two raced door-to-door for two laps before Earnhardt lost control off the second turn.

Earnhardt side-swiped Allison, knocking him into the infield. Kyle Petty punched the nose of Earnhardt's Chevrolet and piled into the backstretch wall.

Irvan cruised to victory under caution as Sterling Marlin finished second. Earnhardt somehow recovered and finished fifth.

Irvan had won NASCAR's biggest event in an upset. A year earlier, he had been without a full-time ride.

SWERVIN' IRVAN

Irvan had earned his spurs as an aggressive driver. Many compared him to Earnhardt.

Aggressiveness had given Morgan-McClure their first victory at Bristol in 1990. The Daytona 500 win elevated the team from that of mere potential to an authentic winner.

Irvan's style on the track did not waver. There was no mistaking the fury in which he drove. He was fast and strong and he played with a feverish intensity and constant daring.

Kim Novasat

A message on one of the cars after Pocono's big 14-car crash.

All of those attributes got his squarely mixed up in a multi-car crash on the backstretch of Talladega Superspeedway during the Winston 500 in May.

Shortly before the mid-way point in the race, Irvan wheeled his car in between Kyle Petty and Mark Martin. Irvan nipped the left-rear bumper of Petty's Pontiac, setting off the melee. Martin's Ford was nearly launched skyward.

Many of the drivers involved blamed Irvan. "He is totally out of control, and you can quote me on that," said Dale Jarrett.

"There are certain guys who would rather wreck than let off the gas," claimed Martin. "And Ernie will always have an excuse."

Buddy Baker: "He may be tough on a small track, but he's out of control here. Someone needs to tell him he's in the big leagues now."

"He (Irvan) had no business where he was. It was a real big mess."

Darrell Waltrip: "It looks like this is the kind of guy who can hurt you."

Irvan shook off the criticisms and went about his business.

A couple months later, Irvan was close to another huge pile-up which occurred at Pocono.

Many drivers claimed Irvan was at fault. Irvan denied all charges and said, "Every time I'm within five car lengths of somebody who has trouble, I get blamed for it."

The 23rd annual Talladega DieHard 500 was the next race on the schedule. About two hours before the start of the race, Irvan held a press conference which was attended by most of his fellow drivers:

"I've talked with a few of the drivers this week and some of the car owners, and I've lost the respect of a lot of the drivers and car owners in this garage area. And that hurts.

"I've drove a little bit over-aggressive some, and I'm going to work on trying to be a little more patient. And I want to earn everybody's respect back. I like to be liked in the garage area and I would appreciate maybe if you guys give me a shot at it. I definitely want to be everybody's friend in here."

Later, Irvan would say that it was one of the most embarrassing things he ever had to do.

Car owner Larry McClure stood by his driver. "Ernie is aggressive, he really is," he remarked. "I feel like he can do things with a race car other people would like to do but can't. Yes, he's made mistakes. Everyone has. But what I want is for everyone to realize that when they are made, we're racing.

"I know what it's like to have a car torn up. No one has to tell me. Ernie also knows he's made mistakes and that he needs to be more patient. If I ever thought Ernie wrecked another car intentionally, NASCAR wouldn't have to park him. I would. I mean that."

In the Talladega 500, Irvan was involved in another big crash, but this time it started when another driver knocked him in the rear and spun him in the face of oncoming traffic.

McDuffie Coll.

J.D. McDuffie working on his car the morning of the day in which he lost his life.

TRAGEDY AT WATKINS GLEN

The Winston Cup series next stop was at Watkins Glen International, a road course in upstate New York. The 18th event on the 1991 Winston Cup schedule had attracted 40 cars. One of the entrants was John Delphus McDuffie.

McDuffie Coll.

J.D. McDuffie 1938-1991

McDuffie's dark blue tow trailer was parked in the far side of the garage. It was scarcely noticeable because of all the expensive big rigs used by virtually every other team.

The 1991 season had been tough on McDuffie, one of the last of the independents – drivers and owners who race with worn out parts and very little finances. He had made only four races. Most of the others he had failed to earn a starting berth in qualifying.

But J.D. McDuffie was never discouraged; never complained about his plight. He towed his ragged Pontiac to each and every stop on the Winston Cup schedule because he loved to race.

McDuffie made the field at Watkins Glen. He had qualified 35th in the field of 40.

The night before, McDuffie had been invited to participate in a celebrity race at Shangri-La Speedway in Owego, N.Y. He was racing against members of the RCR Enterprises pit crew team.

Starting in the second row, J.D. drove to the front immediately and went on to win the race. It was was on his proudest moments as the spectators cheered him as a winner.

The next day, he strapped himself into his Pontiac for the Budweiser At The Glen. It was his 653rd start in a NASCAR Winston Cup race.

In the fifth lap, McDuffie's Pontiac slid off the race course and slammed into a retaining barrier. He died instantly.

SALUTE TO J.D.

Some men try to conquer life in a number of ways. Race car drivers are courageous men who try to conquer life and death and they calculate the risks. J.D. McDuffie was aware of the risks, but more importantly, he was aware of the joys racing had given him over the years.

J.D. was both serious and frivolous. He was fun and a wonderful gentleman. On the race track, he was a familar presence. While success didn't follow with glowing statistics, J.D. was a winner.

They say that it is God's will to lose J.D. and we must accept our loss. In a sense, we are all speeding toward death at the rate of 60 minutes per hour. The difference is that we don't know how to speed faster, but J.D.did.

Since death has a thousand or more doors, J.D. exited this earth in a race car. Racing was his first love – we must assume that's the way he would have wanted it.

Racing will continue, but without J.D. McDuffie.

ALLISON, GANT COME ON STRONG

Dale Earnhardt had taken the lead in the Winston Cup standings as of the ninth race of the season at Talladega. He would never relinquish his grip on first place. Ricky Rudd ran second most of the way, but he never was able to make a charge.

Harry Gant and Davey Allison were the swiftest competitors in the late season rush, but they had buried themselves into a hole early in the year and were unable to catch up in the point race.

Gant, in his third year with team owner Leo Jackson, hit stride in September, winning four straight races. He also won a pair of Busch Grand National events during the string.

The 51 year-old Gant scored at Darlington, outrunning runner-up Ernie Irvan by nearly 11 seconds. The event marked the competitive return for Kyle Petty, who had been out of action since May with injuries he suffered at Talladega. Kyle was running fourth late in end. We just had to leave it like it was.

"We also had an oil cooler that was almost jammed into the wheel, and that was a concern, too. We had a brake duct knocked loose. It took a lot of time to get that off the car. We knew we couldn't go back on the track dragging it or NASCAR would have black-flagged us."

Gant restarted the race in 12th place. Nobody thought he had a chance to win.

But Handsome Harry began picking off his rivals one by one. In less than 50 miles, he scrubbed by Brett Bodine and led the rest of the way.

Gant's late season success drew national attention. A 51-year-old man was outrunning all of his younger adversaries. Rarely had he ever called on relief. He could withstand the summer's heat as well as anybody.

Through the Modern Era record-tying streak, Gant's hat size never grew.

Tony Head, a resident in Gant's hometown of Taylorsville, N.C., said, "Harry Gant is the only big league racer I know who celebrates Sunday by mowing his yard on Monday."

Gant finished the season with five victories, tying Davey Allison for first in that category.

He also won the most Busch Grand National races, becoming the first driver to ever win the most races in a season in NASCAR's two premier divisions.

Brian Czobat

Harry Gant's smiling face in Victory Lane was a common occurrence in late 1991.

the race when his engine blew.

Gant then went to Richmond and scampered past Allison with 19 laps remaining. He led the final 240 laps to score a resounding victory at Dover. And then he captured the Martinsville event despite being involved in a wreck past the half-way point.

Gant had led for 111 straight laps at Martinsville before Rusty Wallace tapped him into a spin. Morgan Shepherd hit Gant's car, mashing in the front end.

Gant's express was derailed, but he didn't give up. "It bent the front wheel out a whole lot and that really affected the car going into the corner," explained Gant.

"We had a lot of stuff rubbing the tires," he added. "We had a lot of stuff knocked loose that we had to get off the car. The main thing was my crew couldn't do anything in the time we had as far as resetting the front

Race #1

Ernie Earns Daytona 500 Trophy; Earnhardt Wipes Out

DAYTONA BEACH, FL (Feb. 19) – A rash of crashes in the final 15 laps stirred up stock car racing's biggest pot and Ernie Irvan emerged as the surprise winner of the 33rd annual Daytona 500 By STP before a packed house of 145,000 at Daytona International Speedway.

NASCAR's new pit rules, which prohibit changing of tires under yellow without penalty, had produced a confusing event until the final stages. Pole winner Davey Allison was leading in the final stages but Darrell Waltrip, the only driver in the lead lap who did not need another fuel stop, appeared likely to win the race until Robby Gordon and Richard Petty tangled in the third turn on lap 185. That two car crash set the stage for two other crashes and a finish that would end under the yellow flag.

Rusty Wallace, making his first start in a Roger Penske Pontiac, led briefly after the Gordon-Petty crash. With all the front-runners racing on worn out tires, the inevitable began to unfold.

Dale Earnhardt, who was an overwhelming favorite to bag his first Daytona 500, scampered past Wallace with 12 laps to go. Irvan slipped into second place.

Moments later, Kyle Petty skated into the side of Wallace, setting off a chain-reaction crash that also eliminated Darrell Waltrip, Harry Gant, defending champion Derrike Cope and Hut Stricklin.

When the green flag came out on lap 195, Irvan surprised the entire audience by streaking past Earnhardt. Allison, who had lined up fifth on the restart, bolted past Earnhardt to take second for an instant. But Earnhardt fought back and battled side-by-side with Allison. Meanwhile, Irvan was slipping away from all challengers.

In the 198th lap, Earnhardt's Chevrolet wagged its tail and spun into Allison in the second turn. Allison's Ford bounced off the wall and darted into the infield. As Earnhardt twirled around, Joe Ruttman and Sterling Marlin snaked their way to safety, but Kyle Petty slugged Earnhardt head on. Miraculously, Earnhardt was able to continue, but Allison and Petty were left stranded on the backstretch.

ISC

Hut Stricklin #12, Harry Gant #33 and Derrike Cope #10 were involved in a late race crash in the Daytona 500.

Winston Cup Series Race No. 1
200 Laps at Daytona Int'l Speedway
Daytona Beach, FL
"Daytona 500 By STP"
500 Miles on 2.5-mile Superspeedway
February 19, 1991

Fin	St	No.	Driver	Team / Car	Laps	Money	Status
1	2	4	Ernie Irvan	Morgan-McClure Chevrolet	200	$233,000	Running
2	12	22	Sterling Marlin	Junior Johnson Ford	200	133,925	Running
3	14	75	Joe Ruttman	RahMoc Racing Olds	200	111,450	Running
4	7	1	Rick Mast	Precision Products Olds	200	100,900	Running
5	4	3	Dale Earnhardt	RCR Enterprises Chevrolet	200	113,850	Running
6	17	21	Dale Jarrett	Wood Brothers Ford	199	74,900	Running
7	36	27	Bobby Hillin,Jr.	Dick Moroso Olds	199	50,925	Running
8	27	7	Alan Kulwicki	AK Racing Ford	199	52,450	Running
9	9	5	Ricky Rudd	Hendrick Motorsports Chevy	199	52,600	Running
10	20	68	Bobby Hamilton	Tri-Star Motorsports Olds	199	43,500	Running
11	28	66	Dick Trickle	Cale Yarborough Pontiac	199	39,525	Running
12	40	23	Eddie Bierschwale	Don Bierschwale Olds	199	31,550	Running
13	31	94	Terry Labonte	Billy Hagan Olds	198	34,355	Running
14	30	19	Chad Little	Chuck Little Ford	198	29,540	Running
15	1	28	Davey Allison	Robert Yates Ford	197	77,350	Running
16	6	42	Kyle Petty	SabCo Racing Pontiac	197	41,580	Crash
17	38	24	Mickey Gibbs	Team III Pontiac	197	24,560	Running
18	35	90	Robby Gordon	Junie Donlavey Ford	196	23,740	Running
19	3	43	Richard Petty	Petty Enterprises Pontiac	195	43,120	Running
20	29	73	Phil Barkdoll	Barkdoll Racing Olds	194	24,160	Running
21	18	6	Mark Martin	Roush Racing Ford	193	31,955	Running
22	41	26	Brett Bodine	King Motorsports Buick	193	23,400	Running
23	21	89	Jim Sauter	Mueller Brothers Pontiac	192	21,845	Running
24	10	17	Darrell Waltrip	DarWal Chevrolet	190	25,540	Crash
25	11	33	Harry Gant	Leo Jackson Olds	190	26,385	Crash
26	33	10	Derrike Cope	Bob Whitcomb Chevrolet	189	28,180	Crash
27	8	2	Rusty Wallace	Roger Penske Pontiac	188	26,425	Crash
28	15	9	Bill Elliott	Melling Performance Ford	188	28,670	Running
29	5	12	Hut Stricklin	Bobby Allison Buick	185	33,865	Crash
30	37	55	Ted Musgrave	RaDiUs Pontiac	180	18,710	Running
31	24	25	Ken Schrader	Hendrick Motorsports Chevy	176	22,330	Running
32	19	11	Geoff Bodine	Junior Johnson Ford	150	28,150	Oil Leak
33	26	8	Rick Wilson	Stavola Brothers Buick	137	21,545	Running
34	34	15	Morgan Shepherd	Bud Moore Eng. Ford	70	23,490	Piston
35	42	71	Dave Marcis	Marcis Auto Racing Chevy	40	19,185	Valve
36	22	51	Jeff Purvis	James Finch Oldsmobile	37	18,380	Heating
37	16	88	Buddy Baker	Osterlund / Malloch Pontiac	35	18,800	Engine
38	13	30	Michael Waltrip	Bahari Racing Pontiac	35	21,520	Piston
39	39	52	Jimmy Means	Means Racing Pontiac	29	17,660	Crash
40	23	98	Jimmy Spencer	Travis Carter Chevrolet	29	20,200	Fire
41	32	20	Sammy Swindell	Dick Moroso Olds	28	16,500	Crash
42	25	18	Greg Sacks	Sacks Chevrolet	20	17,450	Crash

Time of Race: 3 hours, 22 minutes, 30 seconds
Average Speed: 148.148 mph
Pole Winner: Davey Allison – 195.955 mph
Lap Leaders: Davey Allison 1, Dale Earnhardt 2-13, Allison 14-26, Earnhardt 27-32, Kyle Petty 33-36, Sterling Marlin 37-38, K.Petty 39-42, Earnhardt 43-64, Joe Ruttman 65-74, Allison 75-84, Marlin 85-89, Rick Mast 90-103, K.Petty 104-123, Ruttman 124, Ernie Irvan 125-133, Darrell Waltrip 134-146, K.Petty 147-169, Irvan 170-183, Allison 184-185, Rusty Wallace 186-188, Earnhardt 189-194, Irvan 195-200.
21 lead changes among 9 drivers
Cautions: 9 for 36 laps Margin of Victory: Under Caution

Brian Czobat

Ernie Irvan grabbed his biggest win in Daytona 500.

The ninth and final caution flag came out and the race ended under the yellow flag. The suspense wasn't quite over as Irvan was having a fuel pick-up problem on the high banks and ran the final two laps on the apron.

Marlin finished second in his first effort with the Junior Johnson Ford, which has expanded into a two car team for 1991. Joe Ruttman was third in the RahMoc Oldsmobile. Curiously, the first and third finishing cars had been formerly driven by Rick Wilson.

Fourth place went to Rick Mast in the Precision Products Olds and somehow Earnhardt finished fifth.

The final crash left everyone but Irvan in a sour mood. "I passed him (Earnhardt) clean on the outside, but then I got hit," huffed Allison, who was left with a 15th place finish. "I ain't happy. I had a shot to win the race. Racing is a business where you have to use your head. I was using mine. Somebody else wasn't."

"What burns me up," added Allison, "is that he is so dad-blame lucky. He always comes out smelling like a rose. He still finished fifth and we're here with a torn up race car."

Kyle Petty said the new rules were responsible for the wreck more than anything. "We were all running on worn out tires," said Kyle, who led the most laps – 51 – in the race. "The (rule) change was too much for us. For 475 years we've all been pitting for new tires under the cautions. Now we can't. Everybody spent all

Brian Czobat

Alan Kulwicki races with Richard Petty at Daytona. Kulwicki finished eighth while Petty wound up 19th after starting third.

winter testing and preparing for this race, but it comes down to something like this." Rules were heavily altered in light of the pit road crash which killed Michael Ritch at Atlanta last November.

"Earnhardt didn't mean to take Davey out," Kyle continued. "Nor did he mean to take me out. I'll tell you, the rules worked – nobody got hurt on pit road. But because of the rules, 40 drivers nearly got killed on the track."

Earnhardt, winless in stock car racing's biggest event in 12 attempts, said, "I just lost the air off my rear spoiler. I was just racing, trying to win the Daytona 500. We weren't leading, so we were trying to get to the front. I was lucky to get my car turned around to finish fifth."

Wallace was teed off with the younger Petty. "I'm big time (expletive) off at Petty," growled Wallace. "We worked so hard all winter and had a sure top five finish ruined by that character."

While a number of top contenders were releasing steam from under their collars, Ernie Irvan was basking in the glorious confines of Victory Lane. "I feel like I've just won the biggest race in the world," said the 32 year-old California native. "Right before I passed Dale, I was debating whether to stay behind him or try to get away from him and Davey. I got such a good run off the fourth corner, I went ahead and passed him. I looked in my mirror the whole time and thought they both would catch me. But they never did," said Irvan, who collected $233,000 for his second career Winston Cup victory.

Ruttman, whose career got a reprieve when Butch Mock asked him to drive the team's Oldsmobile, was passed by Marlin in the final green flag lap when he had to lift momentarily to avoid the Earnhardt-Allison tangle. "I was lucky to get through the wreck," said Ruttman. "A hole kind of opened up. But in that instant

Brian Czobat

Darrell Waltrip, making his first start in his own DarWal Chevrolet, leads eventual winner Ernie Irvan mid-way through the Daytona 500.

Brian Czobat

Jim Sauter #89 and Richard Petty #43 pace a gaggle of cars through the high banks of Daytona.

I had to lift, Sterling got by me."

During the afternoon, there were 21 lead changes. But most drivers said they did not know where they were running or who the leader was. Earnhardt got behind when he pitted to have the remains of a sea gull removed from his grill. While he was in the pits, he could not change tires.

Hut Stricklin, who ran third in Thursday's qualifying race, had one of the quickest cars, but he cut down two tires when he spun after a nudge from Earnhardt. Stricklin ran around the track tossing bits of debris but finally had to pit for tires. NASCAR penalized him a lap. "That took us out of the race," said Stricklin. "I became an innocent victim. I got some help when I spun. We still could have been in the lead lap, but we had to get tires."

Other drivers didn't care for the rules either. Brett Bodine flat-spotted a tire when he had to get on the binders to avoid the spinning Sammy Swindell. He came down pit road and his King Motorsports team checked the tires. Crew chief Larry McReynolds noticed the tires needed replacing but couldn't do so.

Two laps after the green, Bodine's tire blew and he slapped the wall. "That rule bit us," complained McReynolds. "These people (NASCAR) need to wake up before they hurt somebody with this rule. It's real dangerous."

Greg Fielden

California newcomer Robby Gordon drove Junie Donlavey's Ford at Daytona.

Richard Petty, who started third but dropped back in the early going, said, "these rules led to a lot of good cars getting torn up on the track. It might have made the pits safer, but it was more dangerous on the track. They're going to have to make a trade-off somewhere."

Dick Beaty, Winston Cup director, said the new system went extremely well. I don't forsee any changes in the rules. But we'll critique it and get some opinions from the race teams."

Finishing sixth was Dale Jarrett in the Wood Brothers Ford. Bobby Hillin, Jr., who landed a back-up Dick Moroso Oldsmobile in the eleventh hour, ran a supurb race and wound up seventh. Alan Kulwicki, in an Army colored Ford, was eighth. He had been unable to land a sponsor in the off-season although he thought Maxwell House was in his pocket. Ricky Rudd and rookie Bobby Hamilton rounded out the top 10.

Race #2

Earnhardt Nips Rudd at Richmond; Pit Woes Foil Kulwicki Again

RICHMOND, VA (Feb. 24) – Dale Earnhardt held off Ricky Rudd in a three lap dash to the finish and won the Pontiac Excitement 400 at Richmond International Raceway. The triumph was the 49th of Earnhardt's career.

Winston Cup Series Race No. 2
400 Laps at Richmond Int'l Raceway
Richmond, VA
"Pontiac Excitement 400"
300 Miles on .75-mile Short Track
February 24, 1991

Fin	St	No.	Driver	Team / Car	Laps	Money	Status
1	19	3	Dale Earnhardt	RCR Enterprises Chevrolet	400	$67,950	Running
2	4	5	Ricky Rudd	Hendrick Motorsports Chevy	400	45,675	Running
3	6	33	Harry Gant	Leo Jackson Olds	400	25,500	Running
4	20	2	Rusty Wallace	Roger Penske Pontiac	400	13,050	Running
5	2	7	Alan Kulwicki	AK Racing Ford	400	19,025	Running
6	14	6	Mark Martin	Roush Racing Ford	400	15,450	Running
7	17	17	Darrell Waltrip	DarWal Chevrolet	400	5,650	Running
8	21	15	Morgan Shepherd	Bud Moore Eng. Ford	399	11,550	Running
9	11	22	Sterling Marlin	Junior Johnson Ford	398	5,150	Running
10	5	25	Ken Schrader	Hendrick Motorsports Chevy	398	11,700	Running
11	23	43	Richard Petty	Petty Enterprises Pontiac	398	7,750	Running
12	1	28	Davey Allison	Robert Yates Ford	398	15,350	Running
13	7	11	Geoff Bodine	Junior Johnson Ford	397	11,500	Running
14	18	94	Terry Labonte	Billy Hagan Olds	397	7,200	Running
15	10	66	Dick Trickle	Cale Yarborough Pontiac	396	7,660	Running
16	29	19	Chad Little	Chuck Little Ford	395	5,225	Running
17	15	30	Michael Waltrip	Bahari Racing Pontiac	394	6,525	Running
18	22	8	Rick Wilson	Stavola Brothers Buick	394	6,375	Running
19	33	55	Ted Musgrave	US Racing Pontiac	393	5,500	Running
20	28	20	Bobby Hillin,Jr.	Dick Moroso Olds	392	5,525	Running
21	13	21	Dale Jarrett	Wood Brothers Ford	392	5,825	Running
22	26	12	Hut Stricklin	Bobby Allison Buick	391	5,750	Crash
23	25	24	Mickey Gibbs	Team III Pontiac	391	3,375	Running
24	3	26	Brett Bodine	King Motorsports Buick	390	6,575	Crash
25	9	42	Kyle Petty	SabCo Racing Pontiac	390	5,475	Running
26	35	90	Robby Gordon	Junie Donlavey Ford	388	3,525	Running
27	8	4	Ernie Irvan	Morgan-McClure Chevrolet	379	8,950	Running
28	32	68	Bobby Hamilton	Tri-Star Motorsports Olds	372	3,225	Running
29	27	75	Joe Ruttman	RahMoc Racing Olds	367	6,250	Running
30	24	9	Bill Elliott	Melling Performance Ford	365	9,870	Running
31	31	52	Jimmy Means	Means Racing Pontiac	356	3,750	Engine
32	12	10	Derrike Cope	Bob Whitcomb Chevrolet	309	10,225	Running
33	34	71	Dave Marcis	Marcis Auto Racing Chevy	256	4,610	Axle
34	30	98	Jimmy Spencer	Travis Carter Chevrolet	236	4,600	Steering
35	16	1	Rick Mast	Precision Products Olds	221	4,600	Running

Time of Race: 2 hours, 50 minutes, 47 seconds
Average Speed: 105.937 mph
Pole Winner: Davey Allison – 120.428 mph
Lap Leaders: Davey Allison 1-20, Alan Kulwicki 21, Allison 22-33, Kulwicki 34, Allison 35-40, Kulwicki 41-53, Ricky Rudd 54-62, Kulwicki 63-72, Harry Gant 73, Kulwicki 74, Gant 75-76, Kulwicki 77-97, Rudd 98-103, Kulwicki 104, Dale Earnhardt 105-107, Darrell Waltrip 108-109, Rudd 110-208, Earnhardt 209-210, Rusty Wallace 211-212, Rudd 213-251, Earnhardt 252-253, Rudd 254, Earnhardt 255-321, Wallace 322, D.Waltrip 323-324, Earnhardt 325-400.
25 lead changes among 7 drivers.
Cautions: 6 for 23 laps Margin of Victory: 1.5 car lengths

Brian Czobat

Jimmy Spencer spins his Chevrolet as Mickey Gibbs gets by unscathed.

Earnhardt started 19th in the field, but it took him less than 80 laps to get to the front. The driver of the RCR Enterprises Chevrolet had built up a healthy margin over Rudd in the late stages until a crash between Brett Bodine and Hut Stricklin bunched the field up in the final laps.

Earnhardt peeled off to a quick advantage but fishtailed in the final lap. That allowed Rudd to poke the nose of his Hendrick Motorsports Chevrolet under Earnhardt as the two sped through the first turn.

Rudd was able to inch ahead in the second turn, but Earnhardt fought back on the high side down the backstretch. Although Rudd had the advantageous low line

Brian Czobat

Hut Stricklin makes a pit stop in Richmond 400.

Kim Novosat

Davey Allison runs just ahead of Dale Earnhardt at Richmond.

through the final turn, Earnhardt prevailed by making a strong run to the outside. He won by a car length and a half.

"I felt like I could get a good run at him off the second turn a keep a fender ahead," explained Earnhardt. "I got the same shot off the fourth turn and beat him."

Rudd, who has had a number of fender rubbing incidents with Earnhardt, didn't go for the killer punch in the final lap. "It came down to a case of whether to knock or not to knock," smiled Rudd. "I ran real right going into the third turn and my car pushed. If not for that, I might have beat him. But I ran him clean."

Earnhardt acknowledged that Rudd eased out of solid shot at victory. "Ricky raced me strong but clean. I'll remember this and give Ricky room the next time I get under him."

Harry Gant finished in third place with Rusty Wallace fourth and Alan Kulwicki fifth.

Kulwicki, who has had victory snatched from his grasp more than once at Richmond, lost another golden opportunity to give his sponsorless team a much needed win. The Ford driver led on seven different occasions during the first 104 laps, but did not get a full tank of gas on his first green flag pit stop. "I don't know what happened in the pits," he lamented. "First, there was something wrong with the catch can on the refueling overflow, and then we had a penalty for too many people over the pit wall. That got us behind and out of sequence. The rest of the race, I had 30 more laps on my tires than the rest of the guys."

Six caution flags would have normally allowed Kulwicki to keep fresh tires on his car, but the new NASCAR rules prohibited that.

Rudd gained the upper hand when Kulwicki faltered and wound up leading the most laps – 154. But in the final analysis, it was Earnhardt that proved strongest as the race wore on. He led all but four of the final 149 laps.

Earnhardt took a 22-point lead over Rudd in the Winston Cup standings. Sterling Marlin ranks third and Kulwicki fourth.

Ernie Irvan qualified eighth but struggled to a 27th place finish.

Davey Allison started on the pole and led 38 of the first 40 laps, but he steadily dropped back after that and would only manage a 12th place finish. After the race, he had blisters on his hands. "The car steered so badly I couldn't race with anybody," said Allison, who was two laps off the pace.

Mark Martin wound up sixth but never challenged. It appeared a rift was brewing between him and car owner Jack Roush. "About half way through the race, we had a car that could have been adjusted and gone faster," said Roush. "It got to the point where we wanted to come in and make the adjustments but he (Martin) didn't want us to make them. I guess he just didn't like the car."

Race #3

Kyle Waxes Rockingham Rivals; Wins Goodwrench 500

ROCKINGAHM, NC (March 3) – Kyle Petty clearly dominated the Goodwrench 500 for the second year in a row, but needed the help of a flurry of yellow flags to score his fourth career win.

NASCAR's mandated controversial rules governing pit stops had left Ken Schrader with a lap ahead of

Petty. Caution flags brought out by separate spins by Joe Ruttman and Harry Gant gave Petty a crucial assist. Petty stormed past Schrader with 11 laps remaining and won by 1.0 second. Schrader, who was never a factor until the confusing series of events in the last 100 miles, settled for second place. Gant recovered from his late spin to grab third. Ricky Rudd was fourth and Bill Elliott came in fifth.

Petty, who led for 380 of the 492 laps, had only Rusty Wallace to worry about throughout the race. In a twinkling of the eye, Schrader went from nearly a lap down to over a lap ahead.

Schrader was running a distant third when he pitted for tires and fuel in the 430th lap. Rick Mast's blown engine brought out the yellow flag, but Schrader was permitted to finish his tire change since he had already been in the pits.

Petty and Wallace pitted for fuel during the caution flag, but were not allowed to change their badly worn tires. "We had planned on pitting for tires a couple laps after the yellow came out," said Kyle. "But with these rules, we were forced to go back on the track and restart with worn out tires."

With the benefit of fresh tires, Schrader lined up on the inside of Petty and Wallace. He quickly dashed off and unlapped himself. Petty scooted up the track and nearly whacked the wall on the restart. Two laps later, he pitted for new tires under green and was over a lap behind.

Wallace led for 10 laps, but he, too, had to pit for new tires. That left Schrader with a lap on the field.

Winston Cup Series Race No. 3
492 Laps at N.C. Motor Speedway
Rockingham, NC
"GM Goodwrench 500"

500.364 Miles on 1.017-mile Superspeedway
March 3, 1991

Fin	St	No.	Driver	Team / Car	Laps	Money	Status
1	1	42	Kyle Petty	SabCo Racing Pontiac	492	$131,450	Running
2	2	25	Ken Schrader	Hendrick Motorsports Chevy	492	34,575	Running
3	4	33	Harry Gant	Leo Jackson Olds	491	23,950	Running
4	5	5	Ricky Rudd	Hendrick Motorsports Chevy	491	20,250	Running
5	12	9	Bill Elliott	Melling Performance Ford	491	21,275	Running
6	15	4	Ernie Irvan	Morgan-McClure Chevrolet	490	15,900	Running
7	6	30	Michael Waltrip	Bahari Racing Pontiac	490	12,400	Running
8	13	3	Dale Earnhardt	RCR Enterprises Chevrolet	489	18,850	Running
9	17	17	Darrell Waltrip	DarWal Chevrolet	488	7,700	Running
10	20	15	Morgan Shepherd	Bud Moore Eng. Ford	488	17,500	Running
11	18	21	Dale Jarrett	Wood Brothers Ford	488	11,100	Running
12	7	11	Geoff Bodine	Junior Johnson Ford	488	15,600	Running
13	16	26	Brett Bodine	King Motorsports Buick	487	10,500	Running
14	23	6	Mark Martin	Roush Racing Ford	486	15,400	Running
15	25	43	Richard Petty	Petty Enterprises Pontiac	486	9,900	Running
16	3	28	Davey Allison	Robert Yates Racing Ford	486	14,700	Running
17	8	7	Alan Kulwicki	AK Racing Ford	485	12,800	Running
18	26	20	Bobby Hillin,Jr.	Dick Moroso Olds	485	7,200	Running
19	9	8	Rick Wilson	Stavola Brothers Buick	485	8,650	Running
20	28	24	Mickey Gibbs	Team III Pontiac	484	6,300	Running
21	19	68	Bobby Hamilton	Tri-Star Motorsports Olds	484	5,700	Running
22	27	19	Chad Little	Chuck Little Ford	483	5,950	Running
23	30	71	Dave Marcis	Marcis Auto Racing Chevy	482	7,700	Running
24	35	75	Joe Ruttman	RahMoc Racing Olds	481	7,550	Running
25	40	55	Ted Musgrave	RaDiUs Pontiac	481	5,700	Running
26	36	47	Rich Bickle	Derick Close Olds	480	5,150	Running
27	38	52	Jimmy Means	Means Racing Pontiac	472	5,000	Running
28	10	2	Rusty Wallace	Roger Penske Pontiac	467	15,500	Engine
29	22	66	Dick Trickle	Cale Yarborough Pontiac	448	6,875	Running
30	11	1	Rick Mast	Precision Products Olds	421	6,800	Engine
31	31	12	Hut Stricklin	Bobby Allison Buick	400	7,150	Running
32	37	13	Mike Skinner	Thee Dixon Chevrolet	338	3,900	Running
33	21	22	Sterling Marlin	Junior Johnson Ford	287	3,750	Engine
34	14	10	Derrike Cope	Bob Whitcomb Chevrolet	287	12,100	Engine
35	33	51	Jeff Purvis	James Finch Olds	165	3,600	Camshaft
36	39	04	Bill Meacham	Meacham Racing Olds	115	3,525	Ignition
37	34	49	Stanley Smith	Smith Buick	25	3,475	Heating
38	29	98	Jimmy Spencer	Travis Carter Chevrolet	19	6,060	Crash
39	24	94	Terry Labonte	Billy Hagan Olds	14	5,425	Crash
40	32	29	Andy Hillenburg	FastTrack Buick	6	3,400	Engine

Time of Race: 4 hours, 1 minute, 57 seconds
Average Speed: 124.083 mph
Pole Winner: Kyle Petty – 149.205 mph
Lap Leaders: Kyle Petty 1-89, Ken Schrader 90-91, Bill Elliot 92, Dave Marcis 93, K.Petty 94-173, Rusty Wallace 174-178, Elliott 179-185, K.Petty 186-218, Wallace 219-264, Elliott 265-266, K.Petty 267-433, Wallace 434-443, Schrader 444-481, K.Petty 482-492.
13 lead changes among 5 drivers.
Cautions: 7 for 29 laps Margin of Victory: 1 second

Brian Czobat

Car owner Felix Sabates (right) greets Rockingham winner Kyle Petty.

Brian Czobat

Ken Schrader #25 passes Jimmy Spencer's crunched car at Rockingham.

"I was never concerned about Schrader," Petty said afterwards. "The only person I was concerned with was Rusty. It was a battle between me and him. But Schrader gained a lap due to the rules. I must admit my heart sank."

When Ruttman looped his Oldsmobile and brought out another yellow, Petty was able to bunch up behind Schrader, though still a lap down.

When the green came out with 52 laps to go, Petty quickly ran away from Schrader, but his hopes for victory were next to nothing.

Dick Trickle and Gant tangled on lap 478, which sent Gant spinning. Petty, trailing Schrader by nearly 20 seconds, had received his second stroke of fortune.

Meanwhile, Wallace had departed with a blown engine, leaving Petty and Schrader the only two contestants on the lead lap.

When the green flag came out, Petty breezed past Schrader and easily won. "We were lucky to win, even as well as we ran," admitted Petty.

"We had the third best car and tried to steal one," said Schrader. "If that last yellow didn't come out, we had Kyle. But I'm not disappointed. He deserved this one."

Petty won a $68,400 bonus from Unocal, boosting his day's take to $131,450. The win also moved him to sixth place in the Winston Cup standings.

Dale Earnhardt never got untracked and wound up eighth, three laps off the pace. His point lead dwindled to four points over Rudd.

Wallace was disappointed with the engine failure, which put him out of the race. "It's the same thing that happened to us a lot last year," said Wallace. "I thought it was cured, but we're going to have to change something. We had super pit stops, but something happened under the hood again."

There were only 13 lead changes among five drivers. Car owner Junior Johnson, whose two cars finished 12th and 33rd, said he was disgusted at the new pit rules. "This seems silly," said the legend of Ingle Hollow. "What NASCAR needs to do is simply reduce the speed the cars come down pit road. Not allowing us to change flat-spotted or worn out tires is ridiculous and dangerous."

The start of the race was delayed by about a half hour after heavy rains, high winds and threats of tornados played havoc the morning of the race.

Race #4

Broome's Strategy Allows Ken Schrader to Sweep to Atlanta Win

HAMPTON, GA (March 18) – Team Manager Richard Broome developed nifty strategy at allowed Ken Schrader to end a 17-month winless streak at the Atlanta Motor Speedway.

The Motorcraft 500 was interrupted by rain Sunday after 47 laps. It was completed on Monday.

Schrader and the Hendrick Motorsports team played the winning hand immediately as the race was resumed under yellow on Monday. "These new rules make racing a lot more complex," said Broome. "We decided over breakfast that we would pit under yellow for fuel as soon as they started Monday. Then we would take on tires under green. Cautions – particularly a late one – would have messed us up."

Brian Czobat

Sterling Marlin led the Atlanta 500 until it rained.

Only two cautions interrupted the proceedings on Monday – none in the last 240 miles.

Bill Elliott ran the strongest, but he twice ran out of fuel and made one more stop than Schrader. "Fuel mileage won the race for Schrader and it killed us," said Elliott, who wound up 3.02 seconds behind when the checkered flag fell. Third place went to Dale Earnhardt, who lengthened his point lead to 24 points in the Winston Cup standings. Morgan Shepherd came home fourth and Michael Waltrip was fifth. Ricky Rudd, ranked second in the standings, finished sixth.

Elliott led the most laps but had to pit for fuel in the 284th lap. Sterling Marlin led a lap before he pitted for fuel, leaving Schrader with a 16 second lead over Elliott. During the final 40 laps, Elliott cut into Schrader's lead decisively but ran out of time.

"I didn't have anything to do with the strategy," said Schrader, who won for the third time in his career and received a contract extension from car owner Rick Hendrick. "All I do is drive the car. I quit second-guessing my crew. They know what they're doing."

Earnhardt said Sunday's rain "must have changed the track, because we were a little off. But we got some points on Rudd."

Alan Kulwicki won the pole with a speed of 174.413 mph in his unsponsored Ford. Mark Stahl, who had been carrying the colors of Hooters restaurants, did not

Winston Cup Series Race No. 4
328 Laps at Atlanta Motor Speedway
Hampton, GA
"Motorcraft Quality Parts 500"
499.216 Miles on 1.522-mile Superspeedway
March 18, 1991

Fin	St	No.	Driver	Team / Car	Laps	Money	Status
1	5	25	Ken Schrader	Hendrick Motorsports Chevy	328	$69,250	Running
2	15	9	Bill Elliott	Melling Performance Ford	328	47,675	Running
3	21	3	Dale Earnhardt	RCR Enterprises Chevrolet	328	37,000	Running
4	20	15	Morgan Shepherd	Bud Moore Eng. Ford	328	23,600	Running
5	13	30	Michael Waltrip	Bahari Racing Pontiac	328	21,400	Running
6	11	5	Ricky Rudd	Hendrick Motorsports Chevy	328	17,750	Running
7	4	22	Sterling Marlin	Junior Johnson Ford	328	17,600	Running
8	1	7	Alan Kulwicki	AK Racing Ford	327	20,150	Running
9	16	17	Darrell Waltrip	DarWal Chevrolet	327	7,450	Running
10	3	2	Rusty Wallace	Roger PEnske Pontiac	327	6700	Running
11	9	10	Derrike Cope	Bob Whitcomb Chevrolet	327	14,670	Running
12	31	8	Rick Wilson	Stavola Brothers Buick	326	12,725	Running
13	18	12	Hut Stricklin	Bobby Allison Buick	326	11,930	Running
14	10	4	Ernie Irvan	Morgan-McClure Chevrolet	326	12,710	Running
15	2	26	Brett Bodine	King Motorsports Buick	325	10,230	Running
16	17	98	Jimmy Spencer	Travis Carter Chevrolet	325	11,070	Running
17	6	6	Mark Martin	Roush Racing Ford	325	15,310	Running
18	28	19	Chad Little	Chuck Little Ford	325	8,500	Running
19	12	33	Harry Gant	Leo Jackson Olds	325	8,690	Running
20	22	21	Dale Jarrett	Wood Brothers Ford	325	10,470	Running
21	14	20	Bobby Hillin,Jr.	Dick Moroso Olds	324	5,960	Running
22	24	89	Jim Sauter	Mueller Brothers Pontiac	323	5,800	Running
23	26	11	Geoff Bodine	Junior Johnson Ford	323	13,490	Running
24	29	51	Jeff Purvis	James Finch Olds	321	5,380	Running
25	35	24	Mickey Gibbs	Team III Pontiac	320	5,075	Running
26	33	90	Wally Dallenbach,Jr.	Junie Donlavey Ford	319	4,420	Running
27	38	75	Joe Ruttman	RahMoc Racing Olds	319	7,310	Running
28	27	66	Dick Trickle	Cale Yarborough Pontiac	319	7,175	Running
29	23	1	Rick Mast	Precision Products Olds	319	6,975	Running
30	36	65	Dave Mader III	Clint Folsom Pontiac	318	4,740	Running
31	25	52	Jimmy Means	Means Racing Pontiac	316	4,680	Running
32	37	29	Andy Hillenburg	FasTrack Buick	314	4,120	Running
33	19	68	Bobby Hamilton	Tri-Star Motorsports Olds	290	3,780	Running
34	40	47	Rich Bickle	Derick Close Olds	282	4,445	Engine
35	32	94	Terry Labonte	Billy Hagan Olds	256	6,385	Camshaft
36	39	71	Dave Marcis	Marcis Auto Racing Chevy	240	6,220	Engine
37	34	55	Ted Musgrave	RaDiUs Pontiac	210	4,280	Engine
38	30	43	Richard Petty	Petty Enterprises Pontiac	188	6,240	Engine
39	7	42	Kyle Petty	SabCo Racing Pontiac	173	12,115	Engine
40	8	28	Davey Allison	Robert Yates Racing Ford	56	13,175	Crash

Time of Race: 3 hours, 33 minutes, 14 seconds
Average Speed: 140.470 mph
Pole Winner: Alan Kulwicki – 174.413 mp
Fastest Qualifier: Dale Earnhardt – 175.351 mph
Lap Leaders: Alan Kulwicki 1-8, Sterling Marlin 9-48, Mark Martin 49-69, Kyle Petty 70-106, Bill Elliott 107-120, Geoff Bodine 121, Elliott 122-187, Ken Schrader 188-192, Dale Earnhardt 193-213, Michael Waltrip 214-236, Elliott 237-252, Schrader 253-263, Elliott 264-271, M.Waltrip 272-278, Elliott 279-284, Marlin 285, Schrader 286-328.
16 lead changes among 9 drivers.
Cautions: 4 for 33 laps   Margin of Victory: 3.02 seconds

Brian Czobat

Ken Schrader's third career win came at Atlanta.

make the field. Robert Brooks, CEO of Hooters, struck a deal with Kulwicki. "It's just a one race deal, but maybe it will turn into something that will benefit both of us on down the road," said Kulwicki.

Kulwicki led the first eight laps, then yielded to Marlin. Kulwicki never led again and wound up eighth, a lap down.

Mark Martin, who challenged for the Winston Cup title the past two years, lumbered to a 17th place finish. Team owner Jack Roush became riled up during a botched pit stop. Roush yanked and shoved crewman Ryan Pemberton and grabbed crew chief Robin Pemberton around the neck. Martin ranks 11th in the point standings with only one top 10 finish to the team's credit thus far in the season.

Davey Allison started eighth, but spun off the fourth turn while racing Dale Earnhardt and passing a lapped car. "I got the air taken off my spoiler," said Allison, who has yet to run in the top 10 in1991. "I rode it for as long as I could, but it finally got away from me."

Following the Atlanta race, Jake Elder was released and Larry McReynolds hired from the King Motorsports team. Team owner Robert Yates said a rift had developed between Allison and Yates. "Jake wouldn't talk to Davey at all and Davey blew up, spun the tires in the garage area and almost hit Richard Petty's car," said Yates. "I didn't really blame Davey. Now we've made a change. Jake was always threatening to quit and I don't want to live under those threats. Jake is a good man and can set up a car, but there's more to racing than that."

Wally Dallenbach, Jr. made his first Winston Cup start and finished 26th in Junie Donlavey's Ford. Dallenbach, Jr. has put his plans of an IndyCar career on hold. "Everything is always a big secret in the pit and garage areas at CART races," he said. "Everybody always runs off to their motor homes and won't talk to anybody. NASCAR racing is a whole lot more fun."

Dick Trickle, who had given the Cale Yarborough Pontiac a number of strong runs in the past year, wound up 28th, nine laps off the pace. Trickle was let go by Yarborough and Lake Speed was hired for presumably the rest of the year.

Race #5

Pit Miscue Robs Michael Waltrip; Rudd Wins at Darlington

DARLINGTON, SC (April 7) – Michael Waltrip's strong bid for his first Winston Cup triumph ended with a despairingly long pit stop, and Ricky Rudd seized the opportunity and came out on top of the TranSouth 500 at Darlington Raceway.

Rudd's first win on an oval since 1986 came at the expense of Waltrip's ill-fated pit stop in the 299th lap. An air wrench malfunctioned and the young Owensboro, Kent. Pontiac driver waited on pit road for 37.4-

Bryan Hallman

Dale Jarrett #21 and Harry Gant tangle in early laps at Darlington.

Brian Czobat

Ricky Rudd and wife Linda share Darlington rewards.

seconds. When he returned to the track, he was hopelessly behind. Another pit stop on lap 321 knocked him a lap off the pace.

"We had problems in the pits at Atlanta and we had them again today," said Waltrip, who led for a total of 208 laps. "We've just got to work on it.The guys tried hard and that's all you can ask. We had great pit stops all day until the end, and we really needed it then and didn't get it.

"These guys have stuck with me ever since I started," Michael continued. "I know I've caused them a lot of heartbreak over the years."

Waltrip's malady in the pits left Davey Allison with a half lap lead. But the Alabama Ford driver was destined to pit whereas Rudd's Hendrick Motorsports team had carefully calculated the race with fuel mileage and pit stops.

Rudd went into the lead when Allison pitted with 37 laps remaining. Allison wound up 11.32 seconds behind at the end.

Waltrip managed to get back in the lead lap and was hoping for a late yellow which would have given him a second chance. The much needed caution never came.

Mark Martin scored his first top five finish by coming home fourth. Fifth place went to Rusty Wallace.

There were 15 lead changes, but only three occurred on the track – one of them in the opening lap when Sterling Marlin passed pole sitter Geoff Bodine. Waltrip, who started 10th, clawed his way to the front by

Winston Cup Series Race No. 5
367 Laps at Darlington Raceway
Darlington, SC
"TranSouth 500"
501.322 Miles on 1.366-mile Superspeedway
April 7, 1991

Fin	St	No.	Driver	Team / Car	Laps	Money	Status
1	13	5	Ricky Rudd	Hendrick Motorsports Chevy	367	$62,185	Running
2	11	28	Davey Allison	Robert Yates Racing Ford	367	38,860	running
3	10	30	Michael Waltrip	Bahari Racing Pontiac	367	20,320	Running
4	12	6	Mark Martin	Roush Racing Ford	366	22,710	Running
5	21	2	Rusty Wallace	Roger Penske Pontiac	365	10,260	Running
6	15	42	Kyle Petty	SabCo Racing Pontiac	365	16,330	Running
7	3	4	Ernie Irvan	Morgan-McClure Chevrolet	365	15,025	Running
8	23	15	Morgan Shepherd	Bud Moore Eng. Ford	365	14,320	Running
9	1	11	Geoff Bodine	Junior Johnson Ford	365	18,400	Running
10	3	22	Sterling Marlin	Junior Johnson Ford	365	12,060	Running
11	25	98	Jimmy Spencer	Travis Carter Chevrolet	365	10,505	Running
12	17	9	Bill Elliott	Melling Performance Ford	365	13,675	Running
13	16	1	Rick Mast	Precision Products Olds	364	9,695	Running
14	18	8	Rick Wilson	Stavola Brothers Buick	364	9,390	Running
15	27	94	Terry Labonte	Billy Hagan Olds	364	9,735	Running
16	8	26	Brett Bodine	King Motorsports Buick	363	8,815	Running
17	28	20	Bobby Hillin,Jr.	Dick Moroso Olds	361	6,560	Running
18	33	71	Dave Marcis	Marcis Auto Racing Chevy	361	8,225	Running
19	4	25	Ken Schrader	Hendrick Motorsports Chevy	361	7,790	Running
20	34	68	Bobby Hamilton	Tri-Star Motorsports Olds	360	6,560	Running
21	29	55	Ted Musgrave	RaDiUs Pontiac	359	5,540	Running
22	24	24	Mickey Gibbs	Team III Pontiac	359	4,070	Running
23	36	52	Jimmy Means	Means Racing Pontiac	358	4,950	Running
24	35	47	Rich Bickle	Derick Close Olds	356	3,830	Running
25	9	17	Darrell Waltrip	DarWal Chevrolet	356	3,810	Running
26	32	75	Joe Ruttman	RahMoc Racing Olds	355	6,545	Running
27	5	33	Harry Gant	Leo Jackson Olds	347	6,380	Running
28	37	87	Randy Baker	Buck Baker Chevrolet	346	3,470	Running
29	7	3	Dale Earnhardt	RCR Enterprises Chevrolet	332	14,310	Engine
30	40	70	J.D.McDuffie	McDuffie Racing Pontiac	282	3,325	Running
31	20	10	Derrike Cope	Bob Whitcomb Chevrolet	279	11,665	Oil Leak
32	19	12	Hut Stricklin	Bobby Allison Buick	259	5,980	Vibration
33	26	65	Dave Mader III	Clint Folsom Pontiac	197	3,170	Fatigue
34	6	7	Alan Kulwicki	AK Racing Ford	186	11,135	Crash
35	39	36	H.B.Bailey	Bailey Pontiac	172	3,100	Handling
36	31	19	Chad Little	Chuck Little Ford	70	3,065	Crash
37	30	43	Richard Petty	Petty Enterprises Pontiac	52	5,750	Engine
38	38	05	Bill Meacham	Meacham Racing Olds	31	3,010	Flagged
39	14	21	Dale Jarrett	Wood Brothers Ford	30	5,670	Crash
40	22	66	Lake Speed	Cale Yarborough Pontiac	10	5,650	Engine

Time of Race: 3 hours, 41 minutes, 50 seconds
Average Speed: 135.594 mph
Pole Winner: Geoff Bodine – 161.939 mph
Lap Leaders: Sterling Marlin 1-45, Michael Waltrip 46-72, Ricky Rudd 73-74, Ken Schrader 75-79, Morgan Shepherd 80, M.Waltrip 81-135, Hut Stricklin 136-143, Rudd 144-148, M.Waltrip 149-203, Rudd 204-217, M.Waltrip 218-274, Rudd 275-285, M.Waltrip 286-299, Davey Allison 300-330, Rudd 331-367.
15 lead changes among 7 drivers
Cautions: 3 for 19 laps   Margin of Victory: 11.32 seconds

Greg Fielden

Michael Waltrip puts a lap on Dale Earnhardt at Darlington. Only a botched pit stop prevented Waltrip from scoring his first Winston Cup win.

the 46th lap and set sail. He lost the lead only during pit stops.

Rudd and crew chief Waddell Wilson admitted they went into the event not to race but to outsmart the other contestants. "We didn't want to set the pace," said Wilson. "We tried to stretch our pit stops to 74 laps. That would eliminate one pit stop during the race."

"I was pacing myself all day," said Rudd. "I was racing the stopwatch, not anybody on the race track."

Rudd took the Winston Cup point lead by 80 points over Earnhardt, who never contended and eventually blew an engine late in the race. Earnhardt got credit for 29th place.

Only three caution flags slowed the action. The most serious wreck took place early when rookie Bill Meacham crowded Harry Gant into a third turn spin. Gant's Oldsmobile slid down the banking and struck the right rear quarter panel of Dale Jarrett. The contact shoved Jarrett up the track where he nailed the wall head on. The car, one which the Wood Brothers debuted, was demolished.

Meacham was flagged to the pits by NASCAR after the incident.

Junior Johnson team cars started on the front row, but both Geoff Bodine and Sterling Marlin were two laps down at the end.

A crowd of 40,000 watched in warm spring weather but had little to cheer about. Racing writer Benny Phillips said the race was so boring that "it looked like a Formula One race. "There were calculators and computers to figure gas mileage, and any number of theories about tire wear," said Phillips. "But there was little or no racing for position on the track."

Waltrip's Pennzoil sponsored Pontiac forfeited $17,050 in prize money because team owner Chuck Rider did not place all the contingency decals on the car. "Pennzoil wanted a 'clean' car without all the front fender decals.

Sanctioning NASCAR said they would make a change in the pit rules for the next stop at Bristol.

Race #6

Wallace and 'Racing' Return at Bristol; Confusion Still Reigns

BRISTOL, TN (April 14) – Rusty Wallace twice battled back from two laps down, then held off Ernie Irvan in a stirring finish to the Valleydale 500 at Bristol International Raceway. Door-to-door racing also returned to NASCAR's premier touring series, but confusion still held top honors.

Wallace started on the pole and led the first 94 laps until a flat tire sent him to the pits. During the time Wallace was never headed, an "official" 14 lead changes took place. New NASCAR rules allowed teams to change tires under the yellow, but a unique twist was dealt into the regulations.

Under the latest rules, cars are designated 'odd' or 'even' based on their qualifying position. Restarts were double file, with all 'odd' cars lining up on the inside and all 'even' cars lining up to the outside. As it turned out, more 'even' cars were vying for the win than 'odd' cars, which created a giant controversy.

Wallace was running seventh when a caution flag came out. He was allowed to pass five other cars in the lead lap by moving to the inside lane – following the guidelines of the rules. When the leader pitted, Wallace moved to the front and ran away from the field. He never had to pass a single car.

"The rules definitely worked in my favor today," Wallace said with a hint of hesitation. "I'm sure if I was one of the guys that had to sit there and watch me move to the front, my attitude may be a little different. But what do you want me to do? The rules are NASCAR's business and I'm sure they will review them and keep adjusting them like they have been."

Despite questionable regulations, the packed house welcomed the good old fashion tight racing back into the sport. The first five events of the season had resembled IndyCar racing on a street course or Formula One racing.

Bryan Hallman

Ken Schrader gets loose in heavy traffic at Bristol.

Bryan Hallman

Geoff Bodine #11 tags a spinning Richard Petty at Bristol.

Winston Cup Series Race No. 6
500 Laps at Bristol Int'l Raceway
Bristol, TN
"Valleydale Meats 500"
266.5 Miles on .533-mile Short Track
April 14, 1991

Fin	St	No.	Driver	Team / Car	Laps	Money	Status
1	1	2	Rusty Wallace	Roger Penske Pontiac	500	$51,300	Running
2	8	4	Ernie Irvan	Morgan-McClure Chevrolet	500	26,000	Running
3	3	28	Davey Allison	Robert Yates Racing Ford	500	18,950	Running
4	6	6	Mark Martin	Roush Racing Ford	500	18,950	Running
5	4	5	Ricky Rudd	Hendrick Motorsports Chevy	500	37,950	Running
6	22	17	Darrell Waltrip	DarWal Chevrolet	500	7,525	Running
7	18	21	Dale Jarrett	Wood Brothers Ford	500	10,775	Running
8	20	98	Jimmy Spencer	Travis Carter Chevrolet	500	10,175	Running
9	30	94	Terry Labonte	Billy Hagan Olds	500	9,575	Running
10	26	15	Morgan Shepherd	Bud Moore Eng. Ford	498	14,275	Running
11	10	33	Harry Gant	Leo Jackson Olds	498	9,375	Running
12	27	55	Ted Musgrave	RaDiUs Pontiac	498	8,275	Running
13	23	75	Joe Ruttman	RahMoc Racing Olds	498	8,150	Running
14	31	19	Chad Little	Chuck Little Ford	497	6,400	Running
15	19	20	Bobby Hillin,Jr.	Dick Moroso Olds	497	6,800	Running
16	13	12	Hut Stricklin	Bobby Allison Buick	496	7,475	Running
17	33	43	Richard Petty	Petty Enterprises Pontiac	496	7,225	Running
18	9	1	Rick Mast	Precision Products Olds	492	7,025	Running
19	17	24	Mickey Gibbs	Team III Pontiac	492	4,665	Running
20	2	3	Dale Earnhardt	RCR Enterprises Chevrolet	484	15,525	Running
21	12	42	Kyle Petty	SabCo Racing Pontiac	480	10,125	Running
22	7	26	Brett Bodine	King Motorsports Buick	471	6,675	Running
23	25	30	Michael Waltrip	Bahari Racing Pontiac	463	6,550	Running
24	11	11	Geoff Bodine	Junior Johnson Ford	461	11,750	Running
25	24	66	Lake Speed	Cale Yarborough Pontiac	455	6,480	Running
26	5	7	Alan Kulwicki	AK Racing Ford	434	9,875	Running
27	15	22	Sterling Marlin	Junior Johnson Ford	421	5,150	Crash
28	29	9	Bill Elliott	Melling Performance Ford	406	9,800	Running
29	14	25	Ken Schrader	Hendrick Motorsports Chevy	314	6,220	Crash
30	21	34	Dick Trickle	Ken Allen Buick	314	4,025	Ignition
31	28	68	Bobby Hamilton	Tri-Star Motorsports Olds	124	4,275	Engine
32	32	10	Derrike Cope	Bob Whitcomb Chevrolet	80	11,125	Crash
33	16	8	Rick Wilson	Stavola Brothers Buick	78	5,850	Heating

Time of Race: 3 hours, 39 minutes, 37 seconds
Average Speed: 72.809 mph
Pole Winner: Rusty Wallace – 118.051 mph
Lap Leaders: Rusty Wallace 1-19, Ricky Rudd 20-24, Wallace 25-33, Rudd 34-35, Wallace 36-43, Rudd 44-45, Wallace 46-50, Rudd 51-52, Wallace 53, Rudd 54-63, Wallace 64-76, Rudd 77-79, Wallace 80-88, Rudd 89-90, Wallace 91-94, Rudd 95-117, Ernie Irvan 118-160, Harry Gant 161, Ken Schrader 162-168, Rudd 169-257, Chad Little 258-261, Mark Martin 262, Gant 263, Little 264-265, Gant 266-295, Davey Allison 296-303, Rudd 304-305, Allison 306-339, Irvan 340, Allison 341-354, Rudd 355, Allison 356-366, Rudd 367-370, Allison 371-373, Martin 374-414, Irvan 415-438, Allison 439-459, Irvan 460-462, Wallace 463-475, Irvan 476-477, Wallace 478-500.
40 lead changes among 8 drivers.
Cautions: 19 for 133 laps Margin of Victory: 1 foot

Brian Czobat

Davey Allison tapped Darrell Waltrip into a spin in Bristol's Valleydale 500.

Wallace took the lead for the final time with 23 laps to go. He sprinted to a comfortable lead after the day's 19th and final caution flag, but had to sweat out Irvan's gallant charge in the closing laps.

"We hung it out, ran door-to-door, knocked each other on the last lap," said Wallace, who notched his first win with the Roger Penske team. "We had a whale of a race. On the last lap, I went to the bottom of the race track and there he was. I came off the fourth turn sideways and spinning tires. I just barely beat him.

"If I would have touched him, the fans would have shot me and I would have gone home in a funeral wagon or something," added Wallace. "I think he drove me as clean today as I would have driven him."

Davey Allison wound up in third place with Mark Martin fourth and Ricky Rudd fifth.

Sterling Marlin suffered second and third degree burns when his Junior Johnson Ford slammed the first turn wall and exploded into flames on lap 422. Marlin's car had been damaged in an earlier altercation, which had exposed the fuel filler neck. Marlin's car rolled down the banking and the driver was able to unbuckle his safety belts and crawl out.

Davey Allison and Darrell Waltrip locked horns and exchanged angry words after the race. Waltrip had scrubbed past Allison in turn three in the 367th lap. The next time around, Allison popped the rear bumper of Waltrip's Chevrolet, which sent him spinning the length of the front chute. Allison was penalized by NASCAR and was forced to restart the race at the rear of the field. Both recovered. Waltrip finished sixth.

"I got hit nine times out there today," snarled Waltrip, "and one of them was intentional. You don't run into somebody and knock the fire out of them on purpose.

"He must have a problem with me and I don't know what it is. He gave me the finger last week down in Darlington. We're going to have to have a little father-son talk."

Allison's version was – not surprisingly – different. "He came over to me mouthing off about spinning him out in the fourth turn," said Allison. "I didn't spin him

Bristol Int'l

Derrike Cope's Chevrolet skids in front of traffic at Bristol.

out intentionally, but I guess it's all right if he runs all over the side of my car. I've got Western Auto (Waltrip's sponsor) colors all over the side of my car. I guess when you're Darrell Waltrip and do that to people, it's okay."

Dale Earnhardt spun backwards into the wall early in the race and fell many laps behind. He wound up 20th and fell to third in the Winston Cup standings, 142 points behind Rudd. Irvan moved into second, 119 out of first place.

Race #7

Darrell Dodges Crashes in Wilkesboro Brawl

N.WILKESBORO, NC (Apr. 21) – Darrell Waltrip walked away with top honors in the First Union 400 at North Wilkesboro Speedway by exercising patience as a multitude of wrecks depleted the field. It was Waltrip's first win since September of 1989 when he won at Martinsville.

Waltrip started 13th and bided his time until the closing stages. "I've never seen anything like today at a NASCAR race," said the weary winner. There's not a lot of discipline on the race track. NASCAR worked to get discipline in the pits, and now they've got to work to get some out on the track.

"I saws a lot of things that were uncalled for. I can't explain it other than it's just a lack of respect."

For the record, Waltrip beat runner-up Dale Earnhardt, who came back from a mid-race spin, by 0.81-seconds. Third place went to Jimmy Spencer who showed plenty of muscle in Travis Carter's Chevrolet. Morgan Shepherd made up a lap and finished fourth, while fifth place went to Ken Schrader.

A total of 17 caution flags interrupted the proceedings – nearly all caused by crashes. Many of the incidents left drivers hot under the collar.

Pole sitter Brett Bodine, defending champion of the race, led the first 37 laps in his King Racing Buick. After being passed by Harry Gant, Bodine kept his car on the lead lap and remained in contention.

Bodine passed Rusty Wallace in the 153rd lap and led for 66 straight laps until a tap from Ricky Rudd sent him backing into the fourth turn wall.

Winston Cup Series Race No. 7
400 Laps at North Wilkesboro Speedway
N.Wilkesboro, NC
"First Union 400"

250 Miles on .625-mile Short Track
April 21, 1991

Fin	St	No.	Driver	Team / Car	Laps	Money	Status
1	13	17	Darrell Waltrip	DarWal Chevrolet	400	$53,800	Running
2	17	3	Dale Earnhardt	RCR Enterprises Chevrolet	400	35,225	Running
3	14	98	Jimmy Spencer	Travis Carter Chevrolet	400	20,350	Running
4	29	15	Morgan Shepherd	Bud Moore Eng. Ford	400	16,450	Running
5	9	25	Ken Schrader	Hendrick Motorsports Chevy	400	14,725	Running
6	26	28	Davey Allison	Robert Yates Ford	400	13,875	Running
7	21	30	Michael Waltrip	Bahari Racing Pontiac	400	9,280	Running
8	32	9	Bill Elliott	Melling Performance Ford	400	11,800	Running
9	20	6	Mark Martin	Roush Racing Ford	400	12,450	Running
10	22	4	Ernie Irvan	Morgan-McClure Chevrolet	400	13,830	Running
11	11	5	Ricky Rudd	Hendrick Motorsports Chevy	399	10,175	Running
12	7	1	Rick Mast	Precision Products Olds	399	7,575	Running
13	12	66	Lake Speed	Cale Yarborough Pontiac	399	7,300	Running
14	15	12	Hut Stricklin	Bobby Allison Buick	398	6,950	Running
15	18	10	Derrike Cope	Bob Whitcomb Chevrolet	397	11,500	Running
16	33	43	Richard Petty	Petty Enterprises Pontiac	397	6,550	Running
17	28	55	Ted Musgrave	RaDiUs Pontiac	397	5,625	Running
18	3	42	Kyle Petty	SabCo Racing Pontiac	396	9,250	Running
19	23	71	Dave Marcis	Marcis Auto Racing Chevy	395	6,200	Running
20	25	20	Bobby Hillin,Jr.	Dick Moroso Olds	394	5,450	Running
21	27	68	Bobby Hamilton	Tri-Star Motorsports Pontiac	392	3,600	Running
22	31	22	Sterling Marlin*	Junior Johnson Ford	388	3,300	Running
23	4	33	Harry Gant	Leo Jackson Olds	388	7,125	Running
24	10	75	Joe Ruttman	RahMoc Racing Olds	378	5,525	Running
25	6	21	Dale Jarrett	Wood Brothers Ford	369	5,500	Crash
26	16	34	Dick Trickle	Ken Allen Buick	369	3,100	Crash
27	24	8	Rick Wilson	Stavola Brothers Buick	339	5,200	Crash
28	8	11	Geoff Bodine	Junior Johnson Ford	333	10,485	Flagged
29	2	7	Alan Kulwicki	AK Racing Ford	323	8,675	Crash
30	1	26	Brett Bodine	King Motorsports Buick	218	15,300	Crash
31	30	94	Terry Labonte	Billy Hagan Olds	207	5,000	Engine
32	5	2	Rusty Wallace	Roger Penske Pontiac	192	2,925	Crash
33	19	24	Mickey Gibbs	Team III Pontiac	110	2,500	Header

Time of Race: 3 hours, 8 minutes, 26 seconds
Average Speed: 79.604 mph
Pole Winner: Brett Bodine – 116.237 mph
Lap Leaders: Brett Bodine 1-37, Harry Gant 38-103, Dale Earnhardt 104-122, Rusty Wallace 123-152, B.Bodine 153-218, Ken Schrader 219-255, Ernie Irvan 256-278, Jimmy Spencer 279-348, Darrell Waltrip 349-400.
8 lead changes among 8 drivers.
Cautions: 17 for 87 laps   Margin of Victory: 0.81 second
*Relieved by Charlie Glotzbach

Bryan Hallman

Davey Allison spins in front of Dick Trickle #34 and Michael Waltrip at North Wilkesboro.

Brian Czobat

Richard Petty #43 leads Hut Stricklin #12 and Bobby Hillin, Jr. #20 through turn at North Wilkesboro Speedway.

"I can't believe we got spun out like we did," said Bodine. "We went into the third turn and the next thing I know is I'm turned around. And he's not even on the lead lap.

"I used to have respect for him, but I don't anymore," said Bodine.

Bodine dismounted his crumpled machine and shook his fist at Rudd when he drove by the next time.

Rudd, who eventually finished 11th, said, "It's not that big of a deal, really. I'm on the inside and he's on the outside and the only way for him to get spun is that he had to come across my nose. He just hadn't cleared me."

Brett's brother Geoff got into an on-track wrestling match with Davey Allison. In the 333rd lap, Allison and Bodine made contact and both spun around. "He simply ran into the back of me and spun me out," said Bodine.

Allison said, "I was racing Bodine and jumped underneath him going into three. But I saw him coming down so I jumped on the brakes to slow up and give him some room. When I did that, my car started sliding up into his."

After the two cars came to rest on the fourth turn apron, Bodine made contact with Allison again. "We were just trying to get out of each other's way," explained Bodine, tongue in cheek. NASCAR officials parked the Bodine car after the second incident.

Waltrip was following close behind Bodine and Allison. "I knew something like that was going to happen. It was a situation where one of 'em had to give and neither one did. I just had to be prepared to move accordingly."

Dale Jarrett trashed another Wood Brothers Ford in a tangle with Dick Trickle and Ernie Irvan. Afterwards, Jarrett was outraged. "It's not racing anymore; it's just survival. People don't pass you anymore, they just knock you out of the way. Everybody gets frustrated and everybody's going crazy. No patience whatsoever. There are just a bunch of damn idiots out there," said Jarrett.

NASCAR's Dick Beaty had drivers and crew chiefs lined up outside his mobile office afterwards, and in a closed door session, he delivered a number of ultimatums. "This was just the opening round," said Beaty. "Thursday at Martinsville (the next race) will be reserved for tail-chewing. We're going to have more school sessions with these guys than you've ever seen."

Waltrip's victory was his first as an owner-driver since May of 1975 when he won at Nashville, Tenn. "We've been coming close to a win this year, but it takes that little extra to get over the top. I'll tell you what, I was tip-toeing when I passed Spencer on the outside," said Waltrip, describing the decisive pass on lap 349.

Spencer had his best outing in his career, leading for 70 laps. Twice he had to overcome misfortune. He lost a lap when he spun to the infield to miss a skirmish between Kyle Petty and Davey Allison. "I couldn't get the car fired up and I lost a lap," said Spencer. "But we made that lap up pretty easily."

He also was slapped with a speeding violation on pit road. "We still had the car to beat, but our last set of tires were the worst we had all day. We had to borrow them because we ran out. They just didn't match up. I had Darrell beat until that last caution came out."

Brian Czobat

Darrell Waltrip waves from Victory Lane.

Waltrip chased Spencer until making the final pass. "I liked racing with him," said Spencer, who has acquired the nickname 'Mr. Excitement'. "I respected him. I could have put some tire marks up and down the side of his car, but I wouldn't do that."

Spencer lost second to Earnhardt in the final laps. "We got beat by two of the best. We can't complain," said Spencer.

Rudd's 11th place finish enabled him to keep the point lead. He leads Earnhardt by 97 points.

Race #8

Dale's Comeback Nets Martinsville Victory

MARTINSVILLE, VA (April 28) – Dale Earnhardt scrambled past Kyle Petty with 37 laps to go and sped to victory in the Hanes 500 at Martinsville Speedway. The Kannapolis, N.C. driver became the first to win more than one race in the 1991 Winston Cup season.

Earnhardt led most of the way – 351 laps in all – but was fading badly near the end of the race. His RCR Enterprises Chevrolet was logged in fifth place behind Davey Allison, Kyle Petty, Rusty Wallace and Ricky Rudd. He was even in danger of losing a lap.

But you can never count Earnhardt out of any NASCAR race. With less than 30 miles to go, the right front tire let go on Allison's Ford. He kept the car off the wall but collided with Alan Kulwicki while trying to get to his pit on the backstretch. That brought out the final caution flag and presented Earnhardt with a chance to regroup.

Allison fell a lap off the pace and was no longer in contention. One by one, the other drivers who had Earnhardt covered fell by the wayside. The transmission in Wallace's Pontiac broke when he tried to exit his pit under yellow. Rudd encountered trouble with a tire rubbing sheet metal and would be destined to finish 11th, four laps off the pace. And Petty was never able to match his earlier speed in the final run to the checker.

Winston Cup Series Race No. 8
500 Laps at Martinsville Speedway
Martinsville, VA
"Hanes 500"
263 Miles on .526-mile Short Track
April 28, 1991

Fin	St	No.	Driver	Team / Car	Laps	Money	Status
1	10	3	Dale Earnhardt	RCR Enterprises Chevy	500	$63,600	Running
2	17	42	Kyle Petty	SabCo Racing Pontiac	500	29,625	Running
3	16	17	Darrell Waltrip	DarWal Chevrolet	500	16,150	Running
4	15	26	Brett Bodine	King Motorsports Buick	500	15,550	Running
5	2	33	Harry Gant	Leo Jackson Olds	499	17,625	Running
6	29	98	Jimmy Spencer	Travis Carter Chevrolet	499	12,350	Running
7	29	30	Michael Waltrip	Bahari Racing Pontiac	499	11,100	Running
8	26	28	Davey Allison	Robert Yates Racing Ford	499	16,350	Running
9	8	7	Alan Kulwicki	AK Racing Ford	497	12,500	Running
10	21	12	Hut Stricklin	Bobby Allison Buick	496	13,000	Running
11	22	5	Ricky Rudd	Hendrick Motorsports Chevy	496	10,985	Running
12	7	21	Dale Jarrett	Wood Brothers Ford	495	7,900	Running
13	4	1	Rick Mast	Precision Products Olds	495	8,200	Running
14	12	43	Richard Petty	Petty Enterprises Pontiac	495	7,500	Running
15	9	4	Ernie Irvan	Morgan-McClure Chevrolet	491	10,950	Running
16	19	75	Joe Ruttman	RahMoc Racing Olds	487	7,200	Running
17	11	20	Bobby Hillin,Jr.	Dick Moroso Olds	487	5,400	Running
18	27	66	Lake Speed	Cale Yarborough Pontiac	487	7,355	Running
19	20	76	Bill Sedgwick	Glenn Spears Chevrolet	466	3,700	Running
20	18	11	Geoff Bodine	Junior Johnson Ford	460	12,000	Trans
21	5	2	Rusty Wallace	Roger Penske Pontiac	458	3,750	Trans
22	32	8	Rick Wilson	Stavola Brothers Buick	453	5,650	Running
23	3	25	Ken Schrader	Hendrick Motorsports Chevy	444	6,525	Running
24	30	55	Ted Musgrave	RaDiUs Pontiac	442	5,175	Running
25	25	24	Mickey Gibbs	Team III Pontiac	414	3,250	Running
26	14	9	Bill Elliott	Melling Performance Ford	411	9,750	Running
27	6	19	Chad Little	Chuck Little Ford	408	3,650	Running
28	23	22	Sterling Marlin*	Junior Johnson Ford	402	2,900	Running
29	1	6	Mark Martin	Roush Racing Ford	293	13,500	Heating
30	31	15	Morgan Shepherd	Wood Brothers Ford	276	9,450	Trans
31	13	94	Terry Labonte	Billy Hagan Olds	126	4,850	Heating
32	24	34	Dick Trickle	Ken Allen Buick	12	2,750	Heating

Time of Race: 3 hours, 26 minutes, 41 seconds
Average Speed: 75.139 mph
Pole Winner: Mark Martin – 91.949 mph
Lap Leaders: Harry Gant 1-82, Kyle Petty 83-84, Gant 85-93, Dale Earnhardt 94-95, Gant 96-133, Earnhardt 134-166, Davey Allison 167-170, Earnhardt 171-323, Allison 324-337, Earnhardt 338-363, Allison 364-455, K.Petty 456-463, Earnhardt 464-500.
13 lead changes among 4 drivers.
Cautions: 11 for 53 laps — Margin of Victory: 3.34 seconds
*Relieved by Charlie Glotzbach

Brian Czobat

Rick Wilson #8 ducks under a spinning Bobby Hillin, Jr. at Martinsville.

Petty held the lead for eight laps after Allison's demise. Earnhardt raced past on lap 464 and led the rest of the way.

Petty finished second, 3.34 seconds behind Earnhardt. Darrell Waltrip was third, Brett Bodine fourth and Harry Gant fifth.

"I can't believe I gave him a race victory for a birthday present," said Allison. "That Earnhardt! I told you at Daytona he's the luckiest human being out there. Just look at the luck he had."

"I needed that last caution," confessed Earnhardt, whose 50th career victory came a day before his 40th birthday. "We got our car adjusted during the pit stop. And then we only had to run with Kyle."

The race, although broken by 11 caution flags, was calm compared to the unprecedented standards set at North Wilkesboro a week earlier. "I didn't see a lot of cars getting together with each other intentionally," said Earnhardt. "NASCAR has everything under control now. They were very concerned about pit road and got a little lax with what was happening on the race track. Now, they have everything under control again."

Ernie Irvan was the only driver sent to NASCAR's penalty box for rough driving. Irvan spent two laps being reprimanded for hitting Hut Stricklin early in the race. Irvan was able to do no better than 15th place.

Earnhardt bit off a large chunk of his deficit to Rudd in the point race, reducing Rudd's lead to just 42 points.

Mark Martin won the pole but never was a factor. His Roush Racing Ford bit the dust with overheating problems after completing 293 laps.

Winston Cup Series Race No. 9
188 Laps at Talladega Superspeedway
Talladega, AL
"Winston 500"
500.08 Miles on 2.66-mile Superspeedway
May 6, 1991

Fin	St	No.	Driver	Team / Car	Laps	Money	Status
1	2	33	Harry Gant	Leo Jackson Olds	188	$81,950	Running
2	5	17	Darrell Waltrip	DarWal Chevrolet	188	47,400	Running
3	8	3	Dale Earnhardt	RCR Enterprises Chevrolet	188	56,100	Running
4	19	22	Sterling Marlin	Junior Johnson Ford	188	25,450	Running
5	20	30	Michael Waltrip	Bahari Racing Pontiac	188	25,800	Running
6	11	11	Geoff Bodine	Junior Johnson Ford	188	25,350	Running
7	18	25	Ken Schrader	Hendrick Motorsports Chevy	188	19,150	Running
8	9	9	Bill Elliott	Melling Performance Ford	188	21,500	Running
9	29	98	Jimmy Spencer	Travis Carter Chevrolet	188	17,300	Running
10	13	1	Rick Mast	Precision Products Olds	187	17,650	Running
11	16	26	Brett Bodine	King Motorsports Buick	187	13,670	Running
12	14	68	Bobby Hamilton	Tri-Star Motorsports Olds	186	10,040	Running
13	6	5	Ricky Rudd	Hendrick Motorsports Chevy	186	15,860	Running
14	33	15	Morgan Shepherd	Bud Moore Eng. Ford	186	15,480	Running
15	21	24	Mickey Gibbs	Team III Pontiac	186	8,700	Running
16	38	55	Ted Musgrave	RaDiUs Pontiac	186	9,860	Running
17	35	20	Bobby Hillin,Jr.	Dick Moroso Olds	184	8,965	Running
18	41	71	Dave Marcis	Marcis Auto Racing Chevy	184	10,155	Running
19	27	73	Phil Barkdoll	Barkdoll Racing Olds	183	6,665	Running
20	36	52	Jimmy Means	Means Racing Pontiac	180	8,555	Running
21	31	49	Stanley Smith	Smith Buick	168	6,140	Running
22	4	28	Davey Allison	Robert Yates Racing Ford	164	14,720	Running
23	12	12	Hut Stricklin	Bobby Allison Buick	157	8,910	Running
24	28	6	Mark Martin	Roush Racing Ford	151	15,305	Running
25	30	8	Rick Wilson	Stavola Brothers Buick	149	8,775	Running
26	7	2	Rusty Wallace	Roger Penske Pontiac	146	5,645	Running
27	15	7	Alan Kulwicki	AK Racing Ford	136	12,590	Running
28	23	10	Derrike Cope	Bob Whitcomb Chevrolet	118	13,935	Engine
29	34	75	Joe Ruttman	RahMoc Racing Olds	116	8,330	Running
30	39	51	Jeff Purvis	James Finch Olds	94	5,425	Hub
31	10	66	Lake Speed	Cale Yarborough Pontiac	79	8,045	Crash
32	1	4	Ernie Irvan	Morgan-McClure Chevrolet	71	15,740	Crash
33	3	42	Kyle Petty	SabCo Racing Pontiac	70	14,410	Crash
34	32	90	Wally Dallenbach,Jr.	Junie Donlavey Ford	70	5,180	Crash
35	22	21	Dale Jarrett	Wood Brothers Ford	70	7,850	Crash
36	37	88	Buddy Baker	Dick Moroso Oldsmobile	70	5,120	Crash
37	24	94	Terry Labonte	Billy Hagan Olds	70	7,715	Crash
38	17	19	Chad Little	Chuck Little Ford	70	5,635	Crash
39	25	47	Greg Sacks	Derick Close Olds	39	5,555	Piston
40	26	43	Richard Petty	Petty Enterprises Pontiac	2	5,500	Crash
41	40	41	Larry Person	Larry Hedrick Chevrolet	2	4,900	Crash

Time of Race: 3 hours, 1 minute, 10 seconds
Average Speed: 165.620 mph
Pole Winner: Ernie Irvan – 195.186 mph
Lap Leaders: Ernie Irvan 1, Kyle Petty 2-10, Ricky Rudd 11-12, Dale Earnhardt 13-17, Davey Allison 18-19, Earnhardt 20-36, Ted Musgrave 37, Irvan 38-48, Earnhardt 49-51, Irvan 52-57, Earnhardt 58-66, Ken Schrader 67, Earnhardt 68-109, Sterling Marlin 110-113, Earnhardt 114, Michael Waltrip 115, Earnhardt 116-120, Schrader 121-125, Harry Gant 126-132, Earnhardt 133-150, Darrell Waltrip 151-156, Earnhardt 157-168, M.Waltrip 169-170, Schrader 171-177, Gant 178-188.
24 lead changes among 11 drivers.
Cautions: 3 for 18 laps Margin of Victory: 11 seconds

Race #9

Gant Gets Assist From Mast to Win Talladega; Kyle Injured

TALLADEGA, AL (May 6) – Harry Gant ran 149 miles on a tankful of fuel and outdistanced the field to win the Winston 500 at Talladega Superspeedway.

Gant's 12th career victory was disputed by runner-up

Bryan Hallman

Mark Martin's Ford lifts high into the air on the backstretch of Talladega Superspeedway.

Darrell Waltrip and third finisher Dale Earnhardt. Each claimed they should have been declared the winner of the second jewel of the Winston Million races.

Adding to the controversy was a savage 20-car crash in the 71st lap triggered by Ernie Irvan. Kyle Petty was airlifted to the hospital where surgery was performed to piece his badly broken leg back together.

The 188-lap contest around the fastest superspeedway in the world was run on Monday following torrential rains on Sunday. Monday's starting time was delayed almost two hours by additional rains.

When the race finally got underway, pole sitter Irvan led the first lap before falling back in a wild scramble for first place. Petty flexed his muscles early, leading for nine laps, but it was Earnhardt who grabbed command for most of the way. He would lead 112 of the 188 laps.

Many contenders were knocked out of action by a wild wreck which left most fingers pointing at Irvan. The Chevrolet driver was running in the low groove through turn two on lap 72. He moved up on the track, creating a three-wide situation, poking the nose of his Chevrolet between Petty and Mark Martin. As the narrow opening started to squeeze shut, Irvan drifted up and snagged Petty's left rear quarter panel. That sent Kyle spinning into a tightly bunched pack of cars.

In an instant, Martin's Ford lurched high on its nose – then somehow returned to the track on all four wheels. Cars skidded into each other, banged into the concrete retaining barrier and slid off the track into the water-logged infield. Petty's car slid to a halt sideways on the backstretch and was hit broadside by Chad Little's Ford.

Petty was the only driver injured in the melee.

Irvan avoided the blame and said Martin was at fault. "Kyle was up against the wall and Mark kept coming up on me," Irvan told a gathering of news reporters. "They both hit me about the same time. I don't think any of them knew I was there. I got pinched between the two and they started spinning."

Irvan's version of the accident brought a sharp response from Martin. "That's not the way it happened," Martin stressed. "There are certain guys out there who would rather wreck than let off the gas. Ernie turned me around and got into the side of me, but it doesn't matter. Ernie is always going to make excuses.

Bryan Hallman

Is Rick Mast drafting or pushing Harry Gant across Talladega's finish line?

"I closed my eyes when I went into the air," Martin continued. "I don't like getting upside down and I was fixing to. I think everybody saw what happened. It's pretty clear."

Davey Allison's Ford was crippled in the crash, but he was able to get back into the race after lengthy repairs. "Ernie was down in the middle where he had no business being," said the fiesty Allison. "I was behind Sterling and backed off. Maybe it was a good thing because Kyle came back out and hit the wall right behind where Sterling was."

Marlin was able to sneak past the incident. "I was behind Kyle and Ernie hung him in the left rear and then got into the side of Mark. Then there were cars spinning everywhere," he said.

Gant said he sensed something was about to cut loose, so he backed off. "I was running as well as anyone, but I backed out of that situation. I backed up to the rear of the field. I knew something bad was going to happen."

The race was halted for 33 minutes while the wreckage was cleared. When the race got underway, there were no more caution flags.

Gant, who led only 18 laps, made his final pit stop in the 132nd lap. It was doubtful he could go the distance, but he was going to try it.

Earnhardt made his final pit stop on lap 168. He and Waltrip hooked up in a draft but had no chance of catching Gant.

Gant was running in a draft with teammate Rick Mast, who was running 10th a lap down. In the final lap, Gant's car sputtered. "The motor cut off and I was out of gas," said Gant. "Rick gave me a good boot when my car cut off in turn three. He gave me another good push and I was able to make it to the finish line."

Waltrip finished second, 11 seconds behind Gant. He immediately filed a protest.

"You can't push the lead car in on the last lap," said a fired up Waltrip. "If they don't take the win away from him, I'm going to be mad. That's plainly spelled out in the rule book. It's not a judgement call. He (Gant) got help on the last lap and that's against the rules."

While Waltrip was complaining to NASCAR officials, Richard Childress, owner of Earnhardt's car, was complaining about Waltrip's rear spoiler. "Waltrip's spoiler was less than the 30° allowed," he insisted. "We ought to get the win."

It was three hours before NASCAR upheld Gant's victory. "The 33 (Gant) car was tapped by the 1 (Mast)," explained Dick Beaty after studying the film. "But we don't feel it had much to do with the outcome of the race. The 33 car got tapped, not assisted."

Regarding Waltrip's spoiler, Beaty said the angle wasn't checked until after all cars had gone to the garage area. "It looks like we'll have to check 'em all out on pit road before they get to the garage. Anybody could have adjusted that spoiler in the garage area. We'll do things different in Daytona (in July)," said Beaty.

Earnhardt was able to leap to the top of the Winston Cup standings, four points ahead of Ricky Rudd, who finished 13th.

Race #10

Davey Scorches Charlotte; Gets First 1991 Victory For Ford

CONCORD, NC (May 26) – Davey Allison humbled the field and drove his Robert Yates Racing Ford to an overwhelming victory in Charlotte Motor Speedway's Coca-Cola 600. Allison gave the Ford nameplate its first win of the season after starting the campaign 0-for-9.

Allison led a total of 264 of the 400 laps and outran Chevrolet driver Ken Schrader by 1.28 seconds to bag the $137,100 first prize. Dale Earnhardt finished third after losing second place with six laps to go. Harry Gant came home fourth and Dale Jarrett was fifth.

Allison, who dominated The Winston All-Star race a week earlier, started 10th on the grid and bided his time in the early stages. He didn't take the lead until the 51st lap and was hardly threatened thereafter. "The guys put a new engine in the car this morning and I just took it easy the first 50 laps," said Allison. "After I worked it in, I felt pretty confident everything would work out."

Allison's fortunes were enhanced when NASCAR allowed Ford teams to raise their trunk lids an inch. "The Fords have been pretty unstable this year," said Allison. "That is reflected in the number of wins we

Winston Cup Series Race No. 10
400 Laps at Charlotte Motor Speedway
Concord, NC
"Coca-Cola 600"
600 Miles on 1.5-mile Superspeedway
May 26, 1991

Fin	St	No.	Driver	Team / Car	Laps	Money	Status
1	10	28	Davey Allison	Robert Yates Racing Ford	400	$137,100	Running
2	3	25	Ken Schrader	Hendrick Motorsports Chevy	400	84,850	Running
3	14	3	Dale Earnhardt	RCR Enterprises Chevrolet	400	53,650	Running
4	7	33	Harry Gant	Leo Jackson Olds	400	37,700	Running
5	12	21	Dale Jarrett	Wood Brothers Ford	400	27,400	Running
6	30	12	Hut Stricklin	Bobby Allison Buick	400	25,400	Running
7	6	4	Ernie Irvan	Morgan-McClure Chevrolet	399	24,200	Running
8	18	17	Darrell Waltrip	DarWal Chevrolet	399	15,500	Running
9	17	5	Ricky Rudd	Hendrick Motorsports Chevy	399	21,500	Running
10	13	94	Terry Labonte	Billy Hagan Olds	399	21,750	Running
11	4	22	Sterling Marlin	Junior Johnson Ford	398	15,000	Running
12	21	10	Derrike Cope	Bob Whitcomb Chevrolet	398	19,700	Running
13	19	42	Kenny Wallace	SabCo Racing Pontiac	398	17,700	Running
14	20	15	Morgan Shepherd	Bud Moore Eng. Ford	397	17,000	Running
15	2	30	Michael Waltrip	Bahari Racing Pontiac	397	20,200	Running
16	34	97	Tommy Ellis	Flossie/Junior Johnson Ford	396	8,800	Running
17	37	55	Ted Musgrave	RaDiUs Pontiac	395	11,000	Running
18	28	8	Rick Wilson	Stavola Brothers Buick	394	11,255	Running
19	31	20	Bobby Hillin,Jr.	Dick Moroso Olds	390	8,500	Engine
20	24	43	Richard Petty	Petty Enterprises Pontiac	383	10,000	Crash
21	35	75	Joe Ruttman	RahMoc Racing Olds	359	9,200	Running
22	9	2	Rusty Wallace	Roger Penske Pontiac	353	7,000	Engine
23	1	6	Mark Martin	Roush Racing Ford	359	55,400	Engine
24	40	23	Eddie Bierschwale	Don Bierschwale Olds	336	5,600	Running
25	23	19	Chad Little	Chuck Little Ford	329	6,450	Engine
26	11	9	Bill Elliott	Melling Performance Ford	315	13,200	Engine
27	29	68	Bobby Hamilton	Tri-Star Motorsports Olds	310	5,350	Engine
28	5	26	Brett Bodine	King Motorsports Buick	300	9,350	Heating
29	16	66	Lake Speed	Cale Yarborough Pontiac	296	7,650	Engine
30	15	1	Rick Mast	Precision Products Olds	287	8,500	Running
31	33	98	Jimmy Spencer	Travis Carter Chevrolet	278	7,375	Engine
32	25	71	Dave Marcis	Marcis Auto Racing Chevy	270	7,275	Engine
33	41	90	Wally Dallenbach,Jr.	Junie Donlavey Ford	254	4,550	Trans
34	27	24	Mickey Gibbs	Team III Pontiac	251	4,500	Running
35	8	7	Alan Kulwicki	AK Racing Ford	205	11,965	Engine
36	32	49	Stanley Smith	Smith Buick	128	4,435	Brakes
37	36	89	Jim Sauter	Mueller Brothers Pontiac	58	4,415	Cylinder
38	39	52	Jimmy Means	Means Racing Pontiac	32	5,520	Engine
39	26	47	Greg Sacks	Derick Close Olds	21	4,980	Crash
40	38	34	Dick Trickle	Ken Allen Buick	19	4,360	Crash
41	22	41	Larry Pearson	Larry Hedrick Chevrolet	12	4,360	Heating

Time of Race: 4 hours, 19 minutes, 5 seconds
Average Speed: 138.951 mph
Pole Winner: Mark Martin – 174.820 mph
Lap Leaders: Mark Martin 1-3, Michael Waltrip 4-8, Ken Schrader 9-18, M.Waltrip 19-22, Rusty Wallace 23-27, Dale Earnhardt 28-50, Davey Allison 51-84, Schrader 85-98, Allison 99-162, Schrader 163-171, Kenny Wallace 172, Allison 173-179, Schrader 180-200, Allison 201-270, Harry Gant 271-273, Hut Stricklin 274-276, Schrader 277-282, Stricklin 283-298, Gant 299-306, Allison 307-375, Dale Jarrett 376-378, Earnhardt 379-381, Allison 382-400.
22 lead changes among 10 drivers.
Cautions: 9 for 54 laps Margin of Victory: 1.28 seconds

Brian Czobat

Rusty Wallace leads Dale Earnhardt into Charlotte Motor Speedway's first turn.

had – zero. The rule changes don't help us go faster, they help us go straighter. It gives our cars more downforce but creates more drag. It has made our cars safer to drive, though."

Earnhardt, the only two-time winner in the 1991 season, complained about Allison's strength. "It's pretty hard to outrun an *illegal* car," said Earnhardt in a statement he probably wishes nobody heard him say. "They (NASCAR) gave them that new (cylinder) head that still hasn't been approved. That was an illegal car."

NASCAR permitted the use of a cylinder head for which Ford has been campaigning. If NASCAR has okayed the use of the heads, obviously they have been *approved.*

"I have news for him," responded Allison. "Our car is legal, and besides, he's won two races this year and now I've won one. All of a sudden, I am illegal?

What's he talking about?"

Despite Earnhardt's complaints, he stretched his point lead to 36 markers over Ricky Rudd, who never led and finished ninth.

Richard Petty gave his strongest effort of the season by running in the top 10 near the end of the race. But as Petty pushed his STP Pontiac to the high side in an effort to pass Darrell Waltrip for eighth place, the King slipped into the wall. The crash occurred with only 16 laps remaining.

"The car just took off and ran head-on into the wall," was Petty's explanation. "It hurt my pride more than anything."

Along with his damaged pride, Petty was placed on a stretcher and checked out at the infield hospital. "I've got bumps and bruises all up and down my legs and my ankle hurts," he said. "I hurt worse here than I did when I crashed at Daytona (in 1988)."

Until the late wreck, the Petty Enterprises team had been foiled by lousy pit stops. "If we can eliminate the mistakes," said crew chief Robbie Loomis, "we're going to be okay." Petty got credit for 20th in the final rundown.

Kenny Wallace, a Busch Grand National Series driver, filled in for the injured Kyle Petty in the SabCo Pontiac. He led a single lap under the yellow and wound up 13th.

Finishing three positions behind Wallace was Tommy Ellis in the Flossie Johnson Ford #97. Ellis, who was filling in for the injured Geoff Bodine, had driven the car in the All-Star race when NASCAR officials found an illegal oversized engine in the car. Junior Johnson, team owner, and crew chief Tim Brewer were suspended for four races. Johnson pulled the necessary strings in order to allow the car to compete in the 600. He simply listed his wife as new car owner and changed the number of the car.

Brian Czobat

Mark Martin leads the field at the start of the Coca-Cola 600.

Race #11

Schrader Outruns Earnhardt For Dover Victory

DOVER, DE (June 2) – Ken Schrader raced around Dale Earnhardt with 78 laps remaining and hustled to victory in the Budweiser 500 at Dover Downs International Speedway. It was the second win of the season for the Fenton, Mo. Chevrolet driver and the fourth of his career.

Schrader started 19th and spent over half the race just riding around, staying out of trouble that many drivers seem to get into when they come to the 'Monster Mile'. He led for two laps when his Hendrick Motorsports team was able to stretch fuel mileage. It wasn't until well after the halfway point that he began to flex his muscles.

"I've always had a habit of wanting to get to the front in a hurry," said Schrader, who has a history of crunching fenders in his haste to run for the lead. "This time I just wanted to stay on the lead lap. For a long time, I was happy to run fifth even though we didn't have to be running fifth."

Earnhardt had no qualms about running up front – where he always seems comfortable. He was on the point for 173 of the first 214 laps, but a stroke of bad luck knocked him a lap off the pace.

"We had a tire go down and I got a lap behind," said Earnhardt.

Harry Gant became a formidable contender when he drove his Leo Jackson Oldsmobile to the front and held Earnhardt a lap down after a seven lap side-by-side battle with Earnhardt, which drew the record crowd of 77,000 to its collective feet.

Shortly before the 400 lap

Kim Novosat

Harry Gant and Dale Earnhardt battle door-to-door at Dover.

Winston Cup Series Race No. 11
500 Laps at Dover Downs Int'l Speedway
Dover, DE
"Budweiser 500"

500 Miles on 1-mile Superspeedway
June 2, 1991

Fin	St	No.	Driver	Team / Car	Laps	Money	Status
1	19	25	Ken Schrader	Hendrick Motorsports Chevy	500	$64,800	Running
2	10	3	Dale Earnhardt	RCR Enterprises Chevrolet	500	44,275	Running
3	7	33	Harry Gant	Leo Jackson Olds	500	28,800	Running
4	6	4	Ernie Irvan	Morgan-McClure Chevrolet	500	21,750	Running
5	5	6	Mark Martin	Roush Racing Ford	500	23,325	Running
6	12	12	Hut Stricklin	Bobby Allison Buick	500	13,950	Running
7	18	17	Darrell Waltrip	DarWal Chevrolet	499	10,900	Running
8	21	15	Morgan Shepherd	Bud Moore Eng. Ford	498	15,700	Running
9	2	2	Rusty Wallace	Roger Penske Pontiac	498	9,950	Running
10	13	5	Ricky Rudd	Hendrick Motorsports Chevy	497	18,000	Running
11	32	68	Bobby Hamilton	Tri-Star Motorsports Olds	495	9,050	Running
12	27	75	Joe Ruttman	RahMoc Racing Olds	494	9,700	Running
13	17	9	Bill Elliott	Melling Performance Ford	494	13,600	Running
14	4	7	Alan Kulwicki	AK Racing Ford	494	12,300	Running
15	22	22	Sterling Marlin	Junior Johnson Ford	494	7,350	Running
16	11	28	Davey Allison	Robert Yates Racing Ford	494	13,450	Running
17	31	43	Richard Petty	Petty Enterprises Pontiac	494	6,050	Running
18	25	55	Ted Musgrave	RaDiUs Pontiac	494	5,985	Running
19	30	52	Bobby Hillin,Jr.	Means Racing Pontiac	491	4,550	Running
20	3	1	Rick Mast	Precision Products Olds	491	8,600	Running
21	26	97	Tommy Ellis	Flossie/Junior Johnson Ford	491	4,450	Running
22	23	66	Lake Speed	Cale Yarborough Pontiac	491	7,350	Running
23	29	71	Dave Marcis	Marcis Auto Racing Chevy	487	7,200	Running
24	8	94	Terry Labonte	Billy Hagan Olds	483	7,050	Running
25	9	8	Rick Wilson	Stavola Brothers Buick	480	7,050	Running
26	15	42	Kenny Wallace	SabCo Racing Pontiac	478	11,200	Running
27	24	10	Derrike Cope	Bob Whitcomb Chevrolet	399	12,550	Crash
28	14	98	Jimmy Spencer	Travis Carter Chevrolet	369	6,775	Crash
29	34	19	Chad Little	Chuck Little Ford	337	4,050	Engine
30	28	24	Mickey Gibbs	Team III Pontiac	303	4,650	Steering
31	35	70	J.D.McDuffie	McDuffie Racing Pontiac	245	3,950	Crash
32	1	30	Michael Waltrip	Bahari Racing Pontiac	186	10,025	Engine
33	16	26	Brett Bodine	King Motorsports Buick	133	6,450	Camshaft
34	33	14	Bobby Labonte	Terry Labonte Olds	88	3,800	Engine
35	20	21	Dale Jarrett	Wood Brothers Ford	18	5,600	Crash

Time of Race: 4 hours, 9 minutes, 41 seconds
Average Speed: 120.152 mph
Pole Winner: Michael Waltrip – 143.392 mph
Lap Leaders: Michael Waltrip 1-15, Rusty Wallace 16-26, Dale Earnhardt 27-87, Harry Gant 88-89, Ken Schrader 90-91, Darrell Waltrip 92-94, Morgan Shepherd 95-106, Earnhardt 107-170, Gant 171, Shepherd 172-183, D.Waltrip 184-190, Earnhardt 191-238, Mark Martin 239-317, Gant 318-352, Schrader 353-357, Ernie Irvan 358-372, Schrader 373, Gant 374-380, Irvan 381-405, Earnhardt 406-412, Schrader 413-415, Earnhardt 416-422, Schrader 423-500.
22 lead changes among 9 drivers.
Cautions: 6 for 42 laps Margin of Victory: 1.18 seconds

mark, Earnhardt fought his way back into the lead lap and made up the distance when Chad Little's blown engine brought out the yellow flag. "I was lucky to get that lap back," relented Earnhardt.

Gant fell from contention when he missed the opportunity to pit with the cars on the lead lap. "I thought the pits were closed, but everybody behind me pitted," said Gant. "By the time I realized it, I couldn't get in."

Gant pitted twice during the yellow, then was black-flagged by NASCAR for returning to the racing surface above the 'blend' line. "I didn't know they called that on the yellow," said Gant.

That set up an Earnhardt-Schrader battle. Earnhardt swept past Schrader in the 416th lap and led for seven laps. Schrader went to the front for keeps in the 423rd lap.

"I followed him for a few laps," said Schrader, "then I decided it was time to go. Usually, you only get one chance at Earnhardt. I made the best of that chance."

Earnhardt held on for second and increased his Winston Cup lead to 82 points over Ricky Rudd, who finished 10th.

Gant's car started smoking badly in the last 15 laps, but he made it to the finish line to grab third place money. Ernie Irvan wound up fourth as General Motors cars finished 1-2-3-4. Five of the six cars that ran the full 500 miles were GM cars..

Fifth place went to Mark Martin, who was very

Dover Downs

Eventual winner Ken Schrader #25 passes Morgan Shepherd at Dover Downs.

dissatisfied with his team's performance. "If we can't run here, we can't run anywhere," said an unhappy Martin. "That worries me. This is supposed to be our race track. I feel madder running fifth today than I did falling out last week (at Charlotte)."

Michael Waltrip recorded his first career pole in the Bahari Racing Pontiac. The younger Waltrip led the first 15 laps but faded thereafter. He dropped from contention after a bout with the wall and eventually parked his car with a blown engine on lap 195. He was running nine laps behind at the time.

Dale Jarrett crashed the Wood Brothers Ford in the opening laps. "Somebody hit me and I'm getting damn tired of it," huffed Jarrett.

Race #11

Rudd Finishes First; Allison Declared Winner at Sonoma

SONOMA, CA (June 9) – Davey Allison was declared the winner of the Banquet Frozen Foods 300 at Sears Point International Raceway after an unprecedented and controversial finish.

Ricky Rudd led the final two laps and crossed the finish line first, but he was stripped of his 13th career Winston Cup victory when NASCAR officials ruled that he unnecessarily roughed up Allison when the decisive pass took place as the leaders were approaching the white flag.

A flurry of bumping incidents punctuated the final four laps that led to the controversial ending.

Rusty Wallace's picture perfect run to apparent victory was spoiled when his Pontiac dropped a cylinder with just over 10 laps to go. Tommy Kendall, filling in for the injured Kyle Petty, took the Sabco Racing Pontiac to the front in the 60th lap and was poised to score an upset triumph when he tangled with Mark Martin with less than three laps to go.

Martin had swung to the outside of Kendall to take the lead, but spun as Kendall stuck a tire into Martin's door. As Martin spun from contention, Kendall limped around the 2.52-mile road course with a flat tire.

That set up the stage for the dramatic Allison-Rudd confrontation. Allison grabbed the lead with a lap and a half to go and was maintaining a car length advantage when the pair hit the hairpin 11th turn.

At a point on the track when cars gear down to as low as 29 mph, Rudd tapped Allison into a spin. Rudd scampered into the lead as Allison gathered control of his car.

NASCAR official in charge, David Hoots, ordered a stop-and-go penalty for Rudd. The order was relayed to crew chief Waddell Wilson but Rudd, having already received the white flag, raced past the pit road entry in the final lap. As he approached the finish line, he was given the black flag. Four seconds later, Allison crossed the finish line and was given the checkered flag.

Wallace's sputtering car came across the line in third spot. Ernie Irvan and Ken Schrader were next.

"I had the lead on the inside of the turn," said Allison, describing the final lap incident with Rudd. "I didn't

Brian Czobat

Davey Allison whips his Ford into a turn at Sears Point International Raceway.

cut anybody off. (When he hit me), it lifted the wheels of my car off the ground and turned me around. I'm not saying it was intentional, but it could have been avoided. The race was taken away from us in an unsportsmanship fashion and given back to us as justification."

Two hours after the race, Rudd was levied a penalty of five seconds, which repositioned the cars as they had been running before the accident.

"I never seen anything like this," said an angry Rudd. "Everyone was racing hard the last four or five laps. I got into Davey and it was my fault. I put on the brakes and the car started hopping. I came around to take the checkered flag and the black flag was out. I don't understand it. I had completed the last lap."

Brian Czobat

Dale Jarrett #21 and Hershel McGriff pair up at Sonoma.

Rudd hinted that he may quit the premier stock car racing tour. "This will definitely make me take a look at this sport and rethink my future. If you've ever seen the World Federation of Wrestling, this is it.

"NASCAR needed a Ford in victory lane," Rudd continued, alluding to the General Motors domination in the early part of the season, leading Ford 10-1 in wins entering the Sonoma event. "NASCAR makes the rules. I'm fed up with this mess."

Wilson backed up his driver. "It's the rottenist thing I've seen in NASCAR, and I've been around since 1961. They didn't do anything to Kendall or Martin when they wrecked," he said.

Les Richter, Director of the Series, delivered the explanation to the media. "We're trying to maintain law and order," said Richter. "That's what it's all about. Ricky hit Davey in the rear and spun Davey out. He was racing very hard into the corner, racing to win. But there comes a time when you have to call balls and strikes; to make a judgment call."

Point leader Dale Earnhardt finished seventh in a car that was trailing a long line of smoke for most of the race. His lead over Rudd was cut to 53 points.

Overshadowed by the controversial finish was a nasty garage area confrontation between the crews of Chad Little and Ernie Irvan, who got into a fight. Little apparently hit Irvan in the eye during the scuffle.

"I had gotten under Chad in the carousel and he didn't see me so he ended up spinning out," explained Irvan. "The next time I came around, he drilled me into the

Winston Cup Series Race No. 12
74 Laps at Sears Point Int'l Raceway
Sonoma, CA
"Banquet Frozen Foods 300"

186.48 Miles on 2.52-mile Road Course
June 9, 1991

Fin	St	No.	Driver	Team / Car	Laps	Money	Status
1	13	28	Davey Allison	Robert Yates Racing Ford	74	$61,950	Running
2	1	5	Ricky Rudd	Hendrick Motorsports Chevy	74	41,975	Running
3	4	2	Rusty Wallace	Roger Penske Pontiac	74	34,975	Running
4	11	4	Ernie Irvan	Morgan-McClure Chevrolet	74	20,350	Running
5	6	25	Ken Schrader	Hendrick Motorsports Chevy	74	17,225	Running
6	2	94	Terry Labonte	Billy Hagan Olds	74	14,400	Running
7	3	3	Dale Earnhardt	RCR Enterprises Chevrolet	74	19,800	Running
8	12	97	Geoff Bodine	Flossie/Junior Johnson Ford	74	7,650	Running
9	14	6	Mark Martin	Roush Racing Ford	74	16,850	Running
10	8	30	Michael Waltrip	Bahari Racing Pontiac	74	10,600	Running
11	28	26	Brett Bodine	King Motorsports Buick	74	10,100	Running
12	9	66	Lake Speed	Cale Yarborough Pontiac	74	9,600	Running
13	25	73	Bill Schmitt	Sylvia Schmitt Ford	74	7,300	Running
14	32	24	Mickey Gibbs	Team III Pontiac	74	6,600	Running
15	29	76	Bill Sedgwick	Wayne Spears Chevrolet	74	6,400	Running
16	19	8	Rick Wilson	Stavola Brothers Buick	74	7,450	Running
17	7	7	Alan Kulwicki	AK Racing Ford	74	11,275	Running
18	5	42	Tommy Kendall	SabCo Racing Pontiac	74	12,450	Running
19	41	1	Rick Mast	Precision Products Olds	73	7,225	Running
20	26	9	Bill Elliott	Melling Performance Ford	73	13,700	Running
21	33	52	Bobby Hillin,Jr.	Means Racing Pontiac	73	4,100	Running
22	35	68	Bobby Hamilton	Tri-Star Motorsports Olds	73	5,775	Running
23	34	49	Stanley Smith	Smith Buick	73	4,050	Running
24	16	71	Dave Marcis	Marcis Auto Racing Chevy	72	6,830	Running
25	10	17	Darrell Waltrip	DarWal Chevrolet	71	4,820	Running
26	15	22	Sterling Marlin	Junior Johnson Ford	71	4,650	Running
27	23	33	Harry Gant	Leo Jackson Olds	70	6,600	Running
28	27	19	Chad Little	Chuck Little Ford	67	3,850	Running
29	38	98	Jimmy Spencer	Travis Carter Chevrolet	65	6,490	Running
30	30	10	Derrike Cope	Bob Whitcomb Chevrolet	64	12,210	Running
31	17	75	Joe Ruttman	RahMoc Racing Olds	64	6,350	Running
32	22	04	Hershel McGriff	Bob Lipseia Pontiac	61	3,675	Crash
33	31	00	Scott Gaylord	Geoff Burney Oldsmobile	61	3,625	Running
34	39	43	Richard Petty	Petty Enterprises Pontiac	59	5,200	Crash
35	24	12	Hut Stricklin	Bobby Allison Buick	59	5,575	Running
36	18	44	Irv Hoerr	Terry Labonte Olds	58	3,565	Rear End
37	37	55	Ted Musgrave	RaDiUs Pontiac	58	3,795	Running
38	40	99	John Krebs	Krebs Pontiac	57	3,525	Running
39	43	91	Robert Sprague	Larry Rouse Ford	54	3,500	Engine
40	42	23	Mike Chase	Don Freymiller Ford	53	3,475	Trans
41	21	21	Dale Jarrett	Wood Brothers Ford	46	5,475	Ignition
42	20	15	Morgan Shepherd	Bud Moore Eng. Ford	39	10,475	Engine
43	36	09	R.K.Smith	Dick Midgley Pontiac	2	3,475	Engine

Time of Race: 2 hours, 33 minutes, 20 seconds
Average Speed: 72.970 mph
Pole Winner: Ricky Rudd – 90.634 mph
Lap Leaders: Ricky Rudd 1-11, Rusty Wallace 12-16, John Krebs 17, Robert Sprague 18, R.Wallace 19-45, Dale Jarrett 46, R.Wallace 47-59, Tommy Kendall 60-71, Davey Allison 72, Rudd 73-74. (Rudd led lap but was placed in 2nd place in final order)
9 lead changes among 7 drivers.
Cautions: 5 for 14 laps Margin of Victory: 1 second (Estimated by NASCAR)

grass. In the garage area, he was mouthing off about me, but I was ignoring it. Then the crews got involved and it all started."

Little said that he was "taken out early by Ernie. He said he was all the way underneath me, but go look at the car."

Richard Petty was examined at the track infirmary and transfered to a local hospital after a savage crash in turn two. Petty's Pontiac shot off the course in the 59th lap and plowed into a barrier. Doctors said he was "pretty well bruised up," but they would not be keeping him overnight.

A crowd of 62,000 watched Allison average 72.970 mph.

Winston Cup Series Race No. 13
200 Laps at Pocono Int'l Raceway
Long Pond, PA
"Champion Spark Plug 500"
500 Miles on 2.5-mile Superspeedway
June 16, 1991

Fin	St	No.	Driver	Team / Car	Laps	Money	Status
1	13	17	Darrell Waltrip	DarWal Chevrolet	200	$60,650	Running
2	21	3	Dale Earnhardt	RCR Enterprises Chevrolet	200	43,775	Running
3	1	6	Mark Martin	Roush Racing Ford	200	38,875	Running
4	8	33	Harry Gant	Leo Jackson Oldsmobile	200	22,600	Running
5	18	97	Geoff Bodine	Flossie/Junior Johnson Ford	200	15,125	Running
6	3	4	Ernie Irvan	Morgan-McClure Chevrolet	200	17,900	Running
7	7	25	Ken Schrader	Hendrick Motorsports Chevy	200	13,200	Running
8	16	22	Sterling Marlin	Junior Johnson Ford	200	9,900	Running
9	12	15	Morgan Shepherd	Bud Moore Eng.. Ford	200	14,300	Running
10	6	10	Derrike Cope	Bob Whitcomb Chevrolet	200	19,200	Running
11	23	43	Richard Petty	Petty Enterprises Pontiac	200	10,450	Running
12	10	28	Davey Allison	Robert Yates Racing Ford	200	14,800	Running
13	11	8	Rick Wilson	Stavola Brothers Buick	200	9,900	Running
14	27	98	Jimmy Spencer	Travis Carter Chevrolet	200	10,600	Running
15	22	42	Bobby Hillin,Jr.	SabCo Racing Pontiac	200	13,250	Running
16	2	7	Alan Kulwicki	AK Racing Ford	200	12,500	Running
17	19	66	Lake Speed	Cale Yarborough Pontiac	200	9,000	Running
18	5	30	Michael Waltrip	Bahari Racing Pontiac	200	8,600	Running
19	25	21	Dale Jarrett	Wood Brothers Ford	200	8,250	Running
20	4	5	Ricky Rudd	Hendrick Motorsports Chevy	199	13,025	Running
21	14	94	Terry Labonte	Billy Hagan Olds	199	7,750	Running
22	26	75	Joe Ruttman	RahMoc Racing Olds	197	7,600	Running
23	30	19	Chad Little	Chuck Little Ford	197	4,550	Running
24	29	71	Dave Marcis	Marcis Auto Racing Chevy	197	7,350	Running
25	24	1	Rick Mast	Precision Products Olds	196	7,800	Running
26	33	52	Jimmy Means	Means Racing Pontiac	176	4,400	Running
27	32	55	Ted Musgrave	RaDiUs Pontiac	174	5,800	Engine
28	17	12	Hut Stricklin	Bobby Allison Buick	163	6,975	Engine
29	37	13	Randy LaJoie	Linro Motorsports Buick	154	4,250	Sway Bar
30	31	24	Mickey Gibbs	Team III Pontiac	145	4,850	Crash
31	9	2	Rusty Wallace	Roger Penske Pontiac	115	4,775	Engine
32	28	41	Larry Pearson	Larry Hedrick Chevrolet	72	4,100	Camshaft
33	20	26	Brett Bodine	King Motorsports Buick	57	6,600	Oil Pan
34	36	70	J.D.McDuffie	McDuffie Racing Pontiac	49	3,925	Handling
35	34	68	Bobby Hamilton	Tri-Star Motorsports Olds	47	4,100	Crash
36	15	9	Bill Elliott	Melling Performance Ford	44	11,775	Valve
37	35	48	James Hylton	Hylton Engineering Chevrolet	14	3,700	Engine

Time of Race: 4 hours, 4 minutes, 34 seconds
Average Speed: 122.666 mph
Pole Winner: Mark Martin – 161.996 mph
Lap Leaders: Mark Martin 1-6, Ken Schrader 7-9, Ricky Rudd 10-12, Schrader 13-19, Ted Musgrave 20, Schrader 21-26, Ernie Irvan 27-50, Jimmy Means 51, Dale Earnhardt 52-56, Darrell Waltrip 57-71, Sterling Marlin 72-87, Harry Gant 88-91, D.Waltrip 92, Geoff Bodine 93, Davey Allison 94, Marlin 95-105, Gant 106-117, Irvan 118-131, Jimmy Spencer 132-143, Rudd 144-156, Earnhardt 157-166, Michael Waltrip 167-169, Earnhardt 170-182, D.Waltrip 183-200.
23 lead changes among 14 drivers.
Cautions: 7 for 37 laps Margin of Victory: 1.92 seconds

Race #13

Darrell Dusts off Dale For Pocono Win; Spencer Foiled

LONG POND, PA (June 16) – Darrell Waltrip slipped past Dale Earnhardt with 18 laps remaining and galloped to his second win of the season in the Champion Spark Plug 500 at Pocono International Raceway.

Waltrip finished 1.92 seconds in front of Earnhardt to notch his 81st career Winston Cup victory. "Winning races at this point in my career with my own team, and coming back from the injury to put this whole thing together, has been special," said Waltrip.

Waltrip and Earnhardt treated the estimated sell-out audience of over 100,000 to a late race showdown. They led all but 16 of the final 57 laps after the race was interrupted for an hour and 42 minutes by rain. Nearly six hours after the race got underway, flagman Doyle Ford flashed Waltrip the checkered flag.

Earnhardt blamed tire problems for fading late in the race. "It started vibrating, and that's when Darrell got by me," said Earnhardt. "I think I could have held Darrell off if we hadn't had the problem."

Waltrip admitted he was concerned about Earnhardt in the final stretch, but he didn't think his rival's car was affected by tire problems. "It appeared to me that the longer he ran, the handle kind of came off his car," said the winner. "He didn't seem to stay as good and I was able to.

"He went into turn one and actually went up on the curve down there," added Waltrip. "It made his car jump off the track a little bit and it gave me a chance to

Kim Novosat

Mark Martin and Alan Kulwicki duel for first place at Pocono International Raceway.

get beside him. He was a gentleman about that whole thing. I passed him and checked on out."

Mark Martin finished third on Earnhardt's bumper. "We caught Earnhardt in the end. Maybe we needed a couple more laps. But a third today feels great," said Martin.

Harry Gant and Geoff Bodine finished fourth and fifth, respectively.

Ricky Rudd led twice for 16 laps, but fell a lap off the pace and wound up 20th. His tribulations allowed Earnhardt to march out to a 120-point lead in the Winston Cup standings.

For awhile it appeared Jimmy Spencer might end up the winner. Spencer was never in contention, but he had held the Travis Carter Chevrolet on the lead lap. The caution flag came out in the 130th lap for debris on the track. During the yellow flag, all contenders ducked onto pit road for fuel and fresh tires. With storm clouds forming, Carter instructed Spencer to stay on the track.

Spencer took the lead in the 132nd lap and led the slow-down parade when the rain began.

The race was halted on lap 138 with Spencer in front. "We knew we were about a top 15 car, said Spencer after eventually finishing 14th. "I guess I won the 345-mile race today. Now we've got to go back to work and try to come back next time and win a 500-mile race."

Ernie Irvan led the most laps, but a pit miscue cost him a chance to win. "A tire hit the jack and knocked it down. The front tire was up in the fender well and rubbing the fender. We had to come back in to make sure nothing was rubbing," explained Irvan.

Irvan restarted 21st but came back to finish sixth.

Ken Schrader lost two positions in the final lap but held on for seventh. "We blew up and finished seventh," said Schrader. "Something happened to the engine with 20 laps to go. Then it just let go with three laps left."

Schrader was able to keep the car running for the final three laps.

Rusty Wallace started ninth but never led. His Pontiac developed engine problems just past the half-way point and he wound up 31st.

Race #14

Allison, Stricklin Give Alabama Gang 1-2 Finish at Michigan

BROOKLYN, MI (June 23) – Davey Allison led over half the distance and scored a convincing victory in the Miller Genuine Draft 400 at Michigan International Speedway.

The 30 year-old Hueytown, Ala. driver flexed the muscles of his Robert Yates Ford Thunderbird and outran upstart Hut Stricklin by 11.72 seconds to score his third win of the season. The margin of victory was the largest of the 23 runnings of the 400-miler.

The race was run crash-free and the only caution flag was for debris early in the race. Allison showed the packed house of 90,000 he was for real as early as the 15th lap when he passed Mark Martin for the lead. From that point on, Allison was rarely out of the lead except during pit stops. Stricklin posed a stout challenge in the first half of the race by leading for 20 straight laps.

But in the final analysis, Allison had the strength to pull away from all contenders, including Stricklin.

The victory ceremonies was a family celebration with strong lineage. Stricklin was driving a Buick owned by Bobby Allison, the winner's father, who retired after a near-fatal crash at Pocono in 1988. Stricklin is married to Davey Allison's cousin, the daughter of Bobby's brother Donnie.

"I think everybody knows I ran second to the #12 in the Daytona 500 a couple of years ago," Allison

Brian Czobat

Lake Speed pits the Yarborough Motorsports Pontiac at Pocono.

Brian Czobat

Morgan Shepherd #15 and Davey Allison pass Mickey Gibbs #24 at Michigan.

Winston Cup Series Race No. 14
200 Laps at Michigan Int'l Speedway
Brooklyn, MI
"Miller Genuine Draft 400"
400 Miles on 2-mile Superspeedway
June 23, 1991

Fin	St	No.	Driver	Team / Car	Laps	Money	Status
1	4	28	Davey Allison	Robert Yates Racing Ford	200	$90,650	Running
2	9	12	Hut Stricklin	Bobby Allison Buick	200	41,925	Running
3	3	6	Mark Martin	Roush Racing Ford	200	37,650	Running
4	6	3	Dale Earnhardt	RCR Enterprises Chevrolet	200	30,950	Running
5	19	4	Ernie Irvan	Morgan-McClure Chevrolet	200	24,725	Running
6	8	25	Ken Schrader	Hendrick Motorsports Chevy	200	23,550	Running
7	13	17	Darrell Waltrip	DarWal Chevrolet	200	15,300	Running
8	7	5	Ricky Rudd	Hendrick Motorsports Chevy	200	18,600	Running
9	15	15	Morgan Shepherd	Bud Moore Eng. Ford	199	18,750	Running
10	22	33	Harry Gant	Leo Jackson Olds	199	17,450	Running
11	20	9	Bill Elliott	Melling Performance Ford	199	17,300	Running
12	14	21	Dale Jarrett	Wood Brothers Ford	199	12,825	Running
13	10	22	Sterling Marlin	Junior Johnson Ford	199	10,275	Running
14	30	24	Mickey Gibbs	Team III Pontiac	198	9,725	Running
15	17	42	Bobby Hillin,Jr.	SabCo Racing Pontiac	198	15,175	Running
16	16	71	Dave Marcis	Marcis Auto Racing Chevy	198	10,750	Running
17	23	2	Rusty Wallace	Roger Penske Pontiac	198	6,925	Running
18	21	66	Lake Speed	Cale Yarborough Pontiac	198	10,500	Running
19	31	75	Joe Ruttman	RahMoc Racing Olds	197	9,585	Running
20	25	41	Larry Pearson	Larry Hedrick Chevrolet	197	7,270	Running
21	34	55	Ted Musgrave	RaDiUs Pontiac	197	7,800	Running
22	29	68	Bobby Hamilton	Tri-Star Motorsports Olds	197	7,135	Running
23	37	49	Stanley Smith	Smith Buick	196	5,925	Running
24	5	7	Alan Kulwicki	AK Racing Ford	196	12,715	Running
25	26	94	Terry Labonte	Billy Hagan Olds	196	8,555	Running
26	38	19	Chad Little	Chuck Little Ford	196	5,435	Running
27	41	52	Jimmy Means	Means Racing Pontiac	195	5,385	Running
28	33	90	Wally Dallenbach,Jr.	Junie Donlavey Ford	195	5,325	Running
29	12	1	Rick Mast	Precision Products Olds	194	7,965	Running
30	28	20	Buddy Baker	Dick Moroso Olds	193	5,150	Running
31	27	8	Rick Wilson	Stavola Brothers Buick	192	7,720	Running
32	24	98	Jimmy Spencer	Travis Carter Chevrolet	188	7,625	Engine
33	40	36	H.B.Bailey	Bailey Pontiac	187	4,870	Running
34	1	30	Michael Waltrip	Bahari Racing Pontiac	185	10,450	Valve
35	36	43	Richard Petty	Petty Enterprises Pontiac	166	7,360	Valve
36	18	26	Brett Bodine	King Motorsports Buick	121	7,290	Engine
37	32	89	Jim Sauter	Mueller Brothers Pontiac	104	4,660	Piston
38	39	23	Eddie Bierschwale	Don Bierschwale Olds	86	4,635	Rock Arm
39	2	11	Geoff Bodine	Junior Johnson Ford	70	17,910	Oil Pan
40	35	35	Bill Venturini	Venturini Chevrolet	64	4,550	Camshaft
41	11	10	Derrike Cope	Bob Whitcomb Chevrolet	2	12,950	Engine

Time of Race: 2 hours, 29 minutes, 9 seconds
Average Speed: 160.912 mph
Pole Winner: Michael Waltrip – 174.351 mph
Lap Leaders: Geoff Bodine 1-8, Mark Martin 9-12, Davey Allison 13, Martin 14, Allison 15-35, Martin 36-39, Dale Earnhardt 40-48, Martin 49, Earnhardt 50, Martin 51, Earnhardt 52, Allison 53, Earnhardt 54-56, Hut Stricklin 57-76, Allison 77, Stricklin 78-80, Allison 81, Martin 82, Harry Gant 83, Darrell Waltrip 84-85, Ricky Rudd 86-87, Ken Schrader 88-92, Allison 93-124, Michael Waltrip 125, Ernie Irvan 126-128, D.Waltrip 129-138, Schrader 139-170, Stricklin 171-174, Irvan 175, Allison 176-200.
31 lead changes among 11 drivers.
Cautions: 1 for 4 laps   Margin of Victory: 11.72 seconds

said, referring to the day his father won the Daytona 500 in 1988. "That's probably the highlight of my career. Dad doesn't drive it anymore, but this guy (Stricklin) is doing a great job."

The runner-up effort was Stricklin's best in Winston Cup since joining the series in 1987. "Our team has been running good every week," said Stricklin. "Things have been happening out of the ordinary to prevent us from being in position to win. Davey and I have been friends since we were kids. We came up through the short tracks together. But the next time, I want the 1-2 finish to be the other way around."

Mark Martin wound up third, passing Dale Earnhardt in the final laps. Earnhardt got fourth and claimed engine problems kept him from contending for the win. Fifth place went to Ernie Irvan.

Ricky Rudd finished eighth and lost more ground to Earnhardt in the chase for the Winston Cup title. "I was just sliding around, skating in the corners," said Rudd, who fell 138 points behind Earnhardt. "It was a pretty boring day. I think I saw Davey once. He was in another league."

Geoff Bodine led the first eight laps in the Junior Johnson Ford, but his day came to an early end with a leak in the oil pan. Derrike Cope lasted only two laps before the engine blew in his Chevrolet. Brett Bodine and Jimmy Spencer were two other hopefuls sidelined by mechanical problems.

The 400-miler, presented in the close proximity of the manufacturers headquarters, often draws big brass out of Detroit. Herb Fishel, Director of Chevrolet's racing effort, complained about the rule change which recently allowed Ford cars to run a higher deck lid. "For NASCAR to give Ford a technical advantage over Chevrolet at this point, when Chevy teams have their acts together, could create a terrible imbalance later in the season. No one should ever lose sight of the fact that Ford won six of the last seven races last year without the benefit of a raised rear deck or any other NASCAR-mandated advantages."

Buddy Baker returned to action in the Dick Moroso Oldsmobile. Baker started 28th and finished 30th.

Michael Waltrip started on the pole in Chuck Rider's Bahari Racing Pontiac. Waltrip lost the lead at the start and departed late in the race with a blown engine. Only nine cars failed to finish the race.

Race #15

Elliott Ends Skid With Daytona Victory; Waltrip Tumbles

DAYTONA BEACH, FL (July 6) – Bill Elliott overcame a stop-and-go penalty for speeding on pit road and led a Ford 1-2-3 sweep in Daytona International Speedway's Pepsi 400.

Elliott, scoring his first win of the season, pushed his Melling Performance Ford into the lead 13 laps from the finish and held off Geoff Bodine by 0.18-second to snare the $75,000 first prize. Davey Allison was a couple car lengths behind in third place. Ken Schrader and Ernie Irvan, principle leaders during the middle stages, were fourth and fifth in Chevrolets.

Elliott dedicated his 34th career victory to his recently deceased mother and grandmother, and to crewman Michael Ritch, who was killed in a pit road accident last year at Atlanta.

"If there was ever a race that was won for anybody, this is for the three of them," said Elliott. "I just wish they could have been here."

Elliott's mother, Mildred, passed away June 26 following a long illness. His grandmother, Audie Reece, died nine days prior to his mother's death.

The 1-2-3 sweep by Ford brought a cry of sandbagging from Chevrolet drivers, particularly Schrader. "The Fords never showed their hand until the end," said Schrader, who led three times for 21 laps. "I was just holding on at the end. The Fords were just playing with us."

The race was broken by four caution flags, the most serious on lap 121 when Darrell Waltrip flipped nearly a dozen times on the back chute.

Sterling Marlin, who notched his first pole in his career, tapped Alan Kulwicki at the head of a tight pack of cars. Kulwicki's Ford wiggled and darted into the side of Waltrip's car. Waltrip scooped up Joe Ruttman as he slid off the track. Both cars appeared fused until Waltrip caught the lip of a paved chicane on the road course portion of the track, turning over countless times.

"It was a typical jammed-up situation you sometimes get into, " said Kulwicki. "We (he and Marlin) had run side-by-side for a couple of laps. But then Sterling ran into the back of me. It got me all crossed up. We both zig-zagged and then – I don't really know what happened after that. I'm sure we probably touched after I got hit in the back."

Marlin said that he was running behind Kulwicki when "I rubbed up against him. We barely touched, but he wobbled a little bit. I saw Darrell take off and cut across the grass."

Ruttman was an innocent victim. "I think he (Waltrip) had already made contact with somebody else," said Ruttman, who was in the RahMoc Oldsmobile. "He just darted in front of me and I hit him. I got him barrel rolling.

"He seemed to be all right when I got to him," said Ruttman, who ran to the aid of Waltrip after both cars stopped. "He recognized me and was able to grip my hand."

Waltrip was released from Halifax Hospital after a two hour examination.

The crash sidelined Waltrip and Ruttman while

Winston Cup Series Race No. 15
160 Laps at Daytona Int'l Speedway
Daytona Beach, FL
"Pepsi 400"
400 Miles on 2.5-mile Superspeedway
July 6, 1991

Fin	St	No.	Driver	Team / Car	Laps	Money	Status
1	10	9	Bill Elliott	Melling Performance Ford	160	$75,000	Running
2	4	11	Geoff Bodine	Junior Johnson Ford	160	48,325	Running
3	2	28	Davey Allison	Robert Yates Racing Ford	160	36,950	Running
4	22	25	Ken Schrader	Hendrick Motorsports Chevy	160	27,450	Running
5	11	4	Ernie Irvan	Morgan-McClure Chevrolet	160	36,525	Running
6	7	30	Michael Waltrip	Bahari Racing Pontiac	160	17,300	Running
7	12	3	Dale Earnhardt	RCR Enterprises Chevrolet	160	23,200	Running
8	1	22	Sterling Marlin	Junior Johnson Ford	160	17,100	Running
9	13	5	Ricky Rudd	Hendrick Motorsports Chevy	160	16,500	Running
10	32	98	Jimmy Spencer	Travis Carter Chevrolet	160	15,800	Running
11	26	6	Mark Martin	Roush Racing Ford	160	17,090	Running
12	28	2	Rusty Wallace	Roger Penske Pontiac	160	9,600	Running
13	19	20	Buddy Baker	Dick Moroso Olds	160	9,210	Running
14	17	7	Alan Kulwicki	AK Racing Ford	160	14,070	Running
15	25	42	Bobby Hillin,Jr.	SabCo Racing Pontiac	160	14,480	Running
16	15	12	Hut Stricklin	Bobby Allison Buick	160	10,440	Running
17	36	10	Derrike Cope	Bob Whitcomb Chevrolet	160	14,825	Running
18	31	21	Dale Jarrett	Wood Brothers Ford	160	9,810	Running
19	9	1	Rick Mast	Precision Products Olds	160	9,295	Running
20	18	15	Morgan Shepherd	Bud Moore Eng. Ford	159	13,730	Running
21	34	41	Larry Pearson	Larry Hedrick Chevrolet	159	5,510	Running
22	21	43	Richard Petty	Petty Enterprises Pontiac	159	8,490	Running
23	3	33	Harry Gant	Leo Jackson Olds	159	8,470	Running
24	14	8	Rick Wilson	Stavola Brothers Buick	158	8,050	Running
25	39	71	Dave Marcis	Marcis Auto Racing Chevy	157	7,930	Running
26	38	52	Jimmy Means	Means Racing Pontiac	157	4,810	Running
27	35	24	Mickey Gibbs	Team III Pontiac	154	5,440	Running
28	5	68	Bobby Hamilton	Tri-Star Motorsports Olds	153	6,070	Running
29	8	19	Chad Little	Chuck Little Ford	150	4,475	Running
30	29	51	Jeff Purvis	James Finch Olds	144	5,080	Running
31	16	75	Joe Ruttman	RahMoc Racing Olds	125	7,000	Crash
32	20	17	Darrell Waltrip	DarWal Chevrolet	119	5,945	Crash
33	30	14	Mike Chase	Foyt Enterprises Olds	106	4,265	Crash
34	40	90	Wally Dallenbach,Jr.	Junie Donlavey Ford	89	4,585	Ignition
35	37	73	Phil Barkdoll	Barkdoll Racing Olds	84	4,205	Crash
36	23	26	Brett Bodine	King Motorsports Buick	17	6,800	Engine
37	24	55	Ted Musgrave	RaDiUs Pontiac	12	4,745	Crash
38	6	66	Lake Speed	Cale Yarborough Pontiac	12	6,130	Crash
39	33	47	Greg Sacks	Derick Close Olds	12	4,120	Crash
40	27	49	Stanley Smith	Smith Buick	12	4,080	Crash
41	41	94	Terry Labonte	Billy Hagan Olds	8	6,080	Quit

Time of Race: 2 hours, 30 minutes, 50 seconds
Average Speed: 159.116 mph
Pole Winner: Sterling Marlin – 190.331 mph
Lap Leaders: Sterling Marlin 1-2, Davey Allison 3-7, Dale Earnhardt 8-10, Ernie Irvan 11-33, Ken Schrader 34-37, Irvan 38-51, Geoff Bodine 52-55 Jimmy Spencer 56-57, Hut Stricklin 58-59, Earnhardt 60-64, Michael Waltrip 65-68, Irvan 69-89, Schrader 90-104, Irvan 105, Schrader 106-107, Ricky Rudd 108-115, Irvan 116-141, Allison 142-147, Bill Elliott 148-160.
18 lead changes among 11 drivers.
Cautions: 4 for 18 laps Margin of Victory: 0.18 second

Brian Czobat

Bill Elliot broke his victory drought in Daytona's Pepsi 400.

Kulwicki and Marlin were able to continue. Marlin wound up in eighth place. "I knew when I joined Junior Johnson that we could win races and poles," said Marlin. "We got our first pole. We haven't won yet, but we will."

Dale Earnhardt finished seventh and increased his point lead to 144 points over Ricky Rudd, who came home ninth.

Mike Chase was selected to drive an Oldsmobile entered by A.J. Foyt. Chase collided with Rick Mast and hit the wall in the 106th lap. Mast recovered and went on to finish 19th on the lead lap.

Lake Speed had qualified Cale Yarborough's Pontiac sixth on the grid but was involved in a multi-car scramble in the 13th lap. Also sidelined were Ted Musgrave, Greg Sacks and Stanley Smith.

Terry Labonte had to use a provisional spot to get in the race. He drove his Billy Hagan Racing Oldsmobile four laps before parking it. Labonte said there was a bad vibration.

The Hagan crew made adjustments to the car, but Labonte was nowhere to be found when the car was ready to go back onto the track. "I think he (Labonte) was gone before the crew ever got to the car," said car owner Hagan. "When the car was ready, I looked for somebody else to drive it. I tried to find Greg Sacks, but he was also gone. I asked Lake Speed and Brett Bodine (both of whom fell out early), but they drive for other oil companies and couldn't do it. We had to leave the car parked."

Greg Fielden

Rusty Wallace ran 12th at Daytona.

Race #16

Earnhardt Assist Gives Wallace Win at Pocono

LONG POND, PA (July 21) – Rusty Wallace led the final 11 laps – six of them under yellow – and came out on top of the Miller Genuine Draft 500 at Pocono International Raceway.

Wallace's second win of the season was highlighted by a helpful push from Dale Earnhardt, who enabled Wallace to complete the rain-shortened distance without running out of fuel.

The scheduled 500-miler was cut short by 21 laps when rains once again plagued the triangular shaped track.

The field was brought to a halt on lap 176 when rain first doused the raceway. During the two hour delay, leader Wallace was chatting with his buddy Dale Earnhardt, who was running some four laps off the pace. Wallace told Earnhardt that he was low on fuel and would have to give up the lead if the race could be restarted.

Earnhardt quickly offered his assistance. "I'll just push you," he told Wallace. "It's only illegal if you do it on the final lap."

Once the track surface had been sufficiently dried,

Pocono Int'l

Rusty Wallace leads Geoff Bodine into the first turn at Pocono International Raceway.

Winston Cup Series Race No. 16
200 Laps at Pocono Int'l Raceway
Long Pond, PA
"Miller Genuine Draft 500"
500 Miles on 2.5-mile Superspeedway
July 21, 1991

Fin	St	No.	Driver	Team / Car	Laps	Money	Status
1	10	2	Rusty Wallace	Roger Penske Pontiac	179	$34,100	Running
2	3	6	Mark Martin	Roush Racing Ford	179	41,475	Running
3	8	11	Geoff Bodine	Junior Johnson Ford	179	32,350	Running
4	6	12	Hut Stricklin	Bobby Allison Buick	179	21,750	Running
5	11	22	Sterling Marlin	Junior Johnson Ford	179	14,100	Running
6	12	21	Dale Jarrett	Wood Brothers Ford	179	13,700	Running
7	13	4	Ernie Irvan	Morgan-McClure Chevrolet	179	16,700	Running
8	24	26	Brett Bodine	King Motorsports Buick	179	11,500	Running
9	4	9	Bill Elliott	Melling Performance Ford	178	15,000	Running
10	19	75	Joe Ruttman	RahMoc Racing Olds	178	12,650	Running
11	22	68	Bobby Hamilton	Tri-Star Motorsports Olds	178	6,900	Running
12	33	19	Chad Little	Chuck Little Ford	178	5,900	Running
13	31	55	Ted Musgrave	RaDiUs Pontiac	178	7,750	Running
14	5	28	Davey Allison	Robert Yates Racing Ford	178	14,100	Running
15	23	94	Terry Labonte	Billy Hagan Olds	178	9,550	Running
16	1	7	Alan Kulwicki	AK Racing Ford	177	17,425	Running
17	34	47	Greg Sacks	Derick Close Olds	177	5,100	Running
18	27	71	Dave Marcis	Marcis Auto Racing Chevy	177	8,300	Running
19	32	44	Irv Hoerr	Terry Labonte Olds	177	4,850	Running
20	7	5	Ricky Rudd	Hendrick Motorsports Chevy	177	12,725	Running
21	38	52	Jimmy Means	Means Racing Pontiac	176	4,500	Running
22	16	3	Dale Earnhardt	RCR Enterprises Chevrolet	175	15,350	Running
23	2	25	Ken Schrader	Hendrick Motorsports Chevy	171	9,650	Running
24	25	8	Rick Wilson	Stavola Brothers Buick	165	7,250	Running
25	40	70	J.D.McDuffie	McDuffie Racing Pontiac	152	4,300	Running
26	15	33	Harry Gant	Leo Jackson Olds	150	7,100	Running
27	18	1	Rick Mast	Precision Products Olds	145	7,450	Brakes
28	14	42	Bobby Hillin,Jr.	SabCo Racing Pontiac	132	11,050	Running
29	9	17	Darrell Waltrip	DarWal Chevrolet	115	4,750	Crash
30	30	66	Lake Speed	Cale Yarborough Pontiac	99	6,650	Valve
31	17	43	Richard Petty	Petty Enterprises Pontiac	97	6,575	Crash
32	36	53	John Paul, Jr.	Team Ireland Chevrolet	77	3,850	Engine
33	37	64	Gary Wright	Billy White Chevrolet	63	3,750	Trans
34	26	15	Morgan Shepherd	Bud Moore Eng. Ford	38	10,675	Engine
35	29	24	Dick Trickle	Team III Pontiac	29	4,250	Crash
36	21	10	Derrike Cope	Bob Whitcomb Chevrolet	20	12,925	Crash
37	28	98	Jimmy Spencer	Travis Carter Chevrolet	20	6,075	Crash
38	20	30	Michael Waltrip	Bahari Racing Pontiac	14	6,010	Crash
39	39	35	Bill Venturini	Venturini Chevrolet	7	3,375	Dr Train
40	35	13	Gary Balough	Linro Motorsports Buick	2	3,300	Crash

Time of Race: 3 hours, 52 minutes, 33 seconds
Average Speed: 115.459 mph
Pole Winner: Alan Kulwicki – 161.473 mph
Lap Leaders: Alan Kulwicki 1, Ken Schrader 2-42, Hut Stricklin 43-49, Ernie Irvan 50-60, Schrader 61-66, Dave Marcis 67, Irvan 68-72, Mark Martin 73-80, Dale Jarrett 81-83, Irvan 84-103, Davey Allison 104, Jimmy Means 105, Martin 106-118, Rusty Wallace 119-126, Irvan 127, Wallace 128, Irvan 129-131, Wallace 132-140, Martin 141-142, Geoff Bodine 143, Irvan 144-168, Wallace 169-179.
21 lead changes among 11 drivers.
Cautions: 11 for 48 laps Margin of Victory: Under Caution
Race shortened to 447.5 miles due to rain.

NASCAR officials instructed pace car driver Elmo Langley to move the field back onto the track. Wallace started his car, drove out of the pits and followed the pace car for about a mile. On the backstretch, Wallace cut his engine off and Earnhardt pushed him for nearly two laps.

As the field was preparing for a restart, rain fell again, forcing officials to terminate the race.

As the field took the yellow and white flag starting the 179th lap, Wallace cranked his engine and drove the final lap unassisted.

Mark Martin wound up second as the race was flagged to its conclusion. Third place went to Geoff Bodine with Hut Stricklin fourth and Sterling Marlin fifth.

Wallace said the 'push' was Earnhardt's idea. "We were in the NASCAR truck watching the radar screen during the rain delay," said Wallace. "I told him I was getting low on gas, but I didn't want to pit and give up first place. He said he'd push me and I said 'go for it'."

While Wallace was celebrating a slick move with a racing buddy, Ernie Irvan said the whole deal wasn't kosher.

Irvan was in a challenging position had the race been restarted, but he had to pit under the caution and fell back to seventh place. "I had to pit because we couldn't have gone another lap. I guess I could have gotten someone to push me around. But if I won a race that way, I wouldn't want it."

Irvan avoided a wild 10-car crack-up in the 71st lap – an incident in which Irvan became a target of blame. Stricklin looped his car off the third turn, setting off a wild melee. "We raced into the turn and I beat him

Brian Czobat

Dale Earnhardt spins down the front chute at Pocono after getting caught up in big wreck.

(Irvan) there," said Stricklin, who recovered to finish fourth. "When I did, he touched my bumper. At that place, it doesn't take much to get you spinning. I'm not mad because I came away without much damage. But there are a lot of guys who can't say that."

Irvan insisted he never touched Stricklin. "I got close to him and it must have taken the air off his spoiler and he lost it. I'm getting tired of being blamed for wrecks. If I'm within five car lengths of anything that happens, I get blamed for it."

Darrell Waltrip leveled a verbal salvo without names: "Isn't there anybody out there who knows how to drive a race car? Nobody will give anybody a break. There are people driving so far over their heads it's incredible. It seems like every week someone does something that causes a bunch of cars to get torn up. Nobody will respect the other man."

Other cars involved included Richard Petty, Ricky Rudd, Earnhardt, Bobby Hillin, Jr. and pole sitter Alan Kulwicki.

Earnhardt finished 22nd, while Rudd was 20th. Earnhardt's point lead stood at 140 points with 13 races ramaining.

Race #17

Earnhardt Wins Talladega 500 as Ford Team Plan Flops

TALLADEGA, AL (July 28) – Dale Earnhardt withstood a disjointed Ford team effort and prevailed in a last lap thriller in the DieHard 500 at Talladega Superspeedway.

Earnhardt officially led the final 28 laps, but was pressured by a galley of Ford drivers throughout the frantic final laps. Bill Elliott was flagged in second place, a car length behind Earnhardt's Chevrolet. Mark Martin was third in a Ford, with Ricky Rudd's Chevrolet fourth and Sterling Marlin's Ford fifth.

Jay Kainz

Front row starters Alan Kulwicki and Ken Schrader lead field toward the green flag.

Davey Allison, at the head of a Ford freight train, had nosed past Earnhardt to take the lead with two laps to go, but drifted to a ninth place finish when the teamwork ended abruptly when Elliott pulled out of line.

As Ford drivers Allison, Marlin, Elliott and Martin were coming on like gangbusters, Elliott suddenly pulled out of line and slid into an opening between Earnhardt and Rudd. The move by the Dawsonville, Ga. driver seemed to help Earnhardt keep his momentum and foiled Allison's attempt.

Winston Cup Series Race No. 17
188 Laps at Talladega Superspeedway
Talladega, AL
"DieHard 500"
500.08 Miles on 2.66-mile Superspeedway
July 28, 1991

Fin	St	No.	Driver	Team / Car	Laps	Money	Status
1	4	3	Dale Earnhardt	RCR Enterprises Chevrolet	188	$88,670	Running
2	5	9	Bill Elliott	Melling Performance Ford	188	51,185	Running
3	2	6	Mark Martin	Roush Racing Ford	188	46,390	Running
4	18	5	Ricky Rudd	Hendrick Motorsports Chevy	188	29,400	Running
5	1	22	Sterling Marlin	Junior Johnson Ford	188	27,075	Running
6	8	2	Rusty Wallace	Roger Penske Pontiac	188	16,250	Running
7	13	30	Michael Waltrip	Bahari Racing Pontiac	188	16,050	Running
8	40	21	Dale Jarrett	Wood Brothers Ford	188	14,400	Running
9	7	28	Davey Allison	Robert Yates Racing Ford	188	19,120	Running
10	19	75	Joe Ruttman	RahMoc Racing Olds	188	15,800	Running
11	21	42	Bobby Hillin,Jr.	SabCo Racing Pontiac	188	16,330	Running
12	6	19	Chad Little	Chuck Little Ford	188	8,250	Running
13	34	20	Buddy Baker	Dick Moroso Olds	188	9,930	Running
14	22	15	Morgan Shepherd	Bud Moore Eng. Ford	188	14,860	Running
15	14	17	Darrell Waltrip	DarWal Chevrolet	188	10,135	Running
16	10	7	Alan Kulwicki	AK Racing Ford	187	14,550	Running
17	28	41	Larry Pearson	Larry Hedrick Chevrolet	187	7,385	Running
18	20	43	Richard Petty	Petty Enterprises Pontiac	187	10,880	Running
19	33	47	Greg Sacks	Derick Close Olds	186	7,100	Running
20	24	24	Dick Trickle	Team III Pontiac	186	9,160	Running
21	41	71	Dave Marcis	Marcis Auto Racing Chevy	186	9,980	Running
22	32	73	Phil Barkdoll	Barkdoll Racing Olds	185	6,625	Running
23	36	52	Jimmy Means	Means Racing Pontiac	185	6,370	Running
24	35	94	Terry Labonte	Billy Hagan Olds	184	9,215	Running
25	31	14	Mike Chase	Foyt Enterprises Olds	184	6,110	Running
26	27	55	Ted Musgrave	RaDiUs Pontiac	182	7,635	Running
27	39	95	Eddie Bierschwale	Earl Sadler Chevrolet	181	5,865	Running
28	17	1	Rick Mast	Precision Products Olds	166	8,645	Crash
29	15	12	Hut Stricklin	Bobby Allison Buick	150	8,475	Crash
30	11	11	Geoff Bodine	Junior Johnson Ford	150	14,455	Crash
31	23	49	Stanley Smith	Smith Buick	147	5,985	Oil Press
32	29	26	Brett Bodine	King Motorsports Buick	146	8,215	Oil Press
33	3	4	Ernie Irvan	Morgan-McClure Chevrolet	146	13,645	Crash
34	16	68	Bobby Hamilton	Tri-Star Motorsports Olds	130	5,400	Running
35	37	10	Derrike Cope	Bob Whitcomb Chevrolet	117	13,755	Oil Pan
36	12	66	Lake Speed	Cale Yarborough Pontiac	109	7,995	Axle
37	38	98	Jimmy Spencer	Travis Carter Chevrolet	102	7,945	Engine
38	30	8	Rick Wilson	Stavola Brothers Buick	102	7,895	Crash
39	9	33	Harry Gant	Leo Jackson Olds	90	7,815	Crash
40	25	25	Ken Schrader	Hendrick Motorsports Chevy	77	7,150	Valve
41	26	90	Wally Dallenbach,Jr.	Junie Donlavey Ford	2	5,150	Crash

Time of Race: 3 hours, 23 minutes, 35 seconds
Average Speed: 147.383 mph
Pole Winner: Sterling Marlin – 192.085 mph
Lap Leaders: Mark Martin 1-2, Dale Earnhardt 3-16, Bill Elliott 17, Davey Allison 18-19, Sterling Marlin 20, Michael Waltrip 21-22, Hut Stricklin 23, M.Waltrip 24, Marlin 25, Earnhardt 26-49, Rick Mast 50-52, Darrell Waltrip 53, Marlin 54-64, Earnhardt 65-72, Allison 73, Earnhardt 74-81, Stricklin 82-85, Allison 86-92, Mast 93-99, Ricky Rudd 100-101, Martin 102, Marlin 103-120, Chad Little 121-127, M.Waltrip 128, Marlin 129-130, Allison 131, Earnhardt 132-146, Allison 147, Earnhardt 148-151, Dale Jarrett 152-159, Rusty Wallace 160, Earnhardt 161-188.
32 lead changes among 13 drivers.
Cautions: 7 for 43 laps   Margin of Victory: 1.5 car lengths

Brian Czobat

Dale Earnhardt and Richard Childress in Talladega's Victory Lane.

Following the race, Allison vented his rage by punching the wall of his transporter, breaking his hand.

"All we needed was four more inches to clear Earnhardt," said Allison. "But instead we end up ninth. You could see the Chevy drivers working together. If you trust another Ford driver then they leave you hung out to dry, that's pitiful. We were fighting with each other instead of working together."

Brian Czobat

Bill Elliott leads the pack through Talladega's tri-oval.

ISC

Dale Earnhardt leads the field at Talladega.

him," said Baker, who had come from 34th starting spot to mix it up with the leaders.

Prior to the race, Irvan made a public apology to his fellow drivers, saying, "If I have lost your respect, I want it back. I've been over-aggressive and I'm going to be more patient from now on."

Rick Mast authored the day's most spectacular wreck. In the 167th lap, Mast got nicked and spun through the tri-oval. His Oldsmobile became airborne, and Mast slid for several hundred feet upside down. The Rockbridge Baths, Va. driver emerged unhurt. He had led twice for 10 laps and was still in contention for victory.

Earnhardt's victory enabled the four-time champ to pull to a 160 point advantage over Rudd.

"The Ford guys cut their own throats," said Earnhardt. "I was watching behind me as much as in front of me. Ricky and I were trying to work together. I looked up and saw those Fords coming. When they passed Ricky, I knew I had to work them. I dropped low to block them, and that broke the draft with Ricky. I hated to do that, but I had to look after myself."

Marlin, still looking for his first Winston Cup win, had to settle for fifth. "Bill was the first to get out of the inside lane and get in high with Earnhardt," he remarked. "We just got broke up and, after that, it was like a crap shoot – every man for himself."

Martin, who came back from a flat tire late in the race, came from 17th in the final 15 laps to challenge. He claimed that he told his crew via radio the Ford game plan would not work. "They (other Ford drivers) had hung me out to dry all race long. Nobody would run with me. At the end, the Fords wanted me to work with them and I burned them all."

Ernie Irvan, subject of much criticism during the last two years, was the victim of a 10-car crash in the 106th lap. Buddy Baker, driving the Dick Moroso Oldsmobile, nipped the rear bumper of Irvan, who spun in heavy traffic. Jimmy Spencer, Ted Musgrave, Rick Wilson, Stanley Smith, Lake Speed, Richard Petty, Terry Labonte and Bobby Hamilton were also involved.

"Ernie came straight across the track and I tapped

Race #18

Irvan Wins at Watkins Glen; McDuffie Killed in Crash

WATKINS GLEN, NY (Aug. 11) – Ernie Irvan withstood a last lap challenge from Mark Martin and drove his Chevrolet to victory in the Budweiser At The Glen – a tragic event that took the life of veteran J.D. McDuffie.

McDuffie, a regular on the Winston Cup Series since 1963, died instantly when his Pontiac smashed into a retaining barrier in the dangerous fifth turn of the 2.428-mile road course. The race was halted for an hour and 48 minutes while repairs were made to a guard rail and for rescue workers to remove McDuffie from the demolished car.

The tragic crash occurred in the fifth lap when

Steve Crumbacker

J.D. McDuffie's Pontiac sails high into the air after striking a tire barrier at Watkins Glen. McDuffie died in the crash.

McDuffie lost a tire and hit the Pontiac driven by Jimmy Means. Both cars sailed off the track. McDuffie hit a row of protective tires strapped to the steel barrier and flipped into the air. Means shot directly under the airborne McDuffie and also struck the barrier.

The 52 year-old McDuffie, competing in his 653rd big league NASCAR event, was killed instantly. It took over an hour for rescue workers to remove his body.

Means was uninjured. He climbed from his car and ran to McDuffie's overturned car but quickly pulled out. "It looked like he didn't have any brakes," said Means. "I saw him lose a wheel and he was up in the air before I got to the fence."

Jim Derhaag, an SCCA Trans-Am regular, was behind McDuffie and Means. "When he (McDuffie) got into the braking area, I saw some smoke," said Derhaag. "Like maybe a brake line had ruptured and fluid got on the headers. He just never slowed down."

Irvan passed Ken Schrader with 22 laps to go and was never headed, although Martin made a bold stab at first place in the final lap.

Irvan, who led 39 laps, was leading Martin and third place Davey Allison by inches as they took the white flag. Entering the right first turn, Martin ducked low and established the low line. But Irvan swung to the inside to block Martin's move.

Martin twitched the steering wheel to keep from hitting Irvan and spun his car. Allison looped his car to avoid Martin, which allowed Irvan to scoot away uncontested.

Irvan finished 7.0-seconds ahead of runner-up Ricky Rudd, who was driving a car rebuilt from a practice crash. Martin was able to recover to finish third. Rusty Wallace and Dale Jarrett rounded out the top five.

After the race, winner Irvan dedicated the victory to the fallen McDuffie. "After all I've been through, this is a great victory," said Irvan. "But winning is tempered by J.D.'s death. I dedicate this victory to him. Every time we went through the turn where he crashed, I thought about

Kim Novasat

Dale Earnhardt hugs Darrell Waltrip's rear bumper at Watkins Glen.

Kim Novosat

Terry Labonte spins at Watkins Glen.

him. I've known what it is like to struggle in this sport without a sponsor like he did, and I'll always remember him."

Irvan also tipped his hat to Martin. "He was trying to pass me clean on the last lap," said Irvan. "We were going for the same place at the same time. My hat's off

Kim Novosat

Dale Jarrett loops his Ford at the Glen. He recovered to finish in fifth place.

to him because he could have spun me out."

Martin said he was "within three inches of Ernie when I spun. If I'd kept going, I would have taken him out. I don't race that way. I spun because my line wasn't right. I couldn't get around him."

Allison, who fell to 10th after his spin, said he indicated a last lap scramble. "I knew a wreck was coming and I was where I wanted to be. I thought I was in the right position. When Ernie hit the curb, I thought he would go over it and I could go around him. But he kept his line and Mark spun. I didn't have anywhere to go and spun to keep from hitting him. I just can't believe our dad-gum luck right now."

Winston Cup Series Race No. 18
90 Laps at Watkins Glen Int'l
Watkins Glen, NY
"Budweiser At The Glen"

218.52 Miles on 2.428-mile Road Course
August 11, 1991

Fin	St	No.	Driver	Team / Car	Laps	Money	Status
1	3	4	Ernie Irvan	Morgan-McClure Chevrolet	90	$64,850	Running
2	22	5	Ricky Rudd	Hendrick Motorsports Chevy	90	37,325	Running
3	2	6	Mark Martin	Roush Racing Ford	90	31,440	Running
4	21	2	Rusty Wallace	Roger Penske Pontiac	90	16,680	Running
5	14	21	Dale Jarrett	Wood Brothers Ford	90	18,565	Running
6	7	17	Darrell Waltrip	DarWal Chevrolet	90	11,600	Running
7	19	9	Bill Elliott	Melling Performance Ford	90	16,030	Running
8	30	12	Hut Stricklin	Bobby Allison Buick	90	11,320	Running
9	31	43	Richard Petty	Petty Enterprises Pontiac	90	11,640	Running
10	9	28	Davey Allison	Robert Yates Racing Ford	90	18,100	Running
11	23	19	Chad Little	Chuck Little Ford	90	5,590	Running
12	28	22	Sterling Marlin	Junior Johnson Ford	90	7,250	Running
13	26	10	Derrike Cope	Bob Whitcomb Chevrolet	90	13,560	Running
14	29	75	Joe Ruttman	RahMoc Racing Olds	90	8,720	Running
15	8	3	Dale Earnhardt	RCR Enterprises Chevrolet	90	16,180	Running
16	27	53	John Paul,Jr.	Team Ireland Chevrolet	90	4,610	Running
17	11	24	Dorsey Schroeder	Team III Pontiac	90	6,840	Running
18	16	42	Bobby Hillin,Jr.	SabCo Racing Pontiac	89	11,370	Running
19	17	8	Rick Wilson	Stavola Brothers Buick	89	7,515	Running
20	38	54	Jim Derhaag	Hakes-Welliver Olds	88	5,120	Running
21	40	30	Michael Waltrip	Bahari Racing Pontiac	88	6,995	Running
22	4	11	Geoff Bodine	Junior Johnson Ford	86	12,575	Running
23	12	7	Alan Kulwicki	AK Racing Ford	82	10,680	Radiator
24	39	13	Oma Kimbrough	Linro Motorsports Buick	80	3,620	Oil Line
25	18	26	Brett Bodine	King Motorsports Buick	77	6,685	Engine
26	34	55	Ted Musgrave	RaDiUs Pontiac	76	4,725	Running
27	33	98	Jimmy Spencer	Travis Carter Chevrolet	72	6,265	Engine
28	15	33	Harry Gant	Leo Jackson Oldsmobile	71	6,105	Running
29	32	68	Bobby Hamilton	Tri-Star Motorsports Olds	70	3,995	Running
30	6	25	Ken Schrader	Hendrick Motorsports Chevy	68	6,660	Camshaft
31	37	20	Kim Campbell	Dick Moroso Olds	64	3,725	Crash
32	5	90	Wally Dallenbach,Jr.	Junie Donlavey Ford	58	3,010	Steering
33	10	66	Lake Speed	Cale Yarborough Pontiac	55	5,575	Rear End
34	1	94	Terry Labonte	Billy Hagan Olds	47	9,490	Engine
35	24	1	Rick Mast	Precision Products Olds	41	4,830	Trans
36	25	15	Morgan Shepherd	Bud Moore Eng. Ford	33	9,800	Engine
37	20	71	Dave Marcis	Marcis Auto Racing Chevy	11	4,745	Brakes
38	13	44	Irv Hoerr	Terry Labonte Olds	8	2,710	Engine
39	36	52	Jimmy Means	Means Racing Pontiac	4	2,655	Crash
40	35	70	J.D.McDuffie	McDuffie Racing Pontiac	4	2,595	Crash

Time of Race: 2 hours, 12 minutes, 28 seconds
Average Speed: 98.977 mph
Pole Winner: Terry Labonte – 121.652 mph
Lap Leaders: Terry Labonte 1-19, Ernie Irvan 20-22, Ted Musgrave 23, Geoff Bodine 24-26, Irvan 27-35, Ken Schrader 36, Dale Earnhardt 37, Schrader 38-41, Davey Allison 42-43, Irvan 44-47, Allison 48, Ricky Rudd 49-59, Dorsey Schroeder 60-62, Schrader 63-67, Irvan 68-90.
14 lead changes among 9 drivers.
Cautions: 5 for 11 laps Margin of Victory: 7 seconds

By running second, Rudd reduced his deficit to 108 points behind Winston Cup point leader Dale Earnhardt, who spun with Geoff Bodine early and encountered two penalties for pit road violations. Earnhardt was able to finish 15th on the lead lap.

The fifth turn, where McDuffie's crash occurred, was the subject of much discussion before and after the race. Earlier in the week, other drivers crashed in the same area. Among those were Alan Kulwicki, Rudd, Harry Gant, Ken Schrader, Michael Waltrip, Dave Marcis and Hut Stricklin. Waltrip suffered a broken shoulder in his mishap.

Track president John Saunders said, "Modifications will have to be made at that turn after the end of the season."

Race #19

Jarrett Nips Allison for 10 Inch Victory in Michigan's 400

BROOKLYN, MI (Aug. 18) – Dale Jarrett squeezed past Davey Allison in the final hundred yards and notched his first career Winston Cup victory in the Champion Spark Plug 400 at Michigan International Speedway.

Jarrett and Allison drove the final two laps side-by-side. The cars slapped together several times in the final lap as Jarrett got to the finish line 10 inches ahead. The triumph was the first for the famed Wood Brothers team since Kyle Petty won the 1987 World 600 at Charlotte.

The epic duel at the end put a feather in the finish of an otherwise dull race. Jarrett had not been a factor – leading a single lap during an exchange of pit stops – until the final 10 laps. The fourth and final caution was waved with 12 laps to go for removal of a tailpipe on the backstretch. Allison was holding a four second lead when the final caution came out.

Most of the leaders pitted for fresh tires in preparation for the nine lap shoot-out, but Jarrett took on fuel only and returned to the track with the lead.

"The car was driving absolutely great (before the yellow)," said Jarrett. "It wouldn't have made any sense for us to change tires and take a risk of getting a set that wouldn't have worked as well. All the credit goes to the crew for making the call to get a splash of gas and see if we could hold them off at the end."

Jarrett held the lead when the green flag waved starting the 192nd lap. Allison, who had led for a total of 61 laps, charged up from the pack and moved in to challenge Jarrett.

With two laps to go, Allison moved to the high side, and the two cars stayed abreast for the final four miles. "I was just going to try to hold my line," said Jarrett, whose initial Winston Cup victory came in his 129th start. "I stayed down low because we were good down there. We touched a few times on that last lap, but I'm sure Davey understands with me going for my first win."

For the third straight week, Allison was foiled by a late race turn of events. "I don't like second worth a

Winston Cup Series Race No. 19
200 Laps at Michigan Int'l Speedway
Brooklyn, MI
"Champion Spark Plug 400"
400 Miles on 2-mile Superspeedway
August 18, 1991

Fin	St	No.	Driver	Team / Car	Laps	Money	Status
1	11	21	Dale Jarrett	Wood Brothers Ford	200	$74,150	Running
2	3	28	Davey Allison	Robert Yates Racing Ford	200	47,700	Running
3	9	2	Rusty Wallace	Roger Penske Pontiac	200	23,600	Running
4	2	6	Mark Martin	Roush Racing Ford	200	30,050	Running
5	4	9	Bill Elliott	Melling Performance Ford	200	26,600	Running
6	14	33	Harry Gant	Leo Jackson Olds	200	17,200	Running
7	5	4	Ernie Irvan	Morgan-McClure Chevrolet	200	18,850	Running
8	1	7	Alan Kulwicki	AK Racing Ford	200	21,000	Running
9	21	30	Michael Waltrip	Bahari Racing Pontiac	200	14,850	Running
10	18	25	Ken Schrader	Hendrick Motorsports Chevy	199	16,500	Running
11	12	5	Ricky Rudd	Hendrick Motorsports Chevy	199	15,850	Running
12	8	22	Sterling Marlin	Junior Johnson Ford	199	10,450	Running
13	22	20	Buddy Baker	Dick Moroso Olds	199	9,850	Running
14	17	12	Hut Stricklin	Bobby Allison Buick	198	11,350	Running
15	27	66	Lake Speed	Cale Yarborough Pontiac	198	11,350	Running
16	25	94	Terry Labonte	Billy Hagan Olds	198	10,050	Running
17	15	55	Ted Musgrave	RaDiUs Pontiac	198	8,450	Running
18	30	1	Rick Mast	Precision Products Olds	198	9,450	Running
19	36	68	Bobby Hamilton	Tri-Star Motorsports Olds	198	7,400	Running
20	33	71	Dave Marcis	Marcis Auto Racing Chevy	197	9,750	Ignition
21	31	24	Dick Trickle	Team III Pontiac	196	6,575	Running
22	34	90	Wally Dallenbach,Jr.	Junie Donlavey Ford	196	5,775	Running
23	23	43	Richard Petty	Petty Enterprises Pontiac	195	8,350	Running
24	26	3	Dale Earnhardt	RCR Enterprises Chevrolet	194	16,425	Running
25	16	19	Chad Little	Chuck Little Ford	194	5,525	Running
26	10	15	Morgan Shepherd	Bud Moore Eng. Ford	193	12,975	Running
27	35	52	Jimmy Means	Means Racing Pontiac	193	5,175	Running
28	39	36	H.B.Bailey	Bailey Pontiac	186	5,125	Running
29	38	14	Mike Chase	Foyt Enterprises Olds	156	5,025	Heating
30	32	75	Joe Ruttman	RahMoc Chevrolet	143	7,625	Running
31	37	89	Jim Sauter	Mueller Brothers Pontiac	140	4,825	Crash
32	7	17	Darrell Waltrip	DarWal Chevrolet	134	5,400	Valve
33	20	42	Bobby Hillin,Jr.	SabCo Racing Pontiac	134	11,725	Engine
34	19	10	Derrike Cope	Bob Whitcomb Chevrolet	125	13,075	Engine
35	6	11	Geoff Bodine	Junior Johnson Ford	123	13,925	Engine
36	13	98	Jimmy Spencer	Travis Carter Chevrolet	99	7,200	Engine
37	28	26	Brett Bodine	King Motorsports Buick	57	6,575	Engine
38	40	44	Bobby Labonte	Terry Labonte Olds	40	4,550	Engine
39	29	8	Rick Wilson	Stavola Brothers Buick	39	6,525	Fuel Pres
40	24	49	Stanley Smith	Smith Buick	30	4,475	Ignition

Time of Race: 2 hours, 51 minutes, 34 seconds
Average Speed: 142.972 mph
Pole Winner: Alan Kulwicki – 173.431 mph
Lap Leaders: Alan Kulwicki 1, Mark Martin 2-11, Davey Allison 12-23, Geoff Bodine 24, Jimmy Means 25, Morgan Shepherd 26-40, Allison 41-48, G.Bodine 49-73, Ken Schrader 74-80, Allison 81-90, Bill Elliott 91-117, Ernie Irvan 118, Dale Jarrett 119, Michael Waltrip 120, Allison 121-126, Elliott 127-135, Martin 136, Elliott 137-148, Martin 149, Harry Gant 150-163, Allison 164-187, Martin 188, Jarrett 189-198, Allison 199, Jarrett 200.
24 lead changes among 12 drivers.
Cautions: 4 for 22 laps Margin of Victory: 10 inches

Brian Czobat

Dale Jarrett gives the thumbs up signal after narrowly beating Davey Allison at Michigan.

flip," said the fiery Alabama driver. "I did everything I could, but he got me. It was a close finish, but I knew he had won."

NASCAR officials checked the television tape of the race and confirmed Jarrett had won.

Third place went to Rusty Wallace with Mark Martin fourth and Bill Elliott fifth.

Ricky Rudd finished 11th, a lap off the pace, but still lopped a sizable chunk off of Dale Earnhardt's point lead. Earnhardt wound up 24th and saw his Winston Cup lead reduced to 69 points.

Earnhardt was fortunate he didn't lose more. A tire blew on his RCR Enterprises Chevrolet in the 23rd lap. Although the backstretch was littered with pieces of rubber, NASCAR did not throw the caution until Earnhardt came down pit road. With the yellow out, Earnhardt went by his pits and back onto the track to stay on the lead lap. The extra time on the track did considerable damage to his car.

Earnhardt pitted five times during the yellow flag, which lasted seven laps. Other teams complained that it should not have taken seven laps to clean up the rubber off the backstretch.

Earnhardt went behind the wall for additional repairs and returned to the track losing minimal time. He was six laps in arrears when the race ended.

Alan Kulwicki won the pole position but led only the first lap. The Greenfield, Wisc. driver eventually finished eighth.

Dave Marcis had one of his finer runs going until ignition problems knocked him out in the final two laps. He received credit for 20th place after starting 33rd.

Allison became a mild threat in the Winston Cup chase, moving up to third place, 137 points off the top.

Winston Cup Series Race No. 20
500 Laps at Bristol Int'l Raceway
Bristol, TN
"Bud 500"
266.5 Miles on .533-mile Short Track
August 24, 1991

Fin	St	No.	Driver	Team / Car	Laps	Money	Status
1	5	7	Alan Kulwicki	AK Racing Ford	500	$61,400	Running
2	14	22	Sterling Marlin	Junior Johnson Ford	500	30,275	Running
3	27	25	Ken Schrader	Hendrick Motorsports Chevy	500	22,950	Running
4	10	6	Mark Martin	Roush Racing Ford	499	19,700	Running
5	17	5	Ricky Rudd	Hendrick Motorsports Chevy	499	16,450	Running
6	18	15	Morgan Shepherd	Bud Moore Eng. Ford	498	13,125	Running
7	13	3	Dale Earnhardt	RCR Enterprises Chevrolet	498	16,025	Running
8	3	17	Darrell Waltrip	DarWal Chevrolet	498	9,275	Running
9	28	94	Terry Labonte	Billy Hagan Olds	493	9,225	Running
10	32	26	Brett Bodine	King Motorsports Buick	493	11,875	Running
11	23	66	Lake Speed	Cale Yarborough Pontiac	492	8,425	Running
12	30	43	Richard Petty	Petty Enterprises Pontiac	491	8,125	Running
13	6	68	Bobby Hamilton	Tri-Star Motorsports Olds	490	7,125	Running
14	4	19	Chad Little	Chuck Little Ford	489	5,025	Running
15	11	98	Jimmy Spencer	Travis Carter Chevrolet	489	20,375	Running
16	19	55	Ted Musgrave	RaDiUs Pontiac	488	5,925	Running
17	24	75	Joe Ruttman	RahMoc Racing Olds	483	6,975	Running
18	26	4	Ernie Irvan	Morgan-McClure Chevrolet	449	10,775	Running
19	25	33	Harry Gant	Leo Jackson Olds	436	6,865	Running
20	12	8	Rick Wilson*	Stavola Brothers Buick	409	7,750	Suspension
21	1	9	Bill Elliott	Melling Performance Ford	404	13,575	Running
22	9	12	Hut Stricklin	Bobby Allison Buick	403	6,450	Running
23	22	71	Dave Marcis	Marcis Auto Racing Chevy	400	6,375	Running
24	7	28	Davey Allison	Robert Yates Racing Ford	377	11,550	Engine
25	31	30	Michael Waltrip	Bahari Racing Pontiac	350	6,205	Running
26	8	1	Rick Mast	Precision Products Olds	344	5,575	Crash
27	21	24	Dick Trickle	Team III Pontiac	313	4,050	Ignition
28	16	21	Dale Jarrett	Wood Brothers Ford	253	5,500	Crash
29	20	10	Derrike Cope	Bob Whitcomb Chevrolet	239	11,075	Engine
30	15	42	Bobby Hillin,Jr.	SabCo Racing Pontiac	220	9,625	Running
31	29	11	Geoff Bodine	Junior Johnson Ford	183	11,425	Crash
32	2	2	Rusty Wallace	Roger Penske Pontiac	88	4,425	Crash

Time of Race: 3 hours, 14 minutes, 56 seconds
Average Speed: 82.028 mph
Pole Winner: Bill Elliott – 116.957 mph
Lap Leaders: Rusty Wallace 1-15, Darrell Waltrip 16-50, Davey Allison 51-61, Wallace 62, D.Waltrip 63-65, Michael Waltrip 66-79, Terry Labonte 80-112, Jimmy Spencer 113-317, Sterling Marlin 318-319, Spencer 320, Marlin 321-323, D.Waltrip 324-326, Marlin 327-363, Alan Kulwicki 364-500.
14 lead changes among 8 drivers.
Cautions 11 for 81 laps Margin of Victory: 9 seconds
*Relieved by Bobby Labonte

Race #20

Kulwicki Survives Bristol Bash as Tires Blow and Cars Crash

BRISTOL, TN (Aug. 24) – Alan Kulwicki gamely battled back from a two lap deficit and won the Bud 500 at Bristol International Raceway going away.

The 500-lap contest around Bristol's steeply-banked oval was an evening of horror for most drivers, who repeatedly had tire failures as the track surface peeled and came apart.

Kulwicki was one of the first to encounter tire problems. In the 53rd lap, Kulwicki pitted for new tires and dropped two laps off the pace. Crumbling pavement and ruptured tires sent a number of contenders into the wall and forced many behind the wall for lengthy repairs.

Kulwicki got back into the lead lap on lap 300 and took the lead for keeps 64 laps later. He outran Sterling Marlin by 9.0 seconds to score his third career victory. Ken Schrader finished third, the only other car on the lead lap. Mark Martin was fourth and Ricky Rudd fifth.

Rudd gained nine points on Dale Earnhardt, who finished seventh. The difference between Earnhardt and Rudd is 60 points.

Jimmy Spencer emerged as the prime contender for victory. The Berwick, Penn. driver assumed command in the 113th lap and led through the 317th lap – 205 straight laps. But throttle linkage problems and a penalty for bumping Mark Martin put Spencer well off the pace. He eventually finished 15th, 11 laps off the pace.

"Who would have thought the throttle linage would break," said Spencer, who was driving Travis Carter's Chevrolet. "It wasn't our time to win tonight."

Spencer howled about the penalty for his on-track confrontation with Martin. "Martin did me dirty," claimed Spencer. "He put me in the wall while I was leading the race. He was trying to make up a lap. Then I bump him back a little. And then NASCAR brought me in the pits for rough driving. Well, what do you call what he did to me?"

Ricky Rudd gained little ground in the championship race.

With Spencer's demise, Kulwicki and Marlin were left to battle it out. Marlin led for 37 laps before Kulwicki made the decisive pass.

"We've been down and out," said Kulwicki, the 12th different winner of the 1991 campaign. "We know we can win. We've run well week after week. I hope winning like this gets us over the hump."

Kulwicki said sanctioning NASCAR ought to look into the track conditions at Bristol. "I love to race on this track when it's right. But tonight it was breaking up. We shouldn't have to come back and race on this surface. Winston Cup is supposed to be tops in professional racing, but this track isn't up to par."

Bill Elliott started on the pole but never led.

Bristol Int'l

Dale Jarrett gets sideways on the front stretch at Bristol.

After an assortment of problems, Elliott finished 21st, 96 laps off the pace.

Davey Allison led for 11 laps early in the race but fell victim to engine failure and wound up 24th. The misfortune dropped him to fourth in the standings, 187 points behind Earnhardt.

Bobby Labonte performed an admirable job of relief driving for Rick Wilson. Labonte ran the Stavola Brothers Buick in impressive fashion before suspension problems knocked him out of the race. "Bobby Labonte is a smart kid," said Tim Brewer, crew chief for the Junior Johnson team. "He showed it tonight."

Winston Cup Series Race No. 21
367 Laps at Darlington Raceway
Darlington, SC
"Heinz Southern 500"
501.322 Miles on 1.366-mile Superspeedway
September 1, 1991

Fin	St	No.	Driver	Team / Car	Laps	Money	Status
1	5	33	Harry Gant	Leo Jackson Olds	367	$179,450	Running
2	6	4	Ernie Irvan	Morgan-McClure Chevrolet	367	40,525	Running
3	9	25	Ken Schrader	Hendrick Motorsports Chevy	367	26,940	Running
4	17	10	Derrike Cope	Bob Whitcomb Chevrolet	366	24,330	Running
5	23	94	Terry Labonte	Billy Hagan Olds	366	19,515	Running
6	15	22	Sterling Marlin	Junior Johnson Ford	365	12,875	Running
7	4	11	Geoff Bodine	Junior Johnson Ford	365	18,230	Running
8	3	3	Dale Earnhardt	RCR Enterprises Chevrolet	365	20,470	Running
9	32	75	Joe Ruttman	RahMoc Chevrolet	365	11,990	Running
10	21	68	Bobby Hamilton	Tri-Star Motorsports Olds	364	14,250	Running
11	24	1	Rick Mast	Precision Products Olds	364	11,015	Running
12	1	28	Davey Allison	Robert Yates Racing Ford	363	21,120	Running
13	22	8	Rick Wilson	Stavola Brothers Buick	363	10,930	Running
14	27	26	Brett Bodine	King Motorsports Buick	363	9,940	Running
15	18	5	Ricky Rudd	Hendrick Motorsports Chevy	363	14,100	Running
16	30	43	Richard Petty	Petty Enterprises Pontiac	363	9,380	Running
17	26	12	Hut Stricklin	Bobby Allison Buick	363	9,110	Running
18	2	9	Bill Elliott	Melling Performance Ford	362	13,935	Running
19	11	15	Morgan Shepherd	Bud Moore Eng. Ford	361	12,755	Running
20	31	55	Ted Musgrave	RaDiUs Pontiac	360	7,785	Running
21	33	47	Greg Sacks	Derick Close Olds	358	5,260	Running
22	16	42	Kyle Petty	SabCo Racing Pontiac	357	12,140	Engine
23	14	24	Dick Trickle	Team III Pontiac	354	5,770	Running
24	12	17	Darrell Waltrip	DarWal Chevrolet	351	5,605	Running
25	8	21	Dale Jarrett	Wood Brothers Ford	350	7,545	Running
26	35	87	Randy Baker	Buck Baker Chevrolet	343	4,585	Running
27	29	30	Michael Waltrip	Bahari Racing Pontiac	333	7,150	Running
28	34	52	Jimmy Means	Means Racing Pontiac	309	4,365	Engine
29	10	6	Mark Martin	Roush Racing Ford	303	14,255	Engine
30	19	41	Larry Pearson	Larry Hedrick Chevrolet	244	4,195	Engine
31	20	98	Jimmy Spencer	Travis Carter Chevrolet	220	6,660	Valve
32	13	2	Rusty Wallace	Roger Penske Pontiac	214	5,045	Engine
33	36	71	Dave Marcis	Marcis Auto Racing Chevy	173	6,455	Engine
34	25	66	Lake Speed	Cale Yarborough Pontiac	156	5,820	Engine
35	7	7	Alan Kulwicki	AK Racing Ford	148	10,710	Engine
36	28	19	Chad Little	Chuck Little Ford	123	3,650	Engine
37	37	82	Mark Stahl	Stahl Racing Ford	14	3,580	Flagged
38	38	48	James Hylton	Hylton Engineering Buick	12	3,540	Flagged

Time of Race: 3 hours, 45 minutes, 18 seconds
Average Speed: 133.508 mph
Pole Winner: Davey Allison – 162.506 mph
Lap Leaders: Davey Allison 1-35, Ted Musgrave 36, Dale Earnhardt 37-39, Mark Martin 40-44, Allison 45-56, Ernie Irvan 57-70, Darrell Waltrip 71, Bobby Hamilton 72-73, Earnhardt 74-75, Allison 76-89, Earnhardt 90-106, Allison 107-133, Martin 134-138, Dale Jarrett 139, Hamilton 140-142, Rick Mast 143-150, Harry Gant 151-199, Martin 200-201, Gant 202-234, Allison 235-297, Gant 298-367.
20 lead changes among 10 drivers.
Cautions: 8 for 33 laps Margin of Victory: 10.97 seconds

Race #21

Gant Bags $100,000 Bonus With Southern 500 Victory

DARLINGTON, SC (Sept. 1) – Harry Gant outlasted Davey Allison and Dale Earnhardt and won the Heinz Southern 500 At Darlington Raceway for his second win of the season.

Gant bagged a $100,000 bonus for winning two of the four crown jewel races designated by R.J.Reynolds in their Winston Million package. Gant was victorious in the Winston 500 at Talladega in May.

Gant took the lead from Allison with 70 laps to go and outran runner-up Ernie Irvan by 10.97 seconds to snare the $179,450 first prize, including the bonus. Ken Schrader never led but wound up third. Derrike Cope got a lap down early but turned in his best performance of the year by taking fourth spot. Fifth place went to Terry Labonte.

Gant's road to Victory Lane was paved by misfortune in the Robert Yates Racing camp. Davey Allison started on the pole and appeared to be in control to cash in on the $114,000 Unocal bonus. Allison led for 151 laps before his Ford developed problems. Although he was able to maintain first place for a few laps after the car started sputtering, Allison was destined to make several unscheduled pit stops.

Kim Novasat

Alan Kulwicki whips off Darlington's second turn just ahead of Mark Martin.

Brian Czobat

Harry Gant and wife Peggy share accolades at Darlington.

Car owner Yates said two rivets which held a cowling around an air breather came loose and caused Allison's trouble. The cowling fell into the throttle linkage, causing the linkage to jam.

"I couldn't push the throttle all the way open," explained Allison. "It was sticking down and it was sticking up, and I couldn't get it to full throttle. We were running so good until it happened."

Gant breezed past Allison in the 298th lap and was never headed.

Dale Earnhardt posed as a threat to Gant. The current Winston Cup point leader was whittling Gant's lead down when an axle broke on his RCR Enterprises Chevrolet with 30 laps remaining.

Earnhardt rode the rest of the way at reduced speed and finished in eighth place, two laps behind. Ricky Rudd could do no better than 15th and fell 89 points behind Earnhardt in the chase for the Cup.

Rudd blamed Earnhardt for a mid-race crash that took his car out of contention. "Earnhardt just turned Shepherd sideways," Rudd said afterwards. "Morgan came down right in front of me and it knocked my front end out. I think it is kind of ironic, kind of strange and kind of convenient – for Dale's situation, anyway."

Rudd finished four laps off the pace.

Gant was confident going into the race. With a new set-up under his Leo Jackson Motorsports Oldsmobile – many crews felt Gant had a cambered rear end – the 51 year-old Taylorsville, N.C. driver was near the front all afternoon. "We thought we had 'em covered, but I wasn't sure what the tires were going to do so I held back in the early going," said Gant. "When I decided everything was going to work, I went right to the front."

Gant felt Allison's demise did not affect the outcome

Davey Allison and Bill Elliott duel through Darlington's tight third turn.

of the race. "All afternoon, I caught him and caught him – and I would have caught him again and passed him if he was still in there. I don't think he could have beaten me today."

Gant made no mention of the slick rear-end gadget, nor a possible detractor that it causes extra strain on the axle components.

Engine problems knocked many strong contenders out. Alan Kulwicki started seventh, but retired with a blown engine after completing 148 laps. Rusty Wallace was plagued with continuing engine woes. Mark Martin and Jimmy Spencer also went down with mechanical problems.

Kyle Petty made his first appearance since suffering leg injuries at Talladega in May. Kyle had the SabCo Racing Pontiac in fourth place with 10 laps to go when the engine blew.

"It feels good to get back in and run a race, but I had no rhythm at the start. The car was off and I was off, and I couldn't think about what to change and not to change. Four months out of the car makes a difference," said Petty.

Petty's run was even more impressive when you consider the SabCo team had not logged a single top 10 finish since Petty had been hurt.

Race #22

Harry Hot Under Richmond's Lights; Snares Miller 400

RICHMOND, VA (Sept. 7) – Harry Gant slipped past Davey Allison with 19 laps to go and hustled to victory in the Miller Genuine Draft 400 at Richmond International Raceway. The 300-mile contest was the first event presented under the lights at the 3/4-mile facility.

Gant finished about four car lengths in front of runner-up Allison. Third place went to Rusty Wallace, who led long stretches. Ernie Irvan came home fourth and Ricky Rudd was fifth.

After the final caution flag slowed the action with less than 75 laps remaining, Gant began to pressure Allison for the lead. The standing room only crowd of 65,000 rose to their collective feet as the two leaders engaged in a ferocious fight.

The decisive moment came with less than 20 laps to go. Gant ducked under Allison and was able to trap his rival behind the lapped car of Terry Labonte. Gant whizzed into the lead and kept Allison at bay for the final 19 laps.

"Davey was awfully, awfully hard to beat," said Gant after winning two consecutive races for the first time in his career. "I tried as hard as I could for several laps to pass him. I didn't make it and backed off to save my tires for one last try. He started sliding a little in the corners and I got beside him. When we came up on Labonte, he was in front of me instead of Davey. I saw it was going to be tight.

"Somebody had to slow down first, and Davey did. I would have if he hadn't because I didn't want someone else to win because of us wrecking. As it turned out, I got by pretty clean."

Allison said, "I want to thank Harry for running a clean race. We ran a lot of laps side-by-side and he

Winston Cup Series Race No. 22
400 Laps at Richmond Int'l Raceway
Richmond, VA
"Miller Genuine Draft 400"
300 Miles on .75-mile Short Track
September 7, 1991

Fin	St	No.	Driver	Team / Car	Laps	Money	Status
1	13	33	Harry Gant	Leo Jackson Olds	400	$63,650	Running
2	3	28	Davey Allison	Robert Yates Racing Ford	400	39,425	Running
3	1	2	Rusty Wallace	Roger Penske Pontiac	400	21,700	Running
4	6	4	Ernie Irvan	Morgan-McClure Chevrolet	400	20,800	Running
5	7	5	Ricky Rudd	Hendrick Motorsports Chevy	400	18,125	Running
6	2	7	Alan Kulwicki	AK Racing Ford	400	13,550	Running
7	9	17	Darrell Waltrip	DarWal Chevrolet	400	9,750	Running
8	10	25	Ken Schrader	Hendrick Motorsports Chevy	400	8,750	Running
9	14	9	Bill Elliott	Melling Performance Ford	400	11,950	Running
10	15	22	Sterling Marlin	Junior Johnson Ford	399	9,700	Running
11	16	3	Dale Earnhardt	RCR Enterprises Chevrolet	398	13,750	Running
12	5	68	Bobby Hamilton	Tri-Star Motorsports Olds	398	6,400	Running
13	27	8	Rick Wilson	Stavola Brothers Buick	397	7,000	Running
14	18	11	Geoff Bodine	Junior Johnson Ford	397	11,500	Running
15	17	98	Jimmy Spencer	Travis Carter Chevrolet	397	7,350	Running
16	22	10	Derrike Cope	Bob Whitcomb Chevrolet	397	10,925	Running
17	28	66	Lake Speed	Cale Yarborough Pontiac	397	6,425	Running
18	21	26	Brett Bodine	King Motorsports Buick	396	5,175	Running
19	20	94	Terry Labonte	Billy Hagan Olds	396	6,000	Running
20	25	21	Dale Jarrett	Wood Brothers Ford	396	6,925	Running
21	11	12	Hut Stricklin	Bobby Allison Buick	396	5,800	Running
22	35	55	Ted Musgrave	RaDiUs Pontiac	395	4,475	Running
23	32	15	Morgan Shepherd	Bud Moore Eng. Ford	394	9,175	Running
24	19	43	Richard Petty	Petty Enterprises Pontiac	393	5,550	Running
25	26	90	Wally Dallenbach,Jr.	Junie Donlavey Ford	391	3,500	Running
26	8	42	Kyle Petty	SabCo Racing Pontiac	388	9,075	Running
27	12	1	Rick Mast	Precision Products Olds	377	5,480	Running
28	34	75	Joe Ruttman	RahMoc Olds	374	5,325	Running
29	33	71	Dave Marcis	Marcis Auto Racing Chevy	370	4,800	Running
30	31	30	Michael Waltrip	Bahari Racing Pontiac	361	4,750	Engine
31	29	24	Kenny Wallace	Team III Pontiac	348	3,200	Rear End
32	23	47	Greg Sacks	Derick Close Olds	256	3,175	Heating
33	4	6	Mark Martin	Roush Racing Ford	253	11,870	Running
34	30	19	Chad Little	Chuck Little Ford	55	3,150	Crash
35	36	52	Jimmy Means	Means Racing Pontiac	36	3,150	Engine
36	24	41	Larry Pearson	Larry Hedrick Chevrolet	9	3,150	Crash

Time of Race: 2 hours, 57 minutes, 35 seconds
Average Speed: 101.361 mph
Pole Winner: Rusty Wallace – 120.590 mph
Lap Leaders: Rusty Wallace 1-57, Richard Petty 58, Dale Earnhardt 59-63, Alan Kulwicki 64-72, Ernie Irvan 73-136, Davey Allison 137-218, Harry Gant 219-226, R.Wallace 227-291, Ricky Rudd 292, R.Wallace 293-294, Irvan 295-308, Kulwicki 309, Irvan 310-311, Ken Schrader 312-313, Allison 314-381, Gant 382-400.
15 lead changes among 9 drivers.
Cautions: 9 for 43 laps Margin of Victory: 4 car lengths

Kim Novosat

Larry Pearson tagged the wall early at Richmond.

could have muscled me out of the way if he wanted to."

Allison and Wallace were handed down penalties by NASCAR for pit road violations. Allison had gone from first to 11th when a crewman had trouble with a balky lug nut during a pit stop on lap 218. He had managed to get back into second place – behind Wallace – when both were sent to the rear for speeding on pit road. "We had a fast pit stop and beat everybody out," said a disgusted Allison, "and we get black-flagged for running too fast. I thought I was doing what I was supposed to do."

Wallace said his penalty, which took place with just over 100 laps remaining, voided his attempt to capture the $122,600 Unocal bonus money. After winning the pole, Wallace led three times for 124 laps – but he was never able to lead after his penalty. "NASCAR messed up when they said we came down pit road too fast," claimed Wallace. "I couldn't have been speeding because I stayed even with the pace car and never passed it. I thought I had the race won. Trying to come from dead last really killed me. I had to use a good set of tires up trying to catch up. I was just too far behind."

Ernie Irvan took over the lead after Wallace and Allison were flagged to the rear. The Modesto, Calif. Chevrolet driver engaged in a tight duel with Alan Kulwicki until the two crashed on lap 312. Kulwicki eased into the side of Irvan's car, causing both to spin. Gant, running close behind, took the low groove but made contact with Morgan Shepherd, sending both of them into a spin. Gant was able to recover quickly. Kulwicki and Irvan were also able to get back in the running without losing a lap.

Rudd was able to close to within 54 points of Winston Cup leader Dale Earnhardt, who lost a cylinder with about 100 laps to go and limped home 11th. Earnhardt was fortunate that four yellow flags in the final 75 miles caused him to lose only two laps.

Car owner Richard Childress was elated with

Kim Novosat

Terry Labonte leads Brett Bodine and Geoff Bodine through Richmond's fourth turn.

finishing 11th. "When we lost the cylinder, I told Dale to keep running as hard as he could," said Childress. "We took a gamble by having him not take it easy. We could have blown up and finished last."

Darrell Waltrip, who finished seventh, praised the Childress team. "That's why it's so hard to beat them for the championship. I've seen them have trouble time after time, and they end up in better shape than most of us when we don't have trouble. It's amazing," said Waltrip.

Winston Cup Series Race No. 23
500 Laps at Dover Downs Int'l Speedway
Dover, DE
"Peak AntiFreeze 500"
500 Miles on 1-mile Superspeedway
September 15, 1991

Fin	St	No.	Driver	Team / Car	Laps	Money	Status
1	10	33	Harry Gant	Leo Jackson Olds	500	$67,100	Running
2	3	11	Geoff Bodine	Junior Johnson Ford	499	42,225	Running
3	21	15	Morgan Shepherd	Bud Moore Eng. Ford	499	31,250	Running
4	19	12	Hut Stricklin	Bobby Allison Buick	499	20,350	Running
5	13	30	Michael Waltrip	Bahari Racing Pontiac	498	17,625	Running
6	11	24	Dick Trickle	Team III Pontiac	496	11,850	Running
7	24	5	Ricky Rudd	Hendrick Motorsports Chevy	493	15,800	Running
8	16	68	Bobby Hamilton	Tri-Star Motorsports Olds	493	10,950	Running
9	20	1	Rick Mast	Precision Products Olds	493	11,450	Running
10	31	71	Dave Marcis	Marcis Auto Racing Chevy	490	13,050	Running
11	30	9	Bill Elliott	Melling Performance Ford	498	14,400	Running
12	18	42	Kyle Petty*	SabCo Racing Pontiac	470	12,900	Crash
13	33	75	Joe Ruttman	RahMoc Racing Olds	463	9,200	Running
14	17	55	Ted Musgrave	RaDiUs Pontiac	454	6,850	Running
15	12	3	Dale Earnhardt	RCR Enterprises Chevrolet	447	16,700	Running
16	25	19	Chad Little	Chuck Little Ford	443	5,950	Running
17	9	22	Sterling Marlin	Junior Johnson Ford	429	5,750	Running
18	34	98	Jimmy Spencer	Travis Carter Chevrolet	402	7,485	Crash
19	14	17	Darrell Waltrip	DarWal Chevrolet	395	5,300	Camshaft
20	29	43	Richard Petty	Petty Enterprises Pontiac	389	6,200	Engine
21	4	6	Mark Martin	Roush Racing Ford	366	13,450	Heating
22	32	49	Stanley Smith	Smith Buick	364	4,400	Heating
23	35	52	Jimmy Means	Means Racing Pontiac	345	4,350	Heating
24	1	7	Alan Kulwicki	AK Racing Ford	323	15,800	Crash
25	7	2	Rusty Wallace	Roger Penske Pontiac	322	5,025	Crash
26	23	94	Terry Labonte	Billy Hagan Olds	302	6,850	Engine
27	37	90	Steve Perry	Junie Donlavey Ford	244	4,150	Engine
28	5	4	Ernie Irvan	Morgan-McClure Chevrolet	202	11,100	Heating
29	22	8	Rick Wilson	Stavola Brothers Buick	165	6,675	Crash
30	15	41	Larry Pearson	Larry Hedrick Chevrolet	159	4,000	Steering
31	2	28	Davey Allison	Robert Yates Racing Ford	115	14,200	Engine
32	26	26	Brett Bodine	King Motorsports Buick	115	6,500	Crash
33	6	25	Ken Schrader	Hendrick Motorsports Chevy	68	5,850	Crash
34	8	21	Dale Jarrett	Wood Brothers Ford	68	5,800	Crash
35	27	66	Lake Speed	Cale Yarborough Pontiac	67	5,600	Crash
36	28	10	Derrike Cope	Bob Whitcomb Chevrolet	67	11,975	Crash
37	39	48	James Hylton	Hylton Engineering Buick	54	3,550	Flagged
38	38	56	Jerry Hill	Willie Tierney Pontiac	39	3,500	Vibration
39	36	58	Brian Ross	Ross Racing Chevrolet	37	3,475	Steering
40	40	59	Andy Belmont	Pat Rissi Ford	11	3,450	Flagged

Time of Race: 4 hours, 32 minutes, 17 seconds
Average Speed: 110.179 mph
Pole Winner: Alan Kulwicki – 146.825 mph
Lap Leaders: Davey Allison 1-114, Alan Kulwicki 115-122, Rusty Wallace 123, Dale Earnhardt 124-144, R.Wallace 145-169, Ricky Rudd 170, Harry Gant 171-256, R.Wallace 257-258, Geoff Bodine 259-260, Gant 261-500.
10 lead changes among 7 drivers.
Cautions: 9 for 70 laps Margin of Victory: 1 lap & 2.75 seconds
*Relieved by Davey Allison

Kim Novosat

Harry Gant engaged in a close battle with Geoff Bodine before pulling away to a one-lap victory.

Race #23

Gant Laps Field at Dover; Rudd Inches Closer to Earnhardt

DOVER, DE (Sept. 15) – Harry Gant led all but four of the final 330 laps and cruised to an easy triumph in the Peak AntiFreeze 500 at Dover Downs International Speedway. It was the third straight win and the 15th in the career for the 51 year-old Taylorsville, N.C. Oldsmobile driver.

Gant started 10th on the grid in his car he dubbed as the "X-1 Project". He picked his way around the mechanical carnage and hustled into the lead for the first time on lap 171. By that time, many of the contenders were sidelined because of wrecks – and a number of others were behind the wall for lengthy repairs.

The biggest collision of the afternoon came on the backstretch of the 69th lap. Geoff Bodine and lap-behind Chad Little collided following a restart, setting off a wild scramble that involved Ken Schrader, Dale Jarrett, Derrike Cope, Lake Speed, Larry Pearson, Ernie Irvan and Sterling Marlin.

Bodine recovered to finish second, a lap behind the

Kim Novosat

Sterling Marlin guides his badly crunched Ford down Dover's pit road.

winner. It was the first Winston Cup event where a driver lapped the entire field since Kyle Petty won the 1987 World 600 at Charlotte by over a lap.

Third place went to Morgan Shepherd, who enjoyed his finest run of the season. Hut Stricklin came home fourth and Michael Waltrip was fifth.

Dale Earnhardt was involved in a crash when he hit a spinning Alan Kulwicki in the 325th lap. "The engine blew going into the third turn with no warning," said Kulwicki. "I hit the wall pretty hard and then somebody else hit me after that. I think I'm okay. That's racing."

Rusty Wallace, who was running in third place, slammed into the wall with Kulwicki. "We went into the corner and Alan blew a motor and that threw oil everywhere. I took a big slide in the oil and got into the wall," explained Wallace.

Earnhardt had been in position to increase his point lead until contact with Kulwicki's Ford sent him to the garage for a half hour. "I thought I was getting ready to pick up a bunch of points on Rudd," said Earnhardt. "But then the wreck got us. I just want to get out of here and go on to the next race."

Earnhardt managed to finish 15th as only 17 cars were around at the finish. Rudd battled an ill-handling car to seventh place, seven laps off the pace. Earnhardt left Dover with a 36 point lead in the Winston Cup standings.

Kyle Petty, making his third start since returning from his Talladega injuries, had to call on relief help from Davey Allison in the middle stages. Petty returned to the seat late in the race, but a tire let go on his SabCo Racing Pontiac sending him hard into the wall. Petty was placed on a stretcher and examined at the infield hospital. He said he had bruised his left leg, the same leg that was broken at Talladega.

Allison led the first 114 laps from his outside front row starting position before a blown engine put his Robert Yates Racing Ford out of the hunt.

Steve Crumbacker

Dale Earnhardt nails Alan Kulwicki in savage crash at Dover.

With the high rate of attrition, a number of lesser known drivers were able to record good finishes. Dick Trickle gave the Team III effort headed by Sam McMahon its best finish. Trickle was able to bring the unsponsored Pontiac home sixth.

Rookie Bobby Hamilton finished in eighth place. Veteran driver Dave Marcis came from 31st starting spot to finish 10th.

Race #24

Gant Grips Goody's 500 Gold Despite Crash With Wallace

MARTINSVILLE, VA (Sept. 22) – In spite of a late race collision with Rusty Wallace, Harry Gant's September winning streak remained intact, authoring a dramatic comeback victory in Martinsville Speedway's Goody's 500. It was the fourth consecutive win for the Oldsmobile driver.

Gant had assumed command for the first time in the 196th lap – and would remain on top for 177 of the next 179 laps. His domination ended when Wallace knocked him into a spin while trying to move into first place.

Gant's car spun backwards into the wall and was clipped by Morgan Shepherd and Derrike Cope. Miraculously, Gant was able to stay on the lead lap and he pitted several times for repairs during the seven lap caution.

"I don't think Rusty spun me intentionally," said Gant. "He went into the corner too hard. I guess he thought he could make it, but there's no way you can go that hard into a corner and keep from drifting up into somebody. It upset me at first, but I cooled down and ran some consistent laps after that."

Gant restarted the race in 12th place. "I was just hoping that somehow we could get a top five finish out of it," added Gant. "But when I moved into the top five, I noticed that none of the other cars were running away from me. I started thinking about winning again."

Bryan Hallman

Michael Waltrip, Darrell Waltrip and Davey Allison in tight quarters at Martinsville Speedway.

Gant was able to dispose of leader Brett Bodine in the 454th lap and led the rest of the way. Bodine was second at the finish, one second behind the winner. Dale Earnhardt took third place with Ernie Irvan fourth and pole sitter Mark Martin fifth.

Wallace wound up in seventh place as the top 10 finishers all completed the 500 laps. "I guess I drove too hard into the turn," Wallace said of the tangle with Gant. "I had felt it was time for me to go for it. After the wreck, something happened to the car. I couldn't accelerate off the corners."

Brett Bodine started second and ran among the leaders throughout the race. He led four times for a total of 95

Brian Czobat

Richard Petty, a 13-time winner at Martinsville, gets his Pontiac loose and whacks the wall in Goody's 500.

Winston Cup Series Race No. 24
500 Laps at Martinsville Speedway
Martinsville, VA
"Goody's 500"
262.5 Miles on .525-mile Short Track
September 22, 1991

Fin	St	No.	Driver	Team / Car	Laps	Money	Status
1	12	33	Harry Gant	Leo Jackson Olds	500	$64,000	Running
2	2	26	Brett Bodine	King Motorsports Buick	500	36,625	Running
3	5	3	Dale Earnhardt	RCR Enterprises Chevrolet	500	30,350	Running
4	13	4	Ernie Irvan	Morgan-McClure Chevrolet	500	19,300	Running
5	1	6	Mark Martin	Roush Racing Ford	500	24,575	Running
6	26	94	Terry Labonte	BILLY Hagan Olds	500	12,900	Running
7	7	2	Rusty Wallace	Roger Penske Pontiac	500	11,500	Running
8	4	5	Ricky Rudd	Hendrick Motorsports Chevy	500	15,300	Running
9	9	25	Ken Schrader	Hendrick Motorsports Chevy	500	10,700	Running
10	18	24	Jimmy Hensley	Team III Pontiac	500	11,300	Running
11	10	15	Morgan Shepherd	Bud Moore Eng. Ford	499	12,135	Running
12	8	42	Kyle Petty	SabCo Racing Pontiac	499	11,150	Running
13	16	1	Rick Mast	Precision Products Olds	499	8,150	Running
14	31	22	Sterling Marlin	Junior Johnson Ford	499	6,450	Running
15	3	17	Darrell Waltrip	DarWal Chevrolet	497	7,900	Running
16	14	12	Hut Stricklin	Bobby Allison Buick	497	7,450	Running
17	11	68	Bobby Hamilton	Tri-Star Motorsports Olds	497	6,950	Running
18	20	21	Dale Jarrett	Wood Brothers Ford	496	6,755	Running
19	23	10	Derrike Cope	Bob Whitcomb Chevrolet	495	12,250	Running
20	32	55	Ted Musgrave	RaDiUs Pontiac	495	6,025	Running
21	28	71	Dave Marcis	Marcis Auto Racing Chevrolet	492	6,125	Running
22	6	7	Alan Kulwicki	AK Racing Ford	485	9,550	Running
23	19	11	Geoff Bodine	Junior Johnson Ford	484	11,050	Running
24	24	19	Chad Little	Chuck Little Ford	480	3,500	Running
25	17	30	Michael Waltrip	Bahari Racing Pontiac	458	5,650	Running
26	22	8	Rick Wilson	Stavola Brothers Buick	447	5,400	Running
27	15	9	Bill Elliott	Melling Performance Ford	437	9,950	Running
28	21	98	Jimmy Spencer	Travis Carter Chevrolet	429	5,150	Running
29	25	28	Davey Allison	Robert Yates Racing Ford	402	10,350	Running
30	29	43	Richard Petty	Petty Enterprises Pontiac	348	4,500	Crash
31	30	75	Joe Ruttman	RahMoc Racing Olds	271	4,500	Crash
32	27	66	Lake Speed	Cale Yarborough Pontiac	239	4,500	Brakes

Time of Race: 3 hours, 31 minutes, 42 seconds
Average Speed: 74.535 mph
Pole Winner: Mark Martin - 93.171 mph
Lap Leaders: Mark Martin 1-13, Ricky Rudd 14-15, Brett Bodine 16-25, Alan Kulwicki 26-44, Chad Little 45-52, B.Bodine 53-88, Jimmy Spencer 89-124, Rusty Wallace 125-138, Dale Earnhardt 139-145, R.Wallace 146-195, Harry Gant 196-210, Dave Marcis 211, Gant 212-263, Hut Stricklin 264, Gant 265-375, Earnhardt 376-377, Ernie Irvan 378-439, B.Bodine 440-447, Gant 448, B.Bodine 449-453, Gant 454-500.
20 lead changes among 12 drivers.
Cautions: 15 for 81 laps Margin of Victory: 1 second

laps. "We did as good as we could against a guy who can do no wrong," said the Buick driver. "I ran out of brakes, out of engine and out of driver. I gave it all I had. Harry was the class of the field. We ran decent enough but not good enough to win."

Jimmy Hensley was tabbed to drive the Pontiac fielded by the Team III unit which has struggled all year. Hensley got into the top five late in the race before fading to 10th in the final laps.

"We almost pulled off a miracle and got a top five finish," said Hensley, who has been running Winston Cup races off and on since 1972. "But having to pit on the backstretch killed us. We had to start in the back every single time we pitted under the yellow."

Earnhardt was able to pad his Winston Cup lead to 59

Brian Czobat

Alan Kulwicki led early at Martinsville but fell to a 22nd place finish.

points over Ricky Rudd, who finished eighth.

Rudd survived a tangle and spin with Richard Petty when the two ran up on the disabled car manned by Michael Waltrip. "When Michael broke, I went to the left and Richard went to the right," said Rudd. "When we got to the turn, I don't guess Richard knew I was there." Rudd lost a lap, but was able to make it up during the Gant-Wallace spin.

Race #25

10¢ Part Costs Gant $170,000; Earnhardt Wins Wilkesboro

N.WILKESBORO, NC (Sept. 29) – Harry Gant's September winning streak came to a disheartening end at North Wilkesboro Speedway as Dale Earnhardt captured the Tyson Holly Farms 400. It was Earnhardt's first tour win since July.

Gant started on the pole and led for 350 of the 400 laps, but brake failure – caused by a malfunctioning 'O'-ring valued at 10¢ – interrupted his bid to become the first driver to win five races in a row in the Modern Era.

"The brake peddle went swoosh – all the way to the floor," said Gant, who was in line to pocket the $144,400 Unocal bonus, plus first place money. "I didn't say anything to my crew on the radio because I didn't want any of Earnhardt's crew to become aware that we were having trouble. With 10 laps to go, I had zero brakes. I had to let him (Earnhardt) go because we would have wrecked if I tried to race him. I don't do people like that."

Gant had the field covered from the start. Winning his first pole since 1987 was an indication. He also jumped out of the box and led the first 252 laps. Morgan Shepherd led 41 laps before Gant went ahead again. The Taylorsville, N.C. driver led until Earnhardt made the decisive pass with nine laps to go.

Gant was able to hold on to second and wound up 1.47 seconds behind Earnhardt at the finish line. Shepherd was third followed by Davey Allison and Mark Martin.

Earnhardt was able to pad his Winston Cup lead to 112 points over Ricky Rudd, who struggled once again and could only manage a 12th place finish. "It's a two man race now for the championship," said Earnhardt. "With our run of bad luck lately, the pressure has been on us. Now, I think the heat is on Rudd."

Brian Czobat

Joe Ruttman slips toward the wall at North Wilkesboro.

Despite Gant's incredible string of successes, he has virtually no hope of challenging for the Winston Cup title. The point system used to determine the champion puts little emphasis on winning races. Gant has won five times more races and has three more top five finishes than Rudd, but trails second place Rudd by 252 points.

Eight caution periods broke the action. Rick Wilson sent Joe Ruttman into the wall in the 94th lap, bringing out the first yellow flag. Later, in the 241st lap, Ruttman returned the favor, putting Wilson nose-first into the wall. Ruttman was held for five laps in NASCAR's penalty box for rough driving. After the race, officials had to separate Wilson and Ruttman as they and their

Winston Cup Series Race No. 25
400 Laps at North Wilkesboro Speedway
N.Wilkesboro, NC
"Tyson Holly Farms 400"
250 Miles on .625-mile Short Track

September 29, 1991

Fin	St	No.	Driver	Team / Car	Laps	Money	Status
1	16	3	Dale Earnhardt	RCR Enterprises Chevrolet	400	$69,350	Running
2	1	33	Harry Gant	Leo Jackson Olds	400	40,575	Running
3	9	15	Morgan Shepherd	Bud Moore Eng. Ford	400	25,375	Running
4	2	28	Davey Allison	Robert Yates Racing Ford	400	19,600	Running
5	3	6	Mark Martin	Roush Racing Ford	400	18,875	Running
6	7	2	Rusty Wallace	Roger Penske Pontiac	400	8,950	Running
7	11	26	Brett Bodine	King Motorsports Buick	400	9,280	Running
8	10	25	Ken Schrader	Hendrick Motorsports Chevy	400	8,425	Running
9	5	21	Dale Jarrett	Wood Brothers Ford	400	7,975	Running
10	4	7	Alan Kulwicki	AK Racing Ford	400	13,355	Running
11	27	24	Jimmy Hensley	Team III Pontiac	399	5,975	Running
12	22	5	Ricky Rudd	Hendrick Motorsports Chevy	399	9,959	Running
13	20	22	Sterling Marlin	Junior Johnson Ford	398	5,500	Running
14	19	94	Terry Labonte	Billy Hagan Olds	398	6,750	Running
15	14	11	Geoff Bodine	Junior Johnson Ford	398	12,050	Running
16	21	42	Kyle Petty	SabCo Racing Pontiac	397	9,550	Running
17	17	12	Hut Stricklin	Bobby Allison Buick	397	6,475	Running
18	13	68	Bobby Hamilton	Tri-Star Motorsports Olds	397	5,375	Running
19	33	43	Richard Petty	Petty Enterprises Pontiac	396	5,875	Running
20	15	17	Darrell Waltrip	DarWal Chevrolet	395	5,350	Running
21	25	19	Chad Little	Chuck Little Ford	394	3,450	Running
22	30	55	Ted Musgrave	RaDiUs Pontiac	394	4,375	Running
23	12	98	Jimmy Spencer	Travis Cater Chevrolet	393	5,425	Running
24	8	9	Bill Elliott	Melling Performance Ford	392	9,925	Running
25	18	1	Rick Mast	Precision Products Olds	391	5,400	Running
26	31	66	Chuck Bown	Cale Yarborough Pontiac	391	5,225	Running
27	28	30	Michael Waltrip	Bahari Racing Pontiac	391	4550	Running
28	32	52	Jimmy Means	Means Racing Olds	390	2,985	Running
29	26	75	Joe Ruttman	RahMoc Chevrolet	353	4,450	Running
30	23	10	Derrike Cope	Bob Whitcomb Chevrolet	320	10,075	Running
31	24	71	Dave Marcis	Marcis Auto Racing Chevy	315	4,400	Rear End
32	29	8	Rick Wilson	Stavola Brothers Buick	240	4,425	Crash
33	6	4	Ernie Irvan	Morgan-McClure Chevrolet	164	9,225	Crash

Time of Race: 2 hours 39 minutes, 23 seconds
Average Speed: 94.113 mph
Pole Winner: Harry Gant – 116.871 mph
Lap Leaders: Harry Gant 1-252, Morgan Shepherd 253-293, Gant 294-391, Dale Earnhardt 392-400.
3 lead changes among 3 drivers.
Cautions: 8 for 43 laps   Margin of Victory: 1.47 seconds

Bryan Hallman

Richard Petty's Pontiac gets on top of Chad Little's Ford at North Wilkesboro.

Brian Czobat

Eventual winner Dale Earnhardt passes King Richard at North Wilkesboro.

respective crews went at each other.

Ernie Irvan, third ranking driver in the standings, clobbered the wall after a tire let go in the 165th lap. He wound up dead last and saw any fleeting hopes of making a run at the championship disappear.

Chuck Bown took the wheel of Cale Yarborough's Pontiac in the 400-lapper. Lake Speed, driver since March, was released. Jeff Gordon, talented driver in the Busch Grand National ranks, turned down Yarborough's offer to drive the car.

Bown had to take a provisional spot to get in the race, and he finished 26th. The Yarborough Motorsports car has not had a top 10 finish all season.

A 33-car field made up the starting grid. Jimmy Means accepted the second provisional spot and Richard Petty took a champion's spot and lined up 33rd. Petty finished 19th, four laps behind the winner.

Race #26

Bodine Ends Skid at Charlotte; Crews Question Size of Fuel Tank

CONCORD, NC (Oct. 6) – Geoff Bodine ran the final 114 miles without refueling and won the disputed Mello Yello 500 at Charlotte Motor Speedway. It was the first win for Bodine and his Junior Johnson team in the 1991 campaign - and it gave Johnson at least one victory in each of his last 26 seasons as a car owner.

But controversy stirred as soon as the race ended when Bodine pulled to the refueling tanks. NASCAR officials said they wanted to check the size of the fuel tank which carried the winner to Victory Lane.

For the record, Bodine finished 11.28 seconds ahead of Davey Allison. Alan Kulwicki finished third in a 1-2-3 sweep for Ford Thunderbirds. Harry Gant came across the stripe in fourth place with Sterling Marlin fifth.

Bodine took the lead for keeps with 17 laps to go when Allison had to pit for fuel. Virtually every rival crew chief expected Bodine to pit or run out of gas in the final laps. But Bodine feathered the throttle during the final 10 laps and coasted home unchallenged.

"We knew we couldn't outrun Allison," said Bodine after his 11th career Winston Cup triumph. "My hat's off to my crew. They knew we could top off our tank during that last caution (on lap 257) and we would have enough fuel to make it to the end."

Brian Czobat

Bill Elliott, taking one of his final rides in the Melling Performance Ford, leads the way into Charlotte's first turn.

Brian Czobat

Crew chief Tim Brewer and Mello Yello 500 winner Geoff Bodine enjoy their first trip to Victory Lane in 1991.

Winston Cup Series Race No. 26
334 Laps at Charlotte Motor Speedway
Concord, NC
"Mello Yello 500"

501 Miles on 1.5-mile Superspeedway
October 6, 1991

Fin	St	No.	Driver	Team / Car	Laps	Money	Status
1	6	11	Geoff Bodine	Junior Johnson Ford	334	$92,200	Running
2	2	28	Davey Allison	Robert Yates Racing Ford	334	69,350	Running
3	3	7	Alan Kulwicki	AK Racing Ford	333	47,250	Running
4	17	33	Harry Gant	Leo Jackson Olds	333	31,350	Running
5	13	22	Sterling Marlin	Junior Johnson Ford	331	25,100	Running
6	24	94	Terry Labonte	Billy Hagan Olds	330	20,300	Running
7	11	30	Michael Waltrip	Bahari Racing Pontiac	330	17,700	Running
8	19	26	Brett Bodine	King Motorsports Buick	330	16,000	Running
9	12	17	Darrell Waltrip	DarWal Chevrolet	329	12,500	Running
10	27	19	Chad Little	Chuck Little Ford	329	12,300	Running
11	9	9	Bill Elliott	Melling Performance Ford	329	16,700	Running
12	39	43	Richard Petty	Petty Enterprises Pontiac	329	11,400	Running
13	18	1	Rick Mast	Precision Products Olds	329	10,600	Running
14	31	55	Ted Musgrave	RaDiUs Pontiac	328	9,050	Running
15	7	42	Kyle Petty	SabCo Racing Pontiac	327	13,625	Running
16	32	75	Joe Ruttman	RahMoc Racing Olds	326	8,200	Running
17	23	8	Rick Wilson	Stavola Brothers Buick	325	7,800	Running
18	35	53	Bobby Hillin,Jr.	Team Ireland Chevrolet	324	4,600	Running
19	41	90	Wally Dallenbach,Jr.	Junie Donlavey Ford	323	4,700	Running
20	25	24	Jimmy Hensley	Team III Pontiac	323	6,150	Running
21	38	99	Brad Teague	Ralph Ball Chevrolet	322	4,175	Running
22	30	49	Stanley Smith	Smith Chevrolet	321	4,050	Running
23	33	98	Jimmy Spencer	Travis Carter Chevrolet	319	6,700	Ignition
24	29	52	Jimmy Means	Means Racing Pontiac	313	3,850	Ignition
26	15	3	Dale Earnhardt	RCR Enterprises Chevrolet	302	22,460	Valve
26	22	21	Dale Jarrett	Wood Brothers Ford	302	6,388	Valve
27	8	2	Rusty Wallace	Roger Penske Pontiac	296	4,775	Running
28	20	15	Morgan Shepherd	Bud Moore Eng. Ford	292	10,525	Crash
29	14	68	Bobby Hamilton	Tri-Star Motorsports Olds	283	4,100	Engine
30	4	4	Ernie Irvan	Morgan-McClure Chevrolet	263	12,875	Crash
31	21	47	Greg Sacks	Derick Close Olds	252	3,300	Engine
32	10	5	Ricky Rudd	Hendrick Motorsports Chevy	232	10,550	Crash
33	26	10	Derrike Cope	Bob Whitcomb Chevrolet	225	5,825	Crash
34	28	71	Dave Marcis	Marcis Auto Racing Chevy	225	11,575	Crash
35	1	6	Mark Martin	Roush Racing Ford	212	70,955	Engine
36	16	12	Hut Stricklin	Bobby Allison Buick	135	5,740	Piston
37	37	95	Kerry Teague	Earl Sadler Chevrolet	124	3,125	Crash
38	5	25	Ken Schrader	Hendrick Motorsports Chevy	59	6,615	Piston
39	34	27	Gary Balough	Gene Isenhour Pontiac	42	3,110	Camshaft
40	40	13	Mike Skinner	Thee Dixon Chevrolet	12	3,105	Oil Line
41	36	66	Dorsey Schroeder	Cale Yarborough Pontiac	2	5,105	H Gasket

Time of Race: 3 hours, 36 minutes, 17 seconds
Average Speed: 138.984 mph
Pole Winner: Mark Martin – 176.499 mph
Lap Leaders: Mark Martin 1-65, Geoff Bodine 66-69, Martin 70, G.Bodine 71-72, Dale Earnhardt 73-74, Martin 75-204, Earnhardt 205-209, Martin 210-211, Earnhardt 212-260, Davey Allison 261-317, G.Bodine 318-334.
10 lead changes among 4 drivers.
Cautions: 6 for 38 laps Margin of Victory: 11.28 seconds

Allison's Robert Yates Racing crew weren't so sure. "It's awful good gas mileage, ain't it," said runner-up Allison. "We sure couldn't get that kind of mileage."

Stirring up the controversy even more was the manner in which the post-race tank capacity was conducted by NASCAR. News reporters were ushered out of the area and a number of the Johnson crewmen stood in front of the gas pump, obscuring view of the pump meter.

Larry McReynolds, crew chief for Allison, peeked around several bodies and said he got a clear shot of the pump meter. He even wrote down the figures. McReynolds said the meter showed 18,176.6 gallons when the refueling began and 18,199.8 when it ended, indicating 23.2 gallons of fuel went into the tank. The maximum capacity under NASCAR specifications is 22 gallons.

"He can't run that far on 22 gallons," McReynolds said matter-of-factly. "Our best is 66 laps (97.5 miles). Thing is, if you get beat by a lap or two, that's one thing. But you don't get by with 17 laps with a legal car."

Tim Brewer, crew chief for Bodine, said their Ford was running a conservative rear end gear that made the difference in gas mileage.

In response to questioning, a NASCAR official said they had "forgot" exactly how many gallons went into the Bodine car, "but it was less than 22 gallons."

The controversy surrounding Bodine's victory might never have occurred if Mark Martin had stayed in the race. The Batesville, Ark. driver, who challenged for the 1990 title but is winless thus far in 1991, started on the pole and made a mockery of the event for the first 350 miles. He led 198 of the first 211 laps before the engine expired in his Roush Racing Ford. "The car was awesome," said Martin. "I've never had an advantage like that in Winston Cup racing. We were running so bad and our luck has been so bad. I kind of figured something would happen to mess it up."

The Winston Cup title chase played into the hands of Dale Earnhardt, who blew an engine and wound up

25th. Despite the DNF, Earnhardt padded his lead to 138 points over Ricky Rudd, who was sidelined by a crash after completing 232 laps.

Rudd's demise came when he was rear-ended by Derrike Cope after Morgan Shepherd and Dave Marcis tangled in the third turn. Shepherd dismounted from his car and got into a 'heated' discussion with Marcis.

Afterward, Shepherd said he asked Marcis why he had just wrecked him. "It's the same old story," said Shepherd. "Marcis was several laps down trying to race me into the corner. We went into the turn and he wrecked me."

Marcis said Michael Waltrip was the cause of the crash. "I was down in the low groove like I had been all day," said Marcis. "I know I was down some laps, but those guys (Shepherd, Rudd and Cope) weren't on the lead lap either. Michael hit me in the rear and I spun into Morgan."

Ernie Irvan was sidelined when he ran into a spinning Kerry Teague early in the race. Teague's Chevrolet spun in turn four and slid down the banking. Irvan, trying to squeeze under Teague, clipped the spinning car, shearing off the front end of both automobiles. "My spotter told me to go high and I went low," said a dejected Irvan. "I can't seem to do anything right."

Winston Cup Series Race No. 27
500 Laps at N.C. Motor Speedway
Rockingham, NC
"AC Delco 500"
500.364 Miles on 1.017-mile Superspeedway
October 20, 1991

Fin	St	No.	Driver	Team / Car	Laps	Money	Status
1	10	28	Davey Allison	Robert Yates Racing Ford	492	$66,050	Running
2	13	33	Harry Gant	Leo Jackson Olds	492	34,675	Running
3	3	6	Mark Martin	Roush Racing Ford	492	29,350	Running
4	11	11	Geoff Bodine	Junior Johnson Ford	492	26,450	Running
5	6	25	Ken Schrader	Hendrick Motorsports Chevy	491	17,325	Running
6	21	68	Bobby Hamilton	Tri-Star Motorsports Olds	490	11,650	Running
7	4	3	Dale Earnhardt	RCR Enterprises Chevrolet	490	19,250	Running
8	24	22	Sterling Marlin	Junior Johnson Ford	490	10,000	Running
9	1	42	Kyle Petty	SabCo Racing Pontiac	499	22,950	Running
10	12	2	Bill Elliott	Melling Performance Ford	490	18,500	Running
11	9	2	Rusty Wallace	Roger Penske Pontiac	489	9,000	Running
12	5	5	Ricky Rudd	Hendrick Motorsports Chevy	489	13,800	Running
13	30	12	Hut Stricklin	Bobby Allison Buick	486	11,000	Running
14	29	24	Jimmy Hensley	Team III Pontiac	486	8,700	Running
15	15	10	Derrike Cope	Bob Whitcomb Chevrolet	485	15,050	Running
16	31	43	Richard Petty	Petty Enterprises Pontiac	485	9,700	Running
17	19	15	Morgan Shepherd	Bud Moore Eng. Ford	485	22,400	Running
18	27	1	Rick Mast	Precision Products Olds	485	8,900	Running
19	18	30	Michael Waltrip	Bahari Racing Pontiac	484	11,000	Running
20	25	8	Rick Wilson	Stavola Brothers Buick	484	9,200	Running
21	32	55	Ted Musgrave	RaDiUs Pontiac	483	6,100	Running
22	28	98	Jimmy Spencer	Travis Carter Chevrolet	482	7,650	Running
23	33	19	Chad Little	Chuck Little Ford	481	6,025	Running
24	23	66	Randy LaJoie	Cale Yarborough Pontiac	479	7,300	Running
25	8	21	Dale Jarrett	Wood Brothers Ford	479	7,275	Running
26	7	71	Dave Marcis	RCR Enterprises Chevrolet	479	7,050	Running
27	26	75	Joe Ruttman	RahMoc Racing Chevrolet	473	6,925	Running
28	22	94	Terry Labonte	Billy Hagan Olds	471	6,850	Running
29	14	47	Greg Sacks	Derick Close Olds	470	4,200	Running
30	20	26	Brett Bodine	King Motorsports Buick	401	9,250	Engine
31	2	4	Ernie Irvan	Morgan-McClure Chevrolet	365	12,700	Crash
32	17	17	Darrell Waltrip	DarWal Chevrolet	362	3,900	Engine
33	16	7	Alan Kulwicki	AK Racing Ford	318	10,750	Engine
34	34	20	Ricky Craven	Dick Moroso Olds	221	3,750	Engine
35	35	52	Jimmy Means	Means Racing Pontiac	203	3,600	Ignition
36	36	82	Mark Stahl	Stahl Racing Ford	16	3,525	Flagged
37	39	35	Keith VanHouten	Jenny VanHouten Pontiac	13	3,475	Flagged
38	37	56	Jerry Hill	Willie Tierney Pontiac	13	3,475	Flagged
39	40	77	Gary Brooks	Brooks Oldsmobile	11	3,425	Flagged
40	38	48	James Hylton	Hylton Engineering Buick	7	3,400	Engine

Time of Race: 3 hours, 55 minutes, 51 seconds
Average Speed: 127.292 mph
Pole Winner: Kyle Petty – 149.461 mph
Lap Leaders: Kyle Petty 1-47, Harry Gant 48-50, K.Petty 51, Gant 52, K.Petty 53-68, Ken Schrader 69-83, Mark Martin 84-87, Gant 88-93, Davey Allison 94-111, Gant 112-114, Allison 115-116, Gant 117-200, Allison 201-203, Geoff Bodine 204-210, Harry Gant 211-266, Allison 267, Gant 268-269, Allison 270, Gant 271, Allison 272-286, G.Bodine 287-295, Allison 296-338, Gant 339-387, G.Bodine 388-398, Gant 399-451, Martin 452-475, Allison 476-492.
26 lead changes among 6 drivers
Cautions: 5 for 24 laps Margin of Victory: 0.91 second

Race #27

Botched Pit Stop Ruins Gant's Bid; Allison Wins Rockingham

ROCKINGHAM, NC (Oct. 20) – Davey Allison took the lead 17 laps from the finish when a botched pit stop halted the Harry Gant express, and finished first in the AC Delco 500 at North Carolina Motor Speedway. It was the fourth win of the season for the Hueytown, Ala. Ford driver.

Gant had once again dominated the race – leading for 290 of the 492 laps – and had matters well in hand until his final routine pit stop 40 miles from the finish. Gant was leading Allison by 10 seconds when he pitted for tires and fuel.

An air wrench wielded by crew chief Andy Petree malfunctioned, delaying a tire change that eventually took 30.8 seconds. By the time Gant returned to the track, he was trailing Allison by eight seconds. Mark Martin had assumed command when Gant pitted, but he still had another pit stop to make.

In the final laps, Gant whittled Allison's lead every lap

Brian Czobat

Andy Petree, crew chief for Harry Gant.

Brian Czobat

Dave Marcis pits at Rockingham. Car owner Richard Childress gave Marcis a ride in one of the RCR Enterprises Chevrolets.

Earnhardt admitted he entered the race on a conservative note. "I won't lie," Earnhardt said, reflecting the importance in the Winston Cup point system which doesn't reward drivers who run for the win. "We were conservative on the engine. We had about a 10th place car. That's all we needed."

Rudd, who has missed a truckload of opportunities to cut into Earnhardt's point lead, took his loss in stride. "We played with tire matching, but nothing worked. The car was really bad. We lost some more ground today, but there are still two races left."

Ricky Craven, youngster from the Busch North Series, made his first Winston Cup start in the Dick Moroso Oldsmobile. Craven started 34th and wound up 34th when engine failure sidelined him after 221 laps.

Eleven cars failed to finish – four of those were flagged off the track for not maintaining racing speed.

and was 0.91-second behind when the checkered flag fell. Martin got third place with Geoff Bodine fourth and Ken Schrader fifth.

"The (air wrench) gun just quit working," said Petree. "I thought it was going to start working again, but it didn't. Maybe I shouldn't have waited so long to get another one."

Gant took the defeat philosophically. "We had 'em whipped, but things went a little whacky."

Allison said he kept an eye in the mirror for the fast closing Gant in the final laps. "I kept looking and seeing that old man getting closer," said Allison. "And I ran into the back of Derrike Cope when he was slowing down to pit. It made my car a little twitchy. I gave myself a lecture for not paying attention. Today things just went our way. We were due for some decent luck."

Kyle Petty, recent King of the Rock, started on the pole and led the first 47 laps but faded thereafter. He eventually finished ninth, two laps off the pace.

"We looked good at first," said Kyle, looking for his first win since being injured at Talladega in May. "But once the tires went away, we struggled. We never hit on the right racing set-up."

Dale Earnhardt finished seventh – two laps down – but came away with a 157 point lead over Ricky Rudd, who finished 12th. "Several down and two to go," said an elated Earnhardt afterwards. "We ran all day and didn't hit nothing and nothing hit us. It feels good to pick up some more points on Rudd."

Race #28

Davey Dazzling in the Desert; Earnhardt Assured of Title

PHOENIX, AZ (Nov. 3) – Davey Allison led 161 of the final 166 laps and breezed to victory in the Pyroil 500 at Phoenix International Raceway. It was the fifth win of the season for the Ford driver, vaulting him into second place in the Winston Cup standings.

Dale Earnhardt spun midway in the race and could do no better than ninth, but still locked up his fifth

Winston Cup championship. Entering the season finale at Atlanta, Earnhardt needs only to crank his engine to wrap up the title. Under NASCAR rules, the event officially gets underway when the drivers roll onto the pace lap. Points are automatically awarded once a car starts to roll under its own power.

All Earnhardt has to do is show up in Atlanta to wrap up the title. He is assured of making the field at Atlanta – even if he does not qualify for the race. Provisional spots for champions guarantee he will make the Atlanta field.

Allison's fortitude on race day was a surprise – especially to Allison. "We were very concerned about this race," admitted Allison, who leaped over Ricky Rudd into second place in the Winston Cup standings. "We struggled all day Friday and Saturday. We just weren't where we needed to be. We made some adjustments on race morning. I was surprised I whipped the field. To be as far off as we were in practice and be as good as we were in the race is just unbelievable."

Brian Czobat

Dale Earnhardt steers his Chevrolet down low to pass Hut Stricklin at Phoenix. Earnhardt all but clinched the 1991 championship.

Allison beat runner-up Darrell Waltrip by 11.44 seconds. Sterling Marlin wound up third with Alan Kulwicki fourth and Rusty Wallace fifth.

Rudd, who has had only one top five finish in the last eight races, had another mediocre day and finished 11th. "There's no doubt about it, NASCAR wants Ford to win," said the Chevy-driving Rudd. "If we could hurry up and build a Ford, we might have something going. The rules are currently imbalanced, and we're racing for second or third place." General Motors holds a significant advantage over Ford in wins this year (19-9) and has also clinched the manufacturers title.

Earnhardt started in 12th place but never challenged. The RCR Enterprises team prepared a car that was more bullet-proof than fleet. "We were a little soft on the engine," admitted Richard Childress, car owner for Earnhardt. "We were probably 25 or 30 horsepower off from what we ran the majority of the year when we were running good and winning."

Brian Czobat

The three Wallace brothers – Kenny, Mike and Rusty – all competed at Phoenix. They became the first triple brother act in the same Winston Cup race since 1961.

Earnhardt said he was relieved that he has locked up the title. "We wanted to wrap it up here," said Dale. "Richard Childress might just lock me up to make sure I get to Atlanta. I've got a lot of deer hunting to do. If I don't fall out of a tree, we'll be all right."

Harry Gant suffered his first rash of sour luck in over a month. He was involved in a mid-race spin with Dave Marcis and Richard Petty. Gant eventually finished 23rd, five laps off the pace.

Kenny and Mike Wallace joined big brother Rusty in the starting field. It was the first time three brothers had started the same race since Dub, Sherman and Layman Utsman drove in the same race at Bristol in 1961.

Kenny Wallace only ran one lap before retiring with steering problems. After the race, Junior Johnson and Barry Dodson, crew chief for the Team III Pontiac driven by Wallace, engaged in a scuffle. Johnson was fined $500 by NASCAR.

Allison reported he had a close call en route to Phoenix. "The trip started out scary," said Allison, who related an emergency landing after the cabin of his plane filled with smoke during a November 6 flight to Phoenix. "Some insulation fell against the heater, but it was a blessing in disguise. When we got on the ground, we discovered an engine had an oil leak. If we had flown much longer, we would have had only one engine working."

Winston Cup Series Race No. 28
312 Laps at Phoenix Int'l Raceway
Phoenix, AZ
"Pyroil 500"

312 Miles on 1-mile Superspeedway
November 3, 1991

Fin	St	No.	Driver	Team / Car	Laps	Money	Status
1	13	28	Davey Allison	Robert Yates Racing Ford	312	$78,500	Running
2	11	17	Darrell Waltrip	DarWal Chevrolet	312	37,225	Running
3	9	22	Sterling Marlin	Junior Johnson Ford	312	25,000	Running
4	5	7	Alan Kulwicki	AK Racing Ford	312	22,600	Running
5	10	2	Rusty Wallace	Roger Penske Pontiac	312	16,475	Running
6	15	4	Ernie Irvan	Morgan-McClure Chevrolet	312	18,100	Running
7	26	98	Jimmy Spencer	Travis Carter Chevrolet	311	12,850	Running
8	1	11	Geoff Bodine	Junior Johnson Ford	311	19,050	Running
9	12	3	Dale Earnhardt	RCR Enterprises Chevrolet	311	18,200	Running
10	19	15	Morgan Shepherd	Bud Moore Eng. Ford	311	16,750	Running
11	14	5	Ricky Rudd	Hendrick Motorsports Chevy	311	13,250	Running
12	35	94	Terry Labonte	Billy Hagan Olds	311	9,750	Running
13	40	68	Bobby Hamilton	Tri-Star Motorsports Olds	311	8,100	Running
14	8	26	Brett Bodine	King Motorsports Buick	311	9,050	Running
15	22	8	Rick Wilson	Stavola Brothers Buick	311	9,000	Running
16	6	10	Derrike Cope	Bob Whitcomb Chevrolet	311	12,950	Running
17	7	25	Ken Schrader	Hendrick Motorsports Chevy	310	7,750	Running
18	21	55	Ted Musgrave	RaDiUs Pontiac	310	5,700	Running
19	3	6	Mark Martin	Roush Racing Ford	310	13,550	Running
20	18	42	Kyle Petty	SabCo Racing Pontiac	309	12,225	Running
21	24	76	Bill Sedgwick	Wayne Spears Chevrolet	308	5,050	Running
22	27	75	Joe Ruttman	RahMoc Racing Olds	308	6,925	Running
23	4	33	Harry Gant	Leo Jackson Olds	307	7,050	Running
24	30	30	Michael Waltrip	Bahari Racing Pontiac	307	6,725	Running
25	2	9	Bill Elliott	Junior Johnson Ford	307	12,450	Running
26	32	14	Mike Chase	Freymiller Chevrolet	305	3,825	Running
27	43	04	Hershel McGriff	Bob Lipseia Pontiac	300	3,800	Running
28	25	1	Rick Mast	Precision Products Olds	259	6,525	Running
29	42	23	Butch Gilliland	Laurie Gilliland Pontiac	299	3,750	Running
30	28	19	Chad Little	Chuck Little Ford	298	4,925	Running
31	38	52	Mike Wallace	Means Racing Pontiac	246	3,700	Running
32	29	66	Randy LaJoie	Cale Yarborough Pontiac	203	6,100	Engine
33	31	41	Larry Pearson	Larry Hedrick Chevrolet	178	3,400	Crash
34	36	72	Mark Reed	Jim Reed Chevrolet	177	3,375	Valve
35	17	21	Dale Jarrett	Wood Brothers Ford	151	6,000	Engine
36	33	49	Stanley Smith	Smith Buick	150	3,325	Crash
37	39	73	Bill Schmitt	Sylvia Schmitt Ford	136	3,305	Crash
38	34	51	Jeff Purvis	Clint Folsom Chevrolet	127	3,295	Engine
39	16	12	Hut Stricklin	Bobby Allison Buick	105	5,910	Crash
40	23	71	Dave Marcis	Marcis Auto Racing Chevy	91	5,850	A Frame
41	20	43	Richard Petty	Petty Enterprises Pontiac	89	3,250	Crash
42	37	29	Gary Collins	Marion Collins Oldsmobile	61	3,250	Crash
43	41	24	Kenny Wallace	Team III Pontiac	1	3,000	Steering

Time of Race: 3 hours, 15 minutes, 31 seconds
Average Speed: 95.746 mph
Pole Winner: Geoff Bodine – 127.589 mph
Lap Leaders: Geoff Bodine 1-23, Mark Martin 24-29, G.Bodine 30-43, Martin 44-57, G.Bodine 58-73, Alan Kulwicki 74, Rick Wilson 75-84, Darrell Waltrip 85-108, Stanley Smith 109-120, Dale Jarrett 121-139, Davey Allison 140, Kyle Petty 141-142, Jimmy Spencer 143-146, Allison 147-257, D.Waltrip 258, Ernie Irvan 259-260, Brett Bodine 261, Bobby Hamilton 262, Allison 263-312.
18 lead changes among 13 drivers.
Cautions: 10 for 55 laps Margin of Victory: 11.44 seconds

Winston Cup Series Race No. 29
328 Laps at Atlanta Motor Speedway
Hampton, GA
"Hardee's 500"

499.216 Miles on 1.522-mile Superspeedway
November 17, 1991

Fin	St	No.	Driver	Team / Car	Laps	Money	Status
1	4	6	Mark Martin	Roush Racing Ford	328	$88,950	Running
2	3	4	Ernie Irvan	Morgan-McClure Chevrolet	328	39,025	Running
3	1	9	Bill Elliott	Melling Performance Ford	328	36,950	Running
4	9	33	Harry Gant	Leo Jackson Olds	328	21,250	Running
5	5	3	Dale Earnhardt	RCR Enterprises Chevrolet	328	27,825	Running
6	25	15	Morgan Shepherd	Bud Moore Eng. Ford	328	17,050	Running
7	11	22	Sterling Marlin	Junior Johnson Ford	327	11,150	Running
8	2	11	Geoff Bodine	Junior Johnson Ford	327	16,850	Running
9	8	7	Alan Kulwicki	AK Racing Ford	326	16,000	Running
10	22	17	Darrell Waltrip	DarWal Chevrolet	326	11,600	Running
11	29	5	Ricky Rudd	Hendrick Motorsports Chevy	326	12,800	Running
12	27	71	Dave Marcis	Marcis Auto Racing Chevy	326	9,675	Running
13	18	12	Hut Stricklin	Bobby Allison Buick	325	9,575	Running
14	33	41	Larry Pearson	Larry Hedrick Chevrolet	324	5,300	Running
15	17	94	Terry Labonte	Billy Hagan Olds	324	9,750	Running
16	10	21	Dale Jarrett	Wood Brothers Ford	324	8,750	Running
17	6	28	Davey Allison	Robert Yates Racing Ford	324	16,850	Running
18	16	68	Bobby Hamilton	Tri-Star Motorsports Olds	323	7,200	Running
19	12	42	Kyle Petty	SabCo Racing Pontiac	322	11,650	Running
20	40	75	Joe Ruttman	RahMoc Racing Chevrolet	322	8,800	Running
21	20	19	Chad Little	Chuck Little Ford	320	4,425	Running
22	30	43	Richard Petty	Petty Enterprises Pontiac	319	7,425	Running
23	31	24	Kenny Wallace	Team III Pontiac	319	5,225	Running
24	15	10	Derrike Cope	Bob Whitcomb Chevrolet	318	12,525	Engine
25	26	49	Stanley Smith	Smith Buick	318	4,375	Running
26	35	47	Greg Sacks	Derick Close Olds	310	3,975	Engine
27	37	95	Eddie Bierschwale	Earl Sadler Chevrolet	310	3,875	Running
28	28	1	Rick Mast	Precision Products Olds	271	6,775	Valve
29	23	26	Brett Bodine	King Motorsports Buick	269	6,575	Valve
30	19	55	Ted Musgrave	RaDiUs Pontiac	257	4,675	Heating
31	34	66	Randy LaJoie	Cale Yarborough Pontiac	244	6,225	Valve
32	21	53	Bobby Hillin,Jr.	Team Ireland Chevrolet	230	6,375	Block
33	32	8	Rick Wilson	Stavola Brothers Buick	207	6,075	Valve
34	24	2	Rusty Wallace	Roger Penske Pontiac	197	4,025	Crash
35	38	89	Jim Sauter	Mueller Brothers Pontiac	195	3,350	Crash
36	39	90	Wally Dallenbach,Jr.	Junie Donlavey Ford	173	3,325	Engine
37	13	25	Ken Schrader	Hendrick Motorsports Chevy	86	5,945	Crash
38	14	98	Jimmy Spencer	Travis Carter Chevrolet	71	5,915	Head
39	36	52	Mike Wallace	Means Racing Pontiac	69	3,300	Crash
40	7	30	Michael Waltrip	Bahari Racing Pontiac	26	5,275	Crash

Time of Race: 3 hours, 37 minutes, 6 seconds
Average Speed: 137.968 mph
Pole Winner: Bill Elliott – 177.937 mph
Lap Leaders: Bill Elliott 1-29, Bobby Hamilton 30, Mark Martin 31-43, Ernie Irvan 44-49, Martin 50-74, Ted Musgrave 75-76, Martin 77-84, Irvan 85-89, Bobby Hillin, Jr. 90-99, Davey Allison 100-123, Dale Earnhardt 124-149, Harry Gant 150-152, Darrell Waltrip 153-156, Geoff Bodine 157-159, Martin 160-167, Earnhardt 168-177, Martin 178-217, Morgan Shepherd 218-222, Earnhardt 223-225, Martin 226-273, Gant 274-280, Martin 281-328.
21 lead changes among 12 drivers
Cautions: 6 for 37 laps Margin of Victory: 10.44 seconds

Race #29

Martin Ends Famine at Atlanta; Earnhardt Champ for 5th Time

HAMPTON, GA (Nov. 17) – Mark Martin put the brakes on a personal skid and emerged with his first win of the season in the Hardee's 500 at Atlanta Motor Speedway. Dale Earnhardt finished fifth and wrapped up his fifth Winston Cup driving championship by 195 points over Ricky Rudd.

Martin led 190 of the 328 laps, including the final 48, and finished 10.44 seconds ahead of runner-up Ernie Irvan. Bill Elliott finished in third place. Harry Gant was fourth and Earnhardt fifth.

Davey Allison lost second place in the Winston Cup points when his Ford spent seven laps on pit road for replacement of a dead battery. Once Allison got back on the track, he made up three lost laps and finished 17th.

The race for the championship was anti-climactic as Earnhardt clinched the title simply by starting his engine. Under NASCAR's point system, he received a minimum of 43 points for starting his engine. "I'm just glad all we had to do was fire the engine to win it," said Earnhardt. "Our goal is to win it again and be the first team since Junior Johnson (with driver Cale Yarborough in 1976, 1977 and 1978) to win three straight.

Bryan Hallman

Jimmy Means tags the wall at Atlanta.

"And I do not think it is so far-fetched to start thinking about matching Richard Petty with seven titles," continued Earnhardt. "But even if I do, there will still be one king of stock car racing – Richard Petty."

Martin avoided the goose egg in the victory column with a resounding triumph. "We never needed a win worse than we did today," he said. "We can live off this momentum all winter. This was the first day of the

Kim Novasat

Ken Schrader's Chevrolet slugged the wall at Atlanta and came to rest against the outside retaining barrier.

rest of our careers.

"Maybe now that we have our bad luck behind us, we can put our name on that championship trophy. We can't let Earnhardt win 'em all," said Martin.

Bill Elliott started on the pole and led the first 29 laps. It was his final appearance in the Melling Performance Ford. The Dawsonville, Ga. driver has said he will move to the Junior Johnson team in 1992.

Most of the race belonged to Martin and Irvan, but Martin clearly had the upper hand in terms of speed. "It was a boring race and that's the way we wanted it," said Martin. "Our plan was to run as strong as we could and get as far out in front in case something happened."

Something did happen. Martin had to make an unscheduled pit stop to replace a tire in the 134th lap. That stop put him a lap off the pace, but he was able to make it up 20 laps later. A caution came out that put him back in pit stop sequence with the other teams.

Mike Wallace suffered a broken shoulder blade when his Jimmy Means Pontiac slammed into the wall in the 73rd lap. Michael Waltrip was knocked woozy when his Pontiac clobbered the wall in the 27th lap. When rescue workers arrived to check on Waltrip, the first thing he asked was, "How did I qualify?"

Other victims of wrecks included Ken Schrader and Rusty Wallace. Schrader wiped out the Hendrick Motorsports Chevrolet in a solo crash in the 89th lap. He was shaken but uninjured.

Brian Czobat

Dale Earnhardt with his fifth Winston Cup championship trophy.

1991 NASCAR Season
Final Point Standings - Winston Cup Series

Rank	Driver	Points	Starts	Wins	Top 5	Top 10	Winnings
1	Dale Earnhardt	4,287	29	4	14	21	$2,416,685
2	Ricky Rudd	4,092	29	1	9	17	1,093,765
3	Davey Allison	4,088	29	5	12	16	1,712,924
4	Harry Gant	3,985	29	5	15	17	1,194,033
5	Ernie Irvan	3,925	29	2	11	19	1,079,017
6	Mark Martin	3,914	29	1	14	17	1,039,991
7	Sterling Marlin	3,839	29	0	7	16	633,690
8	Darrell Waltrip	3,711	29	2	5	17	604,854
9	Ken Schrader	3,690	29	2	10	18	772,434
10	Rusty Wallace	3,582	29	2	9	14	502,073
11	Bill Elliott	3,535	29	1	6	12	705,605
12	Morgan Shepherd	3,438	29	0	4	14	521,147
13	Alan Kulwicki	3,354	29	1	4	11	595,614
14	Geoff Bodine	3,277	27	1	6	12	625,256
15	Michael Waltrip	3,254	29	0	4	12	440,812
16	Hut Stricklin	3,199	29	0	3	7	426,524
17	Dale Jarrett	3,124	29	1	3	8	444,256
18	Terry Labonte	3,024	29	0	1	7	348,898
19	Brett Bodine	2,980	29	0	2	6	376,220
20	Joe Ruttman	2,938	29	0	1	4	361,661
21	Rick Mast	2,918	29	0	1	3	344,020
22	Bobby Hamilton	2,915	28	0	0	4	259,105
23	Ted Musgrave	2,841	29	0	0	0	200,910
24	Richard Petty	2,817	29	0	0	1	268,035
25	Jimmy Spencer	2,790	29	0	1	6	283,620
26	Rick Wilson	2,723	29	0	0	0	241,375
27	Chad Little	2,678	28	0	0	1	184,190
28	Derrike Cope	2,516	28	0	1	2	419,380
29	Dave Marcis	2,374	27	0	0	1	219,760
30	Bobby Hillin, Jr.	2,317	22	0	0	1	251,645
31	Kyle Petty	2,078	18	1	2	4	413,727
32	Lake Speed	1,742	20	0	0	0	149,300
33	Jimmy Means	1,562	20	0	0	0	111,210
34	Mickey Gibbs	1,401	15	0	0	0	100,360
35	Dick Trickle	1,258	14	0	0	1	129,125
36	Stanley Smith	893	12	0	0	0	56,915
37	Larry Pearson	848	11	0	0	0	56,570
38	Wally Dallenbach,Jr.	803	11	0	0	0	54,020
39	Greg Sacks	791	11	0	0	0	84,215
40	Buddy Baker	552	6	0	0	0	58,060
41	Jimmy Hensley	488	4	0	0	1	32,125
42	Eddie Bierschwale	431	5	0	0	0	55,025
43	Jim Sauter	423	6	0	0	0	47,395
44	Kenny Wallace	412	5	0	0	0	58,325
45	Jeff Purvis	399	6	0	0	0	42,910
46	Phil Barkdoll	364	4	0	0	0	41,655
47	Mike Chase	356	5	0	0	0	22,700
48	J.D.McDuffie	335	5	0	0	0	19,795
49	Bill Sedgwick	324	3	0	0	0	15,150
50	Randy LaJoie	304	4	0	0	0	23,875

1992 Winston Cup Season

The King Retires, The Founder Dies; And the Underdog Wins the Title

PLAYING THE POINT GAME

For years, NASCAR race teams rarely concerned themselves with the point standings during the early portions of a season. A common remark heard from drivers and team owners was, "We're going to race and let the points fall where they may."

Throughout the lengthy tenure of NASCAR Winston Cup racing, teams would lock out any prescribed strategy in the point race until things became more focused in the final months. It was at that point that most teams would map their strategy, whether it was to adopt a conservative approach or run like gangbusters in an effort to make up sizable deficits.

In 1963, Fred Lorenzen had a banner year on NASCAR's premier stock car racing series. While concentrating on the major races and passing up the 100 and 125-mile short track events, Lorenzen virtually rewrote the record book. He became the first driver to top $100,000 in winnings for a single season. He won six major races. By the time the autumn months rolled around, someone on his Holman-Moody team realized he was running in the top five in points despite missing over half the races.

Kim Novosat

King Richard Petty announced that 1993 would be his final year as a driver.

At that point, Lorenzen began competing in a number of the short track races since he had an outside shot at winning the championship. But by then, it was too late to change the outcome of the 1963 title race.

Lorenzen finished third in the point standings despite running only 29 of the 55 races. Had he and his team been keeping an eye on the point race earlier in the season, Lorenzen could very well have won the title.

In 1970, Bobby Allison missed the Richmond race in March. Allison wanted to make a run at the championship, but he didn't have everything mapped out early in the year. He wound up losing the title by 51 points. Had Allison been a little more concerned about the championship early in the year, he would have certainly won the championship ring. All he had to do was finish 25th (next to last in the 26-car field) at Richmond and he would have been the 1970 national champion.

THE CURRENT POINT SYSTEM

NASCAR adopted a new point system in 1975 – the same structure which determines the champion today.

Richard Petty mopped up in 1975, winning 13 races and finishing over 700 points in front of runner-up Dave Marcis. But a few of the numbers conveyed a message that winning races and running near the front was not necessarily the key to placing high in the point standings. In 1975, James Hylton finished third in the points while having zero wins and only two top five finishes in his 30 starts. Benny Parsons won the Daytona 500 and had 11 top five efforts in his full 30-race schedule but was nearly 100 points behind Hylton.

The tell-tale factor in Hylton's finishing ahead of Parsons was the number of DNF's. Hylton had only three; Parsons endured 13.

Brian Czobat

Car owner Junior Johnson watched as his driver Bill Elliott won four of the first five races, but was not leading the point standings. Later in the year, Elliott built up a big lead but squandered it away with late season failures.

NASCAR's point systems have always been defined as a structure which rewards consistency rather than winning races. The key to winning the Winston Cup championship is to avoid trouble and guard against falling out of a race early. The biggest determining factor in the NASCAR point system is not winning the most races or how strong a team runs, it boils down to the simple fact of how many DNF's a team has.

In 1991, Ricky Rudd finished second in the point standings. He won only one race while Davey Allison and Harry Gant each won five times, but Rudd had only one DNF. Therein lies the thread of success.

In the last 10 years, many drivers have complained about the NASCAR point system. Darrell Waltrip has been one of the most outspoken opponents of the system. In 1984, Waltrip won seven races, but wound up a distant fifth in the standings. Two-time winner Terry Labonte won it.

The following year, Waltrip won three races and the championship by a wide margin in spite of Bill Elliott's 11-win, record setting season. Waltrip still spoke out against the point system. "There's not enough incentive to winning races," Waltrip has claimed. "Bill really deserved to be the Winston Cup champion in 1985."

Tim Richmond won seven races and drew the most attention in 1986, but he finished third in the point standings behind Earnhardt and Waltrip.

WIN 29 RACES AND YOU MAY LOSE THE TITLE

Under the current format, it is possible for a driver to *win* 29 races and finish *second* in the other event, and still *lose* the Winston Cup championship by 15 points.

That's because bonus points for leading a race can offset on track performance. Dozens of times the winner of a race has not earned any more points than the second place finisher. Carried to extremes, a driver would win all but one race and never have first place to himself.

While most Winston Cup teams concentrated on racing during the early season events, more and more teams were keeping a careful eye focused on the development of the point race. It matters not whether a costly DNF occurs early in the year or in the final championship stretch. All races carry the same point value and the same importance.

One of the best teams at handling the pressures of the point race is Dale Earnhardt and his RCR Enterprises crew. When trouble strikes, Earnhardt is a master at keeping the car running – sometimes at reduced speed. This enables him to steer clear of many DNF's. Quite often, the championship has been won with a mediocre finish in a certain crucial race, while other contenders have fallen out early or were not as prepared to keep a car running in the face of adversity.

For the 1992 season, many other teams were concen-

Dick Beaty stepped down as NASCAR Director of Competition.

trating on the point race right out of the blocks. "We're going to keep the championship in mind every race this year," said Allison, who was bitten by sour luck at the start of the 1991 campaign and could not make up the deficit despite five race wins. "You can't afford to bury yourself in a hole. We know that. Now we must go out and keep from doing it."

NELSON'S ACTIVE WHISTLE

When the teams began arriving at Daytona for the season-opening Speedweeks events, there were a few changes. Most notably was Gary Nelson handling the technical inspections. Dick Beaty had slipped into the more comfortable confines of retirement and NASCAR had solicited the services of Nelson, who was one of the more ingenious crew chiefs in racing history.

Nelson promised to be strict but fair to the NASCAR teams. "NASCAR had to hire a thief to catch a thief," one crew chief said.

Teams got a taste of Nelson's strict hand in pre-race inspections. Only four cars made it through initial inspection. Six drivers would be fined for stepping outside NASCAR's specifications.

Harry Gant's Leo Jackson team was fined $750 and his fifth fastest qualifying time on pole day was disallowed. Officials said Gant's Oldsmobile had copper spacers which flattened during high speed runs.

"I couldn't give them a good explanation for it," said Andy Petree, Gant's crew chief. "We went through pre-qualifying inspection as low as possible and didn't consider there would be no tolerance in post-qualifying inspection."

Jimmy Means and Jimmy Spencer were fined for illegal rear air foils. Spencer's device, rigged by car owner Travis Carter, had a spoiler mounted so it would bend below the 35-degree minimum when air rushed against it at speed. Means was fined for having a similar gadget.

"We didn't do anything Gary Nelson hasn't done," reasoned Means. "That's why he caught us. But for every one thing they find, there are 10 things they don't find."

Rick Mast, A.J. Foyt and Stanley Smith were also fined for illegal additions to their cars. NASCAR blew the whistle on Smith when it was discovered his car had eight feet more fuel line than permitted.

THE KING'S FINAL HURRAH

King Richard Petty announced in late 1991 that the 1992 Winston Cup season would be his 34th and final one. Petty would call it his *'Fan Appreciation Tour'*. "It's not a farewell tour or anything like that," said Petty. "Heck, I ain't going nowhere. This will be our way of telling the fans how much we appreciate their support over the last 34 years. Without the fans, I wouldn't have had a job."

Petty's 200th and most recent win came at Daytona in 1984. Since then, his statistics have slipped. No top five finishes since 1988.

"Not winning races, not finishing races, not doing the things I am capable of doing – all of it adds up," said Petty. "God might have given me 25 years of good luck and I might be trying to stretch it to 35. Maybe He's trying to tell me something, like, 'Hey, you'd better get out of this thing before something happens to you and I can't look out for you no more'."

Petty confessed that thoughts of retirement entered his mind in late 1990. But he didn't air his convictions until a year later. He told his family first – in a private moment at his home in Level Cross, N.C. "They had mixed emotions at first," said Petty. "They all wanted me to quit, but they know how I love it so much that they hurt for me because they know I'm going to have to get out of it. It was pretty emotional around there for about 10 minutes."

Chris Economaki, noted auto racing publisher and television commentator, said Petty has been responsible for a large part of the growth of NASCAR racing. "He set an example that really has made NASCAR the popular sport it is today," said Economaki. "Stock car drivers in general and NASCAR drivers in particular are the most open and the most accessible drivers in the world. In all other forms of motorsports, they're secluded. They rush to their motor homes, they close the door and the fans stand outside and never really have a

Brian Czobat

Joe Gibbs unveiled his Interstate Batteries Chevrolet at Daytona.

chance at them.

"Richard Petty was the pioneer in the style that has caught on with the other NASCAR drivers," said Economaki.

JOE GIBBS COMES TO NASCAR

Joining the Speedweeks festivities as an active participant was Joe Gibbs, highly successful head coach of the NFL Washington Redskins. Hot off his third Super Bowl win, Gibbs was a mere rookie in Winston Cup racing.

He had hired Dale Jarrett as driver and Jimmy Makar as crew chief. "I had to get a good quarterback and I think Dale is the obvious choice," said Gibbs.

Gibbs said he wanted to become involved directly in the race team and not play the role of a hands-off owner. "I think you have to be an auto racing fan to understand how I feel," said Gibbs. "It is an intense emotional high.

"Coaching football is a lot like running an emotional marathon. It's not only the 11 years I've been doing it, but the 20 I fought to get there. When I got the chance to get into racing, it gave me an opportunity to get excited about life in general," said Gibbs.

The new owner was in the pits during Speedweeks. "They gave me headphones but didn't teach me how to talk," he said with a grin. "I think that means keep your mouth shut, try to learn and stay out of the way. They probably don't want me coaching Dale right into the wall."

Jarrett had his problems at Daytona, crashing a car in the Twin 125, and another in the Daytona 500.

ELLIOTT A STORM IN THE SPRING

Bill Elliott had left the Harry Melling team to join Junior Johnson in 1992. Johnson had won six Winston Cup championships from 1976-1985 and he wanted the taste of champagne again. "I had tried to hire Elliott about six or seven years ago," said Johnson. "But things were never right for it to happen. It took a long time to get him, but this time things were right."

Johnson and Elliott would have master crew chief Tim Brewer at the helm. "Junior's a pretty open-minded guy," said Brewer, who joined the Johnson team in 1978. "He'll let Bill and I pretty much do as we please. But if he sees us going off in left field, we'd better duck because we know there's a foot coming through."

Johnson had his eyes locked on the championship trophy – even before the season began. "Bill is the right kind of driver to win championships," said Johnson. "There's nothing wrong with Dale's (Earnhardt) style – I approve of it – but he's not going to be able to continue roughing people up and get away with it. I'd rather have a guy who uses finesse. I think I've got the right driver."

Elliott qualified second in the Daytona 500, his first official effort with Johnson. Sterling Marlin, in Johnson's other Ford, won the pole.

Elliott and Marlin led most of the early laps in the Daytona 500. Then a crash occurred shortly before the half-way point when Elliott, Marlin and Ernie Irvan were battling for first place.

Elliott's car was heavily damaged, but he got back in the race and eventually finished 27th. Davey Allison held off Morgan Shepherd by two car lengths to win the Daytona 500. He also took an early lead in the

Winston Cup point standings.

But Elliott hit stride the next four races. He won at Richmond, nipping a surging Alan Kulwicki by less than a foot. He pulled away from the field to win at Rockingham. He also won at Atlanta when he was seemingly out of contention. By utilizing excellent fuel mileage and a timely late caution flag, Elliott found himself nearly a lap up on the entire field. He coasted to victory.

Elliott won at Darlington, unpressured by rivals. He had won all four races in March. He had won 80 percent of the races, but a not-so-funny thing happened.

Greg Crisp

Davey Allison's Ford was a streak at certain times during the 1992 season.

He was *not* leading the Winston Cup point standings. No driver had ever won four of the first five races to start off the year. It is hard to imagine that he wouldn't be leading the point standings.

The point system drew criticism again, but the teams were aware of the structure and understood it. "It doesn't do any good to complain about it," said Tim Brewer. "We know how it works. But one thing we all need to concern ourselves with is to make sure we put that 3 team (Dale Earnhardt and the RCR Enterprises unit) down some points here early in the year. So many times they get off to a big lead and we all find ourselves trying to catch up. You don't necessarily catch up by winning. And you don't want to ever get into a situation where you have to rely on them having trouble."

ALLISON'S TRAVAILS

While Bill Elliott was stringing a chain of victories together, Davey Allison held the Winston Cup point lead. The Ford driver from Alabama had finished in the top five in the season's first five events. Allison scored 98 points more than Elliott in the Daytona 500. But Elliott was only able to chop 50 points off of Allison's point lead while winning four in a row.

Dale Earnhardt started the year off slowly and was holding down eighth place in the point standings after the fifth race of the year. He trailed by 207 points.

Allison and Elliott both tapered off on the short tracks. Elliott recorded finishes of 20th, 20th and 10th in races at Bristol, North Wilkesboro and Martinsville.

Allison crashed hard at Bristol, suffering a shoulder injury. The following week he won North Wilkesboro, but crashed again at Martinsville, finishing 26th.

Allison continued to lead the standings as Elliott fell to fourth. Alan Kulwicki had been quietly accumulating points and was fifth after eight races.

Allison rebounded at Talladega, winning the Winston 500. He had bagged the first two races of the Winston Million and was an even bet to become the second driver in history to capture the million dollar bonus from Winston.

But Allison didn't consider the Winston Million as his prime objective. "I want to keep focused on our goal, the Winston Cup championship," said Allison. "We want to be at the head table in New York (at the NASCAR awards ceremony. We want to have a big party in December."

ALL STAR RACE UNDER THE STARS

During The Winston, the all-star race that annually precedes the Coca-Cola 600, Allison had a sturdy and reliable Ford Thunderbird at his disposal. Nicknamed '007', the formidable car had taken Allison to great heights at the Charlotte mile-and-a-half.

Allison led all the way in the 1991 The Winston, and backed that up a week later with a triumph in the 600. In the fall, Allison wound up second in the Mello Yello 500, losing only to Geoff Bodine's wonderful fuel mileage.

Now he and the Robert Yates team were back at Charlotte with their best buggy. And Allison had shaken off his early season injury at Bristol.

The Winston was staged under the lights at Charlotte, becoming the first time NASCAR has sanctioned a superspeedway race under artificial lights since 1955.

Billed as "One Hot Night", Charlotte Motor Speedway's lighting system was the brainchild of General Manager Humpy Wheeler, Track President Bruton Smith and Musco Corp., an Iowa firm specializing in the lighting of sporting events.

The project was so enormous that it took 24 semi-trailers to haul all the equipment from Iowa to Charlotte.

The lighting system cost $1.7 million. It consisted of 1,200 fixtures, 56 poles from 70 to 110 feet tall, 160 tons of steel, 1,700 mirrors, 75 miles of wire, 520 tons of concrete, and 11 and a half tons of glass.

The system cost about $140 per hour to operate.

THE DEMISE OF '007'

Allison earned the pole for The Winston in '007'. He led the first 30-lap segment from start-to-finish. Starting positions were reversed in order of finish, and Kyle Petty led most of the second segment and started on the pole in the final 10-lap dash.

Dale Earnhardt hustled past Petty with seven laps to go and led until he spun in the third turn of the final lap.

Petty ducked under Earnhardt's errant car and took the lead out of the fourth turn. Allison caught Petty just before the finish line and swooped to the low side and won by a bumper.

The two leaders slapped doors and Allison's car slid driver's door-first into the concrete retaining wall. Allison was knocked out in the crash. He was transported to the hospital suffering from a concussion, a bruised lung and minor leg injuries. For the second time this year, Allison had taken a serious hit.

"I remember everything until we crossed the finish line," Allison said after he was released from the hospital. "I knew I beat Kyle and I remember getting turned around. Then the lights went out."

Kim Novosat

Too many times Davey Allison's car was dragged back to the garage by a wrecker.

Allison's trusty '007' had been wiped out. He would have to use a back-up car in the Coca-Cola 600. Neil Bonnett, sidelined since April of 1990, was summoned by Allison to shake down the back-up car while Allison recuperated from his latest injuries.

Allison was able to qualify 17th on pole day; and he led twice for 33 laps en route to a fourth place finish. He held onto the point lead by 111 points over Elliott. Kulwicki, the underdog of the title contenders, held fourth place, 132 points behind Allison. Sneaking up was Coca-Cola 600 winner Dale Earnhardt, who was only 12 points behind Kulwicki.

A late penalty for speeding on pit road knocked Allison down to 12th at Dover. An off-track excursion on the road course at Sonoma, Calif. left him with a 28th place. Allison's point lead had dwindled to just 28 points – and Earnhardt had moved into second place. Through a dozen races, the top five in the standings were separated by only 83 points.

It was turning out to be a very interesting point race.

ANOTHER HARD LICK FOR ALLISON

Allison rebounded and won big at Michigan and finished 10th at Daytona. He was able to open a 46-point lead over Elliott in the battle for the national championship.

At the July event at Pocono International Raceway , Allison was clearly the class of the field. He had led all but 24 of the first 139 laps, but got pinned back in the field by a slow pit stop under yellow.

Two laps after the restart, Allison was jockeying for position when he and Darrell Waltrip tapped bumpers. Allison's Ford shot off the track, flipped backwards and tumbled itself into a mass of twisted iron, spitting off clumps of sheet metal.

Allison was removed from the car and transported by helicopter to LeHigh Valley Hospital in Allentown, Penn. He suffered two fractures in the right forearm, a broken right wrist, a broken collar bone and a contusion over his left eye.

"There are times you over-extend yourself or under-protect yourself," Allison said afterwards. "Not only does it cost us a win, it cost us a lot of points in the championship race. There are a lot of negatives to it, but I have no animosity toward Darrell."

Cifford Allison, younger brother of Davey, was killed at Michigan International Speedway while practicing for the Busch Grand National race.

Allison had fallen nine points behind Elliott in the Winston Cup standings, the first time he has been out of first place since the start of the year.

Surgical pins put Allison's arm back together. He was fitted with a special cast in order to grip the steering wheel. He had all intentions of running the Talladega DieHard 500 a week later.

Bobby Hillin, Jr. qualified Allison's car in third place at Talladega. Allison started the race and let Hillin, Jr. take over on the first caution period. Hillin, Jr. brought Allison's car home third – and gave him a one point lead in the standings. It would be a short-lived point lead.

Allison and road racing relief driver Dorsey Schroeder wound up a disappointing 20th at Watkins Glen. That put him 17 points behind Elliott. Kulwicki had been keeping the leaders in sight. He trailed by only 94 points.

Dale Earnhardt had fallen from the point race with last place finishes at Daytona and Talladega. He had dropped to eighth in the standings, 336 points out of first place. Earnhardt would never be a factor.

THE LOSS OF A BROTHER

After Watkins Glen, the Winston Cup touring pros headed for Michigan International Speedway.

On Friday August 13, 27 year-old Clifford Allison died from injuries he suffered when his car spun into the concrete retaining barrier in the fourth turn. According to officials, Allison died en route to W.A. Foote Hospital in Jackson, Mich. Cause of death was severe head injuries.

A distraught Davey Allison mourned the loss of his brother, but went ahead and showed a great deal of strength by qualifying third. "Davey says that deep in his heart, he knows that Clifford would want him to go ahead and drive," said Brian VanDercook, spokesman for the Robert Yates team. "He'd want him to go out there and try his best to win."

Crew chief Larry McReynolds was also shaken by the news of Clifford's death. "I told Davey, 'I'm not only your crew chief, but you're my best friend. And I'm here if you need a shoulder to cry on, or somebody to yell at. I can't say how I know you feel because I've never lost a brother. But I'm not here just to set your race car up'.

"We've got to keep him pumped up and let him know that this will pass," added McReynolds. "It will take time, but it will pass."

Allison drove the full 400-miles at Michigan and finished in fifth place. Allison excused himself from the media afterwards and left to go back home.

"Obviously, I'm going to miss him tremendously," said Allison a couple of weeks later. "But Clifford is gone. And there is nothing I can say or do or nothing anybody can say or do to change that.

"The thing to do now is retain memories and try to prepare ourselves to live every day the best we can. Sometimes we have to play with the cards we are dealt."

Allison added that for himself, all he wanted was to "be able to provide for my family a good family atmosphere, raise my kids and know that should the day come along that I'm in the same position Clifford is, they'll be taken care of when I'm gone."

ELLIOTT INCREASES POINT LEAD

Elliott logged three straight top 10 efforts at Michigan, Bristol and Darlington and took a 119-point lead over Allison. Kulwicki was hanging in the chase, 161 points behind Elliott.

At Dover, Kulwicki crashed early after rubbing fenders with a lapped car. His car was so badly damaged that repairs could not be made. He wound up 34th and fell 278 points behind Elliott with just six races remaining.

"Realistically, that probably finishes us off in the championship deal," said Kulwicki. "I don't like to give up, but I know it will be hard to come back now."

Elliott finished second in the Dover race and had Allison on the ropes. The margin between first and second in the Winston Cup standings was 154 points – a fairly comfortable lead.

POINT LEAD SLIPS AWAY

But Elliott consistency went awry in the next three races. At Martinsville, Elliott's Ford fell out early with engine problems, leaving him with a 30th place finish in the 31-car field. Allison failed to take full advantage of Elliott's departure, finishing 16th. He was able to pull to within 112 points of the point leader.

Crew chief Tim Brewer and driver Bill Elliott built up a healthy point lead only to watch it slip away at the end of the season.

Kulwicki finished in fifth place and crept to within 191 points of Elliott.

At North Wilkesboro a week later, Elliott never got untracked and was lapped eight times. He finished 26th as only one car fell out of the race.

Allison finished 11th, three laps off the pace while Kulwicki wound up 12th. Elliott now led Allison by 67 points and Kulwicki by 144 points.

At Charlotte, Elliott had ample opportunity to put a lid on the Winston Cup point race. Allison had struggled all day, running outside the top 20. Kulwicki was dicing for the lead as Elliott ran comfortably in the top 10.

But late in the race, Elliott grazed the wall and broke a track bar. The incident forced Elliott behind the wall and allowed not only Allison and Kulwicki to get back into immediate title contention, but he also left the door open for Mark Martin, Harry Gant and Kyle Petty.

Only 114 points separated the top six. Allison had drawn within 39 points of Elliott while Kulwicki trailed by only 47 points.

Elliott authored a brief turnaround at Rockingham, finishing a strong fourth while Allison registered a 10th place finish and Kulwicki finished 12th. With two races remaining on the 1992 slate, Elliott led Allison and Kulwicki by 70 and 85 points respectively.

At Phoenix, Elliott's car started smoking early and after several lengthy and unscheduled pit stops, he could only manage a 31st place finish. He also managed to drop from first to third in the point standings as Allison won and Kulwicki finished fourth.

Allison took a 30 point lead over Kulwicki into the season finale at Atlanta. Kulwicki was 10 points ahead of Elliott.

A TITLE RACE TO REMEMBER

For only the second time since 1979, there would be an all-out *race* in the final event for the

Winston Cup championship. The last few years, the battle for the Winston Cup championship had been an anti-climatic stage play. A year ago, Earnhardt received enough points to clinch the title simply by starting his car. In 1989, Rusty Wallace tip-toed to a 15th place finish and held off Dale Earnhardt's late surge.

The year before that, Elliott had admittedly stroked his way to the championship, lumbering to an 11th place finish.

This time, no stroking would be allowed. With three drivers separated by 30 points, the title contenders would have to abandon any thoughts of conservative strategy. It set the stage for one of the most memorable finales, and no one at Atlanta Motor Speedway would leave disappointed. They saw one heck of a race.

Paul Andrews kept tab of the number of laps Alan Kulwicki had led at Atlanta and simple arithmetic contributed greatly to Kulwicki's Winston Cup championship.

Richard Petty was commanding as much attention as the contenders for the Cup. Atlanta Motor Speedway would be the site for King Richard's last race as a driver.

Petty was caught up in an early wreck, and his Petty Enterprises crew spent the rest of the day repairing the car so the King could finish the last couple of laps at a greatly reduced speed.

None of the challengers would qualify in the top 10. Elliott posted an 11th place starting spot, while Kulwicki earned the 14th position. Allison started 17th.

Allison needed a fifth place finish to lock up the championship. Elliott and Kulwicki needed to win and get some help.

ALLISON CRASHES

On lap 253, Ernie Irvan spun his Chevrolet directly in the path of Allison. The cars collided with a clap of thunder, thus ending Allison's bid. True to his form, Allison was a class act in a heartbreaking defeat. "That's the way it goes sometimes," said Allison, who was holding down fifth place when the crash occurred. "We were just trying to run a smart race.

"It looked like Ernie must have had a flat tire or something. The car just got away from him. That's the way it goes.

"We appreciate all the support everybody has shown us," Allison continued. "The fans have been great (with) all the letters of encouragement. We want to tell everybody we appreciate that. It just wasn't our year.

"We knew we were going to have to race hard. That's what we came to do. I just hate that our race came to an end the way it did."

When Allison's championship hopes were dashed by the wreck, Kulwicki was leading with Elliott second. With Allison out of the scenario, the championship took an interesting twist. There was a distinct possibility that the championship could end in a tie – and for the first time in history, the tie-breaker would have to be used to determine the Winston Cup champion.

SIMPLE ARITHMETIC

Elliott, by virtue of leading Kulwicki four-to-two in the number of victories entering the race, held the tie-breaker. Both drivers had led a lap in the race – and Elliott and Kulwicki were vying to lead the most laps. If Elliott could lead the most laps, he would pick up five additional bonus points on Kulwicki. And if he could win the race and Kulwicki run second, both drivers would tie for the point lead. Elliott would win on the tie-breaker.

The battle for the most coveted award in NASCAR

Brian Czobat

1992 Winston Cup champion Alan Kulwicki holds NASCAR's most important trophy.

had boiled down to the privateer, determined to build his own team running against the heralded team for which he twice shunned offers to drive.

Paul Andrews, Kulwicki's crew chief, was keeping tabs of the number of laps each driver led. He knew it was going to be close. He was in constant communication with his driver and told him that if he could lead until the 310th lap, all he would have to do is finish second to wrap up the title. He would no longer have to beat Elliott to win.

Kulwicki stretched his fuel mileage and led through the 310th lap. That was the 103rd lap that Kulwicki had led. If Elliott led the remaining 18 laps, they would both lead 103 laps and both receive the five point bonus for leading the most laps.

Kulwicki pitted for fuel only on lap 311. Elliott took the lead and pitted three laps later for fuel. Terry Labonte led the 315th lap, which clinched the bonus for Kulwicki. That lap really did not have a bearing on the outcome of the championship race.

Kulwicki came into the pits at a cautious clip, making sure he didn't exceed the pit road speed limit. Elliott approached his pit at a normal speed and when he returned to the track, he was leading by 4.3-seconds.

"I had been told by the guys (on his pit crew) I needed to lead until lap 310," said Kulwicki. "I knew then that even if I finished second, I would win the championship. All I wanted to do for the last laps was be smart and not do anything foolish. It would have been tough to lose the championship that way."

Elliott went on to win the 500-miler at Atlanta, beating Kulwicki by 8.06-seconds. But Kulwicki had climbed the mountain as Winston Cup champion.

A GRACIOUS CHAMPION

"I thank God for the fortune to be here and to be an American and compete on the Winston Cup circuit," Kulwicki said as he climbed out of his car. "When I moved down South years ago, this was my dream. I came here in a pick-up truck and a trailer. I want to thank the many people who helped me along the way.

"I nicknamed this Ford the 'Underbird' because we were going into this race as the underdog. I'm really proud of the whole team. I couldn't have done it without my crew. This is a storybook ending. It's really wonderful.

"The money is nice, but there is the prestige that comes with the championship. They can never take that away from you.

"If you were to bet money back in '86 that I'd be where I am today, the odds were slim. When you consider everything it took to get here from there, you'd say it couldn't be done.

"But you can't look at it that way. I didn't. Obstacles are what you see when you take your eyes off the goal line," said a gracious Kulwicki.

BIG BILL PASSES AWAY

On the morning of June 7, 1992, William Henry Getty France, the founder of NASCAR, died in his sleep in Ormond Beach, Fla. He was 82. He had been in declining health for eight years and seriously ill the past two years. He suffered from Alzheimer's Disease, a memory-afflicting ailment generally attributed to genetic factors and advancing age.

France was born on September 26, 1909 in Washington, D.C., the son of a Virginia farmer. In 1931, he married North Carolina native Anne Bledsoe, his wife until she died earlier in the year.

Big Bill had migrated to Florida in 1934 and worked as a mechanic at a service station.

He promoted stock car races on the old Beach and Road course at Daytona, and formed NASCAR in 1947.

"He was a disciplinarian," said NASCAR's Les Richter. "But he had a dream and he pursued it. This vision of Bill France was to build superspeedways, and without Bill France, there would be no Daytona, Talladega or Michigan. He meant something to everybody, and he's left something with us all."

Junior Johnson, who had verbally sparred with France over the years, paid salute to "The Tall Man".

"He was a great innovator as far as having the foresight into racing, what he was after and what he was trying to accomplish," said Johnson. "He had a dream and he stood by that dream. His efforts are what we see in our sport today. There have been a lot of heroes come through this sport driverwise, ownerwise, trackwise, stuff like that. But Bill France, Sr. is the hero of our sport."

Graham Niven

Bill France, Sr. and son Bill, Jr. in a photo taken in 1985.

"He had more foresight than anyone could have imagined," said Glen Wood, who was a pioneer driver when France formed NASCAR. "He was a whale of a man. He certainly got stock car racing going when no one else considered it."

Richard Childress said he watched how Big Bill handled himself in business ventures. "I tried to adopt his style," said Childress. "Everything he did, he did right. And he took care of everybody. He didn't just look out for himself. That's the thing I admire most about him."

Race #1

14 Car Crash Depletes Daytona 500 Field; Allison Wins

DAYTONA BEACH, FL (Feb. 16) – Davey Allison avoided a 14-car crash just before the half-way point and motored to victory in the 34th annual Daytona 500 by STP at Daytona International Speedway.

Allison snaked through the mechanized scramble on the backstretch in the 92nd lap. The crash knocked out or crippled nine of the 16 cars that were on the lead lap at the time.

Allison kept his Robert Yates Racing Ford in the lead for all but five of the final 103 laps and beat runner-up Morgan Shepherd by two car lengths. Third place went to Geoff Bodine, who passed Alan Kulwicki in the final lap. Dick Trickle's sterling performance in an unsponsored RahMoc Racing Oldsmobile netted him fifth place.

The race started out as one of the speediest and most serene of all time. The race was caution free until a light rain shower forced the yellow flag on lap 84. The field restarted in the 90th lap with Elliott and Marlin, both in Junior Johnson Fords, leading the chase.

Ernie Irvan made a move off the second turn and pulled to the low side down the backstretch. Marlin shifted from behind his teammate and created a three-abreast situation down the long chute. Within an instant, all three leaders were nosing into each other – with Marlin in the middle.

The wreck brought out a lot of emotions and finger pointing from the drivers involved. Most blamed Ernie Irvan although television replays seemed to indicate he received a bum rap on this one.

"Ernie never gave Sterling any room," said Elliott, who had led 23 of the first 91 laps. "I think Sterling just got caught in the middle of a bad situation. It does seem like every time something goes on, Ernie's right in the middle of it."

Greg Fielden

Richard Petty drove in his 32nd and final Daytona 500.

Marlin's version: "I just kind of got sandwiched. We were just racing hard, Ernie got loose and came up the track a little. I got out of the gas and almost missed it. He hung my front end and I got into Bill."

Other drivers involved included Rusty Wallace, Dale Earnhardt, Mark Martin, Dale Jarrett, Bobby Hillin,Jr., Chad Little, Darrell Waltrip, Hut Stricklin, Ken Schrader and Kulwicki. Kulwicki was able to drive off with minimal damage.

Wallace said he "can't understand how it's possible to wreck in a straightaway, but it happens week in and week out. And it seems like it's always the same faces involved. It's upsetting."

Irvan insisted he had "cleared Sterling, but then I got hit in the rear quarter-panel. That wasn't the first three-abreast move all day and I don't think I made that one three-abreast.

ISC

Dale Earnhardt limps back to the pits after big 92nd lap crash.

Winston Cup Race No. 1
200 Laps at Daytona Int'l Speedway
Daytona Beach, FL
"Daytona 500 By STP"

500 Miles on 2.5-mile Superspeedway
February 16, 1992

Fin	St	No.	Driver	Team / Car	Laps	Money	Status
1	6	28	Davey Allison	Robert Yates Racing Ford	200	$244,050	Running
2	4	21	Morgan Shepherd	Wood Brothers Ford	200	161,300	Running
3	16	15	Geoff Bodine	Bud Moore Eng. Ford	200	116,250	Running
4	41	7	Alan Kulwicki	AK Racing Ford	200	87,500	Running
5	28	75	Dick Trickle	RahMoc Racing Olds	200	78,800	Running
6	33	42	Kyle Petty	SabCo Racing Pontiac	200	67,700	Running
7	34	94	Terry Labonte	Billy Hagan Olds	199	58,575	Running
8	40	55	Ted Musgrave	RaDiUs Chevrolet	199	52,750	Running
9	3	3	Dale Earnhardt	RCR Enterprises Chevrolet	199	87,000	Running
10	19	9	Phil Parsons	Melling Performance Ford	199	49,150	Running
11	24	47	Buddy Baker	Derick Close Olds	199	38,275	Running
12	11	33	Harry Gant	Leo Jackson Olds	199	51,100	Running
13	13	1	Rick Mast	Precision Products Olds	199	40,355	Running
14	9	41	Greg Sacks	Larry Hedrick Chevrolet	199	36,790	Running
15	37	16	Wally Dallenbach,Jr.	Roush Racing Ford	198	29,700	Running
16	32	43	Richard Petty	Petty Enterprises Pontiac	198	32,530	Running
17	25	73	Phil Barkdoll*	Barkdoll Racing Olds	198	27,960	Running
18	10	30	Michael Waltrip	Bahari Racing Pontiac	197	37,140	Flagged
19	31	90	Dorsey Schroeder	Junie Donlavey Ford	196	25,750	Running
20	23	71	Dave Marcis	Marcis Auto Racing Chevy	195	26,210	Running
21	39	14	A.J.Foyt	Don Bierschwale Olds	195	23,055	Running
22	30	49	Stanley Smith	Smith Chevrolet	195	24,150	Running
23	38	8	Rick Wilson	Stavola Brothers Ford	195	24,045	Running
24	42	12	Hut Stricklin	Bobby Allison Chevrolet	188	27,740	Running
25	27	0	Delma Cowart	H.L.Waters Ford	188	23,285	Running
26	12	17	Darrell Waltrip	DarWal Chevrolet	180	33,580	Running
27	2	11	Bill Elliott	Junior Johnson Ford	178	60,255	Running
28	7	4	Ernie Irvan	Morgan-McClure Chevrolet	166	43,370	Handling
29	5	6	Mark Martin	Roush Racing Ford	162	49,675	Running
30	29	77	Mike Potter	Steve Balogh Chevrolet	151	21,710	Fuel Pump
31	17	2	Rusty Wallace	Roger Penske Pontiac	150	30,455	Running
32	22	68	Bobby Hamilton	Tri-Star Motorsports Olds	125	27,350	Piston
33	21	03	Kerry Teague	Teague Oldsmobile	122	22,445	Crash
34	20	10	Derrike Cope	Bob Whitcomb Chevrolet	120	23,15	Radiator
35	1	22	Sterling Marlin	Junior Johnson Ford	91	34,435	Crash
36	35	18	Dale Jarrett	Joe Gibbs Chevrolet	91	19,780	Crash
37	15	25	Ken Schrader	Hendrick Motorsports Chevy	91	30,500	Crash
38	26	31	Bobby Hillin,Jr.	Team Ireland Chevrolet	91	20,370	Crash
39	14	66	Chad Little	Cale Yarborough Ford	90	22,760	Crash
40	8	5	Ricky Rudd	Hendrick Motorsports Chevy	79	34,350	Engine
41	18	26	Brett Bodine	King Motorsports Ford	13	25,150	Distrib
42	36	95	Bob Schacht	Earl Sadler Olds	7	18,250	Engine

Time of Race: 3 hours, 7 minutes, 12 seconds
Average Speed: 160.256 mph
Pole Winner: Sterling Marlin – 192.213 mph
Lap Leaders: Sterling Marlin 1-5, Bill Elliott 6-19, Marlin 20-47, Elliott 48, Darrell Waltrip 49, Ken Schrader 50-55, Davey Allison 56-83, Elliott 84-91, Allison 92, Morgan Shepherd 93-97, Allison 98-144, Shepherd 145, Allison 146-166, Shepherd 167, Michael Waltrip 168-170, Allison 171-200.
15 lead changes among 7 drivers
Cautions: 4 for 22 laps Margin of Victory: 2 car lengths
*Relieved by Jim Sauter

Brian Czobat

Davey Allison hoists winner's trophy in Daytona's Victory Lane.

We were only two abreast when I made my move.

"You have to do things during the race that help you end up where you end up, whether it be on lap 50 or lap 100," continued Irvan. "I have to go out and race hard. I was just trying to win the race."

Jarrett was making his first official start in the Chevrolet owned by Super Bowl Washington Redskins head coach Joe Gibbs. Jarrett trashed one car in the 125-mile qualifier and wiped another one out in the 500. "My guys made $36,000 each for winning the Super Bowl," Gibbs chided his driver. "You cost me that much in one race."

The crash cleared the way for Allison and Shepherd to battle for top honors in stock car racing's most celebrated prize.

"I veered to the outside lane and gave it the gas," said Allison referring to how he missed the crash. "All hell broke loose behind me. A year ago I probably would have been right in the middle of it. Maybe I've grown up a little. But it feels good to miss a wreck like that, especially after getting my car all torn up last year by Dale Earnhardt."

Allison kept Shepherd at bay in the final laps and bagged $244,050 for his 14th career win. His best

ISC

Mark Martin #6 and Rusty Wallace #2 drive their battle-scarred cars after backstretch wreck.

race and it was to us," said a dejected Waltrip. "My car was strong. It would have been a real interesting finish."

Earnhardt failed for the 14th time to bag the Daytona 500. He finished ninth, a lap off the pace after being involved in the big crash. "Every year I just seem to have one of those days. I don't know what to say other than it's the Daytona Blues, I reckon."

King Richard Petty, making his final Daytona 500 start, qualified 10th on pole day. He

previous finish in the Daytona 500 was in 1988 when he ran second to his dad Bobby. "That second place is still the most special day of my career," said Davey. "This is the biggest victory of my career, but it's not as special as finishing second to my dad."

was involved in an early crash in the Twin 125-mile qualifying race, which sent him back to the 32nd starting position.

Petty gave the command to start the engines. Rather than the usual 'Gentlemen, Start Your Engines'

Shepherd gave the Wood Brothers Ford a strong run. "I could hang with him, but I didn't have enough power to move out and pass him. We'll just have to settle for second place," said Shepherd.

Kulwicki's fourth place run came from 41st starting spot. He had not finished well enough in the 125-mile qualifier or logged a quick enough qualifying time to get in the race. Hut Stricklin claimed the other provisional.

Michael Waltrip posed as a serious threat in the late laps, running as high as second. But the engine in his Bahari Racing Pontiac went sour in the final five laps. NASCAR blackflagged him with three laps to go due to excessive smoke and running at a dangerously reduced speed. "The Daytona 500 can be a cruel

Brian Czobat

Davey Allison leads Wally Dallenbach, Jr., Bobby Hamilton and Rick Wilson at Daytona.

command, Petty delivered a unique command. "Okay guys, let's go. Crank 'em up."

Petty finished in 16th place, two laps off the pace. "I'm disappointed," said Petty. "I felt really good while we were out there running. But then I got a lap down and we had the wreck and I got hit from behind."

Race #2

Elliott Rips Field at the Rock; Allison Has Healthy Point Lead

ROCKINGHAM, NC (March 1) – Bill Elliott led the final 213 laps and romped to an easy victory in the GM Goodwrench 500 at North Carolina Motor Speedway. The 14-second triumph was the 35th in Elliott's career and his first in two starts for car owner Junior Johnson.

"I had heard a lot of different reactions to me joining forces with Junior Johnson," said Elliott. "I felt all along I made the right decision. Today sort of reinforced that belief."

Elliott started second on the grid and took the lead as early as the 11th lap. Davey Allison drove to the front in the middle stages and was able to keep comfortably ahead of Elliott and the rest of the challengers.

After keeping to a pre-determined pace for a couple hundred miles, Elliott poked the nose of his red Thunderbird into the lead and shook off the challenges from Allison.

NCMS

Bill Elliott ducked under Davey Allison and sprinted to victory at Rockingham.

Winston Cup Race No. 2
492 Laps at N.C. Motor Speedway
Rockingham, NC
"GM Goodwrench 500"
500.364 Miles on 1.017-mile Superspeedway
March 1, 1992

Fin	St	No.	Driver	Team / Car	Laps	Money	Status
1	2	11	Bill Elliott	Junior Johnson Ford	492	$57,800	Running
2	10	28	Davey Allison	Robert Yates Racing Ford	492	48,875	Running
3	13	33	Harry Gant	Leo Jackson Olds	492	31,600	Running
4	14	30	Michael Waltrip	Bahari Racing Pontiac	491	18,650	Running
5	9	25	Ken Schrader	Hendrick Motorsports Chevy	491	21,650	Running
6	3	6	Mark Martin	Roush Racing Ford	490	20,575	Running
7	21	94	Terry Labonte	Billy Hagan Olds	490	15,200	Running
8	4	26	Brett Bodine	King Motorsports Ford	490	14,700	Running
9	15	12	Hut Stricklin	Bobby Allison Chevrolet	490	14,400	Running
10	24	17	Darrell Waltrip	DarWal Chevrolet	490	19,900	Running
11	6	4	Ernie Irvan	Morgan-McClure Chevrolet	489	18,400	Running
12	19	1	Rick Mast	Precision Products Olds	489	13,300	Running
13	22	21	Morgan Shepherd	Wood Brothers Ford	489	13,000	Running
14	12	15	Geoff Bodine	Bud Moore Eng. Ford	489	12,600	Running
15	25	22	Sterling Marlin	Junior Johnson Ford	489	12,150	Running
16	29	43	Richard Petty	Petty Enterprises Pontiac	488	11,700	Running
17	28	55	Ted Musgrave	RaDiUs Oldsmobile	486	11,400	Running
18	20	68	Bobby Hamilton	Tri-Star Motorsports Olds	486	12,150	Running
19	26	10	Derrike Cope	Bob Whitcomb Chevrolet	482	8,375	Running
20	27	98	Jimmy Spencer	Travis Carter Chevrolet	480	10,950	Running
21	34	16	Wally Dallenbach,Jr.	Roush Racing Ford	480	5,650	Running
22	30	66	Chad Little	Cale Yarborough Ford	475	7,200	Running
23	32	13	Mike Skinner	Thee Dixon Chevrolet	470	6,150	Running
24	8	3	Dale Earnhardt	RCR Enterprises Chevrolet	469	16,850	Running
25	38	87	Randy Baker	Buck Baker Chevrolet	459	8,700	Running
26	5	2	Rusty Wallace	Roger Penske Pontiac	442	13,100	Wtr Pump
27	40	56	Jerry Hill	Willie Tierney Pontiac	440	5,250	Running
28	23	5	Ricky Rudd	Hendrick Motorsports Chevy	437	12,950	Running
39	1	42	Kyle Petty	SabCo Racing Pontiac	430	12,375	Camshaft
30	33	9	Phil Parsons	Melling Performance Ford	368	9,325	Running
31	7	7	Alan Kulwicki	AK Racing Ford	356	9,075	Running
32	31	49	Stanley Smith	Smith Chevrolet	332	4,500	Running
33	35	52	Jimmy Means	Means Racing Pontiac	269	5,850	Engine
34	16	41	Greg Sacks	Larry Hedrick Chevrolet	232	4,300	Engine
35	36	0	Delma Cowart	H.L.Waters Ford	210	4,200	Brakes
36	11	8	Dick Trickle	Stavola Brothers Ford	113	4,125	Wtr Pump
37	18	18	Dale Jarrett	Joe Gibbs Chevrolet	73	4,075	Camshaft
38	39	59	Andy Belmont	Pat Rissi Ford	27	4,060	Engine
39	17	71	Dave Marcis	Marcis Auto Racing Chevy	22	5,525	Engine
40	37	53	John McFadden	Means Racing Pontiac	8	4,000	Quit

Time of Race: 3 hours, 58 minutes, 2 seconds
Average Speed: 126.125 mph
Pole Winner: Kyle Petty – 149.926 mph
Lap Leaders: Kyle Petty 1-10, Bill Elliott 11-28, Rusty Wallace 29, K.Petty 30-43, Davey Allison 44-52, R.Wallace 53-68, Allison 69-130, Morgan Shepherd 131, Allison 132-247, Elliott 248-276, Allison 277-279, Elliott 280-492.
11 lead changes among 5 drivers
Cautions: 7 for 28 laps Margin of Victory: 14 seconds

Allison ran second and opened a 56 point lead over Morgan Shepherd in the chase for the Winston Cup title. Shepherd finished in 13th place, three laps behind.

Third place went to Harry Gant, who was nearly a lap behind. Michael Waltrip finished in fourth with Ken Schrader fifth.

Five-time champion Dale Earnhardt suffered through brake trouble and a collision with Alan Kulwicki and finished 24th. He currently is logged in a tie for 13th place in the point standings.

Brian Czobat

Lenny and Julie Batycki present Bill Elliott with winner's trophy at Rockingham.

Kyle Petty started the SabCo Racing Pontiac on the pole and led 24 of the first 43 laps. Rated as an overwhelming favorite to pocket the $190,000 Unocal bonus, the two time defending champion surprisingly faded and was never a factor. A series of problems and an eventual engine failure put him out of the race. "We had six or seven problems and finally narrowed it down to one," cracked Petty about the blown engine.

Dale Jarrett made his second outing in the Joe Gibbs Chevrolet, but he wasn't around very long. Engine problems sent the Hickory, N.C. driver to the showers after just 73 laps.

"This is about as tough a start you can get," said Gibbs. "When you're tested, you find out what you're made of. I think we're being tested right now."

Dick Trickle took over the Stavola Brothers Ford ride in place of the released Rick Wilson. A broken water pump put him out just past the 100-mile mark.

Michael Waltrip rebounded from his Daytona disappointment with a fine top five run. "This race is a marathon," said the younger Waltrip. "Along about 400 laps I started noticing things aching that I didn't even know I had."

Wally Dallenbach, Jr., driving the second entry from the Roush Racing shops, was making his first appearance at The Rock. "The 24-hour race at Daytona is a piece of cake compared to this," said Dallenbach, Jr., who finished 21st. "I ache all over."

King Richard Petty ran a steady race and finished 16th. He moved up to a tie for 11th in the Winston Cup standings.

Rusty Wallace started fifth and led briefly in the early going. Wallace was holding down a position in the top five when a broken water pump put him out in the final 50 miles.

Bryan Hallman

Ricky Rudd's Chevrolet billows smoke after at Rockingham.

Race #3

Elliott Hits Mother Lode; Wins $272,700 at Richmond

RICHMOND, VA (March 8) – Bill Elliott held off a fast closing Alan Kulwicki by inches and won the Pontiac Excitement 400 at Richmond International Raceway. Elliott stuffed $272,700 in the pockets of his lanky overalls – including $197,600 from the Unocal bonus.

An overflow crowd of 65,200 watched Elliott vault

from the pole and lead 217 of the first 218 laps. Davey Allison and Darrell Waltrip led a total of four laps during exchanges of pit stops before Harry Gant drove to the front for 48 laps. Elliott battled past Gant in the 270th lap and was never headed.

Kulwicki overcame misfortune in the pits to make it a race in the end. Gant claimed third spot with Allison fourth and Waltrip fifth.

Kim Novosat

Davey Allison #28 races with Bill Elliott #11 and Sterling Marlin at Richmond.

Winston Cup Race No. 3
400 Laps at Richmond Int'l Raceway
Richmond, VA
"Pontiac Excitement 400"
300 Miles on .75-mile Short Track
March 8, 1992

Fin	St	No.	Driver	Team / Car	Laps	Money	Status
1	1	11	Bill Elliott	Junior Johnson Ford	400	$272,700	Running
2	5	7	Alan Kulwicki	AK Racing Ford	400	36,525	Running
3	6	33	Harry Gant	Leo Jackson Olds	400	31,950	Running
4	2	28	Davey Allison	Robert Yates Racing Ford	400	25,100	Running
5	18	17	Darrell Waltrip	DarWal Chevrolet	400	21,775	Running
6	27	5	Ricky Rudd	Hendrick Motorsports Chevy	400	16,050	Running
7	4	22	Sterling Marlin	Junior Johnson Ford	399	13,700	Running
8	19	94	Terry Labonte	Billy Hagan Olds	399	12,250	Running
9	8	12	Hut Stricklin	Bobby Allison Chevrolet	399	11,950	Running
10	11	21	Morgan Shepherd	Wood Brothers Ford	399	13,600	Running
11	29	3	Dale Earnhardt	RCR Enterprises Chevrolet	399	16,600	Running
12	16	98	Jimmy Spencer	Travis Carter Chevrolet	398	10,650	Running
13	21	18	Dale Jarrett	Joe Gibbs Chevrolet	398	4,800	Running
14	13	25	Ken Schrader	Hendrick Motorsports Chevy	397	13,700	Running
15	10	4	Ernie Irvan	Morgan-McClure Chevrolet	397	14,360	Running
16	14	15	Geoff Bodine	Bud Moore Eng. Ford	397	12,225	Running
17	12	2	Rusty Wallace	Roger Penske Pontiac	396	12,425	Running
18	17	1	Rick Mast	Precision Products Olds	396	9,875	Running
19	26	10	Derrike Cope	Bob Whitcomb Chevrolet	396	5,550	Running
20	3	42	Kyle Petty	SabCo Racing Pontiac	395	9,325	Running
21	25	43	Richard Petty	Petty Enterprises Pontiac	395	9,875	Running
22	22	8	Dick Trickle	Stavola Brothers Ford	394	9,100	Running
23	23	66	Chad Little	Cale Yarborough Ford	393	5,925	Running
24	31	16	Wally Dallenbach,Jr.	Roush Racing Ford	393	4,150	Running
25	32	55	Ted Musgrave	RaDiUs Oldsmobile	393	8,750	Running
26	35	90	Charlie Glotzbach	Junie Donlavey Ford	392	5,675	Running
27	34	49	Stanley Smith	Smith Chevrolet	392	4,050	Running
28	28	71	Dave Marcis	Marcis Auto Racing Chevy	389	5,600	Running
29	30	88	Jeff Fuller	Fuller Pontiac	386	4,000	Wtr Pump
30	15	6	Mark Martin	Roush Facing Ford	363	11,970	Running
31	24	68	Bobby Hamilton	Tri-Star Motorsports Olds	353	9,500	Rear End
32	20	41	Greg Sacks	Larry Hedrick Chevrolet	342	3,925	Running
33	9	26	Brett Bodine	King Motorsports Ford	267	9,435	Axle
34	7	30	Michael Waltrip	Bahari Racing Pontiac	259	8,400	Engine
35	33	52	Jimmy Means	Means Racing Pontiac	93	4,400	Engine

Time of Race: 2 hours, 52 minutes, 27 seconds
Average Speed: 104.378 mph
Pole Winner: Bill Elliott – 121.337 mph
Lap Leaders: Bill Elliott 1-123, Davey Allison 124, Elliott 125-218, Darrell Waltrip 219-221, Harry Gant 222-269, Elliott 270-400.
5 lead changes among 4 drivers.
Cautions: 4 for 23 laps Margin of Victory: 18 inches

NASCAR listed the official margin of victory at 18 inches.

"I saw Alan coming on and I knew he was going to be the man to beat," said Elliott after his 36th career triumph. "I knew he was going to have to take the bottom of the race track to beat me. Coming off the last turn, Alan got in the throttle real quick and came up against me. I almost scraped the wall. He wasn't going to back off and I wasn't either. I knew I wouldn't be roughed up by Alan because he doesn't drive that way.

"I knew what kind of money was at stake," continued Elliott. "But I would have raced Alan just as hard for a dollar."

Kulwicki said he was "deeply disappointed" at losing the photo finish. "We were so close. One of us could have taken the other out if he wanted to, but we raced

Kim Novosat

Harry Gant passes Stanley Smith #49 at Richmond. Gant finished third, while Smith was 27th.

Kim Novosat

Alan Kulwicki #7 zips past Dale Earnhardt en route to a second place finish at Richmond.

clean. We didn't touch until the last hundred feet or so."

Paul Andrews, Kulwicki's crew chief, accepted blame for the pit stops. "Pit stops killed us today," said Andrews. "We kept coming in second or third and coming out fourth or fifth. That was mainly because I'm so slow changing rear tires. We're looking for a replacement for me in that position."

Sterling Marlin started fourth, but fell a lap off the pace near the half way point. He was poised to get one of his laps back – running just a car length behind teammate Elliott – when a caution came out. Pit road occupants were surprised Elliott didn't let his running mate back in the lead lap. Mike Beam, crew chief for Marlin, couldn't understand the lack of teamwork.

Kim Novosat

Richmond International Raceway President Paul Sawyer chats with NASCAR President Bill France, Jr.

Car owner Johnson said that "if I had been on Bill's (radio) frequency, I would have told him to let Sterling go by. But things happened kind of fast."

In the final laps, Marlin was still pressing Elliott when car owner Johnson got on the radio and told him to back off. "Sterling was a lap down and there wasn't any sense in him racing up there," said Johnson.

Kulwicki was riding behind the dueling Johnson Fords, buι kept his composure. "I've got to commend Sterling," said Kulwicki. "He could have tried to mess me up. He held me up a little, but that was expected. He moved over and played fair. He didn't do anything dirty."

Allison retained his lead in the Winston Cup standings by a 73 point cushion over Gant. Elliott climbed to third, but still trails by 78 points despite winning two out of three races. "If you have any trouble at all, it can offset two or three wins," said Elliott, accenting the point structure. "It's still early in the year."

Dale Earnhardt couldn't get the handle on his RCR Enterprises Chevrolet and finished 11th, a lap off the pace. He had qualified 29th. He ranks 11th, 166 points behind leader Allison.

Michael Waltrip and Brett Bodine, both of whom qualified in the top 10, went out early with mechanical problems. Waltrip seized an engine on lap 259 and Bodine went out with a broken axle a few laps later.

Race #4

Late Caution Flag is Gift For Elliott in Atlanta 500

HAMPTON, GA (March 15) – Bill Elliott was buried deep in the pack virtually all the way in Atlanta Motor Speedway's Motorcraft 500, but a timely caution flag late in the running left the Georgia red head nearly a lap up on the field.

Elliott breezed the final 40 laps and wound up 18.25

Gregg Feistman

Bill Elliott drove his Junior Johnson Ford to his third straight win at Atlanta.

seconds in front of runner-up Harry Gant. Dale Earnhardt came in third with Davey Allison fourth and Dick Trickle fifth.

Elliott was running ninth when the leaders starting making their final scheduled pit stops. Alan Kulwicki, running fifth at the time, zipped down pit road for fresh tires and a supply of fuel. With Kulwicki forcing everybody's hand, other cars came in the following lap, leaving Elliott in front. On lap 285 Mike Wallace, driving Dick Moroso's Oldsmobile, spun his car off the second turn. The caution came out, leaving Elliott a full lap on the field.

During the slowdown, Elliott pitted and returned to the track behind the other contenders, who were all nearly a lap behind. From that point on, Elliott merely had to keep his Junior Johnson Ford between the fences.

"Boy, they just give this one to us," said a startled Elliott when he pulled into Victory Lane. "I've lost a bunch of races with crazy stuff – like this race last year. This might be the first one I've won like this."

Wallace almost felt like looking for a place to hide after the race ended. "I came off the corner exactly like I had all day," he said after finishing 33rd. "The rear end just snapped loose on me. I'm glad it wasn't one of my brothers or a General Motors car that I helped. If it had been that way, people sure would be looking real hard at me."

Elliott acknowledged Wallace's crucial assist. "I wish somebody would give him a hug and a kiss for me," said Elliott.

Allison had led the most laps – 160 in all – and seemed destined to rack up his second win of the season. "Losing like this is dejecting," muttered Allison. "You can't beat luck. He was lucky and we weren't. At least a Ford won."

Kulwicki, the great calculator, opted to pit early to get new tires on his car for the final stretch run. Curiously, neither Kulwicki nor any of the leaders were running low on fuel. "Everybody was trying to split the difference," explained Kulwicki. "I figured if I could pit early and the race stayed green, I would get an advantage with new tires. But then all the other leaders followed our lead. Elliott was so far back he didn't have anything to lose by staying out. He was out of it, or so we all thought."

"Alan set the stage," said Larry McReynolds,

Jim Ahmay

Dick Trickle drove the Stavola Brothers Ford to an impressive fifth place finish at Atlanta.

Allison's crew chief. "When he pitted, we all had to. We couldn't stand around and let him gain a half second per lap on us with those new tires."

Earnhardt lumbered around most of the day, running between sixth and 10th. But a final spurt vaulted him into third place.

Trickle qualified second and gave the Stavola Brothers Ford its strongest run in three years. Although he never officially led a lap, Trickle was dicing it out with the leaders all afternoon. Twice, he made miraculous saves when the car broke loose and got out of shape.

Winston Cup Race No. 4
328 Laps at Atlanta Motor Speedway
Hampton, GA
"Motorcraft Quality Parts 500"
499.216 Miles on 1.522-mile Superspeedway
March 15, 1992

Fin	St	No.	Driver	Team / Car	Laps	Money	Status
1	4	11	Bill Elliott	Junior Johnson Ford	328	$71,000	Running
2	10	33	Harry Gant	Leo Jackson Olds	328	45,875	Running
3	7	3	Dale Earnhardt	RCR Enterprises Chevrolet	328	36,850	Running
4	25	28	Davey Allison	Robert Yates Racing Ford	328	32,550	Running
5	2	8	Dick Trickle	Stavola Brothers Ford	328	28,125	Running
6	23	15	Geoff Bodine	Bud Moore Eng. Ford	328	18,600	Running
7	8	7	Alan Kulwicki	AK Racing Ford	328	20,850	Running
8	15	42	Kyle Petty	SabCo Racing Pontiac	328	15,650	Running
9	3	94	Terry Labonte	Billy Hagan Olds	328	17,150	Running
10	14	21	Morgan Shepherd	Wood Brothers Ford	328	16,000	Running
11	17	18	Dale Jarrett	Joe Gibbs Chevrolet	328	7,670	Running
12	24	5	Ricky Rudd	Hendrick Motorsports Chevy	328	15,425	Running
13	1	6	Mark Martin	Roush Racing Ford	328	19,230	Running
14	28	10	Derrike Cope	Bob Whitcomb Chevrolet	328	9,810	Running
15	12	2	Rusty Wallace	Roger Penske Pontiac	327	14,980	Running
16	32	43	Richard Petty	Petty Enterprises Pontiac	327	12,470	Running
17	6	22	Sterling Marlin	Junior Johnson Ford	327	15,660	Running
18	30	90	Charlie Glotzbach	Junie Donlavey Ford	326	6,600	Running
19	16	55	Ted Musgrave	RaDiUs Chevrolet	326	13,990	Running
20	9	26	Brett Bodine	King Motorsports Ford	325	11,920	Running
21	36	31	Bobby Hillin,Jr.	Team Ireland Chevrolet	323	6,260	Running
22	11	1	Rick Mast	Precision Products Olds	323	13,050	Running
23	29	66	Chad Little	Cale Yarborough Ford	322	9,590	Running
24	19	68	Bobby Hamilton	Tri-Star Motorsports Olds	321	13,130	Running
25	22	4	Ernie Irvan*	Morgan-McClure Chevrolet	317	16,725	Running
26	38	32	Jimmy Horton	Active Racing Chevrolet	316	6,820	Running
27	27	16	Wally Dallenbach,Jr.	Roush Racing Ford	316	6,460	Running
28	21	30	Michael Waltrip	Bahari Racing Pontiac	298	12,740	Engine
29	26	12	Hut Stricklin	Bobby Allison Chevrolet	281	10,100	Engine
30	31	71	Dave Marcis	Marcis Auto Racing Chevy	277	8,940	Running
31	18	41	Greg Sacks	Larry Hedrick Chevrolet	268	5,330	Running
32	34	49	Stanley Smith	Smith Chevrolet	261	5,270	Oil Leak
33	35	20	Mike Wallace	Dick Moroso Olds	251	5,180	Running
34	39	83	Lake Speed	Speed Chevrolet	218	5,135	Crash
35	41	9	Dorsey Schroeder	Melling Performance Ford	176	10,385	T Chain
36	37	47	Buddy Baker	Derick Close Olds	172	5,070	Engine
37	20	98	Jimmy Spencer	Travis Carter Chevrolet	91	9,555	Engine
38	42	52	Jimmy Means	Means Racing Pontiac	87	5,040	Engine
39	13	17	Darrell Waltrip	DarWal Chevrolet	79	15,715	Oil Press
40	40	23	Eddie Bierschwale	Don Bierschwale Olds	71	4,975	Valve
41	5	25	Ken Schrader	Hendrick Motorsports Chevy	38	13,975	Crash
42	33	13	Bob Schacht	Earl Sadler Chevrolet	23	5,225	Valve

Time of Race: 3 hours, 22 minutes, 44 seconds
Average Speed: 147.746 mph
Pole Winner: Mark Martin – 179.923 mph
Lap Leaders: Terry Labonte 1-12, Alan Kulwicki 13-39, T.Labonte 40, Darrell Waltrip 41-43, T.Labonte 44-53, Kulwicki 54-79, Davey Allison 80-136, Harry Gant 137-179, D.Allison 180-282, Bill Elliott 283-328.
10 lead changes among 6 drivers
Cautions: 7 for 29 laps Margin of Victory: 18.25 seconds
*Relieved by Bobby Labonte

"I wrecked a couple of times, but the car didn't know it," cracked Trickle. "Our last set of tires really tightened up the car. When it came time to ring the bell, the harder I ran the more it wanted to skate up the track. We would have liked to finish better, but we're happy with our performance."

Bobby Labonte drove in relief for Ernie Irvan, who was injured the day before in the Busch Grand National race. Labonte, following instructions from his Morgan-McClure team, drove conservatively and finished 25th, nine laps down.

The Ford nameplate captured its eighth Winston Cup win in a row – including the final four races of the 1991 season.

Despite winning three of the first four races – 75% of the races run in 1992 – Elliott finds himself only in a tie for second in the Winston Cup point standings. It has to be one of the real head-scratchers of all time.

Allison holds a 58 point lead over Elliott and Gant in the standings.

Race #5

Elliott Now 4 for 5 But Still Isn't Leading Point Standings

DARLINGTON, SC (March 29) – Harry Gant needed a few more laps to pull off the TranSouth 500, but it was Bill Elliott who racked up his fourth win of the season at Darlington Raceway.

Elliott led the final 45 laps and held on to beat the fast-closing Gant. His triumph gave the Ford Thunderbirds their ninth win in a row. Mark Martin finished in third place with Davey Allison fourth and Ricky Rudd fifth. Only three cars completed the full 501 miles.

Bryan Hallman

Rusty Wallace's Pontiac breaks loose at Darlington after a tap from Brett Bodine.

Jim Ahmay

Bill Elliott enjoyed another flawless run at Darlington.

Winston Cup Race No. 5
367 Laps at Darlington Raceway
Darlington, SC
"TranSouth 500"

501.322 Miles on 1.366-mile Superspeedway
March 29, 1992

Fin	St	No.	Driver	Team / Car	Laps	Money	Status
1	2	11	Bill Elliott	Junior Johnson Ford	367	$64,290	Running
2	11	33	Harry Gant	Leo Jackson Olds	367	40,715	Running
3	14	6	Mark Martin	Roush Racing Ford	367	29,375	Running
4	5	28	Davey Allison	Robert Yates Racing Ford	366	35,315	Running
5	18	5	Ricky Rudd	Hendrick Motorsports Chevy	366	21,020	Running
6	4	26	Brett Bodine	King Motorsports Ford	366	16,290	Running
7	16	8	Dick Trickle	Stavola Brothers Ford	365	14,160	Running
8	12	15	Geoff Bodine	Bud Moore Eng. Ford	365	13,130	Running
9	21	94	Terry Labonte	Billy Hagan Olds	365	13,150	Running
10	8	3	Dale Earnhardt	RCR Enterprises Chevrolet	365	20,570	Running
11	19	2	Rusty Wallace	Roger Penske Pontiac	364	14,665	Running
12	15	25	Ken Schrader	Hendrick Motorsports Chevy	364	15,435	Running
13	13	21	Morgan Shepherd	Wood Brothers Ford	364	11,155	Running
14	24	30	Michael Waltrip	Bahari Racing Pontiac	363	10,850	Running
15	22	55	Ted Musgrave	RaDiUs Pontiac	363	10,745	Running
16	26	10	Derrike Cope	Bob Whitcomb Chevrolet	362	9,175	Running
17	27	1	Rick Mast	Precision Products Olds	362	9,720	Running
18	25	7	Alan Kulwicki	AK Racing Ford	358	10,385	Engine
19	32	95	Bob Schacht	Earl Sadler Oldsmobile	356	6,500	Running
20	34	52	Jimmy Means	Means Racing Pontiac	347	7,670	Running
21	9	18	Dale Jarrett	Joe Gibbs Chevrolet	328	4,950	Running
22	1	22	Sterling Marlin	Junior Johnson Ford	307	11,555	Running
23	20	68	Bobby Hamilton	Tri-Star Motorsports Olds	306	9,460	Engine
24	6	17	Darrell Waltrip	DarWal Chevrolet	264	13,950	Heating
25	33	71	Dave Marcis	Marcis Auto Racing Chevy	260	6,120	Engine
26	3	4	Ernie Irvan	Morgan-McClure Chevrolet	257	14,030	Head
27	17	42	Kyle Petty	SabCo Racing Pontiac	256	7,890	Heating
28	7	41	Greg Sacks	Larry Hedrick Chevrolet	249	4,230	Engine
29	23	12	Hut Stricklin	Bobby Allison Chevrolet	233	7,720	Valve
30	31	16	Wally Dallenbach,Jr.	Roush Racing Ford	187	4,085	Engine
31	36	77	Mike Potter	Steve Balogh Chevrolet	183	4,025	Steering
32	30	43	Richard Petty	Petty Enterprises Pontiac	161	7,540	Piston
33	29	66	Chad Little	Cale Yarborough Ford	133	5,455	Valve
34	10	9	Dave Mader III	Melling Performance Ford	90	7,645	Engine
35	39	56	Jerry Hill	Willie Tierney Pontiac	31	3,860	Handling
36	28	98	Jimmy Spencer	Travis Carter Chevrolet	28	5,825	Head
37	35	53	John McFadden	Means Racing Pontiac	17	3,810	Quit
38	37	90	Kerry Teague	Junie Donlavey Ford	15	3,790	Quit
39	38	48	James Hylton	Hylton Engineering Pontiac	7	3,760	Flagged

Time of Race: 3 hours, 35 minutes, 50 seconds
Average Speed: 139.364 mph
Pole Winner: Sterling Marlin – 163.067 mph
Lap Leaders: Bill Elliott 1-15, Davey Allison 16-26, Bob Schacht 27-28, Allison 29-78, Brett Bodine 79-86, Allison 87, Elliott 88-90, Hut Stricklin 91, Alan Kulwicki 92, B.Bodine 93-100, Allison 101-147, Elliott 148, Kulwicki 149-153, Harry Gant 154-175, D.Allison 176-222, Stricklin 223, Allison 224-227, Gant 228-275, Elliott 276-304, Gant 305-322, Elliott 323-367.
21 lead changes among 7 drivers.
Cautions: 4 for 21 laps Margin of Victory: 7.8 seconds

Elliott is batting a phenominal .800 – winning four of the five races – but is still looking up in the Winston Cup title chase. Elliott still trails Allison by 48 points in one of the weirdest quirks in professional sports history.

Gant's Leo Jackson team had developed a unique but risky game plan – to make an *extra* pit stop during the race. "We found out that the tires started going away as early as 40 laps," said Gant. "So we pitted every 45 laps. The others were pitting around 65 laps. We had to make an extra pit stop, but we were hoping to make up for it on the track with fresher tires."

The strategy nearly worked. Gant had made a pit stop in the 287th lap of the 367-lap event. Elliott's final pit stop came on lap 304. Gant pitted one last time on lap 322 and by the time he got back on the track, he was a lap and two seconds behind Elliott.

Eight laps later, Gant passed Elliott to get back in the lead lap and ran like a banshee the final laps. When the checkered flag fell, Gant trailed by only 7.8 seconds.

"Harry probably had the fastest car here," admitted Elliott after his 38th career Winston Cup win. "But we stuck to our own plan and we won because we were patient. Patience is a critical thing here. I'll let the other guys race each other all day here. Our strategy was to race the race track until it came time to make a move."

Winning crew chief Tim Brewer lauded his driver. "Bill's smart. He knows you don't win at Darlington running wide open the first 200 laps."

Allison led the most laps for the third time this season, but he faded in the end.

Only four cautions broke the action. Pole sitter Sterling Marlin walloped the third turn wall in the 26th lap. Repairs were made to the Junior Johnson Ford and Marlin managed to finish 22nd, 60 laps off the pace.

Brett Bodine was involved in two skirmishes that resulted in yellow flags. He tapped Rusty Wallace into a spin after the half-way point, and Dick Trickle popped Bodine into a spin on lap 243. Bodine still was able to finish sixth – his best effort of the season.

Dale Earnhardt finished in 10th place, two laps off the pace. He failed to lead a lap and had not led a lap all year. "We tested down here and everything went fine. But then we get here and NASCAR has thrown us these new spoiler rules," he said, blaming an increased

Brian Czobat

Davey Allison finished fourth at Darlington and retained his Winston Cup point lead.

spoiler area mandated by NASCAR.

Alan Kulwicki had driven his Ford up to second place with nine laps to go but lost the engine in his AK Racing Ford. The late engine failure left him with an 18th place finish. Kulwicki is logged in seventh place in the Winston Cup standings, 200 points behind leader Allison.

"There was so much junk on the race track that the grille of my car was caked," said Kulwicki. "The engine started to overheat, but what are you going to do in the last laps? With 10 laps to go, it just blew up. It's a shame. We had second in the bag."

Darrell Waltrip and Geoff Bodine tangled in the 174th lap, bringing out the second caution of the day. "(Bodine) just ran me over," complained Waltrip. "You have to give and take, and I gave the man plenty of room. But I guess he decided he needed a little more."

Bodine, who went on to finish eighth, said, "I got a run on him down the front straightaway and I guess he didn't see me. We just bumped. I guess I'd be mad, too, if I had just wrecked."

Race #6

Kulwicki Nips Jarrett at the Line to Win at Bristol

BRISTOL, TN (April 5) – Alan Kulwicki maneuvered past Dale Jarrett with 25 laps to go and won a thrilling two-car shoot-out in the Food City 500 at Bristol International Raceway. It was the first win for the 37 year-old Wisconsin driver since he won at this same track in the summer of 1991.

Kulwicki started on the pole and led four times for 282 laps. Jarrett, giving the Joe Gibbs team its finest outing, battled door-to-door with Kulwicki for the final 50 laps, but settled for second.

Third place went to Ken Schrader, the only other driver on the lead lap. Terry Labonte came in fourth and Dick Trickle was fifth.

Kulwicki said a well handling car and his decision not to change tires on every caution flag, contributed to his victory. "We didn't get lucky this time," said Kulwicki after his fourth career win. "This came down to handling more than anything else.

Kulwicki also adopted a slice of strategy that most observers felt was unusual. "Twice, we didn't take on tires under the yellow," said Kulwicki. "We felt being at or near the front was important, the way the wrecks were occurring in the back of the pack. We made the right decisions today."

A total of 10 cautions interrupted the race for 78 laps. Most were due to crashes.

Point leader Davey Allison suffered his first DNF of the season. His Robert Yates Ford took a hard shot into

Brian Czobat

Alan Kulwicki waves from Victory Lane at Bristol.

the wall when an oil fitting broke loose, spilling oil under his wheels. "I took a pretty good shot on the shoulder blade," said Allison, who was relieved by Sterling Marlin once repairs were made. "I'm going back to Birmingham and have it X-rayed."

Allison's wreck came moments after a one lap penalty for a pit road violation. NASCAR judged Allison's right sided wheels were outside the pit stall, and held him a lap. That took him out of the lead and off the leader lap.

Car owner Yates and crew chief Larry McReynolds protested so loudly that Competition Director Dick Beaty, observing from the control tower, threatened to park the car.

Allison finished in 28th place but still held onto his point lead.

Bill Elliott, seeking his fifth straight win, never got untracked. He spun in the 31st lap and fell a lap behind. Later, he went behind for repairs after being involved in a crash with Ted Musgrave. Despite finishing 20th, Elliott made a significant gain in the point standings – more of a move than he did when winning three of his four races. He trails Allison by 29 points. Kulwicki moved into fifth place, 99 points out of first place.

Brett Bodine had worked his way into contention, but was penalized a lap for passing the lapped car of Dick Trickle on a restart.

Dale Earnhardt led twice for 28 laps but fell two laps off the pace with a tire problem. The Kannapolis, N.C. Chevrolet driver hustled his way back into the lead lap and was pressuring Kulwicki when a tire blew in the 434th lap, sending him into the wall. After repairs, Earnhardt finished in 18th place. He held onto eighth in the point standings, 177 points behind Allison.

Winston Cup Race No. 6
500 Laps at Bristol Int'l Raceway
Bristol, TN
"Food City 500"

266.5 Miles on .533-mile Short Track
April 5, 1992

Fin	St	No.	Driver	Team / Car	Laps	Money	Status
1	1	7	Alan Kulwicki	AK Racing Ford	500	$83,360	Running
2	4	18	Dale Jarrett	Joe Gibbs Chevrolet	500	29,835	Running
3	8	25	Ken Schrader	Hendrick Motorsports Chevy	500	29,410	Running
4	15	94	Terry Labonte	Billy Hagan Olds	499	20,010	Running
5	22	8	Dick Trickle	Stavola Brothers Ford	499	18,410	Running
6	17	5	Ricky Rudd	Hendrick Motorsports Chevy	497	16,485	Running
7	13	21	Morgan Shepherd	Wood Brothers Ford	496	13,685	Running
8	5	12	Hut Stricklin	Bobby Allison Chevrolet	495	13,185	Running
9	3	2	Rusty Wallace	Roger Penske Pontiac	494	15,280	Running
10	31	10	Derrike Cope	Bob Whitcomb Chevrolet	494	11,630	Running
11	2	26	Brett Bodine	King Motorsports Ford	494	12,680	Running
12	27	15	Geoff Bodine	Bud Moore Eng. Ford	494	11,730	Running
13	29	41	Greg Sacks	Larry Hedrick Chevrolet	492	6,055	Running
14	24	55	Ted Musgrave	RaDiUs Oldsmobile	492	11,105	Running
15	9	6	Mark Martin	Roush Racing Ford	488	13,905	Running
16	25	9	Dave Mader III	Melling Performance Ford	487	11,430	Running
17	10	30	Michael Waltrip	Bahari Racing Pontiac	478	10,530	Running
18	18	3	Dale Earnhardt	RCR Enterprises Chevrolet	471	18,130	Running
19	23	42	Kyle Petty	SabCo Racing Pontiac	471	10,420	Running
20	11	11	Bill Elliott	Junior Johnson Ford	470	14,230	Running
21	26	52	Brad Teague	Means Racing Pontiac	456	7,080	Running
22	32	16	Wally Dallenbach,Jr.	Roush Racing Ford	446	5,280	Running
23	20	66	Chad Little	Cale Yarborough Ford	439	4,880	Running
24	7	4	Ernie Irvan	Morgan-McClure Chevrolet	415	14,755	Crash
25	16	17	Darrell Waltrip	DarWal Chevrolet	382	24,505	Running
26	28	68	Bobby Hamilton	Tri-Star Motorsports Olds	379	10,680	Running
27	14	43	Richard Petty	Petty Enterprises Pontiac	354	9,630	Running
28	6	28	Davey Allison*	Robert Yates Racing Ford	335	15,205	Running
29	12	33	Harry Gant	Leo Jackson Olds	277	14,975	Engine
30	30	1	Rick Mast	Precision Products Olds	122	9,480	Crash
31	21	71	Dave Marcis	Marcis Auto Racing Chevy	92	6,455	Engine
32	19	22	Sterling Marlin	Junior Johnson Ford	16	9,430	Crash

Time of Race: 3 hours, 5 minutes, 15 seconds
Average Speed: 86.316 mph
Pole Winner: Alan Kulwicki – 122.474 mph
Lap Leaders: Alan Kulwicki 1-95, Dale Earnhardt 96-99, Kulwicki 100-156, Earnhardt 157-180, Davey Allison 181-229, Darrell Waltrip 230-252, Allison 253, Brett Bodine 254-312, Ken Schrader 313-332, Kulwicki 333-435, Dale Jarrett 436-473, Kulwicki 474-500.
11 lead changes among 7 drivers.
Cautions: 10 for 75 laps Margin of Victory: 0.72 second
*Relieved by Sterling Marlin

Winston Cup Race No. 7
400 Laps at North Wilkesboro Speedway
N.Wilkesboro, NC
"First Union 400"

250 Miles on .625-mile Short Track
April 12, 1992

Fin	St	No.	Driver	Team / Car	Laps	Money	Status
1	7	28	Davey Allison	Robert Yates Racing Ford	400	$51,740	Running
2	5	2	Rusty Wallace	Roger Penske Pontiac	400	29,140	Running
3	2	5	Ricky Rudd	Hendrick Motorsports Chevy	400	23,465	Running
4	11	15	Geoff Bodine	Bud Moore Eng. Ford	400	22,665	Running
5	16	33	Harry Gant	Leo Jackson Olds	400	19,590	Running
6	9	3	Dale Earnhardt	RCR Enterprises Chevrolet	400	32,540	Running
7	1	7	Alan Kulwicki	AK Racing Ford	400	21,990	Running
8	10	22	Sterling Marlin	Junior Johnson Ford	400	11,835	Running
9	3	94	Terry Labonte	Billy Hagan Olds	400	11,085	Running
10	8	26	Brett Bodine	King Motorsports Ford	400	12,965	Running
11	6	8	Dick Trickle	Stavola Brothers Ford	400	10,610	Running
12	14	21	Morgan Shepherd	Wood Brothers Ford	400	10,260	Running
13	4	4	Ernie Irvan	Morgan-McClure Chevrolet	400	13,935	Running
14	22	10	Derrike Cope	Bob Whitcomb Chevrolet	399	6,860	Running
15	25	17	Darrell Waltrip	DarWal Chevrolet	399	13,735	Running
16	12	6	Mark Martin	Roush Racing Ford	399	11,960	Running
17	24	18	Dale Jarrett	Joe Gibbs Chevrolet	399	3,885	Running
18	29	12	Hut Stricklin	Bobby Allison Chevrolet	399	9,835	Running
19	13	55	Ted Musgrave	RaDiUs Oldsmobile	398	9,010	Running
20	20	11	Bill Elliott	Junior Johnson Ford	398	12,410	Running
21	19	41	Greg Sacks	Larry Hedrick Chevrolet	397	3,660	Running
22	18	25	Ken Schrader	Hendrick Motorsports Chevy	397	12,610	Running
23	27	1	Rick Mast	Precision Products Olds	396	8,460	Running
24	26	71	Dave Marcis	Marcis Auto Racing Chevy	396	5,310	Running
25	32	66	Bobby Hillin,Jr.	Cale Yarborough Ford	393	5,260	Running
26	21	98	Jimmy Spencer	Travis Carter Chevrolet	393	8,060	Running
27	23	68	Bobby Hamilton	Tri-Star Motorsports Olds	393	8,885	Running
28	15	42	Kyle Petty	SabCo Racing Pontiac	367	7,770	Running
29	17	30	Michael Waltrip	Bahari Racing Pontiac	347	9,735	Running
30	31	16	Wally Dallenbach,Jr.	Roush Racing Ford	346	3,060	Running
31	28	43	Richard Petty	Petty Enterprises Pontiac	234	8,610	Handling
32	30	52	Jimmy Means	Means Racing Pontiac	219	4,535	Engine

Time of Race: 2 hours, 45 minutes, 28 seconds
Average Speed: 90.653 mph
Pole Winner: Alan Kulwicki – 117.242 mph
Lap Leaders: Alan Kulwicki 1-135, Dale Earnhardt 136-140, Kulwicki 141-187, Earnhardt 188-205, Brett Bodine 206-224, Earnhardt 225-237, Geoff Bodine 238-265, Rusty Wallace 266-312, Davey Allison 313-400.
8 lead changes among 6 drivers.
Cautions: 9 for 55 laps Margin of Victory: 0.15 second

Race #7

Allison Shakes off Injuries to Win at North Wilkesboro

N.WILKESBORO, NC (April 12) – Davey Allison survived a fender bender, a spin-out, shook off nagging injuries and outran Rusty Wallace to win the First Union 400 at North Wilkesboro Speedway. It was the second win of the season for the Hueytown, Ala. Ford driver.

Allison led the final 88 laps and finished about two car lengths ahead of Rusty Wallace's Pontiac.

"I didn't know if I was going to make it," said Allison, who suffered muscle and cartilage damage to his ribs and shoulder in a crash a week earlier at Bristol. "My left leg started hurting first and I didn't know if I was going to be able to hold the brake pedal down when I needed to. Then the right one started cramping. All that and having Rusty Wallace breathing down our necks really made it rough. We had to fight for it."

Wallace, who led 47 laps, said he wasn't too sure about all of Allison's 'cramps'. "Obviously he wasn't hurting that bad – the way he was driving," he said. "One little bump and it could have been mine. GM really needs a win, but we don't need it bad enough to start

Bryan Hallman

Davey Allison increased his Winston Cup point lead with a win at North Wilkesboro.

wrecking people. I think this erases any doubt that the GM cars are capable of winning."

Ricky Rudd finished in third place with Geoff Bodine fourth and Harry Gant fifth.

Allison stretched his Winston Cup point lead to 86 points over Gant, who moved past Bill Elliott into second place. Elliott finished 20th, 30 laps behind and fell to third, 106 points behind Allison.

Allison, who let substitute driver Jimmy Hensley qualify his car, grabbed the lead from Wallace in the pits on lap 313 after a collision between Bobby Hillin, Jr. and Kyle Petty brought out the final caution flag.

Hillin, Jr., serving a temporary assignment in the Yarborough Motorsports Ford in light of Chad Little's release, snagged Kyle Petty's rear bumper, sending him into a spin. NASCAR officials put Hillin, Jr. in the 'penalty box' for five laps for rough driving. During the time Hillin, Jr. was held, Felix Sabates, owner of Kyle's Pontiac, lashed out verbally

Brian Czobat

Alan Kulwicki started on the pole and finished seventh at North Wilkesboro.

at Hillin, Jr. Ironically, Hillin, Jr. was one of the drivers who filled in for Kyle in 1991 when he was injured at Talladega.

The Hillin-Petty yellow set up the pit road battle, which Allison's Yates team won. "I've got the best pit crew in racing," claimed Allison. "They gave me the lead and all I had to do was keep it."

Allison survived a spin with Petty in the 128th lap. "Kyle hooked me and didn't let off," said Allison. "I thought I was going into the infield. He couldn't help it. We were racing for position and ran together."

Only two cars failed to finish. Jimmy Means went out after completing 219 laps with a blown engine. Richard Petty departed on lap 234 with handling woes.

Pole sitter Alan Kulwicki started on the pole and led the first 135 laps. He led for another 47 lap stretch before falling back. "After that, it was a question of track position," said Kulwicki. "We couldn't pass many people after that. It seemed like everybody stayed in the position they were in. Track position was everything."

Dale Earnhardt had another strong run which resulted in a sixth place finish. "That's the most fun I've had in a long time," said Earnhardt, who got into some close racing with Wallace before being warned by NASCAR officials. "They probably would have hit anybody else with a penalty," said Wallace. "But they know how Dale and I like to race together. It was just good racing, that's all."

Davey Allison in Victory Lane at North Wilkesboro.

Brian Czobat

Race #8

Mark Wins at Martin's Ville; Cambered Rear Ends Foil Leaders

MARTINSVILLE, VA (April 26) – Mark Martin led the final 27 laps and outran a faltering Sterling Marlin to win the Hanes 500 at Martinsville Speedway. It was the 12th straight victory for Ford and Martin's first of the season.

Martin exercised patience and capitalized on the

Winston Cup Race No. 8
500 Laps at Martinsville Speedway
Martinsville, VA
"Hanes 500"
262.5 Miles on .525-mile Short Track
April 26, 1992

Fin	St	No.	Driver	Team / Car	Laps	Money	Status
1	12	6	Mark Martin	Roush Racing Ford	500	$59,300	Running
2	22	22	Sterling Marlin	Junior Johnson Ford	500	32,775	Running
3	1	17	Darrell Waltrip	DarWal Chevrolet	499	30,700	Running
4	19	94	Terry Labonte	Billy Hagan Olds	499	19,700	Running
5	15	33	Harry Gant	Leo Jackson Olds	498	22,875	Running
6	20	21	Morgan Shepherd	Wood Brothers Ford	498	16,400	Running
7	18	25	Ken Schrader	Hendrick Motorsports Chevy	498	17,700	Running
8	3	26	Brett Bodine	King Motorsports Ford	498	15,850	Running
9	2	3	Dale Earnhardt	RCR Enterprises Chevrolet	497	22,550	Running
10	10	11	Bill Elliott	Junior Johnson Ford	497	16,900	Running
11	26	12	Hut Stricklin	Bobby Allison Chevrolet	495	11,835	Running
12	25	41	Greg Sacks	Larry Hedrick Chevrolet	495	5,450	Running
13	31	68	Bobby Hamilton	Tri-Star Motorsports Olds	494	11,050	Running
14	11	1	Rick Mast	Precision Products Olds	490	10,850	Running
15	6	66	Jimmy Hensley	Cale Yarborough Ford	488	8,950	Running
16	9	7	Alan Kulwicki	AK Racing Ford	464	25,200	Running
17	27	8	Dick Trickle	Stavola Brothers Ford	464	10,050	Running
18	17	42	Kyle Petty	SabCo Racing Pontiac	450	9,455	Crash
19	30	16	Wally Dallenbach,Jr.	Roush Racing Ford	450	4,150	Running
20	28	55	Ted Musgrave	RaDiUs Oldsmobile	440	9,650	Running
21	24	9	Dave Mader III	Melling Performance Ford	438	9,050	Running
22	4	10	Derrike Cope	Bob Whitcomb Chevrolet	434	6,100	Running
23	5	5	Ricky Rudd	Hendrick Motorsports Chevy	426	11,850	Running
24	13	71	Dave Marcis	Marcis Auto Racing Chevy	406	5,150	Axle
25	16	4	Ernie Irvan	Morgan-McClure Chevrolet	386	14,000	Axle
26	23	28	Davey Allison	Robert Yates Racing Ford	383	13,500	Crash
27	8	30	Michael Waltrip	Bahari Racing Pontiac	358	4,850	Running
28	21	18	Dale Jarrett	Joe Gibbs Chevrolet	351	5,225	Running
29	29	43	Richard Petty	Petty Enterprises Pontiac	286	7,600	Engine
30	32	52	Jimmy Means	Means Racing Pontiac	232	4,525	Handling
31	7	2	Rusty Wallace	Roger Penske Pontiac	176	11,000	Valve
32	12	15	Geoff Bodine	Bud Moore Eng. Ford	104	8,000	Engine

Time of Race: 3 hours, 22 minutes, 5 seconds
Average Speed: 78.086 mph
Pole Winner: Darrell Waltrip – 92.956 mph
Lap Leaders: Dale Earnhardt 1-60, Dave Mader III 61-67, Alan Kulwicki 68-286, Ernie Irvan 287-302, Earnhardt 303-313, Irvan 314-362, Earnhardt 363-457, Mark Martin 458-463, Earnhardt 464, Brett Bodine 465-473, Martin 474-500.
11 lead changes among 6 drivers.
Cautions: 11 for 59 laps   Margin of Victory: 12.125 seconds

Greg Fielden

Mark Martin was the survival of the fittest at Martinsville.

failure of Alan Kulwicki, Ernie Irvan and Dale Earnhardt - all of whom fell victim to broken axles – to move to the front.

Many of the front runners were using a new trick, angling axles slightly to bring rear wheels inward at the top. Cambered rear ends give the tires a wider 'footprint' on the track.

"The problem," said Martin, "is that bending the axles increases pressure on the splines which attach the axle to the wheels. Either the teeth in the splines and hubs strip out or the axle breaks. We weren't running an axle bent to the degree that some of the others had. I'd say our axle was bent about half as much as some of the others."

While Martin's Ford passed the durability test, the fleet cars of Kulwicki, Irvan and Earnhardt were foiled while leading.

Kulwicki led for a stretch of 219 laps and appeared to have the race well in hand until his Ford slowed with a broken rear end on lap 287. "It was a race decided by cambered rear ends," he said after finishing 16th, 36 laps off the pace. "We were forced to start using them since they give you better traction. Everybody thought they had the pieces figured out to make it work, but it backfired on most of us."

Irvan led most of the laps following Kulwicki's failure until he, too, ran into the same problem. "We broke a rear end, plain and simple," said Irvan. "But to have a realistic chance of winning, you had to take the risk."

Irvan's car owner Larry McClure, complained that NASCAR had not approved proper components which would enhance durability. "NASCAR thinks they're saving us a lot of money by not approving the stuff to make the cambered axle work. If NASCAR keeps saving me money, pretty soon I'm going to be broke."

Earnhardt took the lead in the 363rd lap and was pulling away when his car slowed with 44 laps to go. Earnhardt was able to salvage a ninth place finish.

Earnhardt angrily answered reporters questions for a few minutes before leaving the track. "We just haven't

Brian Czobat

Alan Kulwicki rounds the corner at Martinsville. He held onto fifth place in the Winston Cup standings despite a 16th place finish.

got no luck at all," he said. "I didn't know if it was going to last or not. It almost did. We wanted to win bad and we had to try something. I thought we had 'em all beat except for Kulwicki. I certainly don't think Mark could have beaten us if we'd been around at the end."

Brett Bodine was poised for his second victory – leading with 28 laps to go – but his run was derailed when a suspension part broke as he headed into the first turn.

Martin took the lead on lap 474 and led the rest of the way. "Maybe I didn't have the sheer car to go out there and whip 'em," said Martin, after giving Ford it's 12th straight Winston Cup win. "But I thought we had a shot if we played it smart. We anticipated there would be some trouble with these trick rear ends."

Sterling Marlin finished second for the sixth time in his career. He finished 12 seconds behind Martin after his Ford slipped off the pace in the closing laps. "We picked up a miss in the engine with about 80 laps to go," remarked Marlin. The Junior Johnson Ford also had one of the cambered rear ends, but experienced no trouble. "We had more camber in our rear end than anybody here and ours didn't break," said Mike Beam, Marlin's crew chief. "I guess we were finally lucky for a change."

Darrell Waltrip started on the pole and wound up in third place, a lap behind. Terry Labonte came from 19th to finish fourth and Harry Gant came home fifth.

Point leader Davey Allison started 23rd and never led. A tire blew on his Ford, sending him into the wall on lap 387. "I bruised my ribs a little bit," said Allison, "but I'm okay."

Allison's point lead was shaved to 16 points by Gant. Bill Elliott, who finished 10th, fell to fourth in the standings despite still winning half the races.

Kyle Petty escaped injury when his Pontiac slapped the backstretch wall and burst into flames. Geoff Bodine, who had fallen out of the race a few laps earlier, ran across the track with a fire extinguisher to assist Petty and helped put out the fire.

"I just ran out of brakes," said Petty. "I tore the walls down and tore up the race car."

Winston Cup Race No. 9
188 Laps at Talladega Superspeedway
Talladega, AL
"Winston 500"
500.08 Miles on 2.66-mile Superspeedway
May 3, 1992

Fin	St	No.	Driver	Team / Car	Laps	Money	Status
1	2	28	Davey Allison	Robert Yates Racing Ford	188	$189,325	Running
2	5	11	Bill Elliott	Junior Johnson Ford	188	56,225	Running
3	10	3	Dale Earnhardt	RCR Enterprises Chevrolet	188	46,970	Running
4	3	22	Sterling Marlin	Junior Johnson Ford	188	45,470	Running
5	1	4	Ernie Irvan	Morgan-McClure Chevrolet	188	35,840	Running
6	20	7	Alan Kulwicki	AK Racing Ford	188	25,315	Running
7	15	18	Dale Jarrett	Joe Gibbs Chevrolet	188	19,215	Running
8	21	6	Mark Martin	Roush Racing Ford	188	22,765	Running
9	6	21	Morgan Shepherd	Wood Brothers Ford	188	19,065	Running
10	9	42	Kyle Petty	SabCo Racing Pontiac	188	17,665	Running
11	18	2	Rusty Wallace	Roger Penske Pontiac	188	18,530	Running
12	29	10	Derrike Cope	Bob Whitcomb Chevrolet	188	15,050	Running
13	32	15	Geoff Bodine	Bud Moore Eng. Ford	188	15,420	Running
14	11	16	Wally Dallenbach,Jr.	Roush Racing Ford	188	9,240	Running
15	17	43	Richard Petty	Petty Enterprises Pontiac	188	14,660	Running
16	8	26	Brett Bodine	King Motorsports Ford	188	14,070	Running
17	14	1	Rick Mast	Precision Products Olds	188	13,055	Running
18	23	9	Dave Mader III	Melling Performance Ford	188	13,365	Running
19	28	8	Dick Trickle	Stavola Brothers Ford	188	12,325	Running
20	34	68	Bobby Hamilton	Tri-Star Motorsports Olds	187	13,765	Running
21	13	55	Ted Musgrave	RaDiUs Chevrolet	187	11,650	Running
22	12	12	Hut Stricklin	Bobby Allison Chevrolet	187	11,430	Running
25	35	25	Ken Schrader	Hendrick Motorsports Chevy	187	15,670	Running
24	24	33	Harry Gant	Leo Jackson Olds	186	16,565	Running
25	16	66	Jimmy Hensley	Cale Yarborough Ford	186	8,340	Running
26	4	5	Ricky Rudd	Hendrick Motorsports Chevy	186	16,005	Running
27	37	71	Dave Marcis	Marcis Auto Racing Chevy	184	7,925	Running
28	27	31	Bobby Hillin,Jr.	Team Ireland Chevrolet	192	6,295	Running
29	33	17	Darrell Waltrip	DarWal Chevrolet	180	15,640	Running
30	31	95	Bob Schacht	Earl Sadler Oldsmobile	180	6,185	Running
31	36	47	Buddy Baker	Derick Close Olds	176	6,055	W Bearing
32	26	98	Jimmy Spencer	Travis Carter Chevrolet	175	10,550	Suspension
33	22	49	Stanley Smith	Smith Chevrolet	116	5,970	Crash
34	38	52	Jimmy Means	Means Racing Pontiac	101	7,465	Engine
35	30	41	Greg Sacks	Larry Hedrick Chevrolet	92	5,910	Engine
36	7	94	Terry Labonte	Billy Hagan Ford	77	10,380	Engine
37	19	90	Charlie Glotzbach	Junie Donlavey Ford	75	5,800	Crash
38	25	30	Michael Waltrip	Bahari Racing Pontiac	63	8,745	Engine
39	39	50	Clay Young	Young Pontiac	40	5,690	Engine
40	40	53	John McFadden	Means Racing Pontiac	5	5,660	Quit

Time of Race: 2 hours, 59 minutes, 1 second
Average Speed: 167.609 mph
Pole Winner: Ernie Irvan – 192.831 mph
Lap Leaders: Davey Allison 1-5, Ernie Irvan 6, Allison 7-10, Sterling Marlin 11-19, Dale Earnhardt 20-23, Marlin 24-48, Mark Martin 49-50, Allison 51-72, Marlin 73-77, Irvan 78-81, Allison 82-89, Marlin 90-96, Earnhardt 97-102, Bill Elliott 103-106, Marlin 107-117, Allison 118-188.
16 lead changes among 5 drivers.
Cautions: 5 for 21 laps Margin of Victory: 2 car lengths

Race #9

Ford's Streak Continues as Allison Wins at Talladega

TALLADEGA, AL (May 3) – Davey Allison held his Ford in front of a tight pack of cars for the final 71 laps and galloped to victory in the Winston 500 at Talladega Superspeedway. The 31 year-old Hueytown, Ala. driver clinched at least a $100,000 bonus for winning two of the four crown jewel races that make up the Winston Million. He has a chance to earn the remainder of the bonus with a victory at either Charlotte or Darlington.

Allison held his line and outran Bill Elliott by two car lengths to post his 16th career Winston Cup triumph. Dale Earnhardt was abreast of Elliott and finished third. Sterling Marlin nipped Ernie Irvan at the stripe to get fourth place.

Allison's victory ran Ford's winning streak to 13 races, including the final four in the 1991 season.

ISC

The Winston Cup stars race two, three and sometimes four abreast on Talladega's high banks.

Allison led on five occasions for a total of 110 laps as a crowd of 142,500 watched the dramatic finish, which came down to a predicted Ford vs. Chevy battle.

"I knew the Chevrolets weren't going to go where the Fords went," said Allison. "The only one I was really concerned about was Bill. After I got a gap between everyone, Earnhardt and Irvan went after Bill. I stayed down (in the groove) trying to assist Bill with the draft as much as possible. I was staying low in the draft to help Bill beat those two Chevys – as long as he finished behind me."

Allison also gave credit to his Robert Yates Racing pit crew. "We stayed up front by not changing tires on our last two pit stops. That was critical because the leader controlled the action," said Allison.

In the final lap, Elliott seemed more concerned with keeping Earnhardt behind him than running Allison for the win. Elliott blocked an Earnhardt move in the first turn and both narrowly averted a collision. "We were in the right place at the wrong time," said Elliott.

Irvan, who started on the pole and led only one lap, said he got lost in the shuffle. "I was trying to work with Dale. I knew he wasn't going where the Fords went. But I got to racing Sterling and couldn't quite get up there to help him."

Morgan Shepherd had worked his way into fourth place, but got hammered out of the lead pack after a shunt with Marlin. "I guess the buddy system is out," said Shepherd, who fell back to ninth place. "If we had worked together, Irvan wouldn't have passed us and we would have had a chance to win. Instead, Sterling almost crashed

ISC

Pole Sitter Ernie Irvan leads the 40-car Talladega field on the pace lap.

me twice."

Allison's victory enabled him to pull out to a 67-point lead over Elliott in the Winston Cup standings.

Jimmy Spencer took an eerie ride in Travis Carter's Chevrolet late in the race. Spencer got tapped in a tight traffic situation and slid off the backstretch. The rear of his car lifted high into the air. After sailing several hundred feet, miraculously the car made a four-point landing without tipping over. "If you think it was scary from where you were, you should have been in my seat," said a shaken Spencer. "I've never experienced anything like it. Things got absolutely quiet. The motor stalled and it sounded like I was gliding. I'd like to say I guided it back to a four-wheel landing, but brother, I had nothing to do with it."

Spencer drove his car back to the pit area. He pulled out with suspension damage when his car slammed back down on the ground.

Kyle Petty said the incident with Spencer was his fault. "I hit Wally (Dallenbach,Jr.) and it was my fault. I knew I was close on him and I wanted to be so I could help him get through. When Spencer got beside him, the air stopped on Wally's car. A little bit was all it took. It slowed him up and I hit just hard enough to jerk him into Spencer."

Charlie Glotzbach had given the Junie Donlavey Ford a strong run until he spun off the backstretch in the 76th lap.

Mark Martin had qualified third, but his time was disallowed when NASCAR found that the car failed the ground clearance test. He requalified and started 21st. Martin finished eighth in the race.

Stanley Smith had qualified a surprising sixth, but his time was also disallowed. NASCAR said Smith's fuel color was different from the series' mandated Unocal gasoline.

Smith said the color variation was caused by a small amount of synthetic fuel remaining in his car from a test session the previous week. Smith started 22nd and retired after completing 116 laps when he tagged the wall.

Terry Labonte, who had run in the top 10 in each of the eight previous races, drove a Ford from the Billy Hagan shops. Engine failure put him out after 77 laps.

Alan Kulwicki finished sixth and moved into fourth place in the point standings, 118 points behind Allison.

Winston Cup Race No. 10
400 Laps at Charlotte Motor Speedway
Concord, NC
"Coca-Cola 600"
600 Miles on 1.5-mile Superspeedway
May 24, 1992

Fin	St	No.	Driver	Team / Car	Laps	Money	Status
1	13	3	Dale Earnhardt	RCR Enterprises Chevrolet	400	$125,100	Running
2	11	4	Ernie Irvan	Morgan-McClure Chevrolet	400	67,275	Running
3	2	42	Kyle Petty	SabCo Racing Pontiac	400	60,900	Running
4	17	28	Davey Allison	Robert Yates Racing Ford	400	45,750	Running
5	26	33	Harry Gant	Leo Jackson Olds	400	35,800	Running
6	14	94	Terry Labonte	Billy Hagan Olds	400	27,100	Running
7	8	7	Alan Kulwicki	AK Racing Ford	400	39,850	Running
8	16	55	Ted Musgrave	RaDiUs Motorsports Ford	399	23,150	Running
9	3	5	Ricky Rudd	Hendrick Motorsports Chevy	398	30,100	Running
10	10	8	Dick Trickle	Stavola Brothers Ford	398	22,800	Running
11	20	66	Jimmy Hensley	Cale Yarborough Ford	398	17,250	Running
12	23	18	Dale Jarrett	Joe Gibbs Chevrolet	397	15,400	Running
13	24	31	Bobby Hillin,Jr.	Team Ireland Chevrolet	397	11,800	Running
14	1	11	Bill Elliott	Junior Johnson Ford	396	57,600	Running
15	35	71	Dave Marcis	Marcis Auto Racing Chevy	394	12,975	Running
16	27	41	Greg Sacks	Larry Hedrick Chevrolet	390	9,750	Running
17	30	10	Derrike Cope	Bob Whitcomb Chevrolet	388	11,150	Running
18	7	2	Rusty Wallace	Roger Penske Pontiac	386	18,050	Engine
19	36	83	Lake Speed	Speed Ford	385	7,650	Running
20	4	26	Brett Bodine	King Motorsports Ford	378	15,780	Running
21	22	68	Bobby Hamilton	Tri-Star Motorsports Olds	377	13,120	Engine
22	9	22	Sterling Marlin	Junior Johnson Ford	364	12,160	Running
23	31	1	Rick Mast	Precision Products Olds	348	11,450	Running
24	39	61	Randy Porter	Porter Racing Pontiac	322	6,340	Engine
25	15	30	Michael Waltrip	Bahari Racing Pontiac	321	10,880	Running
26	6	25	Ken Schrader	Hendrick Motorsports Chevy	309	16,845	Crash
27	37	98	Jimmy Spencer	Travis Carter Chevrolet	288	10,465	Engine
28	38	16	Wally Dallenbach,Jr.	Roush Racing Ford	279	5,710	Engine
29	25	21	Morgan Shepherd	Wood Brothers Ford	252	10,230	Crash
30	29	49	Stanley Smith	Smith Chevrolet	248	5,555	No Tires
31	40	95	Bob Schacht	Thee Dixon Chevrolet	245	5,725	Engine
32	19	15	Geoff Bodine	Bud Moore Eng. Ford	244	9,975	Engine
33	5	6	Mark Martin	Roush Racing Ford	234	14,850	Engine
34	28	12	Hut Stricklin	Bobby Allison Chevrolet	220	9,850	Crank
35	32	20	Joe Ruttman	Dick Moroso Olds	213	5,250	Crash
36	42	90	Charlie Glotzbach	Junie Donlavey Ford	194	5,200	Piston
37	33	89	Jim Sauter	Mueller Brothers Pontiac	194	5,165	Ignition
38	18	17	Darrell Waltrip	DarWal Chevrolet	185	14,540	Piston
39	21	9	Dave Mader III	Melling Performance Ford	184	10,145	Crash
40	34	27	Gary Balough	Linro Motorsports Chevrolet	131	5,100	Crash
41	12	43	Richard Petty	Petty Enterprises Pontiac	115	10,600	Crash
42	41	52	Jimmy Means	Means Racing Pontiac	8	5,100	Engine

Time of Race: 4 hours, 30 minutes, 43 seconds
Average Speed: 132.980 mph
Pole Winner: Bill Elliott – 175.479 mph
Lap Leaders: Ricky Rudd 1-8, Kyle Petty 9-16, Rudd 17-29, Alan Kulwicki 30, Ken Schrader 31-59, Kulwicki 60-62, Mark Martin 63-66, K.Petty 67-74, Dale Jarrett 75, Jimmy Spencer 76, Kulwicki 77, Rudd 78-89, Kulwicki 90-106, Davey Allison 107-121, Greg Sacks 122-127, Jimmy Hensley 128-138, Rusty Wallace 139-161, Kulwicki 162-168, Allison 169-186, Kulwicki 187-200, K.Petty 201-204, Geoff Bodine 205-208, K.Petty 209-227, R.Wallace 228-242, K.Petty 243-288, Ernie Irvan 289-290, K.Petty 291-346, Dale Earnhardt 347-400.
27 lead changes among 14 drivers
Cautions: 12 for 62 laps Margin of Victory: 0.41 second

Race #10

Rivals Howl as Speedy Run in Pits Nets Victory for Earnhardt

CONCORD, NC (May 24) – Dale Earnhardt snookered Kyle Petty and Ernie Irvan with a quick pit stop and a quicker trip down pit road, and emerged victorious in the Coca-Cola 600 at Charlotte Motor Speedway. Earnhardt, who started 13th, ended Ford's winning streak at 13 and ended a personal 13-race losing streak.

Earnhardt ran with the leaders most of the day, but

Crew chiefs Kirk Shelmerdine and Jeff Hammond relax at Charlotte. Shelmerdine got his 46th win as a crew chief when Dale Earnhardt captured the Coca-Cola 600.

never led until he took the lead for good with 54 laps remaining. Kyle Petty, the race's biggest leader with 141 laps on the point, and Ernie Irvan, who battled back from two laps down, were the two main factors until Earnhardt's late bid.

Petty and Irvan were running first and second when they pitted together in the 346th lap. Observing the 55 mph speed limit on pit road, both drivers came into their respective pits together. Irvan got four new tires and fuel in 20.2 seconds, while Petty received the same service in 19.9 seconds. Petty got back on the track a few car lengths ahead of Irvan.

Earnhardt, who had been trailing the leaders by nearly three seconds, pitted a lap later. He zipped down pit road at an alarming rate and locked up his brakes, skidding the length of two pit stalls. He stopped perfectly in his pit where the RCR Enterprises crew went to work. In 19.1-seconds, Earnhardt was on his way.

When the three leaders reached racing speeds, Earnhardt was 1.27 seconds ahead and never looked back.

Irvan passed Petty and began closing on Earnhardt in the final laps but could not make the pass. Earnhardt beat Irvan by 0.41-second to win the $125,100 first prize.

Petty fell off the pace and wound up third. Davey Allison's bid for the Winston Million came up short by finishing fourth. Fifth place went to Harry Gant.

Petty and Irvan questioned the legality of Earnhardt's last pit stop. "There's no way a man can be over two seconds behind you on the race track and everybody pits at about the same time, and he comes out over a second ahead," growled Petty. "I don't care what anybody says. Unless he had a 13 second pit stop, there's no way he should have been up there where he was. The only place he could have gotten that advantage was

Dick Trickle #8 spins in foreground as Ken Schrader, Darrell Waltrip, Bobby Hillin, Jr. and Dave Mader III mix it up in Charlotte's fourth turn.

CMS

Dale Jarrett's Chevrolet and Sterling Marlin's Ford fuse together in accident at Charlotte.

plce, only 12 points behind Kulwicki.

Dick Trickle survived a spin with Ken Schrader and Michael and Darrell Waltrip. He came back to move into fifth place until mechanical problems dropped him two laps off the pace. He eventually finished 10th.

Michael Waltrip, bitten by sour luck for yet another time, got back in the race after repairs and finished 25th, 79 laps behind. "I know God has a plan for all of this," said Waltrip. "I just wish He would let me in on it."

Gary Balough and Greg Sacks tangled in the early going, knocking Balough out of the race. The fiery Florida driver marched down to Sacks' Larry Hedrick crew and got into an argument with one of the pit crewmen. After taking a swing at one person, NASCAR officials escorted Balough out of the area.

speeding down pit road."

Irvan said he couldn't understand "how he gained one second in the pits, but it came out to five seconds on the race track. I guess I should have run a little faster down pit road like Dale did," said Irvan.

Earnhardt said he "got in real quick and flat-footed it on the return lane. I fudged all I could on the speed limit without getting penalized."

Despite gaining an unfair advantage on pit road, there were plenty of laps left for the others to make up ground.

Irvan made a strong run from a two lap deficit. In the 16th lap, Irvan pitted with a bad misfire in the engine. The Morgan-McClure pit crew thought it was a loose plug wire, but a quick diagnosis revealed a bad carburetor. "The guys fixed the problem incredibly fast," said Irvan. "The bad carburetor almost cooked the engine though. It ran like a V-6 engine down the straightaways, but the car was handling good. We were very fortunate to make up two laps."

Earnhardt said he knew he had Irvan's number in the final laps. "I ran my line, and for Ernie to pass me he'd have to move me or move his line. He raced me hard but clean. I was a little surprised at that. But Ernie's coming around. He's becoming a pretty good driver."

Bill Elliott started on the pole but never led. He struggled and finished 14th, four laps off the pace. Elliott held onto second in the Winston Cup standings, but fell 111 points behind Allison.

Alan Kulwicki led six times, but a mis-matched set of tires cost him dearly. He wound up seventh, the final car on the lead lap. Kulwicki ranks fourth in the standings, 132 points off the top. Earnhardt moved into fifth

Race #11

Gasless Gant Grabs Dover; Moves to 2nd in Point Race

DOVER, DE (May 31) – Harry Gant overcame a series of early pit stops and coasted to victory in the Budweiser 500 at Dover Downs International Speedway for his first win of the season.

Gant drove the final 98 laps without a pit stop and ran out of fuel in the final lap. The 52 year-old Taylorsville, N.C. driver had built up a big enough cushion so that he could cross the finish line nearly a lap in front of runner-up Dale Earnhardt.

Rusty Wallace finished in third place with Ernie Irvan fourth and Darrell Waltrip fifth.

Waltrip's bid was foiled when he ran out of gas with two laps to go.

Gant started in 15th place and was never a factor until the late going. A stroke of luck allowed him to make over a dozen pit stops during the second caution of the day to correct a tow-in problem after he and Davey

Allison collided on pit road. The yellow flag was out for 19 laps while repair crews welded the steel inside retaining barrier after Derrike Cope and Wally Dallenbach, Jr. crashed hard.

"I pulled out of the pits and Davey knocked my front wheel in," explained Gant. "It wasn't a big lick, but it caught my tire. The crew adjusted the front end alignment as best they could, but it was still off."

Gant was forced to work his way up from the rear, and timely caution flags kept him in the hunt when he was in danger of going a lap down.

During an 82 lap stretch of green flag conditions, most of the front-runners had made pit stops. Many of the contenders were trapped a lap behind the leader when the sixth caution came out. Gant moved into immediate contention by getting superior fuel mileage.

In the final analysis, Gant was able to employ his Leo Jackson team's strength once again. He pitted for the final time in the 402nd lap. Waltrip was the last of the leaders to make his pit stop on lap 405. Every other contender had to make an additional stop in the waning laps.

"The crew told me it would be real close on fuel and I shouldn't run too hard," said Gant after his 17th career Winston Cup win. "That's why I followed Darrell so long."

Gant drove past Waltrip with 41 laps to go and led the rest of the way. Waltrip was within striking distance when his engine sputtered with two miles to go. "We thought we could go the distance," said Waltrip. "I'm disappointed we ran out when we were so close to the end. I thought we could go further than Harry did because we pitted three laps later. I don't know how to explain it."

Winning crew chief Andy Petree was holding his breath the final laps. "We goofed a little on the last stop," said Petree. "We only got 18 gallons (out of a capacity of 22 gallons) in the car on the last stop. Leo

Dover Downs

Harry Gant #33 coasts across the finish line at Dover. Gant ran the final 98 miles on one tankful of fuel and made it home on fumes.

Winston Cup Race No. 11
500 Laps at Dover Downs Int'l Speedway
Dover, DE
"Budweiser 500"

500 Miles on 1-mile Superspeedway
May 31, 1992

Fin	St	No.	Driver	Team / Car	Laps	Money	Status
1	15	33	Harry Gant	Leo Jackson Olds	500	$65,145	Running
2	24	3	Dale Earnhardt	RCR Enterprises Chevrolet	500	43,720	Running
3	14	2	Rusty Wallace	Roger Penske Pontiac	499	25,795	Running
4	9	4	Ernie Irvan	Morgan-McClure Chevrolet	499	29,445	Running
5	4	17	Darrell Waltrip	DarWal Chevrolet	499	25,140	Running
6	13	5	Ricky Rudd	Hendrick Motorsports Chevy	498	21,215	Running
7	23	12	Hut Stricklin	Bobby Allison Chevrolet	498	26,490	Running
8	12	66	Jimmy Hensley	Cale Yarborough Ford	498	13,140	Running
9	20	8	Dick Trickle	Stavola Brothers Ford	498	14,340	Running
10	7	21	Morgan Shepherd	Wood Brothers Ford	498	18,040	Running
11	21	28	Davey Allison	Robert Yates Racing Ford	497	17,090	Running
12	37	7	Alan Kulwicki	AK Racing Ford	497	14,590	Running
13	8	11	Bill Elliott	Junior Johnson Ford	496	14,290	Running
14	10	22	Sterling Marlin	Junior Johnson Ford	496	11,890	Running
15	3	30	Michael Waltrip	Bahari Racing Pontiac	495	11,690	Running
16	26	55	Ted Musgrave	RaDiUs Motorsports Ford	495	11,390	Running
17	5	15	Geoff Bodine	Bud Moore Eng. Ford	494	10,940	Running
18	29	68	Bobby Hamilton	Tri-Star Motorsports Olds	494	11,525	Running
19	27	41	Greg Sacks	Larry Hedrick Chevrolet	491	7,240	Running
20	17	43	Richard Petty	Petty Enterprises Pontiac	489	10,790	Running
21	18	94	Terry Labonte	Billy Hagan Oldsmobile	474	9,990	Running
22	31	32	Jimmy Horton	Active Racing Chevrolet	474	5,090	Running
23	6	25	Ken Schrader	Hendrick Motorsports Chevy	470	14,040	Running
24	2	6	Mark Martin	Roush Racing Ford	470	13,890	Running
25	19	71	Dave Marcis	Marcis Auto Racing Chevy	435	6,690	Crash
26	25	9	Chad Little	Melling Performance Ford	412	7,890	Trans
27	28	18	Dale Jarrett	Joe Gibbs Chevrolet	308	6,490	Engine
28	33	77	Mike Potter	Steve Balogh Buick	266	4,790	Valve
29	16	42	Kyle Petty	SabCo Racing Pontiac	252	9,340	Crash
30	1	26	Brett Bodine	King Motorsports Ford	247	12,765	Engine
31	32	52	Jimmy Means	Means Racing Pontiac	201	4,640	Engine
32	22	1	Rick Mast	Precision Products Olds	190	9,140	Crash
33	11	10	Derrike Cope	Bob Whitcomb Chevrolet	145	6,065	Crash
34	30	16	Wally Dallenbach,Jr.	Roush Racing Ford	143	5,990	Crash
35	39	48	James Hylton	Hylton Engineering Pontiac	118	4,290	Flagged
36	34	65	Jerry O'Neil	Alan Aroneck Oldsmobile	59	4,265	Handling
37	35	59	Andy Belmont	Pat Rossi Ford	59	4,490	Engine
38	36	56	Jerry Hill	Willie Tierney Pontiac	39	4,190	Ignition
39	40	85	D.K.Ulrich	Alan Aroneck Chevrolet	21	4,165	Quit
40	38	53	Graham Taylor	Means Racing Pontiac	14	4,140	Quit

Time of Race: 4 hours, 34 minutes, 5 seconds
Average Speed: 109.456 mph
Pole Winner: Brett Bodine – 147.408 mph
Lap Leaders: Brett Bodine 1-18, Mark Martin 19-43, Ricky Rudd 44-101, Martin 102-122, Dale Earnhardt 123-129, Martin 130-147, Alan Kulwicki 148-150, Earnhardt 151-195, Ernie Irvan 196-205, Hut Stricklin 206-263, Irvan 264-268, Morgan Shepherd 269-287, Darrell Waltrip 288-302, Shepherd 303-314, D.Waltrip 315-379, Shepherd 380-400, D.Waltrip 401-404, Terry Labonte 405-408, Irvan 409-439, D.Waltrip 440-459, Harry Gant 460-500.
20 lead changes among 11 drivers
Cautions: 7 for 98 laps Margin of Victory: 26 seconds

Kim Novasat

Ernie Irvan shares a quiet moment with NASCAR's Chip Williams before the Dover 500-miler.

said I had a chewing-out coming if we didn't win."

Gant was able to move into second place in the Winston Cup title chase, 70 points behind Allison, who was penalized for speeding on pit road late in the race. The reprimand knocked Allison three laps off the pace and he wound up 11th.

"I made a conscious effort not to go too fast," said a perturbed Allison. "I ran the same speed on pit road all day and they call me in and penalize me. They let Earnhardt run the speed he wanted to at Charlotte and he went on and won the race."

Morgan Shepherd led three times for 52 laps and was holding a comfortable lead when a botched pit stop ruined his chances. A balky lug nut on a routine pit stop forced the Wood Brothers to take 43 seconds to get the car serviced. Shepherd fell off the lead lap during the stop. He made a strong run at the end to nab 10th place.

"The lug nut didn't strip, it just wouldn't break loose," explained Shepherd. "They finally had to take a big 'ol bar and bust it lose."

Alan Kulwicki scored a moral victory by bringing his Ford home 12th. He had wiped out two cars in practice and qualifying and a third car had to be shipped in from North Carolina. "The car snapped twice," said Kulwicki. "I mean, it was a different situation both times. Something is wrong here because I just don't go out and wreck in practice."

Many drivers complained about the asphalt sealer used to cure the track.

Race #12

Irvan Wins at Sears Point; NASCAR Founder France Dies

SONOMA, CA (June 7) – Ernie Irvan overcame an opening lap penalty, roared back from the rear of the field and won the Save Mart 300-kilometer race at Sears Point International Raceway. Irvan's victory was tempered with news earlier in the day that NASCAR

Winston Cup Race No. 12
74 Laps at Sears Point Int'l Raceway
Sonoma, CA
"Save Mart 300K"
186.48 Miles on 2.52-mile Road Course
June 7, 1992

Fin	St	No.	Driver	Team / Car	Laps	Money	Status
1	2	4	Ernie Irvan	Morgan-McClure Chevrolet	74	$61,810	Running
2	6	94	Terry Labonte	Billy Hagan Oldsmobile	74	36,685	Running
3	8	6	Mark Martin	Roush Racing Ford	74	28,185	Running
4	1	5	Ricky Rudd	Hendrick Motorsports Chevy	74	25,710	Running
5	5	11	Bill Elliott	Junior Johnson Ford	74	32,585	Running
6	12	3	Dale Earnhardt	RCR Enterprises Chevrolet	74	21,910	Running
7	13	2	Rusty Wallace	Roger Penske Pontiac	74	18,110	Running
8	4	17	Darrell Waltrip	DarWal Chevrolet	74	18,610	Running
9	13	25	Ken Schrader	Hendrick Motorsports Chevy	74	17,360	Running
10	15	15	Geoff Bodine	Bud Moore Eng. Ford	74	16,360	Running
11	33	1	Rick Mast	Precision Products Olds	74	13,460	Running
12	19	42	Kyle Petty	SabCo Racing Pontiac	74	12,960	Running
13	14	52	Tommy Kendall	Means Racing Pontiac	74	6,755	Running
14	7	7	Alan Kulwicki	AK Racing Ford	74	14,255	Running
15	16	26	Brett Bodine	King Motorsports Ford	74	11,905	Running
16	11	22	Sterling Marlin	Junior Johnson Ford	74	11,405	Running
17	24	33	Harry Gant	Leo Jackson Olds	74	15,530	Running
18	20	10	Derrike Cope	Bob Whitcomb Chevrolet	74	6,345	Running
19	32	75	Bill Sedgwick	Wayne Spears Chevrolet	74	9,080	Running
20	26	30	Michael Waltrip	Bahari Racing Pontiac	74	11,155	Running
21	17	43	Richard Petty	Petty Enterprises Pontiac	74	11,055	Running
22	31	55	Ted Musgrave	RaDiUs Motorsports Olds	73	10,230	Running
23	27	71	Dave Marcis	Marcis Auto Racing Chevy	73	7,155	Running
24	34	9	Bill Schmitt	Sylvia Schmitt Ford	73	8,235	Running
25	9	16	Wally Dallenbach,Jr.	Roush Racing Ford	73	6,975	Running
26	28	8	Dick Trickle	Stavola Brothers Ford	73	9,855	Running
27	37	12	Hut Stricklin	Bobby Allison Chevrolet	73	9,780	Running
28	10	28	Davey Allison	Robert Yates Racing Ford	73	16,305	Running
29	21	21	Morgan Shepherd	Wood Brothers Ford	72	9,670	Running
30	22	66	Jimmy Hensley	Cale Yarborough Ford	72	5,815	Running
31	40	99	John Krebs	Diamond Ridge Pontiac	72	6,530	Running
32	17	92	Ron Hornaday,Jr.	Bob Fisher Chevrolet	72	4,930	Running
33	29	09	R.K.Smith	Dick Midgley Pontiac	70	4,880	Engine
34	25	68	Bobby Hamilton	Tri-Star Motorsports Olds	70	10,380	Running
35	39	60	Mike Chase	Kaylan Young Pontiac	69	6,330	Running
36	42	51	Rick Scribner	Scribner Chevrolet	68	4,820	Running
37	38	37	Rick Carelli	Marshall Chesrown Chevrolet	57	4,800	Rear End
38	36	24	Butch Gilliland	Gilliland Pontiac	55	4,780	Handling
39	23	18	Dale Jarrett	Joe Gibbs Chevrolet	52	4,750	Trans
40	43	44	Jack Sellers	Adele Emerson Buick	48	4,725	Trans
41	18	0	Irv Hoerr	Precision Products Olds	12	4,725	Engine
42	35	50	Hershel McGriff	John Strauser Chevrolet	19	4,725	Trans
43	41	41	Greg Sacks	Larry Hedrick Chevrolet	2	4,725	Engine

Time of Race: 2 hours, 17 minutes, 26 seconds
Average Speed: 81.413 mph
Pole Winner: Ricky Rudd – 90.985 mph
Lap Leaders: Ricky Rudd 1-9, Alan Kulwicki 10-14, Rusty Wallace 15-26, Harry Gant 27-28, Bill Elliott 29-50, Mark Martin 51, Terry Labonte 52-66, Ernie Irvan 67-74.
7 lead changes among 8 drivers.
Cautions: 3 for 7 laps Margin of Victory: 3.6 seconds

Brian Czobat

Richard Petty wheels his Pontiac around the Sears Point International Raceway en route to a 21st place finish.

founder Bill France, Sr. had passed away in his Ormond Beach, Fla. home at the age of 82.

France had been in declining health for about eight years and seriously ill for the past 24 months.

Irvan, who started second, jumped pole sitter Ricky Rudd at the green flag and was black-flagged for a stop and go penalty. The stop put Irvan at the rear of the 43 car field in the second lap.

"I didn't know I did anything wrong," said Irvan after his fourth career victory. "Doyle Ford waved the green flag and I took off. I thought that was the way we raced. But even after I came into the pits, I still thought we could win.

"I think Rudd was messing with me," added Irvan. "I think he held back at the start on purpose."

To complicate matters, the transmission in Irvan's Morgan-McClure Chevrolet stuck in fourth gear as early as the fifth lap. He was able to get that repaired when the first caution came out when Davey Allison slammed into a stack of tires in the 10th lap.

Irvan moved into fifth place after 35 laps and had moved into second place on lap 62, passing Rudd. Terry Labonte had built up a five-second lead in the closing stages, but Irvan ran him down in five laps.

Irvan took the lead from Labonte with eight laps to go and sprinted to a 3.6-second victory before a record turn-out of 83,000. It was his first Winston Cup win in his home state.

"I could see fans in every corner with signs supporting me," said Irvan. "This is like winning a game for the home town football team. When I was catching Terry, I could see the fans getting into it. It was a thrill."

Runner-up Labonte admitted he was no match for Irvan. "I didn't figure there was any point in blocking him," said Labonte, who was attempting to win his first race since 1989. "His car was quicker than anything else out there."

Third place finisher Mark Martin was foiled when he skidded off course on lap 58 while battling with Rudd. "I had a car capable of winning, but I got over anxious trying to get around Ricky. I got off course and nearly tore the car up," he said.

Rudd finished in fourth place and Bill Elliott was fifth.

Dale Earnhardt came home sixth and moved into second place in the Winston Cup standings. He trails leader Allison by only 28 points despite having two fewer victories and half as many top five finishes as Allison. Four-time winner Elliott trails Earnhardt by three points.

Allison was unable to finish higher than 28th due to his off-track excursion. "I was over my head and didn't realize it," said Allison, who also spun out late in the race. "I'm not really thinking about the points right now. That's three races we've crashed in and been out of the top 10 and one that NASCAR penalized us out of the top 10."

The triumph was the fourth in a row for General Motors cars after Ford won the first nine events. "We finally quit whining and went to work," said eighth place finisher Darrell Waltrip, who drove a Chevrolet. "We worked on the whole package and now we're racing again."

Alan Kulwicki finished 14th after being penalized for speeding in the pits. The Wisconsin native ranks fifth in the point standings, 83 points behind Allison.

Race #13

Special K Leads Ford's Romp at Pocono; Moves to 3rd in Standings

LONG POND, PA (June 14) – Alan Kulwicki took the lead for the final time with 11 laps to go and drove to a 2.34 second victory over Mark Martin in the Champion Spark Plug 500 at Pocono International Raceway. It was the second win of the season for Kulwicki and the fifth of his career.

Bill Elliott finished third in a 1-2-3 sweep for Ford Thunderbirds. Chevrolet driver Ken Schrader, who won the pole, wound up fourth. Davey Allison finished fifth.

Dale Earnhardt, who entered the race in second place in the Winston Cup standings, tumbled to fifth place after engine problems hampered him most of the day.

Kulwicki, who led seven times for 58 laps, lost the lead 15 laps from the finish when he nearly slugged the wall. "(James) Hylton was right in the groove and I couldn't slow quick enough to follow him through the turn," said Kulwicki. "Sometimes when you're going 40 mph faster than someone, they don't realize how quick you're going to catch them. I got up into the marbles and almost hit the wall. What I said then is unprintable."

Despite the detour, Kulwicki came back and ran down Elliott on lap 190. "I regrouped and kept my cool. I felt I had an edge on Bill because I had gotten four tires on my last pit stop and I knew he had gotten only two. I thought he would race me clean and he did," he remarked.

Martin got around Elliott in the last couple of laps to take second. He had to overcome a 68th lap pit stop

Brian Czobat

Alan Kulwicki flashes across the finish line to win Pocono's Champion Spark Plug 500.

Winston Cup Race No. 13
500 Laps at Pocono Int'l Raceway
Long Pond, PA
"Champion Spark Plug 500"
500 Miles on 2.5-mile Superspeedway
June 14, 1992

Fin	St	No.	Driver	Team / Car	Laps	Money	Status
1	6	7	Alan Kulwicki	AK Racing Ford	200	$74,255	Running
2	4	6	Mark Martin	Roush Racing Ford	200	39,480	Running
3	3	11	Bill Elliott	Junior Johnson Ford	200	32,355	Running
4	1	25	Ken Schrader	Hendrick Motorsports Chevy	200	32,980	Running
5	18	28	Davey Allison	Robert Yates Racing Ford	200	27,175	Running
6	5	42	Kyle Petty	SabCo Racing Pontiac	200	18,150	Running
7	19	22	Sterling Marlin	Junior Johnson Ford	200	15,750	Running
8	8	26	Brett Bodine	King Motorsports Ford	200	14,650	Running
9	23	66	Jimmy Hensley	Cale Yarborough Ford	200	11,800	Running
10	12	94	Terry Labonte	Billy Hagan Olds	200	15,600	Running
11	26	41	Greg Sacks	Larry Hedrick Chevrolet	199	10,000	Running
12	14	10	Derrike Cope	Bob Whitcomb Chevrolet	199	9,650	Running
13	24	17	Darrell Waltrip	DarWal Chevrolet	199	16,150	Running
14	27	15	Geoff Bodine	Bud Moore Eng. Ford	199	12,050	Running
15	15	30	Michael Waltrip	Bahari Racing Pontiac	199	11,550	Running
16	21	43	Richard Petty	Petty Enterprises Pontiac	198	11,400	Running
17	29	68	Bobby Hamilton	Tri-Star Motorsports Olds	198	12,050	Running
18	32	71	Dave Marcis	Marcis Auto Racing Chevy	196	7,900	Running
19	16	4	Ernie Irvan	Morgan-McClure Chevrolet	194	16,000	Running
20	31	77	Mike Potter	Steve Balogh Buick	191	6,475	Running
21	35	65	Jerry O'Neil	Alan Aroneck Olds	188	5,750	Running
22	7	18	Dale Jarrett	Joe Gibbs Chevrolet	187	10,150	Running
23	28	33	Harry Gant	Leo Jackson Olds	186	15,300	Engine
24	10	2	Rusty Wallace	Roger Penske Pontiac	185	13,250	Running
25	2	21	Morgan Shepherd	Wood Brothers Ford	180	9,860	Running
26	39	48	James Hylton	Hylton Engineering Pontiac	178	5,150	Running
27	13	16	Wally Dallenbach,Jr.	Roush Racing Ford	177	5,100	Clutch
28	17	3	Dale Earnhardt	RCR Enterprises Chevrolet	148	16,600	Engine
29	20	8	Dick Trickle	Stavola Brothers ford	146	6,600	Engine
30	30	1	Rick Mast	Precision Products Olds	141	9,525	Engine
31	11	12	Hut Stricklin	Bobby Allison Chevrolet	116	9,450	Engine
32	37	85	Bobby Gerhart	Gerhart Chevrolet	113	4,850	Engine
33	22	55	Ted Musgrave	RaDiUs Motorsports Ford	102	9,275	Engine
34	34	32	Jimmy Horton	Active Racing Chevrolet	49	4,675	Crash
35	33	52	Jimmy Means	Means Racing Pontiac	33	7,100	H Gasket
36	9	5	Ricky Rudd	Hendrick Motorsports Chevy	22	12,515	Engine
37	25	9	Chad Little	Melling Performance Ford	15	4,445	Piston
38	40	56	Jerry Hill	Willie Tierney Pontiac	10	4,405	Engine
39	38	62	Mark Thompson	Henley Gray Ford	8	4,370	Engine
40	36	59	Andy Belmont	Pat Rissi Ford	3	4,295	Engine

Time of Race: 3 hours, 28 minutes, 18 seconds
Average Speed: 144.023 mph
Pole Winner: Ken Schrader – 162.499 mph
Lap Leaders: Ken Schrader 1-10, Mark Martin 11-34, Brett Bodine 35, Bill Elliott 36-37, Harry Gant 38-39, Schrader 40-41, Martin 42-68, Alan Kulwicki 69-70, Ernie Irvan 71-85, Kulwicki 86-107, Rusty Wallace 108, Jimmy Hensley 109-110, Irvan 111-115, Kulwicki 116-121, Davey Allison 122-136, Schrader 137-139, Allison 140-157, Kulwicki 158-159, Allison 160, Kulwicki 161-170, Elliott 171, Darrell Waltrip 172, Hensley 173-175, Elliott 176-180, Kulwicki 181-185, Elliott 186-189, Kulwicki 190-200.
26 lead changes among 11 drivers.
Cautions: 3 for 13 laps Margin of Victory: 2.34 seconds

Pocono Int'l

Rusty Wallace #2 and Hut Stricklin lead the field into Pocono's first turn.

which cost him a lap. An air gun malfunctioned and Martin shot out of the pits with several lug nuts on his tires loose. He stopped at the end of pit road and backed up into his pit to have them tightened.

"After we had the bad pit stop, my guys were great," said Martin. "They had a lot of 19-second pit stops. We made everything up that we lost. We just fell short at the end."

Kulwicki and Martin were using a new Jerico transmission which allows shifting to a higher gear on the track's long front stretch.

"I got beat by the shift," said Elliott, who wound up third. "Everybody that beat me had that shifter."

Fifth place finisher Allison was running in second place late in the race until a botched pit stop ruined his chances with 31 laps remaining. Allison's car fell off the jack and by the time he got back out on the track, 40.6 seconds had elapsed.

"The jack didn't break," said car owner Robert Yates. "The car just slipped off."

Rookie Jimmy Hensley finished ninth in the Yarborough Motorsports Ford. "I had never seen this place until I came here this week," said Hensley. Despite being unfamiliar with the tri-angular track, Hensley led twice for five laps and gave car owner Yarborough his second top 10 finish of the season.

Kulwicki moved into third place in the point standings as the chase for the Winston Cup began taking shape of a wide open scramble. Allison leads Elliott by 21 points with Kulwicki 58 points out of first place.

Pocono Int'l

Alan Kulwicki's sparkling run led him to Victory Lane at Pocono.

Race #14

Allison Dominates Michigan 400; Musgrave Shines

BROOKLYN, MI (June 21) – Davey Allison thoroughly dominated the Miller Genuine Draft 400 at Michigan International Speedway before a packed house of 105,000, and stretched his lead in the Winston Cup point standings.

Winston Cup Race No. 14
200 Laps at Michigan Int'l Speedway
Brooklyn, MI
"Miller Genuine Draft 400"
400 Miles on 2-mile Superspeedway
June 21, 1992

Fin	St	No.	Driver	Team / Car	Laps	Money	Status
1	1	28	Davey Allison	Robert Yates Racing Ford	200	$150,665	Running
2	9	17	Darrell Waltrip	DarWal Chevrolet	200	47,840	Running
3	4	7	Alan Kulwicki	AK Racing Ford	200	38,215	Running
4	17	42	Kyle Petty	SabCo Racing Pontiac	200	25,265	Running
5	12	5	Ricky Rudd	Hendrick Motorsports Chevy	200	25,760	Running
6	2	6	Mark Martin	Roush Racing Ford	200	27,285	Running
7	18	33	Harry Gant	Leo Jackson Olds	200	23,910	Running
8	26	55	Ted Musgrave	RaDiUs Motorsports Ford	199	18,910	Running
9	22	3	Dale Earnhardt	RCR Enterprises Chevrolet	199	23,110	Running
10	3	11	Bill Elliott	Junior Johnson Ford	199	21,260	Running
11	30	15	Geoff Bodine	Bud Moore Eng. Ford	199	16,210	Running
12	19	21	Morgan Shepherd	Wood Brothers Ford	198	15,635	Running
13	10	25	Ken Schrader	Hendrick Motorsports Chevy	198	18,185	Running
14	15	41	Greg Sacks	Larry Hedrick Chevrolet	198	11,635	Running
15	14	43	Richard Petty	Petty Enterprises Pontiac	198	14,285	Running
16	25	90	Charlie Glotzbach	Junie Donlavey Ford	198	7,960	Running
17	5	31	Bobby Hillin,Jr.	Team Ireland Chevrolet	197	7,735	Running
18	31	16	Wally Dallenbach,Jr.	Roush Racing Ford	197	7,510	Running
19	7	26	Brett Bodine	King Motorsports Ford	196	12,995	Running
20	24	8	Dick Trickle	Stavola Brothers Ford	196	10,280	Running
21	32	9	Chad Little	Melling Performance Ford	196	6,860	Running
22	35	10	Derrike Cope	Bob Whitcomb Chevrolet	195	8,945	Running
23	34	52	Jimmy Means	Means Racing Pontiac	192	8,635	Running
24	13	18	Dale Jarrett	Joe Gibbs Chevrolet	191	11,425	Running
25	39	48	James Hylton	Hylton Engineering Chevy	188	6,415	Running
26	40	32	Jimmy Horton	Active Racing Chevrolet	187	6,255	Running
27	41	30	Michael Waltrip*	Bahari Racing Pontiac	186	11,045	Engine
28	28	1	Rick Mast	Precision Products Olds	158	10,885	Engine
29	11	66	Jimmy Hensley	Cale Yarborough Ford	157	8,425	Fly Whee
30	6	4	Ernie Irvan	Morgan-McClure Chevrolet	157	16,560	Running
31	16	68	Bobby Hamilton	Tri-Star Motorsports Olds	156	11,430	Running
32	23	22	Sterling Marlin	Junior Johnson Ford	145	10,335	Engine
33	36	77	Mike Potter	Steve Balogh Chevrolet	112	5,680	Valve
34	38	59	Andy Belmont	Pat Rissi Ford	104	5,860	Clutch
35	27	12	Hut Stricklin	Bobby Allison Chevrolet	91	10,090	Valve
36	33	71	Dave Marcis	Marcis Auto Racing Chevy	75	7,020	Engine
37	8	2	Rusty Wallace	Roger Penske Pontiac	69	13,465	Crank
38	20	94	Terry Labonte	Billy Hagan Olds	41	9,940	Engine
39	29	89	Jim Sauter	Mueller Brothers Pontiac	31	5,415	Clutch
40	21	49	Stanley Smith	Smith Chevrolet	28	5,855	Engine
41	37	36	H.B.Bailey	Bailey Pontiac	8	5,355	Valve

Time of Race: 2 hours, 37 minutes, 12 seconds
Average Speed: 152.672 mph
Pole Winner: Davey Allison – 176.258 mph
Lap Leaders: Alan Kulwicki 1, Davey Allison 2, Kulwicki 3-22, Mark Martin 23-32, Allison 33-42, Kulwicki 43-44, Darrell Waltrip 45, Bill Elliott 46, Harry Gant 47-49, Allison 50-85, D.Waltrip 86-87, Allison 88-125, D.Waltrip 126-127, Allison 128-200.
14 lead changes among 6 drivers.
Cautions: 4 for 13 laps   Margin of Victory: 3.31 seconds
*Relieved by Ben Hess

Brian Czobat

Davey Allison jumps out to an early lead in opening lap at Michigan.

Allison started on the pole and was hardly threatened, leading for 158 of the 200 laps. Darrell Waltrip finished second, a deceiving 3.31-seconds behind the fleet Allison. Alan Kulwicki took third spot with Kyle Petty fourth and Ricky Rudd fifth.

Sophomore driver Ted Musgrave enjoyed a sparkling run. After starting 26th, Musgrave ran steady and moved into the top 10 in the final 100 miles. The Franklin, Wisc. Ford driver began picking off the big names until he was in fourth place. But a pit stop for fuel knocked him down to eighth. "We've got some horsepower now," said Musgrave. "Now we need to work on fuel mileage."

Allison was never threatened after the final caution flag, which ended on lap 155. He moved out quickly to a 12 second lead before coasting the final 50 miles.

"The guys did a great job of giving me a fast, comfortable race car," said Allison, who won for the 17th time in his career. "My job was easy. All I had to do was drive it."

Waltrip held off Kulwicki for runner-up honors. "I had to fight Alan for it," said Waltrip. "Davey was just on cruise control. If we gained a little, he'd stretch it back out. At the end, he was letting us catch up. He could have lapped the field."

Allison's triumph enabled him to pull to a 67-point lead over Bill Elliott, who wound up 10th after running out of gas early and losing a lap. Kulwicki pulled to within six points of Elliott.

Brian Czobat

Davey Allison with wife Liz in Victory Lane after winning Miller 400 at Michigan.

Dale Earnhardt started 22nd and never led. He finished in ninth place, a lap off the pace. "The thing drove like a truck. We used way too high a gear trying to make sure the engine would last."

Ernie Irvan complained that Allison forced him into the second turn wall in the fourth lap while battling for second place. Allison said he slipped in a patch of oil causing him to crowd Irvan.

"I was passing Davey and he must have gotten loose and slid into my quarter-panel," explained Irvan. "I was lucky to hold it against the wall. He could have taken out about 20 cars. He took away our shot at winning. It's

MIS

Davey Allison and Dale Earnhardt at the front of the field for a restart at Michigan.

one thing to get loose and hit somebody and another thing to make up a story about hitting some oil."

Allison said "there was something on the track. Kulwicki (leader at the time) hit it, Ernie hit it, Mark (Martin) hit it and I hit it. We all went for a little ride over there. None of us touched."

Michael Waltrip suffered a broken nose and several bruises in a scary crash in qualifying. Waltrip's Pontiac broke loose and clobbered the third turn wall with a resounding shot.

The Owensboro, Kent. driver made the start on Sunday but was relieved early by Ben Hess. The Bahari Racing Pontiac succumbed to engine problems late in the race and Hess finished 27th.

"All I wanted to do was bring the car home in one piece," said Hess.

Race #15

King Richard's Bid Fizzles; Irvan Captures 400 at Daytona

DAYTONA BEACH, FL (July 4) – Ernie Irvan led the final 24 laps and held off Sterling Marlin to win the Pepsi 400 at Daytona International Speedway, a contest witnessed by a crowd of 80,000 and President George Bush.

Irvan started sixth on the grid but had the lead as early as the eighth lap. The Modesto, Calif. driver kept his Morgan-McClure Chevrolet at or near the front most of the day – leading for a total of 118 of the 160 laps. He took the lead for the final time in the 137th lap when he passed Dale Jarrett.

Marlin won the pole position, knocking King Richard Petty off the coveted inside front row starting spot. Petty started second and led the opening five laps as the crowd roared approvingly.

But Petty would not be a factor in his final appearance as a driver at Daytona. He faded with an ill-handling car and began suffering from heat exhaustion before the half-way point. He pitted in the 82nd lap and called for a relief driver.

Eddie Bierschwale, who had parked his Oldsmobile

ISC

Ernie Irvan won the Pepsi 400 sizzler.

Winston Cup Race No. 15
160 Laps at Daytona Int'l Speedway
Daytona Beach, FL
"Pepsi 400"
400 Miles on 2.5-mile Superspeedway
July 4, 1992

Fin	St	No.	Driver	Team / Car	Laps	Money	Status
1	6	4	Ernie Irvan	Morgan-McClure Chevrolet	160	$86,300	Running
2	1	22	Sterling Marlin	Junior Johnson Ford	160	50,025	Running
3	10	18	Dale Jarrett	Joe Gibbs Chevrolet	160	37,200	Running
4	17	15	Geoff Bodine	Bud Moore Eng. Ford	160	26,075	Running
5	20	11	Bill Elliott	Junior Johnson Ford	160	26,500	Running
6	11	25	Ken Schrader	Hendrick Motorsports Chevy	160	22,625	Running
7	5	5	Ricky Rudd	Hendrick Motorsports Chevy	160	20,875	Running
8	4	6	Mark Martin	Roush Racing Ford	160	19,325	Running
9	29	2	Rusty Wallace	Roger Penske Pontiac	160	18,325	Running
10	3	28	Davey Allison	Robert Yates Racing Ford	160	23,075	Running
11	15	16	Wally Dallenbach,Jr.	Roush Racing Ford	160	8,915	Running
12	7	26	Brett Bodine	King Motorsports Ford	160	14,350	Running
13	13	17	Darrell Waltrip	DarWal Chevrolet	159	17,460	Running
14	12	42	Kyle Petty	SabCo Racing Pontiac	159	13,720	Running
15	23	66	Jimmy Hensley	Cale Yarborough Ford	159	11,280	Running
16	27	55	Ted Musgrave	RaDiUs Motorsports Chevy	159	13,090	Running
17	19	1	Rick Mast	Precision Products Olds	159	12,675	Running
18	24	12	Hut Stricklin	Bobby Allison Chevrolet	159	12,160	Running
19	8	21	Morgan Shepherd	Wood Brothers Ford	159	11,745	Running
20	18	90	Charlie Glotzbach	Junie Donlavey Ford	159	7,180	Running
21	14	94	Terry Labonte	Billy Hagan Ford	158	11,160	Running
22	21	49	Stanley Smith	Smith Chevrolet	158	6,140	Running
23	16	33	Harry Gant	Leo Jackson Olds	158	15,970	Running
24	32	9	Chad Little	Melling Performance Ford	158	5,850	Running
25	34	31	Bobby Hillin,Jr.	Team Ireland Chevrolet	158	5,730	Running
26	31	41	Greg Sacks	Larry Hedrick Chevrolet	157	7,410	Running
27	9	30	Michael Waltrip	Bahari Racing Pontiac	156	10,065	Running
28	35	73	Phil Barkdoll	Barkdoll Racing Olds	156	5,295	Running
29	39	99	Brad Teague	Ralph Ball Chevrolet	147	5,200	Running
30	26	7	Alan Kulwicki	AK Racing Ford	144	13,105	Running
31	37	59	Andy Belmont	Pat Rissi Ford	133	5,300	Running
32	40	71	Dave Marcis	Marcis Auto Racing Chevy	130	6,670	Engine
33	25	68	Bobby Hamilton	Tri-Star Motorsports Chevy	124	10,590	Crash
34	30	10	Derrike Cope	Bob Whitcomb Chevrolet	122	6,535	Crash
35	33	8	Dick Trickle	Stavola Brothers Ford	122	6,480	Crash
36	2	43	Richard Petty*	Petty Enterprises Pontiac	84	10,925	Fatigue
37	36	85	Bobby Gerhart	Gerhart Chevrolet	58	4,870	Fatigue
38	38	23	Eddie Bierschwale	Don Bierschwale Olds	45	4,855	Quit
39	28	52	Jimmy Means	Means Racing Pontiac	24	7,045	W Bearing
40	22	3	Dale Earnhardt	RCR Enterprises Chevrolet	7	16,355	Engine

Time of Race: 2 hours, 20 minutes, 47 seconds
Average Speed: 170.457 mph
Pole Winner: Sterling Marlin – 189.366 mph
Lap Leaders: Richard Petty 1-5, Sterling Marlin 6-7, Ernie Irvan 8-31, Ricky Rudd 32, Irvan 33-47, Dale Jarrett 48-51, Rudd 52, Bill Elliott 53-54, Irvan 55-97, Jarrett 98-105, Elliott 106-107, Irvan 108-109, Alan Kulwicki 110, Irvan 111-119, Davey Allison 120-122, Jarrett 123-136, Irvan 137-160.
17 lead changes among 8 drivers.
Cautions: 2 for 8 laps Margin of Victory: 2 car lengths
*Relieved by Eddie Bierschwale

ISC

Morgan Shepherd's Ford breaks loose on the backstretch at Daytona as Wally Dallenbach, Jr. and Rusty Wallace pass.

after 100 miles, got into Petty's Pontiac but only made two laps. He was unable to adjust to Petty's custom made seat and couldn't reach the floor pedals.

"I started getting hot and I knew I couldn't last another 200 miles," Petty said afterwards. "The best thing for me to do was get out of the car, even if I couldn't find a relief driver. I was getting weak and knew I could cause an accident if I kept going."

ISC

President George Bush and Richard Petty before the Pepsi 400 at Daytona. Bush was on a campaign tour in Florida.

ISC

Sterling Marlin #22 and King Richard Petty on the front row at Daytona International Speedway.

Petty said a hectic schedule of promotional appearances and wearing his driving suit for about two hours in pre-race ceremonies on a hot and humid day contributed to his fatigue.

"All the hullabaloo finally caught up with me," said the King. "I was hyped-up because this is my last race here and because of the President's visit. The crew can get mad at me. The car was fine. I just wasn't mentally or physically ready."

Marlin drop-kicked Petty off the pole position in qualifying on Thursday. He was welcomed with a chorus of boos and jeers from the crowd. "I hated to beat him for the pole," said Marlin, "but we had a job to do and we did it. It was definitely a different feeling to get booed after winning the pole. I've never had that happen before. I'm going to an autograph session in a little while. I wonder if I need to take a security guard with me."

ISC

Ernie Irvan nips Sterling Marlin at the finish line at Daytona.

Irvan exercised patience – a virtue he has rarely used – and put the spurs on his yellow Chevrolet only when he needed to. "Today, I kept remembering something Darrell Waltrip told me," said Irvan after his fifth career win. "He said 'don't let somebody who can't beat you make you run too hard'. That's pretty good advice."

Irvan beat Marlin by two car lengths at the stripe. Third place went to Jarrett with Geoff Bodine and Bill Elliott, who rubbed fenders in the final laps, fourth and fifth respectively.

Dale Earnhardt left the

race with a blown engine after just seven laps. "We must have burnt a piston," said the five-time Winston Cup champ. "The engine misfired as soon as I stepped on the gas. I can't believe this happened."

Earnhardt fell 252 points behind Davey Allison in the Winston Cup title chase. Less than a month earlier he was only 28 points behind. "Falling out of a couple races early can kill you in the point race," Earnhardt affirmed.

Allison finished in 10th place after battling an ill-handling car in the final laps. "We developed a severe push and it was all I could do to hang on," said Allison. "We lost some positions, but we still have the point lead."

Allison's cushion over Elliott was 46 points. Alan Kulwicki, who wound up 30th, still ranks third, but fell 134 points behind.

Despite two victories and five top 5 finishes, Irvan is not in the top 10 in points.

Morgan Shepherd looped his Ford off the second turn in the 125th lap, setting off a multi-car tangle which also involved Bobby Hamilton, Kulwicki, Stanley Smith, Derrike Cope, Ted Musgrave, Greg Sacks and Dick Trickle.

Darrell Waltrip collided briefly with Jimmy Hensley while trying to avoid the crash. Both Waltrip and Hensley continued without becoming involved. "The last two years I've left here on a stretcher," said Waltrip, who eventually finished 13th, one lap off the pace. "I feel pretty good about today. My knees are raw from praying to finish this race in one piece."

Race #16

Darrell Waltrip Wins at Pocono; Allison Survives Nasty Crash

Winston Cup Race No. 16
200 Laps at Pocono Int'l Raceway
Long Pond, PA
"Miller Genuine Draft 500"
500 Miles on 2.5-mile Superspeedway
July 19, 1992

Fin	St	No.	Driver	Team / Car	Laps	Money	Status
1	8	17	Darrell Waltrip	DarWal Chevrolet	200	$63,445	Running
2	22	33	Harry Gant	Leo Jackson Olds	200	40,520	Running
3	10	7	Alan Kulwicki	AK Racing Ford	200	42,095	Running
4	2	5	Ricky Rudd	Hendrick Motorsports Chevy	200	24,695	Running
5	27	55	Ted Musgrave	RaDiUs Motorsports Ford	200	22,365	Running
6	3	6	Mark Martin	Roush Racing Ford	200	19,040	Running
7	13	42	Kyle Petty	SabCo Racing Pontiac	200	15,890	Running
8	12	26	Brett Bodine	King Motorsports Ford	200	14,290	Running
9	20	8	Dick Trickle	Stavola Brothers Ford	200	10,690	Running
10	18	18	Dale Jarrett	Joe Gibbs Chevrolet	200	15,190	Running
11	14	22	Sterling Marlin	Junior Johnson Ford	199	12,640	Running
12	5	25	Ken Schrader	Hendrick Motorsports Chevy	199	15,590	Running
13	16	11	Bill Elliott	Junior Johnson Ford	199	14,390	Running
14	17	66	Jimmy Hensley	Cale Yarborough Ford	199	9,640	Running
15	9	21	Morgan Shepherd	Wood Brothers Ford	199	11,640	Running
16	40	94	Terry Labonte	Billy Hagan Olds	199	11,090	Running
17	26	9	Chad Little	Melling Performance Ford	199	5,790	Running
18	19	2	Rusty Wallace	Roger Penske Pontiac	199	13,690	Running
19	15	10	Derrike Cope	Bob Whitcomb Chevrolet	199	7,540	Running
20	7	43	Richard Petty	Petty Enterprises Pontiac	199	11,015	Running
21	23	12	Hut Stricklin	Bobby Allison Chevrolet	199	10,040	Running
22	24	68	Bobby Hamilton	Tri-Star Motorsports Olds	199	10,840	Running
23	29	3	Dale Earnhardt	RCR Enterprises Chevrolet	199	16,540	Running
24	25	1	Rick Mast	Precision Products Olds	197	9,590	Running
25	30	31	Bobby Hillin,Jr.	Team Ireland Chevrolet	197	4,890	Running
26	28	30	Michael Waltrip	Bahari Racing Pontiac	197	9,440	Running
27	36	77	Mike Potter	Steve Balogh Chevrolet	193	4,790	Running
28	37	59	Andy Belmont	Pat Rissi Ford	193	4,990	Running
29	11	41	Greg Sacks	Larry Hedrick Chevrolet	180	6,265	Running
30	21	15	Geoff Bodine	Bud Moore Eng. Ford	171	9,190	Ignition
31	32	71	Dave Marcis	Marcis Auto Racing Chevy	161	6,115	Engine
32	6	16	Wally Dallenbach,Jr.	Roush Racing Ford	165	4,540	Handling
33	1	28	Davey Allison	Robert Yates Racing Ford	149	21,365	Crash
34	34	32	Jimmy Horton	Active Racing Chevrolet	130	4,365	Rear End
35	33	65	Jerry O'Neil	Alan Aroneck Olds	113	4,290	Oil Leak
36	31	83	Lake Speed	Speed Ford	89	4,215	Engine
37	4	4	Ernie Irvan	Morgan-McClure Chevrolet	74	13,740	Valve
38	35	27	Bob Schacht	Linro Motorsports Chevrolet	58	4,100	Trans
39	38	52	Jimmy Means	Means Racing Pontiac	24	5,565	Steering
40	39	48	James Hylton	Hylton Engineering Pontiac	17	3,990	Quit

Time of Race: 3 hours, 43 minutes, 47 seconds
Average Speed: 134.058 mph
Pole Winner: Davey Allison – 162.022 mph
Lap Leaders: Davey Allison 1-30, Alan Kulwicki 31-34, Harry Gant 35, Bill Elliott 36-37, Allison 38-61, Kulwicki 62-68, Allison 69-95, Kulwicki 96-101, Allison 102-119, Kyle Petty 120-123, Allison 124-139, Kulwicki 140-180, Ted Musgrave 181-188, Darrell Waltrip 189-200.
13 lead changes among 7 drivers.
Cautions: 3 for 23 laps Margin of Victory: 1.31 seconds

LONG POND, PA (July 19) – Darrell Waltrip outran Harry Gant in a battle of speed and fuel consumption to win the Miller Genuine Draft 500 at Pocono International Raceway. Davey Allison, who had dominated the first 150 laps, was involved in a horrific tumble and was transported to an Allentown hospital with multiple injuries.

Allison started on the pole and led 115 of the first 139 laps, but a long pit stop during the second caution of the day put him deep in the pack for a restart on lap 147. While trying to weave his way through traffic and get back to the front, Allison cut in front of Waltrip and the two cars made contact. Allison's Ford slid sideways off the track on the North chute and did a 'reverse flip'. Then Allison's car dug into the grass and bounded high into the air, tumbling onto a steel guard rail inside the turn.

"We were going for the same spot," explained Waltrip. "He cut over and I slowed a little bit. When he cut over again, which I couldn't conceive him doing, I couldn't avoid hitting him. When I came around the next lap and saw what had happened, it almost made me sick to my stomach. I thought back to last year when I turned over at Daytona."

Allison was removed from the wreckage and transported by helicopter to a hospital in Allentown, where he underwent surgery for broken bones in his right forearm, collarbone and wrist. Doctors negated a report that he had suffered a broken eye socket and a skull fracture.

It was the fourth time this year that Allison has suffered injuries in a crash. He had been banged up after wrecks at Bristol, Martinsville and Charlotte earlier. "I don't know how many hits our little driver can take," sid Larry McReynolds, crew chief for the Robert Yates Racing team. "I hope this is the last one. Next Sunday's race at Talladega isn't on my mind. My only concern is Davey's health."

The yellow flag was out from lap 151-160 to clean up the debris from Allison's crash. Alan Kulwicki, who had taken the lead in the 140th lap when Allison had his long pit stop, elected to stay on the speedway and keep track position. Most of the other leaders followed suit.

Waltrip and Gant were the only drivers to pit again during the Allison caution to top off the fuel tank. "We knew to win we had to come in a second time," said Waltrip. "It surprised me that most of the other guys didn't. That old nemesis called track position got them. They wanted to keep it and hope for another caution that would let them stop for fuel."

While Waltrip and Gant started at the rear of the lead cars, Kulwicki hammered his Ford into a solid lead. He led for 41 straight laps until he pitted for fuel in the 180th lap.

Sophomore driver Ted Musgrave made a brilliant charge from 27th starting spot to take over the lead when Kulwicki pitted. The Franklin., Wisc. driver held his RaDiUs Motorsports Ford in the lead until he had to pit in the 188th lap, giving the lead to Waltrip. Gant chased Waltrip the final few laps but settled for second place, 1.31-seconds behind the winner.

Third place went to Kulwicki, who was miffed that Waltrip and Gant did not have to pit. "Everyone else is getting 35 to 37 laps on a tank of fuel," said Kulwicki. "But those two got 41 laps. They pulled the ol' fuel mileage trick again. I thought I had the race won."

Ricky Rudd finished in fourth place and said he didn't understand how Waltrip and Gant could run over 100 miles. "I don't know how those guys can run 41 laps," said Rudd. "We don't run restrictor plates here. I thought you only got that kind of mileage with a Toyota."

Fifth place went to Musgrave, who enjoyed his best finish of his career. "If you keep running near the front, sooner or later you've going

Gregg Feistman

Davey Allison's horrific crash at Pocono.

Greg Crisp

Bill Elliott #11 streaks past Dale Earnhardt en route to 12th place finish at Pocono. Elliott climbed atop the Winston Cup standings for the first time in the 1992 season.

to bust through," said Musgrave. "I drove hard when I was in front, but I should have paced myself more."

Bill Elliott finished in 12th place and took the lead in the Winston Cup point standings. Allison fell nine points behind Elliott – the first time all year that Allison had not held the point lead.

On a curious note, Elliott never led the point standings while he was winning 80% (4 of the first 5 races) of the early season events, but while he has gone winless in the last 11 races, he has moved into the point lead.

Kulwicki ranks third in the title chase, only 47 points behind Elliott. Gant is fourth, only 80 points off the top.

Dale Earnhardt struggled once again and wound up 23rd, one lap off the pace. He fell to sixth place in the point standings.

Race #17

Chevy Teamwork Tops as Irvan Nips Marlin at Talladega

TALLADEGA, AL (July 26) – Ernie Irvan battled back from a lap deficit and used the assistance of fellow Chevrolet driver Ricky Rudd in the final laps to win the Talladega 500 for his third win of the season.

Irvan nipped the Ford of pole-sitter Sterling Marlin by 0.19 second. Bobby Hillin, who relieved Davey Allison in the sixth lap, finished third in a sparkling effort. Rudd and Bill Elliott rounded out the top five.

Irvan's day started on a sour note as he pitted for a flat tire in the fourth lap. NASCAR officials hit him with a penalty as Irvan sped too fast down pit road when getting back up to speed.

The detour didn't deter Irvan, who battled back into the lead lap on lap 69 when a caution was waved for debris on the track in the form of a can thrown from the grandstand by a spectator. "I want to thank whoever threw that can on the track," said Irvan.

Rudd, who started second, led the opening 50 laps – the most a driver has led at the outset of a Talladega race since the track opened in 1969. He gave up the lead in the 51st lap when he made his first pit stop.

Bill Elliott, Hillin, Jr., Dale Jarrett, Marlin and Rusty Wallace swapped the lead before Irvan blasted to the front in the 111th lap. From that point on, it was a

Bryan Hallman

Bobby Hillin, Jr. was Davey Allison's designated relief driver in Talladega's DieHard 500.

battle between Irvan and Marlin.

Elliott and Rudd lost the draft with the two leaders and in the span of about 30 laps, were both lapped. It was one of the most glaring displays of what happens when a driver gets shuffled out of the draft. "I got squeezed out of line and went from third to about 20th," said Rudd. "Once I lost the draft, that was it."

Marlin led all but 16 laps from laps 129-177, but couldn't hold off Irvan in the end. Irvan made his final pit stop on lap 174, giving the lead to Marlin. Marlin and Hillin, Jr. pitted a lap later. Hillin, Jr. lost the tow from Marlin when he made his final pit stop. "I was following Sterling down the pit road, but I thought we were getting too close to the speed limit and I didn't want to get penalized, so I backed off," said Hillin, Jr. "That's the last I saw of Sterling."

Marlin was not flagged for speeding and had a sizable two second lead over Irvan when he returned to the track.

Irvan ran Marlin down in four laps and took the lead in a bold move when he dived under a pack of lapped cars while Marlin was held up. "None of those guys know what the move-over flag means," complained Marlin.

With Irvan in the lead, the lapped car of Rudd latched onto the rear bumper of the new leader. Marlin and the lapped car of Elliott hooked up once they cleared the slower cars.

In the final laps, Marlin had Rudd and Elliott between him and Irvan and didn't get past them until the final lap. He didn't have enough time to muster a challenge for Irvan and settled for his eighth career runner-up finish.

"It didn't look good in the beginning," admitted Irvan, "but in the end, I'm just glad Ricky was in a Chevrolet. He kept us where we could win. He was a big help."

Marlin said that he didn't receive any help from his Ford teammate Elliott. "Ernie was awfully stout," said Marlin. "But you know, the 11 car (Elliott) got to racing with the 42 (Kyle Petty) and I got trapped."

Car owner Junior Johnson was angry that his car ran second. "If I'd have been Sterling, Ernie would never have gotten around me," huffed Johnson. "But I'm not out there driving. All I know is we shouldn't have finished second.

"I heard Sterling say he didn't get any help from his teammate," added Johnson. "Well, he doesn't have a teammate. I have two cars out there and they stand on their own merits."

For Hillin, Jr., it was a shot in the arm for his career. "I've never lost confidence in my ability," said Hillin, Jr., who won the 1986 Talladega 500. "I got Davey the points lead back, but I wanted to win the race."

Hillin, Jr.'s effort put Allison back on top of the Winston Cup point chase by a single point. Allison dropped to the rear of the field for the start and got a break when a light shower brought out the first yellow flag on lap six. Allison watched the remainder of the race from a VIP suite and coached Hillin, Jr. via radio.

Dale Earnhardt finished dead last for the second time in three races. After starting 30th, Earnhardt made one of the most incredible charges up through the pack. He passed 18 cars in the opening lap and had moved up to second place when the engine in his RCR Enterprises Chevrolet let go after 52 laps. "We've definitely got a piston problem, " said Earnhardt. "Same thing that

Winston Cup Race No. 17
188 Laps at Talladega Superspeedway
Talladega, AL
"DieHard 500"

500.08 Miles on 2.66-mile Superspeedway

July 26, 1992

Fin	St	No.	Driver	Team / Car	Laps	Money	Status
1	7	4	Ernie Irvan	Morgan-McClure Chevrolet	188	$81,815	Running
2	1	22	Sterling Marlin	Junior Johnson Ford	188	54,760	Running
3	3	28	Davey Allison*	Robert Yates Racing Ford	188	42,845	Running
4	2	5	Ricky Rudd	Hendrick Motorsports Chevy	187	32,195	Running
5	15	11	Bill Elliott	Junior Johnson Ford	187	27,965	Running
6	6	42	Kyle Petty	SabCo Racing Pontiac	187	20,840	Running
7	9	30	Michael Waltrip	Bahari Racing Pontiac	187	18,640	Running
8	12	9	Chad Little	Melling Performance Ford	187	10,990	Running
9	26	25	Ken Schrader	Hendrick Motorsports Chevy	187	18,960	Running
10	5	26	Brett Bodine	King Motorsports Ford	187	17,530	Running
11	28	2	Rusty Wallace	Roger Penske Pontiac	187	17,220	Running
12	25	55	Ted Musgrave	RaDiUs Motorsports Chevrolet	187	15,640	Running
13	10	21	Morgan Shepherd	Wood Brothers Ford	187	14,520	Running
14	22	16	Wally Dallenbach,Jr.	Roush Racing Ford	187	8,550	Running
15	4	43	Richard Petty	Petty Enterprises Pontiac	187	14,325	Running
16	23	12	Hut Stricklin	Bobby Allison Chevrolet	187	13,740	Running
17	32	33	Harry Gant	Leo Jackson Olds	186	18,075	Running
18	21	94	Terry Labonte	Billy Hagan Ford	186	13,170	Running
19	29	41	Greg Sacks	Larry Hedrick Chevrolet	186	9,790	Running
20	16	6	Mark Martin	Roush Racing Ford	186	16,250	Running
21	8	18	Dale Jarrett	Joe Gibbs Chevrolet	186	12,270	Running
22	24	10	Derrike Cope	Bob Whitcomb Chevrolet	186	9,090	Running
23	13	17	Darrell Waltrip	DarWal Chevrolet	186	16,460	Running
24	31	68	Bobby Hamilton	Tri-Star Motorsports Chevy	185	12,630	Running
25	18	7	Alan Kulwicki	AK Racing Ford	185	14,700	Running
26	17	1	Rick Mast	Precision Products Olds	185	11,275	Running
27	11	49	Stanley Smith	Smith Chevrolet	185	6,555	Running
28	33	8	Dick Trickle	Stavola Brothers Ford	185	8,085	Running
29	35	71	Dave Marcis	Marcis Auto Racing Chevy	184	7,990	Running
30	19	90	Charlie Glotzbach	Junie Donlavey Ford	184	6,345	Running
31	20	66	Jimmy Hensley	Cale Yarborough Ford	184	8,575	Running
32	27	52	Jimmy Means	Means Racing Pontiac	181	7,730	Running
33	39	37	Randy Porter	Porter Pontiac	180	6,135	Running
34	34	85	Bobby Gerhart	Gerhart Chevrolet	179	6,090	Running
35	40	56	T.W.Taylor	Willie Tierney Pontiac	138	6,045	Piston
36	36	13	Stan Fox	Clint Folsom Chevrolet	102	6,010	Engine
37	38	0	Delma Cowart	H.L.Waters Ford	100	5,985	Running
38	14	15	Geoff Bodine	Bud Moore Eng. Ford	76	10,450	Engine
39	37	59	Andy Belmont	Pat Rissi Ford	53	6,155	Engine
40	30	3	Dale Earnhardt	RCR Enterprises Chevrolet	52	18,140	Engine

Time of Race: 3 hours, 5 minutes, 11 seconds

Average Speed: 176.309 mph

Pole Winner: Sterling Marlin – 190.586 mph

Lap Leaders: Ricky Rudd 1-50, Bill Elliott 51-54, Davey Allison 55-58, Elliott 59-60, Rudd 61-64, Dale Jarrett 65-70, Brett Bodine 71-77, Jarrett 78-80, Sterling Marlin 81, Rusty Wallace 82-84, Allison 85-110, Ernie Irvan 111-124, Jarrett 125-128, Marlin 129-157, Irvan 158-173, Marlin 174-177, Irvan 178-188.

17 lead changes among 8 drivers.

Cautions: 2 for 11 laps Margin of Victory: 0.19 second

*Relieved by Bobby Hillin,Jr.

Brian Czobat

Ernie Irvan drove the Morgan-McClure Chevrolet to victory in thriller at Talladega.

happened at Daytona."

Earnhardt dropped to eighth place in the point standings.

Alan Kulwicki could only manage a 25th place finish and fell 120 points behind. Irvan, who has now won three of the last six races, is logged far behind in 12th place in the standings. After winning the race at Sears Point, Irvan was in 10th place in the standings. Despite winning twice since then, he has fallen to 12th.

Race #18

Kyle Petty Ends Famine With Soggy Watkins Glen Win

WATKINS GLEN, NY (Aug. 9) – Kyle Petty scored his first win in 17 months with a soggy victory in the Budweiser At The Glen, an event that started three hours late and was terminated after 51 of the scheduled 90 laps on the twisting road course.

It was the first win for Petty since his triumph at Rockingham in March of 1991. Quick pit work by the Wood Brothers made it possible for Morgan Shepherd to nail down his second runner-up finish of the season. Ernie Irvan finished third with Roush Racing teammates Mark Martin and Wally Dallenbach, Jr. fourth and fifth.

Dale Earnhardt started on the pole and led the first 10 laps. Irvan and Petty swapped the lead the rest of the way – with the exception of a three lap stint led by Dick Trickle.

After a final exchange of pit stops, Petty took the lead from Trickle in the 43rd lap. Trickle had placed track position ahead of a pit stop for fresh tires and restarted at the front of the pack. Rain once again plagued the road course and forced a yellow flag four laps later. Rain, darkness and a slim prospect of getting the race restarted brought a red flag and an official race after 51 laps.

Petty, who qualified second, said pit selection made by crew chief Robin Pemberton was a major factor in the victory. "We were near the end of pit road and I could go straight out onto the track," said Petty after his fourth career win. "Ernie and the rest of the guys had to slow down for cars coming in and out of their pits."

Trickle, who led with nine laps to go, drifted all the way back to 24th position in the final four green flag laps.

Bill Elliott finished a disappointing 14th, but was still able to forge his way into the Winston Cup point lead. He now leads Davey Allison by 17 points.

Kim Novosat

Kyle Petty's Pontiac breezes down Watkins Glen's straightaway en route to his first win of the year.

Allison drove for 18 laps before giving way to road racing specialist Dorsey Schroeder, who kept the car in the lead pack but overshot his pit late in the race. He was forced to go back around and pit again, putting him at the rear of the pack. "I did what I was supposed to do," said Schroeder, "but I made a big mistake, too. I probably cost our team a top 10 finish."

Allison and Schroeder got credit for 20th place – on the lead lap. Alan Kulwicki finished in seventh place and crept to within 94 points of leader Elliott.

Todd Bodine made his Winston Cup debut, joining brothers Geoff and Brett in the same race. The Bodines became the fourth triple-brother act in the same race. Others were Tim, Fonty and Bob Flock; Dub, Sherman and Layman Utsman – who all drove in a race at Bristol in 1961; and Rusty, Mike and Kenny Wallace. Young Todd stuffed his Ford into the wall in the 10th lap. "I just lost it. And I lost my first lesson in Winston Cup. I got into the corner too deep."

Scott Sharp, noted SCCA Trans-Am driver, made his first Winston Cup start in the Jimmy Means Pontiac. Sharp stayed on the lead lap all day and brought the car home 19th.

Greg Sacks, driver of the Larry Hedrick Chevrolet, survived a terrible crash in practice that saw his car leave the facility. "I tried a little different shift pattern," explained Sacks. "It got me out of shape. I ended up locking it down and slid into the wall. The wall then launched me. I tumbled a couple of times. It tore the heck out of the car, but I'm okay."

There was a touching unofficial ceremony conducted in the turn where J.D. McDuffie was killed a year ago. On Thursday night, a fan made his way onto the track and lit a candle in McDuffie's honor at the spot where his life ended. The candle was not spotted by track security and it burned throughout the night.

Winston Cup Race No. 18
90 Laps at Watkins Glen International
Watkins Glen, NY
"Budweiser At The Glen"
220.5 Miles on 2.45-mile Road Course
August 9, 1992

Fin	St	No.	Driver	Team / Car	Laps	Money	Status
1	2	42	Kyle Petty	SabCo Racing Pontiac	51	$50,895	Running
2	16	21	Morgan Shepherd	Wood Brothers Ford	51	48,545	Running
3	10	4	Ernie Irvan	Morgan-McClure Chevrolet	51	35,060	Running
4	5	6	Mark Martin	Roush Racing Ford	51	28,325	Running
5	12	16	Wally Dallenbach,Jr.	Roush Racing Ford	51	13,480	Running
6	8	2	Rusty Wallace	Roger Penske Pontiac	51	18,240	Running
7	17	7	Alan Kulwicki	AK Racing Ford	51	20,095	Running
8	19	94	Terry Labonte	Billy Hagan Olds	51	14,110	Running
9	1	3	Dale Earnhardt	RCR Enterprises Chevrolet	51	22,430	Running
10	3	26	Brett Bodine	King Motorsports Ford	51	15,840	Running
11	23	55	Ted Musgrave	RaDiUs Motorsports Ford	51	12,230	Running
12	15	17	Darrell Waltrip	DarWal Chevrolet	51	15,490	Running
13	4	5	Ricky Rudd	Hendrick Motorsports Chevy	51	14,400	Running
14	6	11	Bill Elliott	Junior Johnson Ford	51	13,660	Running
15	7	18	Dale Jarrett	Joe Gibbs Chevrolet	51	11,420	Running
16	31	22	Sterling Marlin	Junior Johnson Ford	51	11,050	Running
17	28	71	Dave Marcis	Marcis Auto Racing Chevy	51	7,730	Running
18	24	33	Harry Gant	Leo Jackson Olds	51	15,110	Running
19	22	52	Scott Sharp	Means Racing Pontiac	51	7,155	Running
20	11	28	Davey Allison*	Robert Yates Racing Ford	51	15,560	Running
21	13	25	Ken Schrader	Hendrick Motorsports Chevy	51	13,635	Running
22	29	68	Bobby Hamilton	Tri-Star Motorsports Olds	51	10,515	Running
23	14	31	Bobby Hillin,Jr.	Team Ireland Chevrolet	51	4,420	Running
24	35	8	Dick Trickle	Stavola Brothers Ford	51	6,260	Running
25	33	65	Jerry O'Neil	Alan Aroneck Olds	51	5,075	Running
26	32	66	Jimmy Hensley	Cale Yarborough Ford	51	6,365	Running
27	9	15	Geoff Bodine	Bud Moore Eng. Ford	50	8,905	Running
28	18	43	Richard Petty	Petty Enterprises Pontiac	50	8,745	Running
29	30	45	Ed Ferree	Gayle Ferree Chevrolet	50	4,035	Running
30	36	27	Bob Schacht	Linro Motorsports Olds	49	3,975	Running
31	34	41	Greg Sacks	Larry Hedrick Chevrolet	49	5,415	Running
32	27	1	Rick Mast	Precision Products Olds	47	8,825	Running
33	38	77	Mike Potter	Steve Balogh Buick	45	3,690	Running
34	20	10	Derrike Cope	Bob Whitcomb Chevrolet	36	5,130	Engine
35	25	30	Michael Waltrip	Bahari Racing Pontiac	35	8,095	Crash
36	26	12	Hut Stricklin	Bobby Allison Chevrolet	33	8,040	Trans
37	21	34	Todd Bodine	Cicci-Welliver Ford	16	3,485	Crash
38	37	69	Denny Wilson	Dick Bahre Pontiac	9	3,450	Clutch
39	39	48	James Hylton	Hylton Engineering Pontiac	1	3,395	Quit

Time of Race: 1 hour, 27 minutes, 21 seconds
Average Speed: 88.980 mph
Pole Winner: Dale Earnhardt – 116.882 mph
Lap Leaders: Dale Earnhardt 1-10, Ernie Irvan 11-19, Kyle Petty 20-25, Irvan 26-35, K.Petty 36-39, Dick Trickle 40-42, K.Petty 43-51.
6 lead changes among 4 drivers.
Cautions: 3 for 13 laps Margin of Victory: Under Caution
*Relieved by Dorsey Schroeder
Race Shortened to 124.95 Miles by Rain

Kim Novosat

Davey Allison and relief driver Dorsey Schroeder discuss strategy at Watkins Glen.

Race #19

Gasmaster Gant Wins Economy Run at Michigan

BROOKLYN, MI (Aug. 16) – Harry Gant made another one of his fuel economy runs and produced another surprising victory in the Champion Spark Plug 400 at Michigan International Speedway. It was Gant's second win of the season – both of them coming as the result of one fewer pit stop than his rivals.

Winston Cup Race No. 19
200 Laps at Michigan Int'l Speedway
Brooklyn, MI
"Champion Spark Plug 400"
400 Miles on 2-mile Superspeedway
August 16, 1992

Fin	St	No.	Driver	Team / Car	Laps	Money	Status
1	24	33	Harry Gant	Leo Jackson Olds	200	$71,545	Running
2	9	17	Darrell Waltrip	DarWal Chevrolet	200	45,670	Running
3	7	11	Bill Elliott	Junior Johnson Ford	200	45,820	Running
4	5	4	Ernie Irvan	Morgan-McClure Chevrolet	200	28,920	Running
5	3	28	Davey Allison	Robert Yates Racing Ford	200	29,265	Running
6	15	42	Kyle Petty	SabCo Racing Pontiac	200	21,715	Running
7	8	22	Sterling Marlin	Junior Johnson Ford	200	19,515	Running
8	14	18	Dale Jarrett	Joe Gibbs Chevrolet	200	18,265	Running
9	2	6	Mark Martin	Roush Racing Ford	200	19,715	Running
10	6	21	Morgan Shepherd	Wood Brothers Ford	200	18,765	Running
11	4	25	Ken Schrader	Hendrick Motorsports Chevy	200	19,240	Running
12	10	26	Brett Bodine	King Motorsports Ford	200	16,615	Running
13	28	1	Rick Mast	Precision Products Olds	199	15,115	Running
14	1	7	Alan Kulwicki	AK Racing Ford	199	19,915	Running
15	16	68	Bobby Hamilton	Tri-Star Motorsports Ford	199	14,415	Running
16	41	3	Dale Earnhardt	RCR Enterprises Chevrolet	199	19,665	Running
17	31	9	Chad Little	Melling Performance Ford	199	7.,865	Running
18	21	43	Richard Petty	Petty Enterprises Pontiac	199	13,165	Running
19	18	8	Dick Trickle	Stavola Brothers Ford	199	9,665	Running
20	27	16	Wally Dallenbach,Jr.	Roush Racing Ford	199	7,965	Running
21	33	2	Rusty Wallace	Roger Penske Pontiac	198	15,040	Running
22	26	30	Michael Waltrip	Bahari Racing Pontiac	198	11,940	Running
23	13	94	Terry Labonte	Billy Hagan Olds	198	11,740	Running
24	20	12	Hut Stricklin	Bobby Allison Chevrolet	198	11,590	Running
25	35	55	Ted Musgrave	RaDiUs Motorsports Ford	197	11,340	Running
26	30	31	Bobby Hillin,Jr.	Team Ireland Chevrolet	197	6,390	Running
27	36	51	Jeff Purvis	James Finch Chevrolet	197	6,340	Running
28	32	23	Eddie Bierschwale	Don Bierschwale Olds	193	6,290	Running
29	19	66	Jimmy Hensley	Cale Yarborough Ford	191	8,590	Running
30	40	77	Mike Potter	Steve Balogh Chevrolet	175	6,140	Running
31	39	27	Jeff McClure	McClure Chevrolet	173	5,990	Running
32	29	71	Dave Marcis	Marcis Auto Racing Chevy	101	7,540	Engine
33	17	10	Derrike Cope	Bob Whitcomb Chevrolet	96	7,465	Crash
34	34	83	Lake Speed	Speed Ford	87	6,840	Crash
35	23	49	Stanley Smith	Smith Chevrolet	61	5,790	Crash
36	11	5	Ricky Rudd	Hendrick Motorsports Chevy	55	13,765	Crash
37	38	13	Stan Fox	Clint Folsom Chevrolet	44	5,740	Crash
38	22	32	Jimmy Horton	Active Racing Chevrolet	21	5,715	Engine
39	37	52	Jimmy Means	Means Racing Pontiac	8	7,240	Engine
40	12	15	Geoff Bodine	Bud Moore Eng. Ford	4	10,165	Crash
41	25	41	Greg Sacks	Larry Hedrick Chevrolet	4	7,140	Crash

Time of Race: 2 hours, 47 minutes, 46 seconds
Average Speed: 146.056 mph
Pole Winner: Alan Kulwicki – 178.196 mph
Lap Leaders: Alan Kulwicki 1-37, Mark Martin 38-44, Kulwicki 45-52, Bill Elliott 53-87, Brett Bodine 88-94, Elliott 95-128, Ernie Irvan 129, Elliott 130-131, Irvan 132-135, Darrell Waltrip 136, Kulwicki 137, Dale Earnhardt 138-141, Harry Gant 142-149, Irvan 150-179, Elliott 180, D.Waltrip 181-185 Gant 186-200.
16 lead changes among 8 drivers.
Cautions: 5 for 25 laps Margin of Victory: 4.94 seconds

Kim Novosat

Clifford Allison and brother Davey pictured at Pocono a few weeks before Clifford's death at Michigan. The youngest Allison was killed while practicing for Michigan's Busch Grand National race.

Gant outran runner-up Darrell Waltrip by 4.94 seconds. Bill Elliott, who led the most laps, wound up in third place. Ernie Irvan was fourth and Davey Allison's courageous run netted him fifth spot.

Allison, painfully injured at Pocono the previous month, drove the entire race for the first time. His brother Clifford was fatally injured Thursday during practice for a Busch Grand National event.

"I hope everybody understands," Allison told news reporters after the race, "but I'm going to the truck and I'm going home."

Despite the spirited run, Allison dropped 20 points to Elliott in the race for the Winston Cup. He now trails by 37 points.

Car owner Robert Yates said, "Finishing fifth and running all 200 laps with Davey back in the car was like a new beginning. It was difficult for our team to stay focused, but we did. Davey said Friday that this has been the best year of his career and the worst at the

MIS

Bill Elliott runs just ahead of incredibly tight competition at Michigan.

same time. It has been hard for any of us to understand."

Gant started in 24th and was never a factor until it was evident fuel mileage was going to play a major role. He did not lead until the 142nd lap – and he led the final 16 laps when Darrell Waltrip pitted for the final time.

Some of Gant's rivals were complaining that yet another race was won on strategy instead of racing. "It burns me up because me and the others raced so hard," said sixth place finisher Kyle Petty. "The fans deserve to see a good race and all of a sudden, they see a guy who has run 20th all day win the thing. It's not fair to us and it's not fair to the fans."

Sterling Marlin, who finished seventh, said, "Yep, the strokers won it again."

The complaints failed to dim Gant's Victory Lane smile. "That's life," he grinned. "Any time you win, you're stealing one from somebody. We stole one from Darrell at Dover this year, then he stole one from us at Pocono. I like to win 'em this way. You don't have to run hard. All the crew tells you on the radio is, 'Don't run into anybody'."

Gant's strategy was employed before the half-way point. During what amounted to the final yellow of the day from laps 97-98, Gant pitted a second time to top off his fuel tank. He made only one pit stop in the final 2-4 miles. "We had about a half gallon left in the car," said Gant.

Runner-up Waltrip accepted his fate. "I could see what they were doing back on lap 98 – with him topping off," said Waltrip. "I tell people all the time that you win races on ET (elapsed time), not speed. Harry had the best ET today, and he also had the best GM."

Ricky Rudd and Lake Speed suffered minor injuries in crashes. Rudd clobbered the wall in the 57th lap. "I

MIS

Richard Petty pits his Pontiac at Michigan.

rang my bell pretty good," said Rudd. "I was still seeing black spots for awhile."

Lake Speed suffered second degree burns on his hands when his car burst into flames after a tap from Dale Earnhardt sent him into the wall. Speed said the blaze was caused by a ruptured oil cooler damaged in the crash.

Earnhardt started dead last – 41st – after NASCAR officials said his car failed to clear the minimum height rule after qualifying. He had posted the 27th fastest speed on the first day of qualifying and was the fastest of the second round. He had to use a provisional to get in the race.

"We had no motor today at all," said the disgustged Earnhardt. "I don't like being where I am. It's killing me."

Race #20

Darrell Like the Ol' D.W. on Bristol's New Concrete Track

BRISTOL, TN (Aug. 29) – Darrell Waltrip led the final 133 laps and ran away with the Bud 500 on Bristol International Raceway's new concrete racing surface. It was the 83rd win in Waltrip's career and the 12th on the high-banked oval.

Responding to drivers' complaints about the conventional pavement ripping up during races, track president Larry Carrier resurfaced the .533-mile oval with concrete. Following testing a few weeks earlier, many of the teams felt the Saturday night affair would be no different. It was rough, most drivers said. "Well," mused Alan Kulwicki before the race, "we're going to get twice as much mileage out of our tires because they're only going to be on the ground half the time."

Dale Jarrett hinted that he would bring his dentist to the race "so he can put my fillings back in after they're jarred out."

But despite pessimistic predictions, the track passed its test. "The track is rough, but fixable," declared Waltrip. "Running on top of concrete sure beats the alternative – running into it. They've had a heck of a time here with the asphalt breaking up. If they work on it and get it a little smoother, it will be a great place to race."

Waltrip started ninth on the grid and easily

Darrell Waltrip scored his 12th win at Bristol.

Winston Cup Race No. 20
500 Laps at Bristol Int'l Raceway
Bristol, TN
"Bud 500"
266.5 Miles on .533-mile Short Track
August 29, 1992

Fin	St	No.	Driver	Team / Car	Laps	Money	Status
1	9	17	Darrell Waltrip	DarWal Chevrolet	500	$73,050	Running
2	23	3	Dale Earnhardt	RCR Enterprises Chevrolet	500	39,325	Running
3	6	25	Ken Schrader	Hendrick Motorsports Chevy	500	28,350	Running
4	26	42	Kyle Petty	SabCo Racing Pontiac	500	18,000	Running
5	5	7	Alan Kulwicki	AK Racing Ford	499	19,800	Running
6	19	11	Bill Elliott	Junior Johnson Ford	499	18,075	Running
7	12	66	Jimmy Hensley	Cale Yarborough Ford	499	11,775	Running
8	2	5	Ricky Rudd	Hendrick Motorsports Chevy	499	16,875	Running
9	3	26	Brett Bodine	King Motorsports Ford	499	14,225	Running
10	8	2	Rusty Wallace	Roger Penske Pontiac	498	14,575	Running
11	11	15	Geoff Bodine	Bud Moore Eng. Ford	497	14,425	Running
12	17	10	Derrike Cope	Bob Whitcomb Chevrolet	497	9,115	Running
13	15	21	Morgan Shepherd	Wood Brothers Ford	497	11,775	Running
14	22	30	Michael Waltrip	Bahari Racing Pontiac	497	11,525	Running
15	27	22	Sterling Marlin	Junior Johnson Ford	495	11,325	Running
16	30	43	Richard Petty	Petty Enterprises Pontiac	493	10,775	Running
17	14	18	Dale Jarrett	Joe Gibbs Chevrolet	492	10,525	Running
18	31	71	Jim Sauter	Marcis Auto Racing Chevy	491	7,375	Running
19	21	16	Wally Dallenbach,Jr.	Roush Racing Ford	489	5,465	Running
20	29	20	Jimmy Spencer	Dick Moroso Ford	487	6,125	Running
21	28	68	Bobby Hamilton	Tri-Star Motorsports Olds	484	11,075	Running
22	25	55	Ted Musgrave	RaDiUs Motorsports Ford	476	9,925	Running
23	10	8	Dick Trickle	Stavola Brothers Ford	446	6,775	Running
24	32	52	Jimmy Means	Means Racing Pontiac	395	6,650	Running
25	4	6	Mark Martin	Roush Racing Ford	385	13,605	Crash
26	16	33	Harry Gant	Leo Jackson Olds	349	15,475	Crash
27	13	12	Hut Stricklin	Bobby Allison Chevrolet	339	9,525	Crash
28	1	4	Ernie Irvan	Morgan-McClure Chevrolet	285	17,000	Crash
29	24	1	Rick Mast	Precision Products Olds	276	9,425	Crash
30	7	28	Davey Allison	Robert Yates Racing Ford	262	16,025	Crash
31	18	94	Terry Labonte	Billy Hagan Olds	125	9,350	Engine
32	20	41	Dave Marcis	Larry Hedrick Chevrolet	101	6,325	Crash

Time of Race: 2 hours, 55 minutes, 20 seconds
Average Speed: 91.198 mph
Pole Winner: Ernie Irvan – 120,535 mph
Lap Leaders: Ernie Irvan 1-7, Ricky Rudd 8-118, Brett Bodine 119-144, Davey Allison 145-155, Darrell Waltrip 156-194, Mark Martin 195-202, Alan Kulwicki 203-204, D.Waltrip 205-257, Martin 258-272, Kulwicki 273, Harry Gant 274-308, D.Waltrip 309-330, B.Bodine 331-339, Rudd 340-367, D.Waltrip 368-500.
14 lead changes among 8 drivers.
Cautions: 10 for 55 laps Margin of Victory: 9.28 seconds

Bristol Int'l

Track personnel work to place down the concrete surface in the turns at Bristol International Raceway.

outdistanced runner-up Dale Earnhardt by 9.28 seconds. Ken Schrader finished third for the third race in a row at Bristol. Fourth place went to Kyle Petty and Alan Kulwicki ran fifth.

Bill Elliott finished sixth and increased his lead in the Winston Cup standings from 37 to 109 points over Davey Allison, who crashed twice. Third ranking Kulwicki pulled to within 24 points of Allison.

Allison's demise came in the 201st lap when he was running in third place. "I just lost it in turn three," said Allison, who wound up 30th in the 32 car field, "and backed into the wall. I hate it for the guys on the team because we could have come away from here with a decent finish."

Problems continued as Allison thumped the wall while running at reduced speed. "The second time I was just trying to stay out of the way and hit the apron and messed up again. I made the mistakes tonight."

Ernie Irvan, who started on the pole and led the first seven laps, crashed a lap later. "I made a mistake and the car slipped out from under me," said Irvan. He lost 153 laps while his Morgan-McClure Chevrolet was repaired. Irvan would eventually finish 28th after being involved in another crash later.

Ricky Rudd took the lead when Irvan spun and led for 111 straight laps. Rudd managed to stay in contention until an extra pit stop late in the race took him out of the hunt. "It's a shame we had to stop again," said Rudd. "I could run with Darrell until we got our last set of tires. They weren't exactly what we needed, but I thought I had a handle on second place until that last stop." Rudd fell to eighth in the final rundown, a lap off the pace.

Along with Rudd, Harry Gant emerged as one of Waltrip's main contenders late in the race. But he was knocked out of the race when Michael Waltrip nicked the rear of Gant's Oldsmobile, sending him into the wall. "I believe Michael got into my quarter panel a little bit," said Gant, who fell to fourth in the standings, 195 points behind Elliott. "Lapped cars were a problem all night long."

Two other contenders, Mark Martin and Kulwicki, spun in the 341st lap while battling for third place. "I just messed up and got into Alan," admitted Martin. "I cut down when I shouldn't have. I was being aggressive and didn't see Alan until it was too late."

Martin's car was heavily damaged, but Kulwicki was able to continue.

Geoff Bodine had climbed to third place, but two pit stops in the final laps knocked him down to 11th at the finish.

Dave Marcis made his first start with the Larry Hedrick team, but the veteran driver slugged the wall after a tire failure after completing 101 laps.

Race #21

Allison's Bid for $Million Bonus Foiled by Waltrip and Rain

DARLINGTON, SC (Sept. 6) – Rain ended Darrell Waltrip's 19 year drought in Darlington Raceway's Southern 500 and washed away any chance Davey Allison had for the Winston Million bonus, as fuel mileage once again played a major role in the outcome of a race.

Bryan Hallman

Davey Allison led a good part of the Southern 500, but couldn't cash in on the Winston Million bonus.

Waltrip started fifth but never led until the final six laps. While virtually all other contenders pitted under threatening skies, Waltrip and Bill Elliott, who lagged behind the leaders all day, used superior fuel mileage to move into first and third. The rains came on lap 295 and the red flag appeared after 298 of the scheduled 367 laps. NASCAR called the race official two hours later with no hope of resumption.

Mark Martin turned in the most spirited performance of the day – repeatedly coming from the rear of the pack after pitting on the backstretch. He got credit for second place, Elliott wound up third while Brett Bodine was fourth and Allison fifth.

"There may be an asterisk in the record books next to this one," said a smiling Waltrip, whose 84th career victory put him within one of third ranking Bobby Allison, who won 85 races in his career that spanned from 1961-1988. "But I don't care. I'm tickled to finally win this thing."

Elliott increased his point lead to 119 over Allison. He had pitted early for replacement of a flat tire and later had brake problems. "We were lucky, darn lucky," conceded Elliott. "The crew did their best under a difficult situation. We'll take third today."

Martin was the class of the field although he didn't lead the most laps. The Batesville, Ark. Ford driver registered a poor qualifying run, which placed him 25th on the grid. That forced him to pit on the backstretch, which is a monumental disadvantage. Martin had to work his way from the rear of the field after each and every caution flag, but each time he made his presence felt. After building up an eight second lead, Martin made an early pit stop after 288 laps – despite the threatening skies. "It was over for those other guys if the race had stayed green," said Martin.

Brian Czobat

Darrell Waltrip gets quick service from his DarWal pit crew at Darlington.

"But it didn't and we were cooked. We were pitting on the backstretch, so I guess we ought to feel fortunate we finished as good as we did."

Allison led three times for 72 laps, but was foiled by the timing of the weather. "Mark Martin sent us to the pits a little early," said Allison. "He was running so good, we had to pit to keep from losing too much ground. If the race had restarted, we'd have been in pretty good shape. But I didn't and there's nothing we can do about it."

Waltrip said he felt for Allison. "I hate Davey didn't win the million dollars, but I don't apologize to anyone for winning the race or the way we did it. Our strategy was to stay out as long as we could before pitting. We thought if the race went all the way, we could win it by making one less pit stop than everybody else."

Harry Gant's Oldsmobile led the most laps – 91 – but he was sidetracked by having to make an extra pit stop to tighten loose lug nuts and a "bad set of tires". He fell a lap off the pace but made it up before pitting right before the rains hit. Gant wound up in 16th place. "We never could get a yellow when we needed one," lamented Gant.

Dale Earnhardt started 13th and had worked his way into fourth place before having to take an extended stay on pit road for repair of the clutch in his Chevrolet. He eventually finished 29th.

Alan Kulwicki finished eighth and held onto third place in the standings, 161 points behind Elliott.

Sterling Marlin won the pole and led three times for 57 laps, but he lost control of his Junior Johnson Ford and tagged the wall in the 193rd lap. Following repairs, Marlin got back into the race and finished 28th.

Ernie Irvan started second and led the opening 10 laps, but transmission failure eventually sidelined his Chevrolet after completing 266 laps.

Winston Cup Race No. 21
367 Laps at Darlington Raceway
Darlington, SC
"Mountain Dew Southern 500"
501.322 Miles on 1.366-mile Superspeedway
September 6, 1992

Fin	St	No.	Driver	Team / Car	Laps	Money	Status
1	5	17	Darrell Waltrip	DarWal Chevrolet	298	$66,030	Running
2	25	6	Mark Martin	Roush Racing Ford	298	41,355	Running
3	4	11	Bill Elliott	Junior Johnson Ford	298	32,620	Running
4	8	26	Brett Bodine	King Motorsports Ford	298	23,260	Running
5	6	28	Davey Allison	Robert Yates Racing Ford	298	38,845	Running
6	17	18	Dale Jarrett	Joe Gibbs Chevrolet	298	19,055	Running
7	30	42	Kyle Petty	SabCo Racing Pontiac	298	16,310	Running
8	9	7	Alan Kulwicki	AK Racing Ford	298	17,890	Running
9	21	2	Rusty Wallace	Roger Penske Pontiac	298	17,060	Running
10	18	5	Ricky Rudd	Hendrick Motorsports Chevy	297	18,470	Running
11	23	12	Hut Stricklin	Bobby Allison Ford	297	13,985	Running
12	19	10	Derrike Cope	Bob Whitcomb Chevrolet	297	10,690	Running
13	3	25	Ken Schrader	Hendrick Motorsports Chevy	297	16,600	Running
14	15	94	Terry Labonte	Billy Hagan Olds	297	13,210	Running
15	7	66	Jimmy Hensley	Cale Yarborough Ford	297	11,320	Running
16	11	33	Harry Gant	Leo Jackson Olds	297	18,600	Running
17	16	31	Bobby Hillin,Jr.	Team Ireland Chevrolet	297	6,880	Running
18	28	41	Dave Marcis	Larry Hedrick Chevrolet	296	9,205	Running
19	10	15	Geoff Bodine	Bud Moore Eng. Ford	295	11,725	Running
20	31	43	Richard Petty	Petty Enterprises Pontiac	295	12,055	Running
21	24	68	Bobby Hamilton	Tri-Star Motorsports Ford	293	11,920	Running
22	34	52	Jimmy Means	Means Racing Pontiac	284	5,900	Running
23	20	1	Rick Mast	Precision Products Olds	280	10,630	Running
24	12	16	Wally Dallenbach,Jr.	Roush Racing Ford	276	7,355	Running
25	2	4	Ernie Irvan	Morgan-McClure Chevrolet	266	15,395	Trans
26	33	83	Lake Speed	Speed Ford	253	5,335	Running
27	14	8	Dick Trickle	Stavola Brothers Ford	242	6,875	Running
28	1	22	Sterling Marlin	Junior Johnson Ford	241	13,265	Running
29	13	3	Dale Earnhardt	RCR Enterprises Chevrolet	241	16,555	Running
30	29	55	Ted Musgrave	RaDiUs Motorsports Ford	225	9,520	Crank
31	26	21	Morgan Shepherd	Wood Brothers Ford	224	9,310	Crash
32	35	59	Andy Belmont	Pat Rissi Ford	212	4,670	Ignition
33	36	77	Mike Potter	Steve Balogh Buick	164	4,605	Engine
34	27	9	Chad Little	Melling Performance Ford	135	4,570	Crash
35	22	30	Michael Waltrip	Bahari Racing Pontiac	102	8,985	Engine
36	32	71	Jim Sauter	Marcis Auto Racing Chevy	47	5,900	Engine
37	37	48	James Hylton	Hylton Engineering Pontiac	13	4,330	Engine
38	38	53	John McFadden	Means Racing Pontiac	3	4,290	Quit

Time of Race: 3 hours, 9 minutes, 10 seconds
Average Speed: 129.114 mph
Pole Winner: Sterling Marlin – 162.249 mph
Lap Leaders: Ernie Irvan 1-10, Sterling Marlin 11-51, Davey Allison 52-54, Marlin 55-69, Harry Gant 70-91, Marlin 92, Mark Martin 93-94, Ricky Rudd 95, Bill Elliott 96-98, Ted Musgrave 99, Gant 100-132, Martin 133-139, Dale Jarrett 140-149, Gant 150-185, Jarrett 186-194, Allison 195-228, Elliott 229, Allison 230-264, Rusty Wallace 265-271, Martin 272-288, Jarrett 289-290, Rudd 291-292, Darrell Waltrip 293-298.
23 lead changes among 11 drivers.
Cautions: 5 for 28 laps Margin of Victory: Under Caution
Race shortened to 298 laps due to rain

Race #22

Wallace Makes Up Lap Deficit and Romps at Richmond

RICHMOND, VA (Sept. 12) – Rusty Wallace rebounded from a lap deficit, prevailed in a spirited side-by-side battle with Darrell Waltrip and won the Miller Genuine Draft 400 at Richmond International Raceway going away.

The triumph ended Wallace's 34-race winless skid dating back to July of 1991. And it was the first time car owner Roger Penske has seen him win.

"Not winning was starting to wear real, real thin," said Wallace. "I was getting nervous and a little concerned. I knew I had everything in the world to do it with. We had a great car, good engines and a great bunch of people. We just couldn't get all the talent organized until Buddy Parrott came on as crew chief five races ago."

Wallace pushed his Pontiac to a 3.59-second win over runner-up Mark Martin. Waltrip fell back to finish third. Dale Earnhardt overcame a penalty for speeding on pit road to finish fourth and Geoff Bodine came home fifth.

Wallace started third on the grid and snared the lead as early as the 17th lap. He had led all but 33 of the

Kim Novosat

Rusty Wallace #2 ended his winless skid at Richmond as Alan Kulwicki #7 kept his slim hopes alive for the Winston Cup championship.

Winston Cup Race No. 22
400 Laps at Richmond Int'l Raceway
Richmond, VA
"Miller Genuine Draft 400"
300 Miles on .75-mile Short Track
September 12, 1992

Fin	St	No.	Driver	Team / Car	Laps	Money	Status
1	3	2	Rusty Wallace	Roger Penske Pontiac	400	$47,115	Running
2	13	6	Mark Martin	Roush Racing Ford	400	48,365	Running
3	14	17	Darrell Waltrip	DarWal Chevrolet	400	44,360	Running
4	11	3	Dale Earnhardt	RCR Enterprises Chevrolet	400	29,655	Running
5	9	15	Geoff Bodine	Bud Moore Eng. Ford	400	19,980	Running
6	2	5	Ricky Rudd	Hendrick Motorsports Chevy	400	18,205	Running
7	18	21	Morgan Shepherd	Wood Brothers Ford	400	13,055	Running
8	15	33	Harry Gant	Leo Jackson Olds	400	16,255	Running
9	10	25	Ken Schrader	Hendrick Motorsports Chevy	400	15,055	Running
10	26	55	Ted Musgrave	RaDiUs Motorsports Ford	400	14,005	Running
11	1	4	Ernie Irvan	Morgan-McClure Chevrolet	400	18,005	Running
12	17	42	Kyle Petty	SabCo Racing Pontiac	399	10,955	Running
13	7	94	Terry Labonte	Billy Hagan Olds	399	10,805	Running
14	25	11	Bill Elliott	Junior Johnson Ford	399	12,805	Running
15	4	7	Alan Kulwicki	AK Racing Ford	399	12,855	Running
16	30	43	Richard Petty	Petty Enterprises Pontiac	399	10,430	Running
17	6	66	Jimmy Hensley	Cale Yarborough Ford	399	7,980	Running
18	8	26	Brett Bodine	King Motorsports Ford	399	9,980	Running
19	5	28	Davey Allison	Robert Yates Racing Ford	398	15,655	Running
20	12	8	Dick Trickle	Stavola Brothers Ford	398	7,330	Running
21	29	22	Sterling Marlin	Junior Johnson Ford	398	9,380	Running
22	24	12	Jeff Purvis	Bobby Allison Chevrolet	398	9,265	Running
23	21	16	Wally Dallenbach,Jr.	Roush Racing Ford	397	6,130	Running
24	34	41	Dave Marcis	Larry Hedrick Chevrolet	397	6,005	Running
25	16	18	Dale Jarrett	Joe Gibbs Chevrolet	397	8,855	Running
26	22	71	Jim Sauter	Marcis Auto Racing Chevy	394	5,780	Running
27	32	9	Chad Little	Melling Performance Ford	393	4,155	Running
28	19	1	Rick Mast	Precision Products Olds	393	8,705	Running
29	27	52	Jimmy Means	Means Racing Pontiac	392	4,105	Running
30	28	90	Hut Stricklin	Junie Donlavey Ford	389	4,055	Running
31	33	32	Jimmy Horton	Active Racing Chevrolet	387	4,055	Running
32	31	68	Bobby Hamilton	Tri-Star Motorsports Ford	368	9,530	Running
33	23	30	Michael Waltrip	Bahari Racing Pontiac	293	8,500	Crash
34	35	49	Stanley Smith	Smith Chevrolet	257	3,955	Axle
35	20	10	Derrike Cope	Bob Whitcomb Chevrolet	12	5,455	Engine

Time of Race: 2 hours, 51 minutes, 59 seconds
Average Speed: 104.661 mph
Pole Winner: Ernie Irvan – 120.784 mph
Lap Leaders: Ernie Irvan 1-13, Ricky Rudd 14, Irvan 15-16, Rusty Wallace 17-85, Mark Martin 86-102, R.Wallace 103-104, Irvan 105-147, Darrell Waltrip 148-229, Harry Gant 230, D.Waltrip 231-239, R.Wallace 240-260, D.Waltrip 261, R.Wallace 262-400.
12 lead changes among 6 drivers.
Cautions: 3 for 20 laps Margin of Victory: 3.59 seconds

first 104 laps when he made his first scheduled pit stop. Two laps later, Jim Sauter looped his Chevrolet, bringing out the yellow flag. Wallace and many of the other contenders were trapped a lap behind those who had not yet pitted.

"That was the only thing that went wrong the whole night," said Wallace after his 21st career Winston Cup win. "But we passed (leaders) Ernie (Irvan) and Darrell and took off from them. We finally got back into the thick of things."

Wallace took the lead in the 240th lap after running door-to-door with Waltrip for seven laps. From that point on, Wallace only lost the lead for a single lap when he pitted for tires on lap 261.

Bill Elliott was never a factor and finished 14th, a lap behind. He was still able to increase his Winston Cup lead to 134 points over Davey Allison with only seven races remaining. Allison wound up 19th after taking a wild ride through the infield grass on the homestretch. "We had a decent run going until Ernie Irvan spun us out," muttered Allison. Compounding the situation was the fact that NASCAR failed to throw the yellow flag when Allison spun. He finished two laps off the pace.

Alan Kulwicki, who ranks third, kept his faint hopes alive by finishing 15th. He is 164 points behind Elliott.

Wallace said the battle with Waltrip during the middle stages got him pumped up. "It was awesome running like that with Darrell," said Wallace. "We ran side-by-side forever. It was like the races we ran a long time ago on the little old short tracks. We were right on the edge."

Waltrip made a chassis adjustment during the final yellow flag brought out by Michael Waltrip's crash. "We were really running good, but we got greedy," explained Waltrip. "We changed the car around a little bit. We took a little wedge out of it and we went the wrong way."

Martin led for 17 laps and ran with the leaders but was no match for the fleet Wallace. "We had a good car, but Rusty was just out of sight. He was incredible so we ran second."

Wallace collected $47,115 for his win, which was

less than runner-up Martin's $48,365 take. Wallace's Penske Racing team forfeits a large chunk of contengency prizes since they don't put all the decals on the front fenders. "We like a cleaner look," said Wallace.

Jeff Purvis made his first start of the season for the Bobby Allison team. Allison had released Hut Stricklin, who has expressed interest in taking an offer from Junior Johnson for the 1993 campaign. Purvis, former late model dirt track champion, finished 22nd, two laps behind.

Pole sitter Ernie Irvan led three times for 58 laps, but drifted to an 11th place finish.

Winston Cup Race No. 23
500 Laps at Dover Downs Int'l Speedway
Dover, DE
"Peak AntiFreeze 500"
500 Miles on 1-mile Superspeedway
September 20, 1992

Fin	St	No.	Driver	Team / Car	Laps	Money	Status
1	6	5	Ricky Rudd	Hendrick Motorsports Chevy	500	$64,965	Running
2	13	11	Bill Elliott	Junior Johnson Ford	500	51,260	Running
3	16	42	Kyle Petty	SabCo Racing Pontiac	500	27,310	Running
4	29	28	Davey Allison	Robert Yates Racing Ford	499	29,410	Running
5	21	21	Morgan Shepherd	Wood Brothers Ford	498	21,980	Running
6	22	33	Harry Gant	Leo Jackson Olds	497	22,205	Running
7	4	94	Terry Labonte	Billy Hagan Olds	496	15,805	Running
8	17	55	Ted Musgrave	RaDiUs Motorsports Ford	496	15,105	Running
9	31	10	Derrike Cope	Bob Whitcomb Chevrolet	495	11,355	Running
10	23	68	Bobby Hamilton	Tri-Star Motorsports Ford	493	16,805	Running
11	19	4	Ernie Irvan	Morgan-McClure Chevrolet	493	16,905	Running
12	11	18	Dale Jarrett	Joe Gibbs Chevrolet	490	12,505	Running
13	26	6	Jimmy Hensley	Cale Yarborough Ford	487	9,755	Running
14	8	15	Geoff Bodine	Bud Moore Eng. Ford	486	11,405	Running
15	20	90	Hut Stricklin	Junie Donlavey Ford	484	6,155	Running
16	3	2	Rusty Wallace	Roger Penske Pontiac	483	13,830	Running
17	24	30	Michael Waltrip	Bahari Racing Pontiac	483	10,630	Running
18	30	71	Jim Sauter	Marcis Auto Racing Chevy	475	7,415	Running
19	2	6	Mark Martin	Roush Racing Ford	470	13,830	Engine
20	14	17	Darrell Waltrip	DarWal Chevrolet	470	15,480	Running
21	5	3	Dale Earnhardt	RCR Enterprises Chevrolet	470	17,880	Running
22	18	26	Brett Bodine	King Motorsports Ford	430	10,130	Running
23	34	52	Jimmy Means	Means Racing Pontiac	399	5,230	Engine
24	10	1	Rick Mast	Precision Products Olds	398	9,930	Running
25	28	77	Mike Potter	Steve Balogh Buick	382	5,130	Running
26	12	41	Dave Marcis	Larry Hedrick Chevrolet	364	6,730	Handling
27	7	8	Dick Trickle	Stavola Brothers Ford	276	6,630	Crash
28	25	43	Richard Petty	Petty Enterprises Pontiac	272	9,555	Crash
29	32	9	Chad Little	Melling Performance Ford	271	4,930	Crash
30	9	25	Ken Schrader*	Hendrick Motorsports Chevy	263	13,880	Crash
31	27	16	Wally Dallenbach,Jr.	Roush Racing Ford	214	11,260	Engine
32	33	12	Jeff Purvis	Bobby Allison Chevrolet	179	9,305	Crash
33	15	22	Sterling Marlin	Junior Johnson Ford	175	9,230	Engine
34	1	7	Alan Kulwicki	AK Racing Ford	91	17,180	Crash
35	36	48	James Hylton	Hylton Engineering Pontiac	89	4,480	Heating
36	35	53	Graham Taylor	Means Racing Pontiac	3	4,455	Quit

Time of Race: 4 hours, 20 minutes, 13 seconds
Average Speed: 115.289 mph
Pole Winner: Alan Kulwicki – 145.267 mph
Lap Leaders: Alan Kulwicki 1, Mark Martin 2-47, Dale Earnhardt 48, Martin 49-94, Earnhardt 95-175, Bill Elliott 176-256, Harry Gant 257-261, Ernie Irvan 262-271, Gant 272-282, Irvan 283-288, Elliott 289-382, Ricky Rudd 383-389, Elliott 390-475, Rudd 476-500.
13 lead changes among 7 drivers.
Cautions: 9 for 48 laps   Margin of Victory: 0.47 second
*Relieved by Sterling Marlin

Race #23

Rudd Delivers at Dover; Kulwicki Down and Out

DOVER, DE (Sept. 20) – Ricky Rudd held off a fast closing Bill Elliott in the final laps and ended his 46-race void in the Peak AntiFreeze 500 at Dover Downs International Speedway. It was the 13th career Winston Cup win for the Chesapeake, Va. Chevrolet driver.

Elliott led 261 of the 500 laps and had built up a five second advantage when the final green flag pit stops took place in the final 25 miles. Elliott was the first to pit. He brought his Junior Johnson Ford down pit road

Brian Czobat

Ricky Rudd had his game face on before the Dover event.

Kim Novasat

Ken Schrader sends up a smoke screen as he slides through Dover's first turn.

and crew chief Tim Brewer was ready to make a two tire change and add fuel. Car owner Johnson ordered a four tire change. Rudd came in five laps later and got fuel only. He returned to the track with a 6.72 second lead with 20 laps to go.

Elliott rapidly erased the deficit but ran out of laps. At the finish, he was only 0.47-second behind Rudd.

"At first, I saw Bill as a speck in my mirror," said Rudd after winning at least one race in his 10th consecutive season – second among active drivers. "It wasn't long before that speck became awfully big. It was a decision by my crew chief Gary DeHart. We had the advantage of seeing what Elliott's crew did. My guys did the right thing and it worked out for us."

Elliott admitted that "Ricky and them outsmarted us at the end. There weren't enough laps left to catch him."

Brewer said that Johnson over-ruled his decision. "I asked for left-side tires, that's all I wanted," said Brewer. "I said put on two, and he (Johnson) said put on four."

Kyle Petty finished third and said that Elliott's team "gave that one away." Davey Allison took on four tires on his final pit stop and wound up fourth, a lap down. "Goodyear said the left side tires probably wouldn't last," said car owner Robert Yates, "so we put tires on. We've been to the body shop too much this year. Running 30 or so laps on worn tires would have been iffy."

Morgan Shepherd brought the Wood Brothers Ford home in fifth place.

Alan Kulwicki won the pole and led the opening lap before giving way to Mark Martin. Dale Earnhardt battled with Martin most of the early laps and had led for an 81 lap stretch when he pitted on lap 175. The caution flag came out 11 laps later, trapping Earnhardt a lap behind the leaders. A number of other contenders found themselves a lap behind, too.

Elliott traded the lead with Harry Gant and Ernie Irvan before Rudd became a player late in the race.

Kulwicki's day came to an end in the 93rd lap when he tangled with Chad Little, sending Kulwicki's Ford head-on into the wall. "He just ran into me," said Kulwicki. "Realistically, this probably finishes us off in the championship deal. I don't like to give up, but I know it will be hard to come back now."

Little said he gave "Kulwicki plenty of room, but he cut down on me. I guess he thought he had cleared me."

Elliott's runner-up effort enabled him to stretch his Winston Cup lead to 154 points over Allison. Kulwicki fell to fourth place in the standings, 278 points off the top. Only a complete collapse by Elliott can let Allison, Kulwicki and third place Gant back in the hunt.

A total of nine caution flags consumed 48 laps, most of them the result of wrecks. Dale Earnhardt, mired in a slump, caused two of the crashes. While trying to get back on the lead lap, he tagged the rear of Geoff

Steve Crumbacker

Rusty Wallace #2 skids in front of Ernie Irvan #4 at Dover as Dale Jarrett #18 takes the low route.

Bodine's Ford, sending Bodine spinning off the fourth turn in heavy traffic. Miraculously, no one slammed into Bodine.

Bodine spun a few laps later in the second turn. "The second one was my fault," said Bodine. "It just got away from me. The first one wasn't my fault. I got hit."

Dick Trickle had worked his way into the top 10 but was the victim of an Earnhardt shunt just past the half-way point. "I was in line, riding along, when somebody knocked the hell out of me," said Trickle. "I don't know who it was, but he drove a black car with the number 3 on it. I don't mind being pushed, but the car was knocked right out from under me. I got hit so hard that it knocked both my rear tires off the ground. That's not right."

Trickle was bruised and an old back problem was aggravated, but he was otherwise unhurt.

Earnhardt got caught up in a third wreck, not of his making. Rusty Wallace tried a daring three-abreast move into the first turn, taking himself, Brett Bodine and Ernie Irvan out of contention. Earnhardt tagged Wallace's car as he went to the apron to try to miss the incident.

"I don't know what Rusty was thinking," said Bodine. "He must have fallen out of a tree or something."

Wallace admitted he "tried a real gutsy move. If Brett is blaming me for that deal, then all I have to say is that he should have backed off of the gas."

Others wiped out by wrecks included Richard Petty, Jeff Purvis, and Ken Schrader's relief driver Sterling Marlin.

Race #24

Kyle Puts on the Show; But Bodine Best at Martinsville

MARTINSVILLE, VA (Sept. 28) – Geoff Bodine held off a late bid by Rusty Wallace and a determined effort by Kyle Petty and drove to his first win of the season in the Goody's 500 at Martinsville Speedway.

The 500-lap contest on the .525-mile oval was delayed until Monday afternoon by heavy rains. When the race finally began at 2:20 pm, the race resembled a bull fight. "It felt like dirt track racing out there," said the winner. "This was the toughest race I've run here and ended up winning. It was rough."

In all, there were a dozen caution flags – most for spins and crashes. Racing scribe Benny Phillips commented, "After a 26 hour wait, they dropped their guard and beat on each other like road warriors in a street rumble. When it was over, the only unscathed piece of sheet metal was the scoreboard."

Bodine led the final 43 laps and outran Rusty Wallace by 0.19-second to claim his first win for the Bud Moore Ford team. Third place went to Brett Bodine, who lost second place in the final laps. Kyle Petty made up a two lap deficit in a crowd pleasing run and claimed fourth place money. Fifth place went to Alan Kulwicki.

Point leader Bill Elliott never got on track and departed early with engine problems. He wound up 30th in the 31-car field and watched as his lead in the standings was reduced to 112 points over Davey Allison.

Allison squandered a golden opportunity and managed only a 16th place finish after spinning out twice.

Winston Cup Race No. 24
500 Laps at Martinsville Speedway
Martinsville, VA
"Goody's 500"
262.5 Miles on .525-mile Short Track
September 28, 1992

Fin	St	No.	Driver	Team / Car	Laps	Money	Status
1	7	15	Geoff Bodine	Bud Moore Eng. Ford	500	$60,550	Running
2	8	2	Rusty Wallace	Roger Penske Pontiac	500	39,400	Running
3	17	26	Brett Bodine	King Motorsports Ford	500	29,125	Running
4	1	42	Kyle Petty	SabCo Racing Pontiac	500	22,000	Running
5	10	7	Alan Kulwicki	AK Racing Ford	500	23,330	Running
6	29	8	Dick Trickle	Stavola Brothers Ford	500	15,925	Running
7	30	22	Sterling Marlin	Junior Johnson Ford	500	16,350	Running
8	14	6	Mark Martin	Roush Racing Ford	499	16,100	Running
9	4	1	Rick Mast	Precision Products Olds	499	13,800	Running
10	21	5	Ricky Rudd	Hendrick Motorsports Chevy	499	17,200	Running
11	27	94	Terry Labonte	Billy Hagan Olds	498	11,635	Running
12	24	55	Ted Musgrave	RaDiUs Motorsports Ford	498	10,950	Running
13	28	25	Ken Schrader	Hendrick Motorsports Chevy	498	14,240	Running
14	31	16	Wally Dallenbach,Jr.	Roush Racing Ford	497	7,350	Running
15	9	17	Darrell Waltrip	DarWal Chevrolet	496	14,600	Running
16	22	28	Davey Allison	Robert Yates Racing Ford	496	15,150	Running
17	2	66	Jimmy Hensley	Cale Yarborough Ford	495	10,100	Running
18	15	43	Richard Petty	Petty Enterprises Pontiac	495	9,355	Running
19	3	33	Harry Gant	Leo Jackson Olds	495	15,150	Running
20	6	10	Derrike Cope	Bob Whitcomb Chevrolet	492	6,600	Running
21	12	21	Morgan Shepherd	Wood Brothers Ford	488	8,700	Running
22	23	71	Jim Sauter	Marcis Auto Racing Chevy	485	5,500	Running
23	13	18	Dale Jarrett	Joe Gibbs Chevrolet	477	8,150	Running
24	19	90	Hut Stricklin	Junie Donlavey Ford	477	3,500	Running
25	20	41	Dave Marcis	Larry Hedrick Chevrolet	474	4,975	Running
26	26	12	Jeff Purvis	Bobby Allison Chevrolet	468	7,850	Running
27	5	4	Ernie Irvan	Morgan-McClure Chevrolet	428	13,150	Running
28	25	68	Bobby Hamilton	Tri-Star Motorsports Ford	425	8,675	Running
29	18	30	Michael Waltrip	Bahari Racing Pontiac	355	7,550	Crash
30	16	11	Bill Elliott	Junior Johnson Ford	158	12,000	Engine
31	11	3	Dale Earnhardt	RCR Enterprises Chevrolet	111	14,550	Engine

Time of Race: 3 hours, 29 minutes, 13 seconds
Average Speed: 75.424 mph
Pole Winner: Kyle Petty – 92.497 mph
Lap Leaders: Kyle Petty 1-13, Jimmy Hensley 14-19, K.Petty 20-141, Geoff Bodine 142-143, Darrell Waltrip 144-150, Sterling Marlin 151-156, Rusty Wallace 157-162, G.Bodine 163-167, R.Wallace 168-219, Brett Bodine 220-224, R.Wallace 225-308, G.Bodine 309-348, Marlin 349-355, Alan Kulwicki 356-358, G.Bodine 359-397, B.Bodine 398-457, G.Bodine 458-500.
12 lead changes among 8 drivers.
Cautions: 12 for 67 laps Margin of Victory: 0.19 second

Kim Novosat

Alan Kulwicki climbs from his Ford after a practice session at Martinsville.

Kulwicki kept his slim hopes alive and trails Elliott by 191 points.

Petty started on the pole and led the first 135 of the first 141 laps. He ran out of fuel, which put him back in the pack, then lost a lap when he collided with Bodine in the 169th lap.

Kyle scrambled back into the lead lap but got stuck in the wet infield grass trying to avoid the spinning cars of Allison and Wallace. That dropped him two laps off the pace, but he never gave up.

"I had a car and engine that killed them all day," said Petty. "I just couldn't get back into position to win the race. Although I was two laps down with 100 laps to go, I knew I could catch up if the cautions fell right. As well as we ran and as hard as the guys worked, I'm a little disappointed with fourth place."

Wallace knocked Allison into a spin on lap 373 while the two were battling for second place. Wallace claimed Allison "jammed on the brakes and I was getting on the gas. Later he popped me and spun me."

Allison said his Ford developed brake problems. "I tried to conserve them, but all the action started when I challenged for the lead. I wasn't trying anything silly, but the roof caved in."

Allison said his second wreck was caused "when the brake pedal went right to the floor. We gained some points, but it could have been a lot more. We're going to keep working to make a horse race out of it."

Bodine went the final 124 laps without a pit stop. He passed by the opportunity to get new tires during three caution periods during that span. "We didn't stop because we didn't run well on new tires," said Bodine "Besides, we didn't want to give up track position. We took a gamble that the cars with new tires wouldn't improve enough to pass us."

Wallace took on tires in the final caution period with 30 laps to go and had to charge out of the pack. "I thought I would win the thing, but I think we broke a shock or something," said Wallace. "It was hopping real bad and I couldn't get around him (Bodine)."

Michael Waltrip lost his cool when he and Dave Marcis tangled in turn three on lap 363. Both cars spun after making contact. "After the wreck," said Marcis, "I'm strapped in my car and Michael comes over and hits me in the mouth and cuts my lip open. I'm strapped in the race car. How can I defend myself? It's up to NASCAR to handle it now."

Waltrip said the wreck "was hard to take" and left it at that.

NASCAR fined Waltrip $500 for his actions.

Dale Earnhardt dropped out of the top 10 in points when he blew an engine and finished last. It was the third time in the last 10 races he has finished last.

Race #25

Another Rain Delay Results in Another Soggy Win for Bodine

N.WILKESBORO, N.C. (Oct. 5) – Geoff Bodine streaked to his second straight short track win on a Monday and dominated the Tyson Holly Farms 400 at North Wilkesboro Speedway. Bodine's triumph in Bud Moore's Thunderbird clinched the manufacturers title for Ford, its first since 1969.

Bodine started third and chased Alan Kulwicki, Kyle Petty and Rusty Wallace in the early stages. He tasted first place for the first time on lap 67, but once he shot past Petty in the 72nd lap, the lights went out for everyone else. In all, he led four times for a total of 312 laps.

Bodine easily outdistanced runner-up Mark Martin by

Brian Czobat

Title contenders Bill Elliott and Davey Allison run nose-to-tail at North Wilkesboro.

5.34 seconds to post his 13th career Winston Cup victory. Third place went to Petty with Wallace fourth and Sterling Marlin fifth.

It was a day when all of the point leaders suffered problems. Leader Bill Elliott struggled all day with an ill-handling car and was lapped eight times in the caution-free event and finished 26th. "With no cautions," said Elliott, "there wasn't any time to fix the car." By the 100 lap mark, Elliott was already two laps down.

Curiously, the other Ford from the Junior Johnson stable driven by fifth-place Marlin, ran well. "This is a new car," said Marlin. "I wanted to take care of it because we intend on running this car at Charlotte. We were strong on new tires, but after 50 laps or so, it went away."

Davey Allison was lapped three times and finished 11th. "We picked up some points, so it was a good day," said Allison, who now trails Elliott by 67 points. In a weird twist, Allison has picked up nearly 100 points on Elliott without the benefit of a top 10 finish.

Kulwicki won the pole and led the first 34 laps, but he disappeared after that, eventually finishing 12th. "We missed the set up a little bit and never had the chance to adjust it," said Kulwicki, who pulled to within 144 points of Elliott. Kulwicki has gained 134 points on Elliott in the last two races. "The key to the point race is to not spend any time in the garage area," said Kulwicki.

The 400-lapper was the first Winston Cup event to be run without a caution flag since a 400-miler at Michigan in 1984. It was the first time a North Wilkesboro race had been run caution-free since 1971.

Brian Czobat

Kyle Petty passes Richard Petty at North Wilkesboro. It was King Richard's final effort on the .625-mile track where he has won 15 times.

Bodine gave credit to new team manager Travis Carter, who joined the team a few weeks ago. "This has always been a good team," said Bodine, "but Travis has given us a sense of direction. Travis has brought a lot of little things to our attention that needed fixing."

Only one car in the field of 32 failed to finish. Jeff Purvis, new driver for the Bobby Allison team, departed after 35 laps with engine problems. It was the third sour pill Purvis had swallowed during the week. Twice he crashed in practice, resulting in his having to take a provisional to get in the race.

Despite winning the last two races, Bodine has only come from 17th to 16th in the point standings. "We'd like to win the Winston Cup championship for Bud and Ford," said Bodine, "but we dug ourselves too much of a hole in the early part of the season. Once you get behind, it becomes nearly impossible to make it up."

Rich Bickle, a short track specialist out of Edgerton, Wisc. raised some eyebrows as he charged past several top cars. "We passed some cars – some good cars – and beat them," said Bickle, who finished 20th, five laps down. "We sure needed a couple of cautions, though. We lost too much time on those green flag pit stops."

Winston Cup Race No. 25
400 Laps at North Wilkesboro Speedway
N.Wilkesboro, NC
"Tyson Holly Farms 400"
250 Miles on .625-mile Short Track
October 5, 1992

Fin	St	No.	Driver	Team / Car	Laps	Money	Status
1	3	15	Geoff Bodine	Bud Moore Eng. Ford	400	$71,625	Running
2	16	6	Mark Martin	Roush Racing Ford	400	36,475	Running
3	4	42	Kyle Petty	SabCo Racing Pontiac	399	20,325	Running
4	2	2	Rusty Wallace	Roger Penske Pontiac	399	18,600	Running
5	6	22	Sterling Marlin	Junior Johnson Ford	399	20,000	Running
6	8	4	Ernie Irvan	Morgan-McClure Chevrolet	399	19,175	Running
7	11	26	Brett Bodine	King Motorsports Ford	398	13,780	Running
8	7	94	Terry Labonte	Billy Hagan Olds	398	11,225	Running
9	17	17	Darrell Waltrip	DarWal Chevrolet	397	14,350	Running
10	10	18	Dale Jarrett	Joe Gibbs Chevrolet	397	12,755	Running
11	14	28	Davey Allison	Robert Yates Racing Ford	397	14,875	Running
12	1	7	Alan Kulwicki	AK Racing Ford	397	18,950	Running
13	28	33	Harry Gant	Leo Jackson Olds	397	14,300	Running
14	25	55	Ted Musgrave	RaDiUs Motorsports Ford	397	9,850	Running
15	5	5	Ricky Rudd	Hendrick Motorsports Chevy	396	12,275	Running
16	23	30	Michael Waltrip	Bahari Racing Pontiac	396	9,450	Running
17	9	21	Morgan Shepherd	Wood Brothers Ford	396	9,100	Running
18	12	8	Dick Trickle	Stavola Brothers Ford	396	5,825	Running
19	13	3	Dale Earnhardt	RCR Enterprises Chevrolet	395	15,350	Running
20	22	45	Rich Bickle	Gene Isenhour Ford	395	4,450	Running
21	19	1	Rick Mast	Precision Products Olds	395	8,550	Running
22	26	10	Derrike Cope	Bob Whitcomb Chevrolet	394	5,450	Running
23	18	25	Ken Schrader	Hendrick Motorsports Chevy	394	12,450	Running
24	27	16	Wally Dallenbach,Jr.	Roush Racing Ford	393	5,150	Running
25	20	66	Jimmy Hensley	Cale Yarborough Ford	392	4,750	Running
26	15	11	Bill Elliott	Junior Johnson Ford	392	11,300	Running
27	21	43	Richard Petty	Petty Enterprises Pontiac	390	7,825	Running
28	29	41	Dave Marcis	Larry Hedrick Chevrolet	388	4,735	Running
29	32	71	Jim Sauter	Marcis Auto Racing Chevy	386	4,700	Running
30	30	90	Hut Stricklin	Junie Donlavey Ford	384	5,100	Running
31	24	68	Bobby Hamilton	Tri-Star Motorsports Ford	383	8,625	Running
32	31	12	Jeff Purvis	Bobby Allison Chevrolet	35	8,500	Engine

Time of Race: 2 hours, 19 minutes, 43 seconds
Average Speed: 107.360 mph
Pole Winner: Alan Kulwicki – 117.133 mph
Lap Leaders: Alan Kulwicki 1-34, Rusty Wallace 35-37, Kyle Petty 38-66, Geoff Bodine 67, K.Petty 68-71, G.Bodine 72-120, Sterling Marlin 121, K.Petty 122, Darrell Waltrip 123-125 G.Bodine 126-243, Mark Martin 244-245, R.Wallace 246-256, G.Bodine 257-400.
12 lead changes among 7 drivers.
Cautions: None Margin of Victory: 5.34 seconds

Brian Czobat

Geoff Bodine's North Wilkesboro victory wrapped up Ford's first manufacturers' title since 1969.

Race #26

Martin Takes Charlotte; Title Chase Wide Open

CONCORD, NC (Oct. 11) – Mark Martin outran Alan Kulwicki in the final 50 miles and won the Mello Yello 500 at Charlotte Motor Speedway. Bill Elliott's demise in the final laps left the Winston Cup championship chase wide open with six hopefuls.

Elliott enjoyed what was assumed to be an insurmountable point lead a month ago. However, repeated mechanical failures have now left him with a slim 39 point cushion over Davey Allison and only 114 points ahead of sixth place Kyle Petty.

Martin pushed his Ford past Kulwicki with 32 laps to go and sprinted to a 1.88-second triumph – the seventh of his career. Kulwicki claimed second with Kyle Petty, who led the most laps, finishing third. Jimmy Spencer, new driver for the Bobby Allison team, turned in a strong effort that netted fourth place. Ricky Rudd came home fifth.

Kulwicki started on the pole and led the first 39 laps. Petty forged to the front in the 68th lap and set sail –

Winston Cup Race No. 26
334 Laps at Charlotte Motor Speedway
Concord, NC
"Mello Yello 500"
501 Miles on 1.5-mile Superspeedway
October 11, 1992

Fin	St	No.	Driver	Team / Car	Laps	Money	Status
1	4	6	Mark Martin	Roush Racing Ford	334	$101,500	Running
2	1	7	Alan Kulwicki	AK Racing Ford	334	89,000	Running
3	20	42	Kyle Petty	SabCo Racing Pontiac	334	68,600	Running
4	24	12	Jimmy Spencer	Bobby Allison Ford	334	41,200	Running
5	5	5	Ricky Rudd	Hendrick Motorsports Chevy	334	35,550	Running
6	3	4	Ernie Irvan	Morgan-McClure Chevrolet	334	34,150	Running
7	2	25	Ken Schrader	Hendrick Motorsports Chevy	334	32,500	Running
8	18	33	Harry Gant	Leo Jackson Olds	334	25,800	Running
9	17	8	Dick Trickle	Stavola Brothers Ford	333	19,300	Running
10	12	15	Geoff Bodine	Bud Moore Eng. Ford	333	19,600	Running
11	30	55	Ted Musgrave	RaDiUs Motorsports Ford	333	16,200	Running
12	13	94	Terry Labonte	Billy Hagan Chevrolet	333	15,000	Running
13	6	21	Morgan Shepherd	Wood Brothers Ford	333	14,700	Running
14	11	3	Dale Earnhardt	RCR Enterprises Chevrolet	332	19,050	Running
15	26	68	Bobby Hamilton	Tri-Star Motorsports Ford	331	13,450	Running
16	19	22	Sterling Marlin	Junior Johnson Ford	331	11,350	Running
17	14	10	Derrike Cope	Bob Whitcomb Chevrolet	331	16,100	Running
18	9	66	Jimmy Hensley	Cale Yarborough Ford	330	8,450	Running
19	22	28	Davey Allison	Robert Yates Racing Ford	329	15,375	Running
20	35	16	Wally Dallenbach,Jr.	Roush Racing Ford	328	7,550	Running
31	39	71	Jim Sauter	Marcis Auto Racing Chevy	326	6,595	Running
22	37	57	Bob Schacht	Doug Stringer Olds	325	4,700	Running
23	29	30	Michael Waltrip	Bahari Racing Pontiac	325	9,220	Running
24	7	18	Dale Jarrett	Joe Gibbs Chevrolet	324	9,640	Clutch
25	33	45	Rich Bickle	Gene Isenhour Ford	324	4,830	Running
26	15	83	Lake Speed	Speed Ford	323	4,235	Clutch
27	32	43	Richard Petty	Petty Enterprises Pontiac	323	8,720	Running
28	8	26	Brett Bodine	King Motorsports Ford	320	9,105	Running
29	34	65	Jerry O'Neil	Alan Aroneck Olds	314	3,965	Running
30	16	11	Bill Elliott	Junior Johnson Ford	310	13,880	Sway Bar
31	27	97	Hut Stricklin	Junior Johnson Ford	305	3,800	Quit
32	31	90	Pancho Carter	Junie Donlavey Ford	297	3,735	Running
33	25	9	Chad Little	Melling Performance Ford	294	3,670	Heating
34	10	17	Darrell Waltrip	DarWal Chevrolet	215	13,350	Engine
35	23	1	Rick Mast	Precision Products Olds	168	8,155	Engine
36	36	49	Stanley Smith	Smith Chevrolet	141	3,610	Engine
37	21	2	Rusty Wallace	Roger Penske Pontiac	128	11,600	Engine
38	38	52	Jimmy Means	Means Racing Pontiac	89	3,590	Engine
39	40	41	Dave Marcis	Larry Hedrick Chevrolet	57	5,085	Rear End
40	28	31	Bobby Hillin,Jr.	Team Ireland Chevrolet		3,580	Disq.

Time of Race: 3 hours, 15 minutes, 47 seconds
Average Speed: 153.537 mph
Pole Winner: Alan Kulwicki – 179.027 mph
Lap Leaders: Alan Kulwicki 1-39, Mark Martin 40-61, Dick Trickle 62-63, Bill Elliott 64-67, Kyle Petty 68-71, Ken Schrader 72-84, K.Petty 85-126, Mark Martin 127-131, Kulwicki 132-133, Ernie Irvan 134-135, Elliott 136-139, K.Petty 140-186, Martin 187-190. Harry Gant 191-198, Elliott 199-200, K.Petty 201-236, Martin 237, Kulwicki 238-242, Martin 243-285, Kulwicki 286-302, Martin 303-334.
21 lead changes among 8 drivers.
Cautions: 3 for 12 laps   Margin of Victory: 1.88 seconds

Brian Czobat

Mark Martin powered his Roush Racing Ford to a convincing win at Charlotte Motor Speedway.

leading for a total of 130 laps. In the final stages, however, Petty faded and did not contend for the win. "The handling keeps going away late in these races," growled Petty. "Same thing happened here in May. We've got to figure out what's causing it."

Martin flexed his muscles late in the race and denied Kulwicki a chance for his third win of the year. "We're on a hot streak and we're going to keep working on them," said Martin. "I can't believe we were 350-some points down a few weeks ago and now we've got a shot at the championship."

Kulwicki said he "was not disappointed in running second. When we wrecked at Dover, I thought our championship hopes were finished. We've come a long way in the last few weeks and we've got a good chance. That's all I ask for – to have a fighting chance to win the championship." Kulwicki trails Elliott by only 47 points.

For most of the race, it appeared Elliott would all but wrap up the title. He had lapped Allison four times and was holding his own in eighth place when the track bar pulled loose from the frame, making the car impossible to drive. "Something broke, that's all I know," muttered a non-talkative Elliott afterwards. "I'm not going to worry about it. We just had a bad day."

Elliott wound up in 30th place, while Allison struggled to finish 19th. "I don't understand what happened to the car," said Allison. "It was good in practice. Anyway, it's not a two-man race for the championship anymore. There's a bunch of us in it right now."

Martin leaped to fourth in the standings, 91 points behind Elliott. Harry Gant, who finished eighth in the race, moved into fifth spot, 98 points off the top. Petty has a slim chance, 114 points back.

Bobby Hillin, Jr. finished 15th in Martin Birrane's Team Ireland Chevrolet, but NASCAR officials discovered that the engine had illegal cylinders and raised intake ports. Hillin, Jr. was disqualified immediately – the first time NASCAR had disqualified a car since it disqualified Buddy Baker in the 1973 National 500 here at Charlotte.

Birrane said he was unaware of the illegalities since the engine had been leased from Richard Childress. NASCAR allowed Birrane to appeal the issue but did not change its verdict. Birrane then quit the series.

Hut Stricklin drove the third Junior Johnson Ford entry as a prelude to teaming up for the 1993 season. Stricklin was pulled into the pits when Elliott had his problems, saving Elliott another three points from being lost in the point race.

Ricky Rudd's Hendrick Motorsports team was fined $5,000 when NASCAR judged the car too low during technical inspection. It was an unusually heavy fine considering Michael Waltrip received a $500 fine for punching Dave Marcis at Martinsville.

Publisher Hank Schoolfield suggeted that Rudd "go punch somebody in the nose and ask for a $4,500 reduction."

Race #27

Petty Rocks Rockingham; Elliott Pads Lead in Standings

ROCKINGHAM, N.C. (Oct. 25) – Kyle Petty led all but eight laps of the AC Delco 500 at North Carolina Motor Speedway and moved from sixth to fourth in the Winston Cup point standings.

Petty started on the pole and was never passed – losing the lead only when he pitted. A late caution flag allowed Ernie Irvan to move to within striking distance, but he finished 0.91-second behind when the checkered flag fell. Ricky Rudd finished third and Bill Elliott enhanced his bid for the title, finishing fourth. Fifth place went to Sterling Marlin.

Elliott's top five finish was his first in over a month, and he was able to increase his lead to 70 points over Davey Allison.

Allison was lapped twice as he struggled once again. Alan Kulwicki fell three laps off the pace and wound up 12th, dropping 85 points behind Elliott. All Elliott has to do is keep the car running between the fences to sew up his second championship.

Winston Cup Race No. 27
492 Laps at N.C. Motor Speedway
Rockingham, NC
"AC Delco 500"
500.364 Miles on 1.017-mile Superspeedway
October 25, 1992

Fin	St	No.	Driver	Team / Car	Laps	Money	Status
1	1	42	Kyle Petty	SabCo Racing Pontiac	492	$153,100	Running
2	5	4	Ernie Irvan	Morgan-McClure Chevrolet	492	31,225	Running
3	7	5	Ricky Rudd	Hendrick Motorsports Chevy	491	31,225	Running
4	3	11	Bill Elliott	Junior Johnson Ford	491	26,200	Running
5	19	22	Sterling Marlin	Junior Johnson Ford	491	20,075	Running
6	18	33	Harry Gant	Leo Jackson Olds	491	21,450	Running
7	6	26	Brett Bodine	King Motorsports Ford	491	15,200	Running
8	12	3	Dale Earnhardt	RCR Enterprises Chevrolet	490	22,350	Running
9	11	94	Terry Labonte	Billy Hagan Olds	490	14,500	Running
10	15	28	Davey Allison	Robert Yates Racing Ford	490	20,600	Running
11	21	12	Jimmy Spencer	Bobby Allison Ford	489	13,600	Running
12	8	7	Alan Kulwicki	AK Racing Ford	489	15,500	Running
13	13	21	Morgan Shepherd	Wood Brothers Ford	489	13,600	Running
14	24	10	Derrike Cope	Bob Whitcomb Chevrolet	488	9,800	Running
15	27	18	Dale Jarrett	Joe Gibbs Chevrolet	488	12,550	Running
16	14	8	Dick Trickle	Stavola Brothers Ford	487	11,500	Running
17	25	1	Rick Mast	Precision Products Olds	487	11,500	Running
18	23	66	Jimmy Hensley	Cale Yarborough Ford	487	8,950	Running
19	4	68	Bobby Hamilton	Tri-Star Motorsports Ford	487	11,950	Running
20	22	30	Michael Waltrip	Bahari Racing Pontiac	486	11,150	Running
21	9	2	Rusty Wallace	Roger Penske Pontiac	485	16,700	Running
22	20	17	Darrell Waltrip	DarWal Chevrolet	485	15,600	Running
23	30	16	Wally Dallenbach,Jr.	Roush Racing Ford	484	5,400	Running
24	33	9	Chad Little	Melling Performance Ford	483	5,300	Running
25	26	43	Richard Petty	Petty Enterprises Pontiac	482	9,850	Running
26	37	52	Jimmy Means	Means Racing Pontiac	475	6,700	Running
27	34	88	Mike Wallace	Barry Owen Ford	474	5,000	Running
28	32	85	Mike Skinner	Thee Dixon Chevrolet	459	4,900	Running
29	16	55	Ted Musgrave	RaDiUs Motorsports Ford	454	9,375	Running
30	2	6	Mark Martin	Roush Racing Ford	436	15,700	Crash
31	36	80	Dave Blaney	Stan Hover Pontiac	371	4,500	Handling
32	17	25	Ken Schrader	Hendrick Motorsports Chevy	322	22,000	Vibration
33	31	41	Greg Sacks	Larry Hedrick Chevrolet	304	5,850	Rear End
34	28	32	Jimmy Horton	Active Racing Chevrolet	299	4,200	Heating
35	10	15	Geoff Bodine	Bud Moore Eng. Ford	278	8,625	Engine
36	35	83	Lake Speed	Speed Ford	263	4,075	Trans
37	38	65	Jerry O'Neil	Alan Aroneck Olds	233	4,625	Brakees
38	29	71	Dave Marcis	Marcis Auto Racing Chevy	144	5,525	Rear End
39	39	77	Mike Potter	Means Racing Pontiac	7	4,025	Quit
40	40	53	John McFadden	Means Racing Pontiac	4	4,050	Quit

Time of Race: 3 hours, 49 minutes, 37 seconds
Average Speed: 130.748 mph
Pole Winner: Kyle Petty – 149.675 mph
Lap Leaders: Kyle Petty 1-82, Mark Martin 83, Ernie Irvan 84, Bill Elliott 85-86, K.Petty 87-164, Martin 165-166, K.Petty 167-328, Irvan 329, K.Petty 330-492.
9 lead changes among 4 drivers.
Cautions: 2 for 12 laps   Margin of Victory: 0.91 second

NCMS

Kyle Petty and Mark Martin on the front row at Rockingham. Kyle led all but eight laps in a dominating performance.

"We needed this to give us momentum," said Elliott. "Phoenix will tell the tale. A bad race at Phoenix could put any of us out of the title picture."

Tim Brewer, crew chief for Elliott, said, "If we can do this two more times, we'll be spraying champagne and catching roses. We needed to do exactly what we did – gain points. If you try to do any more or try to go out and win the race, you're a fool."

Petty crept to within 94 points of Elliott, but acknowledged his slim hopes of winning the title. "I still think all the planets would have to line up funny or something for us to win the championship," admitted Petty. "Me winning the championship would be like Ross Perot winning the Presidential election. But we're only 24 points out of second place and we'll shoot for that. Regardless of what happens, it's been a good year. I've never won more than one race in a season before."

Mark Martin ran second most of the day, but his afternoon came to an end when he cracked the wall off the fourth turn with 57 laps to go while trying to pass the lapped car of Michael Waltrip. "I just lost it," said Martin, who fell 172 points behind Elliott. "I guess I should have been more patient, but I was trying my guts out and got bit.

"Our championship hopes went from possible to unlikely," Martin added. "It was really a points race we had no business being in. I'm disappointed, but our main objective the second half of the year is to win races."

Kulwicki said his 12th place effort "hurt us, but it didn't kill us. It's three guys about even and one with a cushion. We feel like we can run as good or better than any of 'em at Phoenix and Atlanta."

Allison and his team had words during the race after their lackluster run. "We didn't cover ourselves with glory today," responded crew chief Larry McReynolds. We didn't run very good at all. With the lead Elliott has, all he has to do is ride it out and the championship is his."

Only two caution flags broke the action – and the first one didn't come until the 371st lap. As a result, Petty averaged a record 130.748 mph for the 500-mile trip.

Race #28

Elliott Falters; Allison Wins Phoenix and Takes Point Lead

PHOENIX, AZ (Nov. 1) – Davey Allison snatched the lead in the Winston Cup point standings with a narrow victory over Mark Martin in the Pyroil 500-kilometer event at Phoenix International Raceway.

Allison's fifth win of the year – his first since being involved in a terrible accident at Pocono – left with a 30 point lead over Alan Kulwicki heading into the season finale at Atlanta. Kulwicki finished fourth and leaped over Bill Elliott in the standings.

Elliott never led and slowed as his Ford began smoking in the early laps. After several pit stops failed to correct the problem, Elliott rode at reduced speeds to a 31st place finish. That left him 10 points behind Kulwicki and 40 behind Allison.

Allison finished 3.22 seconds ahead of Mark Martin to record his 18th career Winston Cup victory. Darrell

Waltrip got around Alan Kulwicki in the final three laps to take third. Kulwicki was fourth and Jimmy Spencer fifth.

Allison said he was " surprised when I looked over to pit road and saw smoke coming from Bill's car. I couldn't believe it was happening to that team because they're so good.

"I changed my strategy a little. I started driving less aggressively, shooting for a top five finish."

Allison's big break came with 29 laps left when leader Martin pitted for fuel. Three laps later, Allison was scheduled to come down pit road for his final service. At that point, Jeff Davis spun his car into the wall, bringing out the final caution of the day. "I was already at the entrance to pit road," said Allison. "My spotter hollered for me to stay out. That caution was such a big break that it put us in shock. After getting the advantage, I told myself I had to race smart the rest of the way."

Jim Ahmay

Davey Allison came on strong in the end and won the Phoenix event. He also took the lead in the Winston Cup standings.

Winston Cup Race No. 28
312 Laps at Phoenix Int'l Raceway
Phoenix, AZ
"Pyroil 500K"

312 Miles on 1-mile Superspeedway
November 1, 1992

Fin	St	No.	Driver	Team / Car	Laps	Money	Status
1	12	28	Davey Allison	Robert Yates Racing Ford	312	$65,285	Running
2	8	6	Mark Martin	Roush Racing Ford	312	40,555	Running
3	10	17	Darrell Waltrip	DarWal Chevrolet	312	32,130	Running
4	3	7	Alan Kulwicki	AK Racing Ford	312	25,730	Running
5	6	12	Jimmy Spencer	Bobby Allison Ford	312	22,105	Running
6	9	25	Ken Schrader	Hendrick Motorsports Chevy	312	20,070	Running
7	13	10	Derrike cope	Bob Whitcomb Chevrolet	312	13,220	Running
8	21	68	Bobby Hamilton	Tri-Star Motorsports Ford	312	15,820	Running
9	2	22	Sterling Marlin	Junior Johnson Ford	311	14,720	Running
10	19	3	Dale Earnhardt	RCR Enterprises Chevrolet	311	21,370	Running
11	11	30	Michael Waltrip	Bahari Racing Pontiac	311	13,120	Running
12	15	26	Brett Bodine	King Motorsports Ford	311	12,520	Running
13	27	16	Wally Dallenbach,Jr.	Roush Racing Ford	311	9,120	Running
14	30	33	Harry Gant	Leo Jackson Olds	311	16,220	Running
15	25	41	Hut Stricklin	Larry Hedrick Chevrolet	311	8,370	Running
16	26	94	Terry Labonte	Billy Hagan Olds	311	10,720	Running
17	14	1	Rick Mast	Precision Products Olds	311	10l420	Running
18	31	83	Lake Speed	Speed Ford	310	5,320	Running
19	7	42	Kyle Petty	SabCo Racing Pontiac	309	10,120	Running
20	17	18	Dale Jarrett	Joe Gibbs Chevrolet	309	10,485	Running
21	23	66	Jimmy Hensley	Cale Yarborough Ford	309	7,410	Running
22	24	43	Richard Petty	Petty Enterprises Pontiac	309	9,510	Running
23	33	29	John Krebs	Diamond Ridge Chevrolet	308	6,460	Running
24	16	55	Ted Musgrave	RaDiUs Motorsports Ford	302	9,410	Engine
25	41	92	Ron Hornaday,Jr.	Bob Fisher Chevrolet	301	6,360	Running
26	39	44	Jeff Davis	Davis Ford	299	4,785	Running
27	37	75	Bill Sedgwick	Wayne Spears Chevrolet	299	7,285	Running
28	1	2	Rusty Wallace	Roger Penske Pontiac	295	26,735	Running
29	40	24	Butch Gilliland	Laurie Gilliland Pontiac	292	6,210	Running
30	4	5	Ricky Rudd	Hendrick Motorsports Chevy	288	12,885	Running
31	18	11	Bill Elliott	Junior Johnson Ford	260	13,660	Running
32	38	49	Stanley Smith	Smith Chevrolet	251	4,385	Running
33	35	73	Bill Schmitt	Sylvia Schmitt Ford	209	4,860	Engine
34	5	4	Ernie Irvan	Morgan-McClure Chevrolet	201	13,935	Crash
35	36	71	Dave Marcis	Marcis Auto Racing Chevy	180	4,310	Engine
36	32	51	Jeff Purvis	James Finch Chevrolet	141	4,285	Brakes
37	34	52	Scott Gaylord	Means Racing Pontiac	124	4,265	Engine
38	22	21	Morgan Shepherd	Wood Brothers Ford	85	7,255	Engine
39	20	15	Geoff Bodine	Bud Moore Eng. Ford	69	7,240	Engine
40	29	8	Dick Trickle	Stavola Brothers Ford	68	4,205	Crash
41	42	61	Rick Scribner	Janet Scribner Chevrolet	7	4,205	Engine
42	28	37	Rick Carelli	Marshall Chesrown Chevrolet	1	4,205	Quit

Time of Race: 3 hours, 0 minutes, 12 seconds
Average Speed: 103.885 mph
Pole Winner: Rusty Wallace – 128.141 mph
Lap Leaders: Rusty Wallace 1-66, Sterling Marlin 67-87, Harry Gant 88-92, Alan Kulwicki 93-108, R.Wallace 109-203, Ted Musgrave 204-205, Kulwicki 206-238, Mark Martin 239-282, Davey Allison 283-312.
8 lead changes among 7 drivers.
Cautions: 7 for 34 laps Margin of Victory: 3.22 seconds

Allison was able to retain the lead when all cars pitted for fresh tires. He led the rest of the way and pulled away from Martin in the end.

Allison was able to put a recent string of poor efforts behind him. "Our team's biggest advantage has been the ability to communicate well," said Allison. "Our communications broke down at Rockingham. Some things that were said shouldn't have been said. So we met and decided to work together, no matter how things were going."

Elliott said "we just tore up the engine and that was it. This is not what we needed. We're not out of the championship picture, but we're not in it either."

Kulwicki led the race for 49 laps, but did not contend at the finish. "We changed two tires on most of the stops to keep track position," said Kulwicki. "In the end, we just didn't have it. That's all I can say."

Kulwicki was aware that Elliott had his problems and "that we've got to take advantage of this opportunity. I'm sure back in May people figured we'd fall by the wayside. We've been a little off in some races, but we ran well today. If Allison runs 5th at Atlanta (to clinch

Jim Ahmay

Jimmy Spencer #12 ducks under Ernie Irvan at Phoenix. Spencer delivered another strong performance in Bobby Allison's Ford, finishing fifth.

the title) and I win, we'll just have to accept it. But we've still had a good year."

Rusty Wallace started on the pole and was a bolt of lightning until his battery went dead. "There was no way anybody could touch us," said Wallace. "Then the battery shorts out. We had it won, hands down. That's the third time that has happened to me this year. This year is just trash. It's really frustrating."

Wallace was able to get repairs on his Roger Penske Pontiac, but he was 17 laps down in 28th place when the checkered flag fell.

Race #29

Kulwicki Nips Race Winner Elliott in Closest Title Chase

HAMPTON, GA (Nov. 15) – Bill Elliott led the final 13 laps and won the Hooters 500 at Atlanta Motor Speedway, but lost the 1992 Winston Cup championship to runner-up Alan Kulwicki.

Davey Allison, who needed only a fifth place finish to win the title, was running in that position when Ernie Irvan spun and took him into the wall on lap 254. Extensive repairs put Allison in 27th at the finish and left him a distant third in the point standings.

Kulwicki took the title by 10 points over Elliott – the closest in the 44 year history of NASCAR Winston Cup racing. But it was actually closer than that.

It came down to a matter of not who won, but who led the most laps. A five point bonus goes to the driver leading the most laps.

Kulwicki led three times for 103 laps, while Elliott led seven times for 102 laps. Kulwicki got the five bonus points and the title.

Winston Cup Race No. 29
328 Laps at Atlanta Motor Speedway
Hampton, GA
"Hooters 500"
499.216 Miles on 1.522-mile Superspeedway
November 15, 1992

Fin	St	No.	Driver	Team / Car	Laps	Money	Status
1	11	11	Bill Elliott	Junior Johnson Ford	328	$93,600	Running
2	14	7	Alan Kulwicki	AK Racing Ford	328	56,000	Running
3	8	15	Geoff Bodine	Bud Moore Eng. Ford	328	32,400	Running
4	18	12	Jimmy Spencer	Bobby Allison Ford	328	27,000	Running
5	6	94	Terry Labonte	Billy Hagan Chevrolet	328	22,235	Running
6	15	2	Rusty Wallace	Roger Penske Pontiac	328	20,100	Running
7	12	22	Sterling Marlin	Junior Johnson Ford	327	18,830	Running
8	34	66	Jimmy Hensley	Cale Yarborough Ford	326	15,300	Running
9	22	55	Ted Musgrave	RaDiUs Motorsports Ford	326	16,600	Running
10	32	18	Dale Jarrett	Joe Gibbs Chevrolet	326	16,950	Running
11	9	21	Morgan Shepherd	Wood Brothers Ford	325	14,500	Running
12	27	68	Bobby Hamilton	Tri-Star Motorsports Ford	325	15,750	Running
13	29	33	Harry Gant	Leo Jackson Olds	324	18,350	Running
14	25	30	Michael Waltrip	Bahari Racing Pontiac	324	13,775	Running
15	10	10	Derrike Cope	Bob Whitcomb Chevrolet	322	9,750	Running
16	20	42	Kyle Petty	SabCo Racing Pontiac	320	13,225	Engine
17	35	9	Chad Little	Melling Performance Ford	320	7,680	Running
18	13	83	Lake Speed	Speed Ford	320	6,740	Running
19	40	23	Eddie Bierschwale	Don Bierschwale Olds	319	6,925	Running
20	38	88	Mike Wallace	Barry Owen Ford	317	7,235	Running
21	37	52	Jimmy Means	Means Racing Ford	317	6,145	Running
33	41	71	Dave Marcis	Marcis Auto Racing Chevy	317	7,380	Running
23	24	17	Darrell Waltrip	DarWal Chevrolet	307	14,665	Running
24	36	32	Jimmy Horton	Active Racing Chevrolet	303	5,000	Running
25	16	5	Ricky Rudd	Hendrick Motorsports Chevy	300	12,735	Running
26	3	3	Dale Earnhardt	RCR Enterprises Chevrolet	299	20,670	Running
27	17	28	Davey Allison	Robert Yates Racing Ford	285	16,255	Running
28	1	1	Rick Mast	Precision Products Olds	253	13,140	Running
29	5	4	Ernie Irvan	Morgan-McClure Chevrolet	251	26,425	Crash
30	31	90	Bobby Hillin,Jr.	Junie Donlavey Ford	235	4,350	Engine
31	21	24	Jeff Gordon	Hendrick Motorsports Chevy	164	6,285	Crash
32	4	6	Mark Martin	Roush Racing Ford	160	16,920	Engine
33	28	57	Bob Schacht	Doug Stringer Olds	120	4,155	Ignition
34	26	45	Rich Bickle	Gene Isenhour Ford	97	4,090	Crash
35	39	43	Richard Petty	Petty Enterprises Pontiac	95	8,625	Running
36	23	25	Ken Schrader	Hendrick Motorsports Chevy	94	12,985	Crash
37	7	8	Dick Trickle	Stavola Brothers Ford	94	5,520	Crash
38	30	16	Wally Dallenbach,Jr.	Roush Racing Ford	94	5,455	Crash
39	33	49	Stanley Smith	Smith Chevrolet	60	3,865	Engine
40	2	26	Brett Bodine	King Motorsports Ford	1	8,425	Crash
41	19	41	Hut Stricklin	Larry Hedrick Chevrolet	1	5,300	Crash

Time of Race: 3 hours, 44 minutes, 20 seconds
Average Speed: 133.322 mph
Pole Winner: Rick Mast – 180.183 mph
Lap Leaders: Brett Bodine 1, Dale Earnhardt 2-16, Ernie Irvan 17-31, Earnhardt 32-60, Geoff Bodine 61, Bill Elliott 62-72, Alan Kulwicki 73, Elliott 74-79, Kulwicki 80, Elliott 81-82, Mark Martin 83-85, Davey Allison 86-90, Martin 91-134, Elliott 133-157, Irvan 158-166, Elliott 167-209, Kulwicki 210-310, Elliot 311-314, Terry Labonte 315, Elliott 316-328.
20 lead changes among 9 drivers.
Cautions: 7 for 45 laps Margin of Victory: 8,06 seconds

Kim Novosat

Richard Petty completed his career at Atlanta Motor Speedway in a banged up Pontiac.

Elliott and Kulwicki both were awarded 180 points. Had Elliott led one more lap than Kulwicki, he would have received the 185 points to Kulwicki's 175 and they would have tied for the championship.

The tie breaker is the number of wins by each driver, and Elliott had a 5-2 edge over Kulwicki in that category.

But the championship came down to a finer line than just that. Elliott led 11 laps under the caution flag. Kulwicki led 12 laps under the yellow, so he won the $1.3 million championship by leading one lap under the caution flag.

"I did all I could do," said Elliott. "I went out and won the race, but it wasn't enough."

Kulwicki overcame nearly impossible odds to win the championship at age 37. He turned down a number of top rides, including an offer from Junior Johnson. "I know some people thought I was crazy when I didn't take the Junior Johnson ride," said Kulwicki. "I don't want to flaunt it, but things turned out okay. I feel good about driving for myself. I have tried to keep a low-key attitude and keep my nose clean. I've had to stand hard and fast to my decisions."

Allison led five laps by not pitting until late during the third caution flag. He had run in the top five much of the day and was holding his own in fifth place – a position which would have assured him of the championship.

But Ernie Irvan's Chevrolet broke loose off turn four, crossed up and knocked Allison into the wall. "That's

Kim Novosat

Jeff Gordon made his first Winston Cup start at Atlanta.

Kim Novasat

Alan Kulwicki and Bill Elliott put on one of the most memorable finishes to a Winston Cup season. Kulwicki led one more lap than Elliott in the Atlanta race, which was the difference between first and second in the Winston Cup standings.

just the way it goes sometimes," said a dejected Allison. "We were trying to work our way back up to the front. I saw Ernie lose it, and we ran out of room. It just wasn't meant to happen this year, and our guys deserve better."

Kulwicki and crew chief Paul Andrews had been calculating the number of laps led in the pits – and Kulwicki knew exactly what it would take to lead the most laps. Stretching his fuel supply, Kulwicki led laps 210-310, and pitted on lap 311. That left 14 laps to go. Elliott picked up first place on lap 311 and then pitted after leading the 314th lap.

Terry Labonte stayed on the track to lead the 315th lap, then Elliott assumed command for good when Labonte pitted. Had Elliott led the 315th lap, he and Kulwicki would have both received the five point bonus. Kulwicki would have won the title by five points.

Elliott outran Kulwicki by 8.06 seconds. Third place went to Geoff Bodine with Jimmy Spencer and Labonte rounding out the top five.

Richard Petty drove in his final Winston Cup race and was involved in a fiery crash on lap 95. Trying to avoid the spinning cars of Dick Trickle and Ken Schrader, Petty ran into the back of Darrell Waltrip's car. "It broke the oil line and got oil on the headers," said Petty. "It caught on fire. I figured I'd better find me a fire truck, so I drove on down the track until I found one."

Then the King registered his trademark smile, "I think

Bryan Hallman

Alan Kulwicki did his celebrated Polish victory lap after capturing the championship.

all them cats wanted was an autograph because none of them brought a fire extinguisher. I had to holler at them to bring one."

Repairs were made to the Petty Pontiac and he drove onto the track in the closing laps and coasted across the finish line. He wound up 35th.

Following the race, the huge audience estimated at 162,500 hung around. "That was kind of funny," said Petty. "Nobody left. There was so much going on. You had a race winner, a new champion and me running my last race. I wish we had this much enthusiasm for all the races."

Bryan Hallman

Bobby Hillin, Jr. drove a Junie Donlavey Ford at Atlanta sponsored by Wrangler jeans.

1992 NASCAR Season
Final Point Standings - Winston Cup Series

Rank	Driver	Points	Starts	Wins	Top 5	Top 10	Winnings
1	Alan Kulwicki	4,078	29	2	11	17	$2,322,561
2	Bill Elliott	4,068	29	5	14	17	1,692,381
3	Davey Allison	4,015	29	5	15	17	1,955,628
4	Harry Gant	3,955	29	2	10	15	1,122,776
5	Kyle Petty	3,945	29	2	8	17	1,107,063
6	Mark Martin	3,887	29	2	10	17	1,000,571
7	Ricky Rudd	3,735	29	1	9	18	793,903
8	Terry Labonte	3,674	29	0	4	16	600,381
9	Darrell Waltrip	3,659	29	3	10	13	876,492
10	Sterling Marlin	3,603	29	0	6	13	649,048
11	Ernie Irvan	3,580	29	3	9	11	996,885
12	Dale Earnhardt	3,574	29	1	6	15	915,463
13	Rusty Wallace	3,556	29	1	5	12	657,925
14	Morgan Shepherd	3,549	29	0	3	11	634,222
15	Brett Bodine	3,491	29	0	2	13	495,224
16	Geoff Bodine	3,437	29	2	7	11	716,583
17	Ken Schrader	3,404	29	0	4	11	639,679
18	Ted Musgrave	3,315	29	0	1	7	449,121
19	Dale Jarrett	3,251	29	0	2	8	418,648
20	Dick Trickle	3,097	29	0	3	9	429,521
21	Derrike Cope	3,033	29	0	0	3	277,215
22	Rick Mast	2,830	29	0	0	1	350,740
23	Michael Waltrip	2,825	29	0	1	2	410,545
24	Wally Dallenbach,Jr.	2,799	29	0	1	1	220,245
25	Bobby Hamilton	2,787	29	0	0	2	367,065
26	Richard Petty	2,731	29	0	0	0	348,870
27	Hut Stricklin	2,689	28	0	0	4	336,965
28	Jimmy Hensley	2,410	22	0	0	4	247,660
29	Dave Marcis	2,348	29	0	0	0	218,045
30	Greg Sacks	1,759	20	0	0	0	178,120
31	Chad Little	1,669	19	0	0	1	145,805
32	Jimmy Means	1,531	22	0	0	0	133,160
33	Jimmy Spencer	1,284	12	0	3	3	183,585
34	Bobby Hillin,Jr.	1,135	13	0	0	0	102,160
35	Stanley Smith	959	14	0	0	0	89,650
36	Mike Potter	806	11	0	0	0	74,710
37	Jim Sauter	729	9	0	0	0	56,045
38	Lake Speed	726	9	0	0	0	49,545
39	Jimmy Horton	660	9	0	0	0	50,125
40	Bob Schacht	611	9	0	0	0	58,815
41	Charlie Glotzbach	592	7	0	0	0	48,060
42	James Hylton	476	8	0	0	0	37,910
43	Andy Belmont	467	8	0	0	0	39,820
44	Jeff Purvis	453	6	0	0	0	45,545
45	Dave Mader III	436	5	0	0	0	69,635
46	Jerry O'Neil	429	6	0	0	0	32,370
47	Eddie Bierschwale	277	4	0	0	0	25,995
48	Buddy Baker	255	3	0	0	0	49,500
49	Rich Bickle	252	3	0	0	0	13,370
50	Mike Wallace	249	3	0	0	0	17,415

1993 Winston Cup Season

The Loss of Two Champions; and Earnhardt Steps Into The King's Shadow

STARTING ON A HIGH NOTE

The 1993 NASCAR Winston Cup season had started on such a high note. After such a dramatic conclusion to the Winston Cup title chase in 1992, underdog champion Alan Kulwicki had given renewed hope to every team in NASCAR's garage area.

Kulwicki was the focus of much of the attention at Daytona International Speedway, Bill France's speed palace which annually opens each Winston Cup campaign.

Kulwicki had ridden a most unlikely wave into stock car racing stardom. He started out with a pick-up truck, a trailer, one race car and a bundle of hopes and dreams. Along the way were heart warming accomplishments and heartbreaking defeats. But perseverance overcame all the obstacles and the Wisconsin native had reaped NASCAR's most rewarding award – the Winston Cup championship.

"The ultimate satisfaction is if you can win it on your own," remarked Kulwicki.

Kulwicki said 'tunnel vision' has earmarked his unlikely success. "You can never take your eyes off your goals," said Kulwicki. "You have to be willing to forfeit other things in life if you have to. I haven't had a real vacation since I don't know when. I have quite a few things to look forward to in life.

"I haven't had time to enjoy the money or the championship," Kulwicki added. "I've been working extra hard keeping up with all the demands."

There were not enough hours in the day, or days in the week for Kulwicki to enjoy his winnings for earning the 1992 title. "I haven't really splurged on anything," he said. "The biggest thing I was going to buy was a plane. But it turns out Hooters (his sponsor) has a couple of planes and they have painted one of them orange and white. We're going to use that to fly the team around and perform some personal appearances."

It was one of the few times that Alan Kulwicki didn't do something 'his way'.

Alan Kulwicki's incredible run to the 1992 Winston Cup championship gave hope to many underdog NASCAR teams.

NEW FACES UP FRONT AT DAYTONA

The Daytona 500 front row produced a unique mix. Third generation driver Kyle Petty had earned the pole and second-generation driver Dale

Jarrett qualified second.

"This is a big deal," said young Kyle. "It'll be a big deal for a long time to come. It's one of those things you can look back on in 15 or 20 years and say, 'Hey, my father sat on the pole at Daytona and years later, I did the same thing'. So at least I'm doing some of the things he did."

Joining the Pettys and the Jarretts at Daytona was Al Unser, Jr., whose father Al, Sr. had finished fourth in the 1968 Daytona 500. Unser, Jr. became the first reigning Indianapolis 500 champion to enter the Daytona Speedweeks events since Tom Sneva in 1984.

LITTLE AL AT CENTER STAGE

Unser, Jr. had been a hit in the International Race of Champions (IROC) cars for several years. He is the only IndyCar driver to regularly duke it out with NASCAR drivers in full-bodied stock cars on big oval speedways.

His crew chief was Waddell Wilson, the savvy veteran who had been with a number of Daytona 500 winning teams. "I know people will say Little Al is a rookie being down here," said Wilson. "But after the first hour or so of practice, you'd think I was working with Cale Yarborough. "The way he has adapted to the car is remarkable. I wasn't ready for it. He came in, and instead of me helping him, he's helping me."

Greg Fielden

Al Unser, Jr., winner of the 1992 Indianapolis 500, drove a Hendrick Motorsports Chevrolet in the Twin 125-mile qualifying race and the Daytona 500.

Unser, Jr. said he "always wanted to do the Daytona 500. I've had offers before, but none of them would have been a winning combination. Now, I feel like I can go out and race for the lead with the frontrunners of NASCAR."

Unser, Jr. became the fourth man on the Rick Hendrick team. Ricky Rudd and Ken Schrader were back with Hendrick Motorsports, and rookie Jeff Gordon had signed with Hendrick in late 1992.

Little Al's car was not up to snuff, however. His qualifying speed was only 184.468 mph, which was only 38th quickest on pole day. "Our speed is borderline," said Unser, Jr. "We're going to have to run good enough in the 125-miler to get in the 500.

Unser, Jr. blew a tire and crashed in the Twin 125 but barely made it in the Daytona 500. He would start from the next-to-last row.

GORDON SPARKLES

Jeff Gordon took Speedweeks by storm. He qualified 11th on pole day and started sixth in the opening Twin 125. He moved quickly into second place and forged past Bill Elliott in the 22nd lap to take the lead. He was never headed.

"It was as amazing to me as it was to anybody else in this speedway," said the 21-year-old Gordon. "My wildest expectations would never have brought me to victory circle."

Gordon became the first rookie to win a Twin 125 since Johnny Rutherford won it in 1963. Rutherford was 24-years-old at the time.

Car owner Hendrick said he had watched Gordon closely during his tenure on NASCAR's Busch Grand National tour. "I had watched him at Atlanta (in 1992)," said Hendrick. "He was smoking his tires; he was so loose. I nudged the guy who was standing with me and I told him 'Watch, he's going to bust his tail on the next lap'. I said that for about 20 laps. Finally, I said, 'I can't believe this'. You can see a lot of raw talent when a guy can handle a car when it's that loose. As young as he was and with the experience he has, I was kind of blown away."

Although Gordon was under Ford Motor Co.'s wing throughout his stock car racing career, Hendrick inquired about his contractual status. "When I found out he wasn't under contract, I signed him within five days," said Hendrick.

World of Outlaws Sprint car king Steve Kinser was another of the new faces at Daytona. But the 12-time WoO champ was having his difficulties getting around the Big D. "I really don't know what I'm doing," confessed Kinser, who was driving a Chevrolet entered by Clint Folsom. "We expected to struggle a bit, but not like this. It is really frustrating."

Kinser qualified at a shade over 180 mph. The only driver he beat was A.J. Foyt, who was back for one last fling at Daytona in Bobby Jones' Ford.

Neither Kinser nor Foyt was able to earn a starting berth for the Daytona 500. Kinser crashed out early in the Twin 125 and Foyt departed with mechanical problems.

EARNHARDT BUZZING BIG D AGAIN

Joining the new faces at Daytona was a very familiar one, in a familiar role, trying to quench the same thirst that has left his mouth dry for 14 years. The familiar face belonged to Dale Earnhardt. The familiar quest was the elusive Daytona 500.

Earnhardt was ripping Speedweeks apart again. He won the Busch Clash for the fifth time, putting his signature on another marvelous run from the back of the pack – twice! He started 13th in the 15-car field, but it took him only six laps to gallop past NASCAR's speediest drivers. With the inverted start for the second 10-lap Clash dash, Earnhardt zipped through the field and had the lead by the sixth lap again. His rivals watched in wonder as he streaked to uncontested victory.

Earnhardt waved his magic wand in the Twin 125, winning for the fourth year in a row. He also won the Saturday Busch Grand National 300-miler for the fourth year in a row. It was vintage Earnhardt. But the big prize still lay ahead.

"The whole crew is pumped up this year," said Earnhardt, bouncing back from a disastrous 1992 season. "I'm really fired up for Sunday (Daytona 500). I feel real good about our chances."

Earnhardt's travails had been well documented in NASCAR's biggest annual event. He had lost the lead in the final 10 laps in three of the past four years. "It took Darrell Waltrip 17 years to win his first Daytona 500," Earnhardt said. "We're confident we can win in our 15th start. But if it takes 17 or 20 tries, we'll keep coming back."

Crew chief Jimmy Makar and Dale Jarrett were the big winners at Daytona.

Freshman Gordon led the opening lap. Dale Jarrett drove into the lead for five laps before Earnhardt took over. Dale shoved his black Chevrolet past Jarrett and comfortably rode in first place for most of the race.

Rusty Wallace authored a rather significant distraction to Earnhardt's dominating performance when he flipped down the backstretch on lap 169. Miraculously, Wallace escaped serious injury.

JARRETT UPSETS EARNHARDT AT DAYTONA

Earnhardt once again picked up first place after Wallace's crash and was heading a five-car frenzy into the final lap. Jarrett, who had to work his way up from mid-pack, found homage on Earnhardt's rear bumper in the final laps. The closer Jarrett ran to Earnhardt, the more unstable Earnhardt's car became.

As the group approached the white flag, Jarrett made his move. He took the low groove and muscled his way past Earnhardt in the first turn.

Earnhardt's retaliation was blocked by a swift-moving Geoff Bodine, who momentarily squeezed past Earnhardt into second place.

Earnhardt was able to get back up to second place,

but he had lost another Daytona 500 in the final lap.

"I'm getting tired of winning everything up until the Dayton 500," lamented Earnhardt. "But we got a good start on the championship. We've had other good years when we've lost the Daytona 500. Maybe that will happen again."

Wallace shook off the effects of his Daytona tumble and won the next event at Rockingham. Davey Allison scored at Richmond, Morgan Shepherd stood tall at Atlanta and Earnhardt won at Darlington. Through the first five races, there had been five different winners.

Earnhardt was leading the Winston Cup point standings. Defending champion Alan Kulwicki was in ninth place, having posted a pair of top five finishes in the first five 1993 events.

Brian Czobat

Alan Kulwicki 1954-1993

THE GLITTER IS GONE

But all the glitter of the 1993 season was wiped away on Thursday, April 1 when reigning champion Alan Kulwicki perished in a private plane crash en route to the Bristol International Raceway.

A twin-engine Merlin Fairchild 300, owned by Hooters restuarants, was carrying Kulwicki and three others: Mark Brooks, 26, son of Hooters CEO Robert Brooks, Dan Duncan, 44, Hooters marketing director, and Charlie Campbell, 48, the pilot of the aircraft.

The plane had departed from Knoxville where Kulwicki had signed autographs at a Hooters. He was headed to Bristol where qualifying was to begin the following day for the Food City 500.

The plane fell into a meadow and exploded on impact at about 9:30 p.m., close to a residential area near Blountville, Tenn.. The plane was six miles short of landing at Tri-Cities Regional Airport.

Kulwicki's car was withdrawn from the Bristol race the next day. On a dark, cold and misty afternoon, the AK Racing transporter – with a wreath attached to its grille – made two commemorative laps around the wet Bristol track as contestants and a few spectators stood with heads bowed. The big hauler departed through a gate near turn three.

Fellow drivers mourned the loss of NASCAR's champion. "I'm not in the frame of mind to run," said Wallace, who had competed with Kulwicki on the midwestern ASA tour before coming to NASCAR. "This is a bad deal. Real bad."

Jarrett expressed feelings shared by most contestants. "I don't want to be here this weekend," said the Daytona 500 winner. "It's going to be hard to concentrate on driving a race car. I wish NASCAR would call it off and come back next weekend, but I know they can't do that."

Mark Martin was another Kulwicki comrade on the short tracks before their exodus to the big time. "This is a tragic loss to our sport," said Martin. "I always had a lot of respect for Alan. He was quite a guy, focused and hard-nosed. Alan accomplished what no one thought he could last year. He knew I was real proud of him for winning that championship."

Darrell Waltrip, who had delivered moving eulogies for racing crash victims J.D. McDuffie and Clifford Allison the past two years, had these thoughts: "You try to understand why things like this happen. Here's a guy who worked so hard to accomplish something and finally does it. It looks like he's ready to enjoy the benefits of all his work, and now this..."

Kulwicki became the first reigning NASCAR champion to lose his life since 1962 and 1963 champion Joe Weatherly was fatally injured at

Rusty Wallace drove his Roger Penske Pontiac to 10 victories in 1993 but failed to win the Winston Cup championship.

Riverside, Calif. in 1964.

Curiously, at the time of the deaths of Weatherly and Kulwicki, their statistical line score in their final season was identical: Each had five starts, no wins, two top five finishes and three top 10 efforts.

Kulwicki was a gracious champion. During his acceptance speech at the NASCAR awards ceremony in New York, he closed his eloquent speech by saying, "I hope that in the year to come, I will be a good representative. I hope that when 1993 is over, the people at Winston, the people at NASCAR, and the competitors all look back and say, 'We were proud to have him represent us as our champion'."

The stock car racing fraternity was proud to have Kulwicki represent them as champion. Kulwicki rose to the pinnacle of his chosen profession doing things "his way".

WALLACE ON RAMPAGE

Rusty Wallace went on a victory tear after Kulwicki's death. He won at Bristol and performed a backwards victory lap in honor of the fallen champion. He also won at North Wilkesboro and at Martinsville.

Following the seventh race of the season at North Wilkesboro, Wallace had taken the point lead away from Earnhardt. "We *are* going to win the Winston Cup championship this year," insisted Wallace. "Our team is geared for it, I'm geared for it and nothing is going to stand in our way."

The winning streak continued at Martinsville. Wallace led 409 of the 500 laps and scored his fourth win in eight starts. "I thought we could win three or four races this year," said Wallace. "But I never thought they would come in the first eight races. The way this team has come together, I don't see why we can't win 10 races this year. And if we can win 10 races, we'll win that Winston Cup championship. We're going to beat that ol' redneck this year," added Wallace, poking a playful verbal jab at his friendly rival Dale Earnhardt.

Wallace's Winston Cup title express derailed at Talladega. In a furious last lap battle, Wallace had banged fenders with Mark Martin, Jimmy Spencer and Dale Jarrett in the final lap, then was on the receiving end of a tap from Earnhardt just short of the finish line.

Wallace moved from the high side to the low groove in the tri-oval area in an effort to block Earnhardt's challenge for fourth place. The two cars collided and Wallace sailed across the finish line in a series of sickening tumbles. He received credit for sixth place, and he still held an 86-point lead over Earnhardt in the

Kim Novosat

Dale Earnhardt said he lost sleep following Rusty Wallace's crash at Talladega.

Winston Cup standings. He also suffered a painful broken wrist in the crash.

Both drivers accepted blame for the accident, smoothing over any ill feelings the respective pit crews might have. The air of respect and professionalism on the part of both Earnhardt and Wallace was refreshing.

Earnhardt was genuinely concerned about Wallace's condition. "I lost sleep after that race worrying," said Earnhardt. "I don't want anybody to get hurt. Rusty is one of my best friends in racing. I was more concerned than I usually am.

"I wish there was something I could have done to change that thing. I hate it happened and wish I could take it back and all that. But you can't."

Wallace hit the skids after Talladega. He lost the point lead to Earnhardt in the next race at Sonoma, Calif. He had fallen out of the race late in the going when the transmission went bad. He departed from the Charlotte Coca-Cola 600 with a damaged suspension after a spin. He crashed at Dover after tangling with Mark Martin. Then his engine blew after only four laps at Pocono.

Suddenly, he was buried in fifth place in the Winston Cup standings, nearly 300 points behind Earnhardt. For all intent purposes, the point race was over at that point. Four straight DNF's in a tight championship race usually spells the end for any challenger.

The only thing that could have put Wallace or anybody else back in the point race was for Earnhardt to spend considerable time in the garage area.

The inaugural Winston Cup event at New Hampshire International Speedway was a turning point – or a *re*-turning point – for Wallace. He outran Mark Martin and Davey Allison in a stretch duel on the neatly manicured 1.058-mile oval.

Brian Czobat

Davey Allison 1962-1993

DEMISE OF A YOUNG HERO

Little did anyone know that the 317.4-mile event at New Hampshire would be the last for Davey Allison.

Allison, like his father Bobby, had a love for flying. He was particularly fascinated with helicopters.

Allison had obtained his helicopter's pilot license in July of 1992. He was a capable pilot but yearned for a more powerful craft. On June 21, 1993, he bought a Hughes 369 HS, a powerful craft with turbo-jet engines.

After returning to Alabama from the New Hampshire race, Allison left Birmingham at 2:15 p.m. on Monday, July 12. Destination was the Talladega Superspeedway, a 15-minute trip to the east. Allison and long-time family friend Red Farmer were going to watch Neil Bonnett and his son David practice for the upcoming Winston Cup and Busch Grand National events. The elder Bonnett was shaking down a car in his preparation to return to an active role for the first time since the spring of 1990 when he was severely injured in a crash at Darlington.

Officials said the helicopter was "within six inches of the ground" when it suddenly spiraled high into the air and twisted wildly. It dropped toward the ground and its tail section clipped a chain-link fence surrounding a paved parking lot in the infield.

The aircraft flipped over and landed in a heap on the ground. With its engines whining at full-throttle, Farmer scrambled to safety. Bonnett sprinted to the crash site and helped free the stricken Allison.

Davey Allison, 32-years-old, died at 7:00 a.m. CDT the following morning.

Robert Yates, Allison's car owner, was distraught over the tragic news. He made an announcement concerning his team's racing plans at his shop on

Greg Crisp

The RCR Enterprises crew joins Dale Earnhardt in prayer after winning the Pocono 500-miler in July. It was the first race without an Allison in the starting field since 1975.

Wednesday, July 14.

"I wish I weren't here," said Yates. "Davey meant so much to this racing team." After his brother's death at Michigan eleven months earlier, Yates had asked Davey if, under the circumstances, he preferred not to race in the wake of the tragedy. Davey had told Yates, "Clifford was doing what he wanted to do. He enjoyed that. He would want to race. That's what we're going to do."

Yates said the he would withdraw his car for the upcoming Pocono race. "Preparing a race car for someone to drive at 200 mph is a serious responsibility," said Yates. "I just don't think that we can bury Davey (on Thursday) and be ready to meet that responsibility. We can't race with tears in our eyes."

The Pocono race would be the first Winston Cup event without a member of the Allison family in the starting line-up since 1975.

DALE HAS SPECIAL PRAYER AT POCONO

The Pocono race was every bit as somber as the Bristol event three months earlier. Dale Earnhardt outran Rusty Wallace in a spirited battle in the final lap. After the conclusion of the 500-miler, Earnhardt pulled his car to a halt on the homestretch, before going to Victory Lane. The RCR Enterprises crew members walked onto the track and kneeled down, offering their respects to the late Davey Allison in a moving, silent tribute.

"You lose a good friend, and it's just a bad situation," said Earnhardt. "Neil (Bonnett) is really taking it hard. Our team flew down Wednesday to see Bobby and Judy (Davey's father and mother). Racing just lost two great race drivers, and at such a young age. You won't be able to replace them. It'll take time for the racing community to get past this.

"The times I really enjoyed with Davey were when we and Neil were out fishing and hunting," continued Earnhardt. "When we were off on a lake fishing somewhere, that was the Davey Allison I really knew. He was a quality guy, just a good friend."

FINDING A REPLACEMENT

Robby Gordon drove Yates' Ford at Talladega. The young IndyCar driver, who had made two Winston Cup appearances in 1991, crashed early. Lake Speed drove the car at Watkins Glen, Michigan and Bristol. Meanwhile, Ford Motor Co. had been actively seeking a full-time replacement. Jeff Gordon was their first choice, but he refused the offer, electing to stay with the Hendrick Motorsports Chevrolet team.

Ernie Irvan, in the fourth year of a five-year contract with Larry McClure's Morgan-McClure Chevrolet team, was became Ford's target. With a healthy salary in the offering, Irvan wanted to ease out of the final year of McClure's contract and drive for Yates in 1994.

McClure stood firm and held Irvan to his contractual obligations. Negotiations continued in the weeks leading up to Darlington's Southern 500. Eventually, Irvan was able to purchase the remaining year of his contract with McClure.

Speed had tested the Yates car at Darlington and was looking forward to the Southern 500. His only Winston Cup victory had come at Darlington in 1988. But the last minute developments with Irvan left Speed with no car to drive.

When McClure settled things with Irvan, he unexpectedly gave Irvan the pink slip – effective immediately. "I never asked for my release this year," said Irvan. "All I asked for is my release at the end of the year. But

Greg Fielden

Mark Martin #6 and Jeff Gordon #24 made plenty of headlines during the 1993 season. Martin won four straight races and Gordon copped Rookie of the Year award.

if Larry McClure doesn't want me to drive for him, I guess I'll go somewhere else.

"Originally, I had intentions to staying all five years," Irvan added. "The important thing is I don't feel I was treated as fairly as some of the other drivers, financially, for the things I was doing for the race team. But that's the way my contract was worded."

Jeff Purvis, a part-time Winston Cup racer, was hired to drive the Morgan-McClure entry.

McClure said his parting with Irvan was "a bad situation, but now it's over. It's a shame to break up a championship-caliber team like this. Ernie Irvan was nothing until I gave him a break. But I wish him luck wherever he goes. You don't work with someone for three-and-a-half years and not care for them."

Irvan would finish fifth in his debut with Robert Yates Racing.

Mark Martin won the Darlington race, his fourth straight Winston Cup victory. Martin and his Roush Racing team had been dogged with mind-boggling sour luck throughout the year. He had the spring race at Atlanta won, but a blown engine late in the race sent him to the garage.

He was innocently involved in a couple of early wrecks that tore his car apart. At Michigan, no one could keep up with him, but he lost when he had to make a late pit stop for fuel.

Things finally turned around for the diminutive Arkansas driver at Watkins Glen. Despite a pit road mistake, Martin charged from mid-pack to win in the final laps.

He came back and won at Michigan, Bristol and Darlington. "It's pretty unbelievable," Martin said during his winning streak. "I remember earlier this year when we were saying, 'What have we got to do to win a race?' We certainly didn't need to run any better than we were running. But the team kept its chin up when things weren't going that well, and it's like we can do no wrong now.

"When we walk out of here, we'll be just the same," Martin added. "It is kind of weird because we haven't really changed that much. Just our record has changed."

TESTING THE BRICKYARD

During the summer, the NASCAR Winston Cup

Jim Ahmay

The Winston Cup cars tested at the Indianapolis Motor Speedway in the summer of 1992 and 1993.

pilots engaged in a test session at the Indianapolis Motor Speedway. A special tire test was conducted in 1992 and all systems were go for the first official Winston Cup event to be staged at Indianapolis in August of 1994.

Speeds were in the 165 to 167 mph range, over 50 mph slower than the IndyCars zip around the fabled Brickyard. Many of the IndyCar regulars expressed regret at the prospect that the good ol' boys and their unique style of thunder were entering their sacred grounds.

"I think the IndyCars belong at Indianapolis and the stock cars belong a Daytona," insisted three-time IndyCar champion Bobby Rahal.

Mario Andretti, winner of the 1967 Daytona 500, reflected, "I hate to see it happen because to me, Indianapolis has always been sacred grounds for open-wheel, single-seat thoroughbreds."

Danny Sullivan: "I can understand why NASCAR wants to come to Indy, but maybe that tells us their Daytona 500 isn't as important as they think it is."

Brian Czobat

Dale Earnhardt won his sixth Winston Cup championship in 1993.

A.J. Foyt, on the other hand, was ready to roll out the red carpet. "Those boys put on a hell of a show and so do we, and I don't see any negatives."

Most of the spectators who attended the tests greeted the NASCAR drivers with open arms. And the drivers seemed to spend more time with the fans. One young lad spotted Dale Earnhardt and Bill Elliott and spoke to them through a fence, "Sirs, you all have signed more autographs in the last hour than the IndyCar drivers have signed in their careers."

During a test session on August 17, John Andretti, Indy 500 veteran, lost control of his Billy Hagan Chevrolet, triggering a collision that swept up Mark Martin and Jimmy Spencer.

"I think I got taught a lesson," said Andretti, who planned to join NASCAR full-time in 1994. "I feel bad for our team and the guys who got tangled up in it."

Martin said he wasn't aware that Andretti was behind the wheel of the Chevrolet normally driven by Terry Labonte. "I thought Labonte was in the car," said Martin. "If I'd have known it was someone inexperienced in a 3,500-pound stock car, I wouldn't have been anywhere near him. It takes time to know their limits."

A total of 32 drivers took speed runs around the track, including Richard Petty, who donned a uniform to take a few quick laps. Fastest speed was turned in by Bill Elliott – a 167.467 mph lap. A total of 1,969 laps were turned in by all the competitors during the two day test.

When the drivers broke from the Indy tests, Earnhardt had a 281-point lead over second place Dale Jarrett in the Winston Cup standings. Rusty Wallace was in third place, but he trailed by 341 points.

Wallace was hopelessly behind but apparently it didn't deter his efforts to catch up. In the next seven races, Wallace outran Earnhardt each time. During that span, he won three races. Earnhardt had troubles at Dover and Martinsville, which allowed Wallace to close to within 72 points. But he would never get any closer than that.

Despite winning 10 races, Wallace finished a distant second to Earnhardt in the final standings. It was the first time since 1985 that a driver had won 10 or more races and lost the championship.

Dale Earnhardt wrapped up his sixth championship, placing him just one behind Richard Petty's storied career. The door to the King's palace is slightly ajar – and Dale Earnhardt is peeking inside.

Race #1

Jarrett Prevails in Battle of Dales at Daytona

DAYTONA BEACH, FL (Feb. 14) – Dale Jarrett ran down Dale Earnhardt in the final lap and prevailed in a five car shuffle to score a popular triumph in the 35th annual Daytona 500.

Jarrett's second career win gave car owner Joe Gibbs his first in what is termed the Super Bowl of stock car racing. During his tenure as head coach for the Washington Redskins, Gibbs led his team to three Super Bowl victories. "This is hard to believe," said an elated Gibbs. "I'm one of the most fortunate individuals in the world. I've won three Super Bowls, and now the Super Bowl of motorsports."

Jarrett started second and led for five laps early in the race. Jarrett fell back in the middle stages, but mustered a gallant charge in the closing laps. He broke out of a pack of cars to run down the lead quartet in the final 25 miles.

As Jarrett was making his charge into contention, Earnhardt was sparring with freshman sensation Jeff Gordon, who had won one of Thursday's 125-milers in his first start with Hendrick Motorsports.

Jarrett whipped to the high side of Gordon with two laps to go, then concentrated on Earnhardt. "I was looking for several laps to see where I could get a run on them," said Jarrett. "My car was working good to the outside. I noticed Earnhardt's car was getting loose. I was running wide open through the turns and was able to go low and get a good run on him."

Jarrett ducked under Earnhardt off the fourth turn with the white flag waiting in the tri-oval. Earnhardt had a fender in front as the cars headed into turn one.

ISC

The door-to-door racing action was incredible in the Daytona 500.

Brian Czobat

Dale Jarrett's Joe Gibbs Racing Chevrolet pulled an upset victory in the Daytona 500.

ISC

The 41 car field moments before the green flag for the 35th annual Daytona 500.

Brian Czobat

Dale Jarrett beams from Victory Lane at Daytona International Speedway.

Winston Cup Series Race No. 1
200 Laps at Daytona Int'l Speedway
Daytona Beach, FL
"Daytona 500 By STP"
500 Miles on 2.5-mile Superspeedway
February 14, 1993

Fin	St	No.	Driver	Team / Car	Laps	Money	Status
1	2	18	Dale Jarrett	Joe Gibbs Chevrolet	200	$238,200	Running
2	4	3	Dale Earnhardt	RCR Enterprises Chevy	200	181,825	Running
3	6	15	Geoff Bodine	Bud Moore Eng. Ford	200	141,450	Running
4	18	27	Hut Stricklin	Junior Johnson Ford	200	95,950	Running
5	3	24	Jeff Gordon	Hendrick Motorsports Chevy	200	111,150	Running
6	23	6	Mark Martin	Roush Racing Ford	200	74,625	Running
7	32	21	Morgan Shepherd	Wood Brothers Ford	200	62,350	Running
8	7	25	Ken Schrader	Hendrick Motorsports Chevy	200	64,025	Running
9	14	8	Sterling Marlin	Stavola Brothers Ford	200	54,225	Running
10	22	16	Wally Dallenbach,Jr.	Roush Racing Ford	200	49,125	Running
11	19	14	Terry Labonte	Billy Hagan Chevrolet	200	47,750	Running
12	31	1	Rick Mast	Precision Products Ford	200	43,375	Running
13	30	12	Jimmy Spencer	Bobby Allison Ford	200	42,130	Running
14	13	83	Lake Speed	Speed Ford	200	36,930	Running
15	33	55	Ted Musgrave	RaDiUs Motorsports Ford	200	38,975	Running
16	28	30	Michael Waltrip	Bahari Racing Pontiac	200	37,305	Running
17	20	26	Brett Bodine	King Motorsports Ford	200	36,585	Running
18	26	17	Darrell Waltrip	DarWal Chevrolet	200	40,415	Running
19	39	89	Jim Sauter	Mueller Brothers Ford	199	28,645	Running
20	25	22	Bobby Labonte	Bill Davis Racing Ford	199	29,685	Running
21	37	33	Harry Gant	Leo Jackson Chevrolet	199	36,780	Running
22	16	41	Phil Parsons	Larry Hedrick Chevrolet	199	30,525	Running
23	24	40	Kenny Wallace	SabCo Racing Pontiac	199	27,820	Running
24	17	9	Chad Little	Melling Performance Ford	198	27,965	Running
25	29	32	Jimmy Horton	Active Racing Chevrolet	198	26,560	Running
26	10	7	Alan Kulwicki	AK Racing Ford	197	42,405	Running
27	27	68	Bobby Hamilton	Tri-Star Motorsports Ford	197	27,775	Running
28	11	28	Davey Allison	Robert Yates Racing Ford	197	37,445	Running
29	35	66	Derrike Cope	Cale Yarborough Ford	189	29,165	Running
30	12	5	Ricky Rudd	Hendrick Motorsports Chevy	177	31,285	Running
31	1	42	Kyle Petty	SabCo Racing Pontiac	170	56,580	Crash
32	34	2	Rusty Wallace	Roger Penske Pontiac	168	38,600	Crash
33	41	71	Dave MArcis	Marcis Auto Racing Chevy	164	25,470	Running
34	15	44	Rick Wilson	Petty Enterprises Pontiac	163	26,315	Crash
35	9	90	Bobby Hillin,Jr.	Junie Donlavey Ford	157	28,960	Crash
36	40	46	Al Unser,Jr.	Hendrick Motorsports Chevy	157	23,005	Crash
37	8	4	Ernie Irvan	Morgan-McClure Chevrolet	148	40,275	Crash
38	36	20	Joe Ruttman	Dick Moroso Ford	128	23,395	Engine
39	5	11	Bill Elliott	Junior Johnson Ford	99	52,660	Engine
40	38	52	Jimmy Hensley	Means Racing Ford	11	21,925	Crash
41	21	75	Dick Trickle	Butch Mock Ford	2	23,300	Engine

Time of Race: 3 hours, 13 minutes, 35 seconds
Average Speed: 154.972 mph
Pole Winner: Kyle Petty – 189.426 mph
Lap Leaders: Jeff Gordon 1, Dale Jarrett 2-6, Dale Earnhardt 7-17, Kyle Petty 18-21, Gordon 22, Ken Schrader 23-24, Earnhardt 25-30, Schrader 31-38, Earnhardt 39-47, Schrader 48-49, Geoff Bodine 50, Rick Wilson 51, Hut Stricklin 52, Derrike Cope 53-62, Harry Gant 63-66, Earnhardt 67-69, Bobby Hillin,Jr. 70, Earnhardt 71-77, Schrader 78-79 Earnhardt 80, Hillin,Jr. 81-82, Earnhardt 83-95,, K.Petty 96-100, Davey Allison 101, Stricklin 102-105, Cope 106-112, Gant 113-114, K.Petty 115-124, Earnhardt 125-151, Cope 152-164, Sterling Marlin 165, Stricklin 166, Earnhardt 167, Stricklin 168, Earnhardt 169-176, Jarrett 177-178, Earnhardt 179-199, Jarrett 200.
38 lead changes among 13 drivers.
Cautions: 7 for 30 laps Margin of Victory: 0.16 seconds

Geoff Bodine went low with Jarrett and helped him "draft" past. Gordon was stuck behind Earnhardt, and Hut Stricklin, making his first start with Junior Johnson, was riding in fifth.

Jarrett broke away down the backstretch as Earnhardt battled his way back into second place. Jarrett's Chevrolet nipped Earnhardt by 0.16-seconds at the stripe. Bodine took third in a Ford with Stricklin and Gordon fourth and fifth.

"When you beat Dale Earnhardt you know you've done a good day's work," said Jarrett. "This is the greatest victory a driver can have. Outrunning Earnhardt for it makes it even better."

Earnhardt, who led for 107 of the 200 laps, failed in his 15th attempt to earn a trip to victory lane in NASCAR's most prestigious event. "Big damn deal, I lost another Daytona 500," said Earnhardt. "We've lost this race about every way you can lose it. "We've been out-gassed, out-tired, out-run and out-everythinged. We've come close. There's nothing left to do but come back and try again next year."

Gordon, making his second official Winston Cup start, thrilled the audience of 135,000 by leading the

Brian Czobat

Richard Childress shows concern from the pits as Dale Jarrett runs down Dale Earnhardt near the end of the Daytona 500.

opening lap. He fell back in the middle stages before working his way back to the front. "I wanted to go with Earnhardt," said the 21 year-old Gordon. "I knew if I made a move nobody would go with the rookie. I stuck with him and got shuffled back at the finish."

Rusty Wallace survived a wild tumble on the backstretch near the end of the race. Michael Waltrip squeezed into Derrike Cope coming off the second turn on lap 170. Cope's spinning car clipped Wallace's Pontiac, sending it into a series of turnovers. Miraculously, Wallace suffered only a cut chin.

"Michael Waltrip was at the top of the track and his car broke loose," said Wallace, who flipped in the same spot in 1983 during a 125-mile qualifying race. "But it wasn't his fault. This is really a shame because this is the strongest 500 I had going. I thought I had a top three car today."

The checkered flag waves for Dale Jarrett, who nipped Dale Earnhardt in Daytona 500.

Al Unser, Jr., the 1992 Indianapolis 500 winner, made his first Winston Cup start in a Hendrick Motorsports Chevrolet. After starting at the rear, Unser, Jr. passed half the field before the first pit stop.

He was still in contention when a collision with Earnhardt sent him out of control. Bobby Hillin, Jr. and Kyle Petty were also eliminated. Earnhardt was unaffected by the scrape.

"Earnhardt hit me on the outside of turn three," explained Unser, Jr. "He got up in the gray area. He got me on my right rear quarter-panel and turned me sideways."

Unser, Jr., shot off the track and collided with Bobby Hillin, Jr., who had led briefly in Junie Donlavey's Ford before the crash. Both cars got into the infield grass. Hillin Jr.'s car slid back onto the track in front of Petty, who couldn't avoid contact.

Petty had words with Hillin, Jr. before the two were separated by NASCAR officials. "Kyle was upset," said Hillin, Jr., who had led on two occasions. "There was no need for him to fly off the handle like he did. I wasn't the one who got into the 46 car (Unser, Jr.). I was on the inside, coming up quickly. They just came across the track and ran into me."

About the confrontation with Hillin, Jr., Kyle said, "I told him to shut up and he kept talking. All I said was shut up."

Petty had been offered a million dollar bonus by car owner Felix Sabates if he had won the Daytona 500. A number of other million dollar bonus incentives were available for Petty if he won certain races.

A total of 18 cars finished on the lead lap. Defending Winston Cup champion Alan Kulwicki finished 26th, two laps down. Davey Allison was three laps down in 28th place. A wreck took Ernie Irvan out in the 150th lap.

ISC

Dale Earnhardt #3 took the low side to get around Hut Stricklin #27 and Derrike Cope #66.

Race #2

Rusty Rustles Rivals at The Rock; Earnhardt Takes Point Lead

ROCKINGHAM, NC (Feb. 28) – A bruised and battered Rusty Wallace bounced back from his Daytona crash to dominate the GM Goodwrench 500 at North Carolina Motor Speedway.

Wallace led 203 laps, including the final 70, and finished a half second behind runner-up Dale Earnhardt, who wrestled an ill-handling car most of the way. Third place went to Ernie Irvan who was hugging Earnhardt's bumper. Alan Kulwicki came home fourth and pole sitter Mark Martin was sixth.

"I told everybody all winter that this team was going to be super strong," said Wallace after his 22nd career victory. "We came here and finally ran like we're capable of ."

Earnhardt led three times for 133 laps but couldn't handle Wallace down the stretch. "As the track cooled down, it went to their (Wallace's) advantage," said Earnhardt. "I was driving as hard as I could. The steering joints on the car were smoking when I pulled into the garage."

It was a determined and spirited run by Earnhardt, whose hands were blistered from fighting his car the last part of the race.

While a cooler track may have helped, Wallace directed much of the credit to his pit crew, which consistently beat all rivals in the pits. "Those guys are the ones to be commended," said Wallace. "The pit stops were so doggone fast it's unreal. They've been practicing and exercising. We even hired a couple of trainers."

Pitsiders timed one of the Penske crew's pit stops at 17.4 seconds for four tires and fuel.

Wallace was able to hold Earnhardt at bay for the final stretch run. "Earnhardt didn't get close enough to pressure me," he said. "I looked in the mirror and he was always seven or eight car lengths behind me. He had a strong car, but I was stronger."

Mechanical failures sidelined Kyle Petty and Harry Gant. Petty, who had earned the pole four straight times at the 1.017-mile oval, started 11th and never led. Clutch failure sent him to the pits for 59 laps, but the Pontiac driver was able to make up three laps once

Brian Czobat

Car owner Roger Penske joins winner Rusty Wallace in Rockingham's Victory Lane.

Winston Cup Series Race No. 2
492 Laps at N.C. Motor Speedway
Rockingham, NC
"GM Goodwrench 500"
500.364 Miles on 1.017-mile Superspeedway
February 28, 1993

Fin	St	No.	Driver	Team / Car	Laps	Money	Status
1	10	2	Rusty Wallace	Roger Penske Pontiac	492	$42,735	Running
2	7	3	Dale Earnhardt	RCR Enterprises Chevrolet	492	47,585	Running
3	2	4	Ernie Irvan	Morgan-McClure Chevrolet	492	33,785	Running
4	20	7	Alan Kulwicki	AK Racing Ford	492	28,085	Running
5	1	6	Mark Martin	Roush Racing Ford	492	29,160	Running
6	22	18	Dale Jarrett	Joe Gibbs Chevrolet	492	21,885	Running
7	5	55	Ted Musgrave	RaDiUs Motorsports Ford	492	17,635	Running
8	17	41	Phil Parsons	Larry Hedrick Chevrolet	492	14,135	Running
9	14	15	Geoff Bodine	Bud Moore Eng. Ford	491	18,925	Running
10	21	14	Terry Labonte	Billy Hagan Chevrolet	491	18,535	Running
11	3	11	Bill Elliott	Junior Johnson Ford	491	20,535	Running
12	12	5	Ricky Rudd	Hendrick Motorsports Chevy	490	15,735	Running
13	8	27	Hut Stricklin	Junior Johnson Ford	490	15,435	Running
14	39	28	Davey Allison	Robert Yates Racing Ford	490	19,535	Running
15	23	68	Bobby Hamilton	Tri-Star Motorsports Ford	489	12,085	Running
16	25	12	Jimmy Spencer	Bobby Allison Ford	489	14,335	Running
17	15	44	Rick Wilson	Petty Enterprises Pontiac	489	10,935	Running
18	9	98	Derrike Cope	Cale Yarborough Ford	486	13,635	Running
19	18	90	Bobby Hillin,Jr.	Junie Donlavey Ford	486	8,485	Running
20	29	16	Wally Dallenbach,Jr.	Roush Racing Ford	485	13,585	Running
21	40	71	Dave Marcis	Marcis Auto Racing Chevy	484	9,835	Running
22	6	26	Brett Bodine	King Motorsports Ford	481	12,635	Running
23	32	40	Kenny Wallace	SabCo Racing Pontiac	481	8,835	Running
24	13	25	Ken Schrader	Hendrick Motorsports Chevy	479	12,335	Running
25	34	52	Jimmy Hensley	Means Racing Ford	479	7,635	Running
26	30	30	Michael Waltrip	Bahari Racing Pontiac	478	12,100	Running
27	33	05	Ed Ferree	Gayle Ferree Chevrolet	475	7,425	Running
28	19	8	Sterling Marlin	Stavola Brothers Ford	473	11,925	Cylinder
29	31	75	Dick Trickle	Butch Mock Ford	467	7,200	Running
30	27	17	Darrell Waltrip	DarWal Chevrolet	461	16,950	Running
31	26	33	Harry Gant	Leo Jackson Chevrolet	457	17,450	Oil Pump
32	11	42	Kyle Petty	SabCo Racing Pontiac	436	14,900	Running
33	24	22	Bobby Labonte	Bill Davis Racing Ford	422	7,250	Crash
34	28	24	Jeff Gordon	Hendrick Motorsports Chevy	402	6,700	Engine
35	16	21	Morgan Shepherd	Wood Brothers Ford	386	11,125	Running
36	35	64	John Chapman	Dick Bahre Pontiac	368	6,526	Handling
37	36	77	Mike Potter	Henley Gray Ford	232	6,475	Crash
38	37	56	Jerry Hill	Willie Tierney Chevrolet	215	6,460	Crash
39	4	1	Rick Mast	Precision Products Ford	176	10,925	H Gasket
40	38	48	James Hylton	Hylton Eng. Pontiac	24	6,400	Oil Pan

Time of Race: 4 hours, 1 minute, 10 seconds
Average Speed: 124.486 mph
Pole Winner: Mark Martin – 149.547 mph
Lap Leaders: Mark Martin 1, Ernie Irvan 2-14, Martin 15-63, Dale Earnhardt 64-81, Martin 82-83, Geoff Bodine 84-85, Darrell Waltrip 86-88, Irvan 89-108, Earnhardt 109-157, Martin 158-160, Ted Musgrave 161, Irvan 162-177, Earnhardt 178-243, Irvan 244-274, Rusty Wallace 275-335, Harry Gant 336-338, Alan Kulwicki 339-340, R.Wallace 341-412, Gant 413-419, Musgrave 420-422, R.Wallace 423-492.
20 lead changes among 9 drivers.
Cautions: 7 for 40 laps   Margin of Victory: 0.5 second

Bryan Hallman

Dale Jarrett spins off the fourth turn at Rockingham. He recovered to finish sixth.

repairs had been completed. He wound up in 32nd place.

Gant started back in 26th place and had to pit on the backstretch. Although he made rapid advancements on the track, yellow flag pit stops would leave him near the rear.

Under long stints under the green flag, Gant was able to work his way to the lead by lap 336. A caution flag came out two laps after Gant had taken the lead, ruining his bid.

Gant was able to forge to the front on lap 413 and pitted under green seven laps later. He emerged from the pits about a third of a lap behind. A broken oil pump on lap 457 took Gant out after he had made up a large chunk of the deficit.

Bill Elliott started third but faded and eventually finished 11th.

Wallace's victory enabled him to vault from 32nd to eighth in the Winston Cup point standings. Earnhardt took sole possession of the point lead as Daytona 500 winner Dale Earnhardt finished sixth.

"I've never been so dedicated to anything as I am winning the Winston Cup championship this year," said Wallace, who won the title in 1989. "My team is in good shape now and we're ready to be champions. I'm looking forward to going to Richmond. We can't let ol' Ironhead get too far ahead of the points."

The prospect of an Earnhardt-Wallace battle for title brought a response from the five-time champion.

"It'd be like old times to get into a title deal with Rusty," said Earnhardt. "Neither one of us ran very good last year, but it looks like it could happen this

Bryan Hallman

Bobby Hillin, Jr. #90 leads a three-abreast duel between Alan Kulwicki #7, Mark Martin #6 and Harry Gant #33 at Rockingham.

year."

Davey Allison finished 14th, two laps off the pace. It was his second dismal effort of the young 1993 campaign. "Dad-gum, there's not that much difference between 'great' and 'terrible'," said car owner Robert Yates.

Crew chief Larry McReynolds said he felt like a truck driver that has missed a gear. "We need to pull this ol' rig over to the side of the road and start over in first gear," said McReynolds.

Race #3

Allison Racks Up Richmond as Petty and Wallace Fade

RICHMOND, VA (March 7) – Davey Allison led all but four of the final 157 laps and motored to a convincing triumph in the Pontiac Excitement 400 at Richmond International Raceway.

Allison was not much of a factor in the early stages, but his Robert Yates Racing Ford came to life after the half-way point. "We didn't take any big gambles," said Allison, who won for the 19th time in his career. "We just tried to be consistent and not punish the car. All of a sudden, the race is over and here we are in Victory Lane."

Allison outdistanced Rusty Wallace by 4.38 seconds.

Brian Czobat

Kenny Wallace's Pontiac was badly crunched in last lap crash at Richmond.

Winston Cup Series Race No. 3
400 Laps at Richmond Int'l Raceway
Richmond, VA
"Pontiac Excitement 400"
300 Miles on .75-mile Short Track
March 7, 1993

Fin	St	No.	Driver	Team / Car	Laps	Money	Status
1	14	28	Davey Allison	Robert Yates Racing Ford	400	$70,125	Running
2	13	2	Rusty Wallace	Roger Penske Pontiac	400	31,550	Running
3	6	7	Alan Kulwicki	AK Racing Ford	400	39,225	Running
4	9	18	Dale Jarrett	Joe Gibbs Chevrolet	400	29,050	Running
5	7	42	Kyle Petty	SabCo Racing Pontiac	400	21,600	Running
6	8	24	Jeff Gordon	Hendrick Motorsports Chevy	400	14,700	Running
7	12	6	Mark Martin	Roush Racing Ford	400	18,150	Running
8	5	17	Darrell Waltrip	DarWal Chevrolet	400	18,100	Running
9	34	33	Harry Gant	Leo Jackson Chevrolet	400	17,300	Running
10	11	3	Dale Earnhardt	RCR Enterprises Chevrolet	399	17,000	Running
11	10	4	Ernie Irvan	Morgan-McClure Chevrolet	399	16,800	Running
12	21	15	Geoff Bodine	Bud Moore Eng. Ford	399	13,300	Running
13	24	12	Jimmy Spencer	Bobby Allison Ford	398	12,850	Running
14	3	21	Morgan Shepherd	Wood Brothers Ford	398	12,650	Running
15	15	5	Ricky Rudd	Hendrick Motorsports Chevy	398	13,035	Running
16	28	41	Phil Parsons	Larry Hedrick Chevrolet	398	9,275	Running
17	16	55	Ted Musgrave	RaDiUs Motorsports Ford	397	12,075	Running
18	33	27	Hut Stricklin	Junior Johnson Ford	396	11,825	Running
19	17	98	Derrike Cope	Cale Yarborough Ford	396	11,500	Running
20	1	25	Ken Schrader	Hendrick Motorsports Chevy	396	15,325	Running
21	27	75	Dick Trickle	Butch Mock Ford	395	6,225	Running
22	35	68	Bobby Hamilton	Tri-Star Motorsports Ford	395	8,100	Crash
23	26	30	Michael Waltrip	Bahari Racing Pontiac	394	10,975	Running
24	19	14	Terry Labonte	Billy Hagan Chevrolet	394	10,850	Running
25	18	44	Rick Wilson	Petty Enterprises Pontiac	394	7,700	Running
26	32	40	Kenny Wallace	SabCo Racing Pontiac	394	6,525	Crash
27	22	16	Wally Dallenbach,Jr.	Roush Racing Ford	393	7,600	Running
28	30	90	Bobby Hillin,Jr.	Junie Donlavey Ford	392	5,975	Running
29	20	22	Bobby Labonte	Bill Davis Racing Ford	382	5,950	Running
30	31	83	Lake Speed	Speed Ford	359	5,920	Running
31	23	8	Sterling Marlin	Stavola Brothers Ford	337	10,475	Running
32	4	26	Brett Bodine	King Motorsports Ford	327	10,445	Running
33	25	11	Bill Elliott	Junior Johnson Ford	227	16,260	Engine
34	36	52	Jimmy Hensley	Means Racing Ford	190	5,850	Clutch
35	2	1	Rick Mast	Precision Products Ford	68	11,375	Engine
36	29	71	Dave Marcis	Marcis Auto Racing Chevy	54	7,350	Engine

Time of Race: 2 hours, 47 minutes, 7 seconds
Average Speed: 107.709 mph
Pole Winner: Ken Schrader – 123.164 mph
Lap Leaders: Ken Schrader 1-7, Morgan Shepherd 8-25, Darrell Waltrip 26-59, Kyle Petty 60-67, D.Waltrip 68-69, K.Petty 70-171, Davey Allison 172-174, D.Waltrip 175-184, Geoff Bodine 185, K.Petty 186-243, Allison 244-353, D.Waltrip 354-358, Allison 359-400.
12 lead changes among 6 drivers.
Cautions: 3 for 19 laps Margin of Victory: 4.38 seconds

Third place went to Alan Kulwicki. Dale Jarrett finished fourth and took a one point lead over Dale Earnhardt in the Winston Cup standings. Fifth place went to Kyle Petty, who faded after dominating the first part of the race.

Earnhardt was hit with a 15 second penalty for speeding on pit road. The penalty brought a sharp response from the RCR Enterprises team. "NASCAR screwed us," complained car owner Richard Childress. "We came down pit road the same speed as Kulwicki and they didn't penalize him. That's favoritism. The inspector who clocked us had a Mickey Mouse watch – he held us 18 seconds."

Earnhardt eventually finished 10th, one lap off the

Brian Czobat

Bobby and Davey Allison share Victory Lane accolades at Richmond.

pace. He admitted he may have been fudging. "We were within a couple hundred RPM (of the 40 mph pit road speed). The Gestapo got us. They ought to give us a little leeway. We ain't got speedometers in these things. Just a tach," said Earnhardt.

Petty led the most laps and enjoyed a comfortable lead during laps 70-171. But as pit stops and strategy became factors in the final laps, Petty faded. His SabCo Racing Team opted for a two-tire pit stop to make up distance while most other teams changed all four. "We picked up a bad push, and then we tried that two-tire stop," reflected Petty. "It probably didn't matter. We'd have probably finished fifth either way."

Allison's victory was a big turnaround for his struggling team.This is a big confidence builder for our team," said the 32 year-old Allison. "You can't believe what had been going through my mind and the pressure the crew had on them after we did so badly in the first two races. We made a bigger gain here than I had anticipated."

The race was interrupted by the yellow flag only three times. Bobby Hamilton and Kenny Wallace crashed hard at the finish line. "I got hit from behind," said Hamilton. "We didn't run very well, but we were sure in the most exciting thing that happened all day."

Allison averaged a record 107.709 mph.

Brian Czobat

Ken Schrader leads Richmond field into first turn.

Race #4

Shepherd Overcomes Flat Tire to Win in Snowy Atlanta

HAMPTON, GA (March 20) – Morgan Shepherd overcame a tire failure with 69 laps to go and used good fuel mileage to capture the Motorcraft 500 at Atlanta Motor Speedway. It was the Conover, N.C. driver's fourth career win – three of which have come on the 1.522-mile oval.

Shepherd was able to offset the flat tire by running the final 105 miles without a pit stop. "We were ahead when the tire went down and it got us behind," said Shepherd. "Then we got it back by stretching our fuel mileage. It pretty much evened things up. The Wood

Brothers gave me a great car today."

Shepherd outran runner-up Ernie Irvan by 17.38 seconds to notch his first win since the 1990 season finale. Rusty Wallace flashed across the finish line in third place, but he thought he had won. Rookie Jeff Gordon came home fourth and Ricky Rudd was fifth.

The 500-miler was run on a Saturday after a heavy winter storm and freezing temperatures forced postponement a week earlier.

Wallace earned the pole and led the first 22 laps. He was passed by Mark Martin, who dominated the proceedings until engine failure put him out after 225 laps.

With Martin's departure, the spotlight was focused on Shepherd, Wallace and Gordon.

Shepherd had pulled away from the pack while he led a 29 lap stretch. As Shepherd came off the fourth turn, the right front tire let go. He did a masterful job of keeping the car out of the wall but had to run a full lap at reduced speed. By the time new tires were placed on the Wood Brothers Ford and the fuel tank filled, Shepherd was logged in fourth place, a lap behind.

Irvan, who led briefly after Shepherd pitted, brought his Morgan-McClure Chevrolet into the pits on lap 263.

Wallace led the 264th lap before Gordon pushed his Hendrick Motorsports Chevrolet to the point. Gordon appeared poised to post his first career win in only his fifth Winston Cup start. The young Pittsboro, Ind. driver led from lap 265-316.

Wallace pitted on lap 301 for two tires and enough fuel to go the distance. He fell a lap behind during his stop. Gordon pitted on lap 316, giving the lead to Shepherd. As Gordon came down pit road, he overshot his assigned pit stall. He lost precious moments as he had to back the car up before taking on fuel only.

Shepherd and Irvan were ahead of Wallace and

Winston Cup Series Race No. 4
328 Laps at Atlanta Motor Speedway
Hampton, GA
"Motorcraft Quality Parts 500"
499.216 Miles on 1.522-mile Superspeedway
March 20, 1993

Fin	St	No.	Driver	Team / Car	Laps	Money	Status
1	7	21	Morgan Shepherd	Wood Brothers Ford	328	$70,350	Running
2	5	4	Ernie Irvan	Morgan-McClure Chevrolet	328	45,950	Running
3	1	2	Rusty Wallace	Roger Penske Pontiac	328	41,550	Running
4	4	24	Jeff Gordon	Hendrick Motorsports Chevy	327	32,000	Running
5	14	5	Ricky Rudd	Hendrick Motorsports Chevy	327	26,550	Running
6	21	15	Geoff Bodine	Bud Moore Eng. Ford	327	23,575	Running
7	27	42	Kyle Petty	SabCo Racing Pontiac	327	20,525	Running
8	6	26	Brett Bodine	King Motorsports Ford	327	17,625	Running
9	15	11	Bill Elliott	Junior Johnson Ford	326	21,025	Running
10	18	12	Jimmy Spencer	Bobby Allison Ford	325	22,125	Running
11	2	3	Dale Earnhardt	RCR Enterprises Chevrolet	325	15,595	Running
12	20	8	Sterling Marlin	Stavola Brothers Ford	325	17,575	Running
13	31	28	Davey Allison	Robert Yates Racing Ford	325	19,055	Running
14	22	30	Michael Waltrip	Bahari Racing Pontiac	325	16,635	Running
15	19	90	Bobby Hillin,Jr.	Junie Donlavey Ford	324	9,155	Running
16	26	40	Kenny Wallace	SabCo Racing Pontiac	324	10,895	Running
17	11	98	Derrike Cope	Cale Yarborough Ford	324	14,035	Running
18	17	22	Bobby Labonte	Bill Davis Racing Ford	324	9,915	Running
19	9	55	Ted Musgrave	RaDiUs Motorsports Ford	321	14,755	Running
20	34	27	Hut Stricklin	Junior Johnson Ford	321	14,685	Running
21	16	33	Harry Gant	Leo Jackson Chevrolet	321	17,075	Running
22	37	52	Jimmy Means	Means Racing Ford	321	18,865	Running
23	40	9	Greg Sacks	Melling Performance Ford	320	10,305	Running
24	24	44	Rick Wilson	Petty Enterprises Pontiac	317	9,645	Running
25	36	16	Wally Dallenbach,Jr.	Roush Racing Ford	317	12,540	Running
26	23	68	Bobby Hamilton	Tri-Star Motorsports Ford	316	9,285	Running
27	32	32	Jimmy Horton	Active Racing Chevrolet	309	7,525	Running
28	28	83	Lake Speed	Speed Ford	308	7,455	Running
29	10	25	Ken Schrader	Hendrick Motorsports Chevy	288	12,240	Running
30	13	1	Rick Mast	Precision Products Ford	266	11,780	Running
31	33	18	Dale JArrett	Joe Gibbs Chevrolet	247	15,145	Running
32	3	6	Mark Martin	Roush Racing Ford	225	19,985	Engine
33	8	14	Terry Labonte	Billy Hagan Chevrolet	213	11,540	Running
34	38	71	Dave Marcis	Marcis Auto Racing Chevy	186	8,480	Engine
35	35	17	Darrell Waltrip	DarWal Chevrolet	157	16,720	Camshaft
36	29	7	Alan Kulwicki	AK Racing Ford	133	18,030	Crash
37	12	75	Dick Trickle	Butch Mock Ford	131	6,865	Crash
38	30	20	Joe Ruttman	Dick Moroso Ford	119	6,850	Crash
39	25	41	Phil Parsons	Larry Hedrick Chevrolet	29	8,325	Valve
40	39	57	Bob Schacht	Doug Stringer Olds	6	6,785	Engine

Time of Race: 3 hours, 17 minutes, 26 seconds
Average Speed: 150.442 mph
Pole Winner: Rusty Wallace – 178.749 mph
Lap Leaders: Rusty Wallace 1-23, Mark Martin 24-33, R.Wallace 34-57, Martin 58-60, Ken Schrader 61-63, Geoff Bodine 64-66, Wally Dallenbach,Jr. 67-68, R.Wallace 69-86, Martin 87-135, Kyle Petty 136-140, Martin 141-194, Jeff Gordon 195-196. Morgan Shepherd 197-201, Martin 202-205, R.Wallace 226-230, Shepherd 231-259, Ernie Irvan 260-263, R.Wallace 264, Gordon 265-316, Shepherd 317-328.
19 lead changes among 9 drivers.
Cautions: 4 for 19 laps Margin of Victory: 17.38 seconds

Wood Brothers hustle to replace Morgan Shepherd's flat tire near the end of the 500-miler at Atlanta.

Brian Czobat

The Blizzard of 1993 dumped over a foot of snow on Atlanta Motor Speedway, forcing officials to postpone the race.

Gordon, but most of the eyes of the 82,000 spectators were on the battle for third place. With fresher tires, Wallace ran down Gordon. With six laps to go, Gordon's Chevrolet scooted up the banking in the third turn and popped the wall. Wallace raced into what he thought was the lead.

"I didn't know Morgan and Ernie had gotten way ahead of us on fuel mileage," said Wallace, who thrust his hand out of the window when he crossed the finish line. "It was the weirdest thing. Gordon hit the wall. I passed him and I thought I was winning the race. I took the checkered flag and looked over and the Wood Brothers were celebrating."

Gordon said he "messed up. My tires were worn and I was letting the car slide up the race track in the middle of the turns. I went a little too far when I saw Rusty was gaining on me. I had a first or second place car, but I blew it by making two mistakes."

Greg Fielden

Morgan Shepherd scored his fourth career Winston Cup victory at Atlanta.

Winning crew chief Leonard Wood said he didn't decide to gamble on the fuel until there were only 30 laps remaining. "It was the only way we could win," said Wood after winning for the 12th time at Atlanta. "We knew Irvan would go the rest of the way without stopping. If we had pitted, we'd have finished fourth or fifth."

Dale Jarrett crashed in the 111th lap and lost his point lead. Dale Earnhardt struggled

to an 11th place finish, but took a 19 point lead in the Winston Cup standings.

Geoff Bodine finished in sixth place and moved to second in the standings.

Wallace leaped to third place, only 27 points behind Earnhardt. Jarrett fell to fourth.

Alan Kulwicki was eliminated in a crash when he lost control of his Ford while dicing with Bodine. Dick Trickle ran into Kulwicki after he was tapped from behind by Wally Dallenbach, Jr.

Race #5

Earnhardt Ends Slump With Convincing Darlington Victory

DARLINGTON, SC (March 28) – Dale Earnhardt scrambled from a lap down and outran Mark Martin to end a personal eight month winless skid in the TranSouth 500 at Darlington Raceway. Earnhardt's 54th career triumph tied him with Lee Petty for sixth on the all-time victory list.

Earnhardt led all but one of the final 149 laps and sprinted to a 1.63-second victory over runner-up Mark Martin. Dale Jarrett shook off the effects of pneumonia and grabbed third place. Ken Schrader finished fourth and Rusty Wallace was fifth.

Following a post-race inspection, NASCAR hit Schrader and his Hendrick Motorsports team with a hefty $10,000 fine for using an illegal rear end gadget.

Greg Fielden

Alan Kulwicki finished sixth at Darlington in what turned out to be his final start in a Winston Cup race.

The 501-mile race was a three-car shoot-out from the beginning, with Earnhardt and Martin being challenged by top rookie driver Jeff Gordon. Gordon was running in second place on lap 100 when Michael Waltrip booted him into the first turn wall. Following extensive repairs, Gordon was able to salvage 24th position.

"I'm so frustrated that maybe I shouldn't be talking right now," said Gordon after his crash. "He was on new tires and I was on old tires. How smart do you have to be to know you have to be careful. And how many laps was he down, like he usually is?"

Waltrip admitted he got into the rear of Gordon's Chevrolet. "It was my fault," he said. "I thought he was going to go deeper into the corner. When he let off, I hit him." Waltrip departed with overheating problems after completing 148 laps.

Bryan Hallman

Jimmy Spencer #12 and Bill Elliott #11 cock their Fords sideways at Darlington

Earnhardt and Wallace were in the pits during the Waltrip-Gordon caution and both fell a lap off the pace. Both were able to get back into the lead lap when they beat leader Martin back to the line when the next caution came out on lap 179.

"I drove my butt off to make up that lap," said Earnhardt. "So it was a satisfaction to come from a lap down to win. This is a big win for us. Something feels special about this team and this year.

"I'm only two championships behind Richard Petty," he continued. "And now I'm only two wins behind David Pearson at this track."

Winston Cup Series Race No. 5
367 Laps at Darlington Raceway
Darlington, SC
"TranSouth 500"

501.322 Miles on 1.366-mile Superspeedway
March 28, 1993

Fin	St	No.	Driver	Team / Car	Laps	Money	Status
1	1	3	Dale Earnhardt	RCR Enterprises Chevrolet	367	$64,815	Running
2	6	6	Mark Martin	Roush Racing Ford	367	38,875	Running
3	4	18	Dale Jarrett	Joe Gibbs Chevrolet	367	30,685	Running
4	16	25	Ken Schrader	Hendrick Motorsports Chevy	367	23,125	Running
5	3	2	Rusty Wallace	Roger Penske Pontiac	366	20,400	Running
6	14	7	Alan Kulwicki	AK Racing Ford	366	25,725	Running
7	15	42	Kyle Petty	SabCo Racing Pontiac	366	17,345	Running
8	2	15	Geoff Bodine	Bud Moore Eng. Ford	366	17,515	Running
9	17	14	Terry Labonte	Billy Hagan Chevrolet	366	14,435	Running
10	8	21	Morgan Shepherd	Wood Brothers Ford	365	16,930	Running
11	9	28	Davey Allison	Robert Yates Racing Ford	365	18,325	Running
12	19	26	Brett Bodine	King Motorsports Ford	364	13,995	Running
13	22	16	Wally Dallenbach,Jr.	Roush Racing Ford	363	13,715	Running
14	28	11	Bill Elliott	Junior Johnson Ford	363	17,910	Running
15	31	1	Rick Mast	Precision Products Ford	363	13,505	Running
16	25	17	Darrell Waltrip	DarWal Chevrolet	363	17,135	Running
17	23	98	Derrike Cope	Cale Yarborough ford	360	12,680	Running
18	36	22	Bobby Labonte	Bill Davis Racing Ford	353	8,545	Running
19	13	5	Ricky Rudd	Hendrick Motorsports Chevy	353	12,100	Running
20	32	75	Dick Trickle	Butch Mock Ford	348	7,270	Running
21	18	8	Sterling Marlin	Stavola Brothers Ford	346	11,600	Running
22	7	4	Ernie Irvan	Morgan-McClure Chevrolet	315	16,080	Heating
23	27	68	Bobby Hamilton	Tri-Star Motorsports Ford	311	8,260	Engine
24	5	24	Jeff Gordon	Hendrick Motorsports Chevy	275	7,740	Handling
25	34	71	Dave Marcis	Marcis Auto Racing Chevy	258	7,970	Engine
26	30	44	Rick Wilson	Petty Enterprises Pontiac	250	7,755	Engine
27	35	57	Bob Schacht	Doug Stringer Olds	246	5,940	Rear End
28	10	27	Hut Stricklin	Junior Johnson Ford	234	10,530	Engine
29	11	12	Jimmy Spencer	Bobby Allison Ford	212	10,370	Crash
30	12	55	Ted Musgrave	RaDiUs Motorsports Ford	188	10,310	Engine
31	33	52	Jimmy Means	Means Racing Ford	170	5,675	H Gasket
32	26	40	Kenny Wallace	SabCo Racing Pontiac	169	5,640	H Gasket
33	21	30	Michael Waltrip	Bahari Racing Pontiac	148	10,130	Heating
34	37	48	James Hylton	Hylton Eng. Pontiac	62	5,545	Quit
35	29	90	Bobby Hillin,Jr.	Junie Donlavey Ford	52	5,510	Engine
36	24	41	Phil Parsons	Larry Hedrick Chevrolet	48	7,000	Camshaft
37	20	33	Harry Gant	Leo Jackson Chevrolet	20	14,460	Engine
38	38	53	Mike Potter	Means Racing Ford	4	5,440	Quit
39	39	63	Norm Benning	O'Neal Racing Olds	1	5,410	Quit

Time of Race: 3 hours, 33 minutes, 29 seconds
Average Speed: 139.958 mph
Pole Winner: No Time Trials
Lap Leaders Dale Earnhardt 1-49, Mark Martin 50-52, Jeff Gordon 53, Geoff Bodine 54-55, Dale Jarrett 56, Terry Labonte 57, Darrell Waltrip 58-60, Earnhardt 61-74, Martin 75-101, Alan Kulwicki 102-103, Martin 104-121, Kyle Petty 122-140, Martin 141-163, Ken Schrader 164-165, Martin 166-216, Davey Allison 217, Earnhardt 218-320, Martin 321, Earnhardt 322-367.
18 lead changes among 11 drivers.
Cautions: 3 for 14 laps Margin of Victory: 1.63 seconds

Steve Hmiel, crew chief for Martin's Roush Racing Ford, said "Earnhardt was unbeatable down the stretch. We outran the third place car by 20 seconds and still got beat. We ran great, but Earnhardt was in another time zone. Plus, they killed us on pit stops."

The pit crews for Wallace and seventh-place finishing Kyle Petty said Earnhardt got an unexpected advantage on pit stops by having as many as nine men over pit wall, two over the legal limit. "Maybe that explains it," related Hmiel. "But NASCAR has never said what the penalty is for that, and I guess they won't now either."

Buddy Parrott, crew chief for Wallace, said his crew performed a 16.98-second, four-tire pit stop. "Felix (Sabates, car owner for Petty) leaned over to me and said, 'Nine people over pit wall' for the 3 car," said Parrott. "But that was only a 20-second pit stop for them. I timed 'em."

Wallace said he "ran out of tires" near the end of the race and wound up losing the lap he had fought so hard to make up.

Wallace moved into second place in the Winston Cup standings, 57 points behind Earnhardt.

Alan Kulwicki finished in sixth place in what was destined to be his final Winston Cup appearance. "We were hot and cold, but at least we got sixth," said Kulwicki. "And we're back in this point race, so maybe we can be heard from later this season."

Kulwicki moved into ninth place in the standings, 179 points off the top.

Greg Fielden

Jeff Gordon ran strong at Darlington before getting involved in a wreck with Michael Waltrip.

Race #6

Racing World Mourns Loss of Kulwicki; Wallace Wins Bristol

BRISTOL, TN (April 4) – Rusty Wallace led 376 of the 500 laps and capped an emotional weekend at Bristol International Raceway.

Defending champion of the Food City 500 was Alan Kulwicki, who perished three days earlier in a private airplane crash en route to the track.

Following the eight car length victory, Wallace whipped his Pontiac around and saluted his fallen comrade with a Polish victory lap – a tradition that Kulwicki made famous at Phoenix in 1988. "I found myself thinking during the race about what I was going to do or say if I won," said Wallace, who had competed with Kulwicki in the ASA midwestern short track series before they both graduated to NASCAR's Winston Cup tour. "I was still thinking about Alan and what happened. I couldn't get if off my mind. I thought it was appropriate for what he had done. I know there's a lot of people who don't like Rusty Wallace. But no one was booing me when I did that lap for Alan."

Wallace passed Dale Earnhardt on a restart in the 374th lap and was never headed. Earnhardt finished second with Kyle Petty third. Jimmy Spencer drove Bobby Allison's Ford home fourth and Davey Allison was fifth.

Wallace inched a little closer in the Winston Cup

Brian Czobat

Alan Kulwicki 1954-1993

Winston Cup Series Race No. 6
500 Laps at Bristol Int'l Raceway
Bristol, TN
"Food City 500"
266.5 Miles on .533-mile Short Track
April 4, 1993

Fin	St	No.	Driver	Team / Car	Laps	Money	Status
1	1	2	Rusty Wallace	Roger Penske Pontiac	500	$107,610	Running
2	6	3	Dale Earnhardt	RCR Enterprises Chevrolet	500	47,760	Running
3	14	42	Kyle Petty	SabCo Racing Pontiac	500	31,485	Running
4	28	12	Jimmy Spencer	Bobby Allison Ford	500	26,050	Running
5	10	28	Davey Allison	Robert Yates Racing Ford	500	25,180	Running
6	35	17	Darrell Waltrip	DarWal Chevrolet	500	23,405	Running
7	4	21	Morgan Shepherd	Wood Brothers Ford	499	17,305	Running
8	8	6	Mark Martin	Roush Racing Ford	498	19,055	Running
9	2	26	Brett Bodine	King Motorsports Ford	497	16,150	Running
10	19	1	Rick Mast	Precision Products Ford	497	17,650	Running
11	25	16	Wally Dallenbach,Jr.	Roush Racing Ford	496	14,950	Running
12	12	98	Derrike Cope	Cale Yarborough Ford	494	15,500	Running
13	30	40	Kenny Wallace	SabCo Racing Pontiac	494	9,825	Running
14	15	30	Michael Waltrip	Bahari Racing Pontiac	492	13,875	Running
15	32	55	Ted Musgrave	RaDiUs Motorsports Ford	488	13,825	Running
16	31	52	Jimmy Means	Means Racing Ford	484	8,450	Running
17	21	24	Jeff Gordon	Hendrick Motorsports Chevy	481	9,400	Crash
18	5	15	Geoff Bodine	Bud Moore Eng. Ford	469	16,350	Running
19	27	20	Joe Ruttman	Dick Moroso Ford	467	8,340	Running
20	17	8	Sterling Marlin	Stavola Brothers Ford	443	13,200	Running
21	18	14	Terry Labonte	Billy Hagan Chevrolet	440	12,950	Running
22	34	75	Dick Trickle	Butch Mock Ford	440	8,050	Running
23	3	4	Ernie Irvan	Morgan-McClure Chevrolet	409	17,900	Crash
24	33	22	Bobby Labonte	Bill Davis Racing Ford	397	7,925	Crash
25	24	44	Rick Wilson	Petty Enterprises Pontiac	392	9,630	Running
26	9	5	Ricky Rudd	Hendrick Motorsports Chevy	369	12,500	Crash
27	23	27	Hut Stricklin	Junior Johnson Ford	352	12,425	Running
28	26	33	Harry Gant	Leo Jackson Chevrolet	329	16,775	Running
29	16	83	Lake Speed	Speed Ford	305	7,745	Engine
30	20	11	Bill Elliott	Junior Johnson Ford	303	17,620	Crash
31	29	41	Phil Parsons	Larry Hedrick Chevrolet	254	8,395	Engine
32	22	18	Dale Jarrett	Joe Gibbs Chevrolet	207	15,420	Crash
33	13	90	Bobby Hillin,Jr.	Junie Donlavey Ford	119	6,420	Oil Pump
34	7	25	Ken Schrader	Hendrick Motorsports Chevy	51	10,970	Crash
35	11	68	Bobby Hamilton	Tri-Star Motorsports Ford	27	7,025	Engine

Time of Race: 3 hours, 8 minutes, 43 seconds
Average Speed: 84.730 mph
Pole Winner: Rusty Wallace – 120.938 mph
Lap Leaders: Brett Bodine 1-4, Rusty Wallace 5-53, Morgan Shepherd 54, Michael Waltrip 55-72, Dale Jarrett 73-102, R.Wallace 103-180, Mark Martin 181-210, Davey Allison 211, R.Wallace 212-257, Martin 258-263, Geoff Bodine 264, R.Wallace 265-310, Jimmy Spencer 311-312, R.Wallace 313-343, Shepherd 344-352, Dale Earnhardt 353-360, Martin 361-367, Earnhardt 368-374, R.Wallace 375-500.
19 lead changes among 10 drivers.
Cautions: 17 for 87 laps Margin of Victory: 0.82 second

Bryan Hallman

Bill Elliott's Ford breaks loose on Bristol's high banks.

standings, cutting Earnhardt's lead to 47 points.

Kulwicki, 38, the first Winston Cup champion with a college degree, was killed with two other passengers and the pilot of the Merlin Fairchild twin-engine plane owned by Kulwicki's sponsor Hooters restaurants. Kulwicki had been at an autograph session in Knoxville and was flying to Bristol for the race.

Wallace started on the pole and was clearly the quickest competitor on the .533-mile high-banked oval. Earnhardt pressured his friendly rival in the closing stages. "I was giving Rusty all I had," said Earnhardt. "I didn't like my tires the way they were, and we weren't as fast on restarts. He got a breather on us on that last restart (with 17 laps remaining) and that was all it took."

An array of crashes caused 17 caution flags which consumed 87 laps. Dale Jarrett was livid with Bobby Hillin, Jr. after the two scrubbed fenders in the 207th lap, sending Jarrett into the wall. Jarrett flung his helmet at Hillin, Jr. under caution – and the helmet struck the car with a solid shot. NASCAR officials ejected Jarrett on the spot and would not let the Joe Gibbs crew repair the car.

"It's a shame idiots like that are out there," said the Daytona 500 winner. "He had already been in a wreck and was a bunch of laps down. Why does someone like that try to race you into a corner? This takes us right out of the point race.

"I don't feel bad about what I did," added Jarrett. I'm not saying it was right, but I don't regret showing my

Bryan Hallman

Joe Ruttman #20 leads Kyle Petty #42, Jeff Gordon #24 and Mark Martin #6 at Bristol.

emotions."

Hillin, Jr. denied he was at fault. "I didn't do anything wrong," he said. "I was driving my line, trying to stay out of the way. Jarrett came up beside me on the right and cut into me. It was his fault."

Others sidelined by crashes included Ricky Rudd, Ernie Irvan, Jeff Gordon, Bill Elliott, Ken Schrader and Bobby Labonte.

Rudd blamed Brett Bodine for his wreck on lap 369. "He decided to take a cheap shot and wreck me," huffed Rudd. "I want to discuss it with him, but he doesn't seem to be anywhere around. I don't understand it."

Bodine, who went on to finish ninth, said "I don't know what he's upset about. I think he went into the corner awfully hard. He turned in there tight, we hit and he spun."

Wallace won $107,610 for his 23rd career win. "I won my first NASCAR race at this track, but this victory was much more emotional. It's a big deal to win for my buddy Alan."

Brian Czobat

Back-to-back victories at Bristol and North Wilkesboro put Rusty Wallace on top of the Winston Cup point standings.

Race #7

Wilkesboro Win Puts Wallace in Winston Cup Standings Lead

N.WILKESBORO, NC (April 18) – Rusty Wallace outran Kyle Petty and outlasted Sterling Marlin and won the First Union 400 at North Wilkesboro Speedway. It was the third win in seven races for the St. Louis, Mo. driver and it put him on top of the Winston Cup point standings.

"We're on a roll like (Bill) Elliott was in 1985," said Wallace. "I thought we would win three or four races this year, but I never thought three of them would come in the first seven races. Now I can foresee us winning 10 races this year."

Wallace took an 18-point lead over Dale Earnhardt, who set a new track record in qualifying, but struggled to a 16th place finish, four laps behind. "I don't know when I've had that bad a car," said a disgusted Earnhardt. "I've never had that bad a car here. I didn't know what to tell the crew to fix. We'd run good for about 10 laps, then it was all I could do to keep it between the walls."

Wallace sped past Ken Schrader with 102 laps to go and led the rest of the way. Petty came in second, 1.66-seconds behind as Pontiacs registered a 1-2 finish. Schrader wound up third with Davey Allison fourth and Darrell Waltrip fifth.

Brothers Brett and Geoff Bodine started on the front row. They became the first brother act to start on the front row for a Winston Cup race since Bobby and Donnie Allison in 1979 at Darlington.

The fireworks started early as Geoff Bodine got a tap from Ernie Irvan, causing him to lose control of his Ford. "Somebody turned me around going into the turn," said Bodine. "This place is so tight and everything is so crowded. I got bumped."

Irvan, who started third, said "I was to the inside of him and he came down on my car. Maybe he didn't know I was there. When we got together, I slowed down. Ken Schrader ran into the back of me and I spun."

Bodine ricocheted off the wall and into the path of Mark Martin, whose car lost a wheel and caught on fire. Dick Trickle and Michael Waltrip were also involved. All cars were able to continue.

Jeff Gordon got into the first turn too deep and backed into the first turn wall in the 61st lap. The impact with the concrete retaining barrier broke the fuel cell in Gordon's Chevrolet, which erupted into a blaze. The Pittsboro, Ind. rookie dashed out of his car unhurt.

Sterling Marlin gave the Stavola Brothers Ford a stout ride, leading for 190 laps, including stretches of 86 and 104 laps. "The car came to our chassis set-up early and the car would really turn," said Marlin, still looking for his first Winston Cup win. "After 200 laps, the handling went away and we couldn't get it back the way we wanted."

Marlin eventually finished ninth, the last car to complete all 400 laps.

Morgan Shepherd made a strong run in the closing laps, but wound up a disappointing eighth after a late race shunt with Irvan, who was two laps down.

"He was trying to run blocker for Schrader," said Shepherd. "The Chevys seem to team up on you, even if they're some laps down. I tried to pass him on the outside and he shot into me. I went to the inside on the frontstretch and he cut over and I ran into the side of him."

Irvan denied blame. "I don't know what his problem is," said Irvan, who finished 11th. "I gave him the bottom of the race track, but he tried to take my half, too. It hurt his car worse than mine."

Ricky Rudd and Brett Bodine, who tangled two weeks earlier at Bristol, squared off after the first round of qualifying. Rudd confronted Bodine after Bodine earned the pole position. Reportedly Rudd said to Bodine: "That's a good qualifying run. Too bad it's for no good, because you'll be in the fence in the race."

Rudd apparently took a swing at Bodine, but the two were separated. "If you can't control your emotions any better than that, you shouldn't be in a race car," declared Bodine.

The next morning, NASCAR officials presided over a meeting with the two drivers. NASCAR's Chip Williams reported that "both drivers agreed to let the past remain in the past and move on to the future. Both agreed to show respect to each other on the track."

Rudd said that he "paid good attention in the meeting. I was a good student. It's over."

Winston Cup Series Race No. 7
400 Laps at North Wilkesboro Speedway
N.Wilkesboro, NC
"First Union 400"
250 Miles on .625-mile Short Track
April 18, 1993

Fin	St	No.	Driver	Team / Car	Laps	Money	Status
1	9	2	Rusty Wallace	Roger Penske Pontiac	400	$43,535	Running
2	22	42	Kyle Petty	SabCo Racing Pontiac	400	29,210	Running
3	4	25	Ken Schrader	Hendrick Motorsports Chevy	400	40,235	Running
4	27	28	Davey Allison	Robert Yates Racing Ford	400	28,285	Running
5	23	17	Darrell Waltrip	DarWal Chevrolet	400	25,935	Running
6	6	14	Terry Labonte	Billy Hagan Chevrolet	400	18,235	Running
7	10	5	Ricky Rudd	Hendrick Motorsports Chevy	400	14,960	Running
8	17	21	Morgan Shepherd	Wood Brothers Ford	400	12,805	Running
9	8	8	Sterling Marlin	Stavola Brothers Ford	400	13,880	Running
10	15	11	Bill Elliott	Junior Johnson Ford	398	18,860	Running
11	3	4	Ernie Irvan	Morgan-Mcclure Chevrolet	398	15,780	Running
12	13	7	Jimmy Hensley	AK Racing Ford	398	13,330	Running
13	19	33	Harry Gant	Leo Jackson Chevrolet	398	14,780	Running
14	14	12	Jimmy Spencer	Bobby Allison Ford	397	11,430	Running
15	24	40	Kenny Wallace	SabCo Racing Pontiac	396	6,930	Running
16	21	3	Dale Earnhardt	RCR Enterprises Chevrolet	396	13,130	Running
17	1	26	Brett Bodine	King Motorsports Ford	396	18,355	Running
18	28	41	Phil Parsons	Larry Hedrick Chevrolet	395	7,505	Running
19	25	1	Rick Mast	Precision Products Ford	395	10,330	Running
20	20	30	Michael Waltrip	Bahari Racing Pontiac	394	10,130	Running
21	33	16	Wally Dallenbach,Jr.	Roush Racing ford	394	10,030	Running
22	5	27	Hut Stricklin	Junior Johnson Ford	393	9,855	Running
23	26	44	Rick Wilson	Petty Enterprises Pontiac	393	6,580	Running
24	31	55	Ted Musgrave	RaDiUs Motorsports Ford	393	9,530	Running
25	30	22	Bobby Labonte	Bill Davis Racing Ford	391	5,580	Running
26	32	90	Bobby Hillin,Jr.	Junie Donlavey Ford	388	4,430	Running
27	34	52	Jimmy Means	Means Racing Ford	388	4,755	Running
28	2	15	Geoff Bodine	Bud Moore Eng. Ford	369	13,690	Running
29	29	68	Bobby Hamilton	Tri-Star Motorsports Ford	359	6,255	Running
30	18	98	Derrike Cope	Cale Yarborough Ford	357	8,805	Running
31	12	6	Mark Martin	Roush Racing Ford	340	12,205	Running
32	11	18	Dale Jarrett	Joe Gibbs Chevrolet	311	12,155	Engine
33	16	75	Dick Trickle	Butch Mock Ford	199	4,155	Engine
34	7	24	Jeff Gordon	Hendrick Motorsports Chevy	25	4,180	Crash

Time of Race: 2 hours, 41 minutes, 59 seconds
Average Speed: 92.602 mph
Pole Winner: Brett Bodine – 117.017 mph
Fastest Qualifier: Dale Earnhardt – 117.616 mph
Lap Leaders: Brett Bodine 1-24, Ken Schrader 25-53, Sterling Marlin 54-139, Darrell Waltrip 140, Dale Jarrett 141, Kenny Wallace 142, Ernie Irvan 143-145, Marlin 146-249, Rusty Wallace 250-267, Morgan Shepherd 268, D.Waltrip 269, Schrader 270-298, R.Wallace 299-400.
12 lead changes among 9 drivers.
Cautions: 4 for 38 laps Margin of Victory: 1.66 seconds

Race #8

Wallace Now 4-for-8 After Narrow win at Martinsville

MARTINSVILLE, VA (April 25) – Martinsville Speedway was the site of a spring re-run as Rusty Wallace won again. Geoff Bodine spun out on the first lap again and Dale Earnhardt continued his short track skid in the Hanes 500.

Wallace bagged his fourth win in eight starts and increased his point lead to 101 over Earnhardt in the battle for the Winston Cup championship.

Wallace dominated the event, leading for 409 of the 500 laps. He nipped Davey Allison by less than a car length as they raced back to the caution flag when Morgan Shepherd whacked the wall three laps from the finish.

Dale Jarrett got third place with Darrell Waltrip fourth and Kyle Petty fifth.

Brake failure sent Shepherd's Ford into the wall in turn four while the leaders were working the 497th lap. Wallace and Allison knew the race back to the yellow flag would determine the outcome. "I slowed down and Davey never did," said Wallace. "I saw him out of the corner of my eye and I mashed the gas. It's a tough deal when you've got a wrecked car in the middle of a turn and have to race back to the caution flag."

Allison said he was trying to "sneak up on him, but Rusty saw me a little too soon and accelerated just enough to beat me. My spotter told me where the wreck was and to keep a low line. We almost pulled it off. But Rusty had everybody covered today."

Geoff Bodine earned the pole – his second straight front row starting spot. But for the second week in a row, he spun after a tap in the rear. "Two weeks in a row," said Bodine. "Who did it this time? I sure don't appreciate it."

Fourth starting Kyle Petty nipped Bodine's rear bumper, sending him looping. "I gave him room, but he cut down on me," explained Petty. "He was already half-sideways when we touched."

Bodine was involved in another altercation with Wally Dallenbach, Jr. a short time later. Despite a crinkled car, Bodine finished sixth.

Hut Stricklin led the first 87 laps in his Junior Johnson Ford, but lost the lead to Wallace during caution flag pit stops. Wallace's Roger Penske crew was again the class of the field. Rear gearing failure put Stricklin out after 404 laps.

Jeff Gordon finished in eighth place despite being hit with a one lap penalty for hitting Stricklin's car while

Hut Stricklin led the first 87 laps at Martinsville in Junior Johnson's Ford.

Winston Cup Series Race No. 8
500 Laps at Martinsville Speedway
Martinsville, VA
"Hanes 500"
262.5 Miles on .525-mile Short Track
April 25, 1993

Fin	St	No.	Driver	Team / Car	Laps	Money	Status
1	5	2	Rusty Wallace	Roger Penske Pontiac	500	$45,175	Running
2	6	28	Davey Allison	Robert Yates Racing Ford	500	49,725	Running
3	11	18	Dale Jarrett	Joe Gibbs Chevrolet	500	30,350	Running
4	26	17	Darrell Waltrip	DarWal Chevrolet	500	28,800	Running
5	4	42	Kyle Petty	SabCo Racing Pontiac	499	21,050	Running
6	1	15	Geoff Bodine	Bud Moore Eng. Ford	497	26,150	Running
7	18	26	Brett Bodine	King Motorsports Ford	497	19,425	Running
8	3	24	Jeff Gordon	Hendrick Motorsports Chevy	497	11,975	Running
9	19	14	Terry Labonte	Billy Hagan Chevrolet	497	16,125	Running
10	8	6	Mark Martin	Roush Racing Ford	496	18,525	Running
11	17	1	Rick Mast	Precision Products Ford	496	13,410	Running
12	24	22	Bobby Labonte	Bill Davis Racing Ford	495	7,325	Running
13	7	7	Jimmy Hensley	AK Racing Ford	495	16,025	Running
14	32	75	Dick Trickle	Butch Mock Ford	495	6,525	Running
15	34	71	Dave Marcis	Marcis Auto Racing Chevy	494	9,725	Running
16	10	30	Michael Waltrip	Bahari Racing Pontiac	494	12,225	Running
17	20	44	Rick Wilson	Petty Enterprises Pontiac	490	9,025	Running
18	13	25	Ken Schrader	Hendrick Motorsports Chevy	489	11,530	Trans
19	29	21	Morgan Shepherd	Wood Brothers Ford	489	11,025	Crash
20	28	41	Phil Parsons	Larry Hedrick Chevrolet	484	7,625	Running
21	30	8	Sterling Marlin	Stavola Brothers Ford	482	10,325	Running
22	21	3	Dale Earnhardt	RCR Enterprises Chevrolet	453	10,625	Engine
23	31	90	Bobby Hillin,Jr.	Junie Donlavey Ford	451	4,925	Running
24	15	40	Kenny Wallace	SabCo Racing Pontiac	424	4,875	Rear End
25	27	98	Derrike Cope	Cale Yarborough Ford	408	9,625	Running
26	2	27	Hut Stricklin	Junior Johnson Ford	404	12,425	Rear End
27	16	11	Bill Elliott	Junior Johnson Ford	381	14,825	Running
28	22	55	Ted Musgrave	RaDiUs Motorsports Ford	350	9,175	Running
29	14	5	Ricky Rudd	Hendrick Motorsports Chevy	310	9,025	Running
30	25	12	Jimmy Spencer	Bobby Allison Ford	212	8,950	Engine
31	23	33	Harry Gant	Leo Jackson Chevrolet	200	13,375	Engine
32	12	4	Ernie Irvan	Morgan-McClure Chevrolet	140	13,975	Running
33	9	68	Bobby Hamilton	Tri-Star Motorsports Ford	40	5,925	Oil Pump
34	33	16	Wally Dallenbach,Jr.	Roush Racing Ford	18	8,900	Crash

Time of Race: 3 hours, 18 minutes, 33 seconds
Average Speed: 79.078 mph
Pole Winner: Geoff Bodine – 93.887 mph
Lap Leaders: Hut Stricklin 1-87, Rusty Wallace 88-200, Stricklin 201, R.Wallace 202-287, Dale Earnhardt 288, R.Wallace 289-425, Davey Allison 426, R.Wallace 427-487, Allison 488, R.Wallace 489-500.
10 lead changes among 4 drivers.
Cautions: 8 for 49 laps   Margin of Victory: Under Caution

on pit road. "I was blocked in by him," said Gordon. "He was taking on four tires and I was only getting two. I pulled out and nicked him. I didn't mean to do it. I thought the penalty was a little too severe."

Earnhardt qualified 21st, which forced him to pit on the backstretch – a decided disadvantage. However, NASCAR made a quick change in the rules with the prospect of Earnhardt having to pit to the backstretch.

The new rule allowed pace car driver Elmo Langley to speed up after dropping the cars off at pit road entrance on the front chute instead of maintaining the usual caution speed. By speeding up, Langley permitted the drivers pitting on the backstretch to lessen their disadvantage. Earnhardt actually led a lap under yellow by pitting on the backstretch – the first time that has occurred in recent years.

Wallace was initially credited with a 106 point lead, and leading a total of 410 laps. Later, NASCAR ruled that Earnhardt had led the 288th lap, which gave him a five point bonus for leading a lap. That left him with a 101 point deficit.

A valve spring broke in Earnhardt's Chevrolet, putting him out in the late stages. He received credit for a 22nd place finish.

Race #9

Irvan Wins Talladega Thriller; Wallace Survives Terrible Tumble

TALLADEGA, AL (May 2) – Ernie Irvan won a thrill-packed final lap shoot-out at Talladega Speedway and Rusty Wallace escaped with his life after a horrifying tumble at the finish of the Winston 500.

Irvan came from fourth to first in the frantic last lap which produced the most jockeying for position in a final lap in the history of NASCAR Winston Cup racing.

The breath-taking finish was set up by a brief rain shower and a NASCAR imposed red flag in the final stages. After the track was dried, two laps remained in the 500-mile event.

Irvan was fourth in line behind Dale Earnhardt, Rusty Wallace and Mark Martin when the green flag waved. It took nearly a full lap for the cars to get up to speed.

Martin was the first to make a move. He shot to the outside of Wallace in the tri-oval, but Wallace squeezed Martin into the wall. A cloud of concrete dust billowed as Martin miraculously regained control.

Irvan shot to the low-side and made a daring pass on Earnhardt in the first turn. The two Chevrolet drivers swapped sheet metal as they vied for the top position.

Winston Cup Series Race No. 9
188 Laps at Talladega Superspeedway
Talladega, AL
"Winston 500"
500.08 Miles on 2.66-mile Superspeedway
May 2, 1993

Fin	St	No.	Driver	Team / Car	Laps	Money	Status
1	16	4	Ernie Irvan	Morgan-McClure Chevrolet	188	$85,875	Running
2	2	12	Jimmy Spencer	Bobby Allison Ford	188	56,850	Running
3	3	18	Dale Jarrett	Joe Gibbs Chevrolet	188	44,870	Running
4	1	3	Dale Earnhardt	RCR Enterprises Chevrolet	188	39,870	Running
5	6	20	Joe Ruttman	Dick Moroso Ford	188	25,765	Running
6	24	2	Rusty Wallace	Roger Penske Pontiac	188	28,490	Sailing
7	5	28	Davey Allison	Robert Yates Racing Ford	188	27,710	Running
8	15	98	Derrike Cope	Cale Yarborough Ford	188	22,285	Running
9	29	7	Jimmy Hensley	AK Racing Ford	188	24,285	Running
10	13	30	Michael Waltrip	Bahari Racing Pontiac	188	19,585	Running
11	30	24	Jeff Gordon	Hendrick Motorsports Chevy	188	15,795	Running
12	11	6	Mark Martin	Roush Racing Ford	188	21,715	Running
13	19	1	Rick Mast	Precision Products Ford	188	17,435	Running
14	17	40	Kenny Wallace	SabCo Racing Pontiac	188	11,655	Running
15	9	21	Morgan Shepherd	Wood Brothers Ford	188	16,975	Running
16	4	44	Rick Wilson	Petty Enterprises Pontiac	187	13,285	Running
17	41	90	Bobby Hillin,Jr.	Junie Donlavey Ford	187	9,770	Running
18	21	42	Kyle Petty	SabCo Racing Pontiac	187	18,030	Running
19	39	41	Phil Parsons	Larry Hedrick Chevrolet	187	11,840	Running
20	25	27	Hut Stricklin	Junior Johnson Ford	187	14,880	Running
21	8	25	Ken Schrader	Hendrick Motorsports Chevy	187	13,810	Running
22	10	11	Bill Elliott	Junior Johnson Ford	186	18,890	Running
23	37	33	Harry Gant	Leo Jackson Chevrolet	184	17,580	Running
24	14	8	Sterling Marlin	Stavola Brothers Ford	182	13,375	Running
25	34	53	Ritchie Petty	Maurice Petty Ford	182	8,395	Running
26	33	17	Darrell Waltrip	DarWal Chevrolet	180	18,115	Running
27	31	15	Geoff Bodine	Bud Moore Eng. Ford	174	16,260	Handling
28	23	55	Ted Musgrave	RaDiUs Motorsports Ford	167	13,055	Running
29	7	16	Wally Dallenbach,Jr.	Roush Racing Ford	158	12,900	Running
30	12	26	Brett Bodine	King Motorsports Ford	156	12,745	Crash
31	27	75	Dick Trickle	Butch Mock Ford	148	7,965	Running
32	28	52	Jimmy Means	Means Racing Ford	139	7,910	Engine
33	22	68	Greg Sacks	Tri-Star Motorsports Ford	138	9,480	Crash
34	32	83	Lake Speed	Speed Ford	127	7,850	Crash
35	20	22	Bobby Labonte	Bill Davis Ford	127	7,820	Crash
36	35	32	Jimmy Horton	Active Racing Chevrolet	127	7,790	Crash
37	38	14	Terry Labonte	Billy Hagan Chevrolet	126	13,285	Crash
38	36	45	Rich Bickle	Gene Isenhour Ford	74	7,665	Shocks
39	18	51	Jeff Purvis	James Finch Chevrolet	32	7,600	Engine
40	40	85	Ken bouchard	Thee Dixon Ford	24	7,570	Engine
41	26	5	Ricky Rudd	Hendrick Motorsports Chevy	12	12,120	Camshaft

Time of Race: 3 hours, 13 minutes, 4 seconds
Average Speed: 155.412 mph
Pole Winner: Dale Earnhardt – 192.355 mph
Lap Leaders: Jimmy Spencer 1, Dale Earnhardt 2-18, Rusty Wallace 19-35, Earnhardt 36-46, Dale Jarrett 47-49, Davey Allison 50-52, Mark Martin 53-55, Earnhardt 56-62, Jarrett 63, Earnhardt 64-90, Ernie Irvan 91, Earnhardt 92-94, Jarrett 95-99, Earnhardt 100-116, Jarrett 117-122,Earnhardt 123-133, Irvan 134, Martin 135-137, Jarrett 138-157, R.Wallace 158-178, Earnhardt 179-187, Irvan 188.
22 lead changes among 7 drivers.
Cautions: 4 for 25 laps
Margin of Victory: 2 car lengths

Wallace nipped the rear of Jimmy Spencer's Ford on the backstretch, then brushed the side of Jarrett's Chevrolet in turn three in his frantic efforts to get back to the front. Earnhardt's momentum was broken and he fell to ninth in the final lap before he reached into his bag of horsepower for a final burst.

Irvan led the pack through the homestretch for the final time with Spencer second. Wallace tried to shut the door on Earnhardt as the two battled for fourth place, but Earnhardt snagged Wallace's left-rear bumper,

ISC

Rusty Wallace's Pontiac rips apart as it flips across finish line at Talladega.

turning him around. Wallace's car lifted high into the air and sailed across the finish line flipping.

Irvan nosed out Spencer by two car lengths to score his seventh career win. Dale Jarrett finished third and Earnhardt fourth. Fifth place went to Joe Ruttman, who took several shunts in the final lap.

Wallace got credit for sixth. Finishing seventh through 10th were Davey Allison, Derrike Cope, Jimmy Hensley and Michael Waltrip. Martin fell to 12th in the final shuffle.

Wallace suffered a broken wrist, concussion, facial cuts and a chipped tooth in the crash. Earnhardt drove down to the scene of the crash after the race and assisted rescue workers. "I came down to go under Rusty," explained Earnhardt, who started on the pole and led most of the way. "He blocked me. He had blocked Mark (the lap before) and about put him in the wall. I was going for the hole and he cut down. I hit him in the left rear bumper and it turned him upside down. It was more my fault than anything, but I didn't do it on purpose. Rusty and I are good friends. I can understand why his crew is mad."

Earnhardt drove back to pit road and handed Wallace's gloves to crew chief Buddy Parrott. A number of the Roger Penske crew were irate at Earnhardt when he drove past.

"We will overcome this," said Parrott. "I'm not going to say anything about that number 3 bunch or anybody else. We race hard together and we may not know the whole deal up there."

Surprisingly, Wallace accepted most of the blame for

Bryan Hallman

The field hooked up in three-abreast formation during the early laps of Talladega's Winston 500.

Brian Czobat

Dale Jarrett and Dale Earnhardt ran up front for a good portion of the Winston 500.

the incident in a remarkable display of sportsmanship. "We had both fallen back," said Wallace, "and we were fighting to get back to the front. When I moved over to block Dale, he was going four or five mph faster than I was. If it was anyone's fault, it was mine. The next time I make a move like that, I'll make sure we're going the same speed."

Martin was livid that he lost an opportunity to win. "Somebody (Wallace) didn't want me to pass them, so he pushed me into the wall," said Martin.

Runner-up Spencer said the two-lap shootout was "a bunch of bull ----. I don't care what anybody says, nobody's life is worth what was going on out there in the last lap."

Spencer said he had a feeling something would tear loose in the last lap. "I saw it coming," he noted. "I got hit pretty hard in the quarter panel (by Wallace) on the backstretch. It turned me sideways and I don't know how I saved it. I guess the people (spectators) saw a heck of a finish though."

Before the late race antics, Wallace had worked his way up from 24th starting position. He had assumed command in the 158th lap and led for 21 laps with Earnhardt and Martin in close pursuit. When rain started falling, Earnhardt made a nifty pass to take the lead. He won the race back to the yellow flag – and many presumed it would end under the yellow.

Seven laps were run under the yellow as NASCAR

Brian Czobat

Rusty Wallace ducks under Dale Jarrett as he charges from mid-pack to the front at Talladega.

officials studied the radar, which indicated a brief shower and not a prolonged rain. It took only 12 minutes to dry the track.

"It has always been NASCAR's policy to finish races under the green flag if at all possible," said spokesman Chip Williams.

Many contestants criticized NASCAR for restarting the race. "They should have stopped the race earlier," said Jarrett, who finished third. "As it was, a lot of people did some stupid things with two laps to go. It was a miracle that I finished at all."

Richard Childress, car owner for Earnhardt, suggested that the race was stopped before the finish because his car was leading. "Jamming people together for the last two laps wasn't safe. It was a disaster waiting to happen," he said.

Bobby Allison, who owns Spencer's Ford, didn't share the opinion of most. "These are the best race car drivers in the world," he said. "They should be able to run two laps."

NASCAR found itself in a difficult position. "It was a no-win situation," said Williams. "If we go back to green, we're wrong. If we don't go back to green, we're wrong." In actuality, NASCAR gave the fans a memorable finish – and continued its policy of giving the fans the best show in motorsports.

Irvan was one driver who did not want to see the race end under the yellow flag. "I didn't want it to end and us finish fourth," said Irvan. "I came here to win. I think everybody in the grandstands thought it would be like that. If the five of us who were up front can't put on a good race, then who can?"

Earnhardt narrowed his deficit in the Winston Cup standings to 86 points.

Race #10

Geoff Bodine Captures Slugfest in Road Race at Sears Point

SONOMA, CA (May 16) – Geoff Bodine, who has been caught up in crashes in the last three races, showed a little muscle of his own and prevailed in the Save Mart 300 – a race named for its distance in kilometers – at Sears Point International Raceway.

Bodine put his Bud Moore Ford into the lead in the 53rd lap and led the rest of the way. The Chemung, NY driver held command during a frantic last lap as he edged Ernie Irvan and Ricky Rudd. It was his 14th career Winston Cup triumph and his first on a road course since he won at Riverside in 1984.

Bodine snared first place when erstwhile leader Dale Earnhardt hit a spinning Tommy Kendall. The collision knocked Earnhardt to the rear of the field in 36th place.

From that point on, it was strictly a Bodine, Rudd and Irvan show – and the show was a foot-stomper.

"They did everything they could to spin me out, but I got 'em," declared a happy Bodine in Victory Lane. "I got turned around at North Wilkesboro and Martinsville, but I was ready for that stuff today."

Dorsey Schroeder brought out the fifth and final

Winston Cup Series Race No. 10
74 Laps at Sears Point Int'l Raceway
Sonoma, CA
"Save Mart Supermarkets 300K"
186.48 Miles on 2.52-mile Road Course
May 16, 1993

Fin	St	No.	Driver	Team / Car	Laps	Money	Status
1	3	15	Geoff Bodine	Bud Moore Eng. Ford	74	$66,510	Running
2	4	4	Ernie Irvan	Morgan-McClure Chevrolet	74	41,190	Running
3	2	5	Ricky Rudd	Hendrick Motorsports Chevy	74	29,590	Running
4	28	25	Ken Schrader	Hendrick Motorsports Chevy	74	22,415	Running
5	18	42	Kyle Petty	SabCo Racing Pontiac	74	22,715	Running
6	1	3	Dale Earnhardt	RCR Enterprises Chevrolet	74	27,790	Running
7	7	16	Wally Dallenbach,Jr.	Roush Racing Ford	74	17,465	Running
8	20	44	Rick Wilson	Petty Enterprises Pontiac	74	13,665	Running
9	10	14	Terry Labonte	Billy Hagan Chevrolet	74	17,015	Running
10	36	27	Hut Stricklin	Junior Johnson Ford	74	17,415	Running
11	15	24	Jeff Gordon	Hendrick Motorsports Chevy	74	10,215	Running
12	23	8	Sterling Marlin	Stavola Brothers Ford	74	14,315	Running
13	32	18	Dale Jarrett	Joe Gibbs Chevrolet	74	16,610	Running
14	12	21	Morgan Shepherd	Wood Brothers Ford	74	13,310	Running
15	9	28	Davey Allison	Robert Yates Racing Ford	73	18,160	Running
16	41	22	Bobby Labonte	Bill Davis Ford	73	7,965	Crash
17	17	11	Bill Elliott	Junior Johnson Ford	73	17,590	Running
18	11	98	Derrike Cope	Cale Yarborough Ford	73	12,340	Running
19	35	33	Harry Gant	Leo Jackson Chevrolet	73	16,315	Running
20	38	75	Dick Trickle	Butch Mock Ford	73	7,840	Running
21	43	37	Rick Carelli	Marshall Chesrown Chevrolet	73	7,190	Running
22	33	7	Tommy Kendall	AK - G.E.B. Racing Ford	73	16,565	Running
23	16	30	Michael Waltrip	Bahari Racing Pontiac	73	12,040	Running
24	26	26	Brett Bodine	King Motorsports Ford	73	12,420	Running
25	14	9	P.J.Jones	Melling Performance Ford	73	8,810	Running
26	34	76	Bill Sedgwick	Wayne Spears Chevrolet	73	8,140	Running
27	22	12	Jimmy Spencer	Bobby Allison Ford	73	11,665	Running
28	25	71	Dave Marcis	Marcis Auto Racing Chevy	72	8,540	Running
29	31	1	Rick Mast	Precision Products Ford	72	11,505	Running
30	29	20	Dirk Stephens	Tom Craigen Ford	72	6,900	Running
31	28	73	Bill Schmitt	Sylvia Schmitt Ford	71	6,815	Running
32	27	36	Butch Gilliland	Laurie Gilliland Chevrolet	71	6,765	Running
33	19	68	Dorsey Schroeder	Tri-Star Motorsports Ford	69	8,265	Crash
34	29	29	John Krebs	Diamond Ridge Chevrolet	68	6,690	Trans
35	13	17	Darrell Waltrip	DarWal Chevrolet	67	16,465	Engine
36	21	40	Kenny Wallace	SabCo Racing Pontiac	66	6,665	Running
37	37	41	Phil Parsons	Larry Hedrick Chevrolet	65	8,160	Rear End
38	6	2	Rusty Wallace	Roger Penske Pontiac	64	15,15	Trans
39	24	55	Ted Musgrave	RaDiUs Motorsports Ford	61	11,085	Running
40	5	6	Mark Martin	Roush Racing Ford	57	15,260	Rear End
41	30	90	Bobby Hillin,Jr.	Junie Donlavey Ford	57	6,560	Rear End
42	40	81	Jeff Davis	Davis Ford	46	6,560	Crash
43	42	04	Hershel McGriff	John Strauser Chevrolet	27	6,560	Engine

Time of Race: 2 hours, 25 minutes, 17 seconds
Average Speed: 77.013 mph
Pole Winner: Dale Earnhardt – 91.838 mph
Lap Leaders: Dale Earnhardt 1-16, Geoff Bodine 17-24, Rusty Wallace 25, Michael Waltrip 26-29, Sterling Marlin 30-31, M.Waltrip 32-33, Earnhardt 34-47, Ernie Irvan 48-49, Earnhardt 50-52, G.Bodine 53-74.
9 lead changes among 6 drivers.
Cautions: 5 for 11 laps Margin of Victory: 0.53 second

Brian Czobat

Ricky Rudd leads Geoff Bodine and Ernie Irvan in middle stages of the Sears Point event.

caution flag near the end of the race. The final restart came in the final lap with Bodine leading.

Rudd popped Bodine in the tight fifth turn but let off the gas so Bodine could regain control. "I dug something out of my dirt track days" to keep control, said Bodine.

Irvan squeezed past Rudd in the shuffle and finished in second place, 0.53-seconds behind. Rudd was third followed by Ken Schrader and Kyle Petty. Earnhardt battled back to finish sixth in a mangled car. His run from 36th to sixth went largely unnoticed, but it was one of the finest displays of road racing talent ever seen in NASCAR.

For Bodine, the victory came a few days after he and wife Kathy purchased the Alan Kulwicki racing stable. "This was really an emotional win and it allowed me to take a 'Polish' victory lap in honor of Alan," said Bodine. "I've seen Rusty (Wallace) do that and I finally got to do that myself. The timing was perfect. We wanted to show our respect to Alan."

Rudd said his maneuver to take the lead was foiled "when we all got bottled up in a knot. I backed off because I couldn't tell which way Geoff was going to slide. If I had kept driving by, we both would have wrecked."

Irvan said, "Ricky had Bodine all the way sideways, but didn't finish him off. I guess Ricky didn't want to win by taking him out."

Rudd was stripped of a win at Sears Point in 1991 when he spun Davey Allison from the lead heading into the final lap. "I don't know if that was in the back of his mind or not," said the winner. "Ricky got me quicker than I expected. I don't blame him for the tap. That was just good racing."

The duel for top honors was not the only dicing in the final lap. Fifth place Kyle complained that Earnhardt had jumped from ninth to sixth place on the final restart without penalty. "I was trying to watch Earnhardt, who came all the way up beside me, and then I ran all over Dale Jarrett," said Petty. "It messed a lot of other guys up. It was probably my fault."

Jarrett, Davey Allison and Bobby Labonte had strong runs wiped out in the final lap wreck. Jarrett fell to 13th, Labonte was 15th and Allison 16th.

"If those guys want to race that way, so can I," said a perturbed Jarrett after the race. "We've got plenty of cars at the shop."

Jarrett got his car turned back around and ran into the side of Allison, putting him into the tire wall. "I don't know what happened," said Allison. "Maybe he thought I was the one who spun him. I wasn't. I was well behind them. Earnhardt jumped the restart and they let him get away with it."

Rusty Wallace, driving with a brace on his broken wrist, ran well but was sidelined by transmission failure with 10 laps to go. He was left with a 38th place finish. Earnhardt made up an 86 point deficit to take a 20 point lead. "I didn't have any problems with the wrist," said Wallace. "But I hated to fall out so late. We'll just have to bounce back next time."

Race #11

Earnhardt Overcomes Three Penalties to Win Coca-Cola 600

CONCORD, NC (May 30) – Dale Earnhardt overcame penalties for rough driving, speeding on pit road and for having too many crew members over the wall on a pit stop and roared back to win the Coca-Cola 600 at Charlotte Motor Speedway. It was the 55th career victory for the 42 year-old Kannapolis, NC driver.

Jeff Gordon leads Dale Jarrett and Sterling Marlin at Charlotte Motor Speedway.

Earnhardt was assessed a one-lap penalty for allegedly spinning Greg Sacks out in the 327th lap. Earnhardt had been fading at the time and was in danger of going a lap down to leader Dale Jarrett. Reportedly, officials heard Earnhardt tell his RCR Enterprises pit crew that if a caution was needed, he would make sure one came out. That radio transmission may have had something to do with the penalty.

"We looked at television replays five or six times," said NASCAR spokesman Chip Williams. "We asked the crew chief of the 68 car to ask Greg what happened and Greg said Earnhardt spun him out. There was absolutely no question in our minds. The incident was uncalled for and the penalty was instituted to make up any advantage Earnhardt might have gained."

The penalty lit a fire in Earnhardt, and he was relentless the rest of the way.

Earnhardt insisted that he never touched Sacks' Ford when it slid on the front chute. "When I got behind him, it must have taken the air off his spoiler," Earnhardt claimed. "I may have rubbed against him, but I didn't run up there and bang into him intentionally."

Sacks, who was taking his second ride in the Tri-Star Motorsports Ford, said he "felt like I had a co-pilot coming off turn four. Dale was running right under me for three or four laps. He really got me loose. Replays don't lie, but I don't think it was intentional. Things happen."

Winston Cup Series Race No. 11
400 Laps at Charlotte Motor Speedway
Concord, NC
"Coca-Cola 600"
600 Miles on 1.5-mile Superspeedway
May 30, 1993

Fin	St	No.	Driver	Team / Car	Laps	Money	Status
1	14	3	Dale Earnhardt	RCR Enterprises Chevrolet	400	$156,650	Running
2	21	24	Jeff Gordon	Hendrick Motorsports Chevy	400	79,050	Running
3	32	18	Dale Jarrett	Joe Gibbs Chevrolet	400	73,100	Running
4	1	25	Ken Schrader	Hendrick Motorsports Chevy	400	91,550	Running
5	19	4	Ernie Irvan	Morgan-McClure Chevrolet	400	46,600	Running
6	30	11	Bill Elliott	Junior Johnson Ford	400	35,300	Running
7	27	12	Jimmy Spencer	Bobby Allison Ford	400	28,700	Running
8	13	22	Bobby Labonte	Bill Davis Racing Ford	400	24,300	Running
9	12	21	Morgan Shepherd	Wood Brothers Ford	399	25,250	Running
10	5	15	Geoff Bodine	Bud Moore Eng. Ford	399	32,600	Running
11	31	17	Darrell Waltrip	DarWal Chevrolet	399	26,300	Running
12	22	41	Phil Parsons	Larry Hedrick Chevrolet	398	18,225	Running
13	6	30	Michael Waltrip	Bahari Racing Pontiac	398	18,800	Running
14	35	42	Kyle Petty	SabCo Racing Pontiac	398	21,700	Running
15	10	7	Jimmy Hensley	AK - G.E.B. Racing Ford	398	22,650	Running
16	28	90	Bobby Hillin,Jr.	Junie Donlavey Ford	398	11,570	Running
17	11	68	Greg Sacks	Tri-Star Motorsports Ford	398	10,880	Running
18	25	33	Harry Gant	Leo Jackson Chevrolet	398	19,100	Running
19	36	75	Dick Trickle	Butch Mock Ford	395	9,500	Running
20	26	27	Hut Stricklin	Junior Johnson Ford	394	14,750	Running
21	34	45	Rich Bickle	Gene Isenhour Ford	393	8,650	Running
22	37	66	Mike Wallace	Barry Owen Pontiac	392	8,325	Running
23	24	40	Kenny Wallace	SabCo Racing Pontiac	392	10,000	Running
24	7	8	Sterling Marlin	Stavola Brothers Ford	392	13,200	Running
25	39	32	Jimmy Horton	Active Racing Chevrolet	388	7,480	Running
26	18	55	Ted Musgrave*	RaDiUs Motorsports Ford	376	12,150	Running
27	15	83	Lake Speed	Speed Ford	364	7,150	Running
28	3	6	Mark Martin	Roush Racing Ford	355	20,710	Engine
29	8	2	Rusty Wallace	Roger Penske Pontiac	353	14,880	Crash
30	23	28	Davey Allison	Robert Yates Racing Ford	342	18,750	Running
31	4	1	Rick Mast	Precision Products Ford	334	13,900	Running
32	9	44	Rick Wilson	Petty Enterprises Pontiac	330	8,600	Engine
33	29	14	Terry Labonte	Billy Hagan Chevrolet	273	11,050	Engine
34	38	9	Chad Little	Melling Performance Ford	263	6,900	Rotor
35	40	20	Joe Ruttman	Dick Moroso Ford	231	6,350	Engine
36	16	98	Derrike Cope	Cale Yarborough Ford	182	10,875	Engine
37	20	5	Ricky Rudd	Hendrick Motorsports Chevy	164	11,310	Engine
38	33	52	Jimmy Means	Means Racing Ford	107	6,225	Engine
39	41	71	Dave Marcis	Marcis Auto Racing Chevy	44	6,200	Engine
40	17	16	Wally Dallenbach,Jr.	Roush Racing ford	28	10,700	Engine
41	2	26	Brett Bodine	King Motorsports Ford	5	15,675	Engine

Time of Race: 4 hours, 7 minutes, 25 seconds
Average Speed: 145.504 mph
Pole Winner: Ken Schrader – 177.352 mph
Lap Leaders: Ken Schrader 1-6, Mark Martin 7, Schrader 8-30, Martin 31-43, Geoff Bodine 44-47, Morgan Shepherd 48-52, G.Bodine 53, Ernie Irvan 54, G.Bodine 55-57, Irvan 58, G.Bodine 59, Irvan 60-61, G.Bodine 62-71, Irvan 72-90, Martin 91-97, Dale Earnhardt 98-135, Rich Bickle 136, Earnhardt 137-147, Irvan 148-156, Earnhardt 157-220, Jeff Gordon 221-223, Dale Jarrett 224-292, Bobby Labonte 293-295, Jarrett 296-333, Martin 334, B.Labonte 335, Jarrett 336-342, Schrader 343-351, Irvan 352-361, Earnhardt 362-400.
29 lead changes among 10 drivers.
Cautions: 7 for 33 laps — Margin of Victory: 3.73 seconds
*Relieved by Derrike Cope

Many observers felt the penalty could have been the result of incidents in prior races in which Earnhardt did not draw any penalties.

Earnhardt was able to make the lap up when Rusty Wallace spun in the 350th lap.

It took only eight laps of green flag racing for Earnhardt to come from the rear to snatch the lead from Ernie Irvan, who complained that Earnhardt had roughed him up in the decisive pass.

Earnhardt led the final 39 laps and finished 3.73

CMS

Greg Sacks #68 spins in front of Dale Earnhardt in Charlotte's Coca-Cola 600.

seconds in front of rookie Jeff Gordon as the sun was setting over the 1.5-mile track. Jarrett finished third, Ken Schrader was fourth and Irvan fell to fifth.

Chevrolets swept the first five positions – the first time one make of car had finished 1-2-3-4-5 since Buick swept the top five positions at Atlanta in 1982.

"It was really satisfying to win this race after getting penalized," said Earnhardt, who increased his lead in the Winston Cup standings to 129 points over Wallace.

Earnhardt had fallen a lap down earlier in the race when he made a routine pit stop for fuel and tires. The caution came out a few laps later, leaving Dale Jarrett and rookie Bobby Labonte with a healthy advantage. But Earnhardt sped back into the lead lap within a few laps.

Mark Martin offered a stout challenge, but the engine in his Roush Racing Ford blew late in the race. Wallace wound up in 29th place after parking his Pontiac with suspension problems after his second spin. "When I spun the second time, I took a hard shot," said Wallace. "My wrist hurts like hell, but it'll be okay."

Race #12

Earnhardt Hikes Point Lead With Dover Downs Victory

DOVER, DE (June 6) – Dale Earnhardt staved off a fast closing Dale Jarrett in the final laps and won the Budweiser 500 at Dover Downs International Speedway for his second win in a row. His victory, the 56th of his career, made him an overwhelming favorite to capture his sixth Winston Cup title as he left Dover with a 209 point lead over Rusty Wallace.

Earnhardt led all but one of the final 154 laps and outran Jarrett by 0.38-second. Davey Allison finished third with Mark Martin fourth and Ken Schrader fifth.

Wallace was one of the victims in a crash-strewn affair on the high-banked one-mile oval. While battling Martin for second place on lap 426, Martin lost traction for an instant and banged into Wallace. Wallace slammed into the fourth turn wall, knocking him out of the race. Geoff Bodine and Jimmy Hensley got tangled up behind Wallace and also wrecked. Ironically, Hensley drives the Ford which Bodine recently purchased from the Alan Kulwicki estate.

Dover Downs

Bobby Hamilton #38 finished 10th at Dover in the debut of the Akins-Sutton racing team.

Dover Downs

Eventual winner Dale Earnhardt wipes his windshield clear during caution laps at Dover.

"I thought it would be me and Rusty battling down to the wire," said Earnhardt. "I hated to see him go out because he's had a lot of tough luck lately. But I'm going to get all the points I can while the getting is good. I want a cushion in case of bad luck later on. We're not counting our chickens yet, but we're getting the hen house cleaned up."

Wallace shook off the effects of the crash. "I didn't get hurt and the wrist is fine," he said. "Mark got under me and wrecked me. I don't know what he did, but he drove up beside me and into the wall I went. It was a heck of a wallop."

Martin, who continued after the scrape, accepted blame for the crash. "I got loose, got into Rusty and took him out. I'm disappointed for the both of us. We both had a shot at winning," said Martin.

Dover Downs

Sterling Marlin's Ford was brought back to Dover's garage on the hook.

The Wallace-Martin crash was just one of a dozen. A total of 78 laps were run under the 14 caution flags.

Some of the wrecks occurred before the race got started. Ernie Irvan won the pole but crashed in a late Saturday practice session. He was forced to bring in a back-up car and start at the rear.

Irvan worked his way up to the lead by the 120th lap, but less than 15 miles later, the engine in his Morgan-McClure Chevrolet started sputtering. He left the race after 153 laps with a blown engine.

Of the 17 cars that failed to finish, 12 of them crashed. Greg Sacks brought out the first yellow flag when he crashed before 20 miles had been completed. Others who went out in wrecks included Dave Marcis, who led for eight laps in the early going, Ricky Rudd, P.J. Jones, Sterling Marlin, Derrike Cope, Kyle Petty and Darrell Waltrip.

Waltrip's demise came in the 418th lap when he and Jeff Gordon tangled. Gordon had been involved in a crash earlier and was cruising the lower groove at reduced speed. "There was a certain rookie who blasted my brother for not getting out of the way at Darlington," said a steamed Waltrip. "Evidently, he didn't learn his own lesson very well. He didn't show me very much respect."

Gordon said he was hugging the low groove and the contact was not his fault. "I'll give him this tape to replay," said Gordon, waving a TV tape of the incident from his in-car camera. "He just misjudged the situation. I was on the white line and couldn't go any lower."

Winston Cup Series Race No. 12
500 Laps at Dover Downs Int'l Speedway
Dover, DE
"Budweiser 500"
500 Miles on 1-mile Superspeedway
June 6, 1993

Fin	St	No.	Driver	Team / Car	Laps	Money	Status
1	8	3	Dale Earnhardt	RCR Enterprises Chevrolet	500	$68,030	Running
2	29	18	Dale Jarrett	Joe Gibbs Chevrolet	500	42,435	Running
3	3	28	Davey Allison	Robert Yates Racing Ford	500	38,240	Running
4	9	6	Mark Martin	Roush Racing Ford	500	28,100	Running
5	12	25	Ken Schrader	Hendrick Motorsports Chevy	500	25,330	Running
6	23	1	Rick Mast	Precision Products Ford	500	20,700	Running
7	13	33	Harry Gant	Leo Jackson Chevrolet	499	21,650	Running
8	20	12	Jimmy Spencer	Bobby Allison Ford	499	18,050	Running
9	16	21	Morgan Shepherd	Wood Brothers Ford	498	17,300	Running
10	33	38	Bobby Hamilton	Akins-Sutton Ford	495	13,200	Running
11	5	44	Rick Wilson	Petty Enterprises Pontiac	495	13,050	Running
12	32	16	Wally Dallenbach,Jr.	Roush Racing Ford	491	15,450	Running
13	35	40	Kenny Wallace	SABCo Racing Pontiac	490	12,950	Running
14	25	55	Ted Musgrave	RaDiUs Motorsports Ford	488	14,350	Running
15	37	27	Hut Stricklin	Junior Johnson Ford	486	14,200	Running
16	2	26	Brett Bodine	King Motorsports Ford	459	14,150	Running
17	24	11	Bill Elliott	Junior Johnson Ford	448	18,950	Running
18	21	24	Jeff Gordon	Hendrick Motorsports Chevy	440	11,485	Running
19	19	22	Bobby Labonte	Bill David Racing Ford	439	10,300	Running
20	26	14	Terry Labonte	Billy Hagan Chevrolet	429	13,550	Running
21	4	2	Rusty Wallace	Roger Penske Pontiac	425	17,450	Crash
22	11	7	Jimmy Hensley	AK - G.E.B. Racing Ford	422	17,800	Crash
23	10	15	Geoff Bodine	Bud Moore Eng. Ford	415	16,350	Crash
24	28	17	Darrell Waltrip	DarWal Chevrolet	414	17,950	Crash
25	30	90	Bobby Hillin,Jr.	Junie Donlavey Ford	402	8,100	Running
26	38	52	Jimmy Means	Means Racing Ford	372	8,050	Engine
27	31	30	Michael Waltrip	Bahari Racing Pontiac	370	12,600	Engine
28	34	75	Dick Trickle	Butch Mock Ford	319	7,950	Engine
29	7	42	Kyle Petty	SabCo Racing Pontiac	243	15,900	Crash
30	17	83	Lake Speed	Speed Ford	238	7,850	Engine
31	6	98	Derrike Cope	Cale Yarborough Ford	206	12,375	Crash
32	1	4	Ernie Irvan	Morgan-McClure Chevrolet	153	22,840	Engine
33	22	8	Sterling Marlin	Stavola Brothers Ford	145	12,240	Crash
34	36	9	P.J.Jones	Melling Performance Ford	130	7,640	Crash
35	15	5	Ricky Rudd	Hendrick Motorsports Chevy	121	12,115	Crash
36	18	71	Dave Marcis	Marcis Auto Racing Chevy	110	7,565	Crash
37	14	41	Phil Parsons	Larry Hedrick Chevrolet	104	9,065	Crash
38	27	68	Greg Sacks	Tri-Star Motorsports Ford	18	7,565	Crash

Time of Race: 4 hours, 44 minutes, 6 seconds
Average Speed: 105.600 mph
Pole Winner: Ernie Irvan – 151.541 mph
Lap Leaders: Davey Allison 1-3, Brett Bodine 4-24, Dave Marcis 25-32, Dale Earnhardt 33-68, Mark Martin 69-72, B.Bodine 73-102, Kyle Petty 103-107, Martin 108-119, Ernie Irvan 120-132, Martin 133-137, Earnhardt 138-148, Bobby Labonte 149-157, Allison 158-211, Rusty Wallace 212-286, Allison 287-298, R.Wallace 299-305, Ken Schrader 306-307, Michael Waltrip 308-314, Earnhardt 315-337, Martin 338-340, Earnhardt 341-343, Rick Mast 344-346, Earnhardt 347-436, Martin 437, Earnhardt 438-500.
25 lead changes among 12 drivers.
Cautions: 14 for 78 laps Margin of Victory: 0.38 second

Dover Downs

Derrike Cope skids into Dover's fourth turn wall.

Race #13

Kyle Dominates Pocono; Tipsy Spectator Startles Racers

LONG POND, PA (June 13) – Kyle Petty led 148 of the 200 laps and thoroughly dominated the Champion Spark Plug 500 at Pocono International Raceway for his first win of the season.

Petty took the lead from Sterling Marlin with 16 laps to go and outran runner-up Ken Schrader by 5.08 seconds to take his seventh career Winston Cup victory.

Harry Gant finished a solid third and Jimmy Spencer was fourth. Ted Musgrave made up a lap in the late going and wound up fifth in a strong run.

Petty, who had been on a cross-country motorcycle trip, carried his own video-tape machine to Victory Lane.

The 500-mile race was relatively incident-free. Only Jeff Gordon's trip into the wall early in the race was the only crash. But there was another incident in the 108th lap that left many of the racers startled.

A spectator, 25 year-old Chad Blaine Kohl, leaped over a six foot fence that separates an infield camping

Pocono Int'l

Jeff Gordon's Chevrolet loses its grip in Pocono's third turn.

area from the 2.5-mile triangular track, and ran across the racing surface. Leaders Petty and Davey Allison were approaching rapidly, and the slightly tipsy Kohl dived over the outside retaining barrier.

"I came around the first turn and couldn't believe what I saw," said Petty. "Ever seen a deer frozen in its tracks by headlights? That pretty much describes what he looked like."

Allison radioed to his crew, "Guys, you ain't gonna believe this...there's some nut standing out here on the race track."

Allison continued, "I saw the stupid nut standing there in front of Kyle. He's lucky he's not dead. I never believed anybody could be that dumb."

Authorities said Kohl had told them that he had been drinking beer since 3 a.m. He was arrested on two felony charges and four misdemeanor counts and was held on $20,000 bond.

Allison finished sixth as 11 cars finished the entire 200 laps. He was able to move into second place in the standings as Dale Earnhardt stretched his advantage to 225 points. Rusty Wallace went only four laps before the engine blew in his Pontiac, placing him 39th in the field of 40. He fell to fifth place in the standings, 298 points behind Earnhardt. It will be all but impossible for Wallace to challenge for the Winston Cup title unless Earnhardt falls out of four or five races.

The only doubt cast in Petty's runaway victory was a late caution period which permitted the pack of cars to close the gap. Four cars elected to stay on the track and assume good track position. Morgan Shepherd led during the yellow flag, but Marlin raced past with 21 laps to go.

Marlin held his Ford on the point for five laps before Petty sailed past.

Earnhardt, who led 20 of the first 23 laps, had lost a

Pocono Int'l

Dale Earnhardt at the head of the line at Pocono in what appears to be a 35-car draft.

lap when his crew had to fix an oil leak. He was on the tail end of the lead lap on the final restart when the pack of cars whipped into the first turn.

Earnhardt punched Rick Wilson in the rear, pushing Wilson into the back of Rick Mast's car. Mast spun into the infield. It would have been a golden opportunity for Earnhardt to catch up, but the yellow flag never came. Mast fell from 11th to 16th as a result of the spin.

Trevor Boys, making a return to racing in James Hylton's lightly regarded Pontiac, led the 25th lap under yellow. "Wonder what NASCAR thinks of us leading the race," queried car owner Hylton. "I think the independents are making a comeback."

Boys authored a feat that Bill Elliott has yet to do in the 1993 season – and that is lead a lap. Elliott, who finished 10th, has yet to lead a lap this year.

Winston Cup Series Race No. 13
200 Laps at Pocono Int'l Raceway
Pocono, PA
"Champion Spark Plug 500"
500 Miles on 2.5-mile Superspeedway
June 13, 1993

Fin	St	No.	Driver	Team / Car	Laps	Money	Status
1	8	42	Kyle Petty	SabCo Racing Pontiac	200	$44,960	Running
2	1	25	Ken Schrader	Hendrick Motorsports Chevy	200	58,435	Running
3	26	33	Harry Gant	Leo Jackson Chevrolet	200	38,335	Running
4	9	12	Jimmy Spencer	Bobby Allison Ford	200	31,410	Running
5	15	55	Ted Musgrave	RaDiUs Motorsports Ford	200	24,040	Running
6	7	28	Davey Allison	Robert Yates Racing Ford	200	24,115	Running
7	25	21	Morgan Shepherd	Wood Brothers Ford	200	17,165	Running
8	32	8	Sterling Marlin	Stavola Brothers Ford	200	16,365	Running
9	12	5	Ricky Rudd	Hendrick Motorsports Chevy	200	15,765	Running
10	16	11	Bill Elliott	Junior Johnson Ford	200	22,015	Running
11	5	3	Dale Earnhardt	RCR Enterprises Chevrolet	200	14,815	Running
12	22	44	Rick Wilson	Petty Enterprises Pontiac	199	11,365	Running
13	3	27	Hut Stricklin	Junior Johnson Ford	199	13,865	Running
14	28	41	Phil Parsons	Larry Hedrick Chevrolet	199	10,465	Running
15	31	40	Kenny Wallace	SabCo Racing Pontiac	199	11,615	Running
16	13	1	Rick Mast	Precision Products Ford	199	13,015	Running
17	18	7	Jimmy Hensley	AK - G.E.B. Racing Ford	199	17,465	Running
18	29	68	Greg Sacks	Tri-Star Motorsports Ford	198	7,965	Running
19	21	18	Dale Jarrett	Joe Gibbs Chevrolet	195	15,815	Running
20	23	22	Bobby Labonte	Bill Davis Racing Ford	194	10,490	Running
21	27	30	Michael Waltrip	Bahari Racing Pontiac	190	12,060	Running
22	37	52	Jimmy Means	Means Racing Ford	188	7,310	Running
23	33	71	Dave Marcis	Marcis Auto Racing Chevy	180	8,210	Engine
24	14	15	Geoff Bodine	Bud Moore Eng. Ford	173	15,160	Axle
25	20	16	Wally Dallenbach,Jr.	Roush Racing Ford	150	11,710	Trans
26	38	29	Kerry Teague	Linro Motorsports Chevrolet	135	7,060	Engine
27	11	83	Lake Speed	Speed Ford	127	7,010	Rock Arm
28	4	24	Jeff Gordon	Hendrick Motorsports Chevy	113	8,535	Running
29	6	26	Brett Bodine	King Motorsports Ford	109	11,460	T Chain
30	34	17	Darrell Waltrip	DarWal Chevrolet	89	16,660	Engine
31	2	6	Mark Martin	Roush Racing Ford	85	14,810	Engine
32	30	14	Terry Labonte	Billy Hagan Chevrolet	83	11,285	Engine
33	24	98	Derrike Cope	Cale Yarborough Ford	62	11,660	Clutch
34	17	4	Ernie Irvan	Morgan-McClure Chevrolet	58	16,185	Engine
35	39	48	Trevor Boys	Hylton Eng. Pontiac	38	6,510	Vibration
36	35	75	Dick Trickle	Butch Mock Ford	17	6,435	Engine
37	36	32	Jimmy Horton	Active Racing Chevrolet	16	6,360	Engine
38	19	90	Bobby Hillin,Jr.	Junie Donlavey Ford	4	6,320	Engine
39	10	2	Rusty Wallace	Roger Penske Pontiac	4	14,285	Engine
40	40	53	Graham Taylor	Means Racing Ford	3	6,210	Quit

Time of Race: 3 hours, 37 minutes, 23 seconds
Average Speed: 138.005 mph
Pole Winner: Ken Schrader – 162.816 mph
Lap Leaders: Mark Martin 1, Ken Schrader 2-3, Dale Earnhardt 4-23, Jimmy Means 24, Trevor Boys 25, Ted Musgrave 26, Kyle Petty 27-28, Martin 29-34, K.Petty 35-58, Dale Jarrett 59, Ricky Rudd 60, K.Petty 61-109, Davey Allison 110-115, K.Petty 116-142, Harry Gant 143, Schrader 144-145, K.Petty 146-171, Gant 172, K.Petty 173-176, Morgan Shepherd 177-179, Sterling Marlin 180-184, K.Petty 185-200.
22 lead changes among 13 drivers.
Cautions: 6 for 24 laps Margin of Victory: 5.08 seconds

Greg Crisp

Kyle Petty with winning trophy following Pocono race.

Race #14

Martin Dominates Michigan But Hendrick Cars Run 1-2

BROOKLYN, MI (June 20) – Ricky Rudd took the lead with nine laps remaining when leader Mark Martin ran out of gas and cruised to victory in the Miller Genuine Draft 400 at Michigan International Speedway.

The victory was Rudd's 14th on NASCAR's major league stock car racing tour and he has won at least once in each of the last 11 years.

Jeff Gordon finished 1.74 seconds behind Rudd as Hendrick Motorsports Chevrolets ran 1-2. Chevrolets also took the next two spots with Ernie Irvan placing third and Dale Jarrett fourth. Rusty Wallace's Pontiac took fifth spot.

Rudd led three times for 19 laps, but was not a factor until the end of the race. Martin, who led 141 of the 200 laps, had run away from the field. Five caution flags couldn't even keep the challengers close to the Roush Racing Ford.

However, Martin and many of the teams could forecast the factors which would decide the outcome. The final 198 miles were run without a caution flag and when Martin pitted with 110 miles to go, it was doubtful he could make it the rest of the way without an additional stop for fuel.

Rudd made his final pit stop with 100 miles to go, and it was evident he would try to make it

Martin's fuel tank ran dry while holding a commanding lead of over 10 seconds. He turned the lead over to

Ricky Rudd saddled up before the Michigan 400.

Rudd, who led the rest of the way.

Martin could finish no better than sixth as 12 cars completed the full 400 miles.

Morgan Shepherd had been running second, but he pitted with 12 laps left. He got back on the track and

Winston Cup Series Race No. 14
200 Laps at Michigan Int'l Speedway
Brooklyn, MI
"Miller Genuine Draft 400"
400 Miles on 2-mile Superspeedway
June 20, 1993

Fin	St	No.	Driver	Team / Car	Laps	Money	Status
1	2	5	Ricky Rudd	Hendrick Motorsports Chevy	200	$77,890	Running
2	23	24	Jeff Gordon	Hendrick Motorsports Chevy	200	44,915	Running
3	5	4	Ernie Irvan	Morgan-McClure Chevrolet	200	41,240	Running
4	17	18	Dale Jarrett	Joe Gibbs Chevrolet	200	29,590	Running
5	15	2	Rusty Wallace	Roger Penske Pontiac	200	26,160	Running
6	7	6	Mark Martin	Roush Racing Ford	200	22,925	Running
7	13	21	Morgan Shepherd	Wood Brothers Ford	200	21,460	Running
8	12	8	Sterling Marlin	Stavola Brothers Ford	200	20,860	Running
9	11	11	Bill Elliott	Junior Johnson Ford	200	23,710	Running
10	37	33	Harry Gant	Leo Jackson Chevrolet	200	23,960	Running
11	9	1	Rick Mast	Precision Products Ford	200	17,960	Running
12	29	42	Kyle Petty	SabCo Racing Pontiac	200	19,660	Running
13	28	41	Phil Parsons	Larry Hedrick Chevrolet	199	13,935	Out of Ga
14	6	3	Dale Earnhardt	RCR Enterprises Chevrolet	199	16,385	Running
15	32	55	Ted Musgrave	RaDiUs Motorsports Ford	199	16,235	Running
16	4	25	Ken Schrader	Hendrick Motorsports Chevy	199	15,460	Running
17	18	15	Geoff Bodine	Bud Moore Eng. Ford	199	17,685	Running
18	21	12	Jimmy Spencer	Bobby Allison Ford	199	14,950	Running
19	14	17	Darrell Waltrip	DarWal Chevrolet	199	19,035	Running
20	25	14	Terry Labonte	Billy Hagan Chevrolet	198	14,470	Running
21	16	27	Hut Stricklin	Junior Johnson Ford	198	13,650	Running
22	34	68	Greg Sacks	Tri-Star Motorsports Ford	198	8,685	Running
23	26	7	Jimmy Hensley	AK - G.E.B. Racing Ford	197	17,975	Running
24	36	71	Dave Marcis	Marcis Auto Racing Chevy	197	8,465	Running
25	27	16	Wally Dallenbach,Jr.	Roush Racing Ford	197	13,105	Running
26	39	39	Jim Sauter	Gary Roulo Chevrolet	197	8,195	Running
27	30	98	Derrike Cope	Cale Yarborough Ford	197	12,785	Running
28	41	52	Jimmy Means	Means Racing Ford	197	8,075	Running
29	33	40	Kenny Wallace	SabCo Racing Pontiac	196	9,965	Running
30	8	83	Lake Speed	Speed Ford	190	7,900	Engine
31	35	75	Dick Trickle	Butch Mock Ford	185	7,770	Engine
32	40	36	H.B.Bailey	Bailey Pontiac	184	7,700	Running
33	31	90	Bobby Hillin,Jr.	Junie Donlavey Ford	171	7,20	Engine
34	24	44	Rick Wilson	Petty Enterprises Pontiac	144	9,125	Oil Leak
35	3	28	Davey Allison	Robert Yates Racing Ford	132	18,900	Running
36	19	22	Bobby Labonte	Bill Davis Ford	104	8,985	Engine
37	10	30	Michael Waltrip	BAHARI Racing Pontiac	91	11,930	Valve
38	22	9	P.J.Jones	Melling Performance Ford	64	7,380	H Gasket
39	1	26	Brett Bodine	King Motorsports Ford	22	15,855	Engine
40	38	62	Clay Young	Henley Gray Ford	14	7,295	Cylinder
41	20	32	Jimmy Horton	Active Racing Chevrolet	2	7,295	Crash

Time of Race: 2 hours, 41 minutes, 38 seconds
Average Speed: 148.484 mph
Pole Winner: Brett Bodine – 175.456 mph
Lap Leaders: Ricky Rudd 1-9, Dale Earnhardt 10-12, Mark Martin 13-21, Ernie Irvan 22-24, Earnhardt 25-48, Martin 49-66, Greg Sacks 67, Martin 68-98, Hut Stricklin 99-101, Martin 102-144, Morgan Shepherd 145-146, Irvan 147-148, Rudd 149, Jeff Gordon 150-151, Martin 152-191, Rudd 192-200.
16 lead changes among 8 drivers.
Cautions: 5 for 20 laps Margin of Victory: 1.74 seconds

Quick pit work helped Jeff Gordon finish second at Michigan.

MIS

Pole sitter Brett Bodine #26 and Ricky Rudd lead the charge into Michigan's first turn.

wound up in seventh place.

"It was pretty evident that I wasn't going to outrun the 6 car (Martin)," said Rudd. "It was his race to win or lose. We were able to go further on fuel and that's why we're here (Victory Lane)."

Martin, who was involved in a controversial on-track tussle with Dale Earnhardt on Saturday, said he was "a little irritated right now, but I'll be fine in five minutes. At least we were running good. It would have been worse if we had not run well and run out of gas."

Earnhardt fell a lap off the pace with handling problems, plus an extra pit stop contributed to his 14th place finish. He still wound up increasing his lead in the Winston Cup standings to 213 points over Dale Jarrett.

Davey Allison, who had entered the race second place in the standings, fell to sixth when he was spun into the wall by Rick Wilson. "It was early in the race and he just drove up beside me and spun me out," said a ruffled Allison. "It was foolish for him to do that. He was a lap down."

The Martin-Earnhardt episode in a practice session on Saturday caused minimal damage to both cars, but caused a disturbance and brought a stern warning from Martin.

Earnhardt and Martin were wheel-to-wheel when Earnhardt's car broke loose and skidded into Martin.

"He hasn't seen the last of me," a disturbed Martin said after climbing out of his car. "He's racing for a championship. I haven't got a chance (463 points behind) at the championship. And I can tear up as many cars as I need to.

"I'm not going to stop racing him," he added. "Not in practice, not anytime. Even if it means we have to fix more cars. As to what happened, you'll have to ask the man in black."

Earnhardt slid into the side of Martin rather than easing off the throttle when another car loomed in his path. "Yea, it was my fault," said Earnhardt. "It wasn't intentional. Me and Mark were both out there running hard trying to get our cars ready for the race."

Race #15

Schrader Suspension Lifted; Earnhardt Wins Pepsi 400

DAYTONA BEACH, FL (July 3) – Dale Earnhardt repelled a late challenge from Ken Schrader and emerged victorious in the Pepsi 400 at Daytona International Speedway. The close win put the five-time national champion 251 points ahead in the Winston Cup standings.

Schrader's Hendrick Motorsports Chevrolet was nabbed with a serious illegal carburetor gadget – "a definite, intentional way of bypassing the (carburetor) plate" according to Technical Inspector Gary Nelson – which automatically carried a four-race suspension for car owner and driver. Joe Hendrick, father of Rick Hendrick, is the owner-of-record.

Hendrick Motorsports appealed the ruling and asked for an appeal. The appeal could not be arranged before the holiday weekend, NASCAR said, so Schrader was allowed to race.

He was forced to start in the rear, but charged into

ISC

Jimmy Hensley loops his Ford as rookies Kenny Wallace #40 and Jeff Gordon #24 narrowly avoid contact.

contention before the half-way point. Earnhardt led most of the way – leading for 110 of the 160 laps.

Earnhardt raced past Schrader in the 132nd lap and led the rest of the way. Entering the final lap, Earnhardt led a freight-train of 10 cars.

"My car was pushing a little bit the last two laps," said Earnhardt. "I almost lost it in front of the whole field. I thought we were going to have a heck of a wreck."

Schrader made his stab to make the pass for the lead, but Earnhardt swerved in front of Schrader, pushing him into the wall. "I stuck my nose in there and he kind of wiped it for me," said a distraught Schrader, who has not won a Winston Cup race in over two years. "I got up there and he cut over and we bumped. That let Sterling (Marlin) get beside me, and after that it was all over."

Earnhardt, who won for the 20th time at Daytona, defended his last lap actions. "I swerved to the left and Schrader went to the right. When I swerved back, it pinched him into the wall. I'm still hungry and eager. The fire is hotter than ever, and I'm determined to win races," he said.

Marlin notched his ninth career runner-up finish without having won a race. He was 0.16-second behind Earnhardt when the checkered flag fell.

Schrader took third spot with Ricky Rudd and Jeff Gordon fourth and fifth.

Although whipped by the heat and humidity, Earnhardt was joking about Schrader's pending appeal and possible suspension. "I was glad to see him run good because he needed to get all he can before he goes on vacation."

Marlin almost gave the Stavola Brothers their first win since Bobby Allison

Brian Czobat

Phil Parsons #41 and Bobby Hamilton #20 run side-by-side as Geoff Bodine looks for an opening.

won the 1988 Daytona 500. "I had the momentum to pass Earnhardt on the last lap," said Marlin, "but if I'd have tried it, I'd have ended up in the pond (Lake Lloyd). He cut me off and there wasn't anywhere to go except in the grass. I was hoping Schrader would spin Earnhardt out so I could go on by. I knew if that didn't happen, Earnhardt's car would get awful wide."

Marlin had been in good shape to win until a caution flew for Ritchie Petty's stalled car on lap 122. He and Rudd had pulled out to a nine second advantage over Earnhardt's ill-handling car.

The RCR Enterprises crew made quick adjustments during the slowdown. "We were off that one time," said Earnhardt, "but we got it fixed and it ran good the rest of the way."

Rusty Wallace fell 345 points behind Earnhardt in the Winston Cup title chase by finishing a disappointing 18th.

Winston Cup Series Race No. 15
160 Laps at Daytona Int'l Speedway
Daytona Beach, FL
"Pepsi 400"
400 Miles on 2.5-mile Superspeedway
July 3, 1993

Fin	St	No.	Driver	Team / Car	Laps	Money	Status
1	5	3	Dale Earnhardt	RCR Enterprises Chevrolet	160	$75,940	Running
2	22	8	Sterling Marlin	Stavola Brothers Ford	160	46,000	Running
3	41	25	Ken Schrader	Hendrick Motorsports Chevy	160	37,125	Running
4	10	5	Ricky Rudd	Hendrick Motorsports Chevy	160	28,250	Running
5	27	24	Jeff Gordon	Hendrick Motorsports Chevy	160	24,625	Running
6	18	6	Mark Martin	Roush Racing Ford	160	23,550	Running
7	1	4	Ernie Irvan	Morgan-McClure Chevrolet	160	29,100	Running
8	13	18	Dale Jarrett	Joe Gibbs Chevrolet	160	21,150	Running
9	31	14	Terry Labonte	Billy Hagan Chevrolet	160	18,050	Running
10	14	55	Ted Musgrave	RaDiUs Motorsports Ford	160	19,500	Running
11	9	44	Rick Wilson	Petty Enterprises Pontiac	160	15,490	Running
12	25	90	Bobby Hillin,Jr.	Junie Donlavey Ford	160	10,260	Running
13	8	17	Darrell Waltrip	DarWal Chevrolet	160	19,770	Running
14	20	21	Morgan Shepherd	Wood Brothers Ford	160	14,930	Running
15	23	68	Greg Sacks	Tri-Star Motorsports Ford	160	9,940	Running
16	12	1	Rick Mast	Precision Products Ford	160	14,300	Running
17	30	20	Bobby Hamilton	Dick Moroso Ford	160	9,085	Running
18	17	2	Rusty Wallace	Roger Penske Pontiac	160	16,870	Running
19	16	26	Brett Bodine	King Motorsports Ford	160	13,555	Running
20	6	11	Bill Elliott	Junior Johnson Ford	159	19,140	Running
21	7	33	Harry Gant	Leo Jackson Chevrolet	159	17,170	Running
22	4	30	Michael Waltrip	Bahari Racing Pontiac	159	12,900	Running
23	33	51	Jeff Purvis	James Finch Chevrolet	159	7,880	Running
24	4	98	Derrike Cope	Cale Yarborough Ford	158	13,010	Running
25	35	41	Phil Parsons	Larry Hedrick Chevrolet	158	9,290	Running
26	38	75	Dick Trickle	Butch Mock Ford	158	7,470	Running
27	24	71	Dave Marcis	Marcis Auto Racing Chevy	158	7,325	Running
28	32	40	Kenny Wallace	SabCo Racing Pontiac	157	9,305	Running
29	40	37	Loy Allen,Jr.	Loy Allen Ford	157	7,110	Running
30	36	9	P.J.Jones	Melling Performance Ford	157	7,515	Running
31	3	28	Davey Allison	Robert Yates Racing Ford	149	17,810	Running
32	37	53	Ritchie Petty	Maurice Petty Ford	114	6,930	Ignition
33	2	42	Kyle Petty	SabCo Racing Pontiac	105	15,900	Fatigue
34	19	7	Jimmy Hensley*	AK - G.E.B. Racing Ford	59	17,270	Crash
35	29	16	Wally Dallenbach,Jr.	Roush Racing Ford	55	11,415	Engine
36	34	52	Jimmy Means	Means Racing Ford	37	6,810	Engine
37	21	15	Geoff Bodine	Bud Moore Eng. Ford	30	14,780	Engine
38	39	32	Jimmy Horton	Active Racing Chevrolet	22	6,765	Crash
39	28	12	Jimmy Spencer	Bobby Allison Ford	21	11,305	Crash
40	15	27	Hut Stricklin	Junior Johnson Ford	21	11,240	Crash
41	26	22	Bobby Labonte	Bill Davis Ford	21	8,215	Crash

Time of Race: 2 hours, 38 minutes, 9 seconds
Average Speed: 151.755 mph
Pole Winner: Ernie Irvan – 190.327 mph
Lap Leaders: Ernie Irvan 1-4, Dale Earnhardt 5-8, Kyle Petty 9, Earnhardt 10-23, Dave Marcis 24, Derrike Cope 25-26, Earnhardt 27-36, Cope 37-39, Earnhardt 40-59, Jeff Gordon 60-62, Earnhardt 63, Ken Schrader 64, Earnhardt 65, Dale Jarrett 66-68, Schrader 69, Earnhardt 70-75, Ricky Rudd 76, Earnhardt 77-92, Schrader 93, Earnhardt 94-99, Sterling Marlin 100-109, Darrell Waltrip 110-111, Brett Bodine 112, Marlin 113-122, Mark Martin 123-126, Irvan 127, Earnhardt 128-130, Schrader 131, Earnhardt 132-160.
28 lead changes among 13 drivers.
Cautions: 6 for 22 laps Margin of Victory: 0.16 seconds
*Relieved by Geoff Bodine

Brian Czobat

Sterling Marlin #8, Rusty Wallace and Bill Elliott #11 run three-abreast through Daytona's tri-oval.

Race #16

Wallace Wins New Hampshire Inaugural; Davey 3rd in Final Race

LOUDON, NH (July 11) – Rusty Wallace used snappy pit service to take the lead in the waning stages and won the inaugural Slick 50 300 at the New Hampshire International Speedway. A crowd of 66,000 packed the 1.058-mile facility as promoter Bob Bahre brought NASCAR Winston Cup racing to New England for the first time since 1970.

Wallace took advantage of the sixth and final caution flag to erase a six second deficit. During the pit stops under the slowdown, Wallace's Roger Penske pit crew got him out in 17.1 seconds and he took the lead with 30 laps to go.

Wallace stretched his lead in the final 27 green flag laps and beat runner-up Mark Martin by 1.31 seconds. Davey Allison, who seemed to have the race won until the final yellow, grabbed third place. Dale Jarrett

Brian Czobat

Early wreck scrambled New Hampshire field.

finished fourth and Ricky Rudd was fifth.

Dale Earnhardt struggled to finish 26th and lost 80 points to Jarrett, who now trails by 171 points. Wallace moved back into third place, 250 points off the top.

"We've been in a bit of a slump, which started at Talladega," said Wallace. "My rhythm got broke at Talladega. Lately we've been taking one step forward and two steps back. And when you're on a roll, this thing can turn around on you. We're not giving up on the Winston Cup championship. Alan (Kulwicki) came from 278 points down last year, so I believe we can catch up, too."

Martin wrestled second place away from Allison in the final five laps, while Allison slipped to third. He did complain about the final yellow flag for the debris. "I sure didn't want to see that yellow," said Allison. "But there was a hub cap laying on the track and NASCAR did the right thing. They couldn't leave it there. If that thing had been run over, it could have flown up and hit somebody in the head."

Martin was driving a Ford built by the Roush crew in two weeks. "I tested up here and didn't like the car," said Martin, who started on the pole and led the first 18 laps. "They built me a new car out of sheer grit and determination. It was everything I hoped it would be. Rusty just drove his heart out and was a little better."

The race was run in near 100 degree temperatures as a sweltering heat wave strangled the northeast. Two

Kim Sanders

Davey Allison #28 chases Rusty Wallace in final laps at New Hampshire.

Busch Grand National regulars, Jeff Burton and Joe Nemechek, each made their Winston Cup debut. Burton qualified a Roush Racing Ford in sixth, while Nemechek qualified his own Chevrolet in 15th.

Burton and Ken Schrader swapped door paint in the second lap and both spun. Ernie Irvan then contacted Schrader. All went to the pits for repairs.

Schrader was eliminated in a second collision less than 10 laps later.

Burton departed after 86 laps with damage to his car and relieved Hut Stricklin, who had come down with food poisoning during the race.

Winston Cup Series Race No. 16
300 Laps at New Hampshire Int'l Speedway
Loudon, NH
"Slick 50 300"
317.4 Miles on 1.058-mile Superspeedway
July 11, 1993

Fin	St	No.	Driver	Team / Car	Laps	Money	Status
1	33	2	Rusty Wallace	Roger Penske Pontiac	300	$77,500	Running
2	1	6	Mark Martin	Roush Racing Ford	300	74,800	Running
3	7	28	Davey Allison	Robert Yates Racing Ford	300	44,725	Running
4	9	18	Dale Jarrett	Joe Gibbs Chevrolet	300	33,850	Running
5	10	5	Ricky Rudd	Hendrick Motorsports Chevy	300	25,375	Running
6	2	8	Sterling Marlin	Stavola Brothers Ford	300	25,550	Running
7	3	24	Jeff Gordon	Hendrick Motorsports Chevy	300	19,150	Running
8	19	42	Kyle Petty	SabCo Racing Pontiac	299	20,700	Running
9	18	11	Bill Elliott	Junior Johnson Ford	299	22,800	Running
10	17	22	Bobby Labonte	Bill Davis Racing Ford	299	16,350	Running
11	13	7	Jimmy Hensley	AK - G.E.B. Racing Ford	299	21,800	Running
12	27	15	Geoff Bodine	Bud Moore Eng. Ford	299	20,300	Running
13	23	26	Brett Bodine	King Motorsports Ford	299	18,100	Running
14	14	21	Morgan Shepherd	Wood Brothers Ford	298	17,900	Running
15	8	4	Ernie Irvan	Morgan-McClure Chevrolet	298	22,050	Running
16	26	1	Rick Mast	Precision Products Ford	298	17,350	Running
17	29	33	Harry Gant	Leo Jackson Chevrolet	298	20,550	Running
18	11	12	Jimmy Spencer	Bobby Allison Ford	298	16,950	Running
19	22	17	Darrell Waltrip	DarWal Chevrolet	298	21,150	Running
20	28	90	Bobby Hillin,Jr.	Junie Donlavey Ford	297	11,800	Running
21	25	40	Kenny Wallace	SabCo Racing Pontiac	297	13,150	Running
22	38	98	Derrike cope	Cale Yarborough Ford	297	16,050	Running
23	12	30	Michael Waltrip	Bahari Racing Pontiac	297	15,850	Running
24	20	55	Ted Musgrave	RaDiUs Motorsports Ford	297	15,700	Running
25	32	27	Hut Stricklin*	Junior Johnson Ford	296	15,500	Running
26	24	3	Dale Earnhardt	RCR Enterprises Chevrolet	296	15,300	Running
27	31	16	Wally Dallenbach,Jr.	Roush Racing Ford	293	15,150	Running
28	16	44	Rick Wilson	Petty Enterprises Pontiac	293	12,025	Running
29	35	85	Ken Bouchard	Thee Dixon Ford	286	10,350	Running
30	34	71	Dave Marcis	Marcis Auto Racing Chevy	283	10,250	Running
31	5	14	Terry Labonte	Billy Hagan Chevrolet	280	14,700	Engine
32	30	68	Greg Sacks	Tri-Star Motorsports Ford	280	10,050	Brakes
33	37	75	Dick Trickle	Butch Mock Ford	251	9,950	Handling
34	40	52	Jimmy Means	Means Racing Ford	138	9,850	Rear End
35	21	83	Lake Speed	Speed Ford	130	9,750	Engine
36	15	87	Joe Nemechek	NemCo Chevrolet	119	9,650	Rock Arm
37	6	0	Jeff Burton	Roush Racing Ford	86	9,550	Crash
38	4	25	Ken Schrader	Hendrick Motorsports Chevy	14	14,975	Engine
39	39	41	Phil Parsons	Larry Hedrick Chevrolet	9	10,850	Crash
40	36	65	Jerry O'Neil	Alan Aroneck Chevrolet	9	9,250	Crash

Time of Race: 2 hours, 59 minutes, 45 seconds
Average Speed: 105.947 mph
Pole Winner: Mark Martin – 126.871 mph
Lap Leaders: Mark Martin 1-18, Sterling Marlin 19-27, Martin 28-38, Marlin 39-81, Davey Allison 82-83, Jeff Gordon 84-85, Dale Jarrett 86, Allison 87-93, Marlin 94-164, Allison 165-167, Rusty Wallace 168-243, Gordon 244, Allison 245-270, R.Wallace 271-300.
13 lead changes among 6 drivers.
Cautions: 6 for 27 laps Margin of Victory: 1.31 seconds
*Relieved by Jeff Burton

Howard Hodge

Davey Allison and Ernie Irvan started in the fourth row at New Hampshire. Ironically, Irvan would take the full-time assignment in Robert Yates' Ford after Davey's tragic demise.

Earnhardt never led and fell a lap behind when his transmission locked up during a routine pit stop. By the time the problem was cleared up, Earnhardt was a lap behind.

The Kannapolis, NC Chevrolet driver diced closely with leader Sterling Marlin to get his lap back. After swapping some sheet metal, Earnhardt slid back into the lead lap.

A few moments later, Marlin nudged Earnhardt into a spin off the backstretch. The caution was not waved and Earnhardt fell further off the pace. When the race ended, he was four laps behind.

Marlin led the most laps, but the handling on his Ford went away in the late stages and he wound up sixth. He had started on the front row next to Martin.

"We were just banging around a little bit," Marlin said of his encounter with Earnhardt. "We had fun and even laughed about it when it was all over. I'm going to win one soon, and they all know it."

The third place finish would be Allison's final Winston Cup effort. The following day, he was gravely injured in a helicopter crash at the Talladega Superspeedway. Allison was flying to the track to watch Neil Bonnett test a Winston Cup car in preparation for the upcoming DieHard 500.

Race #17

Earnhardt Earns Pocono Win; Pays Tribute to Fallen Allison

Winston Cup Series Race No. 17
200 Laps at Pocono Int'l Raceway
Long Pond, PA
"Miller Genuine Draft 500"
500 Miles on 2.5-mile Superspeedway
July 18, 1993

Fin	St	No.	Driver	Team / Car	Laps	Money	Status
1	11	3	Dale Earnhardt	RCR Enterprises Chevrolet	200	$66,795	Running
2	18	2	Rusty Wallace	Roger Penske Pontiac	200	35,145	Running
3	2	11	Bill Elliott	Junior Johnson Ford	200	39,720	Running
4	8	21	Morgan Shepherd	Wood Brothers Ford	200	26,345	Running
5	10	26	Brett Bodine	King Motorsports Ford	200	25,940	Running
6	1	25	Ken Schrader	Hendrick Motorsports Chevy	200	28,040	Running
7	15	8	Sterling Marlin	Stavola Brothers Ford	200	17,765	Running
8	23	18	Dale Jarrett	Joe Gibbs Chevrolet	200	19,915	Running
9	21	33	Harry Gant	Leo Jackson Chevrolet	200	19,665	Running
10	27	17	Darrell Waltrip	DarWal Chevrolet	200	22,815	Running
11	3	5	Ricky Rudd	Hendrick Motorsports Chevy	200	15,615	Running
12	13	15	Geoff Bodine	Bud Moore Eng. Ford	200	17,565	Running
13	5	6	Mark Martin	Roush Racing Ford	200	17,365	Running
14	16	30	Michael Waltrip	Bahari Racing Pontiac	200	14,865	Running
15	7	22	Bobby Labonte	Bill Davis Racing Ford	200	12,915	Running
16	32	14	Terry Labonte	Billy Hagan Chevrolet	199	14,065	Running
17	22	16	Wally Dallenbach,Jr.	Roush Racing Ford	199	13,765	Running
18	28	41	Phil Parsons	Larry Hedrick Chevrolet	199	10,565	Running
19	34	38	Bobby Hamilton	Akins-Sutton Ford	199	8,515	Running
20	14	90	Bobby Hillin,Jr.	Junie Donlavey Ford	199	8,940	Running
21	25	44	Rick Wilson	Petty Enterprises Pontiac	198	10,015	Running
22	36	71	Dave Marcis	Marcis Auto Racing Chevy	197	8,065	Running
23	30	40	Kenny Wallace	SabCo Racing Pontiac	197	10,215	Running
24	24	12	Jimmy Spencer	Bobby Allison Ford	195	12,565	Running
25	37	85	Ken Bouchard	Thee Dixon Ford	193	7,865	Running
26	35	32	Jimmy Horton	Active Racing Chevrolet	183	7,815	Crash
27	19	42	Kyle Petty	SabCo Racing Pontiac	174	16,765	Running
28	12	27	Hut Stricklin	Junior Johnson Ford	174	12,315	Running
29	9	98	Derrike Cope	Cale Yarborough Ford	173	12,240	Rear End
30	31	75	Dick Trickle	Butch Mock Ford	171	7,615	Running
31	4	4	Ernie Irvan	Morgan-McClure Chevrolet	157	17,165	Engine
32	26	68	Greg Sacks	Tri-Star Motorsports Ford	103	7,515	Engine
33	17	55	Ted Musgrave	RaDiUs Motorsports Ford	101	11,965	Engine
34	38	29	Kerry Teague	Linro Motorsports Chevrolet	88	7,340	Crash
35	40	99	John Krebs	Diamond Ridge Chevrolet	86	7,265	Crash
36	29	1	Rick Mast	Precision Products Ford	72	11,715	Engine
37	20	24	Jeff Gordon	Hendrick Motorsports Chevy	49	9,615	Engine
38	39	62	Clay Young	Henley Gray Ford	46	7,075	Brakes
39	6	7	Jimmy Hensley	AK - G.E.B. Racing Ford	42	16,440	Engine
40	33	02	T.W.Taylor	Taylor Performance Ford	26	6,965	Clutch

Time of Race: 3 hours, 44 minutes, 59 seconds
Average Speed: 133.343 mph
Pole Winner: Ken Schrader – 162.934 mph
Lap Leaders: Ken Schrader 1-5, Ernie Irvan 6-12, Dale Earnhardt 13-21, Irvan 22, Earnhardt 23-35, Bobby Labonte 36, Michael Waltrip 37-41, Harry Gant 42-50, Darrell Waltrip 51, Kyle Petty 52-71, Dale Jarrett 72, Gant 73-75, Earnhardt 76-90, K.Petty 91-96, Earnhardt 97-104, Jarrett 105-128, Schrader 129, Geoff Bodine 130-132, Jarrett 133-143, Earnhardt 144, Jarrett 145-155, Earnhardt 156-162, Brett Bodine 163-176, Rusty Wallace 177-182, Earnhardt 183-200.
24 lead changes among 12 drivers.
Cautions: 8 for 27 laps Margin of Victory: 0.78 second

LONG POND, PA (July 18) – Dale Earnhardt regained the lead from Rusty Wallace with 18 laps to go and sped to victory in the emotionally-packed Miller Genuine Draft 500 at Pocono International Raceway. The 500-miler was the first event held since the death of Davey Allison in a helicopter crash. The Pocono event was the first Winston Cup race without an Allison in the line-up since the Nov. 2, 1975 race at Bristol, Tenn.

Greg Crisp

The American flag flew at half-staff at Pocono.

Following his 58th career Winston Cup win, Earnhardt pulled to the start-finish line where the RCR

Pocono Int'l

Dale Earnhardt drove a Polish victory lap in honor of Alan Kulwicki while waving a flag with Davey Allison's #28.

Enterprises crew came to the car and was led in prayer by mechanic David Smith. "Everyone was emotional out there," said crewman Danny "Chocolate" Myers. "I've never seen Dale Earnhardt cry until today."

The crew gave Earnhardt a large flag bearing Allison's car number. It was taken from Kyle Petty's car, which had suffered clutch problems in the 129th lap and fell from victory contention. Earnhardt waved the flag as he drove his reverse 'Polish Victory Lap' made famous by the late Alan Kulwicki.

"I was happy about winning the race, but having Davey's death on my mind made it really hard," said Earnhardt, who sat in his car to gather his thoughts before participating in the victory celebrations. "The Allison's are like a part of our family. It's been a bad year, losing Davey and Alan. I wish there was something that could be done to bring them back."

Earnhardt led 71 of the 200 laps, but lost the lead during a late caution period when Jimmy Horton hit the wall. Wallace's pit crew got him in and out of the pits quicker than anyone and he took the lead for the first time in the 177th lap. Earnhardt chased Wallace for three laps before making the decisive pass.

"I'd been outrunning Rusty, but he got better and better," said Earnhardt, who increased his lead in the Winston Cup standings to 209 points over Dale Jarrett, who wound up eighth. "He got good there at the end. I had to race him for a few laps to get by him, and doggone if he didn't race me hard."

Wallace finished second, 0.78-second behind the winner. Bill Elliott finished third, Morgan Shepherd was fourth and Brett Bodine fifth.

Greg Crisp

Bill Elliott pits the Junior Johnson Ford at Pocono. He finished third in the race.

Robert Yates, owner of the Fords that Allison drove, did not enter the race. "We can't race with tears in our eyes," said a subdued Yates.

Runner-up Wallace gave a spirited run in the final laps, but was no match for Earnhardt's Chevrolet. "We wanted to remember the Allison family today," said Wallace. "I just wish I could have been the one to make the reverse victory lap and brought out the #28 flag.

Kyle Petty, who dominated the race here in June, turned in a strong effort, leading twice for 26 laps. Clutch problems developed during a pit stop, which knocked Petty several laps off the pace. He eventually wound up in 27th place, 26 laps behind.

"I could run with Earnhardt and those guys," said Petty, "but I tore the clutch up after leaving the pits. It was simply driver error."

Ken Schrader won the pole – his fourth of the season – but his winless skid reached 26 months as he was only able to salvage a sixth place finish.

Brett Bodine appeared poised for his first career superspeedway triumph, leading from laps 163-176. But the Chemung, NY driver was foiled by a late caution. Following pit stops, Bodine lost the lead and fell to fifth at the finish. "I'm real proud of the (King Racing) team. The car worked flawlessly and we finally finished a race, and in the top five."

Winston Cup Series Race No. 18
188 Laps at Talladega Superspeedway
Talladega, AL
"DieHard 500"
500.08 Miles on 2.66-mile Superspeedway
July 25, 1993

Fin	St	No.	Driver	Team / Car	Laps	Money	Status
1	11	3	Dale Earnhardt	RCR Enterprises Chevrolet	188	$87,315	Running
2	2	4	Ernie Irvan	Morgan-McClure Chevrolet	188	53,210	Running
3	25	6	Mark Martin	Roush Racing Ford	188	40,495	Running
4	4	42	Kyle Petty	SabCo Racing Pontiac	188	31,395	Running
5	15	18	Dale Jarrett	Joe Gibbs Chevrolet	188	301,390	Running
6	7	68	Greg Sacks	Tri-Star Motorsports Ford	188	17,715	Running
7	23	21	Morgan Shepherd	Wood Brothers Ford	188	20,865	Running
8	12	33	Harry Gant	Leo Jackson Chevrolet	188	21,815	Running
9	3	26	Brett Bodine	King Motorsports Ford	188	18,085	Running
10	26	16	Wally Dallenbach,Jr.	Roush Racing Ford	188	19,665	Running
11	1	11	Bill Elliott	Junior Johnson Ford	188	25,745	Running
12	9	27	Hut Stricklin	Junior Johnson Ford	188	16,665	Running
13	29	90	Bobby Hillin,Jr.	Junie Donlavey Ford	188	10,695	Running
14	36	14	Terry Labonte	Billy Hagan Chevrolet	188	16,250	Running
15	41	22	Bobby Labonte	Bill Davis Racing Ford	188	14,350	Coasting
16	33	15	Geoff Bodine	Bud Moore Eng. Ford	188	18,065	Running
17	32	2	Rusty Wallace	Roger Penske Pontiac	188	17,900	Running
18	40	83	Lake Speed	Speed Ford	188	9,795	Running
19	38	75	Dick Trickle	Butch Mock Ford	187	9,615	Running
20	13	30	Michael Waltrip	Bahari Racing Pontiac	187	15,425	Running
21	30	51	Jeff Purvis	James Finch Chevrolet	187	9,195	Running
22	37	41	Phil Parsons	Larry Hedrick Chevrolet	187	11,265	Running
23	10	44	Rick Wilson	Petty Enterprises Pontiac	186	10,885	Running
24	5	5	Ricky Rudd	Hendrick Motorsports Chevy	186	14,155	Running
25	17	52	Jimmy Means	Means Racing Ford	185	8,525	Running
26	18	37	Loy Allen,Jr.	Loy Allen Ford	185	8,450	Running
27	22	8	Sterling Marlin	Stavola Brothers Ford	183	13,730	Running
28	19	7	Jimmy Hensley	AK - G.E.B. Racing Ford	182	17,710	Running
29	42	71	Dave Marcis	Marcis Auto Racing Chevy	179	8,240	Running
30	27	12	Jimmy Spencer	Bobby Allison Ford	174	12,920	Running
31	8	24	Jeff Gordon	Hendrick Motorsports Chevy	148	11,250	Engine
32	28	25	Ken Schrader	Hendrick Motorsports Chevy	143	12,630	Engine
33	21	55	Ted Musgrave	RaDiUs Motorsports Ford	132	12,535	Crash
34	20	31	Neil Bonnett	RCR Enterprises Chevrolet	131	8,915	Crash
35	34	40	Kenny Wallace	SabCo Racing Pontiac	94	9,420	Handling
36	31	98	Derrike Cope	Cale Yarborough Ford	90	12,360	Engine
37	16	17	Darrell Waltrip	DarWal Chevrolet	79	17,610	Engine
38	6	1	Rick Mast	Precision Products Ford	69	12,285	Crash
39	24	32	Jimmy Horton	Active Racing Chevrolet	69	7,730	Crash
40	35	49	Stanley Smith	Smith Chevrolet	68	7,690	Crash
41	39	53	Ritchie Petty	Maurice Petty Ford	68	7,665	Crash
42	14	28	Robby Gordon	Robert Yates Racing Ford	55	17,665	Crash

Time of Race: 3 hours, 15 minutes, 1 second
Average Speed: 153.858 mph
Pole Winner: Bill Elliott – 192.397 mph
Lap Leaders: Bill Elliott 1, Ernie Irvan 2-12, Kyle Petty 13, Dale Earnhardt 14-43, Irvan 44-47, Elliott 48-49, Irvan 50-65, Ricky Rudd 66, Irvan 67, Dale Jarrett 68-70, K.Petty 71-74, Mark Martin 75-83, Jeff Gordon 84-86, Earnhardt 87-97, Morgan Shepherd 98-102, Gordon 103-105, Earnhardt 106-116, Brett Bodine 117-120, Jarrett 121-122, Gordon 123, Earnhardt 124-126, K.Petty 127-130, Irvan 131-146, K.Petty 147-155, Irvan 156-163, K.Petty 164-184, Earnhardt 185-188.
26 lead changes among 10 drives.
Cautions: 5 for 27 laps Margin of Victory: 0.005 second

Race #18

Earnhardt Edges Irvan in Brutal Talladega DieHard 500

TALLADEGA, AL (July 25) – Dale Earnhardt nipped Ernie Irvan by inches in an electrifying finish in the Talladega DieHard 500, an event which sent Alabama driver Stanley Smith to the hospital with critical head injuries.

Smith, making his first Winston Cup start since the 125-mile qualifying race at Daytona in February, was involved in a multi-car pile-up in the 70th lap which sent Jimmy Horton over the first turn wall. That untimely exit – the first time a car had left the confines of the Talladega Superspeedway – left Horton dazed and bruised but otherwise unhurt.

Smith, the 1989 NASCAR All-Pro champion, glanced off Horton's errant car and slugged the concrete wall head-on.

Others involved were Kenny Wallace, Rick Mast, Loy Allen, Jr. and Ritchie Petty.

"I was trying to get away from Kenny Wallace when I got hit," said Horton. "Anytime you get upside down, it's bad. And at 190 mph it's *real* bad. I knew I was in all sorts of trouble when I saw the dirt flying."

That was the first of two scary crashes. Neil Bonnett, ending a three-year retirement, lost control when he was racing in tight quarters with Dick Trickle and Ted Musgrave. Bonnett's RCR Enterprises Chevrolet slipped sideways and became airborne in the tri-oval. The car cleared the ground, flew over Musgrave's hood and plowed into the chain-link fence on the home-

Bobby Labonte #22 passes Rick Wilson #44 at Talladega. Labonte came from the last row to challenge for victory until he ran out of fuel in the final lap.

stretch.

Bonnett crawled out unhurt. Musgrave was also kayoed in the crash. Trickle continued.

Bonnett's crash and damage to the protective fence forced a red flag for an hour and 10 minutes. It was the first time a red flag came at the world's fastest speedway for a wreck since Bobby Allison tore down the fencing in a similar crash in 1987.

Earnhardt scooted past Kyle Petty with four laps to go and held off Irvan in a finish that thrilled the sun-baked crowd of 95,000. The official margin of victory was 0.005-second – the closest on record in motorsports history. Mark Martin finished third, Kyle Petty was fourth and Dale Jarrett fifth.

Earnhardt's sixth win of the season vaulted him to a 234 point lead over Jarrett in the Winston Cup standings. Rusty Wallace, who has rarely excelled at Talladega or Daytona, finished in 17th place, the next-to-last car on the lead lap. He fell 333 points behind Earnhardt.

The sixth win of the season for Earnhardt came in typical manner – outrunning a pack of cars in a photo finish. He allowed Petty to lead for 21 laps before the final shuffle took place. "I stayed behind Kyle for several laps," said Earnhardt after his 59th career win. "His car was a little loose and he seemed to be favoring the throttle. I thought he was holding me up, so I decided to go for the lead."

Irvan made a move on Earnhardt down the backstretch – and the two raced side-by-side from there until the finish line. "It was a see-saw battle and I took the last saw," said Earnhardt.

"I still shake my head when I see what Dale Earnhardt

Brian Czobat

There was plenty of door-to-door racing in the Talladega DieHard 500.

ISC

Neil Bonnett's return to Winston Cup racing ended in a frightening flip at Talladega.

does in a race car," said an admiring Andy Petree, who joined the RCR Enterprises team as crew chief in 1993.

Irvan said he "was surprised Dale made his move that early (with four laps to go). The last lap wasn't what I had planned, but you take the cards you're dealt. He beat me by six or seven inches, maybe a foot, but I knew he beat me. I've won some races on the last lap and I've lost some. Gotta take the good with the bad."

Bonnett was making his first start since the 1990 TranSouth 500 at Darlington. He was carrying an in-car camera for CBS and reported to the television audience via microphone that he was "going to take you for a ride and have some fun."

The fun ran out on lap 132. "I was having a good time until I heard the tires stop squealing and everything got real quiet. I took a real hard lick. I'm just sorry that I tore up Dale's toy. I don't think Richard Childress is going to let me drive another one of his cars."

Robby Gordon was assigned to drive the Robert Yates Racing Ford. After starting 14th, Gordon drifted back in the pack, but was making a strong run when he crashed in the front chute on lap 55.

Bill Elliott won the pole and led the first lap – the first time in the 1993 campaign that he has led - but he finished 11th after scraping the wall while battling with Dale Jarrett on lap 154. "My spotter told me I had cleared him," said Jarrett. "I moved over and got into Bill. I'm sorry it happened."

Bobby Labonte started in the last row, having to use a provisional spot to get in the race. But the young freshman from Texas drove like a veteran as he whipped his Bill Davis Ford as high as second. He was in the lead pack until his fuel tank ran dry on the last lap. He coasted across the finish line in 15th place. "What a heartbreaker," said Labonte. "We were right there. I'm not saying we would have won the race, but we could have given them a run. My car ran great in the draft. Our calculations had us with enough fuel to finish the race. We missed it by a half lap."

Race #19

Earnhardt-Petty Crash Opens Door For Martin's First '93 Win

WATKINS GLEN, NY (Aug. 8) – Mark Martin overcame a misfortune in the pits and roared back in the late stages to win the Budweiser At The Glen for his first win of the 1993 season.

Wally Dallenbach, Jr. enjoyed his finest moment in Winston Cup racing by finishing second, giving car owner Jack Roush his first 1-2 finish in NASCAR Winston Cup racing.

Jimmy Spencer was a close third with Bill Elliott fourth and Ken Schrader fifth.

Steve Crumbacker

Kyle Petty #42 spins in front of Dale Earnhardt near the end of the Watkins Glen race.

Brian Czobat

Ted Musgrave whips his RaDiUs Motorsports Ford through a turn at Watkins Glen.

Martin, who won $166,110 including $98,800 bonus from Unocal, started on the pole and dominated the early portion of the race. He led all but 11 of the first 52 laps, but fell deep into the pack after a lug wrench jammed during a routine pit stop. He fell to 25th place as Dale Earnhardt and Kyle Petty moved to the front. The race was shaping up as a duel to the finish until their shunt with six laps to go.

Petty had passed Earnhardt in the 76th lap of the 90-lap contest. He held his Pontiac in front by a narrow margin until he spun at the entrance to the long backstretch straightaway on lap 85. Earnhardt could not avoid the spinning Petty and hit him in the side.

Martin, who was in ninth place on a restart just three laps earlier, charged through the field and was running third when Petty and Earnhardt crashed. "I just lost it," said Petty, defending champion of the Watkins Glen event. "It was all my fault. I ran up on the curb with my right front, and Dale had no place to go. It was going to be whoever made the mistake, and I was the one who made it."

"Road course luck, I guess," explained Earnhardt, still looking for his first road course win. "I ain't suppose to win on a road course."

Earnhardt managed to right his path and finish 18th on the lead lap. Petty wound up 26th and got a ride back to the pits from Dale Jarrett.

Earnhardt was able to increase his lead in the Winston Cup standings to 281 points over Jarrett, who finished 32nd. Rusty Wallace finished one spot behind Earnhardt and fell 341 points behind with 11 races remaining.

Martin never gave up despite his problems in the pits. "After I got to third place so quickly, I thought I might be able to catch them (Petty and Earnhardt), but I wasn't sure I could pass them.

"The door swung open for us in the end and we sneaked home," continued Martin. "Today we got paid back for all the ugly stuff that's been happening to us – blowing up at Atlanta and running out of gas at Michigan."

Crew chief Steve Hmiel said the race would have "been boring without our lug nut problem. We had a brand new batch of lug nuts and we didn't check them

Winston Cup Series Race No. 19
90 Laps at Watkins Glen International
Watkins Glen, NY
"Budweiser At The Glen"
220.5 Miles on 2.45-mile Road Course
August 8, 1993

Fin	St	No.	Driver	Team / Car	Laps	Money	Status
1	1	6	Mark Martin	Roush Racing Ford	90	$166,110	Running
2	10	16	Wally Dallenbach,Jr.	Roush Racing Ford	90	37,045	Running
3	32	12	Jimmy Spencer	Bobby Allison Ford	90	31,135	Running
4	8	11	Bill Elliott	Junior Johnson Ford	90	28,075	Running
5	2	25	Ken Schrader	Hendrick Motorsports Chevy	90	24,655	Running
6	30	8	Sterling Marlin	Stavola Brothers Ford	90	18,190	Running
7	24	22	Bobby Labonte	Bill Davis Ford	90	14,670	Running
8	29	9	P.J.Jones	Melling Performance Ford	90	10,460	Running
9	19	40	Kenny Wallace	SabCo Racing Pontiac	90	12,210	Running
10	18	33	Harry Gant	Leo Jackson Chevrolet	90	19,990	Running
11	15	98	Derrike Cope	Cale Yarborough Ford	90	13,930	Running
12	26	30	Michael Waltrip	Bahari Racing Pontiac	90	13,490	Running
13	28	39	Scott Lagasse	Gary Roulo Chevrolet	90	7,800	Running
14	25	17	Darrell Waltrip	DarWal Chevrolet	90	17,360	Running
15	12	4	Ernie Irvan	Morgan-McClure Chevrolet	90	17,420	Running
16	16	15	Geoff Bodine	Bud Moore Eng. Ford	90	15,250	Running
17	37	27	Hut Stricklin	Junior Johnson Ford	90	12,330	Running
18	5	3	Dale Earnhardt	RCR Enterprises Chevrolet	90	13,510	Running
19	6	2	Rusty Wallace	Roger Penske Pontiac	90	16,105	Running
20	27	26	Brett Bodine	King Motorsports Ford	89	12,210	Running
21	13	87	Joe Nemechek	NemCo Chevrolet	89	6,535	Running
22	23	44	Rick Wilson	Petty Enterprises Pontiac	89	8,265	Running
23	3	14	Terry Labonte	Billy Hagan Chevrolet	88	11,070	Running
24	9	5	Ricky Rudd	Hendrick Motorsports Chevy	87	10,910	Running
25	33	7	Tommy Kendall	AK - G.E.B. Racing Ford	85	15,625	Running
26	7	42	Kyle Petty	SabCo Racing Pontiac	84	15,165	Crash
27	4	28	Lake Speed	Robert Yates Racing Ford	79	17,055	Running
28	22	21	Morgan Shepherd	Wood Brothers Ford	76	10,595	Running
29	38	52	Scott Gaylord	Oldsmobile	75	5,935	Running
30	34	75	Todd Bodine	Butch Mock Ford	67	5,875	Oil Leak
31	11	24	Jeff Gordon	Hendrick Motorsports Chevy	64	7,290	Engine
32	14	18	Dale Jarrett	Joe Gibbs Chevrolet	61	13,650	Clutch
33	20	41	Phil Parsons	Larry Hedrick Chevrolet	57	7,140	Crash
34	36	55	Ted Musgrave	RaDiUs Motorsports Ford	51	10,055	Trans
35	17	90	Bobby Hillin,Jr.	Junie Donlavey Ford	42	5,470	Engine
36	35	05	Ed Ferree	Gayle Ferree Chevrolet	36	5,440	Crash
37	31	1	Rick Mast	Precision Products Ford	6	9,885	Crash
38	21	68	Dorsey Schroeder	Tri-Star Motorsports Ford	0	5,350	Crash

Time of Race: 2 hours, 36 minutes, 4 seconds
Average Speed: 84.771 mph
Pole Winner: Mark Martin – 119.118 mph
Lap Leaders: Mark Martin 1-20, Dale Earnhardt 21-25, Martin 26-35, Geoff Bodine 36-41, Martin 42-52, G.Bodine 53-54, Earnhardt 55-75, Kyle Petty 76-84, Martin 85-90.
8 lead changes among 4 drivers.
Cautions: 7 for 20 laps Margin of Victory: 3.84 seconds

because the last few batches had been good. We're not quite caught up building race cars. It just shows that you have to use all 24 hours in a day."

Martin finished the race on tires designated for Dallenbach, Jr. Car owner Jack Roush ordered that the two remaining sets of tires be used on Martin's car as he hustled through the pack. Dallenbach, Jr.'s crew went looking for tires and finally got some from the Geoff Bodine-Bud Moore team. After the race, Dallenbach, Jr. and Roush exchanged angry words. A week earlier, Roush had given Dallenbach, Jr. his release effective in 1994.

"Our pit stops were just horrible," said Roush. "Mark and Wally really worked together, and that made it possible to finish 1-2. I'll remember this one forever, It's real special."

One of the first to congratulate Roush was Richard Childress, who owns the cars Dale Earnhardt drives.

Lake Speed took over the Robert Yates Racing Ford and qualified fourth. He was running second when he spun early in the race. "I was trying so hard that I messed up down-shifting," said Speed, who has been running selected races in cars owned by himself prior to landing the Yates ride. "That's about the dumbest thing I've ever done."

Speed charged back into the top five before transmission problems forced him behind the wall for several laps. He wound up 27th, 11 laps off the pace.

Race #20

Martin Master at Michigan; Engine Failure Foils Rudd

BROOKLYN, MI (Aug. 15) – Mark Martin led 83 of the last 91 laps and sprinted to an easy triumph in the Champion Spark Plug 400 at Michigan International Speedway. Martin copped the weekend by sweeping both races. He had won the 200-mile Busch Grand National event on Saturday.

It was Martin's second straight win and the ninth of his career.

Morgan Shepherd finished 1.28-seconds behind Martin as Fords claimed the first two spots. Rookie Jeff Gordon came home third with Dale Jarrett fourth. Ted Musgrave passed Rusty Wallace and Lake Speed in the final lap to take fifth place.

The 400-miler was a reversal of fortune for Martin and Rudd at the 2-mile track located in the Irish Hills of Michigan. Martin dominated the race in June only to run out of gas, leaving Rudd with the victory champagne.

Rudd's Hendrick Motorsports Chevrolet was the class of the field this time, leading for 86 of the first 104 laps. His engine began overheating and after several unsuccessful pit stops, Rudd parked the car after 125 laps.

"This was the most dominant car I have ever been in," said Rudd. "But we started losing water. I think a cylinder head gasket blew and it probably cracked a cylinder. It's disappointing."

Winston Cup Series Race No. 20
200 Laps at Michigan Int'l Speedway
Brooklyn, MI
"Champion Spark Plug 400"
400 Miles on 2-mile Superspeedway
August 15, 1993

Fin	St	No.	Driver	Team / Car	Laps	Money	Status
1	12	6	Mark Martin	Roush Racing Ford	200	$76,645	Running
2	4	21	Morgan Shepherd	Wood Brothers Ford	200	47,320	Running
3	9	24	Jeff Gordon	Hendrick Motorsports Chevy	200	34,745	Running
4	27	18	Dale Jarrett	Joe Gibbs Chevrolet	200	29,045	Running
5	5	55	Ted Musgrave	RaDiUs Motorsports Ford	200	27,990	Running
6	10	2	Rusty Wallace	Roger Penske Pontiac	200	24,115	Running
7	2	28	Lake Speed	Robert Yates Racing Ford	200	25,215	Running
8	11	22	Bobby Labonte	Bill Davis Racing Ford	200	17,565	Running
9	7	3	Dale Earnhardt	RCR Enterprises Chevrolet	200	19,215	Running
10	8	11	Bill Elliott	Junior Johnson Ford	200	25,115	Running
11	18	90	Bobby Hillin,Jr.	Junie Donlavey Ford	200	12,015	Running
12	13	68	Greg Sacks	Tri-Star Motorsports Ford	200	11,615	Running
13	30	17	Darrell Waltrip	DarWal Chevrolet	200	21,015	Running
14	19	26	Brett Bodine	King Motorsports Ford	200	16,615	Running
15	15	7	Jimmy Hensley	AK - G.E.B. Racing Ford	200	20,315	Running
16	28	30	Michael Waltrip	Bahari Racing Pontiac	199	15,960	Running
17	34	8	Sterling Marlin	Stavola Brothers Ford	199	15,240	Running
18	22	42	Kyle Petty	SabCo Racing Pontiac	199	17,540	Running
19	32	41	Phil Parsons	Larry Hedrick Chevrolet	199	11,540	Running
20	25	12	Jimmy Spencer	Bobby Allison Ford	199	14,690	Running
21	17	98	Derrike Cope	Cale Yarborough Ford	199	13,815	Running
22	38	71	Dave Marcis	Marcis Auto Racing Chevy	199	8,815	Running
23	14	40	Kenny Wallace	SabCo Racing Pontiac	199	10,565	Running
24	26	15	Geoff Bodine	Bud Moore Eng. Ford	198	16,615	Running
25	31	52	Jimmy Means	Means Racing Ford	198	8,465	Running
26	39	9	P.J.Jones	Melling Performance Ford	196	8,265	Running
27	1	25	Ken Schrader	Hendrick Motorsports Chevy	193	16,965	Running
28	29	44	Rick Wilson	Petty Enterprises Pontiac	191	9,815	Running
29	41	14	Terry Labonte	Billy Hagan Chevrolet	183	12,665	Running
30	20	33	Harry Gant	Leo Jackson Chevrolet	162	17,015	Crash
31	35	16	Wally Dallenbach,Jr.	Roush Racing Ford	157	12,440	Running
32	24	4	Ernie Irvan	Morgan-McClure Chevrolet	155	17,415	Engine
33	16	1	Rick Mast	Precision Products Ford	150	12,315	Running
34	37	27	Hut Stricklin	Junior Johnson Ford	139	12,240	Crash
35	3	5	Ricky Rudd	Hendrick Motorsports Chevy	125	14,590	Engine
36	33	89	Jim Sauter	Mueller Brothers Ford	108	7,640	Crash
37	21	87	Joe Nemechek	NemCo Chevrolet	95	8,115	Rear End
38	23	32	Jimmy Horton	Active Racing Chevrolet	94	7,590	Engine
39	40	39	Dick Trickle	Gary Roulo Chevrolet	79	7,565	Rear End
40	6	75	Todd Bodine	Butch Mock Ford	15	7,515	Crash
41	36	45	Rich Bickle	Gene Isenhour Ford	10	7,515	Engine

Time of Race: 2 hours, 46 minutes, 1 seconds
Average Speed: 144.564 mph
Pole Winner: Ken Schrader – 180.750 mph
Lap Leaders: Ken Schrader 1, Ricky Rudd 2-18, Lake Speed 19-20, Ernie Irvan 21-25, Rudd 26-66, Schrader 67, Jeff Gordon 68-70, Rudd 71-85, Gordon 86-91, Rudd 92-104, Ted Musgrave 105-107, Mark Martin 108-143, Rusty Wallace 144-147, Martin 148-158, Gordon 159-166, Martin 167-200.
15 lead changes among 8 drivers.
Cautions: 8 for 27 laps Margin of Victory: 1.28 seconds

Brian Czobat

Morgan Shepherd #21 inches ahead of Rusty Wallace, Dave Marcis #71 and low riding Lake Speed #28 at Michigan.

Martin said he knew how Rudd felt. "The deal here in June broke our hearts," said Martin. "We clobbered the field that day (but finished sixth). When you're running that good, you need to capitalize.

"I was more of a maniac this weekend, wanting to win two in a row," continued Martin. "A couple of weeks ago, I said if I could just win one race I'd be satisfied. Now I'm greedy."

Martin has come from 12th to fourth in the point standings since the June race at Michigan, but he acknowledged that he has virtually no hopes of challenging for the championship. "None of us are going to catch Earnhardt unless he spends a heck of a lot of time in the garage area," said Martin, who now trails Earnhardt by 342 points. "You can't catch up unless the leader has trouble."

Earnhardt lost a lap in the early stages but made it up near the finish. He was able to finish ninth as 15 cars finished on the lead lap. "We cut down a tire that cost us a lap," said Earnhardt. "That was unlucky but then we got lucky and finished ninth."

Brian Czobat

Steve Hmiel gets Mark Martin's Ford dialed in before the Michigan 400-miler.

Ken Schrader won his fifth pole of the season, but spun in the late stages and wound up 27th. "I'd traded all the poles for a win," said Schrader, who is now on a 67-race losing skid.

Shepherd gave the Wood Brothers Ford another strong run, which pleased crewman Eddie Wood. "Morgan drove a smart race," said the younger Wood. "He doesn't drive like a 51-year-old, does he? He's just as young as the rest of 'em when the race starts. He's so at ease in the car; you can hear it in his voice. He never gets excited. It's like he's sitting in his living room."

Jarrett trimmed 22 points off of Earnhardt's point lead but still trails by 259 points. Wallace trails by 324 points.

Wallace was concentrating in his battle with Speed on the last lap. "Rusty was a moving roadblock," said Speed, who was taking his second ride in the Robert Yates Ford. "He was holding us up so much it let the other guys catch us. I'm not happy about finishing seventh."

Musgrave had one of his finer runs, coming home fifth. He dived to the apron in the front chute to edge Wallace and Speed for fifth. "I remember that deal in an IROC race," said Musgrave, who announced he will be driving for Jack Roush in 1994. "They (Wallace and Speed) got too busy with themselves, looking at each other, and I just scooted down the banking and got a good run on them."

Race #21

Late Surge by Martin Topples Wallace in Bristol 500

BRISTOL, TN (Aug. 28) – Mark Martin overcame a two-lap deficit and roared past Rusty Wallace in the closing stages to grab his third straight win in the Bud 500 at Bristol International Raceway.

Winston Cup Series Race No. 21
500 Laps at Bristol Int'l Raceway
Bristol, TN
"Bud 500"
266.5 Miles on .533-mile Short Track
August 28, 1993

Fin	St	No.	Driver	Team / Car	Laps	Money	Status
1	1	6	Mark Martin	Roush Racing Ford	500	$80,125	Running
2	2	2	Rusty Wallace	Roger Penske Pontiac	500	31,875	Running
3	19	3	Dale Earnhardt	RCR Enterprises Chevrolet	500	32,325	Running
4	10	33	Harry Gant	Leo Jackson Chevrolet	500	28,150	Running
5	12	1	Rick Mast	Precision Products Ford	500	22,000	Running
6	9	7	Jimmy Hensley	AK - G.E.B. Racing Ford	500	22,075	Running
7	13	26	Brett Bodine	King Motorsports Ford	500	16,925	Running
8	11	15	Geoff Bodine	Bud Moore Eng. Ford	500	18,925	Running
9	23	40	Kenny Wallace*	SabCo Racing Pontiac	499	12,600	Running
10	24	30	Michael Waltrip	Bahari Racing Pontiac	498	17,600	Running
11	14	11	Bill Elliott	Junior Johnson Ford	498	19,300	Running
12	31	90	Bobby Hillin,Jr.	Junie Donlavey Ford	497	8,900	Running
13	16	21	Morgan Shepherd	Wood Brothers Ford	497	14,550	Running
14	25	41	Phil Parsons	Larry Hedrick Chevrolet	497	11,300	Running
15	4	22	Bobby Labonte*	Bill Davis Racing Ford	495	12,500	Running
16	21	28	Lake Speed	Robert Yates Racing Ford	493	18,350	Running
17	29	71	Dave Marcis	Marcis Auto Racing Chevy	484	8,300	Running
18	27	52	Jimmy Means	Means Racing Ford	483	8,250	Running
19	28	68	Greg Sacks***	Tri-Star Motorsports Ford	483	8,240	Running
20	8	24	Jeff Gordon****	Hendrick Motorsports Chevy	466	11,450	Running
21	22	16	Wally Dallenbach,Jr.	Roush Racing Ford	437	13,000	Running
22	3	5	Ricky Rudd	Hendrick Motorsports Chevy	414	13,900	Running
23	30	8	Sterling Marlin	Stavola Brothers Ford	374	12,750	Running
24	26	25	Ken Schrader	Hendrick Motorsports Chevy	354	12,575	Running
25	32	12	Jimmy Spencer	Bobby Allison Ford	325	12,430	Running
26	34	4	Ernie Irvan	Morgan-McClure Chevrolet	316	17,650	Running
27	7	98	Derrike Cope	Cale Yarborough Ford	292	12,325	Handling
28	6	44	Rick Wilson	Petty Enterprises Pontiac	274	9,250	Crash
29	17	17	Darrell Waltrip	DarWal Chevrolet	246	17,450	Running
30	20	42	Kyle Petty	SabCo Racing Pontiac	207	16,600	Handling
31	33	18	Dale Jarrett	Joe Gibbs Chevrolet	199	15,600	Rear End
32	5	27	Hut Stricklin	Junior Johnson Ford	83	12,150	Crash
33	15	20	Bobby Hamilton	Dick Moroso Ford	30	7,600	Crash
34	18	14	Terry Labonte	Billy Hagan Chevrolet	30	12,125	Crash

Time of Race: 3 hours, 1 minute, 21 seconds
Average Speed: 88.172 mph
Pole Winner: Mark Martin – 121.405 mph
Lap Leaders: Mark Martin 1-49, Rusty Wallace 50-80, Martin 81-85, R.Wallace 86-155, Kyle Petty 156-178, R.Wallace 179-347, Rick Mast 348, R.Wallace 349-487, Martin 488-500.
8 lead changes among 4 drivers.
Cautions: 11 for 71 laps Margin of Victory: 0.14 second
*Relieved by Dick Trickle **Relieved by Terry Labonte ***Relieved by Bobby Hamilton
****Relieved by Todd Bodine.

Brian Czobat

Lake Speed #28 takes the high-side at Bristol to pass the crippled car of Jimmy Spencer #12.

Martin took the lead from Wallace with 13 laps to go and held his Ford in front during a frantic final three laps as lapped cars blocked the path for the two contenders. Geoff Bodine, who had fallen from third to eighth in the late stages, was trying desperately to stay on the lead lap and interrupted Martin's run to the flag.

"I'm not too proud of Geoff Bodine right now," said Martin after holding off Wallace by a single car length. "I wouldn't have done that to him. He made the last couple of laps pretty hairy."

Bodine was racing his brother Brett and Jimmy Hensley for position. "I wasn't aware that it was the last lap," he explained. "My spotter said he was yelling for me to get out of their way, but I couldn't hear the radio. I certainly wouldn't have wanted to cost either one of them the race."

Dale Earnhardt came from 19th starting spot to finish third. He retained a healthy advantage in the Winston Cup standings. Wallace moved into second place, 309 points behind.

Fourth place went to Harry Gant with Rick Mast fifth. It was Mast's first career top five finish on a short track.

Martin led twice for 54 laps in the early going, but had to retreat to the pits in the 129th lap when his right-rear wheel started vibrating. He lost two laps while he pitted under green, and from that point on it was a game of catch-up for the Batesville, Ark. driver. "I didn't think we could make up much ground on

Bryan Hallman

Jimmy Spencer #12 rides over the hidden car of Terry Labonte in early crash at Bristol. Sterling Marlin #8 and Darrell Waltrip #17 were also involved.

Wallace," said Martin. "He was awesome and his crew is simply incredible. But we had a lot of laps left and I was going to do the best I could."

Martin got one lap back 60 miles later and broke back into the leader lap before the half-way point. Dick Trickle, who was driving in relief of the injured Kenny Wallace, spun on lap 269, allowing Martin to close the gap.

He chased Wallace the rest of the night before making the winning pass with less than eight miles to go. "Rusty and I were fighting for the same piece of real estate," said Martin. "The low groove was the fastest in the turns and Rusty was trying to guard it. He slipped a little and I squeezed in there to make the pass. It was a heck of a race."

Wallace said effects from his Talladega crash in May took it's toll. "Everything from that wreck is hurting tonight. I just got tired. The driver was the weak link. Mark made a clean pass."

Wallace only picked up 15 points on Earnhardt. "That durn Earnhardt," Wallace fussed in a good-natured manner. "He runs like a John Deere. I was hoping we'd gain more than 15 points."

Morgan Shepherd had third place locked up until a rear axle snapped in the final 10 laps. He limped home 13th.

The race was slowed 11 times by the yellow flag, mostly for wrecks. Rick Wilson started the yellow fever by putting the Petty Enterprises Pontiac into the wall on lap 10. The biggest crash of the day came on lap 31 when Bobby Hamilton's Ford broke loose and he was hit by Sterling Marlin and Terry Labonte. Jimmy Spencer tagged the rear of Labonte's Chevrolet, lifting Spencer high into the air. Darrell Waltrip and Ken Schrader were also involved.

Race #22

Martin Snares 4th Straight in Rain-Delayed Southern 500

DARLINGTON, SC (Sept. 5) – Mark Martin broke out of a three-car struggle and pulled away to win the rain-shortened Mountain Dew Southern 500 at Darlington Raceway. It was the fourth straight Winston Cup win for the diminutive Ford driver.

The 44th running of the granddaddy of superspeedway races was delayed three hours at the start and flagged to a finish 16 laps before it's scheduled conclusion by darkness. Martin led all but three of the final 103 laps and finished 1.51 seconds in front of runner-up Brett Bodine. Rusty Wallace came home third and Dale Earnhardt was fourth. Fifth place went to Ernie Irvan, who was taking his first ride in the Robert Yates Ford.

Irvan had expressed interest in taking Yates' Ford ride but had another full year in his contract with the Morgan-McClure Chevrolet team. After buying out his contract, Morgan-McClure fired him for the remainder of the 1993 season. Irvan was put in the Yates car in an 11th hour move, leaving Lake Speed without a ride.

The first five laps were run under green/yellow conditions to dry off the track after heavy rains pelted the 1.366-mile oval for nearly 24 hours. Only two other yellows broke the action, one of them for a mandatory tire check on lap 31. Irvan's late spin at the entrance to pit road brought out the final caution.

For the first half of the race, Earnhardt, Wallace and

Greg Fielden

Mark Martin and Dale Earnhardt treated the rain-drenched Darlington crowd to a terrific duel.

Martin treated the dampened audience to a terrific duel. The lead often swapped hands three or four times per lap. "Dale was hanging tough there in the beginning," said Martin, who became the sixth driver in the Modern Era to post four straight wins. "I let Ernie go battle Dale for awhile. When Ernie started to fade, I kicked in. It was good, hard racing – nothing underhanded about it. Every time I passed him, he came right back and passed me."

Earnhardt put on a tremendous show in the face of rivals saying he was stroking since he had an insurmountable point lead. "Did it look like I was stroking?" Earnhardt fired at a group of news reporters after the race. "It was a gut-buster. I got waylaid by the wall. I slipped in some water that was coming off the 26 car (Brett Bodine). They should have blackflagged that guy off the track."

The final yellow flag erased an eight second lead Martin had built up. The green flag came out with 10 laps to go and Martin stretched it out again. Earnhardt was battling Bodine for second when he popped the wall. He faded, but still held onto fourth.

Bodine said his car was running a little hot in the late going, "but it didn't hinder us. The way my season has gone, if we'd have been leaking anything, NASCAR would have pulled us in. I think Earnhardt was the only one complaining about it."

Ken Schrader scored his sixth pole of the season and led the first 12 laps – five of them under the yellow. He lost the lead to Earnhardt, who led for a total of 101 laps. Schrader never led again and faded to a ninth place finish.

Wallace picked up only five points in the Winston Cup standings. "No matter how good you run, you

Winston Cup Series Race No. 22
367 Laps at Darlington Raceway
Darlington, SC
"Mountain Dew Southern 500"

501.322 Miles on 1.366-mile Superspeedway
September 5, 1993

Fin	St	No.	Driver	Team / Car	Laps	Money	Status
1	4	6	Mark Martin	Roush Racing Ford	351	$67,765	Running
2	12	26	Brett Bodine	King Motorsports Ford	351	40,690	Running
3	11	2	Rusty Wallace	Roger Penske Pontiac	351	27,495	Running
4	6	3	Dale Earnhardt	RCR Enterprises Chevrolet	351	31,090	Running
5	10	28	Ernie Irvan	Robert Yates Racing Ford	350	28,395	Running
6	16	5	Ricky Rudd	Hendrick Motorsports Chevy	350	16,940	Running
7	2	33	Harry Gant	Leo Jackson Chevrolet	350	19,945	Running
8	21	21	Morgan Shepherd	Wood Brothers Ford	349	16,025	Running
9	1	25	Ken Schrader	Hendrick Motorsports Chevy	349	19,195	Running
10	31	40	Kenny Wallace*	SabCo Racing Pontiac	348	14,255	Running
11	30	16	Wally Dallenbach,Jr	Roush Racing Ford	348	14,405	Running
12	27	18	Dale Jarrett	Joe Gibbs Chevrolet	348	16,510	Running
13	25	30	Michael Waltrip	Bahari Racing Pontiac	348	13,820	Running
14	3	22	Bobby Labonte	Bill Davis Ford	347	12,130	Running
15	14	12	Jimmy Spencer	Bobby Allison Ford	347	13,390	Running
16	28	42	Kyle Petty	SabCo Racing Pontiac	347	15,770	Running
17	5	98	Derrike Cope	Cale Yarborough Ford	347	12,500	Running
18	7	11	Bill Elliott	Junior Johnson Ford	347	17,625	Running
19	32	20	Bobby Hamilton	Dick Moroso Ford	347	7,245	Running
20	29	15	Geoff Bodine	Bud Moore Eng. Ford	346	15,625	Running
21	34	41	Phil Parsons	Larry Hedrick Chevrolet	346	9,090	Running
22	15	24	Jeff Gordon	Hendrick Motorsports Chevy	346	8,870	Running
23	26	7	Jimmy Hensley	AK - G.E.B. Racing Ford	345	15,900	Running
24	19	90	Bobby Hillin,Jr.	Junie Donlavey Ford	345	6,325	Running
25	13	68	Greg Sacks	Tri-Star Motorsports Ford	344	6,215	Running
26	22	4	Jeff Purvis	Morgan-McClure Chevrolet	343	15,655	Running
27	17	75	Todd Bodine	Butch Mock Ford	341	5,945	Running
28	24	17	Darrell Waltrip	DarWal Chevrolet	339	15,635	Running
29	33	71	Dave Marcis	Marcis Auto Racing Chevy	333	5,725	Running
30	35	44	Rick Wilson	Petty Enterprises Pontiac	327	7,315	Running
31	9	8	Sterling Marlin	Stavola Brothers Ford	321	10,080	Running
32	8	1	Rick Mast	Precision Products Ford	316	9,965	Running
33	20	14	Terry Labonte	Billy Hagan Chevrolet	299	9,875	Engine
34	18	55	Ted Musgrave	RaDiUs Motorsports Ford	257	9,815	Engine
35	36	52	Mike Skinner	Means Racing Ford	145	5,180	Engine
36	23	27	Hut Stricklin	Junior Johnson Ford	135	9,620	Engine
37	40	36	H.B.Bailey	Bailey Pontiac	54	5,050	Engine
38	38	99	Brad Teague	Ralph Ball Chevrolet	13	5,010	Vibration
39	39	53	Jimmy Means	Means Racing Ford	11	4,930	Quit
			Bob Schacht	Schacht Racing Olds	-	5,760	DNS

Time of Race: 3 hours, 28 minutes, 34 seconds
Average Speed: 137.932 mph
Pole Winner: Ken Schrader – 161.259 mph
Lap Leaders: Ken Schrader 1-12, Dale Earnhardt 13-27, Mark Martin 28-31, Jimmy Hensley 32, Jeff Purvis 33, Martin 34-36, Earnhardt 37-61, Ernie Irvan 62-93, Harry Gant 94, Jeff Gordon 95-97, Brett Bodine 98-100, Irvan 101-112, Earnhardt 113-129, Martin 130-141, Irvan 142-143, Gant 144, Earnhardt 145-188, Martin 189-247, Brett Bodine 248, Martin 249-299, Rusty Wallace 300-302, Martin 303-351.
21 lead changes among 10 drivers.
Cautions: 3 for 16 laps Margin of Victory: 1.51 seconds
*Relieved by Dick Trickle
Race shortened to 351 laps due to darkness

Bryan Hallman

Ernie Irvan took over the Robert Yates Ford ride for the first time at Darlington.

can't catch up unless the other guy has trouble," said Wallace. "But we're not giving up yet. There's still time to make up ground."

Jeff Purvis, who was hired to replace Irvan in the Morgan-McClure Chevrolet, finished 26th, eight laps off the pace.

Dick Trickle relieved Kenny Wallace in the early laps and finished 10th. It was Trickle's second straight top 10 finish while driving in relief for Wallace, who broke a shoulder in a practice session at Indianapolis Motor Speedway.

Race #23

Wallace Overcomes Penalty and Stops Martin's Streak at Richmond

RICHMOND, VA (Sept. 11) – Rusty Wallace vented his anger over a controversial penalty by charging past Mark Martin to win the Miller Genuine Draft 400 at Richmond International Raceway. It was the sixth win of the season for the St. Louis, Mo. Pontiac driver.

Bill Elliott notched his best finish of the year by taking second place, 0.57-second behind the winner. Dale Earnhardt got third place, Ricky Rudd was fourth and Brett Bodine passed Mark Martin for fifth place in the final lap.

Wallace started third and led all but 23 of the first 95 laps. He was black-flagged to the pits for jumping on the restart after the second caution flag – an unusual ruling since Wallace was leading at the time.

The penalty dropped Wallace back to 26th place. "I had a normal restart and I got pretty mad about the penalty," said Wallace. "I raced on anger for a long time until I wore the tires off my car."

NASCAR officials ruled that Wallace had gained an advantage in the restart by braking, then accelerating quickly as others were recovering from the jostle. NASCAR's Chip Williams explained the ruling to the media: "Those of you who regularly cover the series will know that we've given Rusty several warnings for jumping on the restarts. After Bristol, we told him he was 'on watch' the rest of the season. When we saw him do it again tonight, we brought him in."

As Wallace was trying to forge his way back into contention, Martin moved to the front in his bid to become the first driver to win five races in a row since Richard Petty and Bobby Allison each won five straight in 1971. "We had everybody covered for awhile," said Martin. "But the car started pushing and then I just had to hang on. It's hard to believe we lost because the car was running so perfectly in the middle of the race."

Wallace zipped around Martin with 134 laps to go and led the rest of the way.

Four yellow flags in the final 50 laps kept the field bunched up – and caused some drivers to get hot under the collar. Ricky Rudd tapped Derrike Cope into a spin in the 352nd lap. During the slowdown, Rudd and Earnhardt collided as they left the pits.

"Earnhardt drove right into me," said an angered Rudd. "I can't believe he did that on purpose because he could have knocked the whole nose of his car off. I don't know what he was doing."

A few laps later, Earnhardt nudged Harry Gant into a spin off of turn two. Gant's Chevrolet broke loose and was hit hard by Bobby Hillin, Jr. "I thought I had broken my neck when he (Hillin, Jr.) hit me," said

Gant. "He was going full bore."

Gant was able to continue the rest of the way. Dick Trickle, driving a Chevrolet owned by Gary Roulo, spun with four laps to go which resulted in a quick two lap caution.

On the restart, Wallace got away from Elliott as Earnhardt and Rudd were trapped behind Ken Schrader, who was two laps behind. Earnhardt popped Schrader a couple of times but settled for third place.

Rudd, still seething over the pit road mishap, rubbed Earnhardt's rear bumper after the race had ended.

After the race, Earnhardt parked his car and headed directly for the team's transporter. Car owner Richard Childress handled the media. "It's a shame when you're running for the Winston Cup championship and the manufacturers title that somebody two laps down forgets which side of the bread is buttered on," Childress said, referring to Schrader's tactics in the final two laps. "I don't know what he could have been thinking."

Even Rudd poked a jab at his teammate. "Schrader got in the way and it kept me from passing Dale for third place," said Rudd.

Wallace trimmed 20 points off of Earnhardt's point lead and now trails by 284 points. "I'm doing everything I can to catch him," said Wallace. "I about had him lapped, but the caution came out and he picked up a bunch of positions. He also had to overcome wrecking on pit road. Everything worked for him, but that's the way you win championships."

Rookie Bobby Labonte won the pole position in Bill Davis' Ford. He finished 13th, two laps off the pace.

Brian Czobat

Buddy Parrott, crew chief for Rusty Wallace's Roger Penske team, notched his second straight win in Richmond's race under the lights.

Winston Cup Series Race No. 23
400 Laps at Richmond Int'l Raceway
Richmond, VA
"Miller Genuine Draft 400"
300 Miles on .75-mile Short Track
September 11, 1993

Fin	St	No.	Driver	Team / Car	Laps	Money	Status
1	3	2	Rusty Wallace	Roger Penske Pontiac	400	$49,415	Running
2	26	11	Bill Elliott	Junior Johnson Ford	400	54,665	Running
3	8	3	Dale Earnhardt	RCR Enterprises Chevy	400	35,780	Running
4	17	5	Ricky Rudd	Hendrick Motorsports Chevy	400	26,505	Running
5	16	26	Brett Bodine	King Motorsports Ford	400	21,580	Running
6	10	6	Mark Martin	Roush Racing Ford	400	21,105	Running
7	4	17	Darrell Waltrip	DarWal Chevrolet	400	18,505	Running
8	23	14	Terry Labonte	Billy Hagan Chevrolet	400	14,405	Running
9	11	42	Kyle Petty	SabCo Racing Pontiac	400	16,205	Running
10	22	24	Jeff Gordon	Hendrick Motorsports Chevy	400	14,205	Running
11	5	33	Harry Gant	Leo Jackson Chevrolet	399	16,305	Running
12	12	25	Ken Schrader	Hendrick Motorsports Chevy	398	12,905	Running
13	1	22	Bobby Labonte	Bill Davis Racing Ford	398	13,755	Running
14	13	18	Dale Jarrett	Joe Gibbs Chevrolet	398	14,955	Running
15	30	16	Wally Dallenbach,Jr.	Roush Racing Ford	398	12,805	Running
16	18	4	Jeff Purvis	Morgan-McClure Chevrolet	398	16,380	Running
17	25	27	Hut Stricklin	Junior Johnson Ford	398	11,880	Running
18	6	1	Rick Mast	Precision Products Ford	398	11,630	Running
19	15	30	Michael Waltrip	Bahari Racing Pontiac	397	11,505	Running
20	27	41	Phil Parsons	Larry Hedrick Chevrolet	397	8,980	Running
21	19	7	Jimmy Hensley	AK - G.E.B. Racing Ford	397	15,930	Running
22	35	55	Ted Musgrave	RaDiUs Motorsports Ford	397	11,255	Running
23	33	71	Dave Marcis	Marcis Auto Racing Chevy	396	6,430	Running
24	24	8	Sterling Marlin	Stavola Brothers Ford	395	11,055	Running
25	9	39	Dick Trickle	Gary Roulo Chevrolet	395	6,355	Running
26	31	52	Jimmy Means	Means Racing Ford	391	6,330	Running
27	34	90	Bobby Hillin,Jr.	Junie Donlavey Ford	383	6,305	Crash
28	14	98	Derrike Cope	Cale Yarborough Ford	350	10,880	Running
29	20	44	Rick Wilson	Petty Enterprises Pontiac	303	7,830	Running
30	29	21	Morgan Shepherd	Wood Brothers Ford	284	10,755	Running
31	36	68	Greg Sacks	Tri-Star Motorsports Ford	264	6,155	Engine
32	28	40	Kenny Wallace	Sabco Racing Pontiac	155	7,655	Engine
33	32	75	Todd Bodine	Butch Mock Ford	130	6,125	Crash
34	7	15	Geoff Bodine	Bud Moore Eng. Ford	119	14,105	H Gasket
35	21	12	Jimmy Spencer	Bobby Allison Ford	57	17,105	Engine

Time of Race: 3 hours, 0 minutes, 9 seconds
Average Speed: 99.917 mph
Pole Winner: Bobby Labonte – 122.006 mph
Lap Leaders: Ernie Irvan 1-8, Bobby Labonte 9-11, Rusty Wallace 12-56, Darrell Waltrip 57-68, R.Wallace 69-95, D.Waltrip 96, Mark Martin 97-242, D.Waltrip 243-245, Bill Elliott 246-248, B.Labonte 249-257, Martin 258-266, R.Wallace 267-400.
12 lead changes among 6 drivers.
Cautions: 8 for 47 laps Margin of Victory: 0.57 second

Race #24

Winston Cup Series Race No. 24
500 Laps at Dover Downs Int'l Speedway
Dover, DE
"SplitFire Spark Plug 500"
500 Miles on 1-mile Superspeedway
September 19, 1993

Fin	St	No.	Driver	Team / Car	Laps	Money	Status
1	1	2	Rusty Wallace	Roger Penske Pontiac	500	$77,645	Running
2	10	25	Ken Schrader	Hendrick Motorsports Chevy	500	53,115	Running
3	17	17	Darrell Waltrip	DarWal Chevrolet	500	38,410	Running
4	26	18	Dale Jarrett	Joe Gibbs Chevrolet	500	31,035	Running
5	8	33	Harry Gant	Leo Jackson Chevrolet	500	27,830	Running
6	19	12	Jimmy Spencer	Bobby Allison Ford	500	21,580	Running
7	11	22	Bobby Labonte	Bill Davis Racing Ford	500	16,680	Running
8	27	14	Terry Labonte	Billy Hagan Chevrolet	500	17,980	Running
9	7	21	Morgan Shepherd	Wood Brothers Ford	499	17,230	Running
10	13	11	Bill Elliott	Junior Johnson Ford	498	23,430	Running
11	18	8	Sterling Marlin	Stavola Brothers Ford	498	15,980	Running
12	32	90	Bobby Hillin,Jr.	Junie Donlavey Ford	498	9,680	Running
13	35	4	Jeff Purvis	Morgan-Mcclure Chevrolet	497	18,980	Running
14	15	42	Kyle Petty	SabCo Racing Pontiac	495	17,080	Running
15	33	16	Wally Dallenbach,Jr.	Roush Racing Ford	492	14,580	Running
16	36	40	Kenny Wallace	SabCo Racing Pontiac	489	11,630	Running
17	37	52	Jimmy Means	Means Racing Ford	489	8,530	Running
18	12	1	Rick Mast	Precision Products Ford	477	13,615	Running
19	31	71	Dave Marcis	Marcis Auto Racing Chevy	470	8,305	Running
20	29	68	Greg Sacks	Tri-Star Motorsports Ford	462	8,805	Running
21	22	5	Ricky Rudd	Hendrick Motorsports Chevy	456	13,205	Flagged
22	30	32	Jimmy Horton	Active Racing Chevrolet	440	8,155	Crash
23	24	30	Michael Waltrip	Bahari Racing Pontiac	421	13,005	Flagged
24	3	24	Jeff Gordon	Hendrick Motorsports Chevy	412	11,255	Flagged
25	23	26	Dick Trickle	King Motorsports Ford	407	12,755	Running
26	2	28	Ernie Irvan	Robert Yates Racing Ford	405	19,105	Running
27	9	3	Dale Earnhardt	RCR Enterprises Chevrolet	404	14,555	Flagged
28	21	55	Ted Musgrave	RaDiUs Motorsports Ford	402	12,955	Engine
29	16	27	Hut Stricklin	Junior Johnson ford	368	12,380	Crash
30	4	7	Geoff Bodine	AK - G.E.B. Racing Ford	358	17,155	Crash
31	5	6	Mark Martin	Roush Racing Ford	237	16,705	Crash
32	14	98	Derrike Cope	Cale Yarborough Ford	232	12,205	Crash
33	25	15	Lake Speed	Bud Moore Eng. Ford	232	15,605	Engine
34	6	44	Rick Wilson	Petty Enterprises Pontiac	117	9,080	Crash
35	28	75	Todd Bodine	Butch Mock Ford	60	7,505	Crash
36	34	57	Bob Schacht	Schacht Oldsmobile	20	7,480	Rotor
37	20	41	Phil Parsons	Larry Hedrick Chevrolet	10	8,980	Crash

Time of Race: 4 hours, 59 minutes, 0 seconds
Average Speed: 100.334 mph mph
Pole Winner: Rusty Wallace – 151.564 mph
Lap Leaders: Rusty Wallace 1-69, Ernie Irvan 70-87, R.Wallace 88-99, Jeff Purvis 100-101, R.Wallace 102-160, Jeff Gordon 161-170, R.Wallace 171-175, Gordon 176-216, R.Wallace 217-265, Gordon 266-294, Ken Schrader 295-377, Darrell Waltrip 378-410, Schrader 411-454, D.Waltrip 455-462, Dale Jarrett 463-464, D.Waltrip 465-476, Terry Labonte 477, D.Waltrip 478-479, R.Wallace 480-500.
18 lead changes among 8 drivers.
Cautions: 16 for 103 laps Margin of Victory: 0.41 second

Wallace In Hot Water After Wreck With Earnhardt at Dover

DOVER, DE (Sept. 19) – Rusty Wallace dodged a number of wrecks, initiated the biggest crash of the day and survived the five-hour SplitFire Spark Plug 500 at Dover Down International Speedway.

Wallace's seventh win of the year left him 181 points behind Dale Earnhardt in the Winston Cup standings and a little less popular with many of his comrades, including Earnhardt.

Wallace started on the pole and led all but 20 of the first 160 laps. He was holding down first place in the 265th lap when a blown tire sent him to the pits. He lost two laps getting a replacement.

Flat tires were an acute problem on the high-banked 1-mile oval as 16 caution flags consumed a track record 103 laps. Goodyear tire representatives said a number of the crews were under-inflating their tires for better traction, but it was causing the tires to blow.

Jeff Gordon and Ken Schrader, teammates on the Hendrick Motorsports Chevrolet unit, led much of the way as Wallace was working his way back into contention.

Kim Novosat

There were dozens of shredded tires at Dover.

The big fracas took place in the 371st lap. Wallace had made up one lap and was starting second in line behind Hut Stricklin on the inside groove. Schrader was leading with Earnhardt on his tail.

As the green flag signaled a restart, Wallace shot into the rear of Stricklin, pushing him into the upper groove where he made heavy contact with Earnhardt and Ricky Rudd. Wallace scooted under the pile-up unscathed. The wreck also involved Rick Mast and Gordon.

Rudd was livid at Wallace after the crash. "That was the stupidest thing I've ever seen in my life," said

Kim Novasat

Dale Earnhardt lends a helping hand in repairs of the RCR Enterprises Chevrolet after it was wrecked at Dover.

Rudd. "I don't want to hear Rusty Wallace ever say anything about someone doing something dumb again."

Stricklin said he thought Wallace "was angry that I didn't give him my position on the restart. We were both a lap down. I had a right to be up front on the restart because my crew had beaten his and we got out first. Rusty just got over-anxious. He hit me before I had a chance to get into third gear. I was going from second to third and all of a sudden, bam!"

Junior Johnson, Stricklin's car owner, said, "Rusty just turned Hut straight into Earnhardt and Rudd. They sent a guy down to our pits asking us to let him in front. When we said 'no', I guess he got mad. He sure did make a mess out of a bunch of good cars."

Wallace denied he was upset with Stricklin. "I told my guys to tell Hut to let me in front and I'd open a lane for the both of us to get the lap back. Hut said 'no', and that was fine with me.

"When I launched on the restart, he didn't launch as good as I did. We wrecked. But we're big boys. I didn't get upset when I went around 16 times at Talladega."

NASCAR did not reprimand any drivers. "Change the car numbers and colors and it could happen to anyone," explained NASCAR's Gary Nelson. "The inside pole car (Stricklin) started to accelerate and slowed suddenly."

Earnhardt didn't subscribe to Wallace's theory that Stricklin bobbled on the restart. "Hut stayed right with me, so I know he didn't miss a shift. I don't know

Steve Crumbacker

Mark Martin's Ford goes up in flames after bout with Dover's retaining wall.

what Rusty was thinking about, but he ran right into the back of Hut. It sure made a big mess."

Earnhardt lost nearly a hundred laps and wound up in 24th spot after NASCAR officials flagged him to the garage late in the race. NASCAR was aware that by staying on the track at that point, Earnhardt could not improve his position. NASCAR also flagged Rudd to the garage in the final five laps.

Once Wallace got back on the lead lap, he had to battle Dale Jarrett and Darrell Waltrip for the win. Waltrip was leading with 24 laps to go when NASCAR brought out a yellow for crews to check tire wear. That gave Wallace a chance to close on Waltrip, and he bolted past with 21 laps to go. Schrader finished second, 0.41-second behind. Waltrip held on for third place while Dale Jarrett was fourth and Harry Gant fifth.

Barry Dodson, crew chief on Waltrip's Chevrolet, didn't care for the tire-check yellow, which was the third one of that nature called by sanctioning officials. "We got robbed," complained Dodson. "I think the guy who won the race would have to agree. I couldn't believe they called for another caution period after we checked our tires only 25 laps earlier. The officials in the control tower determined the outcome of this race."

Wallace admitted his crew was one of those under-inflating their tires – a risky move yet one that helped in the victory run. "I told them to drop the tire pressure so it would make the front end stick better," said Wallace. "I'm not going to tell you how low the pressure was because it might scare someone. We had just enough air in it to complete 20 laps. If it had been 22 laps, I'd have been worried."

Geoff Bodine made his first start as owner/driver, but was knocked into a spin by Gordon on lap 360. "I was trying to get back in the lead lap," said Bodine. "Gordon came up from behind and got into me. I don't think it was on purpose, but he did wreck my race car. This is not a good way to start my career as a car owner."

Race #25

Irvan Tops at Martinsville; Wallace Slices Point Deficit

MARTINSVILLE, VA (Sept. 26) – Ernie Irvan led most of the way and drove the Robert Yates Racing Ford to victory in the Goody's 500 at Martinsville Speedway. It was the first win for Irvan, who was making his fourth start in the car left vacant by the tragic death of Davey Allison.

"This is an emotional win for all of us," said Irvan, who survived an unusual summer-like day at the .525-mile oval. "I've been wearing a Davey Allison T-shirt ever since I got in this car. This win is dedicated to him and his whole family. He'll always be a part of this team. We were on a mission. I wanted to get this team back on the winning track. This team is going on from here, remembering the old times and looking forward to the new times."

Irvan started on the pole and led 402 of the 500 laps. He finished 2.77 seconds ahead of runner-up Rusty Wallace, who cut heavily into Dale Earnhardt's point lead. Third place went to Jimmy Spencer with Ricky Rudd fourth and Dale Jarrett fifth.

Winston Cup Series Race No. 25
500 Laps at Martinsville Speedway
Martinsville, VA
"Goody's 500"
262.5 Miles on .525-mile Short Track
September 26, 1993

Fin	St	No.	Driver	Team / Car	Laps	Money	Status
1	1	28	Ernie Irvan	Robert Yates Ford	500	$75,300	Running
2	4	2	Rusty Wallace	Roger Penske Pontiac	500	31,875	Running
3	15	12	Jimmy Spencer	Bobby Allison Ford	500	31,000	Running
4	20	5	Ricky Rudd	Hendrick Motorsports Chevy	500	25,250	Running
5	17	18	Dale Jarrett	Joe Gibbs Chevrolet	499	22,675	Running
6	14	26	Brett Bodine*	King Motorsports Ford	499	18,425	Running
7	29	14	Terry Labonte	Billy Hagan Chevrolet	499	16,075	Running
8	24	30	Michael Waltrip	Bahari Racing Pontiac	499	15,375	Running
9	11	21	Morgan Shepherd	Wood Brothers Ford	498	14,675	Running
10	5	42	Kyle Petty**	SabCo Racing Pontiac	498	16,475	Running
11	25	24	Jeff Gordon	Hendrick Motorsports Chevy	498	13,360	Running
12	22	11	Bill Elliott	Junior Johnson Ford	497	17,075	Running
13	12	25	Ken Schrader	Hendrick Motorsports Chevy	497	12,125	Running
14	2	7	Geoff Bodine	AK - G.E.B. Racing Ford	497	17,925	Running
15	23	40	Kenny Wallace	SabCo Racing Pontiac	496	9,125	Running
16	21	6	Mark Martin	Roush Racing Ford	495	15,275	Running
17	30	4	Jeff Purvis	Morgan-McClure Chevrolet	495	15,825	Running
18	6	17	Darrell Waltrip	DarWal Chevrolet	495	15,630	Running
19	33	41	Phil Parsons	Larry Hedrick Chevrolet	493	7,525	Running
20	18	98	Derrike Cope	Cale Yarborough Ford	492	10,875	Running
21	32	71	Dave Marcis	Marcis Auto Racing Chevy	487	5,325	Running
22	26	90	Bobby Hillin,Jr.	Junie Donlavey Ford	484	5,225	Running
23	16	27	Hut Stricklin	Junior Johnson Ford	483	9,775	Running
24	19	15	Lake Speed	Bud Moore Eng. Ford	478	12,875	Running
25	10	75	Todd Bodine	Butch Mock Ford	468	4,775	Running
26	13	1	Rick Mast	Precision Products Ford	454	9,425	Running
27	31	16	Wally Dallenbach,Jr.	Roush Racing Ford	447	9,275	Running
28	34	68	Greg Sacks	Tri-Star Motorsports	445	4,525	Running
29	7	3	Dale Earnhardt	RCR Enterprises Chevrolet	440	10,525	Rear End
30	3	8	Sterling Marlin	Stavola Brothers Ford	438	10,000	Running
31	28	55	Ted Musgrave	RaDiUs Motorsports Ford	435	8,925	Running
32	9	22	Bobby Labonte	Bill Davis Ford	413	6,400	Running
33	27	33	Harry Gant	Leo Jackson Chevrolet	362	13,375	Trans
34	8	44	Jimmy Hensley	Petty Enterprises Pontiac	292	5,875	Crash

Time of Race: 3 hours, 32 minutes, 57 seconds
Average Speed: 74.102 mph
Pole Winner: Ernie Irvan – 92.583 mph
Lap Leaders: Geoff Bodine 1-32, Ernie Irvan 33-116, Rusty Wallace 117-167, Irvan 168-328, R.Wallace 329-331, Irvan 332-381, R.Wallace 382-388, Irvan 389-421, Jimmy Spencer 422-426, Irvan 427-500.
10 lead changes among 4 drivers.
Cautions: 11 for 73 laps Margin of Victory: 2.77 seconds
*Relieved by Dick Trickle **Relieved by Jimmy Hensley

Bryan Hallman

Ernie Irvan took over the Robert Yates' Ford and won the Goody's 500 at Martinsville. He leads Jimmy Hensley, filling in for the injured Rick Wilson, and Dale Earnhardt into the first turn.

finish.

Jimmy Hensley, driving the Petty Enterprises Pontiac in place of injured Rick Wilson, got tangled up in a crash when Sterling Marlin tapped Darrell Waltrip into a spin in the third lap.

"It's a shame," said Waltrip, who is winless since September of 1992. "We could have had something for them today."

Spencer gave the Bobby Allison Ford a strong run. "Wow, I was impressed with this car today," said the Berwick, Penn. driver. "I sure didn't have anything for Ernie or Rusty. I had a third place car and drove my heart out to finish there. I think it will be a day my car owner Bobby Allison will remember for a long time."

Wallace made another significant leap in the Winston Cup standings when Earnhardt fell victim to rear gearing failure and wound up 29th. "I kept telling everybody it wasn't over," said Wallace, who gained 99 points. "He was due for some bad luck. My team is a legitimate contender and we're going to make it a heck of a battle in the last five races."

Earnhardt said his recent run of foul luck "really stinks. But it wasn't anybody's fault. It was just a bad part. But we're still ahead. We're the ones being chased." Earnhardt left Martinsville with an 82-point lead in the Winston Cup standings.

Irvan only lost the lead during pit stops in the final half of the race. "These are the kind of days I had hoped for when I joined Robert Yates," said Irvan. "I wanted to get in on what I consider the dominant Ford on the circuit. Today it certainly was."

The triumph was a big moral lifter for Yates and crew chief Larry McReynolds. "I wish Davey was here to celebrate with us," said McReynolds. "But I'm sure he's looking down and grinning in that big, wide Allison grin. Davey Allison is our teammate forever. And now he can finally say he won at Martinsville."

Irvan and Geoff Bodine occupied the front row – in cars vacated by Allison and Alan Kulwicki. "Looking at the front row had to be a little eerie for the fans," said Bodine. "I'm sure it evoked a lot of memories. I'm glad Ernie won one for Davey. Now it's up to me to win one for Alan."

Bodine led the first 32 laps but faded to a 13th place

Race #26

Title Contenders Wallace and Earnhardt Run 1-2 at Wilkesboro

N.WILKESBORO, NC (Oct. 3) – Title contenders Rusty Wallace and Dale Earnhardt took center stage at North Wilkesboro and recorded a first and second place finish in the Tyson/Holly Farms 400. Wallace captured his seventh win of the season and finished ahead of Earnhardt for the seventh consecutive race.

Wallace's Pontiac led the final 102 laps and raced across the finish line 1.64-seconds ahead of Earnhardt. The victory was worth only 10 points to Wallace in the Winston Cup title chase and now trails by 72 points.

Wallace has now shaved 273 points off of Earnhardt's lead since the July race at Daytona. "With that 300-point lead, they (Earnhardt and the RCR Enterprises team) pulled the throttle back and put it on cruise," declared Wallace. "I'm sure they never thought in a million years that they'd lose 200 points in two weeks. They got in trouble because they put it on cruise control."

Wallace claimed that Earnhardt utilized the structure in the point system which makes it virtually impossible to cut into a point lead – unless the leader develops

Bryan Hallman

Jeff Purvis #4 and John Andretti #72 tangle in the third turn at North Wilkesboro.

problems. "But now they're going to have to run wide open," said Wallace. "Today, Dale drove a typical Earnhardt race – real aggressive and real hard. I think he's the best driver out there. He's great. And if you can beat the best driver, then you feel good going home."

Wallace said he expected a full-tilt charge from both contenders the rest of the way., "The neat thing about this championship is neither of us can be conservative. We've both got to race our tails off."

Earnhardt conceded the race to Wallace, but was upbeat afterwards. "We'll give this one to him. So we'll give him these 10 points. Hopefully we can go to Charlotte and beat him there."

Only four caution flags interrupted the brisk pace, but one of those took place at the start. Ricky Rudd got the jump on pole-sitter Ernie Irvan, but realizing that he might be penalized, Rudd hit the brakes so he wouldn't beat Irvan to the green flag.

That jammed up the outside lane. "We got the green flag and I started like I should have," said Rudd. "Ernie didn't come up to speed and I wasn't about to pass him and get penalized."

In all, 13 cars were involved and Earnhardt, who started 10th, survived a brush with disaster. With the line stacked up, a chain-reaction bumper banging ensued. The cars of Jeff Gordon, Geoff Bodine, Mark Martin and Morgan Shepherd were heavily damaged.

"That's the second race here this year that I haven't gone one lap before my car got all torn up," said a dejected Martin. "It's ridiculous. Rudd slammed on the brakes. I braked, but (Bill) Elliott hit me in the rear"

"I don't know what happened," said Elliott. "They started and all of a sudden they stopped."

Bryan Hallman

Jeff Gordon's Chevrolet was badly mangled after opening lap crash at North Wilkesboro.

Geoff Bodine suffered another crumpled car. "I can't believe this luck we've had since I started driving my own car. I just hope my luck turns around," he said.

Gordon said he "got turned around and hit from all four sides. I can't believe my luck this year. I haven't made 10 laps at this track before something happened to put me out."

Gordon and Bodine got their cars repaired and got back in the race, but pulled out later with handling problems. They were the only drivers who failed to finish.

John Andretti, the IndyCar star who made his first Winston Cup start, finished 24th after spinning out twice.

Jeff Purvis struggled to finish 25th in the Morgan-McClure Chevrolet, but would lose his ride two days later.

Winston Cup Series Race No. 26
400 Laps at North Wilkesboro Speedway
N.Wilkesboro, NC
"Tyson/Holly Farms 400"
250 Miles on .625-mile Short Track
October 3, 1993

Fin	St	No.	Driver	Team / Car	Laps	Money	Status
1	11	2	Rusty Wallace	Roger Penske Pontiac	400	$46,260	Running
2	10	3	Dale Earnhardt	RCR Enterprises Chevrolet	400	46,285	Running
3	1	28	Ernie Irvan	Robert Yates Racing Ford	400	39,435	Running
4	3	42	Kyle Petty	SabCo Racing Pontiac	400	20,085	Running
5	2	5	Ricky Rudd	Hendrick Motorsports Chevy	399	21,235	Running
6	5	33	Harry Gant	Leo Jackson Chevrolet	398	21,235	Running
7	4	14	Terry Labonte	Billy Hagan Chevrolet	398	15,660	Running
8	13	1	Rick Mast	Precision Products Ford	397	12,805	Running
9	24	18	Dale Jarrett	Joe Gibbs Chevrolet	397	14,455	Running
10	12	25	Ken Schrader	Hendrick Motorsports Chevy	397	14,560	Running
11	7	17	Darrell Waltrip	DarWal Chevrolet	397	15,980	Running
12	20	22	Bobby Labonte	Bill Davis Ford	396	9,730	Running
13	17	12	Jimmy Spencer	Bobby Allison Ford	396	11,480	Running
14	28	30	Michael Waltrip	Bahari Racing Pontiac	396	11,130	Running
15	29	16	Wally Dallenbach,Jr.	Roush Racing Ford	395	11,230	Running
16	6	6	Mark Martin	Roush Racing Ford	395	13,455	Running
17	19	15	Lake Speed	Bud Moore Eng. Ford	395	13,355	Running
18	8	11	Bill Elliott	Junior Johnson Ford	394	15,530	Running
19	9	8	Sterling Marlin	Stavola Brothers Ford	394	10,305	Running
20	27	98	Derrike Cope	Cale Yarborough Ford	391	10,680	Running
21	26	26	Brett Bodine	King Motorsports Ford	390	9,980	Running
22	32	90	Bobby Hillin,Jr.	Junie Donlavey Ford	388	5,080	Running
23	25	75	Todd Bodine	Butch Mock Ford	382	4,930	Running
24	31	72	John Andretti	Billy Hagan Chevrolet	380	7,880	Running
25	33	4	Jeff Purvis	Morgan-McClure Chevrolet	380	14,530	Running
26	30	78	Jay Hedgecock	Wilson-Inman Ford	372	4,780	Running
27	22	40	Kenny Wallace	SabCo Racing Pontiac	364	6,955	Running
28	14	27	Hut Stricklin	Junior Johnson Ford	359	9,290	Running
29	18	55	Ted Musgrave	RaDiUs Motorsports Ford	341	9,230	Running
30	15	41	Dick Trickle	Larry Hedrick Chevrolet	340	5,830	Running
31	23	7	Geoff Bodine	AK - G.E.B. Racing Ford	256	13,605	Handling
32	21	21	Morgan Shepherd	Wood Brothers Ford	252	8,705	Running
33	34	44	Rick Wilson	Petty Enterprises Pontiac	246	5,730	Running
34	16	24	Jeff Gordon	Hendrick Motorsports Chevy	117	5,655	Handling

Time of Race: 2 hours, 34 minutes, 46 seconds
Average Speed: 96.920 mph
Pole Winner: Ernie Irvan – 116.786 mph
Lap Leaders: Ricky Rudd 1-23, Kyle Petty 24-77, Terry Labonte 78-122, Rick Mast 123-124, Dale Jarrett 125-126, Bobby Labonte 127, Wally Dallenbach,Jr. 128, Derrike Cope 129-131, T.Labonte 132-139, Mast 140-159, Rusty Wallace 160-238, Dale Earnhardt 239-292, Petty 293, Earnhardt 294-298, R.Wallace 299-400.
15 lead changes among 10 drivers.
Cautions: 4 for 26 laps Margin of Victory: 1.64 seconds

Race #27

Irvan Routs Charlotte Field by Leading All But 6 Laps

CONCORD, NC (Oct. 10) – The highly anticipated duel at Charlotte Motor Speedway was watered down by an overwhelming performance by Ernie Irvan, who led all but six laps and romped to victory in the Mello Yello 500.

Winston Cup Series Race No. 27
334 Laps at Charlotte Motor Speedway
Concord, NC
"Mello Yello 500"
501 Miles on 1.5 mile Superspeedway
October 10, 1993

Fin	St	No.	Driver	Team / Car	Laps	Money	Status
1	2	28	Ernie Irvan	Robert Yates Racing Ford	334	$147,450	Running
2	7	6	Mark Martin	Roush Racing Ford	334	67,900	Running
3	9	3	Dale Earnhardt	RCR Enterprises Chevrolet	334	56,900	Running
4	21	2	Rusty Wallace	Roger Penske Pontiac	334	42,950	Running
5	1	24	Jeff Gordon	Hendrick Motorsports Chevy	334	56,875	Running
6	15	12	Jimmy Spencer	Bobby Allison Ford	334	32,750	Running
7	31	42	Kyle Petty	SabCo Racing Pontiac	334	28,500	Running
8	8	5	Ricky Rudd	Hendrick Motorsports Chevy	333	24,500	Running
9	4	25	Ken Schrader	Hendrick Motorsports Chevy	332	25,400	Running
10	5	11	Bill Elliott	Junior Johnson Ford	332	29,050	Running
11	36	15	Lake Speed	Bud Moore Eng. Ford	332	20,200	Running
12	13	33	Harry Gant	Leo Jackson Chevrolet	331	20,425	Running
13	3	7	Geoff Bodine	AK - G.E.B. Racing Ford	331	23,150	Running
14	16	21	Morgan Shepherd	Wood Brothers Ford	331	15,050	Running
15	10	26	Brett Bodine	King Motorsports Ford	331	14,800	Running
16	22	14	Terry Labonte	Billy Hagan Chevrolet	331	13,025	Running
17	34	8	Sterling Marlin	Stavola Brothers Ford	331	12,200	Running
18	12	1	Rick Mast	Precision Products Ford	331	11,600	Running
19	24	17	Darrell Waltrip	DarWal Chevrolet	330	16,625	Running
20	37	90	Bobby Hillin,Jr.	Junie Donlavey Ford	330	6,650	Running
21	26	55	Ted Musgrave	RaDiUs Motorsports Ford	329	10,800	Running
22	27	41	Dick Trickle	Larry Hedrick Chevrolet	329	7,575	Running
23	23	27	Hut Stricklin	Junior Johnson Ford	329	10,310	Running
24	33	16	Wally Dallenbach,Jr.	Roush Racing Ford	328	10,050	Running
25	11	4	Joe Nemechek	Morgan-McClure Chevrolet	326	14,880	Running
26	38	18	Dale Jarrett	Joe Gibbs Chevrolet	325	13,160	Running
27	20	30	Michael Waltrip	Bahari Racing Pontiac	324	9,645	Running
28	41	22	Bobby Labonte	Bill Davis Ford	324	7,010	Running
29	30	95	Jeremy Mayfield	Earl Sadler Ford	324	4,830	Running
30	35	52	Mike Wallace	Means Racing Ford	323	4,745	Running
31	40	72	John Andretti	Billy Hagan Chevrolet	323	4,630	Running
32	6	68	Greg Sacks	Tri-Star Motorsports Ford	314	5,250	Running
33	39	19	Chad Little	Pollex-Rypien Ford	314	4,475	Running
34	32	65	Jerry O'Neil	Heidi O'Neil Chevrolet	311	4,450	Oil Press
35	42	40	Kenny Wallace	SabCo Racing Pontiac	304	5,975	Running
36	18	44	Rick Wilson	Petty Enterprises Pontiac	302	5,925	Running
37	28	20	Bobby Hamilton	Dick Moroso Ford	299	4,390	Running
38	29	85	Jim Sauter	Thee Dixon Ford	265	4,380	Engine
39	14	98	Derrike Cope	Cale Yarborough Ford	253	8,870	Engine
40	19	45	Rich Bickle	Gene Isenhour Ford	252	4,365	Handling
41	25	29	Andy Hillenburg	Diamond Ridge Chevrolet	242	4,365	Fatigue
42	17	75	Todd Bodine	Butch Mock Ford	140	5,365	Crash

Time of Race: 3 hours, 14 minutes, 31 seconds
Average Speed: 154.537 mph
Pole Winner: Jeff Gordon – 177.684 mph
Lap Leaders: Ernie Irvan 1-64, Jeff Gordon 65, Irvan 66-161, Dale Earnhardt 162-164, Irvan 165-210, Mark Martin 211, Irvan 212-272, Martin 273, Irvan 274-334.
9 lead changes among 4 drivers.
Cautions: 2 for 11 laps Margin of Victory: 1.83 seconds

The 34-year-old Modesto, Calif. pounded the star-studded field into submission to record his third win of the season – and his second since joining the Robert Yates Racing team.

Irvan had a lead of nearly 14 seconds over second running Mark Martin when a yellow flag was waved with 28 remaining. NASCAR officials said that oil on the backstretch from the car of Rich Bickle was responsible for the yellow. But Bickle had pulled out of the race several laps earlier.

"I didn't see any oil," said Irvan. "They did spread some kitty-litter over there. Maybe a cat had to go to the bathroom. But what the heck, that's what made it a good race in the last laps."

Bryan Hallman

Mark Martin #6 gets sideways during his battle with Dale Earnhardt for second place in final laps of Charlotte's 500-miler.

The final 22-lap sprint kept the audience of 115,000 on its feet. Irvan once again motored away from the pack and crossed the finish line 1.83-seconds ahead of runner-up Martin, who nosed out Dale Earnhardt. Rusty Wallace came in fourth with pole-sitter Jeff Gordon fifth.

In the final green flag run, Earnhardt and Martin engaged in a duel to be remembered. Earnhardt poked the nose of his Chevrolet under the rear bumper of Martin's Ford, and although no contact was ever made, Martin had a handful every time he came off the fourth turn. "He was really causing me some grief," said Martin. "Dale can do that better than anyone. He got a burst of speed and it was some serious racing. I wish we'd have been battling like that for the lead."

Wallace joined the fray and made one stab at Earnhardt but had to settle for fourth.

"We were fender-to-fender with Rusty at the end, weren't we," said Earnhardt, who increased his lead in the Winston Cup standings to 82 points. "Rusty was all over me in the corners and I was all over Mark. It was a lot of fun. My arm is really sore. I was racing hard at the end."

Steve Hmiel, crew chief for Martin, summed up the day for everyone but Irvan. "We brought a knife to a gun-fight," said Hmiel. "The first 300 laps were boring. I almost went to sleep. But I could hardly stand those last 34 laps."

Irvan had the field covered so much that he was able to increase his lead even when his engine started skipping halfway through the race. "We had a miss in the engine, so I started flipping switches," said Irvan. "I didn't know what they were for. It's the same car Davey had here in May. They had the same trouble then, and they never did figure out what it was. I never lost any RPMs and I kept passing cars. So I'm sure they were saying, 'Boy, this is a dummy. He doesn't even know when it's slowing down'."

Irvan averaged a record 154.537 mph as only one other caution slowed the field. He established another record by leading 328 laps, surpassing the 1966 mark of 301 laps led by LeeRoy Yarbrough. "The race may have been stinky for the fans," said Irvan, "but it smelled pretty good to me."

The race was the first under new NASCAR spoiler rules, which drew a major complaint from many drivers, especially the Pontiac teams. "We're in a championship race and they started messin' with the rules," said Wallace. "The Pontiacs got screwed. Our cars have a smaller rear deck width and it hurts us worse than the Chevys or the Fords."

Only six cars fell out of the race. Many drivers had predicted a rash of crashes because of uncertainty about the new rules, which were designed to reduce speeds here and at tracks in Atlanta and Michigan. The rules reduced the height of the rear spoilers from six-and-a-half inches to five; increased the height of the cars about an inch-and-a-half and closed air intakes near windshields.

Todd Bodine looped his Ford on lap 144 in the day's only crash. Seventh-place finisher Kyle Petty said,

"I'm sure everybody drove hard, but there was no side-by-side racing," he said. "If somebody came on you, you just let them go."

Car owner Junior Johnson, whose cars finished 10th (Bill Elliott) and 23rd (Hut Stricklin), said, "There was no racing today. Just a lot of slipping and sliding. It was a game of horsepower."

Jeff Gordon earned his first Winston Cup pole with a run of 177.684 mph in a nighttime qualifying session. He lost the lead to Irvan at the start but was able to lead one lap during the shuffling of pit stops. "My car's handling was off in one corner, okay in the other. We never could get through the corners very well," he said.

Race #28

Rusty Runs Ragged to Rack Up at The Rock

ROCKINGHAM, NC (Oct. 24) – Rusty Wallace fought handling problems for over half the race then sprinted to an easy victory in the AC Delco 500 at North Carolina Motor Speedway. It was the ninth win of the season for Wallace, but he was only able to chip 10 points off Dale Earnhardt's lead in the Winston Cup standings.

Bobby Labonte discusses pre-race strategy with car owner Bill Davis and crew chief Tim Brewer.

Winston Cup Series Race No. 28
492 Laps at N.C. Motor Speedway
Rockingham, NC
"AC Delco 500"
500.364 Miles on 1.017 mile Superspeedway
October 24, 1993

Fin	St	No.	Driver	Team / Car	Laps	Money	Status
1	18	2	Rusty Wallace	Roger Penske Pontiac	492	$52,850	Running
2	22	3	Dale Earnhardt	RCR Enterprises Chevrolet	492	49,550	Running
3	4	11	Bill Elliott	Junior Johnson Ford	492	35,675	Running
4	9	33	Harry Gant	Leo Jackson Chevrolet	492	29,225	Running
5	1	6	Mark Martin	Roush Racing Ford	491	33,150	Running
6	3	28	Ernie Irvan	Robert Yates Racing Ford	491	24,800	Running
7	16	17	Darrell Waltrip	DarWal Chevrolet	491	21,350	Running
8	2	25	Ken Schrader	Hendrick Motorsports Chevy	491	17,900	Running
9	10	41	Dick Trickle	Larry Hedrick Chevrolet	490	14,550	Running
10	19	7	Geoff Bodine	AK - G..E.B. Racing Ford	490	22,500	Running
11	8	21	Morgan Shepherd	Wood Brothers Ford	490	16,150	Running
12	25	8	Sterling Marlin	Stavola Brothers Ford	490	16,350	Running
13	6	42	Kyle Petty	SabCo Racing Pontiac	490	18,250	Running
14	5	5	Ricky Rudd	Hendrick Motorsports Chevy	490	15,350	Running
15	24	14	Terry Labonte	Billy Hagan Chevrolet	489	15,500	Running
16	31	15	Lake Speed	Bud Moore Eng. Ford	489	17,150	Running
17	13	1	Rick Mast	Precision Products Ford	489	14,450	Running
18	29	30	Michael Waltrip	Bahari Racing Pontiac	489	16,050	Running
19	17	98	Derrike Cope	Cale Yarborough Ford	489	13,550	Running
20	15	12	Jimmy Spencer	Bobby Allison Ford	489	14,750	Running
21	7	24	Jeff Gordon	Hendrick Motorsports Chevy	486	11,350	Running
22	12	22	Bobby Labonte	Bill Davis Ford	485	10,150	Running
23	14	4	Joe Nemechek	Morgan-McClure Chevrolet	485	17,400	Running
24	20	27	Hut Stricklin	Junior Johnson Ford	485	14,950	Running
25	23	75	Todd Bodine	Butch Mock Ford	485	7,625	Running
26	28	44	Rick Wilson	Petty Enterprises Pontiac	482	9,100	Running
27	34	71	Dave Marcis	Marcis Auto Racing Ford	478	7,400	Running
28	32	55	Ted Musgrave	RaDiUs Motorsports Ford	469	11,875	Running
29	37	52	Jimmy Means	Means Racing Ford	467	7,200	Running
30	21	18	Dale Jarrett	Joe Gibbs Chevrolet	454	15,675	Rear End
31	30	16	Wally Dallenbach,Jr	Roush Racing Ford	430	11,450	Handling
32	27	68	Greg Sacks	Tri-Star Motorsports Ford	416	6,800	Running
33	38	90	Bobby Hillin,Jr.	Junie Donlavey Ford	415	6,700	Running
34	35	32	Jimmy Horton	Active Racing Chevrolet	304	6,600	Crash
35	11	26	Brett Bodine	King Motorsports Ford	281	15,125	Ignition
36	33	66	Mike Wallace	Barry Owen Ford	246	6,475	Engine
37	41	40	Kenny Wallace	SabCo Racing Pontiac	181	7,950	Handling
38	40	56	Jerry Hill	Willie Tierney Chevrolet	138	6,425	Engine
39	39	72	John Andretti	Billy Hagan Chevrolet	122	6,425	Crash
40	26	02	T.W.Taylor	Taylor Performance Ford	120	6,400	Crash
41	36	37	Loy Allen,Jr.	Allen Racing Ford	8	6,400	Crash

Time of Race: 4 hours, 23 minutes, 16 seconds
Average Speed: 114.036 mph
Pole Winner: Mark Martin – 148.353 mph
Lap Leaders: Mark Martin 1, Ernie Irvan 2-16, Ken Schrader 17, Irvan 18-68, Jimmy Means 69, T.W.Taylor 70, Irvan 71-85, Martin 86-87, Irvan 88-92, Dale Earnhardt 93-97, Jimmy Spencer 98-125, Dave Marcis 126-130, Spencer 131-155, Earnhardt 156-164, Spencer 165-167, Harry Gant 168-214, Schrader 215-217, Dale Jarrett 218, Gant 219-297, Schrader 298, Gant 299-311, Rusty Wallace 312-438, Schrader 439-440, R.Wallace 441-492.
Cautions: 8 for 54 laps Margin of Victory: 3.23 seconds

Wallace's Pontiac outran Earnhardt's Chevrolet by 3.23 seconds to rack up his 30th career triumph. Bill Elliott finished a distant third. Harry Gant, who held command during the middle stages, fell to fourth after encountering poor pit stops. Fifth place went to pole-sitter Mark Martin.

Although basking in Victory Lane, Wallace seemed to sense that the point championship was getting further

Kim Novosat

Rusty Wallace (left) chats with Dale Earnhardt and crew member Will Lind at Rockingham.

out of reach. "This has been a wonderful year," said Wallace, "but we just can't seem to cut into Dale's lead. We've led thousands more laps than anyone, have more top fives, more top 10s, more wins. But those darn DNF's (did not finish) in the middle of the year are still plaguing us. It's frustrating to have the kind of year we're having and still be 72 points behind.

"I'm not giving up on the championship. If he slips just one time, I'll be right there and he knows it," he said.

Wallace had built an 8.5-second lead in the closing stages before Earnhardt began reeling him in. "I still had half a throttle left, so I wasn't worried," declared Wallace.

Earnhardt said a deflating tire cost him any chance to run Wallace down. "It started going flat with about 10 laps to go," said the title-bound Earnhardt. "The car was pretty ornery, but I kept driving it."

Gant made a strong bid to remove the goose-egg from the 1993 victory column. He drove to the front for the first time in the 164th lap, using his patented rim-riding technique. He actually put a lap on Earnhardt before a green flag round of pit stops.

"We lost a lot of time in the pits," said the 53-year-old Gant. "It's unbelievable how much time Wallace and Earnhardt picked up on me in green-flag pit stops. I almost had Earnhardt lapped and he still beat me."

Jimmy Spencer loomed as a possible contender, but he too lost time in the pits. "We looked strong all 500 miles," said Spencer, who led 56 of the first 167 laps. "We had the car today. I really think if everything went right, we'd win, especially after we got into that little duel with Earnhardt and was able to pull away.

"Then we rounded off a lug nut (during a pit stop),"

Bryan Hallman

Richard Petty, crew chief Robbie Loomis and driver Rick Wilson discuss the upcoming Winston Cup race at North Carolina Motor Speedway.

Spencer continued. "It's disappointing, really frustrating to run like this and only finish 20th." Spencer was three laps behind when the checkered flag fell.

Crew chief Jimmy Fennig said he "felt like throwing the thing (lug wrench) through a window or something" when the problem surfaced in the pits.

Rookies Loy Allen, Jr., T.W. Taylor and John Andretti were involved in crashes. No injuries were reported.

Taylor and Andretti were eliminated in a backstretch crash on lap 125. Many of the leaders snaked their way through the scraps of metal laying on the track. "It was raining metal," said Wallace, who was able to avoid the spinning cars. "I saw a wheel and a spindle – and big heavy springs flying in front of me. Man, those cars were shredding parts like an IndyCar.

Race #29

Martin on the Mark at Phoenix; Wallace on the Ropes

PHOENIX, AZ (Oct. 31) – Mark Martin led all but one of the final 96 laps and galloped to a convincing win in the Slick 50 500 at Phoenix International Raceway as Rusty Wallace's title hopes were virtually put to rest.

Martin drove his Ford to an 0.17-second victory over Ernie Irvan to score his fifth win of the season. Kyle Petty came from 27th to finish third. Dale Earnhardt overcame early troubles and survived two bumper-bangers to finish fourth. He stretched his lead over Wallace to 126 points. Fifth place went to Bill Elliott, who started on the pole but failed to lead a lap.

Wallace finished 19th, two laps behind. He was running in fourth place in the 190th lap when a tire peeled and suspension parts were damaged as they scraped the track while Wallace drove to the pits.

The Roger Penske crew replaced the flat tire, but had to wait until a caution flag to make hasty repairs to the suspension. Before the problem developed, Wallace

Dale Earnhardt all but wrapped up the 1993 Winston Cup championship at Phoenix.

Winston Cup Series Race No. 29
312 Laps at Phoenix Int'l Raceway
Phoenix, AZ
"Slick 50 500"
312 Miles on 1-mile Superspeedway
October 31, 1993

Fin	St	No.	Driver	Team / Car	Laps	Money	Status
1	3	6	Mark Martin	Roush Racing Ford	312	$67,035	Running
2	5	28	Ernie Irvan	Robert Yates Racing Ford	312	44,155	Running
3	27	42	Kyle Petty	SabCo Racing Pontiac	312	28,430	Running
4	11	3	Dale Earnhardt	RCR Enterprises Chevrolet	312	29,980	Running
5	1	11	Bill Elliott	Junior Johnson Ford	312	31,655	Running
6	4	5	Ricky Rudd	Hendrick Motorsports Chevy	312	21,120	Running
7	21	17	Darrell Waltrip	DarWal Chevrolet	312	21,820	Running
8	20	22	Bobby Labonte	Bill Davis Ford	312	14,620	Running
9	23	30	Michael Waltrip	Bahari Racing Pontiac	312	16,020	Running
10	13	1	Rick Mast	Precision Products Ford	312	17,770	Running
11	22	21	Morgan Shepherd	Wood Brothers Ford	312	14,820	Running
12	15	33	Harry Gant	Leo Jackson Chevrolet	311	17,520	Running
13	16	15	Lake Speed	Bud Moore Eng. Ford	311	16,220	Running
14	26	14	Terry Labonte	Billy Hagan Chevrolet	311	13,720	Running
15	36	55	Ted Musgrave	RaDiUs Motorsports Ford	311	13,420	Running
16	14	18	Dale Jarrett	Joe Gibbs Chevrolet	311	15,320	Running
17	32	40	Kenny Wallace	SabCo Racing Pontiac	310	9,920	Running
18	35	90	Bobby Hillin,Jr.	Junie Donlavey Ford	310	7,049	Running
19	6	42	Rusty Wallace	Roger Penske Pontiac	310	15,495	Running
20	37	44	Rick Wilson	Petty Enterprises Pontiac	309	9,260	Running
21	25	61	Rick Carelli	Marshall Chesrown Chevy	309	6,685	Running
22	24	76	Ron Hornaday,Jr.	Wayne Spears Chevrolet	307	6,660	Running
23	31	98	Derrike Cope	Cale Yarborough Ford	306	11,535	Running
24	10	39	Chuck Bown	Roulo Brothers Chevrolet	306	6,610	Running
25	30	75	Todd Bodine	Butch Mock Ford	305	6,585	Running
26	40	68	Loy Allen,Jr.	Tri-Star Motorsports Ford	305	6,560	Running
27	17	12	Jimmy Spencer	Bobby Allison Ford	305	11,385	Running
28	12	25	Brett Bodine	King Motorsports Ford	300	11,260	Running
29	18	29	Steve Grissom	Diamond Ridge Chevrolet	260	6,485	Running
30	7	8	Sterling Marlin	Stavola Brothers Ford	255	11,110	Crash
31	2	41	Dick Trickle	Larry Hedrick Chevrolet	254	9,535	Tr. Arm
32	29	4	Jimmy Hensley	Morgan-McClure Chevrolet	242	15,760	Handling
33	8	25	Ken Schrader	Hendrick Motorsports Chevy	236	10,710	Running
34	33	16	Wally Dallenbach,Jr.	Roush Racing Ford	234	10,660	Rear End
35	9	24	Jeff Gordon	Hendrick Motorsports Chevy	195	7,610	Handling
36	28	27	Hut Stricklin	Junior Johnson Ford	157	10,560	Handling
37	41	71	Terry Fisher	Dick Midgley Pontiac	132	6,040	Engine
38	39	86	Rich Woodland,Jr.	Richard Woodland Olds	114	6,030	Engine
39	38	50	Mike Chase	John Strauser Chevrolet	87	6,015	Engine
40	34	72	John Andretti	Billy Hagan Chevrolet	49	5,980	Crash
41	43	58	Wayne Jacks	Jacks Pontiac	48	5,980	Engine
42	42	20	Dirk Stephens	Tom Craigen Ford	24	5,980	Engine
43	19	7	Geoff Bodine	AK - G.E.B. Racing Ford	14	15,380	Crash

Time of Race: 3 hours, 6 minutes, 30 seconds
Average Speed: 100.375 mph
Pole Winner: Bill Elliott – 129.482 mph
Lap Leaders: Dick Trickle 1-3, Mark Martin 4-19, Rusty Wallace 20, Martin 21-38, Martin 39-42, Ernie Irvan 43, Martin 44-73, Jeff Gordon 74-121, Rick Mast 122-127, Kyle Petty 128-136, Martin 137-190, Irvan 191-194, Bill Elliott 195, Dale Earnhardt 198-199, Michael Waltrip 200-201, Harry Gant 202-217, Martin 218-288, Irvan 289, Martin 290-312.
Cautions: 9 for 45 laps Margin of Victory: 0.17-seconds

Mark Martin grabbed his fifth win of the year at Phoenix.

had run in the top five and stayed well ahead of Earnhardt.

"I'm disappointed because we had Dale beat," said Wallace. "He fell back to 14th one time when I was leading. I congratulate him because he did a good job to finish fourth. We had the better car, but when the tire went down, that was it."

Earnhardt's Chevrolet barely made the starting call. A brake caliper was replaced the morning of the race, then the car failed a weight inspection. Weight was added moments before the national anthem was played.

Earnhardt started 11th and advanced into the top 10 as Dick Trickle led the early laps. In the third lap, Earnhardt tapped Ken Schrader into the second turn wall. "Dale drove hard into the turn," said Schrader. "He drove right into me. I guess he was a little over-anxious. It's a shame when it happens so early.

"He's always the one who cries about the manufacturers championship race," Schrader continued, alluding to the Richmond event when members of the RCR Enterprises team said that Schrader had cost Chevrolet some valuable points. "He sure didn't help the Chevrolets out today."

Earnhardt said that he "got into Schrader, but he came down on me a little bit and I bumped him."

Earnhardt was battling Jeff Gordon for eighth place in the 133rd lap when Gordon shot into the fourth turn wall. "Dale went to the left of me on the backstretch and we rubbed a little," explained Gordon. "When we got to the turn, I couldn't believe he got into the side of me again and put me in the wall."

Earnhardt said the two cars "got together, but I had a couple of other close calls, too. We'll take fourth place, considering what happened."

Martin and Irvan put on a dazzling duel late in the event, which had the crowd of 87,000 on its feet. After a few laps running nose-to-tail, Irvan inched ahead in the 289th lap. Martin came back the following lap to take the lead for good.

"I was racing hard those few laps," said Martin. "I got what I expected racing against Ernie. He raced me clean and left me enough room. He can always expect to get the same from me.

"I knew I would be in pretty good shape if I didn't mess up," Martin added. "If he had caught me, he would have had a heck of a time getting past me."

Trickle, driving the Larry Hedrick Chevrolet, qualified a surprising second and led for three laps. Engine problems put him well off the pace and he finally withdrew after spinning to avoid Sterling Marlin's wrecked car on lap 258.

Marlin qualified seventh, but twirled his car after an early bump from Irvan. "I don't know how he didn't see me," said Marlin. "I was right in front of him."

Geoff Bodine continued having a run of terrible luck when he was pinched into the wall while trying to avoid Marlin's spinning car.

Race #30

Earnhardt Wraps Up Title as Wallace Claims Atlanta Finale

HAMPTON, GA (Nov. 14) – Rusty Wallace ran down fuel-conscious Darrell Waltrip in the final four laps and won the Hooters 500 at Atlanta Motor Speedway, but his 10th win of the season wasn't enough to keep Dale Earnhardt from capturing his sixth Winston

Bryan Hallman

Ernie Irvan's Ford kicks up sparks after a tire failure at Atlanta.

Cup championship.

Earnhardt finished 10th and wound up 80 points in front of 10-time winner Wallace. It was the third straight year that the driver who won the most races outright did not win the title.

"To win six championships is really unbelievable," said Earnhardt, who has won three of the last four championships. "When I was growing up, I never dreamed I'd ever be where I'm at today.

"We had a tough year at times," he added. "At times it was a great year, and other times it was a sad year. We lost Davey (Allison) and Alan (Kulwicki). We'll have great memories of them.

"But it's unbelievable that this (RCR Enterprises) team keeps on ticking. Last year we couldn't put it together. Now we've got (crew chief) Andy Petree and we'll have to take him to New York and teach him how to party."

Earnhardt has King Richard Petty's standard of seven championships in his viewfinder. "I want to get two more and have eight championships," said Earnhardt. "But even if I do that, Richard will still be the King. I think I have about eight more good years in this car and I'm going to run 'em wide open. Now we can get ready and try to win the (1994) Daytona 500...again," said the 42-year-old Earnhardt.

Earnhardt clinched the championship when T.W. Taylor hit the wall in the 141st lap. Earnhardt needed only to finish 34th to clinch the title.

Wallace led most of the way and outran Ricky Rudd by 5.66 seconds. Rudd's effort enabled Chevrolet to

Bryan Hallman

Atlanta winner Rusty Wallace and six-time champion Dale Earnhardt give their final salute to Alan Kulwicki and Davey Allison.

Winston Cup Series Race No. 30
328 Laps at Atlanta Motor Speedway
Hampton, GA
"Hooters 500"

499.216 Miles on 1.522-mile Superspeedway
November 14, 1993

Fin	St	No.	Driver	Team / Car	Laps	Money	Status
1	20	2	Rusty Wallace	Roger Penske Pontiac	328	$93,100	Running
2	13	5	Ricky Rudd	Hendrick Motorsports Chevy	328	57,225	Running
3	28	17	Darrell Waltrip	DarWal Chevrolet	328	40,175	Running
4	8	11	Bill Elliott	Junior Johnson Ford	328	34,250	Running
5	18	41	Dick Trickle	Larry Hedrick Chevrolet	328	24,300	Running
6	31	30	Michael Waltrip	Bahari Racing Pontiac	328	21,875	Running
7	29	18	Dale Jarrett	Joe Gibbs Chevrolet	328	23,380	Running
8	4	55	Ted Musgrave	RaDiUs Motorsports Ford	328	20,950	Running
9	22	75	Phil Parsons	Butch Mock Ford	328	11,725	Running
10	19	3	Dale Earnhardt	RCR Enterprises Chevrolet	327	19,300	Running
11	41	42	Kyle Petty	SabCo Racing Pontiac	327	18,575	Running
12	7	28	Ernie Irvan	Robert Yates Racing Ford	327	20,250	Running
13	30	14	Terry Labonte	Billy Hagan Chevrolet	327	15,625	Running
14	32	22	Bobby Labonte	Bill Davis Ford	327	14,500	Running
15	23	66	Mike Wallace	Jack Carney Pontiac	326	10,600	Running
16	5	12	Jimmy Spencer	Bobby Allison Ford	326	14,900	Running
17	34	8	Sterling Marlin	Stavola Brothers Ford	326	14,255	Running
18	37	71	Dave Marcis	Marcis Auto Racing Chevy	326	8,315	Running
19	27	98	Derrike Cope	Cale Yarborough Ford	325	12,925	Running
20	33	6	Mark Martin	Roush Racing Ford	325	16,310	Running
21	6	20	Bobby Hamilton	Dick Moroso Ford	325	7,995	Running
22	42	27	Hut Stricklin	Junior Johnson Ford	323	12,455	Running
23	36	44	Rick Wilson	Petty Enterprises Pontiac	323	8,965	Running
24	26	68	Greg Sacks	Tri-Star Motorsports Ford	322	6,700	Running
25	17	4	Jimmy Hensley	Morgan-McClure Chevrolet	308	16,135	Running
26	10	15	Lake Speed	Bud Moore Eng. Ford	307	14,420	Running
27	21	25	Ken Schrader	Hendrick Motorsports Chevy	293	9,955	Running
28	1	33	Harry Gant	Leo Jackson Chevrolet	225	30,920	Crash
29	24	37	Loy Allen, Jr.	Tri-Star Motorsports Ford	223	6,175	Crash
30	40	40	Kenny Wallace	SabCo Racing Pontiac	214	8,200	Crash
31	15	24	Jeff Gordon	Hendrick Motorsports Chevy	193	8,710	Crash
32	16	21	Morgan Shepherd	Wood Brothers Ford	184	10,720	Engine
33	38	16	Wally Dallenbach,Jr.	Roush Racing Ford	156	10,430	Crash
34	39	02	T.W.Taylor	Taylor Performance Ford	134	5,840	Crash
35	25	61	Rick Carelli	Marshall Chesrown Chevrolet	117	5,775	Vibration
36	9	45	Rich Bickle	Gene Isenhour Ford	113	5,710	Trans
37	3	1	Rick Mast	Richard Jackson Ford	105	10,170	Engine
38	14	32	Jimmy Horton	Active Racing Chevrolet	46	5,640	Crash
39	11	7	Geoff Bodine	AK - G E B Racing Ford	28	15,015	Crash
40	2	26	Brett Bodine	King Motorsports Ford	19	8,600	Crash
41	12	90	Bobby Hillin, Jr.	Junie Donlavey Ford	19	5,600	Crash
42	35	31	Neil Bonnett	RCR Enterprises Chevrolet	3	5,600	Quit

Time of Race: 3 hours, 59 minutes, 12 seconds
Average Speed: 125.221 mph
Pole Winner: Harry Gant – 176.902mph
Lap Leaders: Harry Gant 1-22, Dale Jarrett 23, Gant 24-28, Ricky Rudd 29, Gant 30-80, Rusty Wallace 81-85, Rudd 86-89, R.Wallace 90-106, Michael Waltrip 107, R.Wallace 108-124, Morgan Shepherd 125-126, R.Wallace 127-152, Jeff Gordon 153, R.Wallace 154, Gordon 155-159, Bobby Labonte 160-163, Phil Parsons 164-166, Dale Earnhardt 167-168, Bill Elliott 169-175, R.Wallace 176-219, Darrell Waltrip 220-223, R.Wallace 244-250, Jarrett 251-261, R.Wallace 262-309, M.Waltrip 310, D.Waltrip 311-324, R.Wallace 325-328.
26 lead changes among 12 drivers.
Cautions: 11 for 58 laps Margin of Victory: 5.66 seconds

beat Ford by one point in the coveted Manufacturers' Championship. "I have mixed emotions about finishing second and giving the Manufacturers' title for Chevrolet," said Rudd, who has announced he will switch for Ford for the 1994 season. "I drove for the only Rick Hendrick team that won in the last two years. But Chevrolet wouldn't even offer me any sheet metal for next year. Chevrolet basically doesn't know that I even exist. They wouldn't give me the time of day, but they stepped up and made good offers to other teams. I'm glad I'm going to Ford."

Third place went to Waltrip, who made one less pit stop than the other leaders. Bill Elliott finished fourth and Dick Trickle's superlative run netted him fifth place.

Wallace couldn't hide his disappointment, but he was well prepared for the letdown. "My crew didn't tell me Earnhardt clinched it, but I had a pretty good feeling. I was watching all those cars fall out and I kept count in my head.

"It turned out about the way I thought it would," added Wallace. "I came down here to win and Dale's bunch came down here to win the championship."

Earnhardt crashed in practice and had to start 19th on the grid. He drove a conservative race until he had mathematically locked up the title. As he was making his move to the front, Earnhardt slipped in turn three on lap 223 and hammered Greg Sacks, who did a masterful job of keeping his car out of the wall. "Once eight cars fell out, I felt it was time to go racing. I was trying to win the race and I messed up. I didn't mean to tag him like that," said Earnhardt.

The race was a crash-fest with 11 cautions consuming 58 laps. There were a number of wrecks in practice that had several contestants feeling apprehensive. In the race, Ken Schrader wrecked for the third time in the week. He piled into a spinning Jimmy Spencer. Geoff Bodine, who endured another wreck not of his making, wiped his car out when he hit the inside concrete barrier after glancing off of Schrader.

Other drivers kayoed by crashes included pole-sitter Harry Gant, Jeff Gordon, Kenny Wallace, Brett Bodine, Bobby Hillin, Jr. and Wally Dallenbach, Jr.

Sandy Roach

Harry Gant put his Leo Jackson Motorsports Chevy on the pole for the season finale at Atlanta.

1993 NASCAR Season
Final Point Standings - Winston Cup Series

Rank	Driver	Points	Starts	Wins	Top 5	Top 10	Winnings
1	Dale Earnhardt	4,526	30	6	17	21	$3,353,789
2	Rusty Wallace	4,446	30	10	19	21	1,702,154
3	Mark Martin	4,150	30	5	12	19	1,657,662
4	Dale Jarrett	4,000	30	1	13	18	1,242,394
5	Kyle Petty	3,860	30	1	9	15	914,662
6	Ernie Irvan	3,834	30	3	12	14	1,400,468
7	Morgan Shepherd	3,807	30	1	3	15	782,523
8	Bill Elliott	3,774	30	0	6	15	955,859
9	Ken Schrader	3,715	30	0	9	15	952,748
10	Ricky Rudd	3,644	30	1	9	14	752,562
11	Harry Gant	3,524	30	0	4	12	772,832
12	Jimmy Spencer	3,496	30	0	5	10	686,026
13	Darrell Waltrip	3,479	30	0	4	10	746,646
14	Jeff Gordon	3,447	30	0	7	11	765,168
15	Sterling Marlin	3,355	30	0	1	8	628,835
16	Geoff Bodine	3,338	30	1	2	9	783,762
17	Michael Waltrip	3,291	30	0	0	5	529,923
18	Terry Labonte	3,280	30	0	0	10	531,717
19	Bobby Labonte	3,221	30	0	0	6	395,660
20	Brett Bodine	3,183	29	0	3	9	582,014
21	Rick Mast	3,001	30	0	1	5	568,095
22	Wally Dallenbach, Jr.	2,978	30	0	1	4	474,340
23	Kenny Wallace	2,893	30	0	0	3	330,325
24	Hut Stricklin	2,866	30	0	1	2	494,600
25	Ted Musgrave	2,853	29	0	2	5	458,615
26	Derrike Cope	2,787	30	0	0	1	402,515
27	Bobby Hillin, Jr.	2,717	30	0	0	0	263,540
28	Rick Wilson	2,647	29	0	0	1	299,725
29	Phil Parsons	2,454	26	0	0	2	293,725
30	Dick Trickle	2,224	26	0	1	2	244,065
31	Davey Allison	2,104	16	1	6	8	513,585
32	Jimmy Hensley	2,001	21	0	0	2	368,150
33	Dave Marcis	1,970	23	0	0	0	202,305
34	Lake Speed	1,956	21	0	0	1	319,800
35	Greg Sacks	1,730	19	0	0	1	168,055
36	Jimmy Means	1,471	18	0	0	0	148,205
37	Bobby Hamilton	1,348	15	0	0	1	142,740
38	Jimmy Horton	841	13	0	0	0	115,105
39	Jeff Purvis	774	8	0	0	0	106,045
40	Todd Bodine	715	10	0	0	0	63,245
41	Alan Kulwicki	625	5	0	2	3	165,470
42	P.J. Jones	498	6	0	0	1	53,370
43	Joe Ruttman	417	5	0	1	1	70,700
44	Joe Nemechek	389	5	0	0	0	56,580
45	Loy Allen, Jr.	362	5	0	0	0	34,695
46	Mike Wallace	343	4	0	0	0	30,125
47	Jim Sauter	295	4	0	0	0	48,860
48	Rich Bickle	292	5	0	0	0	36,095
49	Rick Carelli	258	3	0	0	0	19,650
50	John Andretti	250	4	0	0	0	24,915

Special Events 1990-1993

Daytona Twin 125-mile Qualifying Races

The Winston NASCAR All-Star Race

Busch Clash

The Winston Legends

1990
1st Daytona Twin 125
February 15, 1990

Fin	St	No.	Driver	Team / Car	Laps	Money	Status
1	4	11	Geoff Bodine	Junior Johnson Ford	50	$34,000	Running
2	13	33	Harry Gant	Leo Jackson Olds	50	21,000	Running
3	3	6	Mark Martin	Roush Racing Ford	50	14,000	Running
4	2	17	Darrell Waltrip	Hendrick Motorsports Chevy	50	9,000	Running
5	6	43	Richard Petty	Petty Enterprises Pontiac	50	7,000	Running
6	14	14	A.J. Foyt	Foyt Enterprises Olds	50	4,000	Running
7	1	25	Ken Schrader	Hendrick Motorsports Chevy	50	3,800	Run/Crash
8	9	12	Mike Alexander	Bobby Allison Buick	50	3,650	Running
9	20	98	Butch Miller	Travis Carter Chevrolet	50	3,500	Running
10	8	5	Ricky Rudd	Hendrick Motorsports Chevy	50	3,350	Running
11	5	94	Sterling Marlin	Billy Hagan Olds	49	3,200	Running
12	22	47	Jack Pennington	Derick Close Olds	49	3,050	Running
13	12	7	Alan Kulwicki	AK Racing Ford	49	2,900	Running
14	19	32	Joe Ruttman	Chuck Wellings Pontiac	49	2,750	Running
15	26	02	Rich Bickle	Bickle Oldsmobile	49	2,600	Running
16	25	72	Stan Barrett	Phil Barkdoll Olds	49	2,450	Running
17	29	44	Jim Sauter	Group 44 Pontiac	49	2,300	Running
18	11	52	Jimmy Means	Means Racing Pontiac	49	2,150	Running
19	17	68	Hut Stricklin	Tri-Star Motorsports Pontiac	48	2,000	Crash
20	27	71	Dave Marcis	Marcis Auto Racing Chevy	48	1,900	Running
21	21	53	Jerry O'Neil	Alan Aroneck Olds	48	1,800	Running
22	15	19	Chad Little	Chuck Little Ford	47	1,700	Running
23	16	85	Bobby Gerhart	Gerhart Chevrolet	47	1,600	Running
24	30	13	Mike Potter	Thee Dixon Chevrolet	46	1,500	Running
25	23	96	Philip Duffie	Lillian Duffie Buick	46	1,400	Running
26	28	77	Ken Ragan	Marvin Ragan Ford	45	1,300	Running
27	7	26	Brett Bodine	King Racing Buick	26	1,200	Trans
28	18	73	Phil Barkdoll	Barkdoll Racing Olds	11	1,150	Heating
29	10	20	Rob Moroso	Dick Moroso Olds	9	1,475	Trans
30	24	59	Mark Gibson	CoHo Racing Pontiac	1	1,050	Engine

Time of Race: 40 minutes, 05 seconds
Average Speed: 187.110 mph
Pole Winner: Ken Schrader – 196.515 mph
Lap Leaders: Darrell Waltrip 1-6, Ken Schrader 7-27, Richard Petty 28-42, Ricky Rudd 43-48, Geoff Bodine 49-50.
Cautions: None Margin of Victory: 2.02 seconds

1990
2nd Daytona Twin 125
February 15, 1990

Fin	St	No.	Driver	Team / Car	Laps	Money	Status
1	1	3	Dale Earnhardt	RCR Enterprises Chevrolet	50	$34,000	Running
2	2	9	Bill Elliott	Melling Performance Ford	50	21,000	Running
3	17	57	Jimmy Spencer	Rod Osterlund Pontiac	50	14,000	Running
4	4	4	Phil Parsons	Morgan-McClure Olds	50	9,000	Running
5	18	8	Bobby Hillin, Jr.	Stavola Brothers Buick	50	7,000	Running
6	19	10	Derrike Cope	Bob Whitcomb Chevrolet	50	4,000	Running
7	7	83	Lake Speed	Speed Racing Olds	50	3,800	Running
8	8	28	Davey Allison	Robert Yates Racing Ford	50	3,650	Running
9	24	90	Ernie Irvan	Junie Donlavey Ford	50	3,500	Running
10	9	1	Terry Labonte	Richard Jackson Olds	50	3,350	Running
11	10	42	Kyle Petty	SabCo Racing Pontiac	50	3,200	Running
12	12	30	Michael Waltrip	Bahari Racing Pontiac	50	3,050	Running
13	12	16	Larry Pearson	Pearson Racing Buick	50	2,900	Running
14	5	75	Rick Wilson	RahMoc Enterprises Olds	50	2,750	Running
15	20	15	Morgan Shepherd	Bud Moore Eng. Ford	50	2,600	Running
16	13	27	Rusty Wallace	Blue Max Pontiac	50	2,650	Running
17	14	35	Bill Venturini	Venturini Chevrolet	50	2,300	Running
18	21	80	Jimmy Horton	George Smith Ford	50	2,150	Running
19	25	01	Mickey Gibbs	Don Gibbs Ford	49	2,000	Running
20	27	2	Eddie Bierschwale	US Racing Olds	49	1,900	Running
21	30	48	Trevor Boys	Lilly Lusty Buick	49	1,800	Running
22	6	66	Dick Trickle	Cale Yarborough Pontiac	48	1,700	Crash
23	15	37	Dennis Langston	Langston Ford	48	1,600	Running
24	29	0	Delma Cowart	H.L. Waters Ford	48	1,500	Running
25	28	70	J.D. McDuffie	McDuffie Pontiac	46	1,400	Running
26	23	82	Mark Stahl	Stahl Racing Ford	45	1,300	Running
27	26	34	Charlie Glotzbach	Ken Allen Pontiac	37	1,200	Quit
28	31	39	Blackie Wangerin	Wangerin Ford	19	1,150	Cylinder
29	3	21	Neil Bonnett	Wood Brothers Ford	15	1,475	Engine
30	22	89	Rodney Combs	Mueller Brothers Pontiac	8	1,050	Vibration
31	16	29	Joe Booher	Booher Farms Pontiac	0	1,000	Crash

Time of Race: 47 minutes, 42 seconds
Average Speed: 157.123 mph
Pole Winner: Dale Earnhardt – 195.767 mph
Lap Leaders: Dale Earnhardt 1-21, Dick Trickle 22-47, Earnhardt 48-50.
Cautions: 2 for 6 laps Margin of Victory: 0.47 seconds

Fuel Mileage Wins For Bodine

Geoff Bodine ran the full 125-miles without a pit stop and scampered home first in the opening Twin 125-mile qualifying race at Daytona International Speedway.

Bodine, taking his first ride with car owner Junior Johnson, outran runner-up Harry Gant by 2.02 seconds to earn the third starting spot for the Daytona 500. Gant also went the distance without a pit stop.

Mark Martin, Darrell Waltrip and Richard Petty completed the top five.

Petty led for a 15-lap stretch before he pulled his Pontiac into the pits for fuel.

Pole sitter Ken Schrader spun off the fourth turn of the final lap and collided with Hut Stricklin. Schrader's car was heavily damaged, forcing him to bring in a back-up car for the 500.

Bryan Hallman

Alan Kulwicki works on his car prior to Twin 125.

Earnhardt Outduels Trickle

Dale Earnhardt ran down a pesky Dick Trickle with three laps to go and sprinted to victory in the second Twin 125 at Daytona.

Earnhardt beat Bill Elliott by a car length to post his third win in the preliminary qualifying event. Third place went to Jimmy Spencer, who turned in a fine run for the Rod Osterlund team. Phil Parsons finished fourth in his first ride with the Morgan-McClure team. Fifth place went to Bobby Hillin, Jr.

Trickle ran out of gas moments after being passed by Earnhardt. Elliott, chasing Earnhardt, tapped Trickle into a spin on the backstretch when he was unable to avoid the slowing car. He got credit for a 22nd place finish.

1991
1st Daytona Twin 125
February 14, 1991

Fin	St	No.	Driver	Team / Car	Laps	Money	Status
1	1	28	Davey Allison	Robert Yates Racing Ford	50	$35,000	Running
2	7	43	Richard Petty	Petty Enterprises Pontiac	50	22,000	Running
3	9	12	Hut Stricklin	Bobby Allison Buick	50	15,000	Running
4	3	1	Rick Mast	Richard Jackson Olds	50	10,000	Running
5	4	5	Ricky Rudd	Hendrick Motorsports Chevy	50	8,000	Running
6	2	33	Harry Gant	Leo Jackson Olds	50	4,900	Running
7	10	30	Michael Waltrip	Bahari Racing Pontiac	50	4,700	Running
8	6	9	Bill Elliott	Melling Performance Ford	50	4,550	Running
9	8	21	Dale Jarrett	Wood Brothers Ford	50	4,400	Running
10	14	11	Geoff Bodine	Junior Johnson Ford	50	4,150	Running
11	15	89	Jim Sauter	Mueller Brothers Pontiac	50	4,000	Running
12	13	98	Jimmy Spencer	Travis Carter Chevrolet	50	3,850	Running
13	25	18	Greg Sacks	Sacks Chevrolet	50	3,700	Running
14	5	7	Alan Kulwicki	AK Racing Ford	50	3,550	Running
15	16	73	Phil Barkdoll	Barkdoll Racing Olds	50	3,400	Running
16	11	10	Derrike Cope	Bob Whitcomb Chevrolet	50	3,150	Running
17	12	24	Mickey Gibbs	Team III Pontiac	49	3,000	Running
18	18	55	Ted Musgrave	US Racing Pontiac	49	2,850	Running
19	21	47	Rich Bickle	Derick Close Olds	49	2,700	Running
20	27	13	Brian Ross	Thee Dixon Buick	48	2,600	Running
21	33	80	Jimmy Horton	George Smith Chevrolet	48	2,400	Running
22	22	65	Dave Mader III	Clint Folsom Chevrolet	48	2,300	Running
23	20	69	Dorsey Schroeder	Lucky Compton Ford	47	2,200	Crash
24	17	20	Sammy Swindell	Dick Moroso Ford	47	2,100	Crash
25	29	45	Philip Duffie	Bobby Fulcher Olds	35	2,000	Handling
26	19	23	Eddie Bierschwale	Don Bierschwale Olds	24	1,900	Handling
27	24	27	Bobby Hillin, Jr.	Dick Moroso Olds	18	2,300	Handling
28	28	0	Delma Cowart	H.L. Waters Ford	18	1,750	Flagged
29	26	82	Mark Stahl	Stahl Racing Ford	10	1,650	Wtr Pump

Time of Race: 45 minutes, 21 seconds
Average Speed: 165.380 mph
Pole Winner: Davey Allison – 195.955 mph
Lap Leaders: Davey Allison 1-50.
Cautions: 2 for 5 laps   Margin of Victory: Under Caution

1991
2nd Daytona Twin 125
February 14, 1991

Fin	St	No.	Driver	Team / Car	Laps	Money	Status
1	3	3	Dale Earnhardt	RCR Enterprises Chevrolet	50	$35,000	Running
2	1	4	Ernie Irvan	Morgan-McClure Chevrolet	50	22,000	Running
3	10	42	Kyle Petty	SabCo Racing Pontiac	50	15,000	Running
4	8	2	Rusty Wallace	Roger Penske Pontiac	50	10,000	Running
5	5	17	Darrell Waltrip	DARWal Chevrolet	50	8,000	Running
6	2	22	Sterling Marlin	Junior Johnson Ford	50	4,900	Running
7	6	75	Joe Ruttman	RahMoc Enterprises Olds	50	4,700	Running
8	21	89	Buddy Baker	Rod Osterlund Pontiac	50	4,550	Running
9	4	6	Mark Martin	Roush Racing Ford	50	4,400	Running
10	13	68	Bobby Hamilton	Tri-Star Motorsports Olds	50	4,150	Running
11	25	51	Jeff Purvis	James Finch Olds	50	4,000	Running
12	16	25	Ken Schrader	Hendrick Motorsports Chevy	50	3,850	Running
13	19	8	Rick Wilson	Stavola Brothers Buick	50	3,700	Running
14	9	66	DICK Trickle	Cale Yarborough Pontiac	50	3,550	Running
15	12	19	Chad Little	Chuck Little Ford	50	3,400	Running
16	17	90	Robby Gordon	Junie Donlavey Ford	50	3,150	Running
17	18	52	Jimmy Means	Means Racing Pontiac	50	3,000	Running
18	7	94	Terry Labonte	Billy Hagan Oldsmobile	50	2,850	Running
19	15	95	Rick Jeffrey	Earl Sadler Chevrolet	50	2,700	Running
20	22	34	Gary Balough	Ken Allen Chevrolet	50	2,600	Running
21	27	70	J.D. McDuffie	McDuffie Pontiac	50	2,400	Running
22	23	96	Phil Parsons	Italian Connection Chevy	49	2,300	Running
23	26	35	Bill Venturini	Venturini Chevrolet	48	2,200	Running
24	20	72	Chuck Bown	Tex Powell Olds	48	2,100	Running
25	28	99	Brad Teague	Ralph Ball Chevrolet	35	2,000	Engine
26	14	71	Dave Marcis	Marcis Auto Racing Chevy	31	1,900	Wheel
27	24	26	Brett Bodine	King Racing Buick	21	2,300	Crash
28	29	39	Blackie Wangerin	Wangerin Ford	6	1,750	Flagged
29	11	15	Morgan Shepherd	Bud Moore Eng. Ford	1	1,650	Engine

Time of Race: 47 minutes, 50 seconds
Average Speed: 156.794 mph
Pole Winner: Ernie Irvan – 195.639 mph
Lap Leaders: Dale Earnhardt 1-50.
Cautions: 1 for 7 laps   Margin of Victory: 1 car length

Allison,Petty Run 1-2 in First Twin

Davey Allison started on the pole and led all the way to win the first Twin 125-miler. Allison had pulled away from the field and was comfortably ahead when a crash involving Sammy Swindell and Dorsey Schroeder brought out the yellow flag with two laps to go.

Richard Petty nosed his Pontiac ahead of Hut Stricklin in the race back to the flag to take runner-up honors. Stricklin finished third with Rick Mast fourth and Ricky Rudd fifth.

Stricklin, driving Bobby Allison's Buick, broke out of a pack of 20 cars and ran down the leaders in the final 10 laps. "We have the same chassis set up when Bobby won the Daytona 500 in 1988," said Stricklin.

Brian Czobat

Richard Petty ran a strong 2nd in First Twin 125.

Earnhardt Express Routs Field

Dale Earnhardt bolted from the second row, took the lead in the opening lap and was never headed as he easily won the second Twin 125-miler.

Ernie Irvan finished second, on Earnhardt's bumper. The two had bumped on the backstretch in the final lap.

Third place went to Kyle Petty. Rusty Wallace finished fourth and Darrell Waltrip came home fifth.

Brett Bodine escaped serious injury after a tap from Bobby Hamilton sent him crashing into the retaining barrier off the fourth turn. Bodine was knocked out on impact, but received clearance from doctors to drive in the Daytona 500.

A total of 21 cars finished the full 125-miles.

1992
1st Daytona Twin 125
February 13, 1992

Fin	St	No.	Driver	Team / Car	Laps	Money	Status
1	4	3	Dale Earnhardt	RCR Enterprises Chevrolet	50	$35,400	Running
2	2	6	Mark Martin	Roush Racing Ford	50	22,200	Running
3	9	4	Ernie Irvan	Morgan-McClure Chevrolet	50	15,200	Running
4	12	41	Greg Sacks	Larry Hedrick Chevrolet	50	10,200	Running
5	19	33	Harry Gant	Leo Jackson Olds	50	8,200	Running
6	15	1	Rick Mast	Richard Jackson Olds	50	5,100	Running
7	21	25	Ken Schrader	Hendrick Motorsports Chevy	50	4,800	Running
8	16	2	Rusty Wallace	Roger Penske Pontiac	50	4,650	Running
9	39	9	Phil Parsons	Melling Performance Ford	50	4,500	Running
10	27	03	Kerry Teague	Teague Oldsmobile	50	4,250	Running
11	17	71	Dave Marcis	Marcis Auto Racing Chevy	50	4,100	Running
12	24	73	Phil Barkdoll	Barkdoll Racing Olds	50	3,950	Running
13	29	0	Delma Cowart	H.L. Waters Ford	50	3,800	Running
14	23	77	Mike Potter	Steve Balogh Chevrolet	50	3,650	Running
15	22	99	Brad Teague	Ralph Ball Chevrolet	49	3,500	Running
16	28	59	Andy Belmont	Pat Rissi Ford	49	3,250	Running
17	13	12	Hut Stricklin	Bobby Allison Chevrolet	46	3,100	Running
18	8	18	Dale Jarrett	Joe Gibbs Chevrolet	35	2,950	Crash
19	6	42	Kyle Petty	SabCo Racing Pontiac	35	2,800	Crash
20	25	23	Eddie Bierschwale	Don Bierschwale Olds	33	2,700	Running
21	10	16	Wally Dallenbach, Jr.	Roush Racing Ford	21	2,500	Engine
22	1	22	Sterling Marlin	Junior Johnson Ford	19	2,900	Crash
23	5	43	Richard Petty	Petty Enterprises Pontiac	8	2,300	Crash
24	14	7	Alan Kulwicki	AK Racing Ford	4	2,200	Crash
25	7	94	Terry Labonte	Billy Hagan Chevrolet	4	2,100	Crash
26	20	14	A.J.Foyt	Richard Jackson Olds	4	2,000	Crash
27	11	8	Rick Wilson	Stavola Brothers Ford	4	1,900	Crash
28	18	13	Dave Mader III	Clint Folsom Chevrolet	4	1,850	Crash
29	26	62	Ben Hess	Hensley Gray Ford	4	1,750	Crash

Time of Race: 1 Hour,4 minutes, 25 seconds
Average Speed: 116.430 mph
Pole Winner: Sterling Marlin – 192.213 mph
Lap Leaders: Dale Earnhardt 1-13, Sterling Marlin 14-19, Mark Martin 20-40, Earnhardt 41-50.
Cautions: 3 for 20 laps Margin of Victory: 3/4-car length

1992
2nd Daytona Twin 125
February 13, 1992

Fin	St	No.	Driver	Team / Car	Laps	Money	Status
1	1	11	Bill Elliott	Junior Johnson Ford	50	$35,200	Running
2	19	21	Morgan Shepherd	Wood Brothers Ford	50	22,200	Running
3	3	28	Davey Allison	Robert Yates Racing Ford	50	15,200	Running
4	5	5	Ricky Rudd	Hendrick Motorsports Chevy	50	10,200	Running
5	8	30	Michael Waltrip	Bahari Racing Pontiac	50	8,200	Running
6	10	17	Darrell Waltrip	DarWal Chevrolet	50	5,100	Running
7	6	66	Chad Little	Cale Yarborough Ford	50	4,800	Running
8	7	15	Geoff Bodine	Bud Moore Eng. Ford	50	4,650	Running
9	4	26	Brett Bodine	King Racing ford	50	4,500	Running
10	16	10	Derrike Cope	Bob Whitcomb Chevrolet	50	4,250	Running
11	14	68	Bobby Hamilton	Tri-Star Motorsports Olds	50	4,100	Running
12	21	47	Buddy Baker	Derick Close Oldsmobile	50	3,950	Running
13	24	31	Bobby Hillin, Jr.	Team Ireland Chevrolet	50	3,800	Running
14	11	75	Dick Trickle	RahMoc Oldsmobile	50	3,650	Running
15	13	49	Stanley Smith	Smith Racing Chevrolet	50	3,500	Running
16	2	90	Dorsey Schroeder	Junie Donlavey Ford	50	3,750	Running
17	20	83	Lake Speed	Speed Racing Chevrolet	49	3,100	Running
18	15	89	Jim Sauter	Muellerr Brothers Pontiac	49	2,950	Running
19	17	20	Mike Wallace	Dick Moroso Olds	49	2,800	Running
20	12	55	Ted Musgrave	RaDiUs Motorsports Chevy	49	2,700	Running
21	25	98	Jimmy Spencer	Travis Carter Chevrolet	49	2,500	Running
22	26	13	Mike Skinner	Thee Dixon Chevrolet	49	2,400	Running
23	27	88	Joe Booher	Nelson Malloch Pontiac	49	2,300	Running
24	18	50	Clay Young	Atlac Racing Pontiac	49	2,200	Running
25	28	48	James Hylton	Hylton Engineering Chevy	49	2,100	Running
26	23	52	Jimmy Means	Means Racing Pontiac	49	2,000	Running
27	22	97	Mark Gibson	John Collins Olds	46	1,900	Running
28	9	95	Bob Schacht	Earl Sadler Oldsmobile	7	1,850	Engine

Time of Race: 44 minutes, 10 seconds
Average Speed: 169.811 mph
Pole Winner: Bill Elliott – 192.090 mph
Lap Leaders: Bill Elliott 1-40, Davey Allison 41, Elliott 42-50.
Cautions: 1 for 4 laps Margin of Victory: 2 car lengths

Earnhardt Wins Wreck-marred 125

Dale Earnhardt hustled around Mark Martin with 10 laps remaining and sped to his third straight victory in the first Twin 125-mile qualifying race.

Martin had to settle for second place with Ernie Irvan a close third. Greg Sacks' spirited effort netted him fourth place and Harry Gant was fifth.

Sterling Marlin started on the pole, but lost the lead to Earnhardt at the start. Marlin regained stride and took the lead on lap 14. He was holding down first place when a nudge from Earnhardt sent him spinning off the fourth turn. "Earnhardt hit me in the quarter-panel," fumed Marlin. "I don't know why he has to drive that way."

ISC

Rick Wilson was involved in crash early in First 125-mile qualifier.

Elliott Edges Shepherd at the Wire

Bill Elliott led all but one lap and made a successful debut in the Junior Johnson Ford in the second Twin 125-mile qualifier.

Elliott finished two car lengths ahead of Morgan Shepherd, who came from 19th starting position in a gallant charge. Davey Allison came in third with Ricky Rudd fourth and Michael Waltrip fifth.

Elliott deflected a late challenge from Shepherd. "I tried to make my car as wide as I could," he said.

Dorsey Schroeder started second in Junie Donlavey's Ford, but drifted back to a 16th place finish. "Things got a little hairy up front, so I backed off to save the car," said Schroeder.

1993
1st Daytona Twin 125
February 11, 1993

Fin	St	No.	Driver	Team / Car	Laps	Money	Status
1	6	24	Jeff Gordon	Hendrick Motorsports Chevy	50	$35,200	Running
2	2	11	Bill Elliott	Junior Johnson Ford	50	22,200	Running
3	1	42	Kyle Petty	SabCo Racing Pontiac	50	15,200	Running
4	3	25	Ken Schrader	Hendrick Motorsports Chevy	50	10,200	Running
5	5	90	Bobby Hillin, Jr.	Junie Donlavey Ford	50	8,200	Running
6	8	28	Davey Allison	Robert Yates Racing Ford	50	5,100	Running
7	16	83	Lake Speed	Speed Racing Ford	50	4,800	Running
8	14	44	Rick Wilson	Petty Enterprises Pontiac	50	4,650	Running
9	19	9	Chad Little	Melling Performance Ford	50	4,500	Running
9	19	14	Terry Labonte	Billy Hagan Chevrolet	50	4,250	Running
11	18	75	Dick Trickle	Butch Mock Ford	50	4,100	Running
12	12	6	Mark Martin	Roush Racing Ford	50	3,900	Running
13	21	22	Bobby Labonte	Bill Davis Ford	50	3,800	Running
14	15	68	Bobby Hamilton	Tri-Star Motorsports Ford	50	3,650	Running
15	20	32	Jimmy Horton	Active Racing Chevrolet	50	3,500	Running
16	10	20	Joe Ruttman	Dick Moroso Ford	50	3,250	Running
17	7	55	Ted Musgrave	RaDiUs Motorsports Ford	50	3,100	Running
18	13	71	Dave Marcis	Marcis Auto Racing Chevy	50	2,950	Running
19	11	33	Harry Gant	Leo Jackson Chevrolet	50	2,800	Running
20	26	85	Dorsey Schroeder	Thee Dixon Ford	50	2,700	Running
21	4	1	Rick Mast	Richard Jackson Ford	50	2,500	Running
22	22	45	Rich Bickle	Gene Isenhour Ford	49	2,400	Running
23	27	0	Delma Cowart	H.L. Waters Ford	43	2,300	Running
24	9	66	Derrike Cope	Cale Yarborough Ford	38	2,700	Crash
25	23	73	Stanley Smith	Phil Barkdoll Chevrolet	2	2,100	Crash
26	25	31	Steve Kinser	Clint Folsom Chevrolet	2	2,000	Crash

Time of Race: 48 minutes, 56 seconds
Average Speed: 153.270 mph
Pole Winner: Kyle Petty – 189.426 mph
Lap Leaders: Kyle Petty 1, Bill Elliott 2-21, Jeff Gordon 22-50.
Cautions: 2 for 9 laps Margin of Victory: 2 car lengths

1993
2nd Daytona Twin 125
February 11, 1993

Fin	St	No.	Driver	Team / Car	Laps	Money	Status
1	4	3	Dale Earnhardt	RCR Enterprises Chevrolet	50	$35,200	Running
2	16	15	Geoff Bodine	Bud Moore Eng. Ford	50	22,200	Running
3	1	18	Dale Jarrett	Joe Gibbs Chevrolet	50	15,200	Running
4	11	4	Ernie Irvan	Morgan-McClure Chevrolet	50	10,200	Running
5	12	7	Alan Kulwicki	AK Racing Ford	50	8,400	Running
6	3	5	Ricky Rudd	Hendrick Motorsports Chevy	50	5,100	Running
7	18	8	Sterling Marlin	Stavola Brothers Ford	50	4,800	Running
8	20	41	Phil Parson	Larry Hedrick Chevrolet	50	4,650	Running
9	5	27	Hut Stricklin	Junior Johnson Ford	50	4,500	Running
10	8	26	Brett Bodine	King Racing Ford	50	4,250	Running
11	10	16	Wally Dallenbach,Jr.	Roush Racing Ford	50	4,100	Running
12	17	40	Kenny Wallace	SabCo Racing Pontiac	50	3,950	Running
13	9	17	Darrell Waltrip	DarWal Chevrolet	50	3,800	Running
14	7	30	Michael Waltrip	Bahari Racing Pontiac	50	3,650	Running
15	2	12	Jimmy Spencer	Bobby Allison Ford	50	3,500	Running
16	24	48	James Hylton	Stavola Brothers Ford	50	3,250	Running
17	15	89	Jim Sauter	Mueller Brothers Ford	49	3,100	Running
18	13	29	Kerry Teague	Linro Motorsports Chevrolet	49	2,950	Running
19	27	77	Mike Potter	Henley Gray Ford	48	2,800	Running
20	26	99	Brad Teague	Ralph Ball Chevrolet	46	2,700	Running
21	21	51	Jeff Purvis	James Finch Chevrolet	36	2,500	Running
22	23	50	A.J. Foyt	Bobby Jones Ford	33	2,400	Heating
23	14	2	Rusty Wallace	Roger Penske Pontiac	24	2,300	Engine
24	6	21	Morgan Shepherd	Wood Brothers Ford	21	2,200	Engine
25	19	46	Al Unser, Jr.	Hendrick Motorsports Chevy	10	2,600	Crash
26	22	52	Jimmy Hensley	Means Racing Ford	10	2,000	Crash

Time of Race: 47 minutes, 41 seconds
Average Speed: 157.288 mph
Pole Winner: Dale Jarrett – 189.274 mph
Lap Leaders: Dale Earnhardt 1-2, Ricky Rudd 3-17, Earnhardt 18-25, Ernie Irvan 26, Earnhardt 27-50.
Cautions: 2 for 7 laps Margin of Victory: 1.5 car lengths

Rookie Gordon a Flash in 125

Twenty-one-year-old rookie Jeff Gordon drove past Bill Elliott in the 22nd lap and authored a stunning upset in the opening Twin 125-mile qualifying race at Daytona.

Despite being coaxed by crew chief Ray Evernham to "take it easy", Gordon charged to the front and won by two car lengths. Elliott finished in second place with Kyle Petty third, Ken Schrader fourth and Bobby Hillin, Jr. fifth.

Gordon became the first rookie to win a preliminary Twin event since 1963 when 24-year-old Johnny Rutherford won in 1963.

Sprint car ace Steve Kinser and Stanley Smith were eliminated in a crash in the third lap.

Steve Crumbacker

Crew Chief Ray Evernham chats with rookie driver Jeff Gordon before triumph in Daytona 125.

Earnhardt Bags 4th Straight

Dale Earnhardt solidified his role as the Daytona 500 favorite with his fourth straight win in the second Twin 125-miler.

Earnhardt drove to a narrow victory over Geoff Bodine after Ernie Irvan and Ricky Rudd faded in the final laps. Pole sitter Dale Jarrett rebounded from an awkward start to finish third. Irvan nailed down fourth and Alan Kulwicki was fifth.

Rudd, who led 15 laps, faded to sixth place.

Al Unser, Jr., making his NASCAR debut, crashed off the second turn when a tire went down. Unser, Jr. had to bring in a backup Hendrick Motorsports Chevrolet to run in the Daytona 500.

A.J. Foyt finished 22nd and failed to make the Daytona 500 field.

Earnhardt Leads Flag-to-Flag to Win The Winston in Romp

Dale Earnhardt's dominant hand delivered a flag-to-flag triumph in the sixth annual The Winston, NASCAR's version of an All-Star race, at Charlotte Motor Speedway.

Earnhardt started on the pole and led all 70 miles of the 105-mile contest. The format of the special event was broken into two segments, a 50-lapper followed by a 20-lap shootout.

Bill Elliott loomed as Earnhardt's largest threat, finishing second in the opening 50-lapper. Earnhardt and Elliott started on the front row for the shootout, but all hopes of a side-by-side battle were doused when Earnhardt pulled one of his tricks to separate him from the field.

Earnhardt lagged behind Elliott as the field approached the green flag, then accelerated quickly at the head of the front chute. By the time the pack had reached the green flag, Earnhardt had a four car length advantage as Elliott had dropped to sixth place.

"I was following the speed of the pace car and Earnhardt kept slowing up," said Elliott. "We were told in the driver's meeting to maintain the speed of the pace car. I did and I got kicked back."

Earnhardt easily outran Ken Schrader in the final 20 laps to pocket the $325,000 first prize. Mark Martin finished in third place while Elliott had to scramble back up to fourth. Fifth place went to Davey Allison.

Dick Trickle, winner of the Winston Open to gain admission into the All-Star race, finished a strong sixth.

Earnhardt defended his tactics of the controversial restart. "When I got to where I wanted to start, I did. It just caught him by surprise. I thought he'd lay back and wait on me, but he didn't," said the winner.

Earnhardt became the first driver to lead every lap of The Winston and also became the first two-time winner. His other triumph came in 1987 when he survived a bumper-banging battle with Elliott and Geoff Bodine in the late stages. "We had a bad deal when I won in 1987," said Earnhardt. "This is the kind of race I wanted to run and win today. No controversy, no rifts. I wanted to win one of these where I could say I won because I had the best car. I didn't want somebody to claim I had won because I hit somebody else."

1990 The Winston All-Star Race
Charlotte Motor Speedway
May 20, 1990

Fin	St	No.	Driver	Team / Car	Laps	Money	Status
1	1	3	Dale Earnhardt	RCR Enterprises Chevrolet	70	$325,000	Running
2	9	25	Ken Schrader	Hendrick Motorsports Chevy	70	82,500	Running
3	4	6	Mark Martin	Roush Racing Ford	70	62,500	Running
4	6	9	Bill Elliott	Melling Performance Ford	70	57,500	Running
5	2	28	Davey Allison	Robert Yates Racing Ford	70	42,500	Running
6	20	66	Dick Trickle	Cale Yarborough Pontiac	70	26,000	Running
7	11	33	Harry Gant	Leo Jackson Olds	70	23,500	Running
8	8	7	Alan Kulwicki	AK Racing Ford	70	22,500	Running
9	5	15	Morgan Shepherd	Bud Moore Eng. Ford	70	21,500	Running
10	15	8	Bobby Hillin, Jr.	Stavola Brothers Buick	70	21,000	Running
11	10	83	Lake Speed	Speed Racing Olds	70	20,500	Running
12	13	5	Ricky Rudd	Hendrick Motorsports Chevy	70	20,000	Running
13	3	17	Darrell Waltrip	Hendrick Motorsports Chevy	70	24,000	Running
14	17	1	Terry Labonte	Richard Jackson Olds	70	18,000	Running
15	12	42	Kyle Petty	Sabco Racing Pontiac	69	18,000	Running
16	19	11	Geoff Bodine	Junior Johnson Ford	69	18,000	Running
17	18	73	Phil Parsons	Phil Barkdoll Olds	69	18,000	Running
18	7	10	Derrike Cope	Bob Whitcomb Chevrolet	68	18,000	Running
19	16	26	Brett Bodine	King Racing Buick	55	18,000	Running
20	14	27	Rusty Wallace	Blue Max Racing Pontiac	8	18,000	Engine

Time of Race: 38 minutes, 39 seconds
Average Speed: 163.001 mph
Pole Winner: Dale Earnhardt – 134.250 mph (including 11.83 second pit stop)
Lap Leaders: Dale Earnhardt 1-70.
Cautions: None Margin of Victory: 0.34-seconds

Kim Novasat

Dale Earnhardt laps Kyle Petty en route to victory in the 1990 The Winston.

Allison's 'Bird Flies to Victory in The Winston of '91

Davey Allison ran off and hid from a star-studded field, leading from start-to-finish in the seventh annual The Winston at Charlotte Motor Speedway.

Allison bagged a record-tying $325,000 for his triumph, which included $50,000 for winning the opening 50-lap segment, plus a $75,000 award for winning the pole.

Allison put his Robert Yates Racing Ford into the lead in the opening lap and was never threatened. Only Ken Schrader was able to show any strength, coming from sixth to second in seven laps.

Brian Czobat

Davey Allison beams from Victory Lane after winning the 1991 The Winston.

1991 The Winston All-Star Race
Charlotte Motor Speedway
May 19, 1991

Fin	St	No.	Driver	Team / Car	Laps	Money	Status
1	1	28	Davey Allison	Robert Yates Racing Ford	70	$325,000	Running
2	6	25	Ken Schrader	Hendrick Motorsports Chevy	70	92,500	Running
3	3	17	Darrell Waltrip	DarWal Chevrolet	70	82,500	Running
4	7	9	Bill Elliott	Melling Performance Ford	70	32,500	Running
5	16	4	Ernie Irvan	Morgan-McClure Chevrolet	70	27,500	Running
6	18	30	Michael Waltrip	Bahari Racing Pontiac	70	26,000	Running
7	10	2	Rusty Wallace	Roger Penske Pontiac	70	23,500	Running
8	20	12	Hut Stricklin	Bobby Allison Buick	70	22,500	Running
9	2	33	Harry Gant	Leo Jackson Olds	70	36,500	Running
10	4	3	Dale Earnhardt	RCR Enterprises Chevrolet	70	21,000	Running
11	11	5	Ricky Rudd	Hendrick Motorsports Chevy	70	20,500	Running
12	19	22	Sterling Marlin	Junior Johnson Ford	70	20,000	Running
13	13	6	Mark Martin	Roush Racing Ford	70	19,000	Running
14	5	11	Tommy Ellis	Junior Johnson Ford	70	18,000	Running
15	8	15	Morgan Shepherd	Bud Moore Eng. Ford	70	18,000	Running
16	15	26	Brett Bodine	King Racing Buick	69	18,000	Running
17	17	42	Kenny Wallace	SabCo Racing Pontiac	69	18,000	Running
18	9	10	Derrike Cope	Bob Whitcomb Chevrolet	50	18,000	Running
19	14	27	Bobby Hillin, Jr.	Dick Moroso Oldsmobile	26	18,000	Valve
20	12	7	Alan Kulwicki	AK Racing Ford	7	18,000	Engine

Time of Race: 37 minutes, 20 seconds
Average Speed: 168.750 mph
Pole Winner: Davey Allison – 133.704 mph (including 12..68 second pit stop)
Lap Leaders: Davey Allison 1-70.
Cautions: None Margin of Victory: 2.87 seconds

But Schrader was never able to make a run on Allison. In the 20-lap shootout, Allison motored away from his rivals and finished 2.87-seconds in front of Schrader, who finished second for the third year in a row.

Darrell Waltrip came home third with Bill Elliott fourth and Ernie Irvan fifth. Michael Waltrip, who won the Winston Open just before the main event, finished in sixth place.

Three hours after the race ended, NASCAR officials announced that the 14th-place finishing Ford driven by Tommy Ellis was equipped with an oversized engine. Ellis was filling in for Geoff Bodine in the Junior Johnson Ford. Bodine had suffered a punctured lung and three cracked ribs in a practice crash.

The big engine measured 362.351 cubic inches, well over the 358 c.i. limit. With the engine cooled, NASCAR reported the following day that the engine measured 361.856 c.i. NASCAR suspended Johnson, crew chief Tim Brewer and Ellis for four races, but altered the suspensions later in the week.

Allison said his team "plans to have a big ol' party. This crew really works hard. I'm just the lucky guy who gets to turn the steering wheel."

Schrader admitted he had no chance of catching Allison. "If there had been more laps, he would have won by a wider margin," confessed Schrader.

Defending champion Dale Earnhardt started fourth but faded to 10th. "It was a big experiment that didn't go so good," said Earnhardt.

Davey Dashes and Crashes His Way to Victory in The Winston

Davey Allison came from third to first in a frantic last lap and prevailed in an electrifying finish in The Winston – the first superspeedway race to be run at night since 1955.

Allison ducked under a spinning Dale Earnhardt and crossed the finish line inches ahead of Kyle Petty to win the $300,000 first prize. As the two lead cars crossed the finish line, Allison's Ford spun across the track and plowed into the retaining barrier.

Rescue crewmen said Allison was knocked unconscious for a few minutes. He was air-lifted to a hospital by helicopter where a physician said he suffered a concussion, bruised lung and bruised legs. He was released the following day.

The format for NASCAR's All-Star event was changed after the most recent two outings had failed to produce a single lead change. The 70-lap format was divided into two 30-lap segments and a 10-lap shootout.

Allison started on the pole and led all the way to win the first 30-lap dash. Positions were inverted for the second 30-lapper and Geoff Bodine led the first seven laps before being passed by Petty.

Petty easily outdistanced the field in the second 30-lap segment and started on the pole for the 10-lap dash.

He had opened a slight lead when Darrell Waltrip's spin brought out the yellow flag. Dale Earnhardt charged past Petty on the restart and led going into the final lap.

Petty made a move to the low side of Earnhardt down the backstretch, but Earnhardt swerved to block the move. Both cars were running on the inside edge of the track as Allison bided his time in third.

"Earnhardt ran me so far to the inside that we went into the turn at a bad angle," explained Petty. "When he cut his car to get back on a good line, he lost it. I had to ease up to miss Dale. Davey had his momentum built up and got inside of me off the fourth turn."

Earnhardt failed to finish and was awarded 14th position.

"Kyle and I were just racing," said Earnhardt. "He took more room than I wanted to give him. It was good hard racing."

1992 The Winston All-Star Race
Charlotte Motor Speedway
May 16, 1992

Fin	St	No.	Driver	Team / Car	Laps	Money	Status
1	1	28	Davey Allison	Robert Yates Racing Ford	70	$300,000	Running
2	16	42	Kyle Petty	SabCo Racing Pontiac	70	130,000	Running
3	4	25	Ken Schrader	Hendrick Motorsports Chevy	70	50,000	Running
4	9	5	Ricky Rudd	Hendrick Motorsports Chevy	70	30,000	Running
5	3	11	Bill Elliott	Junior Johnson Ford	70	47,000	Running
6	2	2	Rusty Wallace	Roger Penske Pontiac	70	42,500	Running
7	14	7	Alan Kulwicki	AK Racing Ford	70	23,000	Running
8	17	4	Ernie Irvan	Morgan-McClure Chevrolet	70	31,500	Running
9	15	43	Richard Petty	Petty Enterprises Pontiac	70	20,500	Running
10	13	94	Terry Labonte	Billy Hagan Oldsmobile	70	19,500	Running
11	6	17	Darrell Waltrip	DarWal Chevrolet	70	19,000	Running
12	7	33	Harry Gant	Leo Jackson Oldsmobile	70	18,500	Running
13	5	15	Geoff Bodine	Bud Moore Eng. Ford	70	18,000	Running
14	8	3	Dale Earnhardt	RCR Enterprises Chevrolet	69	25,500	Crash
15	19	30	Michael Waltrip	Bahari Racing Pontiac	68	18,000	Running
16	12	9	Dave Mader III	Melling Performance Ford	66	18,000	Handling
17	18	6	Mark Martin	Roush Racing Ford	64	18,000	Running
18	10	18	Dale Jarrett	Joe Gibbs Chevrolet	11	18,000	Crash
19	11	21	Morgan Shepherd	Wood Brothers Ford	4	18,000	Axle
20	20	12	Hut Stricklin	Bobby Allison Chevrolet	2	18,000	Crash

Time of Race: 47 minutes, 29 seconds
Average Speed: 132.678 mph
Pole Winner: Davey Allison – 135.265 mph (including 11.19 second pit stop)
Lap Leaders: Davey Allison 1-30, Geoff Bodine 31-37, Kyle Petty 38-63, Dale Earnhardt 64-69, Allison 70.
Cautions: 1 for 5 laps Margin of Victory: Four Feet

Bryan Hallman

Davey Allison won The Winston in a dazzling finish, but had to celebrate in the hospital.

Quick Starting Earnhardt Snares Controversial The Winston

Dale Earnhardt took the lead with two laps to go and prevailed in a disputed ninth annual running of The Winston. It was the third win in NASCAR's All-Star event for the Kannapolis, N.C. rustler.

The 105-mile event was broken into three segments. Ernie Irvan and Rick Mast sprinted to victory in the first two 30-lappers. Mast started on the pole for the 10-lap shootout but was dropkicked several places as drivers jockeyed for position.

Mark Martin had taken the lead at the start of the 10-lap dash and had built up a healthy lead. Earnhardt had moved into second place when Terry Labonte's engine failure triggered a wreck with Bill Elliott with two laps to go.

Laps under the caution flag were not scored during the final 10-lap segment. For the restart, officials started the cars two-abreast, rather than single-file. That put Martin and Earnhardt on the front row for a two-lap dash for $200,000.

Earnhardt jumped past pole-sitter Martin well before the green flag and had opened a 15-car length lead by the time the cars reached the starting line. Officials ordered a restart with no penalty to Earnhardt for jumping.

An orderly restart followed with Earnhardt surging past Martin in the third turn. He held on to win by 0.16-seconds.

A frustrated Martin had to settle for runner-up honors. Third place went to Ernie Irvan with Ken Schrader fourth and Geoff Bodine fifth.

Earnhardt said he quick-started in an effort to "rattle Martin. I didn't think I'd get away with it, but I thought I'd try it. I didn't think they'd put me in the back of the field. For The Winston, they always restart people in the same position."

Martin said he felt officials would send Earnhardt "to the rear. That's how NASCAR usually handles that situation. But Winston puts up the money and makes the rules for excitement. I don't make the rules."

Irvan was more livid at Earnhardt's quick escape than anyone. "They let him steal the race," said Irvan. "To jump the start and get a second try is like giving a bank robber a second shot. They sent me to the rear last year for jumping the start at Sears Point. I didn't get a second chance."

Sixth-place finisher Darrell Waltrip said he "feels sorry for Martin. He got taken advantage of. We were told in the driver's meeting that normal race procedures would be in effect."

Sterling Marlin scored his third win in the Winston Open race and qualified for the main event. He finished in seventh place. A total of 14 cars finished on the lead lap.

1993 The Winston All-Star Race
Charlotte Motor Speedway
May 2, 1993

Fin	St	No.	Driver	Team / Car	Laps	Money	Status
1	3	3	Dale Earnhardt	RCR Enterprises Chevrolet	70	222,500	Running
2	14	6	Mark Martin	Roush Racing Ford	70	102,500	Running
3	1	4	Ernie Irvan	Morgan-McClure Chevrolet	70	150,000	Running
4	17	25	Ken Schrader	Hendrick Motorsports Chevy	70	30,000	Running
5	10	15	Geoff Bodine	Bud Moore Eng. Ford	70	27,000	Running
6	8	17	Darrell Waltrip	DarWal Chevrolet	70	25,000	Running
7	16	8	Sterling Marlin	Stavola Brothers Ford	70	23,000	Running
8	2	2	Rusty Wallace	Roger Penske Pontiac	70	39,000	Running
9	5	28	Davey Allison	Robert Yates Racing Ford	70	20,500	Running
10	18	26	Brett Bodine	King Racing Ford	70	19,500	Running
11	11	1	Rick Mast	Richard Jackson Ford	70	69,000	Running
12	9	21	Morgan Shepherd	Wood Brothers Ford	70	18,500	Running
13	12	33	Harry Gant	Leo Jackson Chevrolet	70	18,000	Running
14	4	11	Bill Elliott	Junior Johnson Ford	70	18,000	Running
15	13	14	Terry Labonte	Billy Hagan Chevrolet	68	18,000	Crash
16	11	5	Ricky Rudd	Hendrick Motorsports Chevy	43	18,000	Engine
17	15	7	Jimmy Hensley	AK - G.E.B. Racing Ford	32	18,000	Crash
18	19	30	Michael Waltrip	Bahari Racing Pontiac	31	18,000	Crash
19	7	18	Dale Jarrett	Joe Gibbs Chevrolet	31	18,000	Crash
20	6	42	Kyle Petty	SabCo Racing Pontiac	30	18,000	Valve

Time of Race: 45 minutes, 6 seconds
Average Speed: 139.690 mph
Pole Winner: Ernie Irvan – 1337.835 mph (including 10.73 second pit stop)
Lap Leaders: Ernie Irvan 1-30, Morgan Shepherd 31-39, Rick Mast 40-60, Mark Martin 61-68, Dale Earnhardt 69-70.
Cautions: 1 for 7 laps Margin of Victory: 0.16 seconds

CMS

Michael Waltrip #30 spins into the wall during The Winston as Ken Schrader #25 and Jimmy Hensley #7 take evasive action.

1990 Busch Clash
Daytona Int'l Speedway
February 11, 1990

Fin	St	No.	Driver	Team / Car	Laps	Money	Status
1	3	25	Ken Schrader	Hendrick Motorsports Chevy	20	$95,000	Running
2	2	46	Greg Sacks	Hendrick Motorsports Chevy	20	24,000	Running
3	9	28	Davey Allison	Robert Yates Racing Ford	20	18,000	Running
4	5	11	Geoff Bodine	Junior Johnson Ford	20	13,000	Running
5	4	9	Bill Elliott	Melling Performance Ford	20	12,000	Running
6	10	6	Mark Martin	Roush Racing Ford	20	11,500	Running
7	6	7	Alan Kulwicki	AK Racing Ford	20	11,000	Running
8	7	27	Rusty Wallace	Blue MAX Racing Pontiac	20	10,500	Running
9	8	15	Morgan Shepherd	Bud Moore Eng. Ford	20	10,000	Running
10	1	20	Jimmy Hensley	Dick Moroso Oldsmobile	19	10,000	Running

Time of Race: 15 minutes, 36 seconds
Average Speed: 192.308 mph
Lap Leaders: Greg Sacks 1-4, Ken Schrader 5-20..
Cautions: None Margin of Victory: 2 car lengths

Schrader Nips Sacks as Hendrick Motorsports Cars Run 1-2 in Clash

Ken Schrader drove past teammate Greg Sacks in the fifth lap and led the rest of the way to win his second consecutive Busch Clash at Daytona International Speedway.

Sacks, who gained entrance of the 50-lap dash for cash, finished a close second, giving the Hendrick Motorsports team a 1-2 finish. Third place went to Davey Allison with Geoff Bodine fourth and Bill Elliott fifth.

Sacks led the first four laps and fought hard to keep Schrader at bay. After a side-by-side duel for two laps, Schrader went ahead to stay.

Sacks said his pit crew told him to back off and let Schrader lead. "They didn't want us to run door-to-door," said Sacks.

Jimmy Hensley started on the pole but had a disastrous start. "The gear shifter broke on the start," said Hensley, who couldn't make up the distance and finished last in the 10-car field.

1991 Busch Clash
Daytona Int'l Speedway
February 10, 1991

Fin	St	No.	Driver	Team / Car	Laps	Money	Status
1	6	3	Dale Earnhardt	RCR Enterprises Chevrolet	20	$60,000	Running
2	12	6	Mark Martin	Roush Racing Ford	20	31,000	Running
3	10	2	Rusty Wallace	Roger Penske Pontiac	20	24,000	Running
4	13	9	Bill Elliott	Melling Performance Ford	20	26,000	Running
5	2	42	Kyle Petty	SabCo Racing Pontiac	20	17,500	Running
6	4	11	Geoff Bodine	Junior Johnson Ford	20	12,000	Running
7	9	4	Ernie Irvan	Morgan-McClure Chevrolet	20	25,000	Running
8	3	7	Alan Kulwicki	AK Racing Ford	20	11,000	Running
9	5	26	Brett Bodine	King Racing Buick	20	11,500	Running
10	8	18	Greg Sacks	Sacks Chevrolet	20	10,000	Running
11	7	66	Dick Trickle	Cale Yarborough Pontiac	20	10,000	Running
12	11	25	Ken Schrader	Hendrick Motorsports Chevy	12	18,500	Crash
13	14	5	Ricky Rudd	Hendrick Motorsports Chevy	12	13,000	Crash
14	1	10	Derrike Cope	Bob Whitcomb Chevrolet	11	10,500	Crash

Time of Race: 15 minutes, 50 seconds
Average Speed: 189.474 mph
Lap Leaders: Geoff Bodine 1, Dale Earnhardt 2-10, G.Bodine 11, Earnhardt 12-20..
Cautions: 1 Margin of Victory: 2 car lengths

Earnhardt Charges From the Rear Twice to Win Clash of '91

Dale Earnhardt charged from the back of the pack *twice* and won the newly formatted Busch Clash with a resounding exclamation point.

The Clash of '91 was broken into a pair of 10-lap segments, with starting positions for the second half of the dash inverted from the finish of the first race.

Earnhardt came from sixth to first in just over a lap and won the first 10-lap segment in a breeze. Starting 14th in the second race, Earnhardt raced through the pack and had the lead in the second turn of the second lap. He held his RCR Enterprises Chevrolet in front the rest of the way and beat runner-up Mark Martin by two car lengths.

Rusty Wallace, Bill Elliott and Kyle Petty rounded out the top five.

Pole sitter Derrike Cope crashed with Ricky Rudd in the the 12th overall lap. It was the second year in a row that the pole sitter had finished in last place.

Brian Czobat

Dale Earnhardt was simply magnificent in the Busch Clash of 1991.

1992 Busch Clash
Daytona Int'l Speedway
February 8, 1992

Fin	St	No.	Driver	Team / Car	Laps	Money	Status
1	3	15	Geoff Bodine	Bud Moore Eng. Ford	20	$39,000	Running
2	14	4	Ernie Irvan	Morgan-McClure Chevrolet	20	27,000	Running
3	13	6	Mark Martin	Roush Racing Ford	20	24,000	Running
4	15	28	Davey Allison	Robert Yates Ford	20	29,500	Running
5	9	7	Alan Kulwicki	AK Racing Ford	20	16,500	Running
6	10	22	Sterling Marlin	Junior Johnson Ford	20	33,000	Running
7	4	11	Bill Elliott	Junior Johnson Ford	20	11,500	Running
8	6	30	Michael Waltrip	Bahari Racing Pontiac	20	24,500	Running
9	5	5	Ricky Rudd	Hendrick Motorsports Chevy	20	12,000	Running
10	11	66	Chad Little	Cale Yarborough Ford	20	10,000	Running
11	1	26	Brett Bodine	King Racing Ford	20	15,000	Running
12	12	42	Kyle Petty	SabCo Racing Pontiac	20	11,000	Running
13	7	94	Terry Labonte	Billy Hagan Chevrolet	20	12,000	Running
14	2	2	Rusty Wallace	Roger Penske Pontiac	20	10,000	Running
15	8	33	Harry Gant	Leo Jackson Oldsmobile	20	10,000	Running

Time of Race: 15 minutes, 52 seconds
Average Speed: 189.076 mph
Lap Leaders: Brett Bodine 1-5, Sterling Marlin 6-10, Rusty Wallace 11-12, Geoff Bodine 13-20.
Cautions: None Margin of Victory: 2 car lengths

1993 Busch Clash
Daytona Int'l Speedway
February 7, 1993

Fin	St	No.	Driver	Team / Car	Laps	Money	Status
1	13	3	Dale Earnhardt	RCR Enterprises Chevrolet	20	$06,000	Running
2	12	25	Ken Schrader	Hendrick Motorsports Chevy	20	29,000	Running
3	1	4	Ernie Irvan	Morgan-McClure Chevrolet	20	37,500	Running
4	8	6	Mark Martin	Roush Racing Ford	20	21,000	Running
5	11	5	Ricky Rudd	Hendrick Motorsports Chevy	20	16,000	Running
6	15	28	Davey Allison	Robert Yates Racing Ford	20	17,000	Running
7	10	42	Kyle Petty	SabCo Racing Pontiac	20	13,000	Running
8	6	8	Sterling Marlin	Stavola Brothers Ford	20	11,500	Running
9	4	11	Bill Elliott	Junior Johnson Ford	20	10,500	Running
10	5	7	Alan Kulwicki	AK Racing Ford	20	12,000	Running
11	9	17	Darrell Waltrip	DarWal Chevrolet	20	10,000	Running
12	3	2	Rusty Wallace	Roger Penske Pontiac	20	18,500	Running
13	2	26	Brett Bodine	King Racing Ford	20	13,000	Running
14	7	1	Rick Mast	Richard Jackson Ford	20	11,000	Running
15	14	52	Jimmy Means	Means Racing Ford	20	10,000	Running

Time of Race: 16 minutes, 3 seconds
Average Speed: 186.916 mph
Lap Leaders: Ernie Irvan 1-5, Dale Earnhardt 6-10, Bill Elliott 11, Darrell Waltrip 12-13, Elliott 14, Sterling Marlin 15, Earnhardt 16-20.
Cautions: None Margin of Victory: 2 car lengths

Bodine's Strategy Nets Victory in Busch Clash of '92

Geoff Bodine used the Busch Clash format to his advantage and sprinted to victory in the 14th annual Busch Clash at Daytona. It was his first win in the special event for previous season's pole winners.

Bodine lumbered around and finished 13th in the opening 10-lap segment, which placed him near the front for the final 10-lap charge.

Bodine pushed his Bud Moore Engineering Ford past Rusty Wallace in the 13th overall lap and led the rest of the way.

Ernie Irvan finished in second with Mark Martin third, Davey Allison fourth and Alan Kulwicki fifth.

Perennial favorite Dale Earnhardt was not entered. He failed to win a pole in the 1991 season and was not extended an invitation.

ISC

Bill Elliott and Darrell Waltrip up front for second segment of Clash of '93.

Another Double Charge Gives Earnhardt Another Clash Win

Dale Earnhardt scored his fifth Busch Clash win in seven tries by gunning past his rivals twice in a dazzling display of speed and nerve.

Earnhardt came from 13th starting position to first in six laps in the opening 10-lap segment. He was forced to start 15th for the restart but ran down the oppositon in six more laps.

Earnhardt sped across the finish line two car lengths ahead of runner-up Ken Schrader. Ernie Irvan, who led the first five laps, came in third. Mark Martin and Ricky Rudd rounded out the top five.

"The first segment was pretty easy," said Dale. "But I got hung out in the second 10-lapper. I had to wait until I got a good draft and moved on past Marlin."

Tim Flock and Junior Johnson engaged in a good ol' fashioned game of bumper-tag in the Winston Legends race.

Winston Legends Race
Charlotte Motor Speedway
May 19, 1991

Fin	St	No	Driver	Status
1	16	64	Elmo Langley	Running
2	3	11	Cale Yarborough	Running
3	22	99	Paul Goldsmith	Running
4	19	06	Neil Castles	Running
5	7	28	Fred Lorenzen	Running
6	2	14	Coo Coo Marlin	Running
7	17	61	Hoss Ellington	Running
8	1	90	Dick Brooks	Running
9	6	42	Marvin Panch	Running
10	10	300	Tim Flock	Running
11	18	3	Junior Johnson	Running
12	20	3	Richard Childress	Crash
13	23	47	Smokey Yunick	Engine
14	4	59	Tom Pistone	Flagged
15	11	29	Little Bud Moore	Flagged
16	9	1	Donnie Allison	Crash
17	8	72	Benny Parsons	Engine
18	5	6	Cotton Owens	Crash
19	12	87	Buck Baker	Crash
20	13	98	Sam McQuagg	Crash
21	15	76	Larry Frank	Crash
22	14	40	Pete Hamilton	Crash

Lap Leaders: Dick Brooks 1-21, Cale Yarborough 22-29, Elmo Langley 30.
Cautions: Many Margin of Victory: 10 Feet

Elmo Nabs Cale at Finish to Win the Winston Legends Race

Elmo Langley ducked to the low side of Cale Yarborough in the final lap and emerged victorious in the Winston Legends event at Charlotte Motor Speedway. The special event was staged for former NASCAR Grand National and Winston Cup drivers as a prelude to the 1991 running of The Winston.

Twenty-two of yesterday's heroes participated in the special 30-lap event. They drove cars prepared by part-time driver Rodney Combs and financed by sponsoring R.J. Reynolds.

Langley started 16th in the field and worked his way into contention as wrecks depleted the field. He moved into second place near the end of the event and snatched first place from Yarborough with a nifty last-lap pass. Yarborough finished second, less than a car length behind.

Third place went to Paul Goldsmith, who came from 22nd starting spot. Neil Castles was fourth and Fred Lorenzen took fifth place.

Dick Brooks won the pole via a draw and led the first 21 laps. His car was damaged in a four-car tangle which involved Yarborough, Langley and Richard Childress. A flat tire sent Brooks to the rear and out of contention. Yarborough picked up the lead until Langley raced past him in the final lap.

"Man, this is just great," said an elated Langley after the race. "I got Cale on the last lap and I didn't have any reason to back off."

Yarborough said Langley, "caught me napping. I didn't even see him until he passed me."

Junior Johnson was involved in many skirmishes, including one with the pace car, which was driven by NASCAR President Bill France, Jr.

Johnson and Tim Flock snagged bumpers frequently to the delight of the crowd. Johnson eventually finished 11th.

Elmo Langley #64 drove his battered car to a close victory over Cale Yarborough #11 in the Winston Legends special event.

Race Winners & Pole Winners 1949-1993

NASCAR Winston Cup Grand National Series

1949

Race #	Year #	Date	Site	Track	Surface	Miles	Race Winner	Car	Speed	Pole Winner	Car	Speed
1	1	6/19/49	Charlotte NC	0.750	D	150.00	Jim Roper	Lincoln	---	Bob Flock	Hudson	67.958
2	2	7/10/49	Daytona Beach FL	4.150	B-R	166.00	Red Byron	Olds	80-.883	Gober Sosebee	Olds	---
3	3	8/7/49	Hillsboro NC	1.000	D	200.00	Bob Flock	Olds	76.800	---	---	---
4	4	9/11/49	Langhorne PA	1.000	D	200.00	Curtis Turner	Olds	69.403	Red Byron	Olds	77.482
5	5	9/18/49	Hamburg NY	0.500	D	100.00	Jack White	Lincoln	---	---	---	---
6	6	9/25/49	Martinsville VA	0.500	D	100.00	Red Byron (2)	Olds	---	Curtis Turner	Olds	---
7	7	10/2/49	Heidelberg PA	0.500	D	100.00	Lee Petty	Plymouth	57.458	Al Bonnell	Olds	61.475
8	8	10/16/49	N Wilkesboro NC	0.500	D	100.00	Bob Flock (2)	Olds	53.364	Ken Wagner	Lincoln	57.563

1950

Race #	Year #	Date	Site	Track	Surface	Miles	Race Winner	Car	Speed	Pole Winner	Car	Speed
9	1	2/5/50	Daytona Beach FL	4.167	B-R	200.00	Harold Kite	Lincoln	89.894	Joe Littlejohn	Olds	98.840
10	2	4/3/50	Charlotte NC	0.750	D	150.00	Tim Flock	Lincoln	---	Red Byron (2)	Olds	67.839
11	3	4/16/50	Langhorne PA	1.000	D	150.00	Curtis Turner (2)	Olds	69.399	Tim Flock	Lincoln	---
12	4	5/21/50	Martinsville VA	0.500	D	75.00	Curtis Turner (3)	Olds	---	Buck Baker	Ford	54.216
13	5	5/30/50	Canfield OH	0.500	D	100.00	Bill Rexford	Olds	---	Jimmy Florian	Ford	---
14	6	6/18/50	Vernon NY	0.500	D	100.00	Bill Blair	Mercury	---	Chuck Mahoney	Mercury	---
15	7	6/25/50	Dayton OH	0.500	D	100.00	Jimmy Florian	Ford	63.354	Dick Linder	Olds	66.543
16	8	7/2/50	Rochester NY	0.500	D	100.00	Curtis Turner (4)	Olds	50.614	Curtis Turner (2)	Olds	54.974
17	9	7/23/50	Charlotte NC	0.750	D	150.00	Curtis Turner (5)	Olds	---	Curtis Turner (3)	Olds	---
18	10	8/13/50	Hillsboro NC	1.000	D	100.00	Fireball Roberts	Olds	---	Dick Linder (2)	Olds	---
19	11	8/20/50	Dayton OH	0.500	D	97.50	Dick Linder	Olds	None	Curtis Turner (4)	Olds	---
20	12	8/27/50	Hamburg NY	0.500	D	100.00	Dick Linder (2)	Olds	50.747	Dick Linder (3)	Olds	53.113
21	13	9/4/50	Darlington SC	1.250	P	500.00	Johnny Mantz	Plymouth	75.250	Curtis Turner (5)	Olds	82.034
22	14	9/17/50	Langhorne PA	1.000	D	200.00	Fonty Flock	Olds	72.801	Wally Campbell	Olds	---
23	15	9/24/50	N Wilkesboro NC	0.625	D	125.00	Leon Sales	Plymouth	---	Fireball Roberts	Olds	73.266
24	16	10/1/50	Vernon NY	0.500	D	100.00	Dick Linder (3)	Olds	---	Dick Linder (4)	Olds	---
25	17	10/15/50	Martinsville VA	0.500	D	100.00	Herb Thomas	Plymouth	---	Fonty Flock	Olds	54.761
26	18	10/15/50	Winchester IN	0.500	D	100.00	Lloyd Moore	Mercury	---	---	---	---
27	19	10/29/50	Hillsboro NC	1.000	D	200.00	Lee Petty (2)	Plymouth	---	Fonty Flock (2)	Olds	85.898

1951

Race #	Year #	Date	Site	Track	Surface	Miles	Race Winner	Car	Speed	Pole Winner	Car	Speed
28	1	2/11/51	Daytona Beach FL	4.100	B-R	160.00	Marshall Teague	Hudson	82.328	Tim Flock (2)	Lincoln	102.200
29	2	4/1/51	Charlotte NC	0.750	D	112.50	Curtis Turner (6)	Nash	70.545	Fonty Flock (3)	Olds	68.337
30	3	4/8/51	Mobile AL	0.750	D	112.50	Tim Flock (2)	Olds	50.260	No Time Trials	NTT	NTT
31	4	4/8/51	Gardena CA	0.500	D	100.00	Marshall Teague (2)	Hudson	61.047	Andy Pierce	Buick	62.959
32	5	4/15/51	Hillsboro NC	1.000	D	95.00	Fonty Flock (2)	Olds	80.889	Fonty Flock (4)	Olds	88.278
33	6	4/29/51	Phoenix AZ	1.000	D	150.00	Marshall Teague (3)	Hudson	60.153	Fonty Flock (5)	Olds	---
34	7	4/29/51	N Wilkesboro NC	0.625	D	93.75	Fonty Flock (3)	Olds	None	Fonty Flock (6)	Olds	72.184
35	8	5/6/51	Martinsville VA	0.500	D	100.00	Curtis Turner (7)	Olds	---	Tim Flock (3)	Olds	55.062
36	9	5/30/51	Canfield OH	0.500	D	100.00	Marshall Teague (4)	Hudson	49.308	Bill Rexford	Olds	54.233
37	10	6/10/51	Columbus OH	0.500	D	100.00	Tim Flock (3)	Olds	---	Gober Sosebee (2)	Cadillac	57.766
38	11	6/16/51	Columbia SC	0.500	D	100.00	Frank Mundy	Studebaker	50.683	Frank Mundy	Studebaker	57.563
39	12	6/24/51	Dayton OH	0.500	P	100.00	Curtis Turner (8)	Olds	---	Tim Flock (4)	Olds	70.838
40	13	6/30/51	Gardena CA	0.500	D	100.00	Lou Figaro	Hudson	---	Lou Figaro	Hudson	76.988
41	14	7/1/51	Grand Rapids MI	0.500	D	100.00	Marshall Teague (5)	Hudson	---	---	---	---
42	15	7/8/51	Bainbridge OH	0.500	D	100.00	Fonty Flock (4)	Olds	65.753	Fonty Flock (7)	Olds	---
43	16	7/15/51	Heidelberg PA	0.500	D	100.00	Herb Thomas (2)	Olds	None	Fonty Flock (8)	Olds	61.983
44	17	7/29/51	Weaverville NC	0.500	D	100.00	Fonty Flock (5)	Olds	---	Billy Carden	Olds	64.608
45	18	7/31/51	Rochester NY	0.500	D	100.00	Lee Petty (3)	Plymouth	---	Fonty Flock (9)	Olds	---
46	19	8/1/51	Altamont NY	0.500	D	100.00	Fonty Flock (6)	Olds	---	---	---	---
47	20	8/12/51	Detroit MI	1.000	D	250.00	Tommy Thompson	Chrysler	57.588	Marshall Teague	Hudson	69.131
48	21	8/19/51	Toledo OH	0.500	D	100.00	Tim Flock (4)	Olds	50.847	Fonty Flock (10)	Olds	55.521
49	22	8/24/51	Morristown NJ	0.500	D	100.00	Tim Flock (5)	Olds	---	Tim Flock (5)	Olds	58.670
50	23	8/25/51	Greenville SC	0.500	D	100.00	Bob Flock (3)	Olds	---	---	---	---
51	24	9/3/51	Darlington SC	1.250	P	500.00	Herb Thomas (3)	Hudson	76.906	Frank Mundy (2)	Studebaker	84.173
52	25	9/7/51	Columbia SC	0.500	D	100.00	Tim Flock (6)	Olds	---	Tim Flock (6)	Olds	58.843
53	26	9/8/51	Macon GA	0.500	D	100.00	Herb Thomas (4)	Oldsmobile	53.222	Bob Flock (2)	Olds	---

Race #	Year #	Date	Site	Track	Surface	Miles	Race Winner	Car	Speed	Pole Winner	Car	Speed
54	27	9/15/51	Langhorne PA	1.000	D	150.00	Herb Thomas (5)	Hudson	71.043	Fonty Flock (11)	Olds	81.773
55	28	9/23/51	Charlotte NC	0.750	D	150.00	Herb Thomas (6)	Hudson	---	Billy Carden (2)	Olds	66.914
56	29	9/23/51	Dayton OH	0.500	P	100.00	Fonty Flock (7)	Olds	---	Fonty Flock (12)	Olds	---
57	30	9/30/51	Wilson NC	0.500	D	100.00	Fonty Flock (8)	Olds	---	Fonty Flock (13)	Olds	---
58	31	10/7/51	Hillsboro NC	1.000	D	150.00	Herb Thomas (7)	Hudson	72.454	Herb Thomas	Hudson	79.628
59	32	10/21/51	Thompson CT	0.500	P	100.00	Neil Cole	Olds	---	Neil Cole	Olds	59.269
60	33	10/14/51	Shippenville PA	0.500	D	100.00	Tim Flock (7)	Olds	---	---	---	---
61	34	10/14/51	Martinsville VA	0.500	D	100.00	Frank Mundy (2)	Olds	---	Herb Thomas (2)	Hudson	56.109
62	35	10/14/51	Oakland CA	0.625	D	250.00	Marvin Burke	Mercury	---	---	---	---
63	36	10/21/51	N Wilkesboro NC	0.625	D	125.00	Fonty Flock (9)	Olds	67.791	Herb Thomas (3)	Hudson	68.828
64	37	10/28/51	Hanford CA	0.500	D	100.00	Danny Weinberg	Studebaker	---	---	---	---
65	38	11/4/51	Jacksonville FL	0.500	D	100.00	Herb Thomas (8)	Hudson	53.412	Herb Thomas (4)	Hudson	64.818
66	39	11/11/51	Atlanta GA	1.000	D	100.00	Tim Flock (8)	Hudson	59.960	Frank Mundy (3)	Studebaker	74.013
67	40	11/11/51	Gardena CA	0.500	D	100.00	Bill Norton	Mercury	---	Fonty Flock (14)	Olds	---
68	41	11/25/51	Mobile AL	0.750	D	112.50	Frank Mundy (3)	Studebaker	---	Frank Mundy (4)	Studebaker	61.113

1952

Race #	Year #	Date	Site	Track	Surface	Miles	Race Winner	Car	Speed	Pole Winner	Car	Speed
69	1	1/20/52	W Palm Beach FL	0.500	D	100.00	Fim Flock (9)	Hudson	None	Tim Flock (7)	Hudson	67.794
70	2	2/10/52	Daytona Beach FL	4.100	B-R	200.90	Marshall Teague (6)	Hudson	85.612	Pat Kirkwood	Chrysler	110.970
71	3	3/6/52	Jacksonville FL	0.500	D	100.00	Marshall Teague (7)	Hudson	55.197	Marshall Teague (2)	Hudson	60.100
72	4	3/30/52	N Wilkesboro NC	0.625	D	125.00	Herb Thomas (9)	Hudson	58.593	Herb Thomas (5)	Hudson	75.075
73	5	4/6/52	Martinsville VA	0.500	D	100.00	Dick Rathmann	Hudson	42.862	Buck Baker (2)	Hudson	54.945
74	6	4/12/52	Columbia SC	0.500	D	100.00	Buck Baker	Hudson	53.460	Buck Baker (3)	Hudson	---
75	7	4/20/52	Atlanta GA	1.000	D	100.00	Bill Blair (2)	Olds	66.877	Tim Flock (8)	Hudson	71.613
76	8	4/27/52	Macon GA	0.500	D	99.00	Herb Thomas (10)	Hudson	53.853	Jack Smith	Studebaker	54.429
77	9	5/4/52	Langhorne PA	1.000	D	150.00	Dick Rathmann (2)	Hudson	67.669	Herb Thomas (6)	Hudson	76.045
78	10	5/10/52	Darlington SC	1.375	P	100.00	Dick Rathmann (3)	Hudson	83.818	No Time Trials	NTT	NTT
79	11	5/18/52	Dayton OH	0.500	P	100.00	Dick Rathmann (4)	Hudson	65.526	Fonty Flock (15)	Olds	71.884
80	12	5/30/52	Canfield OH	0.500	D	100.00	Herb Thomas (11)	Hudson	48.057	Dick Rathmann	Hudson	58.102
81	13	6/1/52	Augusta GA	0.500	D	100.00	Gober Sosebee	Chrysler	None	Tommy Moon	Hudson	51.561
82	14	6/1/52	Toledo OH	0.500	D	100.00	Tim Flock (10)	Hudson	47.175	Fonty Flock (16)	Olds	57.034
83	15	6/8/52	Hillsboro NC	1.000	D	100.00	Tim Flock (11)	Hudson	81.008	Fonty Flock (17)	Olds	91.977
84	16	6/15/42	Charlotte NC	0.750	D	112.50	Herb Thomas (12)	Hudson	64.820	Fonty Flock (18)	Olds	70.038
85	17	6/29/52	Detroit MI	1.000	D	250.00	Tim Flock (12)	Hudson	59.908	Dick Rathmann (2)	Hudson	70.230
86	18	7/1/52	Niagara Falls ONT	0.500	D	100.00	Buddy Shuman	Hudson	45.620	Herb Thomas (7)	Hudson	52.401
87	19	7/4/52	Owego NY	0.500	D	100.00	Tim Flock (13)	Hudson	56.603	Tim Flock (9)	Hudson	67.669
88	20	7/6/52	Monroe MI	0.500	D	100.00	Tim Flock (14)	Hudson	44.499	Tim Flock (10)	Hudson	57.600
89	21	7/11/52	Morristown NJ	0.500	D	100.00	Lee Petty (4)	Plymouth	59.661	Herb Thomas (8)	Hudson	60.996
90	22	7/20/52	South Bend IN	0.500	D	100.00	Tim Flock (15)	Hudson	41.889	Herb Thomas (9)	Hudson	58.120
91	23	8/15/52	Rochester NY	0.500	D	88.00	Tim Flock (16)	Hudson	None	No Time Trials	NTT	NTT
92	24	8/17/52	Weaverville NC	0.500	D	100.00	Bob Flock (3)	Hudson	57.288	Herb Thomas (10)	Hudson	64.888
93	25	9/1/52	Darlington SC	1.375	P	500.00	Fonty Flock (10)	Olds	74.512	Fonty Flock (19)	Olds	88.550
94	26	9/7/52	Macon GA	0.500	D	150.00	Lee Petty (5)	Plymouth	48.404	Fonty Flock (20)	Olds	50.113
95	27	9/14/52	Langhorne PA	1.000	D	250.00	Lee Petty (6)	Plymouth	72.463	Herb Thomas (11)	Hudson	85.287
96	28	9/21/52	Dayton OH	0.500	P	150.00	Dick Rathmann (5)	Hudson	61.643	Fonty Flock (21)	Olds	72.741
97	29	9/28/52	Wilson NC	0.500	D	100.00	Herb Thomas (13)	Hudson	35.398	Herb Thomas (12)	Hudson	55.883
98	30	10/12/52	Hillsboro NC	1.000	D	150.00	Fonty Flock (11)	Olds	73.489	Bill Blair	Olds	75.901
99	31	10/29/52	Martinsville VA	0.500	D	100.00	Herb Thomas (14)	Hudson	47.556	Perk Brown	Hudson	55.333
100	32	10/26/52	N Wilkesboro NC	0.625	D	125.00	Herb Thomas (15)	Hudson	67.044	Herb Thomas (13)	Hudson	76.013
101	33	11/16/52	Atlanta GA	1.000	D	100.00	Donald Thomas	Hudson	64.853	Donald Thomas	Hudson	72.874
102	34	11/30/52	W Palm Beach FL	0.500	D	100.00	Herb Thomas (16)	Hudson	58.008	Herb Thomas (14)	Hudson	63.716

1953

Race #	Year #	Date	Site	Track	Surface	Miles	Race Winner	Car	Speed	Pole Winner	Car	Speed
103	1	2/1/53	W Palm Beach FL	0.500	D	100.00	Lee Petty (7)	Dodge	60.220	Dick Rathmann (3)	Hudson	65.028
104	2	2/15/53	Daytona Beach FL	4.100	B-R	160.00	Bill Blair (3)	Olds	89.789	Bob Pronger	Olds	115.770
105	3	3/8/53	Spring Lake NC	0.500	D	100.00	Herb Thomas (17)	Hudson	48.826	Herb Thomas (15)	Hudson	51.918
106	4	3/29/53	N Wilkesboro NC	0.625	D	125.00	Herb Thomas (18)	Hudson	71.907	Herb Thomas (16)	Hudson	78.108
107	5	4/5/53	Charlotte NC	0.750	D	112.50	Dick Passwater	Olds	---	Tim Flock (11)	Hudson	71.108
108	6	4/19/53	Richmond VA	0.500	D	100.00	Lee Petty (8)	Dodge	45.535	Buck Baker (4)	Olds	48.465
109	7	4/26/53	Macon GA	0.500	D	100.00	Dick Rathmann (6)	Hudson	56.417	---	---	---
110	8	5/3/53	Langhorne PA	1.000	D	150.00	Buck Baker (2)	Olds	72.743	No Time Trials	---	---
111	9	5/9/53	Columbia SC	0.500	D	100.00	Buck Baker (3)	Olds	53.707	Herb Thomas (17)	Hudson	58.670
112	10	5/9/53	Hickory NC	0.500	D	100.00	Tim Flock (17)	Hudson	---	---	---	---
113	11	5/17/53	Martinsville VA	0.500	D	100.00	Lee Petty (9)	Dodge	---	---	---	---
114	12	5/24/53	Columbus OH	0.500	D	100.00	Herb Thomas (19)	Hudson	56.127	Fonty Flock (22)	Olds	59.288
115	13	5/30/53	Raleigh NC	1.000	P	300.00	Fonty Flock (12)	Hudson	70.629	Slick Smith	Olds	76.230
116	14	6/7/53	Shreveport LA	0.500	D	100.00	Lee Petty (10)	Dodge	53.199	Herb Thomas (18)	Hudson	58.727
117	15	6/14/53	Pensacola FL	0.500	D	70.00	Herb Thomas (20)	Hudson	63.316	Dick Rathmann (4)	Hudson	67.039
118	16	6/21/53	Langhorne PA	1.000	D	200.00	Dick Rathmann (7)	Hudson	64.434	Lloyd Shaw	Jaguar	82.200

Race #	Year #	Date	Site	Track	Surface	Miles	Race Winner	Car	Speed	Pole Winner	Car	Speed
119	17	6/23/53	High Point NC	0.500	D	100.00	Herb Thomas (21)	Hudson	58.186	Herb Thomas (19)	Hudson	66.152
120	18	6/28/53	Wilson NC	0.500	D	100.00	Fonty Flock (13)	Hudson	53.803	---	---	---
121	19	7/3/53	Rochester NY	0.500	D	100.00	Herb Thomas (22)	Hudson	56.939	No Time Trials	NTT	NTT
122	20	7/4/53	Spartanburg SC	0.500	D	100.00	Lee Petty (11)	Dodge	56.934	Buck Baker (5)	Olds	58.027
123	21	7/10/53	Morristown NJ	0.500	D	100.00	Dick Rathmann (8)	Hudson	69.417	Herb Thomas (20)	Hudson	61.016
124	22	7/12/53	Atlanta GA	1.000	D	100.00	Herb Thomas (23)	Hudson	70.685	Herb Thomas (21)	Hudson	72.756
125	23	7/22/53	Rapid City SD	0.500	D	100.00	Herb Thomas (24)	Hudson	57.720	Herb Thomas (22)	Hudson	55.727
126	24	7/26/53	N Platte NE	0.500	D	100.00	Dick Rathmann (9)	Hudson	54.380	Herb Thomas (23)	Hudson	54.397
127	25	8/2/53	Davenport IA	0.500	D	100.00	Herb Thomas (25)	Hudson	62.500	Buck Baker (6)	Olds	54.397
128	26	8/9/53	Hillsboro NC	1.000	D	100.00	Curtis Turner (9)	Olds	75.125	Curtis Turner (6)	Olds	89.078
129	27	8/16/53	Weaverville NC	0.500	D	100.00	Fonty Flock (14)	Hudson	62.434	Curtis Turner (7)	Olds	---
130	28	8/23/53	Norfolk VA	0.500	D	100.00	Herb Thomas (26)	Hudson	51.040	Curtis Turner (8)	Olds	54.200
131	29	8/29/53	Hickory NC	0.500	D	100.00	Fonty Flock (15)	Hudson	---	Tim Flock (12)	Hudson	79.362
132	30	9/7/53	Darlington SC	1.375	P	500.00	Buck Baker (4)	Olds	92.881	Fonty Flock (23)	Hudson	107.893
133	31	9/13/53	Macon GA	0.500	D	100.00	Speedy Thompson	Olds	55.172	Joe Eubanks	Hudson	60.810
134	32	9/20/53	Langhorne PA	1.000	D	250.00	Dick Rathmann (10)	Hudson	67.046	Herb Thomas (24)	Hudson	---
135	33	10/3/53	Bloomsburg PA	0.500	D	100.00	Herb Thomas (27)	Hudson	---	Jim Paschal	Dodge	55.953
136	34	10/4/53	Wilson NC	0.500	D	100.00	Herb Thomas (28)	Hudson	56.022	Herb Thomas (25)	Hudson	56.962
137	35	10/11/53	N Wilkesboro NC	0.625	D	100.00	Speedy Thompson (2)	Olds	71.202	Buck Baker (7)	Olds	78.288
138	36	10/18/53	Martinsville VA	0.500	D	100.00	Jim Paschal	Dodge	56.013	Fonty Flock (24)	Hudson	58.958
139	37	11/1/53	Atlanta GA	1.000	D	100.00	Buck Baker (5)	Olds	63.180	Tim Flock (13)	Hudson	73.580

1954

Race #	Year #	Date	Site	Track	Surface	Miles	Race Winner	Car	Speed	Pole Winner	Car	Speed
140	1	2/7/54	W Palm Beach FL	0.500	D	100.00	Herb Thomas (29)	Hudson	58.958	Dick Rathmann (5)	Hudson	66.371
141	2	2/21/54	Daytona Beach FL	4.100	B-R	160.00	Lee Petty (12)	Chrysler	89.108	Lee Petty	Chrysler	123.410
142	3	3/7/54	Jacksonville FL	0.500	D	100.00	Herb Thomas (30)	Hudson	56.561	Curtis Turner (9)	Olds	63.581
143	4	3/21/54	Atlanta GA	1.000	D	100.00	Herb Thomas (32)	Hudson	60.494	Herb Thomas (26)	Hudson	73.514
144	5	3/28/54	Savannah GA	0.500	D	100.00	Al Keller	Hudson	59.820	Herb Thomas (27)	Hudson	63.202
145	6	3/28/54	Oakland CA	0.500	D	125.00	Dick Rathmann (11)	Hudson	50.692	Hershel McGriff	Olds	55.624
146	7	4/4/54	N Wilkesboro NC	0.625	D	100.00	Dick Rathmann (12)	Hudson	68.545	Gober Sosebee (3)	Olds	78.698
147	8	4/18/54	Hillsboro NC	1.000	D	100.00	Herb Thomas (32)	Hudson	77.386	Buck Baker (8)	Olds	86.767
148	9	4/25/54	Macon GA	0.500	D	100.00	Gober Sosebee (2)	Olds	55.410	Dick Rathmann (6)	Hudson	57.859
149	10	5/2/54	Langhorne PA	1.000	D	150.00	Herb Thomas (33)	Hudson	74.883	Lee Petty (2)	Chrysler	87.217
150	11	5/9/54	Wilson NC	0.500	D	100.00	Buck Baker (6)	Olds	52.279	Jim Paschal (2)	Olds	55.469
151	12	5/16/54	Martinsville VA	0.500	D	100.00	Jim Paschal (2)	Olds	46.153	No Time Trials	NTT	NTT
152	13	5/23/54	Sharon PA	0.500	D	100.00	Lee Petty (13)	Chrysler	None	Dick Rathmann (7)	Hudson	62.090
153	14	5/29/54	Raleigh NC	1.000	P	250.00	Herb Thomas (34)	Hudson	73.909	Herb Thomas (28)	Hudson	76.660
154	15	5/30/54	Charlotte NC	0.750	D	100.00	Buck Baker (7)	Olds	49.805	Al Keller	Hudson	68.947
155	16	5/30/54	Gardena CA	0.500	D	248.00	John Soares	Dodge	53.438	Danny Letner	Hudson	62.849
156	17	6/6/54	Columbia SC	0.500	D	100.00	Curtis Turner (10)	Olds	56.719	Buck Baker (9)	Olds	62.240
157	18	6/13/54	Linden NJ	2.000	P	100.00	Al Keller (2)	Jaguar	77.469	Buck Baker (10)	Olds	80.536
158	19	6/19/54	Hickory NC	0.500	D	100.00	Herb Thomas (35)	Hudson	82.872	Herb Thomas (29)	Hudson	81.669
159	20	6/25/54	Rochester NY	0.500	D	100.00	Lee Petty (14)	Chrysler	52.455	Herb Thomas (30)	Hudson	60.422
160	21	6/27/54	Mechanicsburg PA	0.500	D	100.00	Herb Thomas (36)	Hudson	51.085	Dick Rathmann (8)	Hudson	54.945
161	22	7/3/54	Spartanburg SC	0.500	D	100.00	Herb Thomas (37)	Hudson	59.181	Hershel McGriff (2)	Olds	58.120
162	23	7/4/54	Weaverville NC	0.500	D	100.00	Herb Thomas (38)	Hudson	61.318	Herb Thomas (31)	Hudson	67.771
163	24	7/10/54	Willow Springs IL	0.500	D	100.00	Dick Rathmann (13)	Hudson	72.216	Buck Baker (11)	Olds	75.662
164	25	7/11/54	Grand Rapids MI	0.500	D	100.00	Lee Petty (15)	Chrysler	52.090	Herb Thomas (32)	Hudson	59.055
165	26	7/30/54	Morristown NJ	0.500	D	100.00	Buck Baker (8)	Olds	58.968	Buck Baker (12)	Olds	66.667
166	27	8/1/54	Oakland CA	0.500	D	150.00	Danny Letner	Hudson	53.045	Marvin Panch	Dodge	55.248
167	28	8/13/54	Charlotte NC	0.500	D	100.00	Lee Petty (16)	Chrysler	51.362	Buck Baker (13)	Olds	57.270
168	29	8/22/54	San Mateo CA	1.000	D	250.00	Hershel McGriff	Olds	64.710	Hershel McGriff (3)	Olds	75.566
169	30	8/29/54	Corbin KY	0.500	D	100.00	Lee Petty (17)	Chrysler	63.080	Jim Paschal (3)	Olds	65.789
170	31	9/6/54	Darlington SC	1.375	P	500.00	Herb Thomas (39)	Hudson	95.026	Buck Baker (14)	Olds	108.261
171	32	9/12/54	Macon GA	0.500	D	100.00	Hershel McGriff (2)	Olds	50.526	Tim Flock (14)	Olds	56.907
172	33	9/24/54	Charlotte NC	0.500	D	100.00	Hershel McGriff (3)	Olds	53.167	Hershel McGriff (4)	Olds	54.054
173	34	9/26/54	Langhorne PA	1.000	D	250.00	Herb Thomas (40)	Hudson	71.186	Herb Thomas (33)	Hudson	89.418
174	35	10/10/54	LeHi AR	1.500	D	250.00	Buck Baker (9)	Olds	89.013	Junior Johnson	Cadillac	---
175	36	10/17/54	Martinsville VA	0.500	D	82.50	Lee Petty (18)	Chrysler	44.547	Lee Petty (3)	Chrysler	53.191
176	37	10/24/54	N Wilkesboro NC	0.625	D	98.10	Hershel McGriff (4)	Olds	65.175	Hershel McGriff (5)	Olds	77.612

1955

Race #	Year #	Date	Site	Track	Surface	Miles	Race Winner	Car	Speed	Pole Winner	Car	Speed
177	1	11/7/54	High Point NC	0.500	D	100.00	Lee Petty (19)	Chrysler	62.882	Herb Thomas (34)	Hudson	71.942
178	2	2/6/55	W Palm Beach FL	0.500	D	100.00	Herb Thomas (41)	Hudson	56.013	Dick Rathmann (9)	Hudson	65.454
179	3	2/13/55	Jacksonville FL	0.500	D	100.00	Lee Petty (20)	Chrysler	69.031	Dick Rathmann (10)	Hudson	63.514
180	4	2/27/55	Daytona Beach FL	4.100	B-R	160.00	Tim Flock (18)	Chrysler	91.999	Tim Flock (15)	Chrysler	130.293
181	5	3/6/55	Savannah GA	0.500	D	100.00	Lee Petty (21)	Chrysler	60.150	Dick Rathmann (11)	Hudson	62.805
182	6	3/26/55	Columbia SC	0.500	D	100.00	Fonty Flock (16)	Chevy	None	Tim Flock (16)	Chrysler	---
183	7	3/27/55	Hillsboro NC	1.000	D	100.00	Jim Paschal (3)	Olds	82.304	Tim Flock (17)	Chrysler	91.696

Race #	Year #	Date	Site	Track	Surface	Miles	Race Winner	Car	Speed	Pole Winner	Car	Speed
184	8	4/3/55	N Wilkesboro NC	0.625	D	100.00	Buck Baker (10)	Olds	73.126	Dink Widenhouse	Olds	77.720
185	9	4/17/55	Montgomery AL	0.500	D	100.00	Tim Flock (19)	Chrysler	60.872	Jim Paschal (4)	Olds	64.290
186	10	4/24/55	Langhorne PA	1.000	D	150.00	Tim Flock (20)	Chrysler	72.893	Tim Flock (18)	Chrysler	86.699
187	11	5/1/55	Charlotte NC	0.750	D	100.00	Buck Baker (11)	Buick	52.630	Herb Thomas (35)	Buick	70.184
188	12	5/7/55	Hickory NC	0.500	D	100.00	Junior Johnson	Olds	65.502	Tim Flock (19)	Chrysler	67.748
189	13	5/8/55	Phoenix AZ	1.000	D	100.00	Tim Flock (21)	Chrysler	71.485	Bill Amick	Dodge	75.519
190	14	5/15/55	Tucson AZ	0.500	D	100.00	Danny Letner (2)	Olds	51.428	Bill Amick (2)	Dodge	56.179
191	15	5/15/55	Martinsville VA	0.500	D	100.00	Tim Flock (22)	Chrysler	52.554	Jim Paschal (5)	Olds	58.823
192	16	5/22/55	Richmond VA	0.500	D	100.00	Tim Flock (23)	Chrysler	54.298	No Time Trials	NTT	NTT
193	17	5/28/55	Raleigh NC	0.500	D	100.00	Junior Johnson (2)	Olds	50.522	Tim Flock (20)	Chrysler	58.612
194	18	5/29/55	Winston Salem NC	0.500	D	100.00	Lee Petty (22)	Chrysler	50.583	Fonty Flock (25)	Chrysler	56.710
195	19	6/10/55	New Oxford PA	0.500	D	100.00	Junior Johnson (3)	Olds	65.371	Junior Johnson (2)	Olds	75.853
196	20	6/17/55	Rochester NY	0.500	D	100.00	Tim Flock (24)	Chrysler	57.710	Buck Baker (15)	Chrysler	61.141
197	21	6/18/55	Fonda NY	0.500	D	100.00	Junior Johnson (4)	Olds	58.413	Fonty Flock (26)	Chrysler	61.770
198	22	6/19/55	Plattsburg NY	0.500	D	100.00	Lee Petty (23)	Chrysler	59.074	Lee Petty (4)	Chrysler	55.744
199	23	6/24/55	Charlotte NC	0.500	D	100.00	Tim Flock (25)	Chrysler	51.289	Tim Flock (21)	Chrysler	57.915
200	24	7/6/55	Spartanburg SC	0.500	D	100.00	Tim Flock (26)	Chrysler	49.106	Tim Flock (22)	Chrysler	58.517
201	25	7/9/55	Columbia SC	0.500	D	100.00	Jim Paschal (4)	Olds	55.469	Jimmie Lewallen	Olds	59.741
202	26	7/10/55	Weaverville NC	0.500	D	100.00	Tim Flock (27)	Chrysler	62.739	Tim Flock (23)	Chrysler	69.310
203	27	7/15/55	Morristown NJ	0.500	D	100.00	Tim Flock (28)	Chrysler	58.092	Tim Flock (24)	Chrysler	63.649
204	28	7/29/55	Altamont NY	0.500	D	88.50	Junior Johnson (5)	Olds	None	Tim Flock (25)	Chrysler	56.603
205	29	7/30/55	Syracuse NY	0.500	D	100.00	Tim Flock (29)	Chrysler	76.522	Tim Flock (26)	Chrysler	78.311
206	30	7/31/55	San Mateo CA	1.000	D	252.00	Tim Flock (30)	Chrysler	68.571	Fonty Flock (27)	Chrysler	79.330
207	31	8/5/55	Charlotte NC	0.500	D	100.00	Jim Paschal (5)	Olds	48.806	Tim Flock (27)	Chrysler	57.859
208	32	8/7/55	Winston-Salem NC	0.500	D	100.00	Lee Petty (24)	Dodge	50.111	Tim Flock (28)	Chrysler	59.016
209	33	8/14/55	LeHi AR	1.500	D	250.00	Fonty Flock (17)	Chrysler	89.892	Fonty Flock (28)	Chrysler	99.944
210	34	8/20/55	Raleigh NC	1.000	P	100.00	Herb Thomas (42)	Buick	76.400	Tim Flock (29)	Chrysler	78.722
211	35	9/5/55	Darlington SC	1.375	P	500.00	Herb Thomas (43)	Chevy	92.281	Fireball Roberts (2)	Buick	110.682
212	36	9/11/55	Montgomery AL	0.500	D	100.00	Tim Flock (31)	Chrysler	62.773	Tim Flock (30)	Chrysler	68.728
213	37	9/18/55	Langhorne PA	1.000	D	250.00	Tim Flock (32)	Chrysler	77.888	Tim Flock (31)	Chrysler	92.095
214	38	9/30/55	Raleigh NC	1.000	P	100.00	Fonty Flock (18)	Chrysler	73.289	Fonty Flock (29)	Chrysler	82.098
215	39	10/6/55	Greenville SC	0.500	D	100.00	Tim Flock (33)	Chrysler	57.942	Bob Welborn	Chevy	58.027
216	40	10/9/55	LeHi AR	1.500	D	300.00	Speedy Thompson (3)	Ford	83.898	Fonty Flock (30)	Chrysler	100.390
217	41	10/15/55	Columbia SC	0.500	D	100.00	Tim Flock (34)	Chrysler	55.393	Junior Johnson (3)	Olds	61.728
218	42	10/16/55	Martinsville VA	0.500	P	100.00	Speedy Thompson (4)	Chrysler	59.210	No Time Trials	NTT	NTT
219	43	10/16/55	Las Vegas NV	1.000	D	111.00	Norm Nelson	Chrysler	44.449	Norm Nelson	Chrysler	74.518
220	44	10/23/55	N Wilkesboro NC	0.625	D	100.00	Buck Baker (12)	Ford	72.347	Buck Baker (16)	Ford	79.815
221	45	10/30/55	Hillsboro NC	1.000	D	100.00	Tim Flock (35)	Chrysler	70.465	Tim Flock (32)	Chrysler	81.673

1956

Race #	Year #	Date	Site	Track	Surface	Miles	Race Winner	Car	Speed	Pole Winner	Car	Speed
222	1	10/30/55	Hickory NC	0.500	D	80.00	Tim Flock (36)	Chrysler	56.962	Tim Flock (33)	Chrysler	---
223	2	11/20/55	Charlotte NC	0.750	D	100.00	Fonty Flock (19)	Chrysler	61.825	Fonty Flock (31)	Chrysler	70.496
224	3	11/20/55	Lancaster CA	0.500	D	200.00	Chuck Stevenson	Ford	66.512	Jim Reed	Chevy	76.556
225	4	12/11/55	W Palm Beach FL	0.500	D	100.00	Herb Thomas (44)	Chevy	65.009	Fonty Flock (32)	Chrysler	78.912
226	5	1/22/56	Phoenix AZ	1.000	D	150.00	Buck Baker (13)	Chrysler	64.408	Joe Weatherly	Ford	71.315
227	6	2/26/56	Daytona Beach FL	4.100	B-R	151.70	Tim Flock (37)	Chrysler	90.657	Tim Flock (34)	Chrysler	135.747
228	7	3/4/56	W Palm Beach FL	0.500	D	100.00	Billy Myers	Mercury	68.990	Buck Baker (17)	Dodge	81.081
229	8	3/18/56	Wilson NC	0.500	D	53.00	Herb Thomas (45)	Chevy	46.287	Herb Thomas (36)	Chevy	57.157
230	9	3/25/56	Atlanta GA	1.000	D	100.00	Buck Baker (14)	Chrysler	70.643	Tim Flock (35)	Chrysler	82.154
231	10	4/8/56	N Wilkesboro NC	0.625	D	100.00	Tim Flock (38)	Chrysler	71.034	Junior Johnson (4)	Pontiac	78.370
232	11	4/22/56	Langhorne PA	1.000	D	150.00	Buck Baker (15)	Chrysler	75.928	Buck Baker (18)	Chrysler	104.590
233	12	4/29/56	Richmond VA	0.500	D	100.00	Buck Baker (16)	Dodge	56.232	Buck Baker (19)	Dodge	67.091
234	13	5/5/56	Columbia SC	0.500	D	100.00	Speedy Thompson (5)	Dodge	54.545	Buck Baker (20)	Dodge	63.224
235	14	5/6/56	Concord NC	0.500	D	100.00	Speedy Thompson (6)	Chrysler	61.633	Speedy Thompson	Chrysler	65.241
236	15	5/10/56	Greenville SC	0.500	D	100.00	Buck Baker (17)	Dodge	60.362	Rex White	Chevy	61.100
237	16	5/12/56	Hickory NC	0.400	D	80.00	Speedy Thompson (7)	Chrysler	59.442	Speedy Thompson (2)	Chrysler	67.447
238	17	5/13/56	Hillsboro NC	0.900	D	90.00	Buck Baker (18)	Chrysler	83.720	Buck Baker (21)	Chrysler	89.305
239	18	5/20/56	Martinsville VA	0.500	P	250.00	Buck Baker (19)	Dodge	60.824	Buck Baker (22)	Dodge	66.103
240	19	5/25/56	Abbottstown PA	0.500	D	100.00	Buck Baker (20)	Dodge	69.619	Speedy Thompson (3)	Dodge	76.628
241	20	5/27/56	Charlotte NC	0.750	D	100.00	Speedy Thompson (8)	Chrysler	64.866	Speedy Thompson (4)	Chrysler	76.966
242	21	5/27/56	Portland OR	0.500	P	75.00	Herb Thomas (46)	Chrysler	63.815	John Kieper	Olds	67.239
243	22	5/30/56	Eureka CA	0.625	D	78.10	Herb Thomas (47)	Chrysler	38.814	John Kieper (2)	Olds	66.040
244	23	5/30/56	Syracuse NY	1.000	D	150.00	Buck Baker (21)	Chrysler	86.179	Buck Baker (23)	Chrysler	83.975
245	24	6/3/56	Merced CA	0.500	D	100.00	Herb Thomas (48)	Chrysler	47.325	Herb Thomas (37)	Chrysler	58.234
246	25	6/10/56	LeHi AR	1.500	D	250.00	Ralph Moody	Ford	74.313	Buck Baker (24)	Chrysler	98.504
247	26	6/15/56	Charlotte NC	0.500	D	100.00	Speedy Thompson (9)	Chrysler	56.022	Fireball Roberts (3)	Ford	59.661
248	27	6/22/56	Rochester NY	0.500	D	100.00	Speedy Thompson (10)	Chrysler	57.288	Jim Paschal (6)	Mercury	57.434
249	28	6/24/56	Portland OR	0.500	P	100.00	John Kieper	Olds	62.586	Herb Thomas (38)	Chrysler	65.934
250	29	7/1/56	Weaverville NC	0.500	D	100.00	Lee Petty (25)	Dodge	56.435	Fireball Roberts (4)	Ford	72.260
251	3C	7/4/56	Raleigh NC	1.000	P	250.00	Fireball Roberts (2)	Ford	79.822	Lee Petty (5)	Dodge	82.587
252	31	7/7/56	Spartanburg SC	0.500	D	100.00	Lee Petty (26)	Dodge	50.483	Fireball Roberts (5)	Ford	58.900
253	32	7/8/56	Sacramento CA	1.000	D	100.00	Lloyd Dane	Mercury	74.074	Eddie Pagan	Ford	76.612

Race #	Year #	Date	Site	Track	Surface	Miles	Race Winner	Car	Speed	Pole Winner	Car	Speed
254	33	7/21/56	Chicago IL	0.500	P	100.00	Fireball Roberts (3)	Ford	61.037	Billy Myers	Mercury	---
255	34	7/17/56	Shelby NC	0.500	D	100.50	Speedy Thompson (11)	Dodge	53.699	Ralph Moody	Ford	55.658
256	35	7/29/56	Montgomery AL	0.500	D	100.00	Marvin Panch	Ford	67.252	Marvin Panch (2)	Ford	69.444
257	36	8/3/56	Oklahoma City OK	0.500	D	100.00	Jim Paschal (6)	Mercury	60.100	Speedy Thompson (5)	Dodge	64.655
258	37	8/12/56	Elkhart Lake WI	4.100	P	258.30	Tim Flock (39)	Mercury	73.858	Buck Baker (25)	Dodge	---
259	38	8/17/56	Old Bridge NJ	0.500	P	100.00	Ralph Moody (2)	Ford	65.170	Jim Reed (2)	Chevy	72.028
260	39	8/19/56	San Mateo CA	1.000	D	241.00	Eddie Pagan	Ford	68.161	Eddie Pagan (2)	Ford	81.614
261	40	8/22/56	Norfolk VA	0.500	D	100.00	Billy Myers (2)	Mercury	56.408	Ralph Moody (2)	Ford	58.631
262	41	8/23/56	Spartanburg SC	0.500	D	100.00	Ralph Moody (3)	Ford	54.372	Ralph Moody (3)	Ford	61.433
263	42	8/25/56	Myrtle Beach SC	0.500	D	100.00	Fireball Roberts (4)	Ford	50.576	Ralph Moody (4)	Ford	58.346
264	43	8/26/56	Portland OR	0.500	P	123.00	Royce Haggerty	Dodge	None	John Kieper (3)	Olds	65.861
265	44	9/3/56	Darlington SC	1.375	P	500.00	Curtis Turner (11)	Ford	95.167	Speedy Thompson (6)	Chrysler	118.683
266	45	9/9/56	Montgomery AL	0.500	D	100.00	Buck Baker (22)	Chrysler	60.893	Tim Flock (36)	Ford	64.864
267	46	9/12/56	Charlotte NC	0.500	D	100.00	Ralph Moody (4)	Ford	52.847	Joe Eubanks (2)	Ford	59.464
268	47	9/23/56	Langhorne PA	1.000	D	300.00	Paul Goldsmith	Chevy	70.615	Buck Baker (26)	Chrysler	93.628
269	48	9/23/56	Portland OR	0.500	P	125.00	Lloyd Dane (2)	Ford	None	Royce Haggerty	Dodge	---
270	49	9/29/56	Columbia SC	0.500	D	100.00	Buck Baker (23)	Dodge	61.193	Tim Flock (37)	Ford	61.940
271	50	9/30/56	Hillsboro NC	0.900	D	99.00	Fireball Roberts (5)	Ford	72.734	Speedy Thompson (7)	Chrysler	88.067
272	51	10/7/56	Newport TN	0.500	D	100.00	Fireball Roberts (6)	Ford	61.475	Joe Eubanks (3)	Ford	65.597
273	52	10/14/56	Charlotte NC	0.750	D	100.00	Buck Baker (24)	Chrysler	72.268	Ralph Moody (5)	Ford	75.041
274	53	10/23/56	Shelby NC	0.500	D	100.00	Buck Baker (25)	Chrysler	54.054	Doug Cox	Ford	58.479
275	54	10/28/56	Martinsville VA	0.500	P	200.00	Jack Smith	Dodge	61.136	Buck Baker (27)	Chrysler	67.643
276	55	11/11/56	Hickory NC	0.400	D	100.00	Speedy Thompson (12)	Chrysler	66.420	Ralph Earnhardt	Ford	68.278
277	56	11/18/56	Wilson NC	0.500	D	100.00	Buck Baker (26)	Chrysler	50.579	Buck Baker (28)	Chrysler	60.160

1957

Race #	Year #	Date	Site	Track	Surface	Miles	Race Winner	Car	Speed	Pole Winner	Car	Speed
278	1	11/11/56	Lancaster CA	2.500	P	150.00	Marvin Panch (2)	Ford	78.648	Marvin Panch (3)	Ford	78.596
279	2	12/2/56	Concord NC	0.500	D	100.00	Marvin Panch (3)	Ford	55.883	Curtis Turner (10)	Ford	62.586
280	3	12/30/56	Titusville FL	1.700	P	89.60	Fireball Roberts (7)	Ford	None	Paul Goldsmith	Chevy	69.106
281	4	2/17/57	Daytona Beach FL	4.100	B-R	160.00	Cotton Owens	Pontiac	101.541	Banjo Matthews	Pontiac	134.382
282	5	3/3/57	Concord NC	0.500	D	100.00	Jack Smith (2)	Chevy	59.860	Mel Larson	Ford	62.225
283	6	3/17/57	Wilson NC	0.500	D	100.00	Ralph Moody (5)	Ford	55.079	Fireball Roberts (6)	Ford	59.269
284	7	3/24/57	Hillsboro NC	0.900	D	99.00	Buck Baker (27)	Chevy	82.233	Fireball Roberts (7)	Ford	87.828
285	8	3/31/57	Weaverville NC	0.500	D	100.00	Buck Baker (28)	Chevy	65.693	Marvin Panch (4)	Ford	73.649
286	9	4/7/57	N Wilkesboro NC	0.625	D	100.00	Fireball Roberts (8)	Ford	75.015	Fireball Roberts (8)	Ford	81.521
287	10	4/14/57	Langhorne PA	1.000	D	150.00	Fireball Roberts (9)	Ford	85.850	Paul Goldsmith (2)	Ford	93.701
288	11	4/19/57	Charlotte NC	0.500	D	100.00	Fireball Roberts (10)	Ford	52.083	Marvin Panch (5)	Ford	60.060
289	12	4/27/57	Spartanburg SC	0.500	D	100.00	Marvin Panch (4)	Ford	55.130	Speedy Thompson (8)	Chevy	61.538
290	13	4/28/57	Greensboro NC	0.333	D	83.25	Paul Goldsmith (2)	Ford	49.905	Buck Baker (29)	Chevy	50.120
291	14	4/28/57	Portland OR	0.500	P	50.00	Art Watts	Ford	64.754	Art Watts	Ford	65.813
292	15	5/4/57	Shelby NC	0.500	D	100.00	Fireball Roberts (11)	Ford	54.861	Tiny Lund	Pontiac	57.544
293	16	5/5/57	Richmond VA	0.500	D	100.00	Paul Goldsmith (3)	Ford	62.445	Russ Hepler	Pontiac	64.239
294	17	5/19/57	Martinsville VA	0.500	P	220.50	Buck Baker (29)	Chevy	57.318	Paul Goldsmith (3)	Ford	65.693
295	18	5/26/57	Portland OR	0.500	P	75.00	Eddie Pagan (2)	Ford	64.732	Art Watts (2)	Ford	66.347
296	19	5/30/57	Eureka CA	0.625	D	96.63	Lloyd Dane (3)	Ford	55.957	Parnelli Jones	Ford	63.920
297	20	5/30/57	New Oxford PA	0.500	D	100.00	Buck Baker (30)	Chevy	76.126	Marvin Panch (6)	Ford	78.238
298	21	6/1/57	Lancaster SC	0.500	D	100.00	Paul Goldsmith (4)	Ford	61.622	Buck Baker (30)	Chevy	67.365
299	22	6/8/57	Los Angeles CA	0.500	D	75.00	Eddie Pagan (3)	Ford	None	Eddie Pagan (3)	Ford	67.290
300	23	6/15/57	Newport TN	0.500	D	100.00	Fireball Roberts (12)	Ford	60.687	Speedy Thompson (9)	Chevy	61.813
301	24	6/20/57	Columbia SC	0.500	D	100.00	Jack Smith (3)	Chevy	58.045	Buck Baker (31)	Chevy	64.585
302	25	6/22/57	Sacramento CA	0.500	D	99.50	Bill Amick	Ford	59.580	Art Watts (3)	Ford	69.337
303	26	6/29/57	Spartanburg SC	0.500	D	100.00	Lee Petty (27)	Olds	46.287	Lee Petty (6)	Olds	59.642
304	27	6/30/57	Jacksonville NC	0.500	D	100.00	Buck Baker (31)	Chevy	55.342	Lee Petty (7)	Olds	61.328
305	28	7/4/57	Raleigh NC	1.000	P	250.00	Paul Goldsmith (5)	Ford	75.693	Frankie Schneider	Chevy	83.371
306	29	7/12/57	Charlotte NC	0.500	D	100.00	Marvin Panch (5)	Ford	56.302	Tiny Lund (2)	Pontiac	60.913
307	30	7/14/57	LeHi AR	1.500	D	200.00	Marvin Panch (6)	Pontiac	67.167	Speedy Thompson (10)	Chevy	98.991
308	31	7/14/57	Portland OR	0.500	P	100.00	Eddie Pagan (4)	Ford	64.539	Art Watts (4)	Ford	66.396
309	32	7/20/57	Hickory NC	0.500	D	100.00	Jack Smith (4)	Chevy	58.737	Gwyn Staley	Chevy	66.085
310	33	7/24/57	Norfolk VA	0.500	D	100.00	Buck Baker (32)	Chevy	47.987	Bill Amick (3)	Ford	56.338
311	34	7/30/57	Lancaster SC	0.500	D	100.00	Speedy Thompson (13)	Chevy	66.543	Speedy Thompson (11)	Chevy	67.694
312	35	8/4/57	Watkins Glen NY	2.300	P	101.20	Buck Baker (33)	Chevy	83.064	Buck Baker (32)	Chevy	87.071
313	36	8/4/47	Bremerton WA	0.900	P	72.00	Parnelli Jones	Ford	38.959	Art Watts (5)	Ford	62.657
314	37	8/10/57	New Oxford PA	0.500	D	100.00	Marvin Panch (7)	Ford	77.569	Tiny Lund (3)	Pontiac	80.971
315	38	8/16/57	Old Bridge NJ	0.500	P	100.00	Lee Petty (28)	Olds	65.813	Rex White (2)	Chevy	71.599
316	39	8/26/57	Myrtle Beach SC	0.500	D	100.00	Gwyn Staley	Chevy	50.782	Johnny Allen	Plymouth	58.139
317	40	9/2/57	Darlington SC	1.375	P	500.00	Speedy Thompson (14)	Chevy	100.094	Cotton Owens	Pontiac	117.416
318	41	9/5/57	Syracuse NY	1.000	D	100.00	Gwyn Staley (2)	Chevy	80.591	Gwyn Staley (2)	Chevy	83.045
319	42	9/8/57	Weaverville NC	0.500	P	100.00	Lee Petty (29)	Olds	67.950	Bill Amick (4)	Ford	77.687
320	43	9/8/57	Sacramento CA	1.000	D	100.00	Danny Graves	Chevy	68.663	Danny Graves	Chevy	78.007
321	44	9/15/57	San Jose CA	0.500	D	58.00	Marvin Porter	Ford	None	No Time Trials	NTT	NTT
322	45	9/15/57	Langhorne PA	1.000	D	300.00	Gwyn Staley (3)	Chevy	72.759	Paul Goldsmith (4)	Ford	92.072

Race #	Year #	Date	Site	Track	Surface	Miles	Race Winner	Car	Speed	Pole Winner	Car	Speed
323	46	9/19/57	Columbia SC	0.500	D	100.00	Buck Baker (34)	Chevy	60.514	Buck Baker (33)	Chevy	63.649
324	47	9/21/57	Shelby NC	0.500	D	100.00	Buck Baker (35)	Chevy	53.699	Buck Baker (34)	Chevy	58.177
325	48	10/5/57	Charlotte NC	0.500	D	100.00	Lee Petty (30)	Olds	51.583	Lee Petty (8)	Olds	60.585
326	49	10/6/57	Martinsville VA	0.500	P	250.00	Bob Welborn	Chevy	63.025	Eddie Pagan (4)	Ford	65.837
327	50	10/12/57	Newberry SC	0.500	D	100.00	Fireball Roberts (13)	Ford	50.398	Jack Smith (2)	Chevy	56.514
328	51	10/13/57	Concord NC	0.500	D	100.00	Fireball Roberts (14)	Ford	59.553	Jack Smith (3)	Chevy	65.052
329	52	10/20/57	N Wilkesboro NC	0.625	P	100.00	Jack Smith (5)	Chevy	69.902	Fireball Roberts (9)	Ford	81.640
330	53	10/27/57	Greensboro NC	0.333	D	83.25	Buck Baker (36)	Chevy	38.927	Ken Rush	Ford	48.358

1958

Race #	Year #	Date	Site	Track	Surface	Miles	Race Winner	Car	Speed	Pole Winner	Car	Speed
331	1	11/3/57	Fayetteville NC	0.333	P	50.00	Rex White	Chevy	59.170	Jack Smith (4)	Chevy	62.665
332	2	2/23/58	Daytona Beach FL	4.100	B-R	160.00	Paul Goldsmith (6)	Pontiac	101.113	Paul Goldsmith (5)	Pontiac	140.570
333	3	3/2/58	Concord NC	0.500	D	100.00	Lee Petty (31)	Olds	58.555	Speedy Thompson (12)	Chevy	---
334	4	3/15/58	Fayetteville NC	0.333	P	50.00	Curtis Turner (12)	Ford	56.141	Lee Petty (9)	Olds	62.600
335	5	3/16/58	Wilson NC	0.500	D	100.00	Lee Petty (32)	Olds	48.459	Marvin Panch (7)	Ford	58.901
336	6	3/23/58	Hillsboro NC	0.900	D	99.00	Buck Baker (37)	Chevy	78.502	Buck Baker (35)	Chevy	83.076
337	7	4/5/58	Fayetteville NC	0.333	P	50.00	Bob Welborn (2)	Chevy	50.229	Lee Petty (10)	Olds	60.576
338	8	4/10/58	Columbia SC	0.500	D	100.00	Speedy Thompson (15)	Chevy	None	Possum Jones	Chevy	66.201
339	9	4/12/58	Spartanburg SC	0.500	D	100.00	Speedy Thompson (16)	Chevy	56.613	Speedy Thompson (13)	Chevy	61.412
340	10	4/13/58	Atlanta GA	1.000	D	100.00	Curtis Turner (13)	Ford	79.016	Joe Weatherly (2)	Ford	81.577
341	11	4/18/58	Charlotte NC	0.500	D	100.00	Curtis Turner (14)	Ford	53.254	Curtis Turner (11)	Ford	54.471
342	12	4/20/58	Martinsville VA	0.500	P	250.00	Bob Welborn (3)	Chevy	61.166	Buck Baker (36)	Chevy	66.007
343	13	4/25/58	Manassas VA	0.375	P	56.25	Frankie Schneider	Chevy	67.590	Eddie Pagan (5)	Ford	69.018
344	14	4/27/58	Old Bridge NJ	0.500	P	93.50	Jim Reed	Ford	68.438	Jim Reed (3)	Ford	71.371
345	15	5/3/58	Greenville SC	0.500	D	100.00	Jack Smith (6)	Chevy	62.295	Jack Smith (5)	Chevy	60.484
346	16	5/11/58	Greensboro NC	0.333	D	50.00	Bob Welborn (4)	Chevy	45.628	Bob Welborn (2)	Chevy	46.250
347	17	5/15/58	Roanoke VA	0.250	P	37.50	Jim Reed (2)	Ford	49.504	Jim Reed (4)	Ford	51.963
348	18	5/18/58	N Wilkesboro NC	0.625	P	100.00	Junior Johnson (6)	Ford	78.636	Jack Smith (6)	Chevy	82.056
349	19	5/24/58	Winston-Salem NC	0.250	P	37.50	Bob Welborn (5)	Chevy	40.407	Rex White (3)	Chevy	46.851
350	20	5/30/58	Trenton NJ	1.000	P	500.00	Fireball Roberts (15)	Chevy	84.522	Marvin Panch (8)	Ford	89.020
351	21	6/1/58	Riverside CA	2.631	P	500.00	Eddie Gray	Ford	79.481	Danny Graves (2)	Chevy	---
352	22	6/5/58	Columbia SC	0.500	D	100.00	Junior Johnson (7)	Ford	54.752	Buck Baker (37)	Chevy	64.308
353	23	6/12/58	Bradford PA	0.333	D	50.00	Junior Johnson (8)	Ford	59.840	Bob Duell	Ford	65.831
354	24	6/15/58	Reading PA	0.500	D	100.00	Junior Johnson (9)	Ford	53.763	Speedy Thompson (14)	Chevy	60.687
355	25	6/25/58	New Oxford PA	0.500	D	100.00	Lee Petty (33)	Olds	69.726	Ken Rush (2)	Chevy	82.796
356	26	6/28/58	Hickory NC	0.400	D	100.00	Lee Petty (34)	Olds	62.413	Speedy Thompson (15)	Chevy	68.768
357	27	6/29/58	Weaverville NC	0.500	P	100.00	Rex White (2)	Chevy	73.892	Rex White (4)	Chevy	76.857
358	28	7/4/58	Raleigh NC	1.000	P	250.00	Fireball Roberts (16)	Chevy	73.691	Cotton Owens (2)	Pontiac	83.896
359	29	7/12/58	Asheville NC	0.250	P	37.50	Jim Paschal (7)	Chevy	46.440	Jim Paschal (7)	Chevy	50.336
360	30	7/16/58	Busti, NY	0.333	D	50.00	Shorty Rollins	Ford	47.110	Lee Petty (11)	Olds	---
361	31	7/18/58	Toronto CAN	0.333	P	33.30	Lee Petty (35)	Olds	43.184	Rex White (5)	Chevy	51.406
362	32	7/19/58`	Buffalo NY	0.250	P	25.00	Jim Reed (3)	Ford	46.972	Rex White (6)	Chevy	38.593
363	33	7/25/58	Rochester NY	0.500	D	100.00	Cotton Owens (2)	Pontiac	59.990	Rex White (7)	Chevy	62.871
364	34	7/26/58	Belmar NJ	0.333	P	100.00	Jim Reed (4)	Ford	65.395	Rex White (8)	Chevy	68.936
365	35	8/3/58	Bridgehampton NY	2.850	P	100.00	Jack Smith (7)	Chevy	80.696	Jack Smith (7)	Chevy	82.001
366	36	8/7/58	Columbia SC	0.500	D	100.00	Speedy Thompson (17)	Chevy	54.820	Speedy Thompson (16)	Chevy	64.240
367	37	8/10/58	Nashville TN	0.500	P	100.00	Joe Weatherly	Ford	59/269	Rex White (9)	Chevy	71.315
368	38	8/17/58	Weaverville NC	0.500	P	250.00	Fireball Roberts (17)	Chevy	66.780	Jimmy Massey	Pontiac	76.596
369	39	8/22/58	Winston-Salem NC	0.250	P	50.00	Lee Petty (36)	Olds	39.158	George Dunn	Mercury	46.680
370	40	8/23/58	Myrtle Beach SC	0.500	D	100.00	Bob Welborn (6)	Chevy	60.443	Speedy Thompson (17)	Chevy	66.667
371	41	9/1/58	Darlington SC	1.375	P	500.00	Fireball Roberts (18)	Chevy	102.585	Eddie Pagen (6)	Ford	116.952
372	42	9/5/58	Charlotte NC	0.500	D	100.00	Buck Baker (38)	Chevy	52.280	Lee Petty (12)	Olds	57.879
373	43	9/7/58	Birmingham AL	0.500	D	100.00	Fireball Roberts (19)	Chevy	60.678	Cotton Owens (3)	Pontiac	64.034
374	44	9/7/58	Sacramento CA	1.000	D	100.00	Parnelli Jones (2)	Ford	65.550	Parnelli Jones (2)	Ford	77.922
375	45	9/12/58	Gastonia NC	0.333	D	66.70	Buck Baker (39)	Chevy	47.856	Tiny Lund (4)	Chevy	52.650
376	46	9/14/58	Richmond VA	0.500	D	100.00	Speedy Thompson (18)	Chevy	57.878	Speedy Thompson (18)	Chevy	62.915
377	47	9/29/58	Hillsboro NC	0.900	D	99.00	Joe Eubanks	Pontiac	72.439	Tiny Lund (5)	Chevy	87.308
378	48	10/5/58	Salisbury NC	0.625	D	100.00	Lee Petty (37)	Olds	58.271	Gober Sosebee (4)	Chevy	72.162
379	49	10/12/58	Martinsville VA	0.500	P	175.00	Fireball Roberts (20)	Chevy	64.344	Glen Wood	Ford	67.950
380	50	10/19/58	N Wilkesboro NC	0.625	P	100.00	Junior Johnson (10)	Ford	84.906	Glen Wood (2)	Ford	86.805
381	51	10/26/58	Atlanta GA	1.000	D	150.00	Junior Johnson (11)	Ford	69.570	Glen Wood (3)	Ford	81.522

1959

Race #	Year #	Date	Site	Track	Surface	Miles	Race Winner	Car	Speed	Pole Winner	Car	Speed
382	1	11/9/58	Fayetteville NC	0.333	D	50.00	Bob Welborn (7)	Chevy	56.001	Bob Welborn (3)	Chevy	61.985
383	2	2/20/59	Daytona Beach FL	2.500	P	100.00	Bob Welborn (8)	Chevy	143.198	Fireball Roberts (10)	Pontiac	140.580
384	3	2/22/59	Daytona Beach FL	2.500	P	500.00	Lee Petty (38)	Olds	135.521	Bob Welborn (4)	Chevy	140.120
385	4	3/1`/59	Hillsboro NC	0.900	D	99.00	Curtis Turner (15)	T-Bird	81.612	Curtis Turner (12)	T-Bird	87.544
386	5	3/8/59	Concord NC	0.500	D	100.00	Curtis Turner (16)	T-Bird	59.239	Buck Baker (38)	Chevy	66.420
387	6	3/22/59	Atlanta GA	1.000	D	100.00	Johnny Beauchamp	T-Bird	75.172	Buck Baker (39)	Chevy	77.888
388	7	3/29/59	Wilson NC	0.500	D	100.00	Junior Johnson (12)	Ford	50.300	No Time Trials	NTT	NTT
389	8	3/30/59	Winston-Salem NC	0.250	P	50.00	Jim Reed (5)	Ford	43.562	Rex White (10)	Chevy	46.296
390	9	4/4/59	Columbia SC	0.500	D	100.00	Jack Smith (8)	Chevy	87.343	Jack Smith (8)	Chevy	60.730

Race	Year #	Date	Site	Track	Surface	Miles	Race Winner	Car	Speed	Pole Winner	Car	Speed
391	10	4/5/59	N Wilkesboro NC	0.625	P	100.00	Lee Petty (39)	Olds	71.985	Speedy Thompson (19)	Chevy	85.746
392	11	4/26/59	Reading PA	0.500	D	100.00	Junior Johnson (13)	Ford	53.011	---	---	---
393	12	5/2/59	Hickory, NC	0.400	D	100.00	Junior Johnson (14)	Ford	62.165	Junior Johnson (5)	Ford	68.900
394	13	5/3/59	Martinsville, VA	0.500	P	250.00	Lee Petty (40)	Olds	59.512	Bobby Johns	Chevy	66.030
395	14	5/17/59	Trenton, NJ	1.000	P	150.00	Tom Pistone	T-Bird	87.350	Bob Burdick	T-Bird	88.950
396	15	5/22/59	Charlotte NC	0.500	D	100.00	Lee Petty (41)	Olds	55.300	Bob Welborn (5)	Chevy	57.950
397	16	5/24/59	Nashville TN	0.500	P	100.00	Rex White (3)	Chevy	71.006	Rex White (11)	Chevy	70.890
398	17	5/30/59	Los Angeles CA	0.400	D	200.00	Parnelli Jones (3)	Ford	50.982	Jim Reed (5)	Chevy	53.590
399	18	6/5/59	Spartanburg SC	0.500	D	100.00	Jack Smith (9)	Chevy	55.547	Cotton Owens (4)	Pontiac	63.180
400	19	6/13/59	Greenville, SC	0.500	D	100.00	Junior Johnson (15)	Ford	51.480	Jack Smith (9)	Chevy	65.838
401	20	6/14/59	Atlanta GA	1.000	D	150.00	Lee Petty (42)	Olds	58.499	No Time Trials	NTT	NTT
402	21	6/18/59	Columbia SC	0.500	D	100.00	Lee Petty (43)	Plymouth	58.726	Bob Burdick (2)	T-Bird	64.865
403	22	6/20/59	Wilson NC	0.500	D	100.00	Junior Johnson (16)	Ford	58.065	No Time Trials	NTT	NTT
404	23	6/21/59	Richmond VA	0.500	D	100.00	Tom Pistone (2)	T-Bird	56.881	Buck Baker (40)	Chevy	66.420
405	24	6/27/59	Winston-Salem NC	0.250	P	50.00	Rex White (4)	Chevy	41.228	Lee Petty (13)	Plymouth	47.071
406	25	6/28/59	Weaverville NC	0.500	P	100.00	Rex White (5)	Chevy	72.934	Glen Wood (4)	Ford	76.820
407	26	7/4/59	Daytona Beach FL	2.500	P	250.00	Fireball Roberts (21)	Pontiac	140.581	Fireball Roberts (11)	Pontiac	144.997
408	27	7/21/59	Heidelberg PA	0.250	D	50.00	Jim Reed (6)	Chevy	45.000	Dick Bailey	Plymouth	47.970
409	28	7/26/59	Charlotte NC	0.500	D	100.00	Jack Smith (10)	Chevy	49.553	Buck Baker (41)	Chevy	63.070
410	29	8/1/59	Myrtle Beach SC	0.500	D	100.00	Ned Jarrett	Ford	52.941	Bob Welborn (6)	Chevy	66.470
411	30	8/2/59	Charlotte NC	0.500	D	100.00	Ned Jarrett (2)	Ford	52.794	Bob Welborn (7)	Chevy	62.540
412	31	8/2/59	Nashville TN	0.500	P	150.00	Joe Lee Johnson	Chevy	63.343	Rex White (12)	Chevy	74.044
413	32	8/16/59	Weaverville NC	0.500	P	250.00	Bob Welborn (9)	Chevy	71.833	Rex White (13)	Chevy	77.687
414	33	8/21/59	Winston-Salem NC	0.250	P	50.00	Rex White (6)	Chevy	44.085	Rex White (14)	Chevy	47.443
415	34	8/22/59	Greenville SC	0.500	D	100.00	Buck Baker (40)	Chevy	58.055	Lee Petty (14)	Plymouth	63.313
416	35	8/29/59	Columbia SC	0.500	D	100.00	Lee Petty (44)	Plymouth	48.264	No Time Trials	NTT	NTT
417	36	9/7/59	Darlington SC	1.375	P	500.00	Jim Reed (7)	Chevy	111.836	Fireball Roberts (12)	Pontiac	123.734
418	37	9/11/59	Hicory NC	0.400	D	100.00	Lee Petty (45)	Plymouth	63.380	No Time Trials	NTT	NTT
419	38	9/13/59	Richmond VA	0.500	D	100.00	Cotton Owens (3)	T-Bird	60.382	Cotton Owens (5)	T-Bird	62.674
420	39	9/13/59	Sacramento CA	1.000	D	100.00	Eddie Gray (2)	Ford	54.753	No Time Trials	NTT	NTT
421	40	9/20/59	Hillsboro NC	0.900	D	99.00	Lee Petty (46)	Plymouth	77.868	Jack Smith (10)	Chevy	85.533
422	41	9/27/59	Martinsville VA	0.500	P	250.00	Rex White (7)	Chevy	60.500	Glen Wood (5)	Ford	69.471
423	42	10/11/59	Weaverville NC	0.500	P	100.00	Lee Petty (47)	Plymouth	76.433	Tommy Irwin	T-Bird	78.568
424	43	10/18/59	N Wilkesboro NC	0.625	P	100.00	Lee Petty (48)	Plymouth	74.829	Glen Wood (6)	Ford	86.806
425	44	10/25/59	Concord NC	0.500	D	150.00	Jack Smith (11)	Chevy	54.005	No Time Trials	NTT	NTT

1960

Race	Year #	Date	Site	Track	Surface	Miles	Race Winner	Car	Speed	Pole Winner	Car	Speed
426	1	11/8/59	Charlotte NC	0.500	D	100.00	Jack Smith (12)	Chevy	52.409	Buck Baker (42)	Chevy	64.103
427	2	11/26/59	Columbia SC	0.500	D	100.00	Ned Jarrett (3)	Ford	55.071	Junior Johnson (6)	Dodge	65.217
428	3	2/12/60	Daytona Beach FL	2.500	P	100.00	Fireball Roberts (22)	Pontiac	137.614	Cotton Owens (6)	Pontiac	149.892
429	4	2/12/60	Daytona Beach FL	2.500	P	100.00	Jack Smith (13)	Pontiac	146.520	Jack Smith (11)	Pontiac	148.157
430	5	2/14/60	Daytona Beach FL	2.500	P	500.00	Junior Johnson (17)	Chevy	124.740	Cotton Owens (7)	Pontiac	149.892
431	6	2/28/60	Charlotte NC	0.500	D	100.00	Richard Petty	Plymouth	53.404	Lee Petty (15)	Plymouth	62.110
432	7	3/27/60	N Wilkesboro NC	0.625	P	100.00	Lee Petty (49)	Plymouth	66.347	Junior Johnson (7)	Chevy	83.860
433	8	4/3/60	Phoenix AZ	1.000	D	100.00	John Rostek	Ford	71.889	Mel Larson (2)	Pontiac	78.930
434	9	4/5/60	Columbia SC	0.500	D	100.00	Rex White (8)	Chevy	50.697	Doug Yates	Plymouth	66.030
435	10	4/10/60	Martinsville VA	0.500	P	250.00	Richard Petty (2)	Plymouth	63.943	Glen Wood (7)	Ford	60.150
436	11	4/16/60	Hickory NC	0.500	D	100.00	Joe Weatherly (2)	Ford	66.347	Rex White (15)	Chevy	71.080
437	12	4/17/60	Wilson NC	0.500	D	100.00	Joe Weatherly (3)	Ford	55.113	Emanuel Zervakis	Chevy	60.500
438	13	4/18/60	Winston Salem NC	0.250	P	50.00	Glen Wood	Ford	43.082	Glen Wood (8)	Ford	47.240
439	14	4/23/60	Greenville SC	0.500	D	100.00	Ned Jarrett (4)	Ford	62.337	Curtis Turner (13)	Ford	64.720
440	15	4/24/60	Weavervile NC	0.500	P	83.50	Lee Petty (50)	Plymouth	63.368	Junior Johnson (8)	Ford	78.090
441	16	5/14/60	Darlington SC	1.375	P	301.13	Joe Weatherly (4)	Ford	102.640	Fireball Roberts (13)	Pontiac	127.750
442	17	5/28/60	Spartanburg SC	0.500	D	100.00	Ned Jarrett (5)	Ford	51.843	Jack Smith (12)	Pontiac	64.220
443	18	5/29/60	Hillsboro NC	0.900	D	99.00	Lee Petty (51)	Plymouth	83.583	Richard Petty	Plymouth	88.190
444	19	6/5/60	Richmond VA	0.500	D	100.00	Lee Petty (52)	Plymouth	62.251	Ned Jarrett	Ford	64.560
445	20	6/12/60	Hanford CA	1.500	P	250.00	Marvin Porter (2)	Ford	88.032	Frank Secrist	Ford	93.040
446	21	6/19/60	Charlotte NC	1.500	P	600.00	Joe Lee Johnson (2)	Chevy	107.735	Fireball Roberts (14)	Pontiac	133.904
447	22	6/26/60	Winston-Salem NC	0.250	P	50.00	Glen Wood (2)	Ford	45.872	Lee Petty (16)	Plymouth	47.850
448	23	7/4/60	Daytona Beach FL	2.500	P	250.00	Jack Smith (14)	Pontiac	146.842	Jack Smith (13)	Pontiac	152.129
449	24	7/10/60	Heidelberg PA	0.500	D	94.00	Lee Petty (53)	Plymouth	67.450	Lee Petty (17)	Plymouth	91.650
450	25	7/17/60	Montgomery NY	2.000	P	200.00	Rex White (9)	Chevy	88.626	John Rostek	Ford	96.650
451	26	7/23/60	Myrtle Beach SC	0.500	D	100.00	Buck Baker (41)	Chevy	60.985	Ned Jarrett (2)	Ford	64.610
452	27	7/31/60	Atlanta GA	1.500	P	300.50	Fireball Roberts (23)	Pontiac	112.652	Fireball Roberts (15)	Pontiac	133.129
453	28	8/3/60	Birmingham AL	0.250	P	50.00	Ned Jarrett (3)	Ford	54.463	Ned Jarrett (3)	Ford	55.866
454	29	8/7/60	Nashville TN	0.500	P	166.50	Johnny Beauchamp (2)	Chevy	56.966	Rex White (16)	Chevy	74.810
455	30	8/14/60	Weaverville NC	0.500	P	250.00	Rex White (10)	Chevy	65.024	Jack Smith (14)	Pontiac	77.850
456	31	8/16/60	Spartanburg SC	0.500	D	100.00	Cotton Owens (4)	Pontiac	59.681	Cotton Owens (8)	Pontiac	63.250
457	32	8/18/60	Columbia SC	0.500	D	150.00	Rex White (11)	Chevy	54.265	Tommy Irwin (2)	T-Bird	60.360
458	33	8/20/60	South Boston VA	0.250	D	37.50	Junior Johnson (18)	Chevy	50.732	Ned Jarrett (4)	Ford	51.903
459	34	8/23/60	Winston-Salem NC	0.250	P	50.00	Glen Wood (3)	Ford	44.389	Glen Wood (9)	Ford	46.970
460	35	9/5/60	Darlington SC	1.375	P	500.50	Buck Baker (42)	Pontiac	105.901	Fireball Roberts (16)	Pontiac	125.549

Race	Year #	Date	Site	Track	Surface	Miles	Race Winner	Car	Speed	Pole Winner	Car	Speed
461	36	9/9/60	Hickory NC	0.400	D	100.00	Junior Johnson (19)	Chevy	69.998	Buck Baker (43)	Chevy	71.180
462	37	9/11/60	Sacramento CA	1.000	D	100.00	Jim Cook	Dodge	70.629	Jim Cook	Dodge	78.450
463	38	9/15/60	Sumter SC	0.250	D	50.00	Ned Jarrett (7)	Ford	41.208	David Pearson	Chevy	45.070
464	39	9/18/60	Hillsboro NC	0.900	D	99.00	Richard Petty (3)	Plymouth	80.161	Richard Petty (2)	Plymouth	75.285
465	40	9/25/60	Martinsville VA	0.500	P	250.00	Rex White (12)	Chevy	60.439	Glen Wood (10)	Ford	68.440
466	41	10/2/60	N Wilkesboro NC	0.625	P	200.00	Rex White (13)	Chevy	77.444	Rex White (17)	Chevy	93.399
467	42	10/16/60	Charlotte NC	1.500	P	400.00	Speedy Thompson (19)	Ford	112.905	Fireball Roberts (17)	Pontiac	133.465
468	43	10/23/60	Richmond VA	0.500	D	100.00	Speedy Thompson (20)	Ford	63.739	Ned Jarrett (5)	Ford	64.410
469	44	10/30/60	Atlanta GA	1.500	P	501.00	Bobby Johns	Pontiac	108.408	Fireball Roberts (18)	Pontiac	134.596

1961

470	1	11/6/60	Charlotte NC	0.500	D	100.00	Joe Weatherly (5)	Ford	59.435	Lee Petty (18)	Plymouth	63.581
471	2	11/20/60	Jacksonville FL	0.500	D	100.00	Lee Petty (54)	Plymouth	64.400	Junior Johnson (9)	Pontiac	68.623
472	3	2/24/61	Daytona Beach FL	2.500	P	100.00	Fireball Roberts (24)	Pontiac	133.037	Fireball Roberts (19)	Pontiac	155.709
473	4	2/24/61	Daytona Beach FL	2.500	P	100.00	Joe Weatherly (6)	Pontiac	152.671	Joe Weatherly (3)	Pontiac	154.122
474	5	2/26/61	Daytona Beach FL	2.500	P	500.00	Marvin Panch (8)	Pontiac	149.601	Fireball Roberts (20)	Pontiac	155.709
475	6	3/4/61	Spartanburg SC	0.500	D	100.00	Cotton Owens (5)	Pontiac	59.152	Ned Jarrett (6)	Ford	63.920
476	7	3/5/61	Weaverville NC	0.500	P	100.00	Rex White (14)	Chevy	72.492	Rex White (18)	Chevy	79.295
477	8	3/12/61	Hanford CA	1.400	P	250.00	Fireball Roberts (25)	Pontiac	95.621	Bob Ross	Ford	98.370
478	9	3/26/61	Atlanta GA	1.500	P	501.00	Bob Burdick	Pontiac	124.172	Marvin Panch (9)	Pontiac	135.755
479	10	4/1/61	Greenville SC	0.500	D	100.00	Emanuel Zervakis	Chevy	52.189	Junior Johnson (10)	Pontiac	62.090
480	11	4/2/61	Hillsboro NC	0.900	D	99.00	Cotton Owens (6)	Pontiac	84.695	Ned Jarrett (7)	Chevy	91.836
481	12	4/3/61	Winston-Salem NC	0.250	P	37.50	Rex White (15)	Chevy	45.500	Glen Wood (11)	Ford	48.700
482	13	4/9/61	Martinsville VA	0.500	P	74.50	Fred Lorenzen	Ford	68.366	Rex White (19)	Chevy	70.280
483	14	4/16/61	N Wilkesboro NC	0.625	P	250.00	Rex White (16)	Chevy	83.248	Junior Johnson (11)	Pontiac	95.660
484	15	4/20/61	Columbia SC	0.500	D	100.00	Cotton Owens (7)	Pontiac	51.940	Ned Jarrett (8)	Chevy	64.380
485	16	4/22/61	Hickory NC	0.400	D	100.00	Junior Johnson (20)	Pontiac	66.654	Junior Johnson (12)	Pontiac	74.074
486	17	4/23/61	Richmond VA	0.500	D	100.00	Richard Petty (4)	Plymouth	62.456	Richard Petty (3)	Plymouth	66.667
487	18	4/30/61	Martinsville VA	0.500	P	250.00	Junior Johnson (21)	Pontiac	66.287	Rex White (20)	Chevy	71.320
488	19	5/6/61	Darlington SC	1.375	P	301.13	Fred Lorenzen (2)	Ford	119.520	Fred Lorenzen	Ford	128.965
489	20	5/21/61	Charlotte NC	1.500	P	100.00	Richard Petty (5)	Plymouth	133.554	Fred Lorenzen (2)	Ford	137.509
490	21	5/21/61	Charlotte NC	1.500	P	100.50	Joe Weatherly (7)	Pontiac	115.591	Junior Johnson (13)	Pontiac	136.951
491	22	5/21/61	Riverside CA	2.580	P	100.00	Lloyd Dane (4)	Chevy	82.512	Eddie Gray	Ford	85.210
492	23	5/27/61	Los Angeles CA	0.500	D	100.00	Eddie Gray (3)	Ford	68.833	Danny Weinberg	Ford	71.940
493	24	5/28/61	Charlotte NC	1.500	P	600.00	David Pearson	Pontiac	111.633	Richard Petty (4)	Plymouth	131.611
494	25	6/2/61	Spartanburg SC	0.500	D	100.00	Jim Paschal (8)	Pontiac	55.495	Joe Weatherly (4)	Pontiac	61.250
495	26	6/4/61	Birmingham AL	0.500	D	100.00	Ned Jarrett (8)	Chevy	61.068	Johnny Allen (2)	Chevy	65.910
496	27	6/8/61	Greenville SC	0.500	D	100.00	Jack Smith (15)	Pontiac	58.441	Ned Jarrett (9)	Chevy	65.480
497	28	6/10/61	Winston-Salem NC	0.250	P	50.00	Rex White (17)	Chevy	42.714	Junior Johnson (14)	Pontiac	47.720
498	29	6/17/61	Norwood MA	0.250	P	125.00	Emanuel Zervakis (2)	Chevy	53.827	Rex White (21)	Chevy	55.870
499	30	6/23/61	Hartsville SC	0.333	D	50.00	Buck Baker (43)	Chrysler	46.234	Emanuel Zervakis (2)	Chevy	54.970
500	31	6/24/61	Roanoke VA	0.250	P	37.50	Junior Johnson (22)	Pontiac	49.907	Rex White (22)	Chevy	53.700
501	32	7/4/61	Daytona Beach FL	2.500	P	250.00	David Pearson (2)	Pontiac	154.294	Fireball Roberts (21)	Pontiac	157.150
502	33	7/9/61	Atlanta GA	1.500	P	250.00	Fred Lorenzen (3)	Ford	118.067	Fireball Roberts (22)	Pontiac	136.088
503	34	7/20/61	Columbia SC	0.500	D	100.00	Cotton Owens (8)	Pontiac	62.198	Cotton Owens (9)	Pontiac	67.650
504	35	7/22/61	Myrtle Beach SC	0.500	D	100.00	Joe Weatherly (8)	Pontiac	57.655	Joe Weatherly (5)	Pontiac	66.690
505	36	7/29/61	Bristol TN	0.500	P	250.00	Jack Smith (16)	Pontiac	68.373	Fred Lorenzen (3)	Ford	70.225
506	37	8/6/61	Nashville TN	0.500	P	201.50	Jim Paschal (9)	Pontiac	56.455	Rex White (23)	Chevy	76.600
507	38	8/9/61	Winston-Salem NC	0.250	P	37.50	Rex White (18)	Chevy	42.452	Junior Johnson (15)	Pntiac	48.050
508	39	8/13/61	Weaverville NC	0.500	P	129.00	Junior Johnson (23)	Pontiac	64.704	Jim Paschal (8)	Pontiac	80.430
509	40	8/18/61	Richmond VA	0.500	P	37.50	Junior Johnson (24)	Pontiac	51.605	Junior Johnson (16)	Pontiac	52.630
510	41	8/27/61	South Boston VA	0.250	P	50.00	Junior Johnson (25)	Pontiac	48.348	Cotton Owens (10)	Pntiac	52.630
511	42	9/4/61	Darlington SC	1.375	P	500.50	Nelson Stacy	Ford	117.787	Fireball Roberts (23)	Pontiac	128.680
512	43	9/8/61	Hickory NC	0.400	D	100.00	Rex White (10)	Chevy	67.529	Rex White (24)	Chevy	72.290
513	44	9/10/61	Richmond VA	0.500	D	125.00	Joe Weatherly (9)	Pontiac	61.677	Junior Johnson (17)	Pontiac	65.010
514	45	9/10/61	Sacramento CA	1.000	D	100.00	Eddie Gray (4)	Ford	None	Bill Amick (5)	Pontiac	79.260
515	46	9/17/61	Atlanta GA	1.500	P	400.50	David Pearson (3)	Pontiac	125.384	Fireball Roberts (24)	Pontiac	136.294
516	47	9/24/61	Martinsville VA	0.500	P	250.00	Joe Weatherly (10)	Pontiac	62.586	Fred Lorenzen (4)	Ford	70.730
517	48	10/1/61	N Wilkesboro NC	0.625	P	200.00	Rex White (20)	Chevy	84.675	Junior Johnson (18)	Pontiac	94.540
518	49	10/15/61	Charlotte NC	1.500	P	400.50	Joe Weatherly (11)	Pontiac	119.950	David Pearson (2)	Pontiac	138.577
519	50	10/22/61	Bristol TN	0.500	P	250.00	Joe Weatherly (12)	Pontiac	72.452	Bobby Johns (2)	Pontiac	80.645
520	51	10/28/61	Greenville SC	0.500	D	100.00	Junior Johnson (26)	Pontiac	63.346	Buck Baker (44)	Chrysler	66.667
521	52	10/29/61	Hillsboro NC	0.900	D	148.50	Joe Weatherly (13)	Pontiac	85.249	Joe Weatherly (6)	Pontiac	95.154

1962

522	1	11/5/61	Concord NC	0.500	D	100.00	Jack Smith (17)	Pontiac	59.405	Joe Weatherly (7)	Pontiac	68.543
523	2	11/12/61	Weaverville NC	0.500	P	100.00	Rex White (21)	Chevy	68.467	Joe Weatherly (8)	Pontiac	81.743
524	3	2/16/61	Daytona Beach FL	2.500	P	100.00	Fireball Roberts (26)	Pontiac	156.999	Fireball Roberts (25	Pontiac	155.774
525	4	2/16/62	Daytona Beach FL	2.500	P	100.00	Joe Weatherly (14)	Pontiac	145.395	Darel Dieringer	Pontiac	155.086
526	5	2/18/62	Daytona Beach FL	2.500	P	500.00	Fireball Roberts (27)	Pontiac	152.529	Fireball Roberts (26)	Pontiac	158.774

Race	Year #	Date	Site	Track	Surface	Miles	Race Winner	Car	Speed	Pole Winner	Car	Speed
527	6	2/25/62	Concord NC	0.500	D	39.00	Joe Weatherly (15)	Pontiac	53.161	Joe Weatherly (9)	Pontiac	---
528	7	3/4/62	Weaverville NC	0.500	P	100.00	Joe Weatherly (16)	Pontiac	75.471	Rex White (25)	Chevy	80.460
529	8	3/17/62	Savannah GA	0.500	D	100.00	Jack Smith (18)	Pontiac	58.775	Rex White (26)	Chevy	70.588
530	9	3/18/62	Hillsboro NC	0.900	D	99.00	Rex White (22)	Chevy	86.948	Joe Weatherly (10)	Pontiac	96.588
531	10	4/1/62	Richmond VA	0.500	D	90.00	Rex White (23)	Chevy	51.363	No Time Trials	NTT	NTT
532	11	4/13/62	Columbia SC	0.500	D	100.00	Ned Jarrett (9)	Chevy	56.710	Joe Weatherly (11)	Pontiac	64.423
533	12	4/15/62	N Wilkesboro NC	0.625	P	250.00	Richard Petty (6)	Plymouth	84.737	Junior Johnson (19)	Pontiac	94.142
534	13	4/19/62	Greenville SC	0.500	D	100.00	Ned Jarrett (10)	Chevy	57.480	Ned Jarrett (10)	Chevy	66.568
535	14	4/21/62	Myrtle Beach SC	0.500	D	100.00	Jack Smith (19)	Pontiac	63.036	Ned Jarrett (11)	Chevy	68.939
536	15	4/22/62	Martinsville VA	0.500	P	250.00	Richard Petty (7)	Plymouth	66.425	Fred Lorenzen (5)	Ford	71.287
537	16	4/23/62	Winston-Salem NC	0.250	P	27.00	Rex White (24)	Chevy	43.392	Rex White (27)	Chevy	48.417
538	17	4/29/62	Bristol TN	0.500	P	250.00	Bobby Johns (2)	Pontiac	73.397	Fireball Roberts (27)	Pontiac	81.374
539	18	5/4/62	Richmond VA	0.500	P	66.70	Jimmy Pardue	Pontiac	67.747	Rex White '(28)	Chevy	71.145
540	19	5/5/62	Hickory NC	0.400	D	100.00	Jack Smith (20)	Pontiac	71.216	Jack Smith (15)	Pontiac	74.074
541	20	5/6/62	Concord NC	0.500	D	100.00	Joe Weatherly (17)	Pontiac	57.052	Not Time Trials	NTT	NTT
542	21	5/12/62	Darlington SC	1.375	P	301.13	Nelson Stacy (2)	Ford	117.429	Fred Lorenzen (6)	Ford	129.810
543	22	5/19/62	Spartanburg SC	0.500	D	100.00	Ned Jarrett (11)	Chevy	60.080	Cotton Owens (11)	Pontiac	64.423
544	23	5/27/62	Charlotte NC	1.500	P	600.00	Nelson Stacy (3)	Ford	125.552	Fireball Roberts (28)	Pontiac	140.150
545	24	6/10/62	Atlanta GA	1.500	P	328.50	Fred Lorenzen (4)	Ford	101.983	Banjo Matthews (2)	Pontiac	137.640
546	25	6/16/62	Winston-Salem NC	0.250	P	50.00	Johnny Allen	Pontiac	45.466	Rex White (29)	Chevy	48.179
547	26	6/19/62	Augusta GA	0.500	D	100.00	Joe Weatherly (18)	Pontiac	59.850	Joe Weatherly (12)	Pontiac	63.069
548	27	6/22/62	Richmond VA	0.333	P	99.90	Jim Paschal (10)	Pontiac	66.293	Rex White (30)	Chevy	70.435
549	28	6/23/62	South Boston VA	0.375	P	100.00	Rex White (25)	Chevy	72.540	Jack Smith (16)	Pontiac	79.458
550	29	7/4/62	Daytona Beach FL	2.500	P	250.00	Fireball Roberts (28)	Pontiac	153.688	Banjo Matthews (3)	Pontiac	160.499
551	30	7/7/62	Columbia SC	0.500	D	100.00	Rex White (26)	Chevy	62.370	Jack Smith (17)	Pontiac	66.667
552	31	7/13/62	Asheville NC	0.400	P	100.00	Jack Smith (21)	Pontiac	78.294	Rex White (31)	Chevy	82.885
553	32	7/14/62	Greensville SC	0.500	D	100.00	Richard Petty (8)	Plymouth	62.219	Rex White (32)	Chevy	66.055
554	33	7/17/62	Augusta GA	0.500	D	100.00	Joe Weatherly (19)	Pontiac	55.104	Jack Smith (18)	Pontiac	65.885
555	34	7/20/62	Savannah GA	0.500	D	100.00	Joe Weatherly (20)	Pontiac	67.239	Wendell Scott	Chevy	71.627
556	35	7/21/62	Myrtle Beach SC	0.500	D	100.00	Ned Jarrett (12)	Chevy	64.171	Ned Jarrett (12)	Chevy	68.467
557	37	7/29/62	Bristol TN	0.500	P	250.00	Jim Paschal (11)	Plymouth	75.276	Fireball Roberts (29)	Pontiac	80.321
558	37	8/3/62	Chattanooga TN	0.333	P	66.70	Joe Weatherly (21)	Pontiac	71.145	Richard Petty (5)	Plymouth	73.365
559	38	8/5/62	Nashville TN	0.500	P	250.00	Jim Paschal (12)	Plymouth	64.469	Johnny Allen (3)	Pontiac	77.854
560	39	8/8/62	Huntsville AL	0.250	P	50.00	Richard Petty (9)	Plymouth	54.644	Richard Petty (6)	Plymouth	54.086
561	40	8/12/62	Weaverville NC	0.500	P	250.00	Jim Paschal (13)	Plymouth	77.492	Jack Smith (19)	Pontiac	82.720
562	41	8/15/62	Roanoke VA	0.250	P	50.00	Richard Petty (10)	Plymouth	51.165	Jack Smith (20)	Pontiac	54.086
563	42	8/18/62	Winston-Salem NC	0.250	P	50	Richard Petty (11)	Plymouth	46.88	Jack Smith (21)	Pontiac	48.102
564	43	8/21/62	Spartanburg SC	0.500	D	100.00	Richard Petty (12)	Plymouth	59.870	Richard Petty (7)	Plymouth	61.590
565	44	8/25/62	Valdosta GA	0.500	D	100.00	Ned Jarrett (13)	Chevy	61.454	Richard Petty (8)	Plymouth	59.386
566	45	9/3/62	Darlington SC	1.375	P	500.50	Larry Frank	Ford	117.965	Fireball Roberts (30)	Pontiac	130.246
567	46	9/7/62	Hickory NC	0.400	D	100.00	Rex White (27)	Chevrolet	70.574	Junior Johnson (20)	Pontiac	71.357
568	47	9/9/62	Richmond VA	0.500	D	100.00	Joe Weatherly (22)	Pontiac	64.981	Rex White (33)	Chevy	66.127
569	48	9/11/62	Moyock, NC	0.250	D	62.50	Ned Jarrett (14)	Chevy	43.078	Ned Jarrett (13)	Chevy	45.569
570	49	9/13/62	Augusta GA	0.500	D	100.00	Fred Lorenzen (5)	Ford	60.759	Joe Weatherly (13)	Pontiac	65.421
571	50	9/23/62	Martinsville VA	0.500	P	250.00	Nelson Stacy (4)	Ford	66.874	Fireball Roberts (31)	Pontiac	71.513
572	51	9/30/62	N Wilkesboro NC	0.625	P	200.00	Richard Petty (13)	Plymouth	86.186	Fred Lorenzen (7)	Ford	94.657
573	52	10/14/62	Charlotte NC	1.500	P	400.50	Junior Johnson (27)	Pontiac	132.085	Fireball Roberts (32)	Pontiac	140.287
574	53	10/28/62	Atlanta GA	1.500	P	400.50	Rex White (28)	Chevy	124.740	Fireball Roberts (33)	Pontiac	138.978

1963

575	1	11/4/62	Birmingham AL	0.500	D	100.00	Jim Paschal (14)	Plymouth	68.350	Jim Paschal (9)	Plymouth	73.592
576	2	11/11/62	Tampa FL	0.333	P	66.70	Richard Petty (14)	Plymouth	57.167	Rex White (34)	Chevy	60.090
577	3	11/22/62	Randleman NC	0.250	P	50.00	Jim Paschal (15)	Plymouth	47.544	Glen Wood (12)	Ford	51.933
578	4	1/20/63	Riverside CA	2.700	P	502.20	Dan Gurney	Ford	84.965	Paul Goldsmith (6)	Pontiac	98.809
579	5	2/22/63	Daytona Beach FL	2.500	P	100.00	Junior Johnson (28)	Chevy	164.083	Fireball Roberts (34)	Pontiac	160.943
580	6	2/22/63	Daytona Beach FL	2.500	P	100.00	Johnny Rutherford	Chevy	162.969	Fred Lorenzen (8)	Ford	161.870
581	7	2/24/63	Daytona Beach FL	2.500	P	500.00	Tiny Lund	Ford	151.566	Fireball Roberts (35)	Pontiac	160.943
582	8	3/2/63	Spartanburg SC	0.500	D	100.00	Richard Petty (15)	Plymouth	55.598	Junior Johnson (21)	Chevy	64.670
583	9	3/3/63	Weaverville NC	0.500	P	100.00	Richard Petty (16)	Plymouth	79.664	Junior Johnson (22)	Chevy	82.750
584	10	3/10/63	Hillsboro NC	0.900	D	148.50	Junior Johnson (29)	Chevy	83.129	Joe Weatherly (14)	Pontiac	95.716
585	11	3/17/63	Atlanta GA	1.500	P	500.50	Fred Lorenzen (6)	Ford	130.582	Junior Johnson (23)	Chevy	141.038
586	12	3/24/63	Hickory NC	0.500	D	100.00	Junior Johnson (30	Chevy	67.950	Junior Johnson (24)	Chevy	75.235
587	13	3/31/63	Bristol TN	0.500	P	250.00	Fireball Roberts (29)	Ford	76.910	Fred Lorenzen (9)	Ford	80.681
588	14	4/4/63	Augusta GA	0.500	D	56.00	Ned Jarrett (15)	Ford	60.089	LeeRoy Yarbrough	Mercury	64.610
589	15	4/7/63	Richmond VA	0.500	D	125.00	Joe Weatherly (23)	Pontiac	58.624	Rex White (35)	Chevy	69.151
590	16	4/13/63	Greenville SC	0.500	D	100.00	Buck Baker (44)	Pontiac	54.853	Jimmy Pardue	Ford	66.270
591	17	4/14/63	South Boston VA	0.375	P	150.00	Richard Petty (17)	Plymouth	75.229	Ned Jarrett (14)	Ford	78.720
592	18	4/15/63	Winston-Salem NC	0.250	P	50.00	Jimmy Pardue (16)	Plymouth	46.814	Richard Petty (9)	Plymouth	48.280
593	19	4/21/63	Martinsville VA	0.500	P	250.00	Richard Petty (18)	Plymouth	64.823	Rex White (36)	Chevy	72.000
594	20	4/28/63	N Wilkesboro NC	0.625	P	160.60	Richard Petty (19)	Plymouth	83.302	Fred Lorenzen (10)	Ford	96.150
595	21	5/2/63	Columbia SC	0.500	D	100.00	Richard Petty (20)	Plymouth	51.650	Richard Petty (10)	Plymouth	68.080
596	22	5/5/63	Randleman NC	0.250	P	50.00	Jim Paschal (17)	Plymouth	48.605	Ned Jarrett (15)	Ford	50.856

Race	Year #	Date	Site	Track	Surface	Miles	Race Winner	Car	Speed	Pole Winner	Car	Speed
597	23	5/11/63	Darlington SC	1.375	P	302.50	Joe Weatherly (24)	Pontiac	122.745	Fred Lorenzen (11)	Ford	131.718
598	24	5/18/63	Manassas VA	0.333	P	99.90	Richard Petty (21)	Plymouth	70.275	Richard Petty (11)	Plymouth	71.580
599	25	5/19/63	Richmond VA	0.333	P	99.90	Ned Jarrett (16)	Ford	65.052	Ned Jarrett (16)	Ford	70.642
600	26	6/2/63	Charlotte NC	1.500	P	600.00	Fred Lorenzen (7)	Ford	132.417	Junior Johnson (25)	Chevy	141.148
601	27	6/9/63	Birmingham AL	0.500	D	100.00	Richard Petty (22)	Plymouth	68.195	Jack Smith (22)	Plymouth	71.146
602	28	6/30/63	Atlanta GA	1.500	P	400.50	Junior Johnson (31)	Chevy	121.139	Marvin Panch (10)	Ford	140.753
603	29	7/4/63	Daytona Beach FL	2.500	P	400.00	Fireball Roberts (30)	Ford	150.927	Junior Johnson (26)	Chevy	166.005
604	30	7/7/63	Myrtle Beach SC	0.500	D	100.00	Ned Jarrett (17)	Ford	60.996	Richard Petty (12)	Plymouth	68.700
605	31	7/10/63	Savannah GA	0.500	D	100.00	Ned Jarrett (18)	Ford	59.622	Richard Petty (13)	Plymouth	71.340
606	32	7/11/63	Moyock NC	0.250	D	62.50	Jimmy Pardue (2)	Ford	45.464	Junior Johnson (27)	Chevy	47.120
607	33	7/13/63	Winston-Salem NC	0.250	P	50.00	Glen Wood (4)	Ford	44.390	Glen Wood (13)	Ford	48.387
608	34	7/14/63	Asheville NC	0.333	P	99.90	Ned Jarrett (19)	Ford	63.384	David Pearson (3)	Dodge	67.235
609	35	7/19/63	Old Bridge NJ	0.500	P	100.00	Fireball Roberts (31)	Ford	73.022	Joe Weatherly (15)	Pontiac	75.850
610	36	7/21/63	Bridgehampton NY	2.850	P	99.00	Richard Petty (23)	Plymouth	86.047	Richard Petty (14)	Plymouth	86.301
611	37	7/28/63	Bristol TN	0.500	P	250.00	Fred Lorenzen (8)	Ford	74.844	Fred Lorenzen (12)	Ford	82.229
612	38	7/30/63	Greenville SC	0.500	D	100.00	Richard Petty (24)	Plymouth	62.456	Ned Jarrett (17)	Ford	65.526
613	39	8/4/63	Nashville TN	0.500	P	175.00	Jim Paschal (18)	Plymouth	60.126	Richard Petty (15)	Plymouth	78.878
614	40	8/8/63	Columbia SC	0.500	D	100.00	Richard Petty (25)	Plymouth	55.1598	Richard Petty (16)	Plymouth	60.014
615	41	8/11/63	Weaverville NC	0.500	P	250.00	Fred Lorenzen (9)	Ford	77.673	No Time Trials	NTT	NTT
616	42	8/14/63	Spartanburg SC	0.500	D	100.00	Ned Jarrett (20)	Ford	52.424`	Joe Weatherly (16)	Pontiac	64.958
617	43	8/16/63	Winston-Salem NC	0.250	P	50.00	Junior Johnson (32)	Chevy	46.320	Junior Johnson (28)	Chevy	66.568
618	44	8/18/63	Huntington WV	0.375	P	112.50	Fred Lorenzen (10)	Ford	59.340	Fred Lorenzen (13)	Ford	66.569
619	45	9/2/63	Darlington SC	1.375	P	500.50	Fireball Roberts (32)	Ford	129.784	Fred Lorenzen (14)	Ford	133.648
620	46	9/6/63	Hickory NC	0.400	D	100.00	Junior Johnson (33)	Chevy	62.926	David Pearson (4)	Dodge	72.471
621	47	9/8/63	Richmond VA	0.500	D	150.00	Ned Jarrett (21)	Ford	66.339	Joe Weatherly (17)	Mercury	68.104
622	48	9/22/63	Martinsville VA	0.500	P	250.00	Fred Lorenzen (11)	Ford	67.486	Junior Johnson (29)	Chevy	73.379
623	49	9/24/63	Moyock NC	0.250	D	75.00	Ned Jarrett (22)	Ford	43.000	Joe Weatherly (18)	Mercury	45.988
624	50	9/29/63	N Wilkesboro NC	0.625	P	250.00	Marvin Panch (9)	Ford	89.428	Fred Lorenzen (15)	Ford	96.566
625	52	10/5/63	Randleman NC	0.250	P	50.00	Richard Petty (26)	Plymouth	46.001	Fred Lorenzen (16)	Ford	51.724
626	52	10/13/63	Charlotte NC	1.500	P	400.50	Junior Johnson (34)	Chevy	132.105	Marvin Panch (11)	Ford	142.461
627	53	10/20/63	South Boston VA	0.375	P	150.00	Richard Petty (27)	Plymouth	76.325	Jack Smith (23)	Plymouth	81.081
628	54	10/27/63	Hillsboro NC	0.900	D	150.00	Joe Weatherly (25)	Pontiac	85.559	Joe Weatherly (19)	Pontiac	93.156
629	55	11/3/63	Riverside CA	2.700	P	399.60	Darel Dieringer	Mercury	91.465	Dan Gurney	Ford	101.050

1964

630	1	11/10/63	Concord NC	0.500	D	125.00	Ned Jarrett (23)	Ford	56.897	David Pearson (5)	Dodge	69.257
631	2	11/10/63	Augusta GA	3.000	P	417.00	Fireball Roberts (33)	Ford	86.320	Fred Lorenzen (17)	Ford	88.590
632	3	12/1/63	Jacksonville FL	0.500	D	101.00	Wendell Scott	Chevy	58.252	Jack Smith (24)	Plymouth	70.921
633	4	12/29/63	Savannah GA	0.500	D	100.00	Richard Petty (28)	Plymouth	68.143	Ned Jarrett (18)	Ford	73.529
634	5	1/19/64	Riverside CA	2.700	P	502.20	Dan Gurney (2)	Ford	91.245	Fred Lorenzen (18)	Ford	102.433
635	6	2/21/64	Daytona Beach FL	2.500	P	100.00	Junior Johnson (35)	Dodge	170.777	Paul Goldsmith (7)	Plymouth	173.910
636	7	2/21/64	Daytona Beach FL	2.500	P	100.00	Bobby Isaac	Dodge	169.811	Richard Petty (17)	Plymouth	174.418
637	8	2/23/64	Daytona Beach FL	2.500	P	500.00	Richard Petty (29)	Plymouth	154.334	Paul Goldsmith (8)	Plymouth	174.910
638	9	3/10/64	Richmond VA	0.500	D	125.00	David Pearson (4)	Dodge	60.233	Ned Jarrett (19)	Ford	69.070
639	10	3/22/64	Bristol TN	0.500	P	250.00	Fred Lorenzen (12)	Ford	72.196	Marvin Panch (12)	Ford	80.640
640	11	3/28/64	Greenville SC	0.500	D	100.00	David Pearson (5)	Dodge	57.554	Dick Hutcherson	Ford	66.740
641	12	3/30/64	Winston-Salem NC	0.250	P	50.00	Marvin Panch (10)	Ford	47.796	Marvin Panch (13)	Ford	49.830
642	13	4/5/64	Atlanta GA	1.500	P	500.00	Fred Lorenzen (13)	Ford	134.137	Fred Lorenzen (19)	Ford	146.470
643	14	4/11/64	Weaverville NC	0.500	P	100.00	Marvin Panch (11)	Ford	81.669	Marvin Panch (14)	Ford	84.905
644	15	4/12/64	Hillsboro NC	0.900	D	150.00	David Pearson (6)	Dodge	83.319	David Pearson (6)	Dodge	99.784
645	16	4/14/64	Spartanburg SC	0.500	D	100.00	Ned Jarrett (24)	Ford	58.852	Dick Hutcherson (2)	Ford	69.044
646	17	4/16/64	Columbia SC	0.500	D	100.00	Ned Jarrett (25)	Ford	64.412	David Pearson (7)	Dodge	71.485
647	18	4/19/64	N Wilkesboro NC	0.625	P	250.00	Fred Lorenzen (14)	Ford	81.930	Fred Lorenzen (20)	Ford	94.024
648	19	4/26/64	Martinsville VA	0.500	P	250.00	Fred Lorenzen (15)	Ford	70.098	Fred Lorenzen (21)	Ford	74.472
649	20	5/1/64	Savannah GA	0.500	D	100.00	LeeRoy Yarbrough	Plymouth	70.326	Jimmy Pardue (2)	Plymouth	73.111
650	21	5/9/64	Darlington SC	1.375	P	301.13	Fred Lorenzen (16)	Ford	130.013	Fred Lorenzen (22)	Ford	135.727
651	22	5/15/64	Hampton VA	0.400	D	100.00	Ned Jarrett (26)	Ford	65.300	David Pearson (8)	Dodge	67.542
652	23	5/16/64	Hickory NC	0.400	D	100.00	Ned Jarrett (27)	Ford	69.364	Junior Johnson (30)	Ford	76.882
653	24	5/17/64	South Boston VA	0.333	P	99.90	Richard Petty (30)	Plymouth	72.957	Marvin Panch (15)	Ford	80.023
654	25	5/24/64	Charlotte NC	1.500	P	600.00	Jim Paschal (19)	Plymouth	125.772	Jimmy Pardue (3)	Plymouth	144.346
655	26	5/30/64	Greenville SC	0.500	D	99.50	LeeRoy Yarbrough (2)	Plymouth	56.559	Marvin Panch (16)	Ford	68.050
656	27	5/31/64	Asheville NC	0.333	P	99.90	Ned Jarrett (28)	Ford	66.538	Richard Petty (18)	Plymouth	69.889
657	28	6/7/64	Atlanta GA	1.500	P	400.50	Ned Jarrett (29)	Ford	112.535	Junior Johnson (31)	Ford	145.906
658	29	6/11/64	Concord NC	0.500	D	100.00	Richard Petty (31)	Plymouth	66.352	Richard Petty (19)	Plymouth	68.233
659	30	6/14/64	Nashville TN	0.500	P	100.00	Richard Petty (32)	Plymouth	76.498	David Pearson (9)	Dodge	80.142
660	31	6/19/64	Chattanooga TN	0.333	P	99.90	David Pearson (7)	Dodge	70.051	Richard Petty (20)	Plymouth	75.235
661	32	6/21/64	Birmingham AL	0.500	P	100.00	Ned Jarrett (30)	Ford	67.643	David Pearson (10)	Dodge	72.115
662	33	6/23/64	Valdosta GA	0.500	D	100.00	Buck Baker (45)	Dodge	61.328	Ned Jarrett (20)	Ford	65.146
663	34	6/26/64	Spartanburg SC	0.500	D	100.00	Richard Petty (33)	Plymouth	58.233	David Pearson (11)	Dodge	66.939
664	35	7/4/64	Daytona Beach FL	2.500	P	400.00	A.J. Foyt	Dodge	151.451	Darel Dieringer (2)	Mercury	172.678
665	36	7/8/64	Manassas VA	0.375	P	150.00	Ned Jarrett (31)	Ford	67.652	Ned Jarrett (21)	Ford	73.609
666	37	7/10/64	Old Bridge NJ	0.500	P	100.00	Billy Wade	Mercury	73.891	Billy Wade	Mercury	76.660

Race	Year #	Date	Site	Track	Surface	Miles	Race Winner	Car	Speed	Pole Winner	Car	Speed
667	38	7/12/64	Bridgehampton NY	2.850	P	142.50	Billy Wade (2)	Mercury	87.707	Richard Petty (21)	Plymouth	90.600
668	39	7/15/64	Islip NY	0.200	P	60.00	Billy Wade (3)	Mercury	46.252	Billy Wade (2)	Mercury	51.100
669	40	7/19/64	Watkins Glen NY	2.300	P	151.80	Billy Wade (4)	Mercury	97.988	Billy Wade (3)	Mercury	102.222
670	41	7/21/64	New Oxford PA	0.500	D	100.00	David Pearson (8)	Dodge	82.568	David Pearson (12)	Dodge	86.289
671	42	7/26/64	Bristol TN	0.500	P	250.00	Fred Lorenzen (17)	Ford	78.044	Richard Petty (22)	Plymouth	82.910
672	43	8/2/64	Nashville TN	0.500	P	200.00	Richard Petty (34)	Plymouth	73.208	Richard Petty (23)	Plymouth	80.826
673	44	8/7/64	Myrtle Beach SC	0.500	D	100.00	David Pearson (9)	Dodge	61.750	David Pearson (13)	Dodge	69.659
674	45	8/9/64	Weaverville NC	0.500	P	250.00	Ned Jarrett (32)	Ford	77.600	Junior Johnson (32)	Ford	84.626
675	46	8/13/64	Moyock NC	0.333	P	99.90	Ned Jarrett (33)	Ford	63.965	Ned Jarrett (22)	Ford	67.643
676	47	8/16/64	Huntington WV	0.375	P	218.75	Richard Petty (35)	Plymouth	70.488	Billy Wade (4)	Mercury	79.505
677	48	8/21/64	Columbia SC	0.500	D	100.00	David Pearson (10)	Dodge	61.697	Ned Jarrett (23)	Ford	69.150
678	49	8/22/64	Winston-Salem NC	0.250	P	62.50	Junior Johnson (36	Ford	46.192	Junior Johnson (33)	Ford	49.846
679	50	8/23/64	Roanoke VA	0.250	P	50.00	Junior Johnson (37)	Ford	49.847	Glen Wood (14)	Ford	55.970
680	51	9/7/64	Darlington SC	1.375	P	500.50	Buck Baker (46)	Dodge	117.757	Richard Petty (24)	Plymouth	136.815
681	52	9/11/64	Hickory NC	0.400	D	100.00	David Pearson (11)	Dodge	67.797	David Pearson (14)	Dodge	74.418
682	53	9/14/64	Richmond VA	0.500	D	150.00	Cotton Owens (9)	Dodge	61.955	Ned Jarrett (24)	Ford	66.890
683	54	9/18/64	Manassas VA	0.375	P	187.50	Ned Jarrett (34)	Ford	68.842	David Pearson (15)	Dodge	74.626
684	55	9/20/64	Hillsboro NC	0.900	D	150.30	Ned Jarrett (35)	Ford	86.725	David Pearson (16)	Dodge	89.280
685	56	9/27/64	Martinsville VA	0.500	P	250.00	Fred Lorenzen (18)	Ford	67.320	Fred Lorenzen (23)	Ford	74.196
686	57	10/9/64	Savannah GA	0.500	D	100.00	Ned Jarrett (36)	Ford	68.663	Ned Jarrett (25)	Ford	68.886
687	58	10/11/64	N Wilkesboro NC	0.625	P	250.00	Marvin Panch (12)	Ford	91.398	Junior Johnson (34)	Ford	100.761
688	59	10/18/64	Charlotte NC	1.500	P	400.50	Fred Lorenzen (19)	Ford	134.475	Richard Petty (25)	Plymouth	150.711
689	60	10/25/64	Harris NC	0.300	P	100.20	Richard Petty (36)	Plymouth	59.009	Billy Wade (5)	Mercury	64.787
690	61	11/1/64	Augusta GA	0.500	P	150.00	Darel Dieringer (2)	Mercury	68.641	Ned Jarrett (26)	Ford	82.455
691	62	11/8/64	Jacksonville NC	0.500	D	100.00	Ned Jarrett (37)	Ford	57.535	Doug Yates (2)	Plymouth	64.285

1965

Race	Year #	Date	Site	Track	Surface	Miles	Race Winner	Car	Speed	Pole Winner	Car	Speed
692	1	1/17/65	Riverside CA	2.700	P	502.20	Dan Gurney (3)	Ford	87.708	Junior Johnson (35)	Ford	102.846
693	2	2/12/65	Daytona Beach FL	2.500	P	100.00	Darel Dieringer (3)	Mercury	165.669	Darel Dieringer (3)	Mercury	171.151
694	3	2/12/65	Daytona Beach FL	2.500	P	100.00	Junior Johnson (38)	Ford	111.706	Junior Johnson (36)	Ford	168.444
695	4	2/14/65	Daytona Beach FL	2.500	P	332.50	Fred Lorenzen (20)	Ford	141.539	Darel Dieringer (4)	Mercury	171.151
696	5	2/27/65	Spartanburg SC	0.500	D	100.00	Ned Jarrett (38)	Ford	66.367	Dick Hutcherson (3)	Ford	70.644
697	6	2/28/65	Weaverville NC	0.500	P	100.00	Ned Jarrett (39)	Ford	75.678	Ned Jarrett (27)	Ford	84.230
698	7	3/7/65	Richmond VA	0.500	D	125.00	Junior Johnson (39)	Ford	61.416	Junior Johnson (37)	Ford	67.847
699	8	3/14/65	Hillsboro NC	0.900	D	150.00	Ned Jarrett (40)	Ford	90.663	Junior Johnson (38)	Ford	98.570
700	9	4/11/65	Atlanta GA	1.500	P	501.00	Marvin Panch (13)	Ford	129.410	Marvin Panch (17)	Ford	145.581
701	10	4/17/65	Greenville SC	0.500	D	100.00	Dick Hutcherson	Ford	56.899	Bud Moore	Plymouth	67.695
702	11	4/18/65	N Wilkesboro NC	0.625	P	250.00	Junior Johnson (40)	Ford	95.047	Junior Johnson (39)	Ford	101.033
703	12	4/25/65	Martinsville VA	0.500	P	250.00	Fred Lorenzen (21)	Ford	66.765	Junior Johnson (40)	Ford	74.503
704	13	4/28/65	Columbia SC	0.500	D	62.00	Tiny Lund (2)	Ford	55.591	Ned Jarrett (28)	Ford	71.061
705	14	5/2/65	Bristol TN	0.500	P	250.00	Junior Johnson (41)	Ford	74.937	Marvin Panch (18)	Ford	84.626
706	15	5/8/65	Darlington SC	1.375	P	301.13	Junior Johnson (42)	Ford	111.849	Fred Lorenzen (24)	Ford	138.133
707	16	5/14/65	Hampton VA	0.400	D	100.00	Ned Jarrett (41)	Ford	57.815	Dick Hutcherson (4)	Ford	66.790
708	17	5/15/65	Winston-Salem NC	0.250	P	50.00	Junior Johnson (43)	Ford	47.911	Junior Johnson (41)	Ford	49.261
709	18	5/16/65	Hickory NC	0.400	D	100.00	Junior Johnson (44)	Ford	72.130	G.C. Spencer	Ford	76.312
710	19	5/23/65	Charlotte NC	1.500	P	600.00	Fred Lorenzen (22)	Ford	121.722	Fred Lorenzen (24)	Ford	145.268
711	20	5/27/65	Shelby NC	0.500	D	100.00	Ned Jarrett (42)	Ford	63.909	Dick Hutcherson (5)	Ford	65.862
712	21	5/29/65	Asheville NC	0.333	P	99.90	Junior Johnson (45)	Ford	66.293	Junior Johnson (42)	Ford	70.601
713	22	5/30/65	Harris NC	0.300	P	100.00	Ned Jarrett (43)	Ford	56.851	Paul Lewis	Ford	61.644
714	23	6/3/65	Nashville TN	0.500	P	100.00	Dick Hutcherson (2)	Ford	71.386	Tom Pistone	Ford	79.155
715	24	6/6/65	Birmingham AL	0.500	P	54.00	Ned Jarrett (44)	Ford	56.364	Ned Jarrett (29)	Ford	71.575
716	25	6/13/65	Atlanta GA	1.500	P	400.00	Marvin Panch (14)	Ford	110.120	Fred Lorenzen (25)	Ford	143.407
717	26	6/19/65	Greenville SC	0.500	D	100.00	Dick Hutcherson (3)	Ford	55.274	Ned Jarrett (30)	Ford	65.574
718	27	6/24/65	Myrtle Beach SC	0.500	D	100.00	Dick Hutcherson (4)	Ford	59.701	Dick Hutcherson (6)	Ford	66.421
719	28	6/27/65	Valdosta GA	0.500	D	100.00	Cale Yarborough	Ford	58.862	Dick Hutcherson (7)	Ford	64.540
720	29	7/4/65	Daytona Beach FL	2.500	P	400.00	A.J.Foyt (2)	Ford	150.046	Marvin Panch (19)	Ford	171.510
721	30	7/8/65	Manassas VA	0.375	P	150.00	Junior Johnson (46)	Ford	68.165	Ned Jarrett (31)	Ford	73.569
722	31	7/9/65	Old Bridge NJ	0.500	P	100.00	Junior Johnson (47)	Ford	72.087	Marvin Panch (20)	Ford	77.286
723	32	7/14/65	Islip NY	0.200	P	50.00	Marvin Panch (15)	Ford	43.838	Marvin Panch (21)	Ford	51.246
724	33	7/18/65	Watkins Glen NY	2.300	P	151.80	Marvin Panch (16)	Ford	98.182	No Time Trials	NTT	NTT
725	34	7/25/65	Bristol TN	0.500	P	250.00	Ned Jarrett (45)	Ford	61.826	Fred Lorenzen (26)	Ford	84.348
726	35	7/31/65	Nashville TN	0.500	P	200.00	Richard Petty (37)	Plymouth	72.383	Richard Petty (26)	Plymouth	82.117
727	36	8/5/65	Shelby NC	0.500	D	100.00	Ned Jarrett (46)	Ford	64.748	David Pearson (17)	Dodge	67.797
728	37	8/8/65	Weaverville NC	0.500	P	250.00	Richard Petty (38)	Plymouth	74.343	Richard Petty (27)	Plymouth	86.455
729	38	8/13/65	Maryville TN	0.500	D	100.00	Dick Hutcherson (5)	Ford	65.455	Ned Jarrett (32)	Ford	77.620
730	39	8/14/65	Spartanburg SC	0.500	D	100.00	Ned Jarrett (47)	Ford	56.926	Dick Hutcherson (8)	Ford	66.890
731	40	8/15/65	Augusta GA	0.500	P	100.00	Dick Hutcherson (6)	Ford	71.499	Ned Jarrett (33)	Ford	81.118
732	41	8/19/65	Columbia SC	0.500	D	100.00	David Pearson (12)	Dodge	57.361	Dick Hutcherson (9)	Ford	71.343
733	42	8/24/65	Moyock NC	0.333	P	99.90	Dick Hutcherson (7)	Ford	63.047	Richard Petty (28)	Plymouth	68.493
734	43	8/25/65	Beltsville MD	0.500	P	100.00	Ned Jarrett (48)	Ford	74.165	Ned Jarrett (34)	Ford	79.260
735	44	8/28/65	Winston-Salem NC	0.250	P	62.50	Junior Johnson (48)	Ford	46.632	Richard Petty (29)	Plymouth	50.195
736	45	9/6/65	Darlington SC	1.375	P	500.50	Ned Jarrett (49)	Ford	115.878	Junior Johnson (43)	Ford	137.571

Race #	Year #	Date	Site	Track	Surface	Miles	Race Winner	Car	Speed	Pole Winner	Car	Speed
737	46	9/10/65	Hickory NC	0.400	D	100.00	Richard Petty (39)	Plymouth	74.365	Junior Johnson (44)	Ford	74.766
738	47	9/14/65	New Oxford PA	0.500	D	100.00	Dick Hutcherson (8)	Ford	82.607	Richard Petty (30)	Plymouth	86.705
739	48	9/17/65	Manassas VA	0.375	P	150.00	Richard Petty (40)	Plymouth	67.890	Ned Jarrett (35)	Ford	73.851
740	49	9/18/65	Richmond VA	0.500	D	150.00	David Pearson (13)	Dodge	60.983	Dick Hutcherson (10)	Ford	67.340
741	50	9/26/65	Martinsville VA	0.500	P	250.00	Junior Johnson (49)	Ford	67.056	Richard Petty (31)	Plymouth	74.503
742	51	10/3/65	N Wilkesboro NC	0.625	P	250.00	Junior Johnson (50)	Ford	88.801	Fred Lorenzen (28)	Ford	101.580
743	52	10/17/65	Charlotte NC	1.500	P	400.50	Fred Lorenzen (23)	Ford	119.117	Fred Lorenzen (29)	Ford	147.773
744	53	10/24/65	Hillsboro NC	0.900	D	100.80	Dick Hutcherson (9)	Ford	87.462	Dick Hutcherson (11)	Ford	98.810
745	54	10/31/65	Rockingham NC	1.000	P	500.00	Curtis Turner (17)	Ford	101.942	Richard Petty (32)	Plymouth	116.260
746	55	11/7/65	Moyock NC	0.333	P	99.90	Ned Jarrett (50)	Ford	63.773	Bobby Isaac	Ford	68.143

1966

Race #	Year #	Date	Site	Track	Surface	Miles	Race Winner	Car	Speed	Pole Winner	Car	Speed
747	1	11/14/65	Augusta GA	0.500	P	150.00	Richard Petty (41)	Plymouth	73.569	Richard Petty (33)	Plymouth	82.987
748	2	1/23/66	Riverside CA	2.700	P	502.20	Dan Gurney (4)	Ford	97.952	David Pearson (18)	Dodge	106.078
749	3	2/25/66	Daytona Beach FL	2.500	P	100.00	Paul Goldsmith (7)	Plymouth	160.427	Richard Petty (34)	Plymouth	175.165
750	4	2/25/66	Daytona Beach FL	2.500	P	100.00	Earl Balmer	Dodge	153.191	Dick Hutcherson (12)	Ford	174.317
751	5	2/27/66	Daytona Beach FL	2.500	P	495.00	Richard Petty (42)	Plymouth	160.627	Richard Petty (35)	Plymouth	175.165
752	6	3/13/66	Rockingham NC	1.000	P	500.00	Paul Goldsmith (8)	Plymouth	100.027	Paul Goldsmith (9)	Plymouth	116.684
753	7	3/20/66	Bristol TN	0.500	P	250.00	Dick Hutcherson (10)	Ford	69.952	David Pearson (19)	Dodge	86.248
754	8	3/27/66	Atlanta GA	1.500	P	501.00	Jim Hurtubise	Plymouth	131.247	Richard Petty (36)	Plymouth	147.742
755	9	4/3/66	Hickory NC	0.400	D	100.00	David Pearson (14)	Dodge	68.428	Elmo Langley	Ford	75.117
756	10	4/7/66	Columbia SC	0.500	D	100.00	David Pearson (15)	Dodge	65.574	Tom Pistone (2)	Ford	72.202
757	11	4/9/66	Greenville SC	0.500	D	100.00	David Pearson (16)	Dodge	65.850	Tiny Lund (6)	Ford	68.208
758	12	4/11/66	Winston-Salem NC	0.250	P	50.00	David Pearson (17)	Dodge	51.341	David Pearson (20)	Dodge	54.479
759	13	4/17/66	N Wilkesboro NC	0.625	P	250.00	Jim Paschal (20)	Plymouth	89.045	Jim Paschal (10)	Plymouth	102.693
760	14	4/24/66	Martinsville VA	0.500	P	250.00	Jim Paschal (21)	Plymouth	69.156	Jim Paschal (11)	Plymouth	76.345
761	15	4/30/66	Darlington SC	1.375	P	400.13	Richard Petty (43)	Plymouth	131.993	Richard Petty (37)	Plymouth	140.815
762	16	5/7/66	Hampton VA	0.400	D	100.00	Richard Petty (44)	Plymouth	60.616	Richard Petty (38)	Plymouth	66.812
763	17	5/10/66	Macon GA	0.500	P	100.00	Richard Petty (45)	Plymouth	82.023	Richard Petty (39)	Plymouth	85.026
764	18	5/13/66	Monroe NC	0.500	D	100.00	Darel Dieringer (4)	Ford	60.140	James Hylton	Dodge	65.099
765	19	5/15/66	Richmond VA	0.500	D	125.00	David Pearson (18)	Dodge	66.539	Tom Pistone (3)	Ford	70.978
766	20	5/22/66	Charlotte NC	1.500	P	600.00	Marvin Panch (17)	Plymouth	135.042	Richard Petty (40)	Plymouth	148.637
767	21	5/29/66	Moyock NC	0.333	P	99.90	David Pearson (19)	Dodge	61.913	Richard Petty (41)	Plymouth	69.164
768	22	6/2/66	Asheville NC	0.333	P	99.90	David Pearson (20)	Dodge	64.917	Richard Petty (42)	Plymouth	72.964
769	23	6/4/66	Spartanburg SC	0.500	D	100.00	Elmo Langley	Ford	60.050	David Pearson (21)	Dodge	68.027
770	24	6/9/66	Maryville TN	0.500	D	100.00	David Pearson (21)	Dodge	71.986	Tom Pistone (4)	Ford	78.947
771	25	6/12/66	Weaverville NC	0.500	P	150.00	Richard Petty (46)	Plymouth	81.423	Richard Petty (43)	Plymouth	86.455
772	26	6/15/66	Beltsville MD	0.500	P	100.00	Tiny Lund (3)	Ford	73.409	Richard Petty (44)	Plymouth	80.250
773	27	6/25/66	Greensville SC	0.500	D	100.00	David Pearson (22)	Dodge	66.286	David Pearson (22)	Dodge	69.364
774	28	7/4/66	Daytona Beach FL	2.500	P	400.00	Sam McQuagg	Dodge	153.813	Lee Roy Yarbrough (2)	Dodge	176.660
775	29	7/7/66	Manassas VA	0.375	P	150.00	Elmo Langley (2)	Ford	68.079	Bobby Allison	Chevy	73.973
776	30	8/10/66	Bridgehampton NY	2.850	P	148.20	David Pearson (23)	Dodge	86.949	David Pearson (23)	Dodge	---
777	31	7/12/66	Oxford ME	0.333	P	99.90	Bobby Allison	Chevy	56.782	Bobby Allison (2)	Chevy	65.681
778	32	7/14/66	Fonda NY	0.500	D	100.00	David Pearson (24)	Dodge	61.010	Richard Petty (45)	Plymouth	71.514
779	33	7/16/66	Islip NY	0.200	P	60.00	Bobby Allison (2)	Chevy	47.285	Tom Pistone (5)	Ford	55.919
780	34	7/24/66	Bristol TN	0.500	P	250.00	Paul Goldsmith (9)	Plymouth	77.693	Curtis Turner (14)	Chevy	84.309
781	35	7/28/66	Maryville TN	0.500	D	100.00	Paul Lewis	Plymouth	69.822	Buddy Baker	Dodge	77.821
782	36	7/30/66	Nashville TN	0.500	P	200.00	Richard Petty (47)	Plymouth	71.770	Richard Petty (46	Plymouth	82.493
783	37	8/7/66	Atlanta GA	1.500	P	501.00	Richard Petty (48)	Plymouth	130.244	Curtis Turner (15)	Chevy	148.331
784	38	8/18/66	Columbia SC	0.500	D	100.00	David Pearson (25)	Dodge	66.128	Bobby Allison (3)	Chevy	73.469
785	39	8/21/66	Weaverville NC	0.500	P	250.00	Darel Dieringer (5)	Mercury	76.700	Junior Johnson (45)	Ford	86.831
786	40	8/24/66	Beltsville MD	0.500	P	100.00	Bobby Allison (3)	Chevy	68.899	Bobby Allison (4)	Chevy	79.330
787	41	8/27/66	Winston-Salem NC	0.250	P	62.50	David Pearson (26)	Dodge	45.928	Richard Petty (47)	Plymouth	54.348
788	42	9/5/66	Darlington SC	1.375	P	500.50	Darel Dieringer (6)	Mercury	114.830	LeeRoy Yarbrough (3)	Dodge	140.058
789	43	9/9/66	Hickory NC	0.400	D	100.00	David Pearson (27)	Dodge	70.533	Richard Petty (48)	Plymouth	76.923
790	44	9/11/66	Richmond VA	0.500	D	150.00	David Pearson (28)	Dodge	62.886	David Pearson (24)	Dodge	70.644
791	45	9/18/66	Hillsboro NC	0.900	D	150.00	Dick Hutcherson (11)	Ford	90.603	Dick Hutcherson (13)	Ford	95.716
792	46	9/25/66	Martinsville VA	0.500	P	250.00	Fred Lorenzen (24)	Ford	69.177	Junior Johnson (46)	Ford	75.598
793	47	10/2/66	N Wilkesboro NC	0.625	P	250.00	Dick Hutcherson (12)	Ford	89.012	Junior Johnson (47)	Ford	103.069
794	48	10/16/66	Charlotte NC	1.500	P	501.00	LeeRoy Yarbrough (3)	Dodge	130.576	Fred Lorenzen (30)	Ford	150.533
795	49	10/30/66	Rockingham NC	1.000	P	500.00	Fred Lorenzen (25)	Ford	104.348	Fred Lorenzen (31)	Ford	115.988

1967

Race #	Year #	Date	Site	Track	Surface	Miles	Race Winner	Car	Speed	Pole Winner	Car	Speed
796	1	11/13/66	Augusta GA	0.500	P	150.00	Richard Petty (49)	Plymouth	71.809	Dick Hutcherson (14)	Ford	84.112
797	2	1/22/67	Riverside CA	2.700	P	502.20	Parnelli Jones (4)	Ford	91.080	Dick Hutcherson (15)	Ford	106.951
798	3	2/24/67	Daytona Beach FL	2.500	P	100.00	LeeRoy Yarbrough (4)	Dodge	163.934	Curtis Turner (16)	Chevy	180.831
799	4	2/24/67	Daytona Beach FL	2.500	P	100.00	Fred Lorenzen (26)	Ford	174.587	Richard Petty (49)	Plymouth	179.068
800	5	2/26/67	Daytona Beach FL	2.500	P	500.00	Mario Andretti	Ford	146.926	Curtis Turner (17)	Chevy	180.831
801	6	3/5/67	Weaverville NC	0.500	P	150.00	Richard Petty (50)	Plymouth	83.360	Darel Dieringer (5)	Ford	88.626
802	7	3/19/67	Bristol TN	0.500	P	250.00	David Pearson (29)	Dodge	77.937	Darel Dieringer (6)	Ford	87.124

Race #	Year #	Date	Site	Track	Surface	Miles	Race Winner	Car	Speed	Pole Winner	Car	Speed
803	8	3/25/67	Greenville SC	0.500	D	100.00	David Pearson (30)	Dodge	61.824	Dick Hutcherson (16)	Ford	70.313
804	9	3/27/67	Winston-Salem NC	0.250	P	50.00	Bobby Allison (4)	Chevy	49.248	Bobby Allison (5)	Chevy	53.476
805	10	4/2/67	Atlanta GA	1.500	P	501.00	Cale Yarborough (2)	Ford	131.238	Cale Yarborough	Ford	148.996
806	11	4/6/67	Columbia SC	0.500	D	100.00	Richard Petty (51)	Plymouth	65.455	Dick Hutcherson (17)	Ford	74.166
807	12	4/9/67	Hickory NC	0.400	D	100.00	Richard Petty (52)	Plymouth	69.699	Richard Petty (50)	Plymouth	79.120
808	13	4/16/67	N Wilkesboro NC	0.625	P	250.00	Darel Dieringer (7)	Ford	93.594	Darel Dieringer (7)	Ford	104.603
809	14	4/23/67	Martinsville VA	0.500	P	250.00	Richard Petty (53)	Plymouth	67.446	Darel Dieringer (8)	Ford	77.319
810	15	4/28/67	Savannah GA	0.500	D	100.00	Bobby Allison (5)	Chevy	66.802	John Sears	Ford	72.173
811	16	4/30/67	Richmond VA	0.500	D	125.00	Richard Petty (54)	Plymouth	65.982	Richard Petty (51)	Plymouth	70.038
812	17	5/13/67	Darlington SC	1.375	P	400.13	Richard Petty (55)	Plymouth	125.738	David Pearson (25)	Ford	144.536
813	18	5/19/67	Beltsville MD	0.500	P	100.00	Jim Paschal (22)	Plymouth	71.036	Richard Petty (52)	Plymouth	80.286
814	19	5/20/67	Hampton VA	0.400	D	100.00	Richard Petty (56)	Plymouth	66.704	Richard Petty (53)	Plymouth	68.214
815	20	5/28/67	Charlotte NC	1.500	P	600.00	Jim Paschal (23)	Plymouth	135.832	Cale Yarborough (2)	Ford ·	154.385
816	21	6/2/67	Asheville NC	0.333	P	99.90	Jim Paschal (24)	Plymouth	63.080	Richard Petty (54)	Plymouth	73.710
817	22	6/6/67	Macon GA	0.500	P	150.00	Richard Petty (57)	Plymouth	80.321	Richard Petty (55)	Plymouth	86.538
818	23	6/8/67	Maryville TN	0.500	D	100.00	Richard Petty (58)	Plymouth	72.919	Jim Hunter	Chevy	79.051
819	24	6/10/67	Birmingham AL	0.500	P	100.00	Bobby Allison (6)	Dodge	88.999	Jim Paschal (12)	Plymouth	94.142
820	25	6/18/67	Rockingham NC	1.000	P	500.00	Richard Petty (59)	Plymouth	104.682	Dick Hutcherson (18)	Ford	116.486
821	26	6/24/67	Greenville SC	0.500	D	100.00	Richard Petty (60)	Plymouth	61.781	Richard Petty (56)	Plymouth	69.498
822	27	6/27/67	Montgomery AL	0.500	P	100.00	Jim Paschal (25)	Plymouth	72.435	Richard Petty (57)	Plymouth	77.088
823	28	7/4/67	Daytona Beach FL	2.500	P	400.00	Cale Yarborough (3)	Ford	143.583	Darel Dieringer (9)	Ford	179.802
824	29	7/9/67	Trenton NJ	1.500	P	300.00	Richard Petty (61)	Plymouth	95.322	Richard Petty (58)	Plymouth	101.208
825	30	7/11/67	Oxford ME	0.333	P	99.90	Bobby Allison (7)	Chevy	61.697	James Hylton (2)	Dodge	66.043
826	31	7/13/67	Fonda NY	0.500	D	100.00	Richard Petty (62)	Plymouth	65.826	Richard Petty (59)	Plymouth	72.173
827	32	7/15/67	Islip NY	0.200	P	60.00	Richard Petty (63)	Plymouth	42.428	Richard Petty (60)	Plymouth	51.136
828	33	7/23/67	Bristol TN	0.500	P	250.00	Richard Petty (64)	Plymouth	78.705	Richard Petty (61)	Plymouth	86.621
829	34	7/27/67	Maryville TN	0.500	D	100.00	Dick Hutcherson (13)	Ford	65.765	Dick Hutcherson (19)	Ford	79.540
830	35	7/29/67	Nashville TN	0.500	P	200.00	Richard Petty (65)	Plymouth	70.866	Dick Hutcherson (20)	Ford	84.260
831	36	8/6/67	Atlanta GA	1.500	P	501.00	Dick Hutcherson (14)	Ford	132.286	Darel Dieringer (10)	Ford	150.417
832	37	8/12/67	Winston-Salem NC	0.250	P	62.50	Richard Petty (66)	Plymouth	50.893	Richard Petty (62)	Plymouth	53.160
833	38	8/17/67	Columbia SC	0.500	D	100.00	Richard Petty (67)	Plymouth	64.274	Richard Petty (63)	Plymouth	74.968
834	39	8/25/67	Savannah GA	0.500	D	100.00	Richard Petty (68)	Plymouth	65.041	Richard Petty (64)	Plymouth	71.942
835	40	9/4/67	Darlington SC	1.375	P	500.50	Richard Petty (69)	Plymouth	130.423	Richard Petty (65)	Plymouth	143.436
836	41	9/8/67	Hickory NC	0.400	P	100.00	Richard Petty (70)	Plymouth	71.414	Dick Hutcherson (21)	Ford	86.538
837	42	9/10/67	Richmond VVA	0.500	D	150.00	Richard Petty (71)	Plymouth	57.631	No Time Trials	NTT	NTT
838	43	9/15/67	Beltsville MD	0.500	P	150.00	Richard Petty (72)	Plymouth	76.563	Richard Petty (66)	Plymouth	81.044
839	44	9/17/67	Hillsboro NC	0.900	D	150.00	Richard Petty (73)	Plymouth	81.574	Richard Petty (67)	Plymouth	94.159
840	45	9/24/67	Martinsville VA	0.500	P	250.00	Richard Petty (74)	Plymouth	69.605	Cale Yarborough (3)	Ford	77.386
841	46	10/1/67	N Wilkesboro NC	0.625	P	250.00	Richard Petty (75)	Plymouth	94.837	Dick Hutcherson (22)	Ford	104.312
842	47	10/15/67	Charlotte NC	1.500	P	501.00	Buddy Baker	Dodge	130.317	Cale Yarborough (4)	Ford	154.872
843	48	10/29/67	Rockingham NC	1.000	P	500.00	Bobby Allison (8)	Ford	98.420	David Pearson (26)	Ford	117.120
844	49	11/5/67	Weaverville NC	0.500	P	250.00	Bobby Allison (9)	Ford	76.291	Bobby Allison (6)	Ford	90.407

1968

Race #	Year #	Date	Site	Track	Surface	Miles	Race Winner	Car	Speed	Pole Winner	Car	Speed
845	1	11/12/67	Macon GA	0.500	P	267.00	Bobby Allison (10)	Ford	81.001	LeeRoy Yarbrough (4)	Ford	94.323
846	2	11/26/67	Montgomery AL	0.500	P	100.00	Richard Petty (76)	Plymouth	70.644	Richard Petty (68)	Plymouth	79.694
847	3	1/21/68	Riverside CA	2.700	P	502.20	Dan Gurney (5)	Ford	100.598	Dan Gurney (2)	Ford	110.971
848	4	2/25/68	Daytona Beach FL	2.500	P	500.00	Cale Yarborough (4)	Mercury	143.251	Cale Yarborough (5)	Mercury	189.222
849	5	3/17/68	Bristol TN	0.500	P	250.00	David Pearson (31)	Ford	77.247	Richard Petty (69)	Plymouth	88.582
850	6	3/24/68	Richmond VA	0.500	D	125.00	David Pearson (32)	Ford	65.217	Bobby Isaac (2)	Dodge	67.822
851	7	3/31/68	Atlanta GA	1.500	P	501.00	Cale Yarborough (5)	Mercury	125.564	LeeRoy Yarbrough (5)	Mercury	155.646
852	8	4/7/68	Hickory NC	0.400	P	100.00	Richard Petty (77)	Plymouth	79.435	David Pearson (27	Ford	86.957
853	9	4/13/68	Greenville SC	0.500	D	100.00	Richard Petty (78)	Plymouth	63.347	David Pearson (28)	Ford	67.848
854	10	4/18/68	Columbia SC	0.500	D	100.00	Bobby Isaac (2)	Dodge	71.358	Richard Petty (70)	Plymouth	75.282
855	11	4/21/68	N Wilkesboro NC	0.625	P	250.00	David Pearson (33)	Ford	90.425	David Pearson (29)	Ford	104.993
856	12	4/28/68	Martinsville VA	0.500	P	250.00	Cale Yarborough (6)	Mercury	66.686	David Pearson (30)	Ford	78.230
857	13	5/3/68	Augusta, GA	0.500	P	125.00	Bobby Isaac (3)	Dodge	73.099	Bobby Isaac (3)	Dodge	83.877
858	14	5/5/68	Weaverville NC	0.500	P	150.00	David Pearson (34)	Ford	75.167	David Pearson (31)	Ford	89.708
859	15	5/11/68	Darlington SC	1.375	P	400.13	David Pearson (35)	Ford	132.699	LeeRoy Yarbrough (6)	Ford	148.850
860	16	5/17/68	Beltsville MD	0.500	P	150.00	David Pearson (36)	Ford	74.844	Richard Petty (71)	Plymouth	83.604
861	17	5/18/68	Hampton VA	0.400	P	100.00	David Pearson (37)	Ford	71.457	Richard Petty (72)	Plymouth	80.801
862	18	5/26/68	Charlotte NC	1.500	P	382.50	Buddy Baker (2)	Dodge	104.207	Donnie Allison	Ford	159.223
863	19	5/31/68	Asheville NC	0.333	P	99.90	Richard Petty (79)	Plymouth	64.741	Richard Petty (73)	Plymouth	74.349
864	20	6/2/68	Macon GA	0.500	P	150.00	David Pearson (38)	Ford	79.342	David Pearson (32)	Ford	86.873
865	21	6/6/68	Maryville TN	0.500	P	100.00	Richard Petty (80)	Plymouth	76.743	David Pearson (33)	Ford	88.583
866	22	6/8/68	Birmingham AL	0.500	P	100.00	Richard Petty (81)	Plymouth	89.153	David Pearson (34)	Ford	97.784
867	23	6/16/68	Rockingham NC	1.000	P	500.00	Donnie Allison	Ford	99.338	LeeRoy Yarbrough (7)	Ford	118.644
868	24	6/22/68	Greenville SC	0.500	D	100.00	Richard Petty (82)	Plymouth	64.609	David Pearson (35)	Ford	68.834
869	25	7/4/68	Daytona Beach FL	2.500	P	400.00	Cale Yarborough (7)	Mercury	167.247	Charlie Glotzbach	Dodge	185.156
870	26	7/7/68	Islip NY	0.200	P	60.00	Bobby Allison (11)	Chevy	48.561	Buddy Baker (2)	Dodge	51.873
871	27	7/9/68	Oxford ME	0.333	P	99.90	Richard Petty (83)	Plymouth	63.717	Buddy Baker (3)	Dodge	67.835
872	28	7/11/68	Fonda NY	0.500	P	100.00	Richard Petty (84)	Plymouth	64.935	David Pearson (36)	Ford	73.800

Race #	Year #	Date	Site	Track	Surface	Miles	Race Winner	Car	Speed	Pole Winner	Car	Speed
873	29	7/14/68	Trenton NJ	1.500	P	300.00	LeeRoy Yarbrough (5)	Ford	89.079	LeeRoy Yarbrough (8)	Ford	103.717
874	30	7/21/68	Bristol TN	0.500	P	250.00	David Pearson (39)	Ford	76.310	LeeRoy Yarbrough (9)	Ford	87.421
875	31	7/25/68	Maryville TN	0.500	P	100.00	Richard Petty (85)	Plymouth	72.513	Bobby Isaac (4)	Dodge	86.538
876	32	7/27/68	Nashville TN	0.500	P	151.50	David Pearson (40)	Ford	72.980	Richard Petty (74)	Plymouth	85.066
877	33	8/4/68	Atlanta GA	1.500	P	501.00	LeeRoy Yarbrough (6)	Mercury	127.068	Buddy Baker (4)	Dodge	153.361
878	34	8/8/68	Columbia SC	0.500	D	100.00	David Pearson (41)	Ford	67.039	Buddy Baker (5)	Dodge	74.196
879	35	8/10/68	Winston-Salem NC	0.250	P	62.50	David Pearson (42	Ford	42.940	Richard Petty (75)	Plymouth	53.828
880	36	8/17/68	Weaverville NC	0.500	P	250.00	David Pearson (43)	Ford	73.686	Darel Dieringer (11)	Plymouth	88.409
881	37	8/23/68	South Boston VA	0.375	P	100.13	Richard Petty (86)	Plymouth	75.916	Richard Petty (76)	Plymouth	84.428
882	38	8/24/68	Hampton VA	0.400	P	100.00	David Pearson (44)	Ford	75.582	David Pearson (37)	Ford	78.007
883	39	9/2/68	Darlington, SC	1.375	P	500.50	Cale Yarborough (8)	Mercury	126.132	Charlie Glotzbach (2)	Dodge	144.830
884	40	9/6/68	Hickory NC	0.400	P	100.00	David Pearson (45)	Ford	80.357	Richard Petty (77)	Plymouth	85.868
885	41	9/8/68	Richmond VA	0.500	P	187.50	Richard Petty (87)	Plymouth	85.659	Richard Petty (78)	Plymouth	103.178
886	42	9/13/68	Beltsville MD	0.500	P	150.00	Bobby Isaac (4)	Dodge	71.033	Cale Yarborough (6)	Mercury	81.311
887	43	9/15/68	Hillsboro NC	0.900	P	150.00	Richard Petty (88)	Plymouth	87.681	Richard Petty (79)	Plymouth	93.245
888	44	9/22/68	Martinsville VA	0.500	P	250.00	Richard Petty (89)	Plymouth	64.808	Cale Yarborough (7)	Mercury	77.279
889	45	9/29/68	N Wilkesboro NC	0.625	P	250.00	Richard Petty (90)	Plymouth	94.103	Bobby Allison (7)	Plymouth	104.525
890	46	10/5/68	Augusta GA	0.500	P	100.00	David Pearson (46)	Ford	75.821	Bobby Allison (8)	Plymouth	84.822
891	47	10/20/68	Charlotte NC	1.500	P	501.00	Charlie Glotzbach	Dodge	135.324	Charlie Glotzbach (3)	Dodge	156.060
892	48	10/27/68	Rockingham NC	1.000	P	500.00	Richard Petty (91)	Plymouth	105.060	Cale Yarborough (8)	Mercury	118.717
893	49	11/3/68	Jefferson GA	0.500	P	100.00	Cale Yarborough (9)	Mercury	77.737	David Pearson (38)	Ford	90.694

1969

Race #	Year #	Date	Site	Track	Surface	Miles	Race Winner	Car	Speed	Pole Winner	Car	Speed
894	1	11/17/68	Macon GA	0.500	P	250.00	Richard Petty (92)	Plymouth	85.121	David Pearson (39)	Ford	95.472
895	2	12/8/68	Montgomery AL	0.500	P	100.00	Bobby Allison (12)	Plymouth	73.200	Richard Petty (80)	Plymouth	80.899
896	3	2/1/69	Riverside CA	2.700	P	500.42	Richard Petty (93)	Ford	105.498	A.J.Foyt	Ford	110.323
897	4	2/20/69	Daytona Beach FL	2.500	P	125.00	David Pearson (47)	Ford	152.181	Buddy Baker (6)	Dodge	188.901
898	5	2/20/69	Daytona Beach FL	2.500	P	125.00	Bobby Isaac (5)	Dodge	151.668	Bobby Isaac (5)	Dodge	188.726
899	6	2/23/69	Daytona Beach FL	2.500	P	500.00	LeeRoy Yarbrough (7)	Ford	157.950	Buddy Baker (7)	Dodge	188.901
900	7	3/9/69	Rockingham NC	1.000	P	500.00	David Pearson (48)	Ford	102.569	David Pearson (40)	Ford	119.619
901	8	3/16/69	Augusta GA	0.500	P	100.00	David Pearson (49)	Ford	77.586	Bobby Isac (6)	Dodge	86.901
902	9	3/23/69	Bristol TN	0.500	P	250.00	Bobby Allison (13)	Dodge	81.455	Bobby Isaac (7)	Dodge	88.669
903	10	3/30/69	Atlanta GA	1.500	P	501.00	Cale Yarborough (10)	Mercury	132.191	David Pearson (41)	Ford	156.794
904	11	4/3/69	Columbia SC	0.500	D	100.00	Bobby Isaac (6)	Dodge	68.558	Bobby Isaac (8)	Dodge	73.806
905	12	4/6/69	Hickory NC	0.400	P	100.00	Bobby Isaac (7)	Dodge	79.086	Bobby Isaac (9)	Dodge	85.612
906	13	4/8/69	Greenville SC	0.500	D	100.00	Bobby Isaac (8)	Dodge	64.389	David Pearson (42)	Ford	70.359
907	14	4/13/69	Richamond VA	0.500	P	250.00	David Pearson (50)	Ford	73.752	David Pearson (43)	Ford	82.538
908	15	4/20/69	N Wilkesboro NC	0.625	P	250.00	Bobby Allison (14)	Dodge	95.268	Bobby Isaac (10)	Dodge	106.731
909	16	4/27/69	Martinsville VA	0.500	P	250.00	Richard Petty (94)	Ford	64.405	Bobby Allison (9)	Dodge	78.260
910	17	5/4/69	Weaverville NC	0.500	P	150.00	Bobby Isaac (9)	Dodge	72.581	Bobby Isaac (11)	Dodge	90.361
911	18	5/10/69	Darlington SC	1.375	P	400.13	LeeRoy Yarbrough (8)	Mercury	131.572	Cale Yarborough (9)	Mercury	152.293
912	19	5/16/69	Beltsville MD	0.500	P	150.00	Bobby Isaac (10)	Dodge	73.059	Bobby Isaac (12)	Dodge	83.329
913	20	5/17/69	Hampton VA	0.400	P	150.00	David Pearson (51)	Ford	75.789	David Pearson (44)	Ford	80.236
914	21	5/25/69	Charlotte NC	1.500	P	600.00	LeeRoy Yarbrough (9)	Mercury	134.361	Donnie Allison (2)	Ford	159.296
915	22	6/1/69	Macon GA	0.500	P	150.00	Bobby Isaac (11)	Dodge	73.717	David Pearson (45)	Ford	87.946
916	23	6/5/69	Maryville TN	0.500	P	150.00	Bobby Isaac (12)	Dodge	81.706	David Pearson (46)	Ford	87.976
917	24	6/15/69	Brooklyn MI	2.000	P	500.00	Cale Yarborough (11)	Mercury	139.254	Donnie Allison (3)	Ford	160.135
918	25	6/19/69	Kingsport TN	0.400	P	100.00	Richard Petty (95)	Ford	73.619	Bobby Isaac (13)	Dodge	90.112
919	26	6/21/69	Greenville SC	0.500	D	100.00	Bobby Isaac (13)	Dodge	61.813	Bobby Isaac (14)	Dodge	66.030
920	27	6/26/69	Raleigh NC	0.500	D	100.00	David Pearson (52)	Ford	65.418	Bobby Isaac (15)	Dodge	72.942
921	28	7/4/69	Daytona Beach FL	2.500	P	400.00	LeeRoy Yarbrough (10)	Ford	160.875	Cale Yarborough (10)	Mercury	190.706
922	29	7/6/69	Dover DE	1.000	P	300.00	Richard Petty (96)	Ford	115.772	David Pearson (47)	Ford	130.430
923	30	7/10/69	Thompson CT	0.625	P	125.00	David Pearson (53)	Ford	89.498	David Pearson (48)	Ford	99.800
924	31	7/13/69	Trenton NJ	1.500	P	300.00	David Pearson (54)	Ford	121.008	Bobby Isaac (16)	Dodge	132.668
925	32	7/15/69	Beltsville MD	0.500	P	150.00	Richard Petty (97)	Ford	77.253	Richard Petty (81)	Ford	82.094
926	33	7/20/69	Bristol TN	0.500	P	250.00	David Pearson (55)	Ford	79.737	Cale Yarborough (11)	Mercury	103.432
927	34	7/26/69	Nashville TN	0.500	P	200.00	Richard Petty (98)	Ford	78.740	Richard Petty (82)	Ford	84.918
928	35	7/27/69	Maryville TN	0.500	P	200.00	Richard Petty (99)	Ford	82.417	David Pearson (49)	Ford	87.434
929	36	8/10/69	Atlanta GA	1.500	P	501.00	LeeRoy Yarbrough (11)	Ford	133.001	Cale Yarborough (12)	Mercury	155.413
930	37	8/17/69	Brooklyn MI	2.000	P	330.00	David Pearson (56)	Ford	115.508	David Pearson (50)	Ford	161.714
931	38	8/21/69	South Boston VA	0.500	P	100.00	Bobby Isaac (14)	Dodge	76.906	Bobby Isaac (17)	Dodge	84.959
932	39	8/22/69	Winston-Salem NC	0.250	P	62.50	Richard Petty (100)	Ford	47.458	Richard Petty (83)	Ford	54.253
933	40	8/24/69	Weaverville NC	0.500	P	250.00	Bobby Isaac (15)	Dodge	80.450	Bobby Isaac (18)	Dodge	89.000
934	41	9/1/69	Darlington SC	1.375	P	316.25	LeeRoy Yarbrough (12)	Ford	105.612	Cale Yarborough (13)	Mercury	151.985
935	42	9/5/69	Hickory NC	0.400	P	100.00	Bobby Isaac (16)	Dodge	80.519	Bobby Isaac (19)	Dodge	86.212
936	43	9/7/69	Richmond VA	0.563	P	250.40	Bobby Allison (15)	Dodge	76.388	Richard Petty (84)	Ford	91.257
937	44	9/14/69	Talladega AL	2.660	P	500.08	Richard Brickhouse	Dodge	153.778	Bobby Isaac (20)	Dodge	196.386
938	45	9/18/69	Columbia SC	0.500	D	100.00	Bobby Isaac (17)	Dodge	70.230	Richard Petty (85)	Ford	73.108
939	46	9/28/69	Martinsville VA	0.500	P	250.00	Richard Petty (101)	Ford	63.127	David Pearson (51	Ford	83.197
940	47	10/5/69	N Wilkesboro NC	0.625	P	250.00	David Pearson (57)	Ford	93.429	Bobby Isaac (21)	Dodge	106.032
941	48	10/12/69	Charlotte NC	1.500	P	501.00	Donnie Allison (2)	Ford	131.271	Cale Yarborough (14)	Mercury	162.162
942	49	10/17/69	Savannah GA	0.500	P	100.00	Bobby Isaac (18)	Dodge	78.432	Bobby Isaac (22)	Dodge	86.095

Race #	Year #	Date	Site	Track	Surface	Miles	Race Winner	Car	Speed	Pole Winner	Car	Speed
943	50	10/19/69	Augusta GA	0.500	P	100.00	Bobby Isaac (19)	Dodge	78.740	Bobby Isaac (23)	Dodge	85.689
944	51	10/26/69	Rockingham NC	1.017	P	500.36	LeeRoy Yarbrough (13)	Ford	111.938	Charlie Glotzbach (4)	Dodge	136.972
945	52	11/2/69	Jefferson GA	0.500	P	100.00	Bobby Isaac (20)	Dodge	85.106	David Pearson (52)	Ford	89.565
946	53	11/9/69	Macon GA	0.548	P	274.00	Bobby Allison (16)	Dodge	81.079	Bobby Isaac (24)	Dodge	98.148
947	54	12/7/69	College Station TX	2.000	P	500.00	Bobby Isaac (21)	Dodge	144.277	Buddy Baker (8)	Dodge	176.284

1970

Race #	Year #	Date	Site	Track	Surface	Miles	Race Winner	Car	Speed	Pole Winner	Car	Speed
948	1	1/18/70	Riverside CA	2.700	P	500.42	A.J. Foyt (3)	Ford	97.450	Dan Gurney (3)	Plymouth	112.060
949	2	2/19/70	Daytona Beach FL	2.500	P	125.00	Cale Yarborough (12)	Mercury	183.295	Cale Yarborough (15)	Mercury	194.015
950	**3**	**2/19/70**	**Daytona Beach FL**	**2.500**	**P**	**125.00**	**Charlie Glotzbach (2)**	**Dodge**	**147.734**	**Buddy Baker (9)**	**Dodge**	**192.624**
951	4	2/22/70	Daytona Beach FL	2.500	P	500.00	Pete Hamilton	Plymouth	149.601	Cale Yarborough (16)	Mercury	194.015
952	5	3/1/70	Richmond VA	0.542	P	271.00	James Hylton	Ford	82.044	Richard Petty (86)	Plymouth	89.137
953	6	3/8/70	Rockingham NC	1.017	P	500.36	Richard Petty (102)	Plymouth	116.117	Bobby Allison (10)	Dodge	139.048
954	7	3/15/70	Savannah GA	0.500	P	100.00	Richard Petty (103)	Plymouth	82.418	Richard Petty (87)	Plymouth	85.874
955	8	3/29/70	Atlanta GA	1.522	P	499.22	Bobby Allison (17)	Dodge	139.554	Cale Yarborough (17)	Mercury	159.929
956	9	4/5/70	Bristol TN	0.533	P	266.50	Donnie Allison (3)	Ford	87.543	David Pearson (53)	Ford	107.079
957	10	4/12/70	Talladega AL	2.660	P	500.08	Pete Hamilton (2)	Plymouth	152.321	Bobby Isaac (25)	Dodge	199.658
958	11	4/18/70	N Wilkesboro NC	0.625	P	250.00	Richard Petty (104)	Plymouth	94.246	Bobby Isaac (26)	Dodge	107.041
959	12	4/30/70	Columbia SC	0.500	D	100.00	Richard Petty (105)	Plymouth	62.685	Larry Baumel	Ford	72.329
960	13	5/9/70	Darlington SC	1.366	P	397.51	David Pearson (58)	Ford	129.668	Charlie Glotzbach (5)	Dodge	153.822
961	14	5/15/70	Beltsville MD	0.500	P	150.00	Bobby Isaac (22)	Dodge	76.370	James Hylton (3)	Ford	83.128
962	15	5/18/70	Hampton VA	0.400	P	120.00	Bobby Isaac (23)	Dodge	73.245	Bobby Isaac (27)	Dodge	79.659
963	16	5/24/70	Charlotte NC	1.500	P	600.00	Donnie Allison (4)	Ford	129.680	Bobby Isaac (28)	Dodge	159.277
964	17	5/28/70	Maryville TN	0.520	P	104.00	Bobby Isaac (24)	Dodge	82.558	Bobby Allison (11)	Dodge	92.094
965	18	5/31/70	Martinsville VA	0.525	P	197.90	Bobby Isaac (25)	Dodge	68.584	Donnie Allison (4)	Ford	82.609
966	19	6/7/70	Brooklyn MI	2.040	P	400.88	Cale Yarborough (13)	Mercury	138.302	Pete Hamilton	Plymouth	162.737
967	20	6/14/70	Riverside CA	2.620	P	400.86	Richard Petty (106)	Plymouth	101.120	Bobby Allison (12)	Dodge	111.621
968	21	6/20/70	Hickory NC	0.363	P	100.19	Bobby Isaac (26)	Dodge	68.011	Bobby Isaac (29)	Dodge	79.596
969	22	6/26/70	Kingsport TN	0.337	P	100.09	Richard Petty (107)	Plymouth	65.583	Richard Petty (88)	Plymouth	75.056
970	23	6/27/70	Greenville SC	0.500	P	100.00	Bobby Isaac (27)	Dodge	75.345	Bobby Isaac (30)	Dodge	82.327
971	24	7/4/70	Daytona Beach FL	2.500	P	400.00	Donnie Allison (5)	Ford	162.235	Cale Yarborough (18)	Mercury	191.640
972	25	7/7/70	Malta NY	0.362	P	90.50	Richard Petty (108)	Plymouth	68.589	Bobby Isaac (31)	Dodge	73.213
973	26	7/9/70	Thompson CT	0.542	P	108.40	Bobby Isaac (28)	Dodge	80.296	Bobby Isaac (32)	Dodge	87.029
974	27	7/12/70	Trenton NJ	1.500	P	300.00	Richard Petty (109)	Plymouth	120.724	Bobby Isaac (33)	Dodge	131.749
975	28	7/19/70	Bristol TN	0.533	P	266.50	Bobby Allison (18)	Dodge	84.880	Cale Yarborough (19)	Mercury	107.375
976	29	7/24/70	Maryville TN	0.520	P	104.00	Richard Petty (110)	Plymouth	84.956	Richard Petty (89)	Plymouth	91.264
977	30	7/25/70	Nashville TN	0.596	P	250.32	Bobby Isaac (29)	Dodge	87.943	LeeRoy Yarbrough (10)	Ford	114.115
978	31	8/2/70	Atlanta GA	1.522	P	499.22	Richard Petty (111)	Plymouth	142.712	Fred Lorenzen (32)	Dodge	157.625
979	32	8/6/70	Columbia SC	0.500	D	100.00	Bobby Isaac (30)	Dodge	67.101	Richard Petty (90)	Plymouth	72.695
980	33	8/11/70	Ona WV	0.455	P	131.10	Richard Petty (112)	Plymouth	78.358	Bobby Allison (13)	Ford	150.555
981	34	8/16/70	Brooklyn MI	2.040	P	401.88	Charlie Glotzbach (3)	Dodge	147.571	Charlie Glotzbach (6)	Dodge	157.363
982	35	8/23/70	Talladega AL	2.660	P	500.08	Pete Hamilton (3)	Plymouth	158.517	Bobby Isaac (34)	Dodge	186.834
983	36	8/28/70	Winston-Salem NC	0.250	P	62.50	Richard Petty (113)	Plymouth	51.527	Richard Petty (91)	Plymouth	54.553
984	37	8/29/70	South Boston VA	0.357	P	100.32	Richard Petty (114)	Plymouth	73.060	Richard Petty (92)	Plymouth	81.187
985	38	9/7/70	Darlington SC	1.366	P	501.32	Buddy Baker (3)	Dodge	128.817	David Pearson (54)	Ford	150.555
986	39	9/11/70	Hickory NC	0.363	P	100.19	Bobby Isaac (31)	Dodge	73.365	Bobby Isaac (35)	Dodge	78.411
987	40	9/13/70	Richmond VA	0.542	P	271.00	Richard Petty (115)	Plymouth	81.476	Richard Petty (93)	Plymouth	87.014
988	41	9/20/70	Dover DE	0.500	P	300.00	Richard Petty (116)	Plymouth	112.103	Bobby Isaac (36)	Dodge	129.538
989	42	9/30/70	Raleigh NC	1.000	D	100.00	Richard Petty (117)	Plymouth	68.376	John Sears (2)	Ford	71.380
990	43	10/4/70	N Wilkesboro NC	0.625	P	250.00	Bobby Isaac (32)	Dodge	90.162	Bobby Isaac (37)	Dodge	105.406
991	44	10/11/70	Charlotte NC	1.500	P	501.00	LeeRoy Yarbrough (14)	Mercury	123.246	Charlie Glotzbach (7)	Dodge	147.273
992	45	10/18/70	Martinsville VA	0.525	P	262.50	Richard Petty (118)	Plymouth	72.235	Bobby Allison (14)	Dodge	82.167
993	46	11/8/70	Macon GA	0.548	P	274.00	Richard Petty (119)	Plymouth	83.284	Richard Petty (94)	Plymouth	94.064
994	47	11/15/70	Rockingham NC	1.017	P	500.36	Cale Yarborough (14)	Mercury	117.811	Charlie Glotzbach (8)	Dodge	136.498
995	48	11/22/70	Hampton VA	0.395	P	118.50	Bobby Allison (19)	Dodge	69.585	Benny Parsons	Ford	78.239

1971

Race #	Year #	Date	Site	Track	Surface	Miles	Race Winner	Car	Speed	Pole Winner	Car	Speed
996	1	1/10/71	Riverside CA	2.620	P	500.42	Ray Elder	Dodge	100.783	Richard Petty (95)	Plymouth	107.084
997	2	2/11/71	Dayton Beach FL	2.500	P	125.00	Pete Hamilton (4)	Plymouth	175.029	A.J. Foyt (2)	Mercury	182.744
998	2	2/11/71	Daytona Beach FL	2.500	P	125.00	David Pearson (59)	Mercury	168.278	Bobby Isaac (38)	Dodge	180.050
999	4	2/14/71	Daytona Beach FL	2.500	P	500.00	Richard Petty (120)	Plymouth	144.744	A.J. Foyt (3)	Mercury	182.744
1000	5	2/28/71	Ontario CA	2.500	P	500.00	A.J. Foyt (4)	Mercury	134.168	A.J. Foyt (4)	Mercury	151.711
1001	6	3/7/71	Richmond VA	0.542	P	271.00	Richard Petty (121)	Plymouth	79.838	Dave Marcis	Dodge	87.178
1002	7	3/14/71	Rockingham NC	1.017	P	500.36	Richard Petty (122)	Plymouth	118.696	Fred Lorenzen (33)	Plymouth	133.892
1003	8	3/21/71	Hickory NC	0.363	P	100.19	Richard Petty (123)	Plymouth	67.700	Bobby Allison (15)	Dodge	79.001
1004	9	3/28/71	Bristol TN	0.533	P	266.50	David Pearson (60)	Ford	91.704	David Pearson (55)	Ford	105.525
1005	10	4/4/71	Atlanta GA	1.522	P	499.22	A.J. Foyt (5)	Mercury	131.375	A.J. Foyt (5)	Mercury	155.152
1006	11	4/8/71	Columbia SC	0.500	P	100.00	Richard Petty (124)	Plymouth	76.513	James Hylton (4)	Ford	84.229
1007	12	4/10/71	Greenville SC	0.500	P	100.00	Bobby Isaac (33)	Dodge	78.159	David Pearson (56)	Ford	82.257
1008	13	4/15/71	Maryville TN	0.520	P	104.00	Richard Petty (125)	Plymouth	88.697	Friday Hassler	Chevy	91.464

Race #	Year #	Date	Site	Track	Surface	Miles	Race Winner	Car	Speed	Pole Winner	Car	Speed
1009	14	4/18/71	N Wilkesboro NC	0.625	P	250.00	Richard Petty (126)	Plymouth	98.479	Bobby Isaac (39)	Dodge	106.217
1010	15	4/25/71	Martinsville VA	0.525	P	262.50	Richard Petty (127)	Plymouth	77.707	Donnie Allison (5)	Mercury	82.529
1011	16	5/2/71	Darlington SC	1.366	P	400.24	Buddy Baker (4)	Dodge	130.678	Donnie Allison (6)	Mercury	149.826
1012	17	5/9/71	South Boston VA	0.357	P	100.32	Benny Parsons	Ford	72.271	Bobby Isaac (40)	Dodge	81.548
1013	18	5/16/71	Talladega AL	2.660	P	500.08	Donnie Allison (6)	Mercury	147.419	Donnie Allison (7)	Mercury	185.869
1014	19	5/21/71	Asheville NC	0.333	P	99.90	Richard Petty (128)	Plymouth	71.231	Richard Petty (96)	Plymouth	79.598
1015	20	5/23/71	Kingsport TN	0.337	P	101.10	Bobby Isaac (34)	Dodge	63.242	Bobby Isaac (41)	Dodge	75.167
1016	21	5/30/71	Charlotte NC	1.500	P	600.00	Bobby Allison (20)	Mercury	140.422	Charlie Glotzbach (9)	Chevy	157.788
1017	22	6/6/71	Dover DE	1.000	P	500.00	Bobby Allison (21)	Ford	123.119	Richard Petty (97)	Plymouth	129.486
1018	23	6/13/71	Brooklyn MI	2.000	P	401.88	Bobby Allison (22)	Mercury	149.567	Bobby Allison (16)	Mercury	161.190
1019	24	6/20/71	Riverside CA	2.620	P	40.86	Bobby Allison (23)	Dodge	93.427	Bobby Allison (17)	Dodge	107.315
1020	25	6/23/71	Houston TX	0.500	P	150.00	Bobby Allison (24)	Dodge	73.489	Bobby Allison (18)	Dodge	78.226
1021	26	6/26/71	Greenville SC	0.500	P	100.00	Richard Petty (129)	Plymouth	74.297	Bobby Allison (19)	Ford	81.555
1022	27	7/4/71	Daytona Beach FL	2.500	P	400.00	Bobby Isaac (35)	Dodge	161.947	Donnie Allison (8)	Mercury	183.228
1023	28	7/11/71	Bristol TN	0.533	P	266.50	Charlie Glotzbach (4)	Chevy	101.074	Richard Petty (98)	Plymouth	104.589
1024	29	7/14/71	Malta NY	0.362	P	90.50	Richard Petty (130)	Plymouth	66.748	Richard Petty (99)	Plymouth	74.896
1025	30	7/15/71	Islip NY	0.200	P	46.00	Richard Petty (131)	Plymouth	49.925	Richard Petty (100)	Plymouth	46.133
1026	31	7/18/71	Trenton NJ	1.500	P	300.00	Richard Petty (132)	Plymouth	120.347	Friday Hassler (2)	Chevy	129.134
1027	32	7/24/71	Nashville TN	0.596	P	250.32	Richard Petty (133)	Plymouth	89.667	Richard Petty (101)	Plymouth	114.628
1028	33	8/1/71	Atlanta GA	1.522	P	499.22	Richard Petty (134)	Plymouth	129.061	Buddy Baker (10)	Dodge	155.796
1029	34	8/6/71	Winston-Salem NC	0.250	P	62.50	Bobby Allison (25)	Mustang	44.792	Richard Petty (102)	Plymouth	55.283
1030	35	8/8/71	Ona WV	0.455	P	227.50	Richard Petty (135)	Plymouth	83.805	Bobby Allison (20)	Mustang	84.053
1031	36	8/15/71	Brooklyn MI	2.000	P	401.88	Bobby Allison (26)	Mercury	149.862	Pete Hamilton (2)	Plymouth	161.901
1032	37	8/22/71	Talladega AL	2.660	P	500.08	Bobby Allison (27)	Mercury	145.945	Donnie Allison (9)	Mercury	187.323
1033	38	8/27/71	Columbia SC	0.500	P	102.00	Richard Petty (136)	Plymouth	64.831	Richard Petty (103)	Plymouth	85.137
1034	39	8/28/71	Hickory NC	0.363	P	100.19	Tiny Lund (4)	Camaro	72.937	Dave Marcis (2)	Dodge	80.147
1035	40	9/6/71	Darlington SC	1.366	P	501.32	Bobby Allison (28)	Mercury	131.398	Bobby Allison (21)	Mercury	147.915
1036	41	9/26/71	Martinsville VA	0.525	P	262.50	Bobby Isaac (36)	Dodge	73.681	Bobby Isaac (42)	Dodge	83.635
1037	42	10/10/71	Charlotte NC	1.500	P	357.00	Bobby Allison (29)	Mercury	126.140	Charlie Glotzbach (10)	Chevy	157.085
1038	43	10/17/71	Dover DE	1.000	P	500.00	Richard Petty (137)	Plymouth	123.254	Bobby Allison (22)	Mercury	132.811
1039	44	10/24/71	Rockingham NC	1.017	P	500.36	Richard Petty (138)	Plymouth	113.405	Charlie Glotzbach (11)	Chevy	135.167
1040	45	11/7/71	Macon GA	0.548	P	274.00	Bobby Allison (30)	Ford	80.859	Bobby Allison (23)	Ford	95.334
1041	46	11/14/71	Richmond VA	0.542	P	271.00	Richard Petty (139)	Plymouth	80.025	Bill Dennis	Mercury	---
1042	47	11/21/71	N Wilkesboro NC	0.625	P	250.00	Tiny Lund (5)	Camaro	96.174	Charlie Glotzbach (12)	Chevy	107.558
1043	48	12/12/71	College Station TX	2.000	P	500.00	Richard Petty (140)	Plymouth	144.000	Pete Hamilton (3)	Plymouth	170.830

1972

Race #	Year #	Date	Site	Track	Surface	Miles	Race Winner	Car	Speed	Pole Winner	Car	Speed
1044	1	1/23/72	Riverside CA	2.620	P	387.76	Richard Petty (141)	Plymouth	104.016	A.J. Foyt (6)	Mercury	110.033
1045	2	2/20/72	Daytona Beach FL	2.500	P	500.00	A.J. Foyt (6)	Mercury	161.550	Bobby Isaac (43)	Dodge	186.632
1046	3	2/27/72	Richmond VA	0.542	P	271.00	Richard Petty (142)	Plymouth	76.258	Bobby Allison (24)	Chevy	90.573
1047	4	3/5/72	Ontario CA	2.500	P	500.00	A.J. Foyt (7)	Mercury	127.082	A.J. Foyt (7)	Mercury	153.217
1048	5	3/12/72	Rockingham NC	1.017	P	500/364	Bobby Isaac (37)	Dodge	113.895	Bobby Allison (25)	Chevy	137.539
1049	6	3/26/72	Atlanta GA	1.522	P	499.22	Bobby Allison (31)	Chevy	128.214	Bobby Allison (26)	Chevy	156.245
1050	7	4/9/72	Bristol TN	0.533	P	266.50	Bobby Allison (32)	Chevy	92.826	Bobby Allison (27)	Chevy	106.875
1051	8	4/16/72	Darlington SC	1.366	P	501.32	David Pearson (61)	Mercury	124.406	David Pearson (57)	Mercury	148.209
1052	9	4/23/72	N Wilkesboro NC	0.625	P	250.00	Richard Petty (143)	Plymouth	86.381	Bobby Isaac (44)	Dodge	107.506
1053	10	4/30/72	Martinsville VA	0.525	P	262.50	Richard Petty (144)	Plymouth	72.657	Bobby Allison (28)	Chevy	84.163
1054	11	5/7/72	Talladega AL	2.660	P	500.08	David Pearson (62)	Mercury	134.400	Bobby Isaac (45)	Dodge	192.428
1055	12	5/28/72	Charlotte NC	1.500	P	600.00	Buddy Baker (5)	Dodge	142.255	Bobby Allison (29)	Chevy	158.162
1056	13	6/4/72	Dover DE	1.000	P	500.00	Bobby Allison (33)	Chevy	118.019	Bobby Isaac (46)	Dodge	130.809
1057	14	6/11/72	Brooklyn MI	2.000	P	400.00	David Pearson (63)	Mercury	146.639	Bobby Isaac (47)	Dodge	160.764
1058	15	6/18/72	Riverside CA	2.620	P	400.86	Ray Elder (2)	Dodge	98.761	Richard Petty (104)	Plymouth	108.688
1059	16	6/25/72	College Station TX	2.000	P	500.00	Richard Petty (145)	Plymouth	144.185	Richard Petty (105)	Plymouth	169.412
1060	17	7/4/72	Daytona Beach FL	2.500	P	400.00	David Pearson (64)	Mercury	160.821	Bobby Isaac (48)	Dodge	186.277
1061	18	7/9/72	Bristol TN	0.533	P	266.50	Bobby Allison (34)	Chevy	92.735	Bobby Allison (30)	Chevy	107.279
1062	19	7/16/72	Trenton NJ	1.500	P	300.00	Bobby Allison (35)	Chevy	114.030	Bobby Isaac (49)	Dodge	133.126
1063	20	7/23/72	Atlanta GA	1.522	P	499.22	Bobby Allison (36)	Chevy	131.295	David Pearson (58)	Mercury	158.353
1064	21	8/6/72	Talladega AL	2.660	P	500.08	James Hylton (2)	Mercury	148.728	Bobby Isaac (50)	Dodge	190.677
1065	22	8/20/72	Brooklyn MI	2.000	P	400.00	David Pearson (65)	Mercury	134.416	Richard Petty (106)	Dodge	157.607
1066	23	8/27/72	Nashville TN	0.596	P	250.32	Bobby Allison (37)	Chevy	92.578	Bobby Allison (31)	Chevy	116.932
1067	24	9/4/72	Darlington SC	1.366	P	501.32	Bobby Allison (38)	Chevy	128.124	Bobby Allison (32)	Chevy	152.228
1068	25	9/10/72	Richmond VA	0.542	P	271.00	Richard Petty (146)	Plymouth	75.899	Bobby Allison (33)	Chevy	89.669
1069	26	9/17/72	Dover DE	1.000	P	500.00	David Pearson (66)	Mercury	120.506	Bobby Allison (34)	Chevy	133.323
1070	27	9/24/72	Martinsville VA	0.525	P	262.50	Richard Petty (147)	Plymouth	69.989	Bobby Allison (35)	Chevy	85.890
1071	28	10/1/72	N Wilkesboro NC	0.625	P	250.00	Richard Petty (148)	Plymouth	95.816	Buddy Baker (11)	Dodge	105.922
1072	29	10/8/72	Charlotte NC	1.500	P	501.00	Bobby Allison (39)	Chevy	133.234	David Pearson (59)	Mercury	158.539
1073	30	10/22/72	Rockingham NC	1.017	P	500.36	Bobby Allison (40)	Chevy	118.275	David Pearson (60)	Mercury	127.528
1074	31	11/12/72	College Station TX	2.000	P	500.00	Buddy Baker (6)	Dodge	147.059	A.J. Foyt (8)	Mercury	170.273

1973

Race #	Year #	Date	Site	Track	Surface	Miles	Race Winner	Car	Speed	Pole Winner	Car	Speed
1075	1	1/21/73	Riverside CA	2.620	P	500.00	Mark Donohue	Matador	104.055	David Pearson (61)	Mercury	110.856

Race #	Year #	Date	Site	Track	Surface	Miles	Race Winner	Car	Speed	Pole Winner	Car	Speed
1076	2	2/18/73	Daytona Beach FL	2.500	P	500.00	Richard Petty (149)	Dodge	157.205	Buddy Baker (12)	Dodge	185.662
1077	3	2/25/73	Richmond VA	0.542	P	271.00	Richard Petty (150)	Dodge	74.764	Bobby Allison (36)	Chevy	90.952
1078	4	3/18/73	Rockingham NC	1.017	P	500.36	David Pearson (67)	Mercury	118.649	David Pearson (62)	Mercury	134.021
1079	5	3/25/73	Bristol TN	0.533	P	266.50	Cale Yarborough (15)	Chevy	88.952	Cale Yarborough (20)	Chevy	107.608
1080	6	4/1/73	Atlanta GA	1.522	P	499.22	David Pearson (68)	Mercury	139.351	No Time Trials	NTT	NTT
1081	7	4/8/73	N Wilkesboro NC	0.625	P	250.00	Richard Petty (151)	Dodge	97.224	Bobby Allison (37)	Chevy	106.750
1082	8	4/15/73	Darlington SC	1.366	P	501.32	David Pearson (69)	Mercury	122.655	David Pearson (63)	Mercury	153.463
1083	9	4/29/73	Martinsville VA	0.525	P	262.50	David Pearson (70)	Mercury	70.251	David Pearson (64)	Mercury	86.369
1084	10	5/6/73	Talladega AL	2.660	P	500.08	David Pearson (71)	Mercury	131.956	Buddy Baker (13)	Dodge	193.435
1085	11	5/12/73	Nashville TN	0.596	P	250.32	Cale Yarborough (16)	Chevy	98.419	Cale Yarborough (21)	Chevy	105.741
1086	12	5/27/73	Charlotte NC	1.500	P	600.00	Buddy Baker (7)	Dodge	124.890	Buddy Baker (14)	Dodge	158.051
1087	13	6/3/73	Dover DE	1.000	P	500.00	David Pearson (72)	Mercury	119.745	David Pearson (65)	Mercury	133.111
1088	14	6/10/73	College Station TX	2.000	P	500.00	Richard Petty (152)	Dodge	142.114	Buddy Baker (15)	Dodge	169.248
1089	15	6/17/73	Riverside CA	2.620	P	400.86	Bobby Allison (41)	Chevy	100.215	Richard Petty (107)	Dodge	110.027
1090	16	6/24/73	Brooklyn Mi	2.000	P	400.00	David Pearson (73)	Mercury	153.485	Buddy Baker (16)	Dodge	158.273
1091	17	7/4/73	Daytona Beach FL	2.500	P	400.00	David Pearson (74)	Mercury	158.468	Bobby Allison (38)	Chevy	179.619
1092	18	7/8/73	Bristol TN	0.533	P	266.50	Benny Parsons (2)	Chevy	91.342	Cale Yarborough (22)	Chevy	106.472
1093	19	7/22/73	Atlanta GA	1.522	P	499.22	David Pearson (75)	Mercury	130.211	Richard Petty (108)	Dodge	157.163
1094	20	8/12/73	Talladega AL	2.660	P	500.08	Dick Brooks	Plymouth	145.454	Bobby Allison (39)	Chevy	187.064
1095	21	8/25/73	Nashville TN	0.596	P	250.32	Buddy Baker (8)	Dodge	89.310	Cale Yarborough (23)	Chevy	103.024
1096	22	9/3/73	Darlington SC	1.366	P	501.32	Cale Yarborough (17)	Chevy	134.033	David Pearson (66)	Mercury	150.366
1097	23	9/9/73	Richmond VA	0.542	P	271.00	Richard Petty (153)	Dodge	63.215	Bobby Allison (40)	Chevy	90.245
1098	24	9/16/73	Dover DE	1.000	P	500.00	David Pearson (76)	Mercury	112.852	David Pearson (67)	Mercury	124.649
1099	25	9/23/73	N Wilkesboro NC	0.625	P	250.00	Bobby Allison (42)	Chevy	95.198	Bobby Allison (41)	Chevy	105.619
1100	26	9/30/73	Martinsville VA	0.525	P	252.00	Richard Petty (154)	Dodge	68.831	Cale Yarborough (24)	Chevy	85.922
1101	27	10/7/73	Charlotte NC	1.500	P	501.00	Cale Yarborough (18)	Chevy	145.240	David Pearson (68)	Mercury	158.315
1102	28	10/21/73	Rockingham NC	1.017	P	500.36	David Pearson (77)	Mercury	117.749	Richard Petty (109)	Dodge	135.748

1974

Race #	Year #	Date	Site	Track	Surface	Miles	Race Winner	Car	Speed	Pole Winner	Car	Speed
1103	1	1/26/74	Riverside CA	2.620	P	500.42	Cale Yarborough (19)	Chevy	101.140	David Pearson (69)	Mercury	110.098
1104	2	2/17/74	Daytona Beach FL	2.500	P	450.00	Richard Petty (155)	Dodge	140.894	David Pearson (70)	Mercury	185.817
1105	3	2/24/74	Richmond VA	0.542	P	243.90	Bobby Allison (43)	Chevy	80.095	Bobby Allison (42)	Chevy	90.353
1106	4	3/3/74	Rockingham NC	1.017	P	450.53	Richard Petty (156)	Dodge	121.622	Cale Yarborough (25)	Chevy	134.868
1107	5	3/17/74	Bristol TN	0.533	P	239.85	Cale Yarborough (20)	Chevy	64.533	Donnie Allison (10)	Chevy	107.785
1108	6	3/24/74	Atlanta GA	1.522	P	450.51	Cale Yarborough (21)	Chevy	136.910	David Pearson (71)	Mercury	159.242
1109	7	4/7/74	Darlington SC	1.366	P	450.78	David Pearson (78)	Mercury	117.543	Donnie Allison (11)	Chevy	150.689
1110	8	4/21/74	N Wilkesboro NC	0.625	P	225.00	Richard Petty (157)	Dodge	96.200	Bobby Allison (43)	Chevy	105.669
1111	9	4/28/74	Martinsville VA	0.525	P	236.25	Cale Yarborough (22)	Chevy	70.427	Cale Yarborough (26)	Chevy	84.362
1112	10	5/5/74	Talladega AL	2.660	P	452.20	David Pearson (79)	Mercury	130.220	David Pearson (72)	Mercury	186.086
1113	11	5/11/74	Nashville TN	0.596	P	238.40	Richard Petty (158)	Dodge	84.240	Bobby Allison (44)	Chevy	100.088
1114	12	5/19/74	Dover DE	1.000	P	450.00	Cale Yarborough (23)	Chevy	119.990	David Pearson (73)	Mercury	134.403
1115	13	5/26/74	Charlotte NC	1.500	P	540.00	David Pearson (80)	Mercury	135.720	David Pearson (74)	Mercury	157.498
1116	14	6/9/74	Riverside CA	2.620	P	361.56	Cale Yarborough (24)	Chevy	102.489	George Follmer	Matador	109.093
1117	15	6/16/74	Brooklyn MI	2.000	P	360.00	Richard Petty (159)	Dodge	127.098	David Pearson (75)	Mercury	156.426
1118	16	7/4/74	Daytona Beach FL	2.500	P	400.00	David Pearson (81)	Mercury	138.310	David Pearson (76)	Mercury	180.759
1119	17	7/14/74	Bristol TN	0.533	P	266.50	Cale Yarborough (25)	Chevy	75.430	Richard Petty (110)	Dodge	107.351
1120	18	7/20/74	Nashville TN	0.596	P	250.32	Cale Yarborough (26)	Chevy	76.368	Darrell Waltrip	Chevy	101.274
1121	19	7/28/74	Atlanta GA	1.522	P	499.22	Richard Petty (160)	Dodge	131.651	Cale Yarborough (27)	Chevy	156.750
1122	20	8/4/74	Pocono PA	2.500	P	480.00	Richard Petty (161)	Dodge	115.593	Buddy Baker (17)	Ford	144.122
1123	21	8/11/74	Talladega AL	2.660	P	500.08	Richard Petty (162)	Dodge	148.637	David Pearson (77)	Mercury	184.926
1124	22	8/25/74	Brooklyn Mi	2.000	P	400.00	David Pearson (82)	Mercury	133.045	David Pearson (78)	Mercury	157.946
1125	23	9/2/74	Darlington SC	1.366	P	501.32	Cale Yarborough (27)	Chevy	111.075	Richard Petty (111)	Dodge	150.132
1126	24	9/8/74	Richmond VA	0.542	P	271.00	Richard Petty (163)	Dodge	64.430	Richard Petty (112)	Dodge	88.852
1127	25	9/15/74	Dover DE	1.000	P	500.00	Richard Petty (164)	Dodge	113.640	Buddy Baker (18)	Ford	133.640
1128	26	9/22/74	N Wilkesboro NC	0.625	P	250.00	Cale Yarborough (28)	Chevy	80.782	Richard Petty (113)	Dodge	105.087
1129	27	9/29/74	Martinsville VA	0.525	P	262.50	Earl Ross	Chevy	66.232	Richard Petty (114)	Dodge	84.119
1130	28	10/6/74	Charlotte NC	1.500	P	501.00	David Pearson (83)	Mercury	119.912	David Pearson (79)	Mercury	158.749
1131	29	10/20/74	Rockingham NC	1.017	P	500.36	David Pearson (84)	Mercury	118.493	Richard Petty (115)	Dodge	135.297
1132	30	11/24/74	Ontario CA	2.500	P	500.00	Bobby Allison (44)	Matador	134.963	Richard Petty (116)	Dodge	149.940

1975

Race #	Year #	Date	Site	Track	Surface	Miles	Race Winner	Car	Speed	Pole Winner	Car	Speed
1133	1	1/19/75	Riverside CA	2.620	P	500.42	Bobby Allison (45)	Matador	98.627	Bobby Allison (45)	Matador	110.382
1134	2	2/16/75	Daytona Beach FL	2.500	P	500.00	Benny Parsons (3)	Chevy	153.649	Donnie Allison (12)	Chevy	185.827
1135	3	2/23/75	Richmond VA	0.542	P	271.00	Richard Petty (165)	Dodge	74.913	Richard Petty (117)	Dodge	93.340
1136	4	3/2/75	Rockingham NC	1.017	P	500/364	Cale Yarborough (29)	Chevy	117.588	Buddy Baker (19)	Ford	137.611
1137	5	3/16/75	Bristol TN	0.533	P	266.50	Richard Petty (166)	Dodge	97.053	Buiddy Baker (20)	Ford	110.951
1138	6	3/25/75	Atlanta GA	1.522	P	499.22	Richard Petty (167)	Dodge	133.496	Richard Petty (118)	Dodge	159.029
1139	7	4/6/75	N Wilkesboro NC	0.625	P	250.00	Richard Petty (168)	Dodge	90.009	Darrell Waltrip (2)	Chevy	105.520
1140	8	4/13/75	Darlington SC	1.366	P	501.32	Bobby Allison (46)	Matador	117.597	David Pearson (80)	Mercury	155.433
1141	9	4/27/75	Martinsville VA	0.525	P	262.50	Richard Petty (169)	Dodge	69.282	Benny Parsons (2)	Chevy	85.789
1142	10	5/4/75	Talladega AL	2.660	P	500.08	Buddy Baker (9)	Ford	144.948	Buddy Baker (21)	Ford	189.947
1143	11	5/10/75	Nashville TN	0.596	P	250.32	Darrell Waltrip	Chevy	94.107	Darrell Waltrip (3)	Chevy	103.793

Race #	Year #	Date	Site	Track	Surface	Miles	Race Winner	Car	Speed	Pole Winner	Car	Speed
1144	12	5/19/75	Dover DE	1.000	P	500.00	David Pearson (85)	Mercury	100.820	David Pearson (81)	Mercury	136.612
1145	13	5/25/75	Charlotte NC	1.500	P	600.00	Richard Petty (170)	Dodge	145.327	David Pearson (82)	Mercury	159.353
1146	14	6/8/75	Riverside CA	2.620	P	400.86	Richard Petty (171)	Dodge	101.028	Bobby Allison (46)	Matador	110.353
1147	15	6/15/75	Brooklyn MI	2.000	P	400.00	David Pearson (86)	Mercury	131.398	Cale Yarborough (28)	Chevy	158.541
1148	16	7/4/75	Daytona Beach FL	2.500	P	400.00	Richard Petty (172)	Dodge	158.381	Donnie Allison (13)	Chevy	186.737
1149	17	7/20/75	Nashville TN	0.596	P	250.32	Cale Yarborough (30)	Chevy	89.792	Benny Parsons (3)	Chevy	103.247
1150	18	8/3/75	Pocono PA	2.500	P	500.00	David Pearson (87)	Mercury	111.179	Bobby Allison (47)	Matador	146.491
1151	19	8/17/75	Talladega AL	2.660	P	500.08	Buddy Baker (10)	Ford	130.892	Dave Marcis (3)	Dodge	191.340
1152	20	8/24/75	Brooklyn MI	2.000	P	400.00	Richard Petty (173)	Dodge	107.583	David Pearson (83)	Mercury	159.798
1153	21	9/1/75	Darlington SC	1.366	P	501.32	Bobby Allison (47)	Matador	116.825	David Pearson (84)	Mercury	153.401
1154	22	9/14/75	Dover DE	1.000	P	500.00	Richard Petty (174)	Dodge	111.372	Dave Marcis (4)	Dodge	133.953
1155	23	9/21/75	N Wilkesboro NC	0.625	P	250.00	Richard Petty (175)	Dodge	88.986	Richard Petty (119)	Dodge	105.500
1156	24	9/28/75	Martinsville VA	0.525	P	262.50	Dave Marcis	Dodge	75.819	Cale Yarborough (29)	Chevy	86.199
1157	25	10/5/75	Charlotte NC	1.500	P	501.00	Richard Petty (176)	Dodge	132.209	David Pearson (85)	Mercury	161.071
1158	26	10/12/75	Richmond VA	0.542	P	271.00	Darrell Waltrip (2)	Chevy	81.886	Benny Parsons (4)	Chevy	91.071
1159	27	10/19/75	Rockingham NC	1.017	P	500.36	Cale Yarborough (31)	Chevy	120.129	Dave Marcis (5)	Dodge	132.021
1160	28	11/2/75	Bristol TN	0.533	P	266.50	Richard Petty (177)	Dodge	97.016	Cale Yarborough (30)	Chevy	110.162
1161	29	11/9/75	Atlanta GA	1.522	P	499.22	Buddy Baker (11)	Ford	130.990	Dave Marcis (6)	Dodge	160.662
1162	30	11/23/75	Ontario CA	2.500	P	500.00	Buddy Baker (12)	Ford	140.712	David Pearson (86)	Mercury	153.525

1976

Race #	Year #	Date	Site	Track	Surface	Miles	Race Winner	Car	Speed	Pole Winner	Car	Speed
1163	1	1/18/76	Riverside CA	2.620	P	500.42	David Pearson (88)	Mercury	99.180	Bobby Allison (48)	Matador	112.416
1164	2	2/15/76	Daytona Beach FL	2.500	P	500.00	David Pearson (89)	Mercury	152.181	Ramo Stott	Chevy	183.456
1165	3	2/29/76	Rockingham NC	1.017	P	500.36	Richard Petty (178)	Dodge	113.665	Dave Marcis (7)	Dodge	138.287
1166	4	3/7/76	Richmond VA	0.542	P	216.80	Dave Marcis (2)	Dodge	72.792	Bobby Allison (49)	Mercury	92.715
1167	5	3/14/76	Bristol TN	0.533	P	213.20	Cale Yarborough (32)	Chevy	87.377	Buddy Baker (22)	Ford	110.720
1168	6	3/21/76	Atlanta GA	1.522	P	499.22	David Pearson (90)	Mercury	128.904	Dave Marcis (8)	Dodge	160.709
1169	7	4/4/76	N Wilkesboro NC	0.625	P	250.00	Cale Yarborough (33)	Chevy	96.858	Dave Marcis (9)	Dodge	108.585
1170	8	4/11/76	Darlington SC	1.366	P	501.32	David Pearson (91)	Mercury	122.973	David Pearson (87)	Mercury	154.171
1171	9	4/25/76	Martinsville VA	0.525	P	262.50	Darrell Waltrip (3)	Chevy	71.759	Dave Marcis (10)	Dodge	86.286
1172	10	5/2/76	Talladega AL	2.660	P	500.08	Buddy Baker (13)	Ford	169.887	Dave Marcis (11)	Dodge	189.197
1173	11	5/8/76	Nashville TN	0.596	P	250.32	Cale Yarborough (34)	Chevy	84.512	Benny Parsons (5)	Chevy	104.328
1175	12	5/16/76	Dover DE	1.000	P	500.00	Benny Parsons (4)	Chevy	115.436	Dave Marcis (12)	Dodge	136.013
1176	13	5/30/76	Charlotte NC	1.500	P	600.00	David Pearson (92)	Mercury	137.352	David Pearson (88)	Mercury	159.132
1176	14	6/6/76	Riverside CA	2.620	P	248.90	David Pearson (93)	Mercury	106.279	David Pearson (89)	Mercury	111.437
1177	15	6/13/76	Brooklyn MI	2.000	P	400.00	David Pearson (94)	Mercury	141.148	Richard Petty (120)	Dodge	158.569
1178	16	7/4/76	Daytona Beach FL	2.500	P	400.00	Cale Yarborough (35)	Chevy	160.966	A.J. Foyt (9)	Chevy	183.090
1179	17	7/16/76	Nashville TN	0.596	P	250.32	Benny Parsons (5)	Chevy	86.908	Neil Bonnett	Mercury	103.049
1180	18	8/1/76	Pocono PA	2.500	P	500.00	Richard Petty (179)	Dodge	115.875	Cale Yarborough (31)	Chevy	147.865
1181	19	8/8/76	Talladega AL	2.660	P	500.08	Dave Marcis (3)	Dodge	157.547	Dave Marcis (13)	Dodge	190.651
1182	20	8/22/76	Brooklyn MI	2.000	P	400.00	David Pearson (95)	Mercury	140.078	David Pearson (90)	Mercury	160.875
1183	21	8/29/76	Bristol TN	0.533	P	213.20	Cale Yarborough (36)	Chevy	99.175	Darrell Waltrip (4)	Chevy	110.300
1184	22	9/6/76	Darlington SC	1.366	P	501.32	David Pearson (96)	Mercury	120.534	David Pearson (91)	Mercury	154.699
1185	23	9/12/76	Richmond VA	0.542	P	216.80	Cale Yarborough (37)	Chevy	77.993	Benny Parsons (6)	Chevy	92.460
1186	24	9/19/76	Dover DE	1.000	P	500.00	Cale Yarborough (38)	Chevy	115.740	Cale Yarborough (32)	Chevy	133.377
1187	25	9/26/76	Martinsville VA	0.525	P	178.50	Cale Yarborough (39)	Chevy	75.370	Darrell Waltrip (5)	Chevy	88.484
1188	26	10/3/76	N Wilkesboro NC	0.625	P	250.00	Cale Yarborough (40)	Chevy	96.380	Darrell Waltrip (6)	Chevy	107.449
1189	27	10/10/76	Charlotte NC	1.500	P	501.00	Donnie Allison (7)	Chevy	141.266	David Pearson (92)	Mercury	161.223
1190	28	10/24/76	Rockingham NC	1.017	P	500.36	Richard Petty (180)	Dodge	117.718	David Pearson (93)	Mercury	139.117
1191	29	11/7/76	Atlanta GA	1.522	P	499.22	Dave Marcis (4)	Dodge	127.396	Buddy Baker (23)	Ford	161.652
1192	30	11/21/76	Ontario CA	2.500	P	500.00	David Pearson (97)	Mercury	137.101	David Pearson (94)	Mercury	153.964

1977

Race #	Year #	Date	Site	Track	Surface	Miles	Race Winner	Car	Speed	Pole Winner	Car	Speed
1193	1	1/16/77	Riverside CA	2.620	P	311.78	David Pearson (98)	Mercury	107.038	Cale Yarborough (33)	Chevy	112.686
1194	2	2/20/77	Daytona Beach FL	2.500	P	500.00	Cale Yarborough (41)	Chevy	153.218	Donnie Allison (14)	Chevy	188.048
1195	3	2/27/77	Richmond VA	0.542	P	133.00	Cale Yarborough (42)	Chevy	73.084	Neil Bonnett (2)	Dodge	93.632
1196	4	3/13/77	Rockingham NC	1.017	P	500.36	Richard Petty (181)	Dodge	97.860	Donnie Allison (15)	Chevy	135.387
1197	5	3/20/77	Atlanta GA	1.522	P	499.22	Richard Petty (182)	Dodge	144.093	Richard Petty (121)	Dodge	162.501
1198	6	3/27/77	N Wilkesboro NC	0.625	P	250.00	Cale Yarborough (43)	Chevy	88.950	Neil Bonnett (3)	Dodge	107.537
1199	7	4/3/77	Darlington SC	1.366	P	501.32	Darrell Waltrip (4)	Chevy	128.817	David Pearson (95)	Mercury	151.269
1200	8	4/17/77	Bristol TN	0.533	P	266.50	Cale Yarborough (44)	Chevy	100.989	Cale Yarborough (34)	Chevy	110.168
1201	9	4/24/77	Martinsville VA	0.525	P	201.98	Cale Yarborough (45)	Chevy	77.405	Neil Bonnett (4)	Dodge	88.923
1202	10	5/1/77	Talladega AL	2.660	P	500.08	Darrell Waltrip (5)	Chevy	164.877	A.J. Foyt (10)	Chevy	192.424
1203	11	5/7/77	Nashville TN	0.596	P	250.32	Benny Parsons (6)	Chevy	87.490	Darrell Waltrip (7)	Chevy	103.643
1294	12	5/15/77	Dover DE	1.000	P	500.00	Cale Yarborough (46)	Chevy	123.327	Richard Petty (122)	Dodge	136.033
1205	13	5/29/77	Charlotte NC	1.500	P	600.00	Richard Petty (183)	Dodge	137.676	David Pearson (96)	Mercury	161.435
1206	14	6/12/77	Riverside CA	2.620	P	248.90	Richard Petty (184)	Dodge	105.021	Richard Petty (123)	Dodge	112.432
1207	15	6/19/77	Brooklyn MI	2.000	P	400.00	Cale Yarborough (47)	Chevy	135.033	David Pearson (97)	Mercury	159.175
1208	16	7/4/77	Daytona Beach FL	2.500	P	400.00	Richard Petty (185)	Dodge	142.716	Neil Bonnett (5)	Dodge	187.191
1209	17	7/16/77	Nashville TN	0.596	P	250.32	Darrell Waltrip (6)	Chevy	78.999	Benny Parsons (7)	Chevy	104.210

Race #	Year #	Date	Site	Track	Surface	Miles	Race Winner	Car	Speed	Pole Winner	Car	Speed
1210	18	7/31/77	Pocono PA	2.500	P	500.00	Benny Parsons (7)	Chevy	128.379	Darrell Waltrip (8)	Chevy	147.591
1211	19	8/7/77	Talladega AL	2.660	P	500.08	Donnie Allison (8)	Chevy	162.524	Benny Parsons (8)	Chevy	192.684
1212	20	8/22/77	Brooklyn MI	2.000	P	400.00	Darrell Waltrip (7)	Chevy	137.944	David Pearson (98)	Mercury	160.346
1213	21	8/28/77	Bristol TN	0.533	P	213.00	Cale Yarborough (48)	Chevy	79.726	Cale Yarborough (35)	Chevy	109.746
1214	22	9/5/77	Darlington SC	1.366	P	501/322	David Pearson (99)	Mercury	106.797	Darrell Waltrip (9)	Chevy	153.493
1215	23	9/11/77	Richmond VA	0.542	P	216.80	Neil Bonnett	Dodge	80.644	Benny Parsons (9)	Chevy	92.281
1216	24	9/18/77	Dover DE	1.000	P	500.00	Benny Parsons (8)	Chevy	114.708	Neil Bonnett (7)	Dodge	134.233
1217	25	9/25/77	Martinsville VA	0.525	P	262.50	Cale Yarborough (49)	Chevy	73.447	Neil Bonnett (8)	Dodge	87.637
1218	26	10/2/77	N Wilkesboro NC	0.625	P	250.00	Darrell Waltrip (8)	Chevy	86.713	Richard Petty (124)	Dodge	108.350
1219	27	10/9/77	Charlotte NC	1.500	P	501.00	Benny Parsons (9)	Chevy	142.780	David Pearson (99)	Mercury	160.892
1220	28	10/23/77	Rockingham NC	1.017	P	500.00	Donnie Allison (9)	Chevy	113.584	Donnie Allison (16)	Chevy	138.685
1221	29	11/6/77	Atlanta GA	1.522	P	407.90	Darrell Waltrip (9)	Chevy	110.052	Sam Sommers	Chevy	160.229
1222	30	11/20/77	Ontario CA	2.500	P	500.00	Neil Bonnett (2)	Dodge	128.296	Richard Petty (125)	Dodge	154.905

1978

Race #	Year #	Date	Site	Track	Surface	Miles	Race Winner	Car	Speed	Pole Winner	Car	Speed
1223	1	1/22/78	Riverside CA	2.620	P	311.78	Cale Yarborough (50)	Olds	102.269	David Pearson (100)	Mercury	113.204
1224	2	2/19/78	Daytona Beach FL	2.500	P	500.00	Bobby Allison (48)	Ford	159.730	Cale Yarborough (36)	Olds	187.536
1225	3	2/26/78	Richmond VA	0.542	P	216.80	Benny Parsons (10)	Chevy	80.304	Neil Bonnett (8)	Dodge	93.382
1226	4	3/5/78	Rockingham NC	1.017	P	500.36	David Pearson (100)	Mercury	116.681	Neil Bonnett (9)	Dodge	141.940
1227	5	3/19/78	Atlanta GA	1.522	P	499.22	Bobby Allison (49)	Ford	142.520	Cale Yarborough (37)	Olds	162.006
1228	6	4/2/78	Bristol TN	0.533	P	266.50	Darrell Waltrip (10)	Chevy	92.401	Neil Bonnett (10)	Dodge	110.409
1229	7	4/9/78	Darlington SC	1.366	P	501.32	Benny Parsons (11)	Chevy	127.544	Bobby Allison (50)	Ford	151.862
1230	8	4/16/78	N. Wilkesboro NC	0.625	P	250.00	Darrell Waltrip (11)	Chevy	92.345	Benny Parsons (10)	Chevy	108.510
1231	9	4/23/78	Martinsville VA	0.525	P	262.50	Darrell Waltrip (12)	Chevy	77.971	Lennie Pond	Chevy	88.637
1232	10	5/14/78	Talladega AL	2.660	P	500.08	Cale Yarborough (51)	Olds	159.699	Cale Yarborough (38)	Olds	191.904
1233	11	5/21/78	Dover DE	1.000	P	500.00	David Pearson (101)	Mercury	114.664	Buddy Baker (24)	Chevy	135.452
1234	12	5/28/78	Charlotte NC	1.500	P	600.00	Darrell Waltrip (13)	Chevy	138.355	David Pearson (101)	Mercury	160.551
1235	13	6/3/78	Nashville TN	0.596	P	250.32	Cale Yarborough (52)	Olds	87.541	Lennie Pond (2)	Chevy	105.094
1236	14	6/11/78	Riverside CA	2.620	P	248.90	Benny Parsons (12)	Chevy	104.311	David Pearson (102)	Mercury	112.882
1237	15	6/18/78	Brooklyn MI	2.000	P	400.00	Cale Yarborough (53)	Olds	149.563	David Pearson (103)	Mercury	163.036
1238	16	7/4/78	Daytona Beach FL	2.500	P	400.00	David Pearson (102)	Mercury	154.340	Cale Yarborough (39)	Olds	186.803
1239	17	7/15/78	Nashville TN	0.596	P	250.32	Cale Yarborough (54)	Olds	88.924	Lennie Pond (3)	Chevy	104.257
1240	18	7/30/78	Pocono PA	2.500	P	500.00	Darrell Waltrip (14)	Chevy	142.540	Benny Parsons (11)	Chevy	149.917
1241	19	8/6/78	Talladega AL	2.660	P	500.08	Lennie Pond	Olds	174.700	Cale Yarborough (40)	Olds	192.917
1242	20	8/20/78	Brooklyn MI	2.000	P	400.00	David Pearson (109)	Mercury	129.566	David Pearson (104)	Mercury	164.073
1243	21	8/26/78	Bristol TN	0.533	P	266.50	Cale Yarborough (55)	Olds	88.628	Lennie Pond (4)	Olds	110.958
1244	22	9/4/78	Darlington SC	1.266	P	501.32	Cale Yarborough (56)	Olds	116.828	David Pearson (105)	Mercury	153.685
1245	23	9/10/78	Richmond VA	0.542	P	216.80	Darrell Waltrip (15)	Chevy	79.568	Darrell Waltrip (10)	Chevy	92.964
1246	24	9/17/78	Dover DE	1.000	P	500.00	Bobby Allison (50)	Ford	119.323	J.D. McDuffie	Chevy	135.480
1247	25	9/24/78	Martinsville VA	0.525	P	262.50	Cale Yarborough (57)	Olds	79.185	Lennie Pond (5)	Chevy	86.558
1248	26	10/1/78	N Wilkesboro NC	0.625	P	150.00	Cale Yarborough (58)	Olds	97.847	Darrell Waltrip (11)	Chevy	109.397
1249	27	10/8/78	Charlotte NC	1.500	P	501.00	Bobby Allison (51)	Ford	141.826	David Pearson (106)	Mercury	161.355
1250	28	10/22/78	Rockingham NC	1.017	P	500.36	Cale Yarborough (59)	Olds	117.288	Cale Yarborough (41)	Olds	142.067
1251	29	11/5/78	Atlanta GA	1.522	P	499.22	Donnie Allison (10)	Chevy	124.312	Cale Yarborough (42)	Olds	168.425
1252	30	11/19/78	Ontario CA	2.500	P	500.00	Bobby Allison (52)	Ford	137.783	Cale Yarborough (43)	Olds	156.190

1979

Race #	Year #	Date	Site	Track	Surface	Miles	Race Winner	Car	Speed	Pole Winner	Car	Speed
1253	1	1/14/79	Riverside CA	2.620	P	311.78	Darrell Waltrip (16)	Chevy	107.820	David Pearson (107)	Mercury	113.659
1254	2	2/18/79	Daytona Beach FL	2.500	P	500.00	Richard Petty (186)	Olds	143.977	Buddy Baker (25)	Olds	196.049
1255	3	3/4/79	Rockingham NC	1.017	P	500.36	Bobby Allison (53)	Ford	121.727	Bobby Allison (51)	Ford	136.790
1256	4	3/11/79	Richmond VA	0.542	P	216.80	Cale Yarborough (60)	Olds	83.608	Bobby Allison (52)	Ford	92.957
1257	5	3/18/79	Atlanta GA	1.522	P	499.22	Buddy Baker (14)	Olds	135.136	Buddy Baker (26)	Olds	165.951
1258	6	3/25/79	N Wilkesboro NC	0.625	P	0.63	Bobby Allison (54)	Ford	88.400	Benny Parsons (12)	Chevy	108.136
1259	7	4/1/79	Bristol TN	0.533	P	266.50	Dale Earnhardt	Chevy	91.033	Buddy Baker (27)	Chevy	111.610
1260	8	4/8/79	Darlington SC	1.366	P	501.32	Darrell Waltrip (17)	Chevy	121.721	Donnie Allison (17)	Chevy	154.797
1261	9	4/22/79	Martinsville VA	0.525	P	262.50	Richard Petty (187)	Chevy	76.562	Darrell Waltrip (12)	Chevy	87.383
1262	10	5/6/79	Talladega AL	2.660	P	500.08	Bobby Allison (55)	Ford	154.770	Darrell Waltrip (13)	Olds	195.644
1263	11	5/12/79	Nashville TN	0.596	P	250.32	Cale Yarborough (61)	Olds	88.652	Joe Millikan	Chevy	104.155
1264	12	5/20/79	Dover DE	1.000	P	500.00	Neil Bonnett (3)	Mercury	111.269	Darrell Waltrip (14)	Chevy	136.103
1265	13	5/27/79	Charlotte NC	1.500	P	600.00	Darrell Waltrip (18)	Chevy	136.674	Neil Bonnett (11)	Mercury	160.125
1266	14	6/3/79	College Station TX	2.000	P	400.00	Darrell Waltrip (19)	Chevy	156.216	Buddy Baker (28)	Chevy	167.903
1267	15	6/10/79	Riverside CA	2.620	P	248.90	Bobby Allison (56)	Ford	103.732	Dale Earnhardt	Chevy	113.039
1268	16	6/17/79	Brooklyn MI	2.000	P	400.00	Buddy Baker (15)	Chevy	135.798	Neil Bonnett (12)	Mercury	162.371
1269	17	7/4/79	Daytona Beach FL	2.500	P	400.00	Neil Bonnett (4)	Mercury	172.890	Buddy Baker (20)	Olds	193.196
1270	18	7/14/79	Nashville TN	0.596	P	250.32	Darrell Waltrip (20)	Chevy	92.227	Darrell Waltrip (15)	Chevy	105.430
1271	19	7/30/79	Pocono PA	2.500	P	500.00	Cale Yarborough (62)	Chevy	115.207	Harry Gant	Chevy	148.711
1272	20	8/5/79	Talladega AL	2.660	P	500.08	Darrell Waltrip (21)	Olds	161.229	Neil Bonnett (13)	Mercury	193.600
1273	21	8/19/79	Brooklyn MI	2.000	P	400.00	Richard Petty (188)	Chevy	130.376	David Pearson (108)	Chevy	162.992
1274	22	8/25/79	Bristol TN	0.533	P	266.50	Darrell Waltrip (22)	Chevy	91.493	Richard Petty (126)	Chevy	110.524
1275	23	9/3/79	Darlington SC	1.366	P	501.32	David Pearson (104)	Chevy	126.259	Bobby Allison (52)	Ford	154.880

Race #	Year #	Date	Site	Track	Surface	Miles	Race Winner	Car	Speed	Pole Winner	Car	Speed
1276	24	9/9/79	Richmond VA	0.542	P	216.80	Bobby Allison (57)	Ford	80.604	Dale Earnhardt (2)	Chevy	92.605
1277	25	9/16/79	Dover DE	1.000	P	500.00	Richard Petty (189)	Chevy	114.366	Dale Earnhardt (3)	Chevy	135.726
1278	26	9/23/79	Martinsville VA	0.525	P	262.50	Buddy Baker (16)	Chevy	75.119	Darrell Waltrip (16)	Chevy	88.265
1279	27	10/7/79	Charlotte NC	1.500	P	501.00	Cale Yarborough (63)	Chevy	134.266	Neil Bonnett (14)	Mercury	164.304
1280	28	10/14/79	N Wilkesboro NC	0.625	P	250.00	Benny Parsons (13)	Chevy	91.454	Dale Earnhardt (4)	Chevy	112.783
1281	29	10/21/79	Rockingham NC	1.017	P	500.36	Richard Petty (190)	Chevy	108.356	Buddy Baker (30)	Chevy	141.315
1282	30	11/4/79	Atlanta GA	1.522	P	499.22	Neil Bonnett (5)	Mercury	140.120	Buddy Baker (31)	Chevy	164.813
1283	31	11/18/79	Ontario CA	2.500	P	500.00	Benny Parsons (14)	Chevy	132.822	Cale Yarborough (44)	Olds	154.902

1980

Race #	Year #	Date	Site	Track	Surface	Miles	Race Winner	Car	Speed	Pole Winner	Car	Speed
1284	1	1/19/80	Riverside CA	2.620	P	311.78	Darrell Waltrip (23)	Chevy	94.974	Darrell Waltrip (17)	Chevy	113.404
1285	2	2/17/80	Daytona Beach, FL	2.500	P	500.00	Buddy Baker (17)	Olds	177.602	Buddy Baker (32)	Olds	194.009
1286	3	2/24/80	Richmond VA	0.542	P	216.80	Darrell Waltrip (24)	Chevy	67.703	Darrell Waltrip (18)	Chevy	93.695
1287	4	3/9/80	Rockingham NC	1.017	P	500.36	Cale Yarborough (64)	Olds	108.735	Darrell Waltrip (19)	Chevy	136.765
1288	5	3/16/80	Atlanta GA	1.522	P	499.22	Dale Earnhardt (2)	Chevy	134.808	Buddy Baker (33)	Olds	166.212
1289	6	3/30/80	Bristol TN	0.533	P	266.50	Dale Earnhardt (3)	Chevy	96.977	Cale Yarborough (45)	Chevy	111.688
1290	7	4/13/80	Darlington SC	1.366	P	258.17	David Pearson (105)	Chevy	112.397	Benny Parsons (13)	Chevy	155.866
1291	8	4/20/80	N Wilkesboro NC	0.625	P	250.00	Richard Petty (191)	Chevy	95.501	Bobby Allison (54)	Ford	113.797
1292	9	4/27/80	Martinsville VA	0.525	P	262.50	Darrell Waltrip (25)	Chevy	69.049	Darrell Waltrip (20)	Chevy	88.566
1293	10	5/4/80	Talladega AL	2.660	P	500.08	Buddy Baker (18)	Olds	170.481	David Pearson (109)	Olds	197.704
1294	11	5/10/80	Nashville TN	0.596	P	250.32	Richard Petty (192)	Chevy	89.471	Cale Yarborough (46)	Chevy	106.581
1295	12	5/18/80	Dover DE	1.000	P	500.00	Bobby Allison (58)	Ford	113.866	Cale Yarborough (47)	Chevy	138.814
1296	13	5/15/80	Charlotte NC	1.500	P	600.00	Benny Parsons (15)	Chevy	119.265	Cale Yarborough (48)	Chevy	165.194
1297	14	6/1/80	College Station TX	2.000	P	400.00	Cale Yarborough (65)	Chevy	159.046	Cale Yarborough (49)	Chevy	170.709
1298	15	6/8/80	Riverside CA	2.620	P	248.90	Darrell Waltrip (26)	Chevy	101.846	Cale Yarborough (50)	Chevy	113.792
1299	16	6/15/80	Brooklyn MI	2.000	P	400.00	Benny Parsons (16)	Chevy	131.808	Benny Parsons (14)	Chevy	163.662
1300	17	7/4/80	Daytona Beach FL	2.500	P	400.00	Bobby Allison (59)	Ford	173.473	Cale Yarborough (51)	Olds	194.670
1301	18	7/12/80	Nashville TN	0.596	P	250.32	Dale Earnhardt (4)	Chevy	93.821	Cale Yarborough (52)	Chevy	104.817
1302	19	7/27/80	Pocono PA	2.500	P	500.00	Neil Bonnett (6)	Mercury	124.395	Cale Yarborough (53)	Chevy	151.469
1303	20	8/3/80	Talladega AL	2.660	P	500.08	Neil Bonnett (7)	Mercury	166.894	Buddy Baker (33)	Olds	198.545
1304	21	8/17/80	Brooklyn MI	2.000	P	400.00	Cale Yarborough (66)	Chevy	145.352	Buddy Baker (34)	Chevy	162.693
1305	22	8/23/80	Bristol TN	0.533	P	266.50	Cale Yarborough (67)	Chevy	86.973	Cale Yarborough (54)	Chevy	110.990
1306	23	9/1/80	Darlington SC	1.366	P	501.32	Terry Labonte	Chevy	115.210	Darrell Waltrip (21)	Chevy	153.838
1307	24	9/7/80	Richmond VA	0.542	P	216.80	Bobby Allison (60)	Ford	79.722	Cale Yarborough (55)	Chevy	93.466
1308	25	9/14/80	Dover DE	1.000	P	500.00	Darrell Waltrip (27)	Chevy	116.024	Cale Yarborough (56)	Chevy	137.583
1309	26	9/21/80	N Wilkesboro NC	0.625	P	250.00	Bobby Allison (61)	Ford	75.510	Cale Yarborough (57)	Chevy	111.996
1310	27	9/28/80	Martinsville VA	0.525	P	262.50	Dale Earnhardt (5)	Chevy	69.654	Buddy Baker (35)	Chevy	88.500
1311	28	10/5/80	Charlotte NC	1.500	P	501.00	Dale Earnhardt (6)	Chevy	135.243	Buddy Baker (36)	Buick	165.634
1312	29	10/19/80	Rockingham NC	1.017	P	500.00	Cale Yarborough (68)	Chevy	114.159	Donnie Allison (18)	Chevy	142.648
1313	30	11/2/80	Atlanta GA	1.522	P	499.22	Cale Yarborough (69)	Chevy	131.190	Bobby Allison (55)	Mercury	165.620
1314	31	11/15/80	Ontario CA	2.500	P	500.00	Benny Parsons (17)	Chevy	129.441	Cale Yarborough (58)	Chevy	155.499

1981

Race #	Year #	Date	Site	Track	Surface	Miles	Race Winner	Car	Speed	Pole Winner	Car	Speed
1315	1	1/11/81	Riverside CA	2.620	P	311.78	Bobby Allison (62)	Chevy	95.263	Darrell Waltrip (22)	Chevy	114.711
1316	2	2/15/81	Daytona Beach FL	2.500	P	500.00	Richard Petty (193)	Buick	169.651	Bobby Allison (56)	Pontiac	194.624
1317	3	2/22/81	Richmond VA	0.542	P	216.80	Darrell Waltrip (28)	Buick	76.570	Morgan Shepherd	Pontiac	92.821
1318	4	3/1/81	Rockingham NC	1.017	P	500.36	Darrell Waltrip (29)	Buick	114.594	Cale Yarborough (59)	Buick	140.448
1319	5	3/15/81	Atlanta GA	1.522	P	499.22	Cale Yarborough (70)	Buick	133.619	Terry Labonte	Buick	162.940
1320	6	3/29/81	Bristol TN	0.533	P	266.50	Darrell Waltrip (30)	Buick	85.530	Darrell Waltrip (23)	Buick	112.125
1321	7	4/5/81	N Wilkesboro NC	0.625	P	250.00	Richard Petty (194)	Buick	85.381	Dave Marcis (14)	Chevy	114.647
1322	8	4/12/81	Darlington SC	1.366	P	501.32	Darrell Waltrip (31)	Buick	126.703	Bill Elliott	Ford	153.896
1323	9	4/26/81	Martinsville VA	0.525	P	262.50	Morgan Shepherd	Pontiac	75.019	Ricky Rudd	Buick	89.056
1324	10	5/3/81	Talladega AL	2.660	P	500.08	Bobby Allison (63)	Buick	149.376	Bobby Allison (56)	Buick	195.864
1325	11	5/9/81	Nashville TN	0.596	P	250.32	Benny Parsons (18)	Ford	89.756	Ricky Rudd (2)	Buick	104.409
1326	12	5/17/81	Dover DE	1.000	P	500.00	Jody Ridley	Ford	116.595	David Pearson (110)	Olds	138.475
1327	13	5/24/81	Charlotte NC	1.500	P	600.00	Bobby Allison (64)	Buick	129.326	Neil Bonnett (15)	Ford	158.115
1328	14	6/7/81	College Station TX	2.000	P	400.00	Benny Parsons (19)	Ford	132.475	Terry Labonte (2)	Buick	167.543
1329	15	6/17/81	Riverside CA	2.660	P	248.90	Darrell Waltrip (32)	Buick	93.957	Darrell Waltrip (23)	Buick	114.378
1330	16	6/21/81	Brooklyn MI	2.000	P	400.00	Bobby Allison (65)	Buick	130.589	Darrell Waltrip (24)	Buick	160.471
1331	17	7/4/81	Daytona Beach FL	2.500	P	400.00	Cale Yarborough (71)	Buick	142.588	Cale Yarborough (60)	Buick	192.852
1332	18	7/11/81	Nashville TN	0.596	P	250.32	Darrell Waltrip (33)	Buick	90.052	Mark Martin	Pontiac	104.353
1333	19	7/26/81	Pocono PA	2.500	P	500.00	Darrell Waltrip (34)	Buick	119.111	Darrell Waltrip (25)	Buick	150.148
1334	20	8/2/81	Talladega AL	2.660	P	500.08	Ron Bouchard	Buick	156.737	Harry Gant (2)	Buick	195.897
1335	21	8/16/81	Brooklyn MI	2.000	P	400.00	Richard Petty (195)	Buick	123.457	Ron Bouchard	Buick	161.501
1336	22	8/22/81	Bristol TN	0.533	P	266.50	Darrell Waltrip (35)	Buick	84.723	Darrell Waltrip (26)	Buick	110.818
1337	23	9/7/81	Darlington SC	1.366	P	501.32	Neil Bonnett (8)	Ford	126.446	Harry Gant (3)	Pontiac	152.693
1338	24	9/13/81	Richmond VA	0.542	P	216.80	Benny Parsons (20)	Ford	69.998	Mark Martin (2)	Pontiac	93.435
1339	25	9/20/81	Dover DE	1.000	P	500.00	Neil Bonnett (9)	Ford	119.561	Ricky Rudd (3)	Chevy	136.757
1340	26	9/27/81	Martinsville VA	0.525	P	262.50	Darrell Waltrip (36)	Buick	70.089	Darrell Waltrip (27)	Buick	89.014
1341	27	10/4/81	N Wilkesboro NC	0.625	P	250.00	Darrell Waltrip (37)	Buick	93.091	Darrell Waltrip (28)	Buick	113.065

Race #	Year #	Date	Site	Track	Surface	Miles	Race Winner	Car	Speed	Pole Winner	Car	Speed
1342	28	10/11/81	Charlotte NC	1.500	P	501.00	Darrell Waltrip (38)	Buick	117.483	Darrell Waltrip (29)	Buick	162.744
1343	29	1/1/81	Rockingham NC	1.017	P	500.36	Darrell Waltrip (39)	Buick	107.399	Darrell Waltrip (30)	Buick	136.164
1344	30	11/8/81	Atlanta GA	1.522	P	499.22	Neil Bonnett (10)	Ford	130.391	Harry Gant (4)	Pontiac	163.266
1345	31	11/22/81	Riverside CA	2.620	P	311.78	Bobby Allison (66)	Buick	95.288	Darrell Waltrip (31)	Buick	114.981

1982

Race #	Year #	Date	Site	Track	Surface	Miles	Race Winner	Car	Speed	Pole Winner	Car	Speed
1346	1	2/14/82	Daytona Beach FL	2.500	P	500.00	Bobby Allison (67)	Buick	153.991	Benny Parsons (15)	Pontiac	196.317
1347	2	2/21/82	Richmond VA	0.533	P	135.50	Dave Marcis (5)	Chevy	72.914	Darrell Waltrip (32)	Buick	93.256
1348	3	3/14/82	Bristol TN	0.533	P	266.50	Darrell Waltrip (40)	Buick	94.025	Darrell Waltrip (33)	Buick	111.068
1349	4	3/21/82	Atlanta GA	1.522	P	436.81	Darrell Waltrip (41)	Buick	124.824	Dale Earnhardt (3)	Ford	163.774
1350	5	3/28/82	Rockingham NC	1.017	P	500.36	Cale Yarborough (72)	Buick	108.992	Benny Parsons (16)	Pontiac	141.577
1351	6	4/4/82	Darlington SC	1.366	P	501.32	Dale Earnhardt (7)	Ford	123.554	Buddy Baker (37)	Buick	153.979
1352	7	4/18/82	N Wilkesboro NC	0.625	P	250.00	Darrell Waltrip (42)	Buick	97.646	Darrell Waltrip (34)	Buick	114.801
1353	8	4/25/82	Martinsville VA	0.525	P	262.50	Harry Gant	Buick	75.073	Terry Labonte (3)	Chevy	89.988
1354	9	5/2/82	Talladega AL	2.660	P	500.08	Darrell Waltrip (43)	Buick	156.697	Benny Parsons (17)	Pontiac	200.176
1355	10	5/8/82	Nashville TN	0.596	P	250.32	Darrell Waltrip (44)	Buick	83.502	Darrell Waltrip (35)	Buick	102.773
1356	11	5/16/82	Dover DE	1.000	P	500.00	Bobby Allison (68)	Chevy	120.136	Darrell Waltrip (36)	Buick	139.308
1357	12	5/30/82	Charlotte NC	1.500	P	600.00	Neil Bonnett (11)	Ford	130.058	David Pearson (111)	Buick	162.511
1358	13	6/6/82	Pocono PA	2.500	P	500.00	Bobby Allison (69)	Buick	113.579	No Time Trials	NTT	NTT
1359	14	6/13/82	Riverside CA	2.620	P	248.90	Tim Richmond	Buick	103.816	Terry Labonte (4)	Buick	114.352
1360	15	6/20/82	Brooklyn MI	2.000	P	400.00	Cale Yarborough (73)	Buick	118.101	Ron Bouchard (2)	Buick	162.404
1361	16	7/4/82	Daytona Beach, FL	2.500	P	400.00	Bobby Allison (70)	Buick	163.099	Geoff Bodine	Pontiac	194.721
1362	17	7/10/82	Nashville TN	0.596	P	250.32	Darrell Waltrip (45)	Buick	86.524	Morgan Shepherd (2)	Pontiac	103.959
1363	18	7/25/82	Pocono PA	2.500	P	500.00	Bobby Allison (71)	Buick	115.496	Cale Yarborough (61)	Buick	150.764
1364	19	8/1/82	Talladega AL	2.660	P	500.08	Darrell Waltrip (46)	Buick	168.157	Geoff Bodine (2)	Pontiac	199.400
1365	20	8/22/82	Brooklyn MI	2.000	P	400.00	Bobby Allison (72)	Buick	136.454	Bill Elliott (2)	Ford	162.173
1366	21	8/28/82	Bristol TN	0.533	P	266.50	Darrell Waltrip (47)	Buick	94.318	Tim Richmond	Buick	112.507
1367	22	9/6/82	Darlington SC	1.366	P	501.32	Cale Yarborough (74)	Buick	115.224	David Pearson (112)	Buick	155.739
1368	23	9/12/82	Richmond VA	0.542	P	216.80	Bobby Allison (73)	Chevy	82.800	Bobby Allison (57)	Chevy	93.435
1369	24	9/19/82	Dover DE	1.000	P	500.00	Darrell Waltrip (48)	Buick	107.642	Ricky Rudd (4)	Pontiac	139.384
1370	25	10/3/82	N Wilkesboro NC	0.625	P	250.00	Darrell Waltrip (49)	Buick	98.071	Darrell Waltrip (37)	Buick	113.860
1371	26	10/10/82	Charlotte NC	1.500	P	501.00	Harry Gant (2)	Buick	137.208	Harry Gant (5)	Buick	164.694
1372	27	10/17/82	Martinsville VA	0.525	P	262.50	Darrell Waltrip (50)	Buick	71.315	Ricky Rudd (5)	Pontiac	89.132
1373	28	10/31/82	Rockingham NC	1.017	P	500.36	Darrell Waltrip (51)	Buick	115.122	Cale Yarborough (62)	Buick	143.220
1374	29	11/7/82	Atlanta GA	1.522	P	499.22	Bobby Allison (74)	Buick	130.884	Morgan Shepherd (3)	Buick	166.779
1375	30	11/21/82	Riverside CA	2.620	P	311.78	Tim Richmond (2)	Buick	99.823	Darrell Waltrip (38)	Buick	122.021

1983

Race #	Year #	Date	Site	Track	Surface	Miles	Race Winner	Car	Speed	Pole Winner	Car	Speed
1376	1	2/20/83	Daytona Beach FL	2.500	P	500.00	Cale Yarborough (75)	Pontiac	155.979	Ricky Rudd (6)	Chevy	198.864
1377	2	2/27/83	Richmond VA	0.542	P	216.80	Bobby Allison (75)	Chevy	79.584	Ricky Rudd (7)	Chevy	93.439
1378	3	3/13/83	Rockingham NC	1.017	P	500.36	Richard Petty (196)	Pontiac	113.055	Ricky Rudd (8)	Chevy	143.413
1379	4	3/27/83	Atlanta GA	1.522	P	499.22	Cale Yarborough (76)	Chevy	124.055	Geoff Bodine (3)	Pontiac	167.703
1380	5	4/10/83	Darlington SC	1.366	P	501.32	Harry Gant (3)	Buick	130.406	Tim Richmond (2)	Pontiac	157.818
1381	6	4/17/83	N Wilkesboro NC	0.625	P	250.00	Darrell Waltrip (52)	Chevy	91.436	Neil Bonnett (16)	Chevy	112.332
1382	7	4/24/83	Martinsville VA	0.525	P	262.50	Darrell Waltrip (53)	Chevy	66.460	Ricky Rudd (9)	Chevy	89.910
1383	8	5/1/83	Talladega AL	2.660	P	500.08	Richard Petty (197)	Pontiac	153.936	Cale Yarborough (63	Chevy	202.650
1384	9	5/7/83	Nashville TN	0.596	P	250.32	Darrell Waltrip (54)	Chevy	70.717	Darrell Waltrip (39)	Chevy	103.119
1385	10	5/15/83	Dover DE	1.000	P	500.00	Bobby Allison (76)	Buick	114.847	Joe Ruttman	Buick	139.616
1386	11	5/21/83	Bristol TN	0.533	P	266.50	Darrell Waltrip (55)	Chevy	93.445	Neil Bonnett (17)	Chevy	110.409
1387	12	5/29/83	Charlotte NC	1.500	P	600.00	Neil Bonnett (12)	Chevy	140.707	Buddy Baker (38)	Ford	162.841
1388	13	6/5/83	Riverside CA	2.620	P	248.90	Ricky Rudd	Chevy	88.063	Darrell Waltrip (40)	Chevy	116.421
1389	14	6/12/83	Pocono PA	2.500	P	500.00	Bobby Allison (77)	Buick	128.636	Darrell Waltrip (41)	Chevy	152.315
1390	15	6/19/83	Brooklyn MI	2.000	P	400.00	Cale Yarborough (77)	Chevy	138.728	Terry Labonte (5)	Chevy	161.965
1391	16	7/4/83	Daytona Beach FL	2.500	P	400.00	Buddy Baker (19)	Ford	167.442	Cale Yarborough (64)	Chevy	196.635
1392	17	7/16/83	Nashville TN	0.596	P	250.32	Dale Earnhardt (8)	Ford	85.726	Ron Bouchard (3)	Buick	103.020
1393	18	7/24/83	Pocono PA	2.500	P	500.00	Tim Richmond (3)	Pontiac	114.818	Tim Richmond (3)	Pontiac	151.981
1394	19	7/31/83	Talladega AL	2.660	P	500.08	Dale Earnhardt (9)	Ford	170.611	Cale Yarborough (65)	Chevy	201.981
1395	20	8/21/83	Brooklyn MI	2.000	P	400.00	Cale Yarborough (78)	Chevy	147.511	Terry Labonte (6)	Chevy	162.437
1396	21	8/27/83	Bristol TN	0.533	P	223.33	Darrell Waltrip (56)	Chevy	89.430	Joe Ruttman (2)	Pontiac	111.437
1397	22	9/5/83	Darlington SC	1.366	P	501.32	Bobby Allison (78)	Buick	123.343	Neil Bonnett (18)	Chevy	157.187
1398	23	9/11/83	Richmond VA	0.542	P	216.80	Bobby Allison (79)	Buick	79.381	Darrell Waltrip (42)	Buick	96.069
1399	24	9/18/83	Dover DE	1.000	P	500.00	Bobby Allison (80)	Buick	116.077	Terry Labonte (7)	Chevy	139.573
1400	25	9/25/83	Martinsville VA	0.525	P	262.50	Ricky Rudd (2)	Chevy	76.134	Darrell Waltrip (43)	Chevy	89.342
1401	26	10/2/83	N Wilkesboro NC	0.625	P	250.00	Darrell Waltrip (57)	Chevy	100.716	Darrell Waltrip (44)	Chevy	114.539
1402	27	10/9/83	Charlotte NC	1.500	P	501.00	Richard Petty (198)	Pontiac	139.998	Tim Richmond (4)	Pontiac	163.073
1403	28	10/30/83	Rockingham NC	1.017	P	500.36	Terry Labonte (2)	Chevy	119.324	Neil Bonnett (19)	Chevy	143.876
1404	29	11/6/83	Atlanta GA	1.522	P	499.22	Neil Bonnett (13)	Chevy	137.643	Tim Richmond (5)	Pontiac	168.151
1405	30	11/20/83	Riverside CA	2.620	P	311.78	Bill Elliott	Ford	95.859	Darrell Waltrip (45)	Chevy	116.782

1984

Race #	Year #	Date	Site	Track	Surface	Miles	Race Winner	Car	Speed	Pole Winner	Car	Speed
1406	1	2/19/84	Daytona Beach FL	2.500	P	500.00	Cale Yarborough (79)	Chevy	150.994	Cale Yarborough (66)	Chevy	102.848
1407	2	2/26/84	Richmond VA	0.542	P	216.80	Ricky Rudd (3)	Ford	76.736	Darrell Waltrip (46)	Chevy	95.817
1408	3	3/4/84	Rockingham NC	0.542	P	500.36	Bobby Allison (81)	Buick	122.931	Harry Gant (6)	Chevy	145.084
1409	4	3/18/84	Atlanta GA	1.522	P	499.22	Benny Parsons (21)	Chevy	144.945	Buddy Baker (39)	Ford	166.642
1410	5	4/1/84	Bristol TN	0.533	P	26.50	Darrell Waltrip (58)	Chevy	93.967	Ricky Rudd (10)	Ford	111.390
1411	6	4/8/84	N Wilkesboro NC	0.625	P	250.00	Tim Richmond (4)	Pontiac	97.830	Ricky Rudd (11)	Ford	113.487
1412	7	4/15/84	Darlington SC	1.366	P	501.32	Darrell Waltrip (59)	Chevy	119.925	Benny Parsons (18)	Chevy	156.328
1413	8	4/29/84	Martinsville VA	0.525	P	262.50	Geoff Bodine	Chevy	73.264	Joe Ruttman (3)	Chevy	89.426
1414	9	5/6/84	Talladega AL	2.660	P	500.08	Cale Yarborough (80)	Chevy	172.988	Cale Yarborough (67)	Chevy	202.692
1415	10	5/12/84	Nashville TN	0.596	P	250.32	Darrell Waltrip (60)	Chevy	85.702	Darrell Waltrip (47)	Chevy	104.439
1416	11	5/20/84	Dover DE	1.000	P	500.00	Richard Petty (199)	Pontiac	118.717	Ricky Rudd (12)	Ford	140.807
1417	12	5/27/84	Charlotte NC	1.500	P	600.00	Bobby Allison (82)	Buick	129.233	Harry Gant (7)	Chevy	162.496
1418	13	6/3/84	Riverside CA	2.620	P	248.90	Terry Labonte (3)	Chevy	102.910	Terry Labonte (8)	Chevy	115.921
1419	14	6/10/84	Pocono PA	2.500	P	500.00	Cale Yarborough (81)	Chevy	138.164	David Pearson (113)	Chevy	150.921
1420	15	6/17/84	Brooklyn MI	2.000	P	400.00	Bill Elliott (2)	Ford	134.705	Bill Elliott (3)	Ford	164.339
1421	16	7/4/84	Daytona Beach FL	2.500	P	400.00	Richard Petty (200)	Pontiac	171.204	Cale Yarborough (68)	Chevy	199.743
1422	17	7/14/84	Nashville TN	0.596	P	250.32	Geoff Bodine (2)	Chevy	80.908	Ricky Rudd (13)	Ford	104.120
1423	18	7/22/84	Pocono PA	2.500	P	500.00	Harry Gant (4)	Chevy	121.351	Bill Elliott (4)	Ford	152.184
1424	19	7/29/84	Talladega AL	2.660	P	500.08	Dale Earnhardt (10)	Chevy	155.485	Cale Yarborough (69)	Chevy	202.474
1425	20	8/12/84	Brooklyn MI	2.000	P	400.00	Darrell Waltrip (61)	Chevy	153.863	Bill Elliott (5)	Ford	165.217
1426	21	8/25/84	Bristol TN	0.533	P	266.50	Terry Labonte (4)	Chevy	85.365	Geoff Bodine (4)	Chevy	111.734
1427	22	9/2/84	Darlington SC	1.366	P	501.32	Harry Gant (5)	Chevy	128.270	Harry Gant (8)	Chevy	155.502
1428	23	9/9/84	Richmond VA	0.542	P	216.80	Darrell Waltrip (62)	Chevy	74.780	Darrell Waltrip (48)	Chevy	92.518
1429	24	9/16/84	Dover DE	1.000	P	500.00	Harry Gant (6)	Chevy	111.856	No Time Trials	NTT	NTT
1430	25	9/23/84	Martinsville VA	0.525	P	262.50	Darrell Waltrip (63)	Chevy	75.532	Geoff Bodine (5)	Chevy	89.523
1431	26	10/7/84	Charlotte NC	1.500	P	501.00	Bill Elliott (3)	Ford	146.861	Benny Parsons (19)	Chevy	165.579
1432	27	10/14/84	N Wilkesboro NC	0.625	P	250.00	Darrell Waltrip (64)	Chevy	90.525	Darrell Waltrip (49)	Chevy	113.304
1433	28	10/21/84	Rockingham NC	1.017	P	500.36	Bill Elliott (4)	Ford	112.617	Geoff Bodine (6)	Chevy	144.415
1434	29	11/11/84	Atlanta GA	1.522	P	499.22	Dale Earnhardt (11)	Chevy	134.610	Bill Elliott (6)	Ford	170.198
1435	30	11/18/84	Riverside CA	2.620	P	311.78	Geoff Bodine (3)	Chevy	98.448	Terry Labonte	Chevy	116.714

1985

Race #	Year #	Date	Site	Track	Surface	Miles	Race Winner	Car	Speed	Pole Winner	Car	Speed
1436	1	2/17/85	Daytona Beach FL	2.500	P	500.00	Bill Elliott (5)	Ford	172.265	Bill Elliott (7)	Ford	205.114
1437	2	2/24/85	Richmond VA	0.542	P	216.80	Dale Earnhardt (12)	Chevy	67.945	Darrell Waltrip (50)	Chevy	95.218
1438	3	3/3/85	Rockingham NC	1.017	P	500.36	Neil Bonnett (14)	Chevy	114.953	Terry Labonte (10)	Chevy	145.067
1439	4	3/17/85	Atlanta GA	1.522	P	499.22	Bill Elliott (6)	Ford	140.273	Neil Bonnett (20)	Chevy	170.278
1440	5	4/6/85	Bristol TN	0.533	P	266.50	Dale Earnhardt (13)	Chevy	81.790	Harry Gant (9)	Chevy	112.778
1441	6	4/14/85	Darlington SC	1.366	P	501.32	Bill Elliott (7)	Ford	126.295	Bill Elliott (8)	Ford	157.454
1442	7	4/21/85	N Wilkesboro NC	0.625	P	250.00	Neil Bonnett (15)	Chevy	93.818	Darrell Waltrip (51)	Chevy	111.899
1443	8	4/28/85	Martinsville VA	0.525	P	262.50	Harry Gant (7)	Chevy	73.022	Darrell Waltrip (52)	Chevy	90.279
1444	9	5/5/85	Talladega AL	2.660	P	500.08	Bill Elliott (8)	Ford	186.288	Bill Elliott (9)	Ford	209.398
1445	10	5/19/85	Dover DE	1.000	P	500.00	Bill Elliott (9)	Ford	123.094	Terry Labonte (11)	Chevy	138.106
1446	11	5/26/85	Charlotte NC	1.500	P	600.00	Darrell Waltrip (65)	Chevy	141.807	Bill Elliott (10)	Ford	164.703
1447	12	6/2/85	Riverside CA	2.620	P	248.90	Terry Labonte (5)	Chevy	104.276	Darrell Waltrip (53)	Chevy	115.533
1448	13	6/9/85	Pocono PA	2.500	P	500.00	Bill Elliott (10)	Ford	138.974	Bill Elliott (11)	Ford	152.563
1449	14	6/15/85	Brooklyn MI	2.000	P	400.00	Bill Elliott (11)	Ford	144.724	No Time Trials	NTT	NTT
1450	15	7/4/85	Daytona Beach FL	2.500	P	400.00	Greg Sacks	Chevy	158.730	Bill Elliott (12)	Ford	201.523
1451	16	7/21/85	Pocono PA	2.500	P	500.00	Bill Elliott (12)	Ford	134.008	Darrell Waltrip (54)	Chevy	152.523
1452	17	7/28/85	Talladega AL	2.660	P	500.08	Cale Yarborough (82)	Ford	148.772	Bill Elliott (13)	Ford	107.578
1453	18	8/11/85	Brooklyn MI	2.000	P	400.00	Bill Elliott (13)	Ford	137.430	Bill Elliott (14)	Ford	165.479
1454	19	8/24/85	Bristol TN	0.533	P	266.50	Dale Earnhardt (14)	Chevy	82.388	Dale Earnhardt (6)	Chevy	113.586
1455	20	9/1/85	Darlington SC	1.366	P	501.32	Bill Elliott (14)	Ford	121.254	Bill Elliott (15)	Ford	156.641
1456	21	9/8/85	Richmond VA	0.542	P	216.80	Darrell Waltrip (66)	Chevy	72.508	Geoff Bodine (7)	Chevy	94.535
1457	22	9/15/85	Dover DE	1.000	P	500.00	Harry Gant (8)	Chevy	120.538	Bill Elliott (16)	Ford	141.543
1458	23	9/22/85	Martinsville VA	0.525	P	262.50	Dale Earnhardt (15)	Chevy	70.694	Geoff Bodine (8)	Chevy	90.521
1459	24	9/29/85	N Wilkesboro NC	0.625	P	250.00	Harry Gant (9)	Chevy	95.077	Geoff Bodine (9)	Chevy	113.967
1460	25	10/6/85	Charlotte NC	1.500	P	501.00	Cale Yarborough (83)	Ford	136.761	Harry Gant (10)	Chevy	166.139
1461	26	10/25/85	Rockingham NC	1.017	P	500.36	Darrell Waltrip (67)	Chevy	118.344	Terry Labonte (12)	Chevy	141.841
1462	27	11/3/85	Atlanta GA	1.522	P	499.22	Bill Elliott (15)	Ford	139.597	Harry Gant (11)	Chevy	167.940
1463	28	11/17/85	Riverside CA	2.620	P	311.78	Ricky Rudd (4)	Ford	105.065	Terry Labonte (13)	Chevy	116.938

1986

Race #	Year #	Date	Site	Track	Surface	Miles	Race Winner	Car	Speed	Pole Winner	Car	Speed
1464	1	2/16/86	Daytona Beach FL	2.500	P	500.00	Geoff Bodine (4)	Chevy	148.124	Bill Elliott (17)	Ford	205.039
1465	2	2/23/86	Richmond VA	0.542	P	216.80	Kyle Petty	Ford	71.078	No Time Trials	NTT	NTT
1466	3	3/2/86	Rockingham NC	1.017	P	500.36	Terry Labonte (6)	Olds	120.488	Terry Labonte (14)	Olds	146.348
1467	4	3/16/86	Atlanta GA	1.522	P	499.22	Morgan Shepherd (2)	Buick	132.126	Dale Earnhardt (7)	Chevy	170.713
1468	5	4/6/86	Bristol TN	0.533	P	266.50	Rusty Wallace	Pontiac	89.747	Geoff Bodine ((10)	Chevy	114.850

Race #	Year #	Date	Site	Track	Surface	Miles	Race Winner	Car	Speed	Pole Winner	Car	Speed
1469	6	4/13/86	Darlington SC	1.366	P	501.32	Dale Earnhardt (16)	Chevy	128.994	Geoff Bodine (11)	Chevy	159.197
1470	7	4/20/86	N Wilkesboro NC	0.625	P	250.00	Dale Earnhardt (17)	Chevy	86.408	Geoff Bodine (12)	Chevy	112.419
1471	8	4/27/86	Martinsville VA	0.525	P	262.50	Ricky Rudd (5)	Ford	76.882	Tim Richmond (6)	Chevy	90.716
1472	9	5/4/86	Talladega AL	2.660	P	500.08	Bobby Allison (83)	Buick	157.698	Bill Elliott (18	Ford	212.229
1473	10	5/18/86	Dover DE	1.000	P	500.00	Geoff Bodine (5)	Chevy	115.009	Ricky Rudd (14)	Ford	138.217
1474	11	5/15/86	Charlotte NC	1.500	P	600.00	Dale Earnhardt (18)	Chevy	140.406	Geoff Bodine (13)	Chevy	164.511
1475	12	6/1/86	Riverside CA	2.620	P	248.90	Darrell Waltrip (68)	Chevy	105.083	Darrell Waltrip (55)	Chevy	117.006
1476	13	6/8/86	Pocono PA	2.500	P	500.00	Tim Richmond (5)	Chevy	113.279	Geoff Bodine (14)	Chevy	153.625
1477	14	6/15/86	Brooklyn MI	2.000	P	400.00	Bill Elliott (16)	Ford	138.581	Tim Richmond (7)	Chevy	172.031
1478	15	7/4/86	Daytona Beach FL	2.500	P	400.00	Tim Richmond (6)	Chevy	131.916	Cale Yarborough (70)	Ford	203.519
1479	16	7/20/86	Pocono PA	2.500	P	375.00	Tim Richmond (7)	Chevy	124.218	Harry Gant (12)	Chevy	154.392
1480	17	7/27/86	Talladega AL	2.660	P	500.08	Bobby Hillin Jr	Buick	151.552	Bill Elliott (19)	Ford	209.005
1481	18	8/10/86	Watkins Glen NY	2.438	P	218.52	Tim Richmond (8)	Chevy	90.463	Tim Richmond (8)	Chevy	117.563
1482	19	8/17/86	Brooklyn MI	2.000	P	400.00	Bill Elliott (17)	Ford	135.376	Benny Parsons (20)	Olds	171.924
1483	20	8/23/86	Bristol TN	0.533	P	266.50	Darrell Waltrip (69)	Chevy	86.934	Geoff Bodine (15)	Chevy	114.665
1484	21	8/31/86	Darlington SC	1.366	P	501.32	Tim Richmond (9)	Chevy	121.068	Tim Richmond (9)	Chevy	158.489
1485	22	9/7/86	Richmond VA	0.542	P	216.80	Tim Richmond (10)	Chevy	70.161	Harry Gant (13)	Chevy	93.966
1486	23	9/14/86	Dover DE	1.000	P	500.00	Ricky Rudd (6)	Ford	114.329	Geoff Bodine (16)	Chevy	146.205
1487	24	9/21/86	Martinsville VA	0.525	P	262.50	Rusty Wallace (2)	Pontiac	73.191	Geoff Bodine (17)	Chevy	90.599
1488	25	9/28/86	N Wilkesboro NC	0.625	P	250.00	Darrell Waltrip (70)	Chevy	95.612	Tim Richmond (10)	Chevy	113.447
1489	26	10/3/86	Charlotte NC	1.500	P	501.00	Dale Earnhardt (19)	Chevy	132.403	Tim Richmond (11)	Chevy	167.078
1490	27	10/10/86	Rockingham NC	1.017	P	500.36	Neil Bonnett (16)	Chevy	126.381	Tim Richmond (12)	Chevy	146.948
1491	28	11/2/86	Atlanta GA	1.522	P	499.22	Dale Earnhardt (20)	Chevy	152.523	Bill Elliott (20)	Ford	172.905
1492	29	11/16/86	Riverside CA	2.620	P	311.78	Tim Richmond (11)	Chevy	101.246	Tim Richmond (13)	Chevy	118.247

1987

Race #	Year #	Date	Site	Track	Surface	Miles	Race Winner	Car	Speed	Pole Winner	Car	Speed
1492	1	2/15/87	Daytona Beach FL	2.500	P	500.00	Bill Elliott (18)	Ford	176.263	Bill Elliott (21)	Ford	210.364
1494	2	3/1/87	Rockingham NC	1.017	P	500.36	Dale Earnhardt (21)	Chevy	117.556	Davey Allison	Ford	146.989
1495	3	3/8/87	Richmond VA	0.542	P	216.80	Dale Earnhardt (22)	Chevy	81.420	Alan Kulwicki	Ford	95.153
1496	4	3/15/87	Atlanta GA	1.522	P	499.22	Ricky Rudd (7)	Ford	133.689	Dale Earnhardt (8)	Chevy	175.497
1497	5	3/29/87	Darlington SC	1.366	P	501.32	Dale Earnhardt (23)	Chevy	122.540	Ken Shrader	Ford	158.387
1498	6	4/5/87	N Wilkesboro NC	0.625	P	250.00	Dale Earnhardt (24)	Chevy	94.103	Bill Elliott (22)	Ford	116.003
1499	7	4/12/87	Bristol TN	0.533	P	266.50	Dale Earnhardt (25)	Chevy	75.621	Harry Gant (14)	Chevy	115.674
1500	8	4/26/87	Martinsville VA	0.525	P	262.50	Dale Earnhardt (26)	Chevy	72.808	Morgan Shepherd (4)	Buick	92.355
1501	9	5/3/87	Talladega AL	2.660	P	473.48	Davey Allison	Ford	154.228	Bill Elliott (23)	Ford	212.809
1502	10	5/24/87	Charlotte NC	1.500	P	600.00	Kyle Petty (2)	Ford	131.483	Bill Elliott (24)	Ford	170.901
1503	11	5/31/87	Dover DE	1.000	P	500.00	Davey Allison (2)	Ford	112.958	Bill Elliott (25)	Ford	145.056
1504	12	6/14/87	Pocono PA	2.500	P	500.00	Tim Richmond (12)	Chevy	122.166	Terry Labonte (15)	Chevy	155.502
1505	13	6/21/87	Riverside CA	2.620	P	248.90	Tim Richmond (13)	Chevy	102.183	Terry Labonte (16)	Chevy	117.541
1506	14	6/28/87	Brooklyn MI	2.000	P	400.00	Dale Earnhardt (27)	Chevy	148.454	Rusty Wallace	Pontiac	170.746
1507	15	7/4/87	Daytona Beach FL	2.500	P	400.00	Bobby Allison (84)	Buick	161.074	Davey Allison (2)	Ford	198.085
1508	16	7/9/87	Pocono PA	3.500	P	500.00	Dale Earnhardt (28)	Chevy	121.745	Tim Richmond (14)	Chevy	155.979
1509	17	7/16/87	Talladega AL	2.660	P	500.08	Bill Elliott (19)	Ford	171.293	Bill Elliott (26)	Ford	203.827
1510	18	8/10/87	Watkins Glen NY	2.438	P	218.52	Rusty Wallace (3)	Pontiac	90.682	Terry Labonte (17)	Chevy	117.956
1511	19	8/16/87	Brooklyn MI	2.000	P	400.00	Bill Elliott (20)	Ford	138.648	Davey Allison (3)	Ford	170.705
1512	20	8/22/87	Bristol TN	0.533	P	266.50	Dale Earnhardt (29)	Chevy	90.373	Terry Labonte (18)	Chevy	115.758
1513	21	9/6/87	Darlington SC	1.366	P	275.90	Dale Earnhardt (30)	Chevy	115.520	Davey Allison (4)	Ford	157.232
1514	22	9/13/87	Richmond VA	0.542	P	216.80	Dale Earnhardt (31)	Chevy	67.074	Alan Kulwicki (2)	Ford	94.052
1515	23	9/20/87	Dover DE	1.000	P	500.00	Ricky Rudd (8)	Ford	124.706	Alan Kulwicki (3)	Ford	145.826
1516	24	9/27/87	Martinsville VA	0.525	P	262.50	Darrell Waltrip (71)	Chevy	76.410	Geoff Bodine (18)	Chevy	91.218
1517	25	10/4/87	N Wilkesboro NC	0.625	P	250.00	Terry Labonte (7)	Chevy	96.051	Bill Elliott (27)	Ford	115.196
1518	26	10/11/87	Charlotte NC	1.500	P	501.00	Bill Elliott (20)	Ford	128.443	Bobby Allison (58	Buick	145.609
1519	27	10/25/87	Rockingham NC	1.017	P	500.36	Bill Elliott (21)	Ford	118.258	Davey Allison (5)	Ford	145.609
1520	28	11/8/87	Riverside CA	2.620	P	311.78	Rusty Wallace (4)	Pontiac	98.035	Geoff Bodine (19)	Chevy	117.934
1521	29	11/22/87	Atlanta GA	1.522	P	499.22	Bill Elliott (22)	Ford	139.047	Bill Elliott (28)	Ford	174.341

1988

Race #	Year #	Date	Site	Track	Surface	Miles	Race Winner	Car	Speed	Pole Winner	Car	Speed
1522	1	2/14/88	Daytona Beach, FL	2.500	P	500.00	Bobby Allison (85)	Buick	137.531	Ken Schrader (2)	Chevy	193.823
1523	2	2/21/88	Richmond, VA	0.542	P	216.80	Neil Bonnett (17)	Pontiac	66.401	Morgan Shepherd (5)	Buick	96.645
1524	3	3/6/88	Rockingham, NC	1.017	P	500.36	Neil Bonnett (18)	Pontiac	120.159	Bill Elliott (30)	Ford	146.612
1525	4	3/20/88	Atlanta, GA	1.522	P	499.22	Dale Earnhardt (32)	Chevy	137.588	Geoff Bodine (20)	Chevy	176.623
1526	5	3/27/88	Darlington, SC	1.366	P	501.32	Lake Speed	Olds	131.284	Ken Schrader (3)	Chevy	162.657
1527	6	4/10/88	Bristol, TN	0.533	P	266.50	Bill Elliott (24)	Ford	83.115	Rick Wilson	Olds	117.522
1528	7	4/17/88	N.Wilkesboro, NC	0.625	P	250.00	Terry Labonte (8)	Chevy	99.075	Terry Labonte (19)	Chevy	117.322
1529	8	4/24/88	Martinsville, VA	0.525	P	263.00	Dale Earnhardt (33)	Chevy	74.740	Ricky Rudd (5)	Buick	91.328
1530	9	5/1/88	Talladega, AL	2.660	P	500.08	Phil Parsons	Olds	156.547	Davey Allison (6)	Ford	198.969
1531	10	5/29/88	Charlotte, NC	1.500	P	600.00	Darrell Waltrip (72)	Chevy	124.460	Davey Allison (7)	Ford	173.594
1532	11	6/5/88	Dover, DE	1.000	P	500.00	Bill Elliott (25)	Ford	118.726	Alan Kulwicki (4)	Ford	146.681
1533	12	6/12/88	Riverside, CA	2.620	P	248.90	Rusty Wallace (5)	Pontiac	88.341	Ricky Rudd (16)	Buick	118.484
1534	13	6/19/88	Pocono, PA	2.500	P	500.00	Geoff Bodine (6)	Chevy	126.147	Alan Kulwicki (5)	Ford	158.806

Race #	Year #	Date	Site	Track	Surface	Miles	Race Winner	Car	Speed	Pole Winner	Car	Speed
1535	14	6/26/88	Brooklyn, MI	2.000	P	400.00	Rusty Wallace (6)	Pontiac	153.551	Bill Elliott (31)	Ford	172.687
1536	15	7/2/88	Daytona Beach, FL	2.500	P	400.00	Bill Elliott (26)	Ford	163.302	Darrell Waltrip (55)	Chevy	193.819
1537	16	7/24/88	Pocono, PA	2.500	P	500.00	Bill Elliott (27)	Ford	122.866	Morgan Shepherd (6)	Pontiac	157.153
1538	17	7/31/88	Talladega, AL	2.660	P	500.08	Ken Schrader	Chevy	154.505	Darrell Waltrip (56)	Chevy	196.274
1539	18	8/14/88	Watkins Glen, NY	2.428	P	218.52	Ricky Rudd (9)	Buick	74.096	Geoff Bodine (21)	Chevy	120.501
1540	19	8/21/88	Brooklyn, MI	2.000	P	400.00	Davey Allison (3)	Ford	156.863	Bill Elliott (32)	Ford	174.940
1541	20	8/27/88	Bristol, TN	0.533	P	266.50	Dale Earnhardt (34)	Chevy	78.755	Alan Kulwicki (6)	Ford	116.893
1542	21	9/4/88	Darlington, SC	1.366	P	501.32	Bill Elliott (28)	Ford	128.297	Bill Elliott (33)	Ford	160.827
1543	22	9/11/88	Richmond, VA	0.750	P	300.00	Davey Allison (4)	Ford	95.770	Davey Allison (8)	Ford	122.850
1544	23	9/18/88	Dover, DE	1.000	P	500.00	Bill Elliott (29)	Ford	109.349	Mark Martin (3)	Ford	148.075
1545	24	9/25/88	Martinsville, VA	0.525	P	263.00	Darrell Waltrip (73)	Chevy	74.988	Rusty Wallace (2)	Pontiac	91.372
1546	25	10/9/88	Charlotte, NC	1.500	P	501.00	Rusty Wallace (7)	Pontiac	130.677	Alan Kulwicki (7)	Ford	175.896
1547	26	10/16/88	N.Wilkesboro, NC	0.625	P	250.00	Rusty Wallace (8)	Pontiac	94.192	Bill Elliott (34)	Ford	116.901
1548	27	10/23/88	Rockingham, NC	1.017	P	500.36	Rusty Wallace (9)	Pontiac	111.557	Bill Elliott (35)	Ford	148.359
1549	28	11/6/88	Phoenix, AZ	1.000	P	312.00	Alan Kulwicki	Ford	90.457	Geoff Bodine (22)	Chevy	123.203
1550	39	11/20/88	Atlanta, GA	1.522	P	499.22	Rusty Wallace (10)	Pontiac	129.024	Rusty Wallace (3)	Pontiac	179.499

1989

Race #	Year #	Date	Site	Track	Surface	Miles	Race Winner	Car	Speed	Pole Winner	Car	Speed
1551	1	2/19/89	Daytona Beach, FL	2.500	P	500.00	Darrell Waltrip (74)	Chevy	148.466	Ken Schrader (4)	Chevy	196.996
1552	2	3/5/89	Rockingham, NC	1.017	P	500.36	Rusty Wallace (11)	Pontiac	115.122	Rusty Wallace (4)	Pontiac	148.793
1553	3	3/19/89	Atlanta, GA	1.522	P	499.22	Darrell Waltrip (75)	Chevy	139.684	Alan Kulwicki (8)	ford	176.925
1554	4	3/26/89	Richmond, VA	0.750	P	300.00	Rusty Wallace (12)	Pontiac	86.619	Geoff Bodine (23)	Chevy	120.573
1555	5	4/2/89	Darlington, SC	1.366	P	501.32	Harry Gant (10)	Olds	115.475	Mark Martin (4)	Ford	161.111
1556	6	4/9/89	Bristol, TN	0.533	P	266.50	Rusty Wallace (13)	Pontiac	76.034	Mark Martin (5)	Ford	120.278
1557	7	4/16/89	N.Wilkesboro, NC	0.625	P	250.00	Dale Earnhardt (35)	Chevy	89.937	Rusty Wallace (5)	Pontiac	120.278
1558	8	4/23/89	Martinsville, VA	0.525	P	262.50	Darrell Waltrip (76)	Chevy	79.025	Geoff Bodine (24)	Chevy	93.097
1559	9	5/7/89	Talladega, AL	2.660	P	500.08	Davey Allison (5)	Ford	155.869	Mark Martin (6)	Ford	193.061
1560	10	5/28/89	Charlotte, NC	1.500	P	600.00	Darrell Waltrip (77)	Chevy	144.077	Alan Kulwicki (9)	Ford	173.021
1561	11	6/4/89	Dover, DE	1.000	P	500.00	Dale Earnhardt (36)	Chevy	121.670	Mark Martin (7)	Ford	144.387
1562	12	6/11/89	Sonoma, CA	2.520	P	186.48	Ricky Rudd (10)	Buick	76.088	Rusty Wallace (6)	Pontiac	90.041
1563	13	6/18/89	Pocono, PA	2.500	P	500.00	Terry Labonte (9)	Ford	131.320	Rusty Wallace (7)	Pontiac	157.489
1564	14	6/25/89	Brooklyn, MI	0002	P	400.00	Bill Elliott (30)	Ford	139.023	Ken Schrader (5)	Chevy	174.728
1565	15	7/1/89	Daytona Beach, FL	0003	p	400.00	Davey Allison (6)	Ford	132.207	Mark Martin (8)	Ford	191.861
1566	16	7/23/89	Pocono, PA	0003	p	500.00	Bill Elliott (31)	Ford	117.847	Ken Schrader (6)	Chevy	157.809
1567	17	7/30/89	Talladega, AL	0003	p	500.08	Terry Labonte (10)	Ford	157.354	Mark Martin (9)	Ford	194.800
1568	18	8/13/89	Watkins Glen, NY	0002	p	218.52	Rusty Wallace (14)	Chevy	87.242	Morgan Shepherd (7)	Pontiac	120.456
1569	19	8/20/89	Brooklyn, MI	0002	p	400.00	Rusty Wallace (15)	Pontiac	157.704	Geoff Bodine (25)	Chevy	175.692
1570	20	8/26/89	Bristol, TN	0001	p	266.50	Darrell Waltrip (78)	Chevy	85.554	Alan Kulwicki (10)	Ford	117.043
1571	21	9/3/89	Darlington. SC	0001	p	501.32	Dale Earnhardt (37)	Chevy	135.462	Alan Kulwicki (11)	Ford	160.156
1572	22	9/10/89	Richmond, VA	0.750	P	300.00	Rusty Wallace (16)	Pontiac	88.380	Bill Elliott (36)	Ford	121.136
1573	23	9/17/89	Dover, DE	1.000	P	500.00	Dale Earnhardt (38)	Chevy	122.909	Davey Allison (9)	Ford	146.169
1574	24	9/24/89	Martinsville, VA	0.525	p	262.50	Darrell Waltrip (79)	Chevy	76.571	Jimmy Hensley	Chevy	91.913
1575	25	10/8/89	Charlotte, NC	1.500	p	501.00	Ken Schrader (2)	Chevy	149.863	Bill Elliott (37)	Foprd	174.081
1576	26	10/15/89	N.Wilkesboro, NC	0.625	p	250.00	Geoff Bodine (7)	Chevy	90.289	No Time Trials	NTT	NTT
1577	27	10/22/89	Rockingham, NC	1.017	p	500.36	Mark Martin	Ford	114.079	Alan Kulwicki (12)	Ford	148.624
1578	28	11/5/89	Phoenix, AZ	1.000	p	312.00	Bill Elliott (32)	Ford	105.683	Ken Schrader (7)	Chevy	124.645
1579	29	11/19/89	Atlanta, GA	1.522	P	499.22	Dale Earnhardt (39)	Chevy	140.229	Alan Kulwicki (13)	Ford	179.112

1990

Race #	Year #	Date	Site	Track	Surface	Miles	Race Winner	Car	Speed	Pole Winner	Car	Speed
1580	1	2/18/90	Daytona Beach, FL	2.500	P	500.00	Derrike Cope	Chevy	165.761	Ken Schrader (8)	Chevy	196.515
1581	2	2/25/90	Richmond, VA	0.750	P	300.00	Mark Martin (2)	Ford	92.158	Ricky Rudd (17)	Chevy	119.617
1582	3	3/4/90	Rockingham, NC	1.017	P	500.36	Kyle Petty (3)	Pontiac	122.864	Kyle Petty	Pontiac	148.751
1583	4	3/18/90	Atlanta, GA	1.522	P	499.22	Dale Earnhardt (40)	Chevy	156.849	No Time Trials	NTT	NTT
1584	5	4/1/90	Darlington, SC	1.366	P	501.32	Dale Earnhardt (41)	Chevy	124.073	Geoff Bodine (26)	Ford	162.996
1585	6	4/8/90	Bristol, TN	0.533	P	266.50	Davey Allison (7)	Ford	87.258	Ernie Irvan	Olds	116.157
1586	7	4/22/90	N.Wilkesboro	0.625	P	250.00	Brett Bodine	Buick	83.908	Mark Martin (10)	Ford	117.475
1587	8	4/29/90	Martinsville, VA	0.526	P	263.00	Geoff Bodine (8)	Ford	77.423	Geoff Bodine (27)	Ford	91.726
1588	9	5/6/90	Talladega, AL	2.660	P	500.08	Dale Earnhardt (42)	Chevy	159.571	Bill Elliott (38)	Ford	199.388
1589	10	5/27/90	Charlotte, NC	1.500	P	600.00	Rusty Wallace (17)	Pontiac	137.650	Ken Schrader (9)	Chevy	173.963
1590	11	6/3/90	Dover, DE	1.000	P	500.00	Derrike Cope (2)	Chevy	123.960	Dick Trickle	Pontiac	145.814
1591	12	6/10/90	Sonoma, CA	2.520	P	186.48	Rusty Wallace (18)	Pontiac	69.245	Ricky Rudd (18)	Chevy	99.743
1592	13	6/17/90	Pocono, PA	2.500	P	500.00	Harry Gant (11)	Olds	120.600	Ernie Irvan (2)	Olds	158.750
1593	14	6/24/90	Brooklyn, MI	2.000	P	400.00	Dale Earnhardt (43)	Chevy	150.219	No Time Trials	NTT	NTT
1594	15	7/7/90	Daytona Beach, FL	2.500	P	400.00	Dale Earnhardt (44)	Chevy	160.894	Greg Sacks	Chevy	195.533
1595	16	7/22/90	Pocono, PA	2.500	P	500.00	Geoff Bodine (9)	Ford	124.070	Mark Martin (12)	Ford	158.264
1596	17	7/29/90	Talladega, AL	2.660	P	500.08	Dale Earnhardt (45)	Chevy	174.430	Dale Earnhardt (9)	Chevy	192.513
1597	18	8/12/90	Watkins Glen, NY	2.428	P	218.52	Ricky Rudd (11)	Chevy	92.452	Dale Earnhardt (10)	Chevy	121.190
1598	19	8/19/90	Brooklyn, MI	2.000	P	400.00	Mark Martin (3)	Ford	138.822	Alan Kulwicki (14)	Ford	174.982
1599	20	8/25/90	Bristol, TN	0.533	P	266.50	Ernie Irvan	Olds	91.782	Dale Earnhardt (11)	Chevy	115.604
1600	21	9/2/90	Darlington, SC	1.366	P	501.32	Dale Earnhardt (46)	Chevy	123.141	Dale Earnhardt (12)	Chevy	158.448

Race #	Year #	Date	Site	Track	Surface	Miles	Race Winner	Car	Speed	Pole Winner	Car	Speed
1601	22	9/9/90	Richmond, VA	0.750	P	300.00	Dale Earnhardt (47)	Chevy	95.567	Ernie Irvan (3)	Chevy	119.872
1602	23	9/16/90	Dover, DE	1.000	P	500.00	Bill Elliott (33)	Ford	125.945	Bill Elliott (39)	Ford	144.928
1603	24	9/23/90	Martinsville, VA	0.526	P	263.00	Geoff Bodine (10)	Ford	76.386	Mark Martin (13)	Ford	91.571
1604	25	9/30/90	N.Wilkesboro, NC	0.625	P	250.00	Mark Martin (4)	Ford	93.818	Kyle Petty (2)	Pontiac	116.387
1605	26	10/7/90	Charlotte, NC	1.500	P	501.00	Davey Allison (8)	Ford	137.428	Brett Bodine	Buick	174.385
1606	27	10/21/90	Rockingham, NC	1.017	P	500.36	Alan Kulwicki (2)	Ford	126.452	Ken Schrader (11)	Chevy	147.814
1607	28	11/4/90	Phoenix, AZ	1.000	P	312.00	Dale Earnhardt (48)	Chevy	96.786	Rusty Wallace (8)	Pontiac	124.443
1608	29	11/18/90	Atlanta, GA	1.522	P	499.22	Morgan Shepherd (3)	Ford	140.911	Rusty Wallace (9)	Pontiac	175.222

1991

Race #	Year #	Date	Site	Track	Surface	Miles	Race Winner	Car	Speed	Pole Winner	Car	Speed
1609	1	2/17/91	Daytona Beach, FL	2.500	P	500.00	Ernie Irvan (2)	Chevy	148.148	Davey Allison (10)	Ford	195.955
1610	2	2/24/91	Richmond, VA	0.750	P	300.00	Dale Earnhardt (49)	Chevy	105.397	Davey Allison (11)	Ford	120.428
1611	3	3/3/91	Rockingham, NC	1.017	P	500.36	Kyle Petty (4)	Pontiac	124.083	Kyle Petty (2)	Pontiac	149.205
1612	4	3/18/91	Atlanta, GA	1.522	P	499.22	Ken Schrader (3)	Chevy	140.470	Alan Kulwicki (15)	Ford	174.413
1613	5	4/7/91	Darlington, SC	1.366	P	501.32	Ricky Rudd (12)	Chevy	135.594	Geoff Bodine (28)	Ford	161.939
1614	6	4/14/91	Bristol, TN	0.533	P	266.50	Rusty Wallace (19)	Pontiac	72.809	Rusty Wallace (10)	Pontiac	118.051
1615	7	4/21/91	N.Wilkesboro, NC	0.625	P	250.00	Darrell Waltrip (80)	Chevy	79.604	Brett Bodine (2)	Buick	116.237
1616	8	4/28/91	Martinsville, VA	0.526	P	263.00	Dale Earnhardt (50)	Chevy	75.139	Mark Martin (14)	Ford	91.949
1617	9	5/6/91	Talladega, AL	2.660	P	500.08	Harry Gant (12)	Olds	165.620	Ernie Irvan (4)	Chevy	195.186
1618	10	5/26/91	Charlotte, NC	1.500	P	600.00	Davey Allison (9)	Ford	138.951	Mark Martin (15)	Ford	174.820
1619	11	6/2/91	Dover, DE	1.000	P	500.00	Ken Schrader (4)	Chevy	120.152	Michael Waltrip	Pontiac	143.392
1620	12	6/9/91	Sonoma, CA	2.520	P	186.48	Davey Allison (10)	Ford	72.970	Ricky Rudd (19)	Chevy	90.634
1621	13	6/16/91	Pocono, PA	2.500	P	500.00	Darrell Waltrip (81)	Chevy	122.666	Mark Martin (16)	Ford	161.996
1622	14	6/23/91	Brooklyn, MI	2.000	P	400.00	Davey Allison (11)	Ford	160.912	Michael Waltrip (2)	Pontiac	174.351
1623	15	7/6/91	Daytona Beach, FL	2.500	P	400.00	Bill Elliott (34)	Ford	159.116	Sterling Marlin	Ford	190.331
1624	16	7/21/91	Pocono, PA	2.500	P	447.50	Rusty Wallace (20)	Pontiac	115.459	Alan Kulwicki (16)	Ford	161.473
1625	17	7/28/91	Talladega, AL	2.660	P	500.08	Dale Earnhardt (51)	Chevy	147.383	Sterling Marlin (2)	Ford	192.085
1626	18	8/11/91	Watkins Glen, NY	2.428	P	218.52	Ernie Irvan (3)	Chevy	98.977	Terry Labonte (20)	Olds	121.652
1627	19	8/18/91	Brooklyn, MI	2.000	P	400.00	Dale Jarrett	Ford	142.972	Alan Kulwicki (17)	Ford	173.431
1628	20	8/24/91	Bristol, TN	0.533	P	266.50	Alan Kulwicki (3)	Ford	82.028	Bill Elliott (40)	Ford	116.957
1629	21	9/1/91	Darlington, SC	1.366	P	501.32	Harry Gant (13)	Olds	133.508	Davey Allison (12)	Ford	162.506
1630	22	9/7/91	Richmond, VA	0.750	P	300.00	Harry Gant (14)	Olds	101.361	Rusty Wallace (11)	Pontiac	120.590
1631	23	9/15/91	Dover, DE	1.000	P	500.00	Harry Gant (15)	Olds	110.179	Alan Kulwicki (18)	Ford	146.825
1632	24	9/22/91	Martinsville, VA	0.526	P	263.00	Harry Gant (16)	Olds	74.535	Mark Martin (17)	Ford	93.171
1633	25	9/29/91	N.Wilkesboro, NC	0.625	P	250.00	Dale Earnhardt (52)	Chevy	94.113	Harry Gant (14)	Olds	116.871
1634	26	10/6/91	Charlotte, NC	1.500	P	501.00	Geoff Bodine (11)	Ford	138.984	Mark Martin (18)	Ford	176.499
1635	27	10/20/91	Rockingham, NC	1.017	P	500.36	Davey Allison (12)	Ford	127.292	Kyle Petty (3)	Pontiac	149.461
1636	28	11/3/91	Phoenix, AZ	1.000	P	312.00	Davey Allison (13)	Ford	95.746	Geoff Bodine (29)	Ford	127.589
1637	29	11/17/91	Atlanta, GA	1.522	P	499.22	Mark Martin (5)	Ford	137.968	Bill Elliott (41)	Ford	177.937

1992

Race #	Year #	Date	Site	Track	Surface	Miles	Race Winner	Car	Speed	Pole Winner	Car	Speed
1638	1	2/16/92	Daytona Beach, FL	2.500	P	500.00	Davey Allison (14)	Ford	160.256	Sterling Marlin (3)	Ford	192.213
1639	2	3/1/92	Rockingham, NC	1.017	P	500.36	Bill Elliott (35)	Ford	126.125	Kyle Petty (4)	Pontiac	149.926
1640	3	3/8/92	Richmond, VA	0.750	P	300.00	Bill Elliott (36)	Ford	104.378	Bill Elliott (42)	Ford	121.337
1641	4	3/15/92	Atlanta, GA	1.522	P	499.22	Bill Elliott (37)	Ford	147.746	Mark Martin (19)	Ford	179.923
1642	5	3/29/92	Darlington, SC	1.366	P	501.32	Bill Elliott (38)	Ford	139.364	Sterling Marlin (4)	Ford	163.067
1643	6	4/5/92	Bristol, TN	0.533	P	266.50	Alan Kulwicki (4)	Ford	86.316	Alan Kulwicki (19)	Ford	122.474
1644	7	4/12/92	N.Wilkesboro, NC	0.625	P	250.00	Davey Allison (15)	Ford	90.653	Alan Kulwicki (20)	Ford	117.242
1645	8	4/26/92	Martinsville, VA	0.526	P	263.00	Mark Martin (6)	Ford	78.086	Darrell Waltrip (57)	Chevy	92.956
1646	9	5/3/92	Talladega, AL	2.660	P	500.08	Davey Allison (16)	Ford	167.609	Ernie Irvan (5)	Chevy	192.831
1647	10	5/24/92	Charlotte, NC	1.500	P	600.00	Dale Earnhardt (53)	Chevy	132.980	Bill Elliott (43)	Ford	175.479
1648	11	5/31/92	Dover, DE	1.000	P	500.00	Harry Gant (17)	Chevy	109.456	Brett Bodine (3)	Ford	147.408
1649	12	6/7/92	Sonoma, CA	2.520	P	186.48	Ernie Irvan (4)	Chevy	81.413	Ricky Rudd (20)	Chevy	90.985
1650	13	6/14/92	Pocono, PA	2.500	P	500.00	Alan Kulwicki (5)	Ford	144.023	Ken Schrader (12)	Chevy	162.499
1651	14	6/21/92	Brooklyn, MI	2.000	P	400.00	Davey Allison (17)	Ford	152.672	Davey Allison (13)	Ford	176.258
1652	15	7/4/92	Daytona Beach, FL	2.500	P	400.00	Ernie Irvan (5)	Chevy	170.457	Sterling Marlin (5)	Ford	189.366
1653	16	7/19/92	Pocono, PA	2.500	P	500.00	Darrell Waltrip (82)	Chevy	134.058	Davey Allison (14)	Ford	162.022
1654	17	7/26/92	Talladega, AL	2.660	P	500.08	Ernie Irvan (6)	Chevy	176.309	Sterling Marlin (6)	Ford	190.586
1655	18	8/9/92	Watkins Glen, NY	2.428	P	123.83	Kyle Petty (5)	Pontiac	88.980	Dale Earnhardt (13)	Chevy	116.882
1656	19	8/16/92	Brooklyn, MI	2.000	P	400.00	Harry Gant (18)	Olds	146.056	Alan Kulwicki (21)	Ford	178.196
1657	20	8/29/92	Bristol, TN	0.533	P	266.50	Darrell Waltrip (83)	Chevy	91.198	Ernie Irvan (6)	Chevy	120.535
1658	21	9/6/92	Darlington, SC	1.366	P	501/322	Darrell Waltrip (84)	Chevy	129.114	Sterling Marlin (7)	Ford	162.249
1659	22	9/12/92	Richmond, VA	0.750	P	300.00	Rusty Wallace (21)	Pontiac	104.661	Ernie Irvan (7)	Chevy	120.784
1660	23	9/20/92	Dover, DE	1.000	P	500.00	Ricky Rudd (13)	Chevy	115.289	Alan Kulwicki (22)	Ford	145.267
1661	24	9/28/92	Martinsville, VA	0.525	P	263.00	Geoff Bodine (12)	Ford	75.424	Kyle Petty (5)	Pontiac	92.497
1662	25	10/5/92	N.Wilkesboro, NC	0.625	P	250.00	Geoff Bodine (13)	Ford	107.360	Alan Kulwicki (23)	Ford	117.133
1663	26	10/11/92	Charlotte, NC	1.500	P	501.00	Mark Martin (7)	Ford	153.537	Alan Kulwicki (24)	Ford	179.027
1664	27	10/25/92	Rockingham, NC	1.017	P	500.36	Kyle Petty (6)	Pontiac	130.748	Kyle Petty (6)	Pontiac	149.675
1665	28	11/1/92	Phoenix, AZ	1.000	P	312.00	Davey Allison (18)	Ford	103.885	Rusty Wallace (12)	Pontiac	128.141
1666	29	11/15/92	Atlanta, GA	1.522	P	499.22	Bill Elliott (39)	Ford	133.322	Rick Mast	Olds	180.813

1993

Race #	Year #	Date	Site	Track	Surface	Miles	Race Winner	Car	Speed	Pole Winner	Car	Speed
1667	1	2/14/93	Daytona Beach, FL	2.500	P	500.00	Dale Jarrett (2)	Chevy	154.972	Kyle Petty (7)	Pontiac	189.426
1668	2	2/28/93	Rockingham, NC	1.017	P	500.36	Rusty Wallace (22)	Pontiac	124.486	Mark Martin (20)	Ford	149.547
1669	3	3/7/93	Richmond, VA	0.750	P	300.00	Davey Allison (19)	Ford	107.709	Ken Schrader (13)	Chevy	123.164
1670	4	3/20/93	Atlanta, GA	1.522	P	499.22	Morgan Shepherd (4)	Ford	150.442	Rusty Wallace (13)	Pontiac	178.749
1671	5	3/28/93	Darlington, SC	1.366	P	501.32	Dale Earnhardt (54)	Chevy	139.958	No Time Trials	NTT	NTT
1672	6	4/4/93	Bristol, TN	0.533	P	266.50	Rusty Wallace (23)	Pontiac	84.730	Rusty Wallace (14)	Pontiac	120.938
1673	7	4/18/93	N.Wilkesboro, NC	0.625	P	250.00	Rusty Wallace (24)	Pontiac	92.602	Brett Bodine (4)	Ford	117.017
1674	8	4/25/93	Martinsville, VA	0.526	P	263.00	Rusty Wallace (25)	Pontiac	79.078	Geoff Bodine (30)	Ford	93.887
1675	9	5/2/93	Talladega, AL	2.660	P	500.08	Ernie Irvan (7)	Chevy	155.412	Dale Earnhardt (14)	Chevy	192.355
1676	10	5/16/93	Sonoma, CA	2.520	P	186.48	Geoff Bodine (14)	Ford	77.013	Dale Earnhardt (15)	Chevy	91.838
1677	11	5/30/93	Charlotte, NC	1.500	P	600.00	Dale Earnhardt (55)	Chevy	145.504	Ken Schrader (14)	Chevy	177.352
1678	12	6/6/93	Dover, DE	1.000	P	500.00	Dale Earnhardt (56)	Chevy	105.600	Ernie Irvan (8)	Chevy	151.541
1679	13	6/13/93	Pocono, PA	2.500	P	500.00	Kyle Petty (7)	Pontiac	138.005	Ken Schrader (15)	Chevy	162.816
1680	14	6/20/93	Brooklyn, MI	2.000	P	400.00	Ricky Rudd (14)	Chevy	148.484	Brett Bodine (5)	Ford	175.456
1681	15	7/3/93	Daytona Beach, FL	2.500	P	400.00	Dale Earnhardt (57)	Chevy	151.755	Ernie Irvan (9)	Chevy	190.327
1682	16	7/11/93	Loudon, NH	1.058	P	317.40	Rusty Wallace (26)	Pontiac	105.947	Mark Martin (21)	Ford	126.871
1683	17	7/18/93	Pocono, PA	2.500	P	500.00	Dale Earnhardt (58)	Chevy	133.343	Ken Schrader (16)	Chevy	162.934
1684	18	7/25/93	Talladega, AL	2.660	P	500.08	Dale Earnhardt (59)	Chevy	153.858	Bill Elliott (44)	Ford	192.397
1685	19	8/8/93	Watkins Glen, NY	2.428	P	218.52	Mark Martin (8)	Ford	84.771	Mark Martin (22)	Ford	119.118
1686	20	8/15/93	Brooklyn, MI	2.000	P	400.00	Mark Martin (9)	Ford	144.564	Ken Schrader (17)	Chevy	180.750
1687	21	8/28/93	Bristol, TN	0.533	P	266.50	Mark Martin (10)	Ford	88.172	Mark Martin (23)	Ford	121.405
1688	22	9/5/93	Darlington, SC	1.366	P	479.47	Mark Martin (11)	Ford	137.932	Ken Schrader (18)	Chevy	161.259
1689	23	9/11/93	Richmond, VA	0.750	P	300.00	Rusty Wallace (27)	Pontiac	99.917	Bobby Labonte	Ford	122.006
1690	24	9/19/93	Dover, DE	1.000	P	500.00	Rusty Wallace (28)	Pontiac	100.334	Rusty Wallace (15)	Pontiac	151.464
1691	25	9/26/93	Martinsville, VA	0.526	P	263.00	Ernie Irvan (8)	Ford	74.101	Ernie Irvan (10)	Ford	92.583
1692	26	10/3/93	N.Wilkesboro, NC	0.625	P	250.00	Rusty Wallace (29)	Pontiac	96.920	Ernie Irvan (11)	Ford	116.786
1693	27	10/10/93	Charlotte, NC	1.500	P	501.00	Ernie Irvan (9)	Ford	154.537	Jeff Gordon	Chevy	177.684
1694	28	10/24/93	Rockingham, NC	1.017	P	500.36	Rusty Wallace (30)	Pontiac	114.036	Mark Martin (24)	Ford	148.353
1695	29	10/31/93	Phoenix, AZ	1.000	P	312.00	Mark Martin (12)	Ford	100.375	Bill Elliott (45)	Ford	129.482
1696	30	11/14/93	Atlanta, GA	1.522	P	499.22	Rusty Wallace (31)	Pontiac	125.221	Harry Gant (15)	Chevy	176.902

The Gallery

Above Left: Dale Jarrett pitches the Wood Brothers Ford into the first turn at Charlotte Motor Speedway. (Brian Czobat)

Above: Alan Kulwicki with hardware and software after winning the Winston Cup title at Atlanta in 1992. (Brian Czobat)

Below Left: Sterling Marlin #8 and Terry Labonte #14 crash at Bristol in '93. (Bryan Hallman)

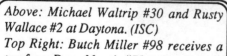

Above: Michael Waltrip #30 and Rusty Wallace #2 at Daytona. (ISC)
Top Right: Butch Miller #98 receives a tap from Dave Marcis #71 at Darlington. (Brian Czobat).
Right: J.D. McDuffie gave his all for the sport he loved. (McDuffie Collection)

Above Left: Alan Kulwicki's Ford leads Ken Schrader's Chevrolet into the first turn at Charlotte Motor Speedway. (Brian Czobat)

Above: Larry McReynolds, one of the top crew chiefs in NASCAR. (Brian Czobat)

Left: Davey Allison and Robert Yates discuss prerace strategy. (Brian Czobat)

Above Left: Sterling Marlin at Daytona in 1992. (Brian Czobat)
Top Right: Rusty Wallace at speed at Darlington. (Greg Fielden)
Left: Dale Earnhardt riding at the 'Rock'. (NCMS)
Above: King Richard Petty. (Brian Czobat)

Top Left: Davey Allison leading the field at Pocono. (Jay Kainz)
Above Right: Jimmy Hensley in deep thought (Brian Czobat)
Lower Left: Harry Gant after '91 Darlington victory (Brian Czobat)
Below: A pack of cars duel on the high banks of Daytona (ISC)

Above: Harry Gant's Oldsmobile at Martinsville. (Brian Czobat)
Above Right: Thumbs up for Kyle Petty. (Kim Novosat)
Below: Jim Sauter #89 cracks the wall at Charlotte as Dale Jarrett spins to the low side. (Brian Czobat)
Below Right: Bill Elliott. (Dover Downs)

Top Left: Neil Bonnett, race driver and TV commentator. (B.Czobat)
Above: The King makes a final lap at Atlanta in 1993. (B.Hallman)
Lower Left: Ernie Irvan in a relaxing moment. (Brian Czobat)
Below: Wallace, Earnhardt and Martin battle at Dover. (B.Czobat)

Above Left: Tight racing in Richmond's first turn. (Brian Czobat)
Above: Lake Speed's Chevrolet at Daytona. (Greg Fielden)
Lower Left: Car owner Junie Donlavey, who was born in the USA a long, long time ago. (Steve Crumbacker)
Below: Brett Bodine at the head of the pack. (B.Czobat)